IGBO IN THE ATLANTIC WORLD

IGBO IN THE ATLANTIC WORLD

AFRICAN ORIGINS AND DIASPORIC DESTINATIONS

EDITED BY Toyin Falola AND Raphael Chijioke Njoku

INDIANA UNIVERSITY PRESS
Bloomington & Indianapolis

This book is a publication of

Indiana University Press
Office of Scholarly Publishing
Herman B Wells Library 350
1320 East 10th Street
Bloomington, Indiana 47405 USA

iupress.indiana.edu

∞ *The paper used in this publication meets the minimum requirements of the American National Standard for Information Sciences—Permanence of Paper for Printed Library Materials, ANSI Z39.48-1992.*

MANUFACTURED IN THE
UNITED STATES OF AMERICA

Library of Congress Cataloging-in-Publication Data

Names: Falola, Toyin, editor. | Njoku, Raphael Chijioke, editor.
Title: Igbo in the Atlantic world : African origins and diasporic destinations / edited by Toyin Falola and Raphael Chijioke Njoku.
Description: Bloomington : Indiana University Press, 2016. | Includes bibliographical references and index.
Identifiers: LCCN 2016024865 (print) | LCCN 2016026274 (ebook) | ISBN 9780253022455 (cl : alk. paper) | ISBN 9780253022578 (e-book)
Subjects: LCSH: Igbo (African people)—Social life and customs. | Igbo (African people)—Ethnic identity. | Igbo diaspora. | Igbo (African people)—United States. | Igbo (African people)—West Indies.
Classification: LCC DT515.45.I33 I4235 2016 (print) | LCC DT515.45.I33 (ebook) | DDC 305.896332—dc23
LC record available at https://lccn.loc.gov/2016024865

1 2 3 4 5 21 20 19 18 17 16

To the memory of Professors

Tekena Tamuno, Adiele Afigbo, Jacob Ade Ajayi,
and Emmanuel Ayandele

CONTENTS

Part III
Cultural Crosscurrents: Dimensions of the Igbo Experience in the Atlantic World

ABBREVIATIONS

AG	Action Group
BBCA	Benue Basin Cultural Area
CCN	Christian Council of Nigeria
CMS	Church Missionary Society
COR	Council of Rivers movement for a Calabar-Ogoja-River statehood
CRCA	Cross River Cultural Area
ICA	Igbo Cultural Area
LTC	Lagos Town Council
NCAST	Nigerian College of Aviation and Technology
NCNC	National Council of Nigeria and Cameroon
NDCA	Niger Delta Cultural Area
NDP	National Democratic Party
NIP	National Independent Party
NPC	Northern People's Congress
NYM	Nigerian Youth Movement
SPILC	Society for Promoting of Igbo Language and Culture
UNCA	Lower Niger Cultural Area
UNN	University of Nigeria, Nsukka

PREFACE AND ACKNOWLEDGMENTS

Despite the fact that Igbo studies in connection with the African diaspora began about 1789 when Olaudah Equiano published *The Interesting Narrative of the Life of Olaudah Equiano*, the dispersed terrains of their civilization is just beginning to unravel. This book contributes to the growing field of the Igbo in the Atlantic world. The primary intent is to examine the Igbo as a people, a culture, a concept, and a global phenomenon in relation to the Atlantic slave trade and diasporic linkages. The scope of enquiry extends from the original Igbo homeland in modern Nigeria and across the Atlantic to the New World.

Tapping from a huge collection of primary and secondary sources reserved in oral data, archives, and depositories in Africa, Europe, and the Americas, the various contributors give accounts of the Igbo involvement in the trans-Atlantic slave trade and the results of that encounter in the mixing of peoples and rise of cultures. The major areas of coverage include remarkably Igbo ways of life in precolonial and indigenous times, interactions with neighbors, migrations and settlements, and their reactions to, and involvement in, international trade—chiefly to the European slave trade which, from the fifteenth century, structured a peculiar order of Euro-African interactions. Other themes extensively covered are those of the Igbo presence in the Atlantic world, slavery, identity, and survival; abolitionism and transition to legitimate or commodity trade. Additionally, attention is paid to the post-abolition world of the Igbo, their arts (including dance, politics, rituals, and religion), and how these intertwined with those of their host societies to produce a hybrid of cultures encountered today across the Atlantic world.

The authors brought their expertise to bear in the interpretations they offer as Igbo identity and culture negotiated with challenges of subjugation, negotiations, adaptation, and survival in the New World encounters. As much as possible, the contributors have tried to use the specific Igbo historical crosscurrents to illuminate common themes of slavery and freedom, culture and tradition, precolonial, colonial, and postcolonial history of the Igbo in particular and Nigeria/Africa/Atlantic in general. This approach has been followed in a tidy manner while avoiding the dangers inherent in romanticizing or even privileging the Igbo over other groups in our interpretation of historical themes. If now and then we come across a bit more Igbo-centric, it is because there is a need to draw attention to the Igbo experience across time and space rather than telling a single story.

It would have been difficult to undertake writing this book without the untiring efforts of several people—not all of whose names we can include here. We must thank Matt Childs for his support for this project. We owe special thanks to many friends and colleagues who read initial drafts of this monograph, including Michael Vickers, Ogechi Anyanwu, and Emily Crumpton. We also thank the Acquisitions Editor for African Studies, Indiana University Press, Ms. Dee Mortensen, for her interest in the manuscript. Above all, we are grateful to our contributors for their persistence as this project dragged on and on. Indeed, they are the true heroes of this volume.

IGBO IN THE ATLANTIC WORLD

1 INTRODUCTION

Raphael Chijioke Njoku and Toyin Falola

This book is about the Igbo (anglicized Ibo) people of southeastern Nigeria and their diasporic connections through the trans-Atlantic slave trade that began in Africa around the mid-fifteenth century. This endeavor followed the expanded Portuguese quest for trade commodities beyond the original attraction to gold, which by then was becoming increasingly scarce. Covering a wide range of topics from the timeless precolonial era through the colonial period and to the present, the various chapters approach the study of Igbo and Igbo/African Diaspora connections from a multidisciplinary perspective. Collectively, the authors provide the most detailed examination to date of the Igbo experience, focusing on indigenous institutions and cultural practices, the Igbo role and agency in the trans-Atlantic slave trade originating from the Bight of Biafra emporium,[1] the sojourns of slavery victims in the Americas, and the return to Africa by those recaptives and émigrés who welcomed the idea of resettling in different parts of nineteenth-century West Africa. Also covered is the impact of the Atlantic exchanges between Africa, Europe, and the Americas (including commerce, missionary evangelism, and colonial rule) on Igbo ways of life in the modern Nigerian setting.

The Igbo are one of the most dynamic and courageous groups in Africa. In particular, their enterprising and entrepreneurial character, resilient spirit, and contradictory reports of their stubbornness and malleability demand further consideration by scholars. The Igbo constituted one of the most predominant ethnic/linguistic groups sucked into the trans-Atlantic slave trade and slavery between the 1650s and the 1800s. Over the past four decades, the fields of Africana studies, African-American studies, Latin-American studies, slave studies, and Atlantic history have attracted a significant amount of scholarly interest as innovative research approaches continue to enhance our knowledge of the multiple and complex processes that created the African Diaspora. Perceptively, *Igbo in the Atlantic World: African Origins and Diasporic Destinations* builds on the insights provided by the methodology and approach of Linda Heywood and coauthors in *Central Africans and Cultural Transformations in the American Diaspora* as well as *The Yoruba Diaspora in the Atlantic World*, edited by Toyin Falola and Matt D. Childs. These works, respectively, focus on the Kongo/Angolan and Yoruba contributions to diasporic cultures by exploring in most part the dynamics of cultural continuities.[2] Similarly, the various chapters here place emphasis on the importance of the Igbo, tracing their historical and cultural contributions in Africa and the African Diaspora from both the perspectives of their Old World origins and the New World destinations.

Until recently, most scholarship interpreted and explained the African Diaspora by using generic descriptions such as "Africa," "Africans," and "Blacks."[3] To cite but a few examples, in 1941, the doyen of modern African studies, Melville Herskovits, fired the cannon of contemporary African and African Diaspora studies with his *The Myth of the Negro Past*, which was widely discussed and debated by scholars across diverse disciplinary divides. Herskovits aimed to counter the erroneous notion that the African slaves arrived in the Americas without their inherited cultural practices.[4] Another study that broadened scholarly debate was Van Sertima's *They Came Before Columbus*,[5] which focused on the earliest mention of Africans and their cultural footprints on the ancient American soil. This was followed by Graham W. Irvin's *Africans Abroad*, which offered a pictorial history of the African presence across different continents. Within the established trend, subsequent works such as Michael L. Conniff and Thomas J. Davis's *Africans in the Americas: A History of the African Diaspora* and *Diasporic Africa*, edited by Michael A. Gomez, focused on African slaves and their descendants from slavery to emancipation in the United States, the Caribbean, and Latin America.[6]

While the extant studies substantially covered the African injection of new cultures in the New World, not all have paid attention to the specific ethnic communities in Africa from where certain observed cultural practices came to the Americas. Consequently, diasporic studies have, by and large, tended to emphasize the universal and common elements of African culture in the Americas and elsewhere rather than underlining the significant cultural, social, and historical diversity that characterized different regions of Africa during the slave trade era.

This study addresses longstanding historiographical lacunae by employing a multidisciplinary perspective from scholars of history, gender studies, anthropology, sociology, religion, literature, and cultural studies to examine both diverse and common experiences of the Igbo in West Africa and the Americas. The volume thus contributes both to the general literature on the diaspora and the specific one of the Igbo ethnic group. By studying in detail how the Igbo became integrated into the Atlantic world through the trans-Atlantic slave trade, this volume highlights the emergence and transformation of Igbo identities and cultures, and how the Igbo and their descendants resiliently adapted, recreated, and reasserted their culture in Africa and the Americas as a strategy of resistance.

Igbo in the Atlantic World is among the first studies to trace the Igbo as a single cultural group from Africa to the New World destinations, and there is no comparable study in English known to the authors at this time. The 2010 award-wining study by G. Ugo Nwokeji, *The Slave Trade and Culture in the Bight of Biafra*, primarily analyzed the internal organization and the aftershocks of the Igbo slave trade on the Bight of Biafra point of embarkation without comparable benefits of a multiple African Diaspora treatment extended to diverse regions of the Caribbean and the Americas.[7] Previous other studies have focused on the Igbo through a single disciplinary lens, and as such, scholars have not been able to gain deeper insights in the manner, for instance, that some Africanists like William Bascom have connected indigenous Yoruba system of divination in Nigeria with its Diaspora adaptations in Haiti and Cuba.[8] Most notably in the field of literature, the Igbo experience in Africa has been covered through Chinua Achebe's writings.[9] Scholars in other disciplines such as history and anthropology have further examined the Igbo in the Bight of Biafra during the era of the trans-Atlantic slave trade.[10] These studies have focused analysis by specialization customary of the academic monograph without accounting for the Igbo people's historical, political, cultural, and economic experiences from about the mid-seventeenth century to the twentieth century. From multiple angles, the present study explores in detail the specific contributions the Igbo have made to the rise of cultures in Africa and the African Diaspora in the Atlantic world. As such, *Igbo in the Atlantic World* is a book on cultural inventions as a by-product of human exchanges in diverse settings. By according agency to the Igbo, the various contributors demonstrate the significant insights gained from focusing historical scholarship on a single cultural group and tracing the Igbo dispersion and influence throughout the Americas.

Several important themes, among them the question of identity, are treated in depth. From their diverse disciplinary expertise, the authors tackled the slippery concept of identity, whether defined as race consciousness, ethnic belonging, common spoken language, material cultural productions, or mannerisms (assumed or real) with uncommon intellectual acuity. This is a positive departure from the familiar culturalist school of thought that has dominated previous studies, a good example of which is Marvin Lewis's *Ethnicity and Identity in Contemporary Afro-Venezuelan Literature*, which explores the concept of Blackness in the African Diaspora as a homogenous ethnic category.[11]

In the present study, the various authors emphasize the heterogeneous nature of Blackness in the African Diaspora, while confirming the long-established nature of identity as a fluid category. In relation to the field, scholars disagree over the relationship of the ethnic label "Igbo" to their shifting social locations. There is no consensus, for instance, over whether the Igbo were a cohesive people in terms of manners and customs prior to the colonial era.[12] This is despite the existence of such philological terms as "Eboe" "Hackbu," or "Heebo" (i.e., Igbo) as encountered in the writings of early European traders and visitors to the Bight of Biafra. In confirming Stephen Cornell and Douglas Hartmann's sociological interpretation of race, ethnicity, and identity, the findings herein lend credence to the fact that the Igbo identity question, like other similar identities appropriated on group belongingness, is fluid and often articulated and claimed when the particular group is confronted with an external threat.[13] An overwhelming body of evidence has revealed that for the Igbo, whereas the preconditions for the rise of an Igbo consciousness were in existence during precolonial times, Igbo elements in the African Diaspora struggled to assert a priori Igbo ethnic identity within the constraints imposed on them by their captivity and enslavement. In similar terms, the Igbo in Africa reacted to the threat posed by British colonial rule and the new sociopolitical and economic order brought by the Europeans with a new spirit staked on a shared history, language, culture, and even skin color.

The identity discourse highlights another important subject of debate: the population of Igbo-speaking people among slave exports from the Bight of Biafra. We are reminded of Philip D. Curtin's 1969 study on the African trans-Atlantic slave trade census, which inspired similar groundbreaking works.[14] The present study advances this kind of thinking. While scholars are in agreement that the precolonial Igbo society kept slaves and that a large proportion of captives that departed to the New World from the eastern Niger Delta came from the Igbo hinterland, there is no consensus over the numbers of Igbo slaves.[15] Using statistics available in 1956, the eminent historian Kenneth O. Dike concluded that Igbo speakers made up the greater part of the American-bound captives dispatched from the Bight of Biafra.[16] This optimism was founded on a source from the 1780s showing that 80 percent of the slaves exported from Bonny, one of the major trading ports in the Niger Delta, were Igbo.[17] In the three decades following the British prohibition of the trans-Atlantic slave trade in 1807 and their effort at policing the seas with Her Majesty's Naval patrols, Sierra Leone registers of rescued slaves reveal that the Igbo composed 60 percent of the captives on ships departing from the Bight of Biafra.[18] If the slave statistics from the eighteenth and nineteenth centuries should serve as a guide, the high proportion of the Igbo slave exports supposes that non-Igbos in their midst would have picked up some of the philology and cultural inventions of the dominant group. In other words, one may therefore hold the assumption that the Igbo influence over slave cargoes from this West African coastal region would have been profound. This book advances this pattern of thinking but cautions that the dynamics of cultural dominance do not always follow the simple logic of majority-versus-minority equations. Otherwise, European cultural imperialism would not have succeeded to the degree observed across the world.

Additionally, *Igbo in the Atlantic World* is important in relation to the wider historiographical debate on the significance of the inherited cultures that enslaved Africans brought to the Americas. In recent years, this issue has polarized scholars into two schools of African and African Diaspora studies at a time when an "Africanist" interpretation that emphasizes the importance of the cultures that enslaved people carried with them to the Americas gains momentum. One of these studies includes Colin Palmer's *The First Passage: Blacks in Americas, 1520–1617*. This engaging social history of early African ethnic groups employed indexes of religion, language, and material culture to account for their landings and promotion of new cultural trends in the Americas.[19] As Northrup noted in a related study, anyone very "familiar with other revisionist movements in history" knows that the passion of Africanists has sometimes led to theoretical and factual errors. Expectedly, "while some have sought to defend their school's position" by attacking those who express doubts over the potency of African slave cultural exports to the Diaspora, the more dexterous Africanists have asserted more nuanced conclusions.[20] For instance, Linda Heywood characterizes the Africanist position as "the view that African ethnicity and identity were important and influenced the process of creolization in the Americas." The insightful nuances of this statement are difficult to dispute. Heywood also correctly observes that another group of scholars "argues that African societies were so fragmented, and the toll of the slave trade and plantation agriculture so destructive, that they precluded the continuation of African culture in the Americas," ascribing such views to Sidney W. Mintz and Richard Price.[21] In line with Heywood, this book moderates between the two extreme polarities with the assertion that no child was born in a state of cultural tabula rasa. Thus, in contrast to John Locke's 1694 theoretical entreaty that gave rise to this thinking,[22] the findings in this book follow Michel Foucault's poststructuralist genealogical investigative approach[23] in showing that culture and identity formation is like a flowing river that creates diverse ecosystems in relation to the environment in diverse settings. In other words, the specific nature that the identity of African elements in the Americas assumed was a function of the nature of politics and exercise of power, mode of production, prevalent religious practices, and the racial/ethnic compositions of the population in that host community, among other determinants.

CHAPTER OUTLINE

This volume consists of twenty-one chapters divided into three parts. Part I, "Igbo Institutions and Customs as Baseline," is composed of three chapters that broadly explore enduring issues of political organization, gender, and values that have been transferred across the Atlantic. In other words, chapters in this part account for the political and socioeconomic climate in the Igbo homeland to better understand their common diasporic origins and adaptations. Chapter 2, Hannah Chukwu's "The Kingless People: The Speech Act as Shield and Sword," presents one of the most feasible political symbols of the Igbo—namely, their inclination toward an indigenously grown republican democratic tradition. If the Igbo are described today as enterprising, fearless, and stubborn, it may be a reflection of this political heritage that was founded on egalitarianism, liberty, and freedom as opposed to the crude practices of slavery, human rights abuses, and oppression that the captives were subjected to in the Americas. This assertion may help shed some useful light on why the story of the historic "Ebo (Igbo) Landing" of 1803 at Dumber Creek in St. Simons Island, Georgia, is essentially a moral resistance to slavery and oppression. It also explains why Toussaint L'Ouverture and his revolutionary comrades put their lives on the line in a heroic defense of freedom and human dignity in late eighteenth-century French Haiti.[24]

As Chukwu notes, Igbo people recognize the dignity and potency in speech and demonstrate the defense and combat strategies imbued in it. Describing themselves as kingless people from their saying, *Igbo enwe eze* (Igbo has no king), the Igbo paradoxically demonstrate true democracy and organization, not represented by an exclusive authority and transcending geographical borders. Speech, being an utterance considered an action, particularly with regard to its intention, purpose, or effect, elucidates the force that drives and moderates life among the Igbo.

Probing further into the characteristics of the indigenous political system, chapter 3, Nwando Achebe's "Igbo Goddesses and the Priests and Male Priestesses Who Serve Them," provides insight into the degree to which Igbo institutions were anchored on the indigenous religion, which made use of the ancestors as the middlemen between the living and the Almighty God in heaven. This study confirms the long-established fact that African traditional religious practices migrated with the enslaved

Africans to the New World.[25] Within the Igbo religious corpus, Ala or Ani (the Earth Goddess) occupied a position of prominence. By extension, women exerted immense power and influence on diverse areas of Igbo life, including politics. In chapter 4, "Gender Relations in Nineteenth- and Early Twentieth-Century Igbo Society," Gloria Chuku continues to illuminate understanding on the diverse and complex patterns of sociopolitical and economic activities as shared between the genders in the Igbo precolonial and colonial settings. According to Chuku, across time and space, Igbo men and women have together resisted docility and consistently demonstrated agency as they are confronted by the sociocultural forces working to reshape the indigenous cultural landscape. Prospectively, this dynamic shaped gender relations and cultural practices in both Old and New World Igbo society as the people came in contact with those internal and external processes that underpinned gender relations and rapid transformations during the nineteenth and early twentieth centuries.

Part II, "The Igbo in the African Diaspora: The Mechanics and Patterns of Migrations, Settlements, and Demographics," contains eight chapters that focus on the processes and patterns of Igbo migration and dispersal in the New World, including the United States, Caribbean, Latin America, and Brazil. Particular emphasis was placed on Igbo involvement in the slave trade originating from the Bight of Biafra and the growth of port cities, such as Old Calabar and New Calabar, that were tied to the trans-Atlantic slave trade. This part maps out the destinations of the Igbo in the Atlantic world from the seventeenth century, when the Aro slavers began to assume control of the Igbo slave trading, through the nineteenth century, when the trade was prohibited by the British.[26] Charting their points of destinations and census, the various chapters highlight the Igbo experience in the Americas. Unifying the divergent experiences of the Igbo throughout the African Diaspora was their attempts to reclaim ties to their ancestral homeland through language, culture, and historical memory while adapting to the horrific conditions of their New World enslavement.

In chapter 5, A. E. Afigbo assumes the difficult task of righting some of the wrongs or unintentional impressions held about the Aro and the roles they played both in the internal and external commodity trade that preceded slave trade of the Bight of Biafra. In many respects, this chapter complements Nwokeji's *The Slave Trade and Culture in the Bight of Biafra*, which shows that the Aro ascendancy was the key factor in the trade expansion.[27] Afigbo critically considers all ramifications of the trade—including geography, economic impact, and ethno-material cultural consequences—with the conclusion that scholars have treated with certain degree of negligence the full impact of the Aro slaving oligarchy in both the Igbo area and the surrounding Efik and Ibibio areas. Afigbo argues that the constant coming and going that Aro businesses entailed for themselves and their associates, and frequent gatherings at regional markets and fairs, helped ensure that the elite of the race and the carriers of Igbo culture continued to speak the same language, no matter what happened. In this process of trading and offering oracular services, the Aro bequeathed the Igbo ethnographic legacies that are often ignored. Overall, Afigbo's exhausting examination of the role of the Aro in the slave trade sets up the foundation for a better understanding of the ethnic origins of the slaves exported from the Bight of Biafra and the infrastructure that handled the logistics of supplies and demographics of those dispatched overseas. If the trans-Atlantic slave trade from the Bight of Biafra sector had started slowly before 1730, for instance, it is because the Aro structures of organization and control were just beginning to take shape. It is the opinion of scholars that it must have been the Aro who first adopted and deployed secret societies like the Ekpe from among the Benue-Congo peoples, especially from among the Efik and the Ibibio, and then planted them in their satellite communities in the course of their business travels.[28] Thus Aro dominance of the slave trade of the hinterland of the Bight of Biafra was not entirely negative and sterile; it also left behind positive impacts, some of which can still be identified today.

In chapter 6, "The Trans-Atlantic Slave Trade from the Bight of Biafra: An Overview,"

Kenneth Morgan identifies a broad context for the other contributions to this volume on the Igbo experience in the Atlantic world by offering an overview of the volume, distribution, and organization of the slave trade from the Bight of Biafra during its entire existence. British domination in this branch of the trade determines that most of the analysis falls upon that specific sector of trans-Atlantic slaving. The chapter is divided into three chronological phases to emphasize changing features of this sector of the slave trade over time. The first phase covers the long period before 1730 when the slave trade from the Bight of Biafra experienced slow beginnings for well over a century followed by a marked rise after the mid-seventeenth century. The second period, from 1730 to 1810, covers the peak years of the slave trade exports from the Bight of Biafra. This was the era when the Bight of Biafra was closely tied to the fortunes of the British slave trade as a whole until the historic abolition of 1807. The eighty years after 1730 was also the period when the commercial organization of the trade in the Niger Delta became highly coordinated. The third phase considers the slave trade from the Bight of Biafra between 1810 and the trade's demise in the 1850s. During this period, Spanish, Portuguese, and French traders tried to pick up the portion of the export dropped by the British and leverage it for profits. But the British naval and diplomatic campaigns hindered the full realization of the Portuguese and French slavers' goals. Morgan's treatment of the history of the trans-Atlantic slave trade in its developmental phases not only enables a deeper comprehension of when and how the Igbo dominated the export trade emanating from the Bight of Biafra, but also where the victims of the slavery ended up.

In chapter 7, "The Igbo and African Backgrounds of the Slave Cargo of the *Henrietta Marie*," John Thornton provides an elaborate "forensic" account involving pieces of evidence indicative that the substantial majority of the ill-fated ship's cargo, which arrived in Jamaica in 1700, were Igbo. The legendary ship, *Henrietta Marie*, had barely dropped off its human consignment when it was caught in a heavy storm and ran aground off of Key West, Florida. If the overall object of the chapter is to prove the "Igbo-ness" of the slaves, it then succeeds in setting up the following chapter.

In chapter 8, "'A Great Many Boys and Girls': Igbo Youth in the British Slave Trade, 1700–1808," Audra A. Diptee gives a blow-by-blow account of the experiences of Igbo youth in the Atlantic slave trade. According to Diptee, in the space of a century, from 1700 to 1808, available evidence reveals that Igbo children were transported on British ships in larger numbers than children of other ethnic groups. The vast majority of these young people ended up in the Caribbean for reasons perhaps connected with demand and adaptability. This finding extends Diptee's other groundbreaking works on this topic while corroborating the findings of both Kenneth Morgan and John Thornton in this volume, that the Igbo slaves were indeed greater in number than other African groups.[29] Contrary to common assumptions that Igbo slaves were difficult to manage and often unprofitable to trade, the Caribbean case study suggests that during this era, ship captains on the African coast and buyers in the Caribbean were more open to purchasing Igbo children than the current scholarship suggests. Diptee contends that the number of Igbo in the British slave trade made it likely that Igbo youth held captive in the Caribbean, compared to other young captives, had more opportunities to interact with persons from their ethnic community. Yet enslaved Igbo children had a range of experiences. The world of slavery was an anomalous space in which lives were characteristically turned upside down and cultural conventions and taboos truncated by human overindulgence, and Diptee quickly adds that slaves who found themselves in the Caribbean were in a world of diverse living and labor conditions and an increasing number of Caribbean-born slave children. How these young captives responded to their enslavement was not only influenced by their circumstances in the Caribbean, but also by their personal histories in Igboland.

As if following up with Diptee's conclusions, albeit in the Niger Delta context, chapter 9, Raphael Chijioke Njoku's "Becoming African: Igbo Slaves and Social Reordering in

Nineteenth-Century Niger Delta," focuses on the process of sociocultural reordering and ethnogenesis among enslaved Igbo who, over time, secured their freedom either through hard work or the changing emphasis from slave export to palm oil export. In this African diaspora within Africa, the liberated Igbo were garnered power and prestige within trading corporations known as "Houses" while exposed to the independence that comes with diligence, membership in the new delta families system, formal education, and Christianity. Simultaneously, the ex-slaves redefined themselves in terms of larger regional, "national," and continental African identities. Njoku's nuanced and detailed treatment of the Igbo in relation to their other Niger Delta and creole neighbors casts useful light on the parallel processes of identity formation among slaves in New World societies. For intellectual historians, Njoku's conclusion throws a useful light on why not all Igbo ex-slaves (including the legendary Africanus Horton resettled in Sierra Leone) returned to their original homeland despite their cursory involvement in some Igbo ethnic associations within the African diaspora.[30]

In chapter 10, "The Clustering of Igbo in the Americas: Where, When, How, and Why?" Gwendolyn Midlo Hall discusses several persistent myths about Igbo in the Americas, including the changing proportions over time of Igbo sent from the Bight of Biafra. One of the most appealing elements of the chapter is Hall's attempt to trace, with precision, where the Igbo slaves ended up across the Americas and why. This is despite the complexities involved in such an exercise given the observed variations in spelling of the word "Igbo." As a result, the purported Igbo slaves were often listed under distinct and sometimes unclear designations in documents housed in the Americas. As Hall notes, although the Igbo slaves' point of embarkation was the Bight of Biafra, the easternmost section of the Lower Guinea Coast, *The Trans-Atlantic Slave Trade* database has no field that could enlighten us about Igbo as opposed to other ethnicities sent from the Bight of Biafra.[31]

In chapter 11, Paul E. Lovejoy's "The Demography of the Bight of Biafra Slave Trade, ca. 1650–1850" tackles the debate over the number of Igbo slaves transplanted to the Americas in the era of the trans-Atlantic slave trade. Given that there are no existing data in form of ship manifests specifically identifying individual slaves as Igbo, the approach was to first tag the total number of human beings exported from the Bight of Biafra, which handled the bulk of the Igbo exports. As Lovejoy notes, over the period of the trade, an estimated 1.5 million people (about 14 percent of the total African exports) were shipped to the Americas from the Bight of Biafra ports. Approximately 1.28 million of them survived the journey across the Atlantic. The difficult question remains: how many of these were actually Igbo? In attempt to determine this, Lovejoy traced the destinations of the slaves departing from the Bight of Biafra to the various European colonies in the Americas, including Jamaica, Barbados, the French Caribbean, as well as independent Brazil and the United States—particularly the Tidewater regions of Virginia and Maryland, Georgia, and the Carolinas. In these disparate locations, the percentage of Igbo elements was calculated from the large number of individual slaves, including Gustavus Vassa (Olaudah Equiano), who self-identified as Igbo.

In chapter 12, "The Igbo Diaspora in the Era of the Slave Trade," Douglas B. Chambers continues to examine the historical geography of the Igbo Diaspora in the era of the slave trade. He argues that this connected particular African and American histories, as the Atlantic Ocean was as much a bridge as a barrier. This is an example of this book's strength in contextualizing nuances of the history of the trans-Atlantic exchanges, avoiding the pitfalls of the previous studies that often focus solely on one part of the story. According to Chambers, Igbo contributed in many ways to slave resistance and to the historical development of early Afro-American cultures in the New World. The extensive social violence of this vast slave trade also had major consequences for Igboland itself, most notably the rise of the Aro slavery, with their network of settlements and powerful *agawhu* (warlords) who controlled the major trade routes to the coast, and the consequent decline and near-collapse of the ancient pacifistic civilization centered at Nri.[32]

In part III, "Cultural Crosscurrents: Dimensions of the Igbo Experience in the Atlantic World," the various chapters explore common themes on the religious, linguistic, social, literary, culinary, dress, familial, artistic, musical, dance, identity, and material influences and legacies of Igbo culture in Africa and the Americas. The nine chapters in this part constitute the heart of the book and cross the most disciplinary, geographic, and chronological boundaries. As culture cannot be isolated in time and space or academic discipline, the various authors demonstrate that it is through these cultural manifestations that the Igbo left their most enduring legacy on diasporic culture as well as the indigenous ways of life. The Igbo gave, borrowed, adopted, reinvented, and incorporated European, American, and other African cultures into their own. In its extension of Njoku's thesis in *African Cultural Values: Igbo Political Leadership in Colonial Nigeria*, this book asserts that the dynamics of cultural change and adaptation highlight the question of identity as it is shaped and reshaped by a shared experience.[33]

Exploring the subject in chapter 13, "The Igbo Diaspora in the Atlantic World: African Origins and New World Formations," Chima J. Korieh explains Igbo identity in the Igbo Diaspora in terms of their Old and New World cultures. Prospectively, Korieh addresses common misconceptions and stereotypes associated with the Igbo and the cultural baggage they brought to the Americas. The chapter emphasizes the fruitfulness of understanding of what Paul Lovejoy and David Trotman have identified as the "interconnectedness of the histories of Africa and the colonial sites where Africans and their descendants lived on the other side of the Atlantic."[34] Korieh's essay, like Thornton's and others' in this volume, found the biography of Olaudah Equiano, published in 1789, to be a useful and perhaps authentic source of information on eighteenth-century Igboland.

However, scholars are beginning to question not only the reliability of Equiano's account but also his true ethnic identity. In chapter 14, "Olaudah Equiano and the Forging of an Igbo Identity," Vincent Carretta introduces one of the most contentious doubts about Equiano's claims to Igbo ancestry and identity. While many might disagree, Carretta argues that acts of appropriation and the combination of sources, imagination, and memory characterize the account Gustavus Vassa or Olaudah Equiano gives us about Africa. Carretta concedes, with some reservations, that evidence suggesting Gustavus Vassa invented the African birth of Olaudah Equiano is inconclusive but insists that a compelling circumstantial case for self-invention can be made. Such a case would be based on what we now know about the evolution of Equiano's claim to an African identity, the timing and context of the publication of his autobiography, his manipulation of dates, his reliance on secondary sources, and his rhetorical shaping of an African past. Carretta accepts that the opening chapters of Equiano's *The Interesting Narrative* remain a classic example of cultural memory, if not history.[35] However, Carretta bravely charges that whether or not he was born an Igbo in Africa, Olaudah Equiano recreated himself as the spokesman for a nation not yet born on a continent still largely unknown during the eighteenth century. In Carretta's view, Equiano anticipated by more than a century the Igbo nationalist and pan-African movements of the twentieth century. He did so to supply the abolitionist cause with the much-needed African voice that Thomas Clarkson wanted—of someone who had "really been there." If the suspicions of Carretta are found to be true, Igbo studies will experience a remarkable, violent somersault, if not a tsunami. This is in realization that much of the existing scholarship on the Igbo is based on Equiano's autobiographical account. A good example is the recent volume edited by Gloria Chuku, which eloquently defended and extolled Equiano's book with a chapter entitled "Olaudah Equiano and the Foundation of Igbo Intellectual Tradition."[36] As the father of the Igbo national identity, Equiano may have earned Afigbo's description of him as "an Igbo man to the marrow."[37] He just may have never actually been in Africa.

In chapter 15, "Olaudah Equiano or Gustavus Vassa: What's in a Name?" Paul E. Lovejoy strongly counters Carretta's assertions that Equiano might have forged his Igbo identity. Employing a diversity of evidence, Lovejoy contends that Equiano was clearly Igbo, born in Essaka or Elese, which is part of Igboland. To buttress his position, for example, Lovejoy cites the evidence of a German ethnographer, Johann Friedrich Blumenbach, who personally met Equiano in London in 1792 and had no little doubt about his African origins. In light of this, Lovejoy asserts that the motive for the dispute over Equiano's birth has more to do with the present clash between literary scholarship and historical interpretation. Thus he warns that the peril in confusing names can lead to misinterpretations and misrepresentations of the past. The controversy over Equiano's Igbo identity will persist until new evidence materializes to tip the pendulum argument to either Carretta's or Lovejoy's position.

If Equiano's Igbo identity is in doubt today, there seems to be less controversy surrounding his fellow traveler and Igbo former slave Aniaso, better known as Archibald Monteith. As Maureen Warner-Lewis clarifies in chapter 16, "Archibald Monteath: Imperial Pawn and Individual Agent," Archibald's identity both contrasts with and complements Carretta's findings.[38] Warner-Lewis shows that Aniaso (a.k.a. Archibald) was actually born in Africa, as acknowledged by the church that designated his burial place alongside a row of spots exclusively reserved for European missionaries and bearing a similar engraving to theirs. It reads: "Archibald Monteith, born in Africa 1800, died July 3 1864."[39] Eschewing the tabula rasa thesis by emphasizing this identity, Warner-Lewis further notes that by the time Aniaso left Igboland, there is every indication that he had developed enough Igbo language skills to have understood the meaning of his name as well as the role of the adult male in Nri culture. He would have absorbed some knowledge of this from adopted Igbo kinsmen in Jamaica.[40] In connection with identity, it is important to note that Aniaso did not hesitate to appropriate symbols of elitism in his host environment to reconstruct his identity, which produced the persona he desired in "Archibald Monteith."

In chapter 17, "Igbo Influences on Masquerading and Drum-Dances in the Caribbean," Robert W. Nicholls prospectively explores the role of material culture and diffusion in the development of Caribbean music and masquerading traditions. Nicholls's essay is captivating because it sheds light on the possible antecedents in West Africa and Western Europe. The term "Afro-Creole," however, recognizes that within the West Indies, people of African descent have been in the majority—a corroboration of findings of similar studies that have explored Igbo masks and masquerades in the African Diaspora.[41] In other words, in the British West Indies, the Afro-Creole prototype of masquerading, like the Creole dialect, emerged at the outset of the plantation economy. Masquerading was recorded by Hans Sloane in Jamaica in the 1680s and probably extends back to the beginning of slavery in Barbados, St. Kitts-Nevis, Antigua, and Montserrat, from whence the early Jamaican planters and slaves migrated.[42] Nicholls's essay demonstrates a quintessential attempt by the Igbo/African elements in the Caribbean to reinvent, although with varied success, an aspect of their inherited culture in the African Diaspora. The particular shape that masquerading assumed in the Caribbean was a function of the sociopolitical and economic climate of the host society.

In Africa, masquerade societies served as an important arm of government, particularly in those places where an elaborate and centralized system of political organization failed to develop. In these areas, including the Igbo, Efik, and Ibibio lands, the affairs of the masquerade societies, which included judicial functions and security services, were conducted with specific secret words and languages. This assertion corroborates Victor Manfredi's findings in "Philological Perspectives on the Southeastern Nigerian Diaspora," which deployed a wide-ranging Igbo syntax, including those connected with masquerading, to provide an engaging discussion on how the Igbo language developed and impacted several aspects of everyday life in the African Diaspora. The narrative shows that some of these lexicons, in their distorted forms, found their ways to the Caribbean and became cornerstones of carnivals and public theaters. As Manfredi preliminarily concludes, there is enough evidence "to believe that existing patterns of linguistic Africanisms in the Americas—as well as of diaspora consciousness—depend, as a historical matter, less on raw demography than widely believed, and more on existing political institutions." Manfredi goes on to assert that "the share of the observed outcomes is due to the intervening factor of E-Language transmission—especially to the institutionalized uses of ritual *lingua franca* in diaspora."[43]

The last four chapters of this book show that cultural transfer obeys the law of dualism—meaning that it is a two-way affair. As the Africans in Diaspora injected elements of their inherited culture in their host societies, so did the European presence in Africa exert enormous life-altering influence on the Africans. In chapter 18, "The Afro-Caribbean Diaspora in Reverse and Its Implications for the Development of Christianity and Education in Igboland, Southeastern Nigeria, 1895–1925," Waibinte E. Wariboko explores the crosscurrents of cultural forces that have contributed in significant ways to transforming the Igbo/African sociopolitical and economic tapestry. This chapter is about the Afro-Caribbean missionaries, one of the most critical catalysts of change in the Igbo society in particular and Africa in general. Unfortunately, their efforts have either been ignored or given very superficial references by scholars interested in reconstructing Igbo responses to Christianity and education. Driven by a sense of race-belonging, these missionaries strived to contribute to the ongoing process of culture change in Igboland under the auspices of the Church Missionary Society (CMS) Niger Mission, the group that, more than any other African group, enthusiastically responded to the back-to-Africa campaign, which commenced in the abolitionist period (with doubts on the part of the liberated slaves) but gained legitimacy and popularity in the 1930s under the advocacy of the esteemed Pan-Africanist, Marcus Mosiah Garvey.[44]

As the new religion permeated the African society, it joined forces with the continuing ravages of slavery and the colonial order that followed to alter social relations and sovereign nationhood in the Nigerian geopolitical areas. In chapter 19, "The Making of Igbo Ethnicity in the Nigerian Setting: Colonialism, Identity, and the Politics of Difference," Raphael Chijioke Njoku examines how the influx of the new trends led to the emergence of a new Igbo identity and how this led to the evolution of exclusionary politics under colonial rule, engendering a conflictual pattern of ethnic structures and violence in postcolonial Nigeria. The politics of exclusion began with the establishment of British colonial rule and the introduction of Western education in the early twentieth century. Among other things, Western education led to the rise of a new class of lettered elite who were exposed to the attractions of neopolitical and neocapitalist systems. The "new world order," established on fault lines of domination and exploitation, pitched the Igbo elite against their neighbors in a heated struggle for access to power and pursuit of economic self-interests. The educated Igbo leaders, like their peers elsewhere in Africa, found writing and political speeches instrumental for mass mobilization and survival in the new sociopolitical milieu that Richard A. Joseph has branded "Prebendal."[45] The result was a gradation of a pattern of conflict at both the regional and national levels, which robbed the precolonial patterns of intergroup relations of its more benevolent aura of innocence. Soon after independence in 1960, interelite struggles for power and privileges coalesced to produce the Nigerian Civil War (1967–1970). Since the end of the war, the place of the Igbo in the Nigerian federation has remained a debate that elucidates fear, bitterness, ethnonationalism, and violence.[46] For most well-meaning Nigerians, the "Igbo problem" must be duly addressed for the nation to move forward.

The intrusion of Western institutions and ways of life further intersected with Igbo art as an expression of ethnic identity. Thus, in chapter 20, "Ethnicity and the Contemporary Igbo Artist: Shifting Igbo Identities in the Post–Civil War Nigerian Art World," Sylvester Okwunodu Ogbechie continues to explore the changing patterns of Igbo identity since 1970 from the perspective of artistic traditions. The primary focus on the implications of adopting ethnicity as a mode of defining contemporary practice in Nigerian art was on the Nsukka school of African art, which the eminent Africanist Simon Ottenberg has described as a loosely affiliated group that has demonstrated the rich and sensitive visage of creativity under the fast-changing African landscape.[47] Like Njoku's essay, Ogbechie's evaluates the historical origins of Igbo identity and its intersection with contemporary politics in the Nigerian civil war and then investigates the ideological nature of such notions of identity within the spaces of practice of specific contemporary Nigerian artists of Igbo (and non-Igbo) origin. By postulating a shift in Igbo identity in post–civil war Nigeria, certain assumptions already circumscribe the boundaries of this analysis. The first assumption deals with the historical question of the nature of Igbo identity within the political entity defined as Nigeria. This entity was formulated by British colonial intervention into the structure of specific indigenous social, political, and cultural entities imbued by fiat with political authority, with origins that are embedded in European paradigms of the nation state. The second assumption concerns the notion of a shifting Igbo identity, which implies a normative space/process of Igbo ethnic identification grounded in biological or social processes of which a deviation in contemporary aesthetic practices becomes identifiable and against which it can be measured and compared. The third assumption concerns the spatiotemporal concept of a "post–civil war Nigeria" and the history of specific interaction between the Igbo and other ethnic constituents of the Nigerian polity. This history exhibits enough cultural and psychological structure to affect the articulation of Igbo ethnic identity and the material culture/production of contemporary Igbo artists.

Finally, in chapter 21, "ỌSỌNDU: Patterns of the Igbo Quest for Jesus Power," Ogbu U. Kalu explores five discourses that explain the direction the quest for spiritual power has assumed in the Igbo/Nigerian context: ecological/culturalist, imaginative/intellectualist, historical, instrumentalist, and religious embedded in the term "Ọsọndu," or literally "the race of life." The Igbo understand the art of living or the passage through life as a long journey that at death will be continued through the ancestral world. To protect, sustain, and enhance the quality of the journey through the human world, individuals and communities literally run to powerful sources to garner the resources for long life with dignity (*nka na nzere*). Since this is a preoccupying endeavor, life itself is often imagined as a long-distance race, a pursuit that involves perseverance, struggle, and a quest for the power and resources that ensure sustainability for a person or community. This is Ọsọndu—a derivative of two words: Ọsọ (race) and *ndu* (life)—which, when combined, stands for "the race of life." Underneath lurks a precarious vision of the human world infested by evil forces that thwart the cherished goal of a prosperous life.

Overall, *Igbo in the Atlantic World*, in its interdisciplinary and wide geographical coverage, touches on varied parts of the mainstream scholarship on African Diaspora studies, slavery and slave studies, and cultural inventions across different settings as well as race, ethnicity, and identity formation on both sides of the Atlantic. It uses a multidimensional treatment of the Igbo experience in the era of the trans-Atlantic slave trade to deepen understanding of the complex roles the Igbo people played in both the internal and external trade and how this fostered new sociocultural and political horizons in both their Old World homeland and the New World destinations.[48]

NOTES

1. The Bight of Biafra roughly embraced the territories from the Lower Guinea region of the River Delta, stretching from the River Nun on the Niger Delta in the west to Cape Lopez in the south.

2. Linda M. Haywood, ed., *Central Africans and Cultural Transformations in the American Diaspora* (Cambridge: Cambridge University Press, 2002); and Toyin Falola and Matt D. Childs, eds., *The Yoruba Diaspora in the Atlantic World* (Bloomington: Indiana University Press, 2005).

3. See John Thornton, *Africa and Africans in the Making of the Atlantic World, 1400–1680* (Cambridge: Cambridge University Press, 1972).

4. Melville Herskovits, *The Myth of the Negro Past* (New York: Harper and Brothers, 1941).

5. Ivan Van Sertima, *They Came Before Columbus* (New York: Random House, 1976).

6. Michael L. Conniff and Thomas J. Davis pioneered African and African Diaspora studies with *Africans in the Americas: A History of the Black Diaspora* (New York: St. Martin's Press, 1994); Michael A. Gomez, ed., *Diasporic Africa* (New York: New York University Press, 2006).

7. G. Ugo Nwokeji, *The Slave Trade and Culture in the Bight of Biafra: An African Society in the Atlantic World* (Cambridge: Cambridge University Press, 2010).

8. William R. Bascom, *Sixteen Cowries: Yoruba Divination from Africa to the New World* (Bloomington: Indiana University Press, 1980).

9. See Chinua Achebe, *Things Fall Apart* (London: Heinemann, 1956); *Arrow of God* (London: Heinemann, 1960); and *No Longer at Ease* (London: Heinemann, 1962). Through his trilogy, Achebe has adequately provided insightful documentation of the Igbo culture and customs.

10. For example, see Femi J. Kolapo, "The Igbo and their Neighbours during the Era of the Atlantic Slave-Trade," *Slavery and Abolition* 25, no. 1 (2004): 114–33; and Douglas B. Chambers, *The Igbo Diaspora in the Era of the Slave Trade* (Glassboro, NJ: Goldline and Jacobs, 2014).

11. See, for instance, Marvin A. Lewis, *Ethnicity and Identity in Contemporary Afro-Venezuelan Literature: A Culturalist Approach* (Colombia: University of Missouri Press, 1992), which focused analysis on four contemporary writers. See also Jane G. Landers, ed., *Against the Odds: Free Blacks in the Free Societies of the Americas* (London: Frank Cass, 1996).

12. See Lorena S. Walsh, *From Calabar to Carter's Grove: The History of a Virginia Slave Community* (Charlottesville: University Press of Virginia, 1997), chap. 2; David Northrup, "Igbo and Myth Igbo: Culture and Ethnicity in the Atlantic World, 1600–1850," *Slavery and Abolition* 21, no. 3 (2000): 1–20. Femi J. Kolapo, "The Igbo and their Neighbours during the Era of the Atlantic Slave-Trade," *Slavery and Abolition* 25, no. 1 (2004): 114–33.

13. Stephen E. Cornell and Douglas Hartmann, *Ethnicity and Race: Making Identities in a Changing World* (Oaks, CA: Pine Forge Press, 2006).

14. Philip D. Curtin, *The Atlantic Slave Trade: A Census* (Madison: University of Wisconsin Press, 1969). For other studies, see, for instance, Philip D. Morgan, "The Cultural Implications of the Atlantic Slave Trade: African Regional Origins, American Destinations, and New World Developments," *Slavery and Abolition* 18, no. 1 (1997): 122–42; David Geggus, "Sex Ratio, Age and Ethnicity in the Atlantic Slave Trade: Data from French Shipping and Plantation Records," *Journal of African History* 30, no. 1 (1989): 23–44; and David Eltis, Stephen D. Behrendt, David Richardson, and Herbert S. Klein, eds., *The Trans-Atlantic Slave Trade: A Database on CD-ROM* (Cambridge: Cambridge University Press, 1999).

15. Victor C. Uchendu, "Slaves and Slavery in Igboland, Nigeria," in *Slavery in Africa: Historical and Anthropological Perspectives*, eds. Suzanne Miers and Igor Kopytoff (Madison: University of Wisconsin Press, 1977), 131.

16. Kenneth Onwuka Dike, *Trade and Politics in the Niger Delta, 1830–1885: An Introduction to the Economic and Political History of Nigeria* (Oxford: Clarendon Press, 1956), 30, 38.

17. John Adams, *Remarks on the Country Extending from Cape Palmas to the River Congo, Including Observations on the Manners and Customs of the Inhabitants. With an Appendix Containing an Account of the European Trade with the West Coast of Africa* (London: G. & W. B. Whittaker, 1823), 116, 129. Douglas B. Chambers, "'My own Nation': Igbo Exiles in the Diaspora," *Slavery and Abolition* 18, no. 1 (1997): 73–77.

18. David Northrup, *Trade without Rulers: Pre-Colonial Economic Development in South Eastern Nigeria* (Oxford: Clarendon Press, 1978), 58–65.

19. Colin A. Palmer, *The First Passage: Blacks in Americas, 1520–1617* (New York: Oxford University Press, 1995).

20. David Northrup, "Becoming African: Identity Formation Among Liberated Slaves in Nineteenth-Century Sierra Leone," *Slavery and Abolition* 27, no. 1 (2006): 1–21.

21. Linda M. Haywood, introduction to *Central Africans and Cultural Transformations in American Diaspora*, ed. Linda M. Heywood (Cambridge: Cambridge University Press, 2002),

13; Sydney W. Mintz and Richard Price, *The Birth of African-American Culture* (Boston: Beacon Press, 1992), viii.

22. John Locke, *An Essay Concerning Human Understanding*, ed. Peter H. Niddich (London: Oxford University Press, 1979).

23. Michel Foucault, "Nietzsche, Genealogy, History," in *Essential Works of Foucault, Vol. 2: Aesthetics, Method & Epistemology*, ed. James D. Faubion (London: Penguin, 1998), 369–92.

24. See Thomas Hoobler, *Toussaint L'Ouverture* (New York: Chelsea House, 1990); and C. L. R. James, *The Black Jacobins: Toussaint L'Ouverture and the San Domingo Revolution* (New York: Vintage Books, 1963).

25. See Patrick Bellegarde-Smith, ed., *Fragments of Bone: Neo-African Religions in a New World* (Urbana: University of Illinois Press, 2005); and George Brandon, *Santeria from Africa to the New World: The Dead Sell Memories* (Bloomington: Indiana University Press, 1993).

26. See A. E. Afigbo, "The Eclipse of the Aro Slaving Oligarchy 1901–1927," *Journal of the Historical Society of Nigeria* 6, no. 1 (1971): 3–23.

27. Nwokeji, *The Slave Trade and Culture in the Bight of Biafra*, i, xviii, 10, 19.

28. A. E. Afigbo, "Igbo Cultural Sub-Areas: Their Rise and Development," in *Groundwork of Igbo History*, ed. A. E. Afigbo (Lagos: Vista Books, 1992), chap. 7.

29. Audra Diptee, "African Children in the British Slave Trade During the Late Eighteenth Century," *Slavery and Abolition* 27, no. 2 (2006): 183–96.

30. See Christopher Fyfe, *Africanus Horton: 1830–1883: West African Scientist and Patriot* (London: Ashgate, 1993).

31. Gwendolyn Midlo Hall, "Africa and Africans in the African Diaspora: The Uses of Relational Databases," *American Historical Review* 115, no. 1 (2010): 136–50.

32. For Aro role in the slave trade, which substantially contributed to the collapse of the region's moral economy, see Nwokeji, *The Slave Trade and Culture in the Bight of Biafra*, chap. 1.

33. For an engaging exposition on this, see Raphael Chijioke Njoku, *African Cultural Values: Igbo Political Leadership in Colonial Nigeria, 1900–1966* (New York: Routledge, 2006), chap. 2.

34. Paul E. Lovejoy and David V. Trotman, "Introduction: Ethnicity and the African Diaspora," in *Trans-Atlantic Dimensions of Ethnicity in the African Diaspora*, ed. Paul E. Lovejoy and David V. Trotman (London: Continuum, 2003).

35. Pierre Nora, "Between Memory and History: *Les Lieux de Mémoire*," *Representations* 26 (1989): 7–25; Ralph A. Austen, "The Slave Trade as History and Memory: Confrontations of Slaving Voyage Documents and Communal Traditions," *William and Mary Quarterly* (2001): 229–44.

36. Gloria Chuku, "Olaudah Equiano and the Foundation of Igbo Intellectual Tradition," in *The Igbo Intellectual Tradition: Creative Conflict in African and African Diaspora Thought*, ed. Gloria Chuku (New York: Palgrave Macmillan, 2013), 33–66.

37. Chuku, "Olaudah Equiano and the Foundation of Igbo Intellectual Tradition," 35.

38. See Maureen Warner-Lewis, *Archibald Monteath: Igbo, Jamaican, Moravian* (Kingston, JM: University of the West Indies Press, 2007), 9–10.

39. This is as found in the church's memoir, "Monteith." Archibald, however, spelled his name in the manner in which his master John and his immediate ancestors spelled theirs.

40. The Igbo youth in the Caribbean may have been schooled in the art of peace negotiation between communities, ritual observances, the conferment of the *ọzọ* title, elements of religious observances such as taboos, the promotion of fertility, etc. See M. Angulu Onuwuejeogwu, *The Social Anthropology of Africa: An Introduction* (London: Heinemann, 1975), 44–46.

41. See, for instance, Raphael Chijioke Njoku, "Symbols and Meanings of Igbo Masquerades and Carnivals of the Black Diaspora," in Toyin Falola, Niyi Afolabi, and Aderonke A. Adesanya, eds., *Migrations and Creative Expressions in Africa and the African Diaspora* (Durham, NC: Carolina Academic Press, 2008), 257–78.

42. See Hans Sloane, *A Voyage to the Islands of Madera, Barbados, and Jamaica*, vol. 1 (London: B. M., 1707), 46–48.

43. Victor Manfredi, "Philological Perspectives on the Southeastern Nigerian Diaspora," *Contours: A Journal of the African Diaspora* 2, no. 2 (2004): 264.

44. Ivor Morrish, *Obeah, Christ, and Rastaman: Jamaica and Its Religion* (Cambridge: James Clark, 1982), 11.

45. Richard A. Joseph, *Democracy and Prebendalism in Nigerian Politics* (Cambridge: Cambridge University Press, 1987).

46. A good example of these forms of reaction is the national/international response that followed the publication of Chinua Achebe's recent memoir, *There Was a Country: A Personal History of Biafra* (London: Penguin, 2012).

47. Simon Ottenberg, ed., *The Nsukka Artists and Nigerian Contemporary Art* (Washington, DC: The Smithsonian National Museum of African Art, 2002).

48. See, for instance, Raphael Chijioke Njoku, "Igbo Slaves and the Transformation of the Niger Delta," in *Aftermath of Slavery: Transitions and Transformations in Southeastern Nigeria*, eds. Chima Korieh and Femi Kolapo (Trenton, NJ: African World Press, 2007), 70–99.

PART I

IGBO INSTITUTIONS AND CUSTOMS AS BASELINE

2 THE KINGLESS PEOPLE

THE SPEECH ACT AS SHIELD AND SWORD

Hannah Chukwu

> The ability to name oneself or one's group in the context of one's culture and experience is essential for psychological, spiritual, and physical empowerment.
>
> —HANNAH CHUKWU

> Igboland "is really quite a small portion of Nigeria . . . but it has been the most troublesome section of any."
>
> —BRITISH SOLDIER BEFORE A LONDON AUDIENCE AS QUOTED IN ELIZABETH ISICHEI

Igbo people recognize the dignity and potency in speech and demonstrate the defense and combat strategies imbued in it. Describing themselves as kingless people from their saying, *Igbo enwe eze* (Igbo has no king), they paradoxically demonstrate true democracy and organization, not represented by an exclusive authority but transcending geographical borders. Speech, being an utterance considered an action, particularly with regard to its intention, purpose, or effect, elucidates the force that drives and moderates life among the Igbos. The common saying, *Igbo enwe eze*, was originally used to differentiate between the different groups, but now the saying has come to describe the political and cultural values of the Igbos that "commemorate collective history and consolidate group identity."[1] The saying also implies that the absence of an exclusive king demonstrates the inalienable and exercisable power of choice among Igbo people and directs attention to the prevalent leadership qualities among the Igbos. Both in their resolved and prolonged resistance to colonial power and survival in the so-called New World, the saying has become a proverb that conceptualizes their values and identity as a people.

Kingship among the Igbos is not isolated and privileged to a few; rather it is open, participatory, and communal. In this chapter, "kingless" does not imply an absolute absence of the concept of kingship among the Igbos; rather, it implies a leadership that is unequivocally of the people, by the people, and for the people. Richard N. Henderson, in his book relevantly titled *The King in Every Man*, writes about an Igbo Society, Onitsha, describing them thus:

> Mostly endogamy even up until now. . . . Pre-colonial Onitsha was a distinctive variant of Ibo social system . . . retain[ing] the character of the autonomous, acephalous village-group communities so typical of its Ibo neighbours. This inchoate village-group kingdom had some remarkable characteristics, for it combined diversely organized associations with highly segmented descent groups, and it contained not just one king but a number of them, related to one another in a complex and ambiguous manner. . . . This kind of socio-political organization combine characteristics of tribal social systems with certain features of the eastern Mediterranean city-states of classical antiquity, societies that in a crucial developmental sense were ancestral to modern social systems.[2]

Having multiple kings instead of an exclusive king and yet possessing a perfectly organized and structured society shows that most Igbo communities have the quality of constituting a complex unity. People's daily life is not guided with numerous promulgated laws but mostly by customs, taboos, conscience, and honor. Judith Van Allen in "'Sitting on a Man': Colonialism and the Lost Political Institutions of Igbo Women" describes the Igbo political system as "diffuse authority, fluid and informal leadership, shared rights of enforcement [. . . different from] 'native administration' derived from colonial experience with chiefs and emirs in northern Nigeria."[3] Kwame Anthony Appiah in *In My Father's House: Africa in the Philosophy of Culture* submits that "no one who knows these places could deny—that there are plenty of room in Africa . . . for all sorts and conditions of men and women; that at each level, Africa is various."[4] Igboland could support every condition of men and women even without an exclusive human source of authority. In the midst of multiplicity of rights and authorities, order is achieved.

This chapter examines the act of speech in terms of sayings or proverbs, storytelling that is made manifest through festivals, and songs. Using these paradigms, the act of speech will be explored to show how it functions as a shield and a sword among the Igbos who have used it to preserve, re-create, resist oppression, and determine their survival in their homeland and in the New World. The proverb, *onye kwe chi ya ekwe*, which means that your attitude toward your destiny transcends even a sealed fate, shows that among the Igbos there are freedom and opportunities for progress and negotiation available to everyone. Other proverbs, such as "A child who washes his or her hands clean deserves to eat with his or her elders" and "No one knows the womb that bears the chief," show that age, birth, or royalty is not an advantage but that excellence can be achieved by anyone. Victor Uchendu in *The Igbo of Southeast Nigeria* observes that "The Igbo saying 'everyone is a chief in his hut' must be understood in its proper context. What is meant is that a dictatorial leader of the Igbo is inconceivable. A leader may be a dictator if he likes, but his leadership must be restricted to his household."[5] As Simon Ottenberg in *Igbo: Religion, Social Life and Other Essays* observes, "While seniority in age is an asset in secular leadership, personal qualities are also important. A secular leader must be aggressive, skilled in oratory, and able to cite past history and precedent."[6] To be able to rise to the level of leadership, great care is taken by the aspirant to learn the culture and to be articulate and also to identify completely with the people; otherwise, such leadership will be disregarded. The Igbos have a concept of kingship that is peculiar to them and sets them apart as literally kingless in comparison to other people.

The Igbo form of leadership is purely traditional yet it is more complex and richer than and superior to modern-day democracy. Further describing the Igbo political institution, Elizabeth Isichei writes:

> Democracy, as it exists today in the Western world, is full of limitations. . . . The average citizen has effectively no power to alter the network of regulations that govern his life. One of the things that struck the first Western visitors to Igboland, [*sic*] was the extent to which democracy was truly practised. An early visitor to a Niger Igbo town said that he felt he was in a free land, among a free people. Another visitor, a Frenchman, said that true liberty existed in Igboland though its name was not inscribed on any monument. Igbo political institutions were designed to combine popular participation with weighting for experience and ability.[7]

The political institutions of the Igbos provide room for individual growth and advancement; nevertheless, the intrusion of the British into the society through slavery and colonialism disorganized them by corrupting their values and destroying their traditional democracy. The Igbos succumbed to slave trade probably because they are a dynamic group with an instinctive flair for commerce, talent for creativity, and a tendency toward materialism. Igbo people's love for materialism is still obvious today, as Dulue Mbachu concurs in "Oil Inflames Nigerian Region Again": "Today, Igbos remain the dominant force in Nigerian commerce, and their prosperity is evident in the new homes in their southern lands which look more well-off than elsewhere in Nigeria."[8]

Despite the Igbo people's dignity and respect for individual rights, slavery thrived among them but not to the extent of Western chattel slavery. Initially, the community sold incorrigible rogues into slavery to help purge the society of miscreants. However, with the desire to acquire Western goods, some collaborators sabotaged their communities and became slave dealers. According to Isichei, "The available evidence all point to one conclusion—that the most important source of slaves was kidnapping and the second most important, war."[9] Further on, Isichei, quoting Captain Adams, writes that within a twenty-year period 370,000 Igbos were sold into slavery.[10] Slavery distorted the values of the Igbo nation, corrupted her people, and made her lose the cream of the society. In spite of the havoc of slavery, their resistance to the British government nearly decimated them because they were resolved to fight the British since foreign domination is repulsive to them.

The engendering of colonization was that, after the abolishment of slavery, the British government diverted its attention to colonialism as another lucrative means that would boost its economy even more than slavery did.[11] Under the cloak of civilization, it embarked upon the program of colonization. The so-called civilization brought by the British in their colonization program for the African nations, in particular Igbo nation, is obviously an extension of savagery and exploitation. Isichei describes colonialism as a "violent phenomenon. It was imposed by violence, and maintained by its potential capacity for violence."[12] An autocratic leader among the Igbos is resented just as a ruling dynasty; much more abominable to them would be a violent foreign domination. Most books written about slavery and colonialism attest that of all the different nations that make up Nigeria as we know it today, it is the Igbo people that were the hardest for the British to conquer. Isichei writes:

> No Nigerian people resisted colonialism more tenaciously than the Igbo. The great Emirates of the north, once conquered, supported the British, with the minor exception of the Satiru rising. The conquest of Igboland took over twenty years of constant military action. What is unquestionable is that the Igbo resisted colonialism, not for months, but for decades, with courage and tenacity of purpose which were undeterred by disaster, and by extraordinary inequality in arms and resources of the adversaries. . . . In 1909, ten years of conflict still lay before the British invaders of Igboland.[13]

Uchendu concurs with that assertion, writing, "Between 1902, when the Aro 'Long Juju' was destroyed, and 1914, when Northern and Southern Nigeria were amalgamated, there were twenty-one British military expeditions into the Igboland. It was not until 1928, when Igbo men were made to pay tax for the first time in their history, that it became clear to them that they were a subject people."[14] Allen further corroborates the resistance of the Igbos by writing, "Southern Nigeria was declared a protectorate in 1900, but it was ten years before the conquest was effective."[15] Don C. Ohadike in *The Ekumeku Movement* asserts that the imperialistic design of the British policy makers "was resisted by the various ethnic groups of Nigeria, the most determined being those organized by the Igbo people."[16] The resistance lasted for over fifty years, according to Ohadike; however, the Igbos were eventually subdued. Nevertheless, Ohadike writes, "Although they were defeated, their descendants still recall with pride that their forebears were brave warriors who resisted British imperialism longer and more stubbornly than most other Nigeria communities."[17] Quoting Julius Nyerere of Tanzania in his description of resistance to colonialism put up by African nations, Ohadike claims that according to Nyerere, the "great rebellion [was] not through fear of a terrorist movement or a superstitious oath, but in response to a natural call, a call of the spirit, ringing in the hearts of all men, and of all times, educated or uneducated, to rebel against foreign domination."[18] The Igbo people's perception of themselves as demonstrated in their speech that embodies their identity is such that they are very different from other nations amalgamated as Nigeria, and that their resistance rises within them as an irresistible force compelling them to resist as long as they can rather than to accept domination easily. They resisted everything including taxation because the goal of taxation was not clear and it was also a further reminder of their subjugation.

The final wars that conquered Igboland, according to Isichei, "were fought primarily by Africans—'imperialism makes its victims its defenders.' The British could not have ruled Igboland in any other way."[19] Ohadike refers to collaborators as indigenous people who assist the British in furthering their goal of colonialism.[20] The British might not have been able to subjugate the people politically if not for the indigenous collaborators and the establishment of an exclusive form of government. For instance, according to Ohadike, after six weeks of severe battle in 1898 between the Otu Ochichi and the soldiers of the Royal Niger Company, "Lieutenant Festing imposed a forced peace on Igbuzo. One of the terms for the peace is 'One king with a council of twelve would be appointed and be responsible to the government, instead of two hundred chiefs then reigning.'"[21] It may seem impossible that two hundred chiefs with equal status will be reigning in a single town peacefully; nevertheless, that is the pattern of the Igbo form of government. It is not only in the death toll as a result of war but also in the direct and forceful removal of the leaders of the people through deceit that helped the British subjugate the people and to destroy Igbo institutions of government. The experience of one Igbo community, Uga, illustrates this point by showing speech in terms of sayings and an annual celebration that tells the story about this community's encounter with the British colonial government.

Uga is a town in Aguata Local Government Area of Anambra state, southeastern Nigeria. It is 640 km east of Lagos and 48 km from Onitsha. "Aguata," as the local government is called, means literally "that which a leopard cannot destroy." They share boundaries with some towns in Imo State. Uga was the name of the first man who with his wife, Ogerioma, settled in the area now known as Uga. They had four sons: Umueze the oldest, followed by Oka, then Umuoru, and the youngest is Awarasi. The names of the children are the names of the main villages of the town. Each village comprises of at least five clans. To show how closely they are related by blood, intermarriage among members of certain clans is still forbidden because of the near blood kinship tie that is still traceable to the fourth generation. There is pride and sense of belonging among Uga people because of their large expanse of land that is very fertile for agricultural purposes. They have many rivers and an acclaimed pure and natural source of drinking water, Obizi Spring Water, which supplies drinking water to Uga and its environs. A common first name among women born in Uga is "Ugadinma" (Uga is good), which typifies pride in the women and affirms their love for the land and desire to marry within the town.

According to the book, *Uga Crisis (1995–2005): The Efforts of U-44 at Resolving it*, Uga being one of the most populous towns in the local government area of more than four hundred thousand people "is inhabited by very hardworking, self reliant and upright people, who are very proud of their place of birth."[22] Their bitter encounter with the British government is a microcosm of the Igbo experience with the British. Their clash with the British colonial masters resulted in their twenty-six leaders being taken as captives through treachery. The British government resorted to deception to be able to disarm and subdue Uga people. Even though Uga people's resistance is not uncommon among other Igbo people, the role they played during the Nigerian civil war (1967–1970) marks them out for further examination in the issue of the Igbo world in the diaspora. According to Dulue Mbachu, "During the three-year secessionist war, in which an estimated 1 million people died and footage of starving children with swollen bellies filled the West's TV screens, Uga played an important role. It had an airstrip that helped sustain the rebellion with arms and supplies, flown in by whomever the Biafran leadership could hire for the perilous job."[23] They provided a formidable base for the Igbo soldiers who were fighting to secede from Nigeria because they found no identity among them and they detested the Nigerian domination. Uga demonstrated the concept of the Igbo in their detestation of an imposed rule and subjugation through the role they played during the secessionist war. Uga's concept of itself is in the saying, *Uga anahagba oso mmiri ma ozughu ha ahu* ("Uga do not run from the rain except it drenches them") holds true not only in the role they played during Nigerian civil war but also in their encounter with the British government. That perception of themselves in their saying demonstrates their audacity to resist as fearless warriors. Their philosophy about combat might be fatalistic but it shows that they confront domination until they determine their fate through their acts. Their dignity as a people is inbred in them, and their right to make choices is inalienable. Though in their resistance they lacked the technological sophistication of warfare, they were not inferior to their oppressors in terms of resoluteness and dauntlessness.

Further, they describe themselves as *Uga ntutuakwu ebe teghete*, which means that they are a hard-working and populous group of people. They pride themselves as leaders who are "not known for violence and murderous tendencies. [They are] magnanimous in victory. The story has it that in the distant past when Uga waged a war which inflicted heavy causalities on a neighboring town, she decided to compensate the town with liberal marriage contracts between [the town's] men and maidens from Uga."[24] The fact is that Igbo wars were fought differently because "deliberate efforts were made to keep the number of casualties as low as possible," according to Ohadike, but when that is not achieved, the losers are compensated after negotiations.[25] Therefore, Uga's magnanimity betrays the Igbo people's attitude toward warfare.

The missionaries decided to settle first in Uga because of its size and resources so that they could reach other smaller towns from there. Uga people resisted both the British and missionary presence violently through uprisings. Finally, the British government representative in charge of the area decided to invite the elders, leaders of the people, to a purported meeting to discuss their grievances and to negotiate an agreement. Twenty-six able-bodied men attended the meeting believing that it was to be an open and fair discussion and not a war. Those men were not seen again. They were taken as captives not in war but in deception since they agreed to lay down their weapons for the meeting. The news was devastating to the people and put them in a state of a dilemma because they were not sure whether further violence would release the captives or whether negotiation would achieve the desired result. Their self-esteem was badly shaken. All the efforts made to trace the whereabouts of these leaders yielded no fruit. The people became more alienated from the British colonial government; hence, the British government had to transfer their headquarters to another town for fear of retaliation. The annual remembrance of this event is commemorated in a festival known as "Obuofo Uga." The word, "Obuofo," according to Igbo tradition, means that the innocent will always go free; therefore, Uga people, by naming the festival so, are invoking nemesis upon the British. They believe that their leaders were innocent and that, though their captors had moved away, justice will still catch up with them.

The Uga people protest through "Obuofo Uga" festival is registered through the act of storytelling because it affords every Uga person the opportunity to learn the facts about Uga's encounter with the British. The yearly celebration of the festival provides an opportunity for the younger generation to understand the history, as the elders recount the facts of the encounter to ensure that the facts are indelibly imprinted on the people's hearts. The significance of stories enacted through events is that they keep the collective memory of the people alive and composed. For instance, Obioma Nnaemeka, quoting Achebe in *A World of Ideas*, says, "But you also have the storyteller who recounts the events—and this is one who survives, who outlives all the others. It is the storyteller, in fact, who makes us what we are, who creates history. The storyteller creates the memory that the survivors must have—otherwise their surviving would have no meaning."[26] Every Uga person by participating or witnessing the reenactment of the event is a storyteller, shaping the memory that Uga people should have so that their surviving and the heroic resistance of their forebears will continue to be reenacted.

Obuofo Uga festival is held annually every December 26 to coincide with the Christian Boxing Day. The Western Boxing Day began to be celebrated officially in England in the middle of the nineteenth century under the rule of Queen Victoria. It is a time when employers give gifts in boxes to their employees. However, among the Uga people the celebration is considered as a day streaked with sorrow but with hope. They are democratizing the Christian message by portraying themselves as God's chosen people who were being destroyed by the murderous and ambitious King Herod as represented by the British people. As noted by Finis Dake in *Dake's Annotated Reference Bible*, when Herod the Great, who was made the king of Judea in 37 BC, heard that there was a king (Jesus Christ) born, he decided to kill all males two years and under in the hope of destroying Jesus (1 N.T.). The Bible notes: "In Rama was there a voice heard, lamentation, and weeping, and great mourning, Rachel weeping for her children, and would not be comforted, because they are not" (Matt. 2: 18). "Obuofo Uga" annual festival is celebrated in the same spirit of mourning for the innocent and refusing to be comforted because they are no more. Appearing only once a year on December 26, twenty-six masquerades, corresponding to the number of the men that were taken away, emerge usually as discontented spirits or gods from the underworld in fierce anger and with much lamentation. Masquerades and people gather in the town square for a ceremony to remember those leaders who were abducted by the British colonial government and have never been seen again in Uga. Boxing Day is actually celebrated in Uga as a fight game and not just a gift-exchange day. Though connecting Herod's slaughter of infants (in his bid to stop Jesus from being the King) with the kidnapping of Uga's twenty-six elders may sound syncretic, the point is that rather than joy and peace attendant to the Christian good news, the British government inflicted loss and casualty on the people. According to Isichei, "The many deaths, the looted farms and livestock, the houses razed, the trees cut down, are adequately documented even in British records, and are remembered with poignant emphasis in the traditions of the Igbo community concerned. The people of Ameke in Item still annually observe the day, in 1916, of conflict with the British—'the blackest time of Item' when one of the four principal villages was turned into a desert."[27] They keep their collective memory alive so that their surviving will continue to have relevance throughout their generations.

Among the Uga people, Britain has become synonymous with deceit and manipulation. The same tactics of deception and lies that insidiously destroy a people, as demonstrated in Uga, is reminiscent of the British kind of diplomacy in other parts of southeastern Nigeria. For example, Isichei writes about King Ja Ja of Opobo, who was a well-established ruler of the sovereign state of Opobo from 1869 to 1887 and owned a trading empire. He was originally sold into slavery but obtained his freedom and wealth through hard work and shrewd business dealing so that he became a king in another southeastern community of not strictly-Igbo-speaking people. (His becoming a king after having been a slave differentiates the southeastern Nigeria form of slavery from that of American chattel slavery.) The acting Vice-Consul, Harry Johnston, made sure he overthrew him through deception. According to Isichei,

> Johnston invited Ja Ja on board the gun-boat *Goshawk* for a discussion of their differences, promising him a safe conduct: 'I have summoned you to attend in a friendly spirit. I hereby assure you that whether you accept or reject my proposals tomorrow, no restraint whatever will be put on you. You will be free to go as soon as you have heard the message of the Government. . . . If you attend tomorrow, I pledge you my word that you will be free to come and go.'[28]

"Solemn as this word may be," according to Isichei, "Ja Ja never returned to Opobo. . . . At Johnston's insistence, he was deported to the West Indies, like so many of his Igbo fellow-countrymen in the past."[29] The great evil about colonialism and slavery was that it concentrated on stealing or luring away the strong and leading group so that the people would have neither an established body of leaders nor available human resource persons to guide the people during this dark period of their history. It is also ridiculous that the act of speech among the British is at variance with that of the Igbos. Unlike the Igbo traditional society where solemn utterances are sacred and binding, the British colonial government has no culture of truth and integrity. Their speech is neither a shield nor a sword but empty without the substance of truth and integrity.

Uga people lost their leaders and that weakened them. Other leaders could have emerged, but since there was no answer as to what had happened to the other representatives, the people found no room for such an alternative arrangement. The rain indeed drenched them as they were inundated with a coordinated sabotage. The British government was able to establish a Warrant Chief whom the people resisted, but their resistance was weak since the rain had figuratively drenched them with the sudden disappearance of their elders.

Leaders from Uga were obviously among those Igbos deported to the New World. These Igbos continued to live and to act in the consciousness that foreign intrusion must always be resisted and, like Uga people's perception of themselves, they will often not surrender until they are no longer able to resist. Even though the resistance Uga people and the Igbo nation put up was eventually quelled, it is still significant that they dared to resist and refused to surrender in fear like some other Nigerian groups or people.[30] They continued to combat subjugation even in the New World. For instance, *The Penguin Book of Caribbean Verse in English*, anthologized by Paula Burnett, has a section on "Work-songs." The spirit of resistance is obvious in the work-song, "Song of the King of the Eboes": "Buckra in this country no make we free: / What Negro for to do? What Negro for to do? / Take force by force! Take force by force!"[31] Then the chorus says, "To be sure! To be sure! To be sure!" The name "Eboes" in this song is most likely a variant spelling of Igbos, and the message of resistance in the song is clear. Ohadike, quoting Frantz Fanon in *The Wretched of the Earth*, reiterates, "In Fanon's view, violence is a means of achieving freedom, a cleansing and unifying force, binding the oppressed together as a whole against the colonizer's violence."[32] Therefore, whether the people resisted their oppressors in their homeland or in the New World, their identity as lovers of true freedom and dignity as a people with the inherent right to make choices continues to manifest itself wherever they are. They are willing to employ force even in their captivity.

The Igbo slaves taken to the New World continued their act of resistance to servitude. They preferred death to slavery; hence, some of them starved, tried mutiny, or suicide. Paule Marshall in *Praise Song for the Widow* presents an account of the Igbos and their exploits in the New World when they arrived to Tatem, a place known as Ibo Landing in the novel. She explores the power of the mind, the spiritual being that defies all odds to achieve victory. The first weapon the captured Igbos employed upon arrival, according to the narrator, is calculated silence in the sense that this silence was not as a result of confusion but a perceptive and spirited silence. In order words, it means that in the New World, speech is not as sacred as in the native country; therefore, silence is the best response. She describes the silence of the Igbo slaves: "A good long look. Not saying a word. Just studying the place real good. Just taking their time and studying on it."[33] They are further described in terms that ascribe a degree of divinity to them because they possess a fourth-dimensional eye that sees beyond what ordinary people see. The Igbos on arrival were able to perceive the chattel slavery that they would be subjected to and they were deeply repulsed and walked out:

> And when they got through sizing up the place real good and seen what was to come, they turned . . . and looked at the white folks what brought 'em here. Took their time again and gived them the same long hard look. . . . And when they got through studying 'em, when they *knew* just from looking at 'em how those folks was gonna do. . . . They just turned . . . and walked on back down to the edge of the river here. Every las' man, woman and chile. . . . They just kept walking right on out over the river.[34]

The people staged their revolt and, though without a king, they were so organized that there was no dissenter among them, showing a unity of purpose that transcends physical authority. As the Igbos were walking back over the water to return to where they came from, they were singing. In the Igbo world view, the land of the living and the dead are not separated. Even if those Igbo slaves accidentally drowned, the belief system suggests that they will join their ancestors and will continue their life from there. An Igbo poet, Catherine Acholonu, in her collection *The Spring's Last Drop* examines in the poem "the message" the idea of death in Igbo tradition. In the poem, the poet celebrates death as life by emphasizing the perpetual quality of life in the traditional sense. In another poem, "life's head," she paradoxically ends the poem with the submission that "death is life" and should be accepted joyfully as a "blessing" received from God.[35] Christopher Okigbo, another black African (Igbo) poet, also describes such tendencies as "an attempt to reconcile the universal opposites of life and death in a live-die proposition: one is the other and either is both."[36] Whether the Igbo slaves who walked out on slavery on water died before reaching their homeland or were able to reach their homeland to continue their life means the same thing. In death a blessing attenuates its pain.

The slaves were not only walking back on water but they were also singing songs. The singing of songs by the Igbo slaves is another example of how the kingless people use lyrics as a shield and a sword. Singing songs is reminiscent of the resilient spirit of resistance, preservation of identity, and assertion of cultural values among the Igbos. Dennis Osadebey, an Igbo artist, quoted in Okumba Miruka, *Encounter with Oral Literature*, describes black people as a singing race who sing when happy or sad; in this particular case, singing was applied as a tool to rarefy the pain of chattel slavery and to keep hope alive.[37] Singing songs became the act of speech that shielded their soul from despondency and formed part of the tools that helped them fight slavery and to flee servitude figuratively. Commenting on the action taken by the Igbos when they landed at Tatem, Susan Rogers in "Embodying Cultural Memory in Paule Marshall's Praisesong for the Widow" comments, "The magnitude of their defiance is communicated in mythical terms of corporeal transcendence."[38] As for Cuney in the novel, Rogers states, "her faith amounts to a literal belief in the Ibos' story, the belief that it is possible to defy the body's limitations and, in so doing, to escape the bonds of enslavement. Cuney's grandmother, however, saw the legend as describing spiritual release."[39] The efficacy of the Ibo rebellion is that it can still act as a bulwark against the psychological assault on the personhood of a black person to the extent that as soon as Avey Johnson was able to believe the story she gained emotional strength, inspiration, and psychological cleansing to meet her physical and material needs at that time. Resistance stems from self-image and belief; therefore, the resistance put up by the Igbos demonstrates their perception of themselves as kings in their own rights and their perception of slavery and colonialism as unacceptable intrusions. It is in believing such an account that dignity and hope are maintained.

Further on, Isichei elaborates on the point about documented evidence of Igbo resistance in the diaspora by stating, "In the New World, the Igbo did not take kindly to servitude, and were unpopular among planters for this reason."[40] In all, they were part of the many heroic deeds of the slaves who won their freedom or fought for their freedom. Isichei succinctly states, "Doubtless, for instance, there were Igbos among the gallant slaves who won their freedom, and established the independent African Republic of Palmares in north-east Brazil, which kept its independence from 1605 to 1695, despite many attempts to conquer it" In summary, Isichei describes the resistance as the "triumphs of the human spirit against great odds,"[41] Parker J. Palmer, in "Teaching with Heart and Soul: Reflections on Spirituality in Teacher Education," refers to the power of the heart and soul in bringing about a change and sustaining a people during difficult times. He writes, "powerless people managed to ferment deep-reaching social change in so many parts of the globe . . . by drawing upon and deploying the only power that cannot be taken from us: the power of the human soul, the human spirit, the human heart. Far from being socially and politically regressive, 'heart and soul' language, rightly understood, is one of the most radical rhetoric we have."[42] The act of speech in sayings such as proverbs, events that tell stories, and songs embodies the potency of a "heart and soul" speech that was powerful to keep alive the resistant spirit among the slaves and to grasp the hope that sustains. The efficacy of the act of speech is still relevant among the Igbo people today, and its power is continually being harnessed.

The survival of black Africans in the New World bears on the power of the unseen—the act of speech based on the force of the spirit. The power of spoken words has always been potent because humans are made in God's image, and Igbo people recognize that. For instance, Jesus, in the Holy Bible, speaking to His disciples says, "The words that I speak unto you, they are spirit, and they are life" (Jn. 6:63b). Mary Stewart Van Leeuwen, Annelies Knoppers, Margaret Koch, Douglas Schuurman, and Helen Sterk affirm that "Naming and defining are two of the most powerful acts of human speech. When something is named, it takes on a fuller reality. It can be talked about. It has presence."[43] Igbo leadership is distinguished by the ability to articulate and communicate truth. The power to articulate is still highly valued, even among world leaders today as has always been among the Igbos. According to Allen:

> The main Igbo political institution seems to have been the village assembly, a gathering of all adults in the village who chose to attend. . . . [T]he leaders were people who had the ability to persuade. The mode of political discourse was that of proverb, parable and metaphor drawn from the body of Igbo tradition. . . . Influential speech was the creative and skilful use of tradition to assure others that a certain course of action was both a wise and right thing to do. . . . The leaders of Igbo society were men and women who combined wealth and generosity with 'mouth'—the ability to speak well.[44]

Allen's observation is similar to what Afua Cooper in *Utterances and Incantations* refers to as the power of spoken word: she describes the foremothers of Dub poetry by claiming that they all "work in the realm of the word."[45] She mentioned different spheres, such as folk culture, religion, and metaphysics, where values are passed on and the community is strengthened; she asserts, "These jobs required one to have an intimate relationship with the word, for a correct and crucial use of the word was required in order to have a successful outcome."[46] To show the potency of the act of speech (word) for protection and for aggression, Cooper referred to the legendary Queen Nanny. She writes, "An Akan Jamaican Maroon priestess leader, anti-slavery fighter, Black Liberation warrior and strategist, and renowned sorceress, she often relied upon, and used words to beat down the British Babylonian slavery system that sought to destroy her and her people."[47] Nanny of the Maroons (1700–1740) was "a shrewd military tactician and the spiritual leader of the Windward Maroons, providing the group with military and religious stability. . . . In addition to being a brilliant military strategist and fearless leader, Nanny played an important role psychologically by not only instilling confidence and courage in her followers but persevering loyalty by administering oaths of secrecy." The people kept their oaths, their word of honor, because of who they are and that helped them be focused to resist and to fight their common enemy. According to Cooper, Dub poets, "as word mistresses, use their language and performance to beat down a system that oppress [*sic*] them, their psychic selves, their well-being, their families, their kinfolk. Their poetry is both a call to arms and a sounding of the drums of victory."[48] Their poetry is their shield and sword and a celebration of their identity as a people.

From Igboland to the New World, the act of speech is imbued with the potency to create life or death. The act of speech among the Igbos who are described as kingless but who possess a superior understanding of democracy authenticates the transcendental and active force imbedded in utterances that continue to be harnessed even in the present time. The soul of the Igbo community is the integrity of the speech act that has always produced meaning, identity, and empowerment for the people.

NOTES

1. Patrick Taylor, "Dancing the Nation: An Introduction," in *Nation Dance: Religion, Identity, and Cultural Difference in the Caribbean*, ed. Patrick Taylor (Bloomington: Indiana University Press, 2001), 12.

2. Richard N. Henderson, *The King in Every Man* (New Haven: Yale University Press, 1972), xiii–xiv.

3. Judith Van Allen, "'Sitting on a Man': Colonialism and the Lost Political Institutions and the Lost Political Institutions of Igbo Women." *Canadian Journal of African Studies* 6, no. 2 (1972): 171.

4. Kwame Anthony Appiah, introduction to *In My Father's House: Africa in the Philosophy of Culture* (New York: Oxford University Press, 1992), vii–xi.

5. Victor C. Uchendu, *The Igbo of Southeast Nigeria* (New York: Holt, Rinehart and Winston, 1965), 20.

6. Simon Ottenberg, *Igbo: Religion, Social Life and Other Essays*, ed. Toyin Falola (Trenton, NJ: Africa World Press, 2006), 186.

7. Elizabeth Isichei, *A History of the Igbo People* (London: Macmillan, 1976), 21.

8. Dulue Mbachu, "Oil Inflames Nigerian Region Again," Associated Press, January 6, 2007, http://www.washingtonpost.com/wp-dyn/content/article/2007/01/06/AR2007010600474.html.

9. Isichei, *A History of the Igbo People*, 45.

10. The period referred to is approximately 1800–1820. See Isichei, *A History of the Igbo People*, 43; Nkem Hyginus M. V. Chigere, *Foreign Missionary Background and Indigenous Evangelization of Igboland* (Munster: Lit Verlag, 2001), 113.

11. According to Chigere, *Foreign Missionary Background*, there were many reasons for colonization but the "most outstanding is the quest by European nations for trade routes and markets, which in effect gave rise to the acquisition and preservation of colonies in order to secure their limited and finite resources" (199). He further quoted Ogbu Kalu, "Christianity and Colonial Society," in *The History of Christianity in West Africa*, ed. Ogbu U. Kalu (London: Longman, 1980). stating succinctly that the "rationale for colonization [is] in the guised coat of civilization" (199).

12. Isichei, *A History of the Igbo People*, 119.

13. Isichei, *A History of the Igbo People*, 119, 121.

14. Uchendu, *The Igbo of Southeast Nigeria*, 4.

15. See Uchendu, *The Igbo of Southeast Nigeria*, 171.

16. Don C. Ohadike, *The Ekumeku Movement: Western Igbo Resistance to the British Conquest of Nigeria, 1883–1914* (Athens: Ohio University Press, 1991), 1.

17. Ohadike, *The Ekumeku Movement*, 2.

18. Ohadike, *The Ekumeku Movement*, 3.

19. Isichei, *A History of the Igbo People*, 143.

20. Ohadike, *The Ekumeku Movement*, 5.

21. Ohadike, *The Ekumeku Movement*, 87.

22. U-44, *Uga Crisis (1995–2005): The Efforts of U-44 at Resolving it* (Enugu: Gostak Printing and Publishing, 2005), 1.

23. Mbachu, "Oil Inflames Nigerian Region Again."

24. U-44, *Uga Crisis (1995–2005)*, 2.

25. Ohadike, *The Ekumeku Movement*, 12.

26. Obioma Nnaemeka, "Introduction: Imag(in)ing Knowledge, Power, and Subversion in the Margins," in *The Politics of (M)Othering: Womanhood, Identity, and Resistance in African Literature*, ed. Obioma Nnaemeka (London: Routledge, 1997), 7.

27. Isichei, *A History of the Igbo People*, 137.

28. Isichei, *A History of the Igbo People*, 99.

29. Isichei, *A History of the Igbo People*, 99.

30. Chigere, *Foreign Missionary Background*, submits: "Unlike the West, and the rest of men in Hausa and Yoruba countries who are under the dominance and monarchic system of government of the Emirs and Obas etc., the Igbo were regarded as free men replete with full liberty in character, expressions, and activities. They have ever enjoyed a unique due free democratic organization of government structured according to local harmony and patrilineal order. They never practiced a centralized form of government. Their system was quite peculiar, complex

in nature and challenged the West a good deal. That was why it became so difficult for them to subjugate the Igbo people into any form of indirect rule as in other areas in entirety" (203–4).

31. Paula Burnett, "Introduction," in *The Penguin Book of Caribbean Verse in English*, ed. Paula Burnett (Harmondsworth: Penguin, 1986), 4–6.

32. Ohadike, quoting Frantz Fanon in *The Wretched of the Earth* (New York: Grove Press, 1963), 6.

33. Paule Marshall, *Praisesong for the Widow* (New York: G. P. Putnam's Sons, 1983), 37.

34. Marshall, *Praisesong for the Widow*, 38.

35. Catherine Acholonu, *The Spring's Last Drop* (Owerri: Totan, 1985), 11–13.

36. Christopher Okigbo, introduction to *Labyrinths: with Path of Thunder* (London: Heinemann, 1971).

37. Okumba Miruka, *Encounter with Oral Literature* (Kenya: East African Publishers, 1994), 87.

38. Susan Rogers, "Embodying Cultural Memory in Paule Marshall's *Praisesong for the Widow*—Critical Essay," *African American* Review 34, no. 1 (2000): 77–93.

39. Rogers, "Embodying Cultural Memory," 3.

40. Isichei, *A History of the Igbo People*, 44.

41. Isichei, *A History of the Igbo People*, 44.

42. Parker J. Palmer, "Teaching with Heart and Soul: Reflections on Spirituality in Teacher Education." *Journal of Teacher Education* 54, no. 5 (2003), 378.

43. Mary Stewart Van Leeuwen, ed., *After Eden: Facing the Challenge of Gender Reconciliation* (Grand Rapids, MI: William B. Eerdmans, 1993), 345.

44. Allen, "'Sitting on a Man,'" 165–81.

45. Afua Cooper, *Utterances and Incantations: Women, Poetry and Dub* (Toronto: Sister Vision, 1999), 4.

46. Cooper, *Utterances and Incantations*, 4.

47. Cooper, *Utterances and Incantations*, 4.

48. Cooper, *Utterances and Incantations*, 8.

3 IGBO GODDESSES AND THE PRIESTS AND MALE PRIESTESSES WHO SERVE THEM

Nwando Achebe

One afternoon, *oge gbo*,[1] a loud noise was heard from the heavens. It sounded like the furious clapping of thunder during a tropical rainstorm. With each crashing reverberation, it seemed as though the sky would split open. Soon the troubled skies opened up and something fell from the womb of the firmament onto the earth. It was a beautiful woman.[2] And the place she fell was Ogwashi Ujom village. A few days later, the people living in the village began to worship her. But no sooner did they start worshipping her than they started dying in great numbers. They consequently consulted an *afa*,[3] who revealed that the people had been too hasty in worshipping the female stranger, who had not yet reached her destination. Soon the beautiful woman left the village for her permanent home: the boundary between Mgboko and Umuniyi villages, where her shrine is presently located.[4] Thus goes the creation story of Nimu Kwome, the mother deity of Obukpa, a village group of northern Igbo-speaking peoples inhabiting an expanse of land known as Old Nsukka Division.

The Obukpa people, like all Igbos of eastern Nigeria, recall in various stories the creation of the world by the Great God. In Nsukka Division, this genderless God is called Ezechitoke. S/He is also referred to as *ugo bi n'elu na-akpa uri n'ani* ("the great king/queen that lives in the sky but exerts tremendous influence on earth"). Although Ezechitoke's influence is felt in every corner of the earth, *o tuo aka o ruo Igbo*, Igbo people believe that s/he is too great to worship directly. Thus, they kneel in supplication to Ezechitoke's many helpers—lesser gods and goddesses, who are personifications of natural phenomena.[5]

This chapter explores, primarily through indigenous oral knowledge, the histories of eight female deities in Nsukka Division and the central role that these Ezechitoke helpers—who function variously as creator spirits, leaders, lawmakers, and enforcers of the decrees of their lands—play. This chapter is as much about reconstructing, assessing, and situating the character of these spirits within a number of identified Igbo contexts. Therefore, in sections dedicated to uncovering these perspectives, I will contextualize each deity's influence on particular social institutions in Igboland (e.g., marriage, fertility, slave structures) and the gendered realities of the human workers who function as their *male* priestesses. These issues and more are navigated in this chapter as I attempt to advance an understanding of the female principle[6] in Igbo religion.

THE "BIRTH" OF THE FEMALE DEITY

As witnessed in the tradition of the origin of Obukpa's mother deity, Nimu Kwome (presented at the beginning of this chapter), Igbo communities have historically evoked narratives to explain the presence of the principal deities in their midst. In Nsukka Division, these spirits tended to either be constructed as deified women (such as Nimu Kwome) or medicinal concoctions that had been elevated by the communities into female deities. The goddess Adoro of Alor-Uno is a good example of this phenomenon. A medicine in her original context, she would eventually be elevated by her society to a female deity who was worshipped with sacrifices.[7]

Some traditions offer rationalizations for the emergence of a given deity, often linking it to *oge gbo gbo* ("the beginning of time") or in some renderings, relating its construction to a moment in time in history when that deity's services were needed to solve or eradicate a societal issue. During the interwar period[8] in Nsukka Division, individuals in certain communities lived in fear of being attacked by their enemies and neighbors. The small community of Idoha found itself in this unenviable position.[9] Thus, its members constructed a deity—Efuru—to help protect them from the expansionist aims of neighboring Ukehe and Aku and from the slave-raiding activities of the Nike and Aro.[10] The Alor-Uno people adopted a similar strategy. They first concocted the aforementioned medicine Adoro, which served their community well, protecting its members from the incessant raiding of Aro and Nike headhunters.[11] Next, the people of Alor-Uno needed to repopulate their society, which had been devastated by this raiding. It was at this moment that Adoro was elevated by society to a deity, which would marry wives in a process known as *igo mma ogo* ("becoming the in-law of a deity"). This deity-to-human marriage, thus instituted, enabled Adoro to replenish society with the help of her human wives. The cultural precept that supported these unions could be found in Igbo social constructions of woman-to-woman marriage—a bond that allowed *female* husbands to marry wives, who would in turn bear children for them, with the help of male surrogates. Adoro, Efuru, and Nimu Kwome, principal Nsukka Division deities, all adapted this institution to help repopulate their societies and, in the process, created generations of "slave"[12] children who remained permanently beholden to their spirit parents.[13]

Other traditions offer insight into the rationale behind a community's gendered classification—or reclassification—of a deity. How does a society, for instance, decide what gendered character to attach to a medicine or a new deity? Some societies in Nsukka Division determined this by relating the need that the medicine or deity was created to fulfill to the gendered quality of that need. Thus, a society that required a mother deity to repopulate it (e.g., Adoro, Efuru, and Nimu Kwome) would naturally construct or adopt a female spirit. If a community needed a warrior spirit, the society might be moved to classify their deity as male.[14]

In this section, I present two traditions of spirit creation—passed down from one generation to the next and distinct in purpose and utilization—as I attempt to analyze the reasoning behind societal religious reconstructions and remembering. First, I will discuss a tradition that links the craft of pot making in Nrobo, Nsukka Division, to a defied woman/goddess Ohe, while attempting to explain the presence of certain taboos surrounding the craft and food aversions that continue to be observed by Nrobo people in present-day Nsukka Division. This is the tradition:

> There was once a woman, Ugwunyangwoke. She was from Ora Ugwu [Nrobo], and was a budding potter. *Oge gbo* ["during the olden days"], the main food of Nrobo people was millet. One day Ugwunyangwoke prepared clay with which she would make a pot. She left the clay in the sun while she went out to grind millet for the day's meal. However, before she returned, the clay had over-dried in the sun and spoiled. Disappointed, she tried to add more clay to the mixture, but it made no difference. She thus went to see her friend Ohe, the head chief of her town, and a woman who was regarded as the mother of the Nrobo community. She begged Ohe to teach her how to properly make pots. Ugwunyangwoke promised that if Ohe taught her how to make pots, she would make the biggest pot anyone had ever seen for her. Because Ugwunyangwoke's clay had spoiled when she went to purchase millet, Ohe banned Nrobo people from eating millet, declaring that if anyone broke the law that she would surely kill the offending person. Today, Nrobo people consider it an *nso* ["abomination"] to eat millet. Ohe then taught Ugwunyangwoke the proper way to make pots and a jubilant Ugwunyangwoke immediately set to work constructing the biggest pot known to humankind and presented it to Ohe.
>
> Not too long after, a cow owned by a man by the name of Onoja Attama wandered into Ohe's compound and broke the

> pot. Ohe called a meeting of all the Nrobo people, who came together and rebuilt the pot that Ugwunyangwoke had crafted to its former splendor.
>
> Soon after that, Ohe convened an important meeting at her palace. Representatives from all the surrounding villages were in attendance. There was Isi-eke from Ugbene, Ezeugwu from Abi, Utamazi from Edem, and Adoro from Aro. That same day Ohe brought her pots outside so that the sun could dry them. At the height of the discussions, rain began to fall. Ohe urged the dignitaries gathered to help retrieve her pots from the rain, so that the water would not ruin them. Everybody helped but Isi-eke, who claimed that she did not wish to get herself dirty. An angry Ohe declared for all to hear that since Isi-eke did not wish to get dirty, that she and her Ugbene compatriots would henceforth be forbidden from making pots. Consequently, from that day on, anyone from Ugbene who attempted to mold a pot died a quick death. What was more, all the people of Ugbene were cursed, such that if any of them passed by where a pot was being molded, that pot would surely break. To this day if an Ugbene person happens to pass by an Nrobo pot maker, the potter will exclaim in a loud voice: "*Urururu . . .*" to scare that Ugbene person away.[15]

A shorter telling of the same tradition links the taboos that prevent Ugbene indigenes from participating in pot making to an unspecified falling out between the friends Ohe and Isi-eke. This particular rendering is detailed below:

> It was Ohe Nrobo who crafted the first clay pot ever made in Nrobo. This was a long time ago. Not long afterwards, Ohe had a feast to celebrate with her good friend, Isi-eke, who was from Ugbene. Isi-eke had a splendid time and looked forward to reciprocating in kind. And reciprocate she would, shortly thereafter.
>
> In the middle of Nrobo was a huge river that had drowned many people. Ohe implored her friend Isi-eke to help drive the river away. She assured Isi-eke that if she could help her do that, that she, Ohe [who was a potter] would make a pot for her. Isieke, a weaver by profession, agreed and drove the river away. Consequently, Ohe made a pot for her.
>
> Not too long after that, the two friends had a huge disagreement and parted ways. As a result, people from Isi-eke's town of Ugbene stopped visiting Nrobo. They also stopped observing the people of Nrobo making pots. So great was the disagreement between Ohe and Isi-eke that Isi-eke's people even stopped observing Nrobo potters extract clay from the earth. The taboos, which surround who can or cannot make pots, or view clay, remain in place up to the present day.[16]

So what do these traditions mean? What were they constructed to relate? Why are they passed down from one generation to the next? Most importantly, why are they remembered? I suggest that traditions of creation are constructed by communities, not to represent intricate truths or histories but to explain the world around them. Hence, the traditions presented above can be understood in relation to the meaning that they were constructed to communicate among the people who created them. It is clear from the traditions that there are a number of normative beliefs and customs, attitudes, and conventions that the legends were meant to engender. It would appear that the first version was constructed to explain society's aversion to particular foods: The people of Nrobo to this day do not eat millet. They cannot as a group, however, explain the origin of this taboo, except to say that it has always been so. Therefore, the story of Ugwunyangwoke's experience with hardening clay, the reason behind the ruin, and the subsequent pronunciation by the goddess Ohe as a result of the ruin, work to create and preserve communal explanations for certain taboos.

This tradition could equally have been constructed to explain why certain societies engage in particular crafts/industries and others do not. In a previous discussion, I have argued that Nsukka Division can be divided into four geoeconomic zones: weaving, potting, farming, and trading.[17] As captured in this tradition, Nrobo is well known for pottery, as are Nsukka town, Ukpata, Eha-Ndiagu,[18] Agu-Udele, Iga, Ogurugu, and Eha Amufu. Ugbene is known for producing intricate woven cloths. Other communities known for their weaving activity include Edem-Ani, Ibagwa-Ani, Obukpa, Enugu-Ezike, Ikem, Neke, Aku, and Ukehe/Idoha.[19] Thus, it is not surprising that a society would construct tales to explain why certain gendered industries flourish in some towns and not in others.

The expressed values of the community—a group working together for the good of the group—might be another reason why this tradition was constructed. The value is represented by all of Nrobo coming together to rebuild the pot. It is the seeming lack of community solidarity represented by Isi-eke's refusal to help carry in pots from the rain that leads to the falling out between her and Ohe. Thus, this tradition could be read as an indictment against individuals who fail to follow societal norms and reject communal expectations.

The legend may also have been constructed to explain the familial relationships that exist between one community and another. The goddesses Ohe and Isi-eke, representing their towns of origin, Nrobo and Ugbene, were said to have been great friends. These two towns historically had maintained friendly relations for several generations, as had the towns of Alor-Uno and Edem,[20] which were also mentioned in the tradition as friends. These friendships tended to mitigate warring and unnecessary squabbling between the towns. But perhaps there would come a time when Nrobo and Ugbene would quarrel.[21] This legend could conceivably have been handed down to explain—in mythical terms—the reality of friendly towns falling out: an explanation of how and why familial relationships between communities can sour.

To be sure, Ohe and Isi-eke are the principal deities of their respective communities, Nrobo and Ugbene. Nsukka Division, however, also boasts smaller, less prominent female deities, such as Iye-Ojah of Ogururgu, a personal family god, who eventually evolved into a community spirit. Deities such as she also evoke elaborate traditions that place their creation in history and time. In the passage below, *Attama* Obeta Ogbali recalls the coming of Iye-Ojah, who was said to have descended from the skies, sometime before the first coming of the locusts, to Ogururgu.[22]

> [Pointing to Iye-Ojah's physical representation] The name of this deity is Iye-Oja, meaning, mother of all. The name of my father is Ogbali. It was my father that this deity Iye-Oja met. This meeting occurred before I was born. This is what happened. My father fought with somebody in our village. The person that he fought with looked exactly like my father. When they were sparring, the man said to my father: "*Mazi* ['mister'], you are a fine man and you are fighting. I realize that you are a strong man. But, what if you die, who will incarnate you?" The words that this man uttered so affected my father that he ended the fight, claiming that he had been unfairly cursed by his rival. At the time my father was serving as an apprentice to a well known man in his town. So unhappy was my father that he told his master that he was going to commit suicide at his farm.
>
> The day was *Nkwo*.[23] It was during the first moon of the *Okochi* ["harmattan"] season,[24] a day that Ogurugu people were not allowed to go to farm. My father went to the farm with a rope and a machete. He strung the rope into a loop and then tied it to a tree, thinking as he was doing this, that his rival's curse had surely come to pass: "Truly what the man said to me was the truth. I don't have a child." My father then inserted his head in the loop of the rope. No sooner did he do this, than something incredibly strange happened. It was like a dream. He saw a woman descending from the sky and land in front of him. He stopped what he was doing and stood transfixed.
>
> The woman said to him: "Do not kill yourself because of what some person said to you. God sent me to come and cool your temper." She instructed him to remove the rope from his neck and return to his house. She told him that she was going to give him that child that he so desired. She said, "This

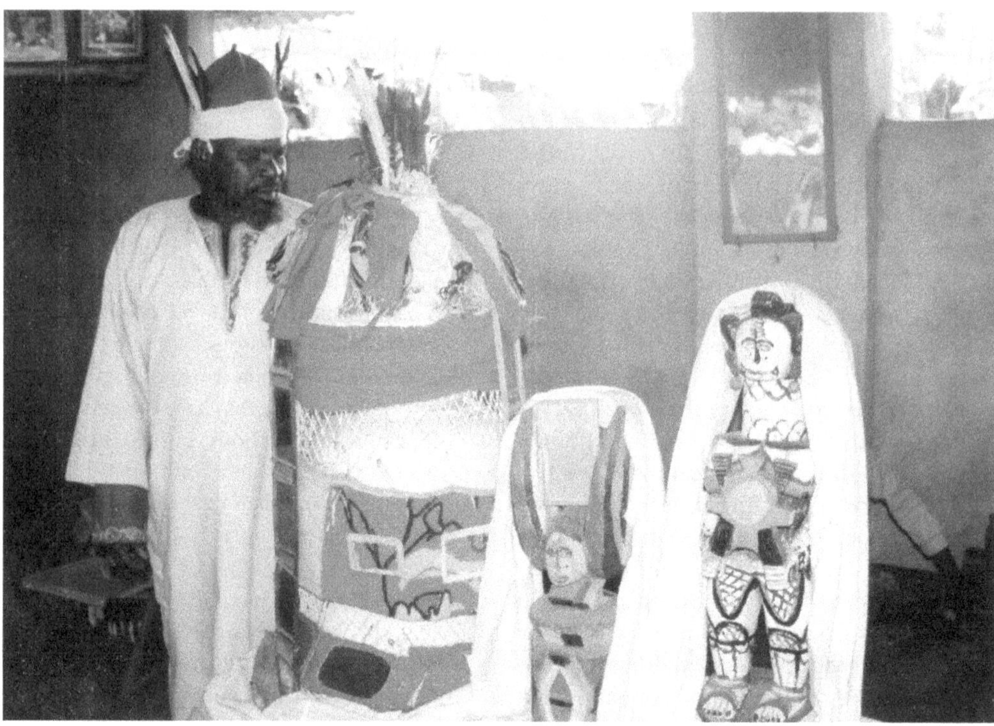

FIGURE 3.1 Goddess Iye-Ojah

> child that this man has cursed you about, you will have." She told him that she was God's helper and that God had sent her to deliver the message to him.
>
> My father consequently removed the rope from his neck. The woman further instructed him to go to the village square and build a house for her there. She told him that he must kill a cow for her in the house that he builds. She promised him that she would give him a male child and that once he received this gift, that he must return and kill another cow for her in her house. She told him that in this world the name of his child would reign forever.[25]
>
> When my father got home, he gathered several friends and told them what had happened. They joined hands to build the house in the village square according to the instructions given by the woman who had descended from the skies. Once they were done, they killed a cow there. My father and mother soon gave birth to me. Then they killed another cow, as the woman requested, in the village square where her house was located.
>
> . . . The promises that the woman, Iye-Ojah, made my father came to pass, because my father gave me life and incarnated into me. I am here because of Iye-Ojah's prophesying. This here [gesticulating], was the house the community built for Iye-Ojah. This place is where Iye-Ojah receives her guests.[26]

The Igbo religious pantheon is large and diverse, consisting of several deities that serve a variety of purposes. The pantheon is also flexible and can be adjusted to fit the needs of members of the society. It would appear that an individual in Ogurugu constructed a savior deity to fulfill such a need in November 1929. The deity was Iye-Ojah, a woman who had miraculously descended from the heavens. The act of descending from the skies is prominent in many other creation legends in Igbo country (e.g., see the Nimu Kwome tradition). However, in this particular telling, Iye-Ojah was said to have descended to save Ogbali from killing himself. Thus, she served as a personal savior spirit: she saved him from death at his own hands—a detail that would have offended Ani, the goddess of the earth, for suicide was a crime against this powerful female deity. Moreover, anyone who died by their own hand would not be buried in Ani's bowels but would be doomed to rot on top of the earth, eventually evolving into an evil spirit.

Iye-Ojah's act of salvation would not be her only act. She would serve as a fertility spirit, promising Ogbali that he would soon give birth to a son. The Iye-Ojah tradition exemplifies the value that this society places on children. It reflects the fact that childlessness is viewed as a curse. This is why Ogbali found it necessary to attempt to kill himself when his rival cursed him with barrenness. The importance of children in Igbo country is also revealed in the names that the people give their children. For instance, Amaechina ("may my path not be closed") and Obiechina ("may my house not be closed") are common names. Thus, in the story of Iye-Ojah, one witnesses the elevation of a spirit from personal savior, redeemer, and deity to a community god that took care of the fertility needs of all members of the society. It is Iye-Ojah that the people of Ogurugu come to when they wish to make sure that their path or house does not close. They offer specific sacrifices to her, and she in turn provides them for children.

DEITIES AS LEADERS AND MAKERS OF LAWS

C. K. Meek argues that the real rulers of Igbo towns were the ancestors or spirits and that the living persons who acted as rulers were merely the agents of these divinities.[27] This assessment is certainly true of the female principle in Nsukka Division. Among these groups, religion was inextricably bound to law, justice, and politics. It was also bound to economics. For example, each Igbo market had a protector spirit and a shrine dedicated to that spirit. The market in Nsukka town had an Ocheg Oye Orba shrine in which market disputes were settled.[28]

In politics there were essentially two political constituencies—one human, one spiritual. The human political constituency was made up of the male and female elders who ruled with the help of the community. The spiritual political constituency—a constituency far superior to the profane one—was made up of supernatural forces that derived their power from the spiritual world. These functionaries included gods and goddesses, male and female masked spirits and medicines, priests, priestesses, and diviners. In the next section, I consider the role of the female principle in Igbo religious politicking.

Ani, mother earth and the goddess of the lands, is considered one of the most powerful deities in Igboland, and as such many societies place her next in rank to the Great God Eze-chitoke. Ani's power is endowed in the fact that the Igbo people are agriculturalists whose lives depend on the fertility of the earth. It is in her honor that new yams are planted and eaten. The Igbo New Year is determined by the cycle of the agricultural season, which is believed to be under the direct control of Ani.

She is also the guardian and supervisor of all morality. The law of the land, *omenani*, is that which the goddess Ani decrees to be either right or wrong. Her prohibitions and taboos are called *nso-ani* and are considered to be abominations against mother earth. These taboos include murder, adultery, incest, food poisoning, and stealing food crops. It is believed that any contravention of her taboos would result in a disturbance of the equilibrium of society—the equilibrium between the living and the dead, for she is the deity in whose bowels the ancestors are buried.[29]

Every living person in the Igbo world submits to the authority of the earth goddess because *ani nna bu ike nwa* ("the strength of the child rests on the integrity and resourcefulness of his or her father's land"). Ani ensures peace and social cohesion among the living and the dead.

The importance of the earth deity is also revealed in the names and proverbs that the Nsukka Igbo people profess. For instance, they say, *ihe igwe na ahughi na ani ga-ahu ya* ("what is not seen by the heavens cannot escape unnoticed on earth"). They also have a saying, *ani bu ishi onodu* ("all human effort or endeavor has the earth as its base and foundation"). Other sayings, *ani ma njo* ("the earth goddess knows all evil intentions") and *ani kwere nwa nkwu omia nri* ("*ani* blesses the person who respects her sacred") also work to articulate this special relationship. Igbo names celebrate the importance of the earth goddess in society as well. Names such as Anibueze ("the goddess of the land is king"), my own surname, Anichebe ("the goddess of the lands protect me"), and Anikwe ("if *ani* permits") all speak to this earth goddess's importance.

Another deity that plays an important role in societal politics and organization is Nimu Kwome. She is the most important deity in Obukpa and the goddess to whom the people attribute their founding (see the introduction, above). They maintain their loyalty and obligations to the goddess to whom they collectively make annual sacrifices.[30] Nimu Kwome is worshipped on three of the four days that make up the Igbo week: Nkwo, Eke, and Afor. This is when believers come to her shrine to pray to her.

Nimu Kwome acts as the society's supreme court of justice. Serious cases and offenses are referred to Nimu and she has the final say on punishment. Lawbreakers are brought before the deity to prove their innocence by swearing in her name.[31] Her chief priest, Attama Nimu, serves as her intermediary and sits in judgment of people who come before Nimu.[32] He acts as a law enforcement agent, collecting fines from individuals and villages and recovering debts owed her.[33]

Nimu is also a goddess of war. In times of emergency, the *igede* Nimu is beaten to alert the people of danger. It is also beaten to inform people of an urgent meeting.[34] Nimu has a horn called *nja* ("the horn of a buffalo") that is also blown to alert people of danger.[35]

Nimu Kwome had female attendants called Umuada Nimu. A special elevated class of women, they were revered by society and greeted with a praise name: Ochebo Nnene Nimu Kwome. They, like Attama Nimu, were law enforcement agents, playing a central role in judging cases involving women.[36] They could also be called in to arbitrate when titled men were unable to settle quarrels among themselves. Umuada Nimu were respected because they were representatives of the Nimu. It was they who organized the festival celebrating the New Year in Obukpa.[37]

The Umuada Nimu would, however, be reined in by society and were seen no more after the early 1950s. Their excesses were curbed by a society that believed that they had gone too far. Their crime was viewing the dreaded masquerade Onyenwe-Ani. As elsewhere in Igboland, masked spirits were constructed as male and represented that which differentiated men from women and full men[38] from ordinary men. Women were supposed to retreat to the background when masked spirits appeared.[39] Moreover, Onyenwe-Ani was feared even by men.

The event that led up to their censoring of the Umuada Nimu occurred one evening when members of the Umuada Nimu viewed the Onyenwe-Ani masquerade as it was returning from the funeral of the oldest man of Amaozalla, Obukpa. Obukpa people believed that any woman who saw Onyenwe-Ani would die. Therefore, the anxious women hurried to the priest of Onyenwe-Ani demanding that he intercede on their behalf. They camped out in his compound and threatened to spend the night if he did not intervene. It was sacrilege for the Umuada Nimu to spend a night in anybody's compound—the act that was tantamount to a symbolic burial of that person, for the only time that the Umuada Nimu spent a night in someone's compound was at that person's funeral. It was, therefore, paramount that the women leave. The priest of Onyenwe-Ani consequently rushed to the home of Eze Obukpa[40] to ask that he serve as mediator. The Eze went with the priest to his home to beg the women to disperse. However, to the surprise of the Eze, the Umuada Nimu left the priest's compound and threatened to move to his compound instead. The women could not, however, penetrate the chief's compound because of the security in place, so they marched instead to his son's house, camped out, and spent the night there. The unspeakable had happened. The foundation of Obukpa had been shaken because of the curse that the Umuada Nimu had put on the son of their chief. The town had to take action. The titled men in Obukpa met and decided that Obukpa would no longer put up with the effrontery of the Umuada Nimu. From that day, the society refused to acknowledge any of the women's powers—the decision was the end of them.[41]

WHEN DEITIES MARRY

Numerous deities in Nsukka Division owned slave communities. These communities were either removed from the rest of the society or were integrated into society in such a way that it was often impossible to tell them apart from *nwa ala* ("sons and daughters of the soil"). The goddess Nimu Kwome owned a community of slaves who lived and worked around the shrine of the goddess. These slaves formed an autonomous village called Umuniyi. The population of this village group was made up of people from different towns and backgrounds that Nimu Kwome had selected—through divination—to serve her. Their bond of unity rested on the fact that they all belonged to Nimu Kwome.[42] Other deities, such as Adoro of Alor-Uno, although having slaves or *igberema* dedicated to her, did not separate them from the larger society.

The institution that encouraged these slave societies to develop was called *igo mma ogo* ("becoming the in-law of a deity") in Nsukka Division. Its roots could be traced to the chaos engendered by the pillaging of souls for the Atlantic slave trade. Even after the so-called abolition, human beings were still being stolen from the Igbo interior to fuel the now-illegal trade in human beings. In the wake of these wars, the fragile Nsukka Division communities were forced to secure protector spirits—deities that would simultaneously protect and repopulate their diminished communities. And, once constructed, these deities wasted no time in fulfilling these aims. They would marry women and, with the aid of male sperm donors, have children with their human wives. These wives were tied to their *female* deity husbands, such that they could not ever marry freeborn men. Instead, they were doomed to be the bearers of children for their deity husbands—children who would in some cases bear the name of their *female* deity father (such as the descendants of the deity Efuru in Idoha Nsukka Division, all of whom bore the name "Nwiyi"); in other cases they would not bear the name of the deity but would still be intricately linked to their parent deity in a slave/master-type relationship.[43]

The wife-marrying goddess Adoro of Alor-Uno and Alor-Agu emerged during the interwar period in Nsukka Division. Initially constructed as a medicine, she was later elevated to a female deity. Adoro had three distinct intermediaries: Attama Adoro,[44] Onyishi Adoro,[45] and Obochi Adoro. The Obochi Adoro was the only priestess among Adoro's functionaries. These intermediaries operated out of an Adoro shrine located in a dense green forest called Uhu.[46]

Adoro was said to have five fingers, each of which was a god in its own right. These included Ngwu Adoro, Nwada Adoro, Okpukuruga, Eze Owo, and Akara Aka. The number five in Igbo cosmology represented completeness, the wholeness of something. The five fingers of Adoro made up a complete goddess, each of which had priests who performed duties on their behalf.

Adoro's wives—*igberema* ("dedicatees")—were essentially human beings who had been enslaved by the deity to bear children for her. This relationship allowed Adoro to become an in-law of the families of her numerous wives. And a strong and powerful in-law she would become, extending her protection to any family whose daughter she had married. Adoro needed to marry wives in order to fulfill the twofold mission for which the Alor-Uno had constructed her—to protect society, which she achieved as a medicine deified, and then to repopulate society. It was this repopulation mission that required the services of females who could bear children for the deity. Over time, Alor-Uno would grow by leaps and bounds, integrating all the women (and their children) that Adoro had married into the community.

WHEN HE IS A SHE: THE MALE PRIESTESS AND THE FEMALE DEITY

Female spirits were arguably the most powerful divinities in the Igbo pantheon. The Igbo ideal of balance, a balance between male and female principles, reveals itself in the biological sex of the human helpers of these female spirits. In Igboland, female deities usually have male priests, and male deities have female priestesses. This reality can be explained by the culture's ideal of a female-male balance of forces, which in turn make up a complete and whole force. As discussed earlier, the Igbo Great God, Ezechitoke, is neither male nor female but a she/he balance of male and female forces. It is this same balance that finds expression in the relationship between deities and their human helpers.

However, there is an exception to this rule, and it occurs very infrequently in Igboland. This is when male would-be ritual initiates transform themselves into females or, more appropriately put, *male* priestesses, in order to serve female deities. Given the Igbo ideal for a balance of forces, why would this happen? How could it happen? The how is easier to answer than the why. And this how can be explained by the complexity Igbo ideas and conceptualizations surrounding gender. In Igboland, sex and gender did not coincide in precolonial society. Gender was fluid and flexible, allowing women to become men and men to become women. Therefore, gendered reclassifications were not uncommon.

Let me now attempt to answer the why: why would male ritual workers transform themselves into women? The answer perhaps can be gleaned from the supreme standing of the spiritual or unseen world. For it is only in this elevated world of spirits that Igbo males transform into females. And it is certainly not surprising that Nsukka men would seek advancement and elevation of their status by transforming themselves into priestesses (gender, not sex) in order to serve this supernatural world as intermediaries.

In this section, I present excerpts from conversations with two men who became priestesses of female deities in Nsukka Division. These individuals are unique because they are socially constructed as females. First, I present excerpts from a 1998 interview with Augustine Ntehe, *male* priestess of the Adani Anunje goddess. He talks about himself, his priesthood, and the origins of his river goddess Anunje:

> You are welcome, you people are welcome. My daughter it will be well with you. What you are looking for, you will get it. . . . I am Augustine Ntehe. I am from Adani. This place is called Amokwe, Amokwe, Adani. My English name is Augustine Ntehe but my Igbo name is Ayogo Nnadozie. I was born a Christian. I joined the army in the year 1939, May 3, 1939. That was the day I was baptized. Since that day I became known as Augustine Ntehe. . . . So as I understand it, I was born and grew up to maturity and acquired knowledge. I met many people and I asked them how the goddess came about. They each informed me that they came to the world and saw her.

The goddess is a personification of a river, and is consulted through divination. In the physical form, she is a piece of cloth that is tied to an *ọfọ*[47] staff and decorated with an *oji* ["metal"] ornament.

> Anunje is a powerful deity. When you consult her, what she demands of you to bring for her, you will bring and she will do what is required of her from her own side. She might demand a pot, fowl, or kolanut. When you complain to her and it is something she will do for you, she will do it.

Anunje is a deified woman. She appears at night to people either as a young or old woman wearing a white cloth tied around her waist. In the next excerpt, Augustine relives the experience of seeing Anunje for the first time:

> When I came back from Hausaland,[48] she would pass through this way [pointing] and I would watch her. That was when her Attama ["priest"] was living here [i.e., in this house]. She would pass here at night and after watching her for sometime, I would go and stay in-

FIGURE 3.2 Male priestess Augustine Ntehe

> side the house. Sometimes she would stop at the house and if no light was lit, she would cry. If she were passing, a fire would be prepared for her to warm herself. If you go there [pointing to the kitchen area], you will see the firewood.

On Anunje's physical appearance, Augustine Ntehe said: "The lady was fair in complexion and she would tie a cloth [around her waist] and would carry a little plate on her head—a small plate like this [shows me]. The plate would contain *odo* ['yellow chalk']."[49] Anunje was also said to appear to individuals, reveal prophesies and tell them what to do:

> She may come to you, assuming you are a child, and tell you what you will do in the future. When the person goes back home, he or she will tell his or her mother what he or she saw. The child would say that he or she saw a mysterious woman and this was her message, or that this is what she told him or her.

Next, Augustine Ntehe elaborates on the process of becoming a (male) priestess of Anunje:

> To become the priestess of this deity is not based on one's wealth. It is not because you are a rich person that you will be invited to become her priestess. If the oldest person in the village dies, somebody will replace him [as Anunje's priestess]. I am the oldest now and someone will take over after I die. Assuming I am a senior to this man [points to my research guide, Erobuike Eze], when I die he will take over my position. He will have to perform some ceremonies and ritual rites. He will cook, buy goats, perform cultural rites. This will indicate that he has become the priestess [of Anunje] and is now in control. This has been the system since the deity came into existence.

He then reveals that he had taken the male title of *ọzọ* before he became the priestess of Anunje. *Ọzọ* is the highest title that Igbo men can take. Ntehe had thus achieved prominence as a man before he did as a woman. He continued:

> I took the *ọzọ* title. Yes, I took the title of men. I took the title before I joined the army. My father was still alive then. In fact, I took the title through my father but I did not wear it [the *ọzọ* symbol] on my feet when I took the title. I started to wear it when I came back [from the war]. . . . Any person that took the *ọzọ* title, if you look at their feet, you will know.

When asked whether there were any apparent distinguishing features of a *male* priestess, Augustine Ntehe said:

> Yes there are. Now . . . this thing I am wearing on my ankle [special beads], it is not everybody that wears it. If it were in the past, it is something like this [points again to his special beads] that is worn on the hands and feet. You will rub this [yellow chalk] on your legs. And anyone you come across will know that you are the Attama of Anunje. A person will not shake hands with you [the Attama] in this way [extends right hand]. I will greet

> you like this [embraces me] because you are my fellow woman. Because he is a man [points to my research guide], I will shake him like this [extends his right hand and asks Erobuike Eze to extend both hands].

There are a number of norms that the *male* priestess of Anunje must observe—mores that set him apart from other men in society and indicate that he has transformed himself into a woman. When asked how he became a woman, Augustine's response was simply: "I did not become a woman, I am a woman." Augustine Ntehe in fact dresses as a woman. He ties his wrapper as a woman would (knotted at the side, as opposed to the front as Igbo men were known to do) and cannot wear clothing that is considered male. Moreover, Ntehe observes societal norms that determine acceptable female behavior, like sitting with both legs tightly closed or crossed. Igbo men readily sit with their legs wide apart. As a *male* priestess, Augustine Ntehe cannot do this. He also cannot have sexual intercourse with his wife during the times that he goes to worship his deity. Augustine Ntehe spoke about these unique features of his priesthood:

> And so I myself that is here, I cannot wear trousers, I cannot wear shorts or trousers except how I tie this cloth. And as I tie this cloth, I will tie it like a woman. I will not tie it like a man because the deity that I answer to is a woman. And she made me a woman.
>
> Any period I am with my wife, I will not go to the deity. I will not go to her because she is a woman. And if Anunje is going to be offered sacrifice today and this person has relationship with a woman [points to my research guide] he will not go there. He will stand outside.

Augustine Ntehe then spoke about the day-to-day worship of Anunje and the individuals who attend to her:

> I offer sacrifices to the deity every Eke day. Just as yesterday was Eke, it is a must that I sacrifice to her. Even if I am traveling to another town, or I am going somewhere, I must wake up early to offer sacrifice to the deity before I leave home. I sacrifice to Anunje on Eke day, unless she requests that someone come and offer sacrifice to her on say, Oye day, then I will do so. But on Eke, I do not fail to offer sacrifices to Anunje.
>
> However, if I am not feeling okay, I will take kolanut and ask a little boy, a boy who does not know women [a virgin] to offer the sacrifice on my behalf. A person that has had sexual intercourse with a woman does not offer sacrifice to Anunje, unless that person is a titled person. I offer sacrifice to Anunje because I am a woman and no longer a man. I was no longer a man the day I took the title [of *male* priestess]. The day I took the title, *odo* ["yellow chalk"], *ushiyi* ["red ointment"], and *ose oji* ["special peppered groundnut sauce"] were used to offer all the necessary sacrifices. They also used a newborn chicken. The newborn chicken meant I had been reborn, that I was no longer a man but a woman.

As the passage above makes clear, men who have not symbolically become women either by being born anew (as in the case of the *male* priestess) or because they are virgin boys (whose virginity distances them from the claim of manhood) cannot offer sacrifices to Anunje. What is more, a *male* priestess who has just had sexual intercourse with a woman is not allowed into her shrine, because that act temporarily displaces his womanhood with manhood. It would appear that Anunje was particular about having only gendered females attend to the intricacies of her daily worship.

Other women who looked after her included the Oboloko, the wife of Anunje's *male* priestess:

> Yes, other women take part in certain rituals concerning the offering of sacrifices to Anunje. The leader of the women that offer sacrifices to the deity is called Oboloko. She is my wife. All the food that is cooked for the deity, or meant for offering sacrifice to the deity is cooked by the Oboloko.

The goddess has many taboos that are observed in her honor. Her color of choice is white, which stands for a purity of body and soul. She detests everything that is black, a color that stands for filth and uncleanliness. This "uncleanliness" informs one of her most powerful taboos—the ostracism of women from her shrine during their menstrual cycles:

> Anything that is black, if you wear black cloth, you will not stand before her presence. You will not enter where she is; you are not supposed to wear black. She forbids black cloth.
>
> ... A woman on her menses will not enter Anunje's shrine. A woman on her menses will not cook for her either. A woman on her menses will stay far from the shrine. This is the way it is.

While the so-called uncleanliness and polluting nature of menstruation are reasons that scholars[50] have pointed to for these types of taboos, in my view, that analysis is limited. It is not so much that menstruation is unclean or pollutes, it is more accurately that in the very act of menstruating, a woman releases that which under different circumstances could have become a living being, a child. And as mother and fertility goddess, Anunje is for the birthing process and must therefore distance herself from any experiential witness of women releasing this exterminational flow.

There are certain foods that she abhors as well:

> This deity detests *okpa* ["bambara nut"]. People don't eat this kind of food in her presence. If you are a practitioner and you eat *okpa*, she will kill you, unless the person ate it mistakenly. But the person has to vomit it, to indicate that it was not a deliberate act.

Anunje is a goddess of morality and moral conduct. She holds her believers to a strict code of behavior, much like the Christian canon, firmly condemning murder and adultery. In fact, she is believed to strike adulterers dead and only the performance of certain absolution rites could save them from this end:

> If you kill a person, you will not enter into the deity's shrine. . . . If a person's crime is very grave such as witchcraft, murder, or adultery . . . if the deity does not kill the person, the person will be exposed for people to know what he or she is doing. The person will be made to confess. That is how Anunje works.
>
> A lady that moves this way [gesticulates, indicating an adulterer], will not enter her shrine. A married woman who moves about, once the deity catches you, you are in trouble. . . . And if you are a woman who has performed the traditional marriage customs and you are living with your husband and you move from one man to another, the deity will invoke her anger on you. . . . The deity abhors this kind of behavior.

There is, however, hope for people who come to the deity in true repentance: "A person who commits evil will confess. He or she will confess the evils he or she has done. . . . Anunje will ask him or her to confess so that they can live."[51]

Adani people have another powerful goddess, a warrior goddess called Nnemuruora, "the mother of all Adani," who is believed to have fought wars of expansion with Nkpologu, Uvuru, Edem, and Ede. Her war strategies included flooding grounds that were previously dry and covering them with grass and leaves, personifying manifestations of natural phenomena like thunder and lightning in order to terrorize her enemies, and turning daylight into nightfall so that Adani's enemies could not see their targets.[52] Ejike Omowo Anthony Eze was the *male* priestess of Nnemuruora in 1998. Like Augustine Ntehe, he is a man that is considered female:

> You people are welcome. . . . My name is Ejike Omowo Anthony Eze. The name of this place is Ajuona, Adani in Uzo Uwani Local Government Area. . . . This deity is a woman and her name is Nnemuruora[53]—the mother that bore Adani. So if you like, you can call her the elderly woman. There are some who call her Inyiukpara. This Inyiukpara that some people call her is because she has a stream. Nnemuruora has a stream. Just as we are here now, if someone tries to do us who

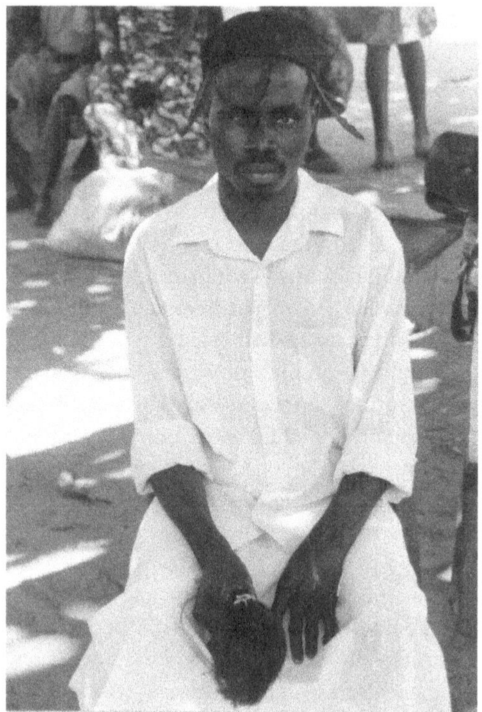

FIGURE 3.3 Male priestess Ejike Omowo Anthony Eze

> are seated here harm, she may flood the road with water and cover it with leaves. . . . So that when the evildoer is coming, he or she will assume that they are walking on solid ground, and the ground will consume them.

Attama Eze then described the physical appearance of Nnemuruora:

> Nnemuruora comes out in the daytime and the night too. When she comes out, you will see her and she will see you too. Just as we are in dry season, you may be a farmer coming back from the farm and you are carrying yams, Nnemuruora may meet you in the form of a human figure. She will dress like a young maiden, with succulent breasts, like a beautiful girl. She will meet you and greet you. She will plead with you to give her some yam. If you are the type of person that refuses to give alms to people, and refuse to give her yam, she will ignore you and keep quiet. And from then on, you will become sick and that sickness will be chicken pox.
>
> Sometimes she will look like an old woman. She will put a plate on her head like this [demonstrates] and will be going about begging for food. She may come just as we are, when she comes, she will be living here. She may ask for water and say that she is thirsty. You will see her, but you will not know her. You will assume that she is a regular human being. At Oye Adani [Adani Market], there is a location where she has her own stall in the market.

As can be discerned from the passage above, Nnemuruora is a deity who believes in the fairness of things. She believes in sharing, in distributing wealth equally between members of the community—an expectation that is revealed in the severity of the punishment: an affliction of chicken pox that she bestows on people for stinginess. Attama Eze described Nnemuruora's duties:

> A woman who has no child, if she comes to Nnemuruora, she will give the woman a child. If a person comes to me and tells me that Nnemuruora has told him or her to bring something to offer a sacrifice to her, so that she will take care of that person's concern, I will first tell the person to go away. I do this to allow me time to carry out my own divining. It is when Nnemuruora reveals her wishes to me, that I will carry out the sacrifice.
>
> Whatever problem you have, when you beg her, she will do it for you. Like deaths, after birth—when you have a baby and the child dies a few weeks or months after delivery, and this pattern is repeated several times, it means that that child is an *ọgbanje*.[54] Nnemuruora may call you to bring the *ọgbanje* child to her, so that she can heal her. When you come, she will heal the child.

Nnemuruora is an organized religion that has an association of female practitioners who meet regularly to discuss their concerns:

> She has an association with members who meet regularly. When her association meeting is about to begin, kolanut is presented.

> Nnemuruora is given her own kolanut. After Nnemuruora's kolanut is taken out of the lot, prayers are said on her behalf. All members present at the meeting will have a share of the kolanut.... It is after the sharing and eating of the kolanut that the meeting will start.

Next Attama Nnemuruora describes the day-to-day operation of Nnemuruora's shrine. Once again he reveals Nnemuruora's articulated desire for equity and fairness among her believers in all things:

> It is on Nkwo or Oye market days that sacrifices are offered to Nnemuruora.... When an animal is killed [for Nnemuruora], it is divided into two halves. I, the Attama [chief priest] will take one half, while the deity owns the other half. And of my own half, my own share, I will give people that come to worship her some of it. Everybody is given the same quantity, whether the person is a little child or a grown up person. Everyone is given an equal share. That is how it works.
>
> Nnemuruora has a river, a forest with everything there, even kolanut trees. So if you want to pluck kolanut, you can. You just have to pick some for her. You can even take the kolanut to the market to sell, provided you share the kolanut equally with her. If your share exceeds hers even by one kola, she will show her wrath by flooding the area with water. So that is how it is.

The goddess has a number of *nso* Nnemurouora ["taboos"] that must be observed by her worshippers. Like Anunje, Nnemuruora rejects all that interrupts the birthing process (e.g., menstrual blood) or is excessively male (e.g., sex with one's wife before consulting her). She also cannot come in contact with a newborn. Attama Eze spoke on this:

> Like you this man [points to my guide Erobuike Eze] if you had sexual intercourse with a woman last night you cannot come into Nnemuruora's shrine. A woman who is on her menses cannot come near Nnemuruora. A woman who has a newborn cannot come in contact with Nnemuruora until that baby is at least 12 days old. Even I cannot visit the mother of a newborn, until that newborn is at least 12 days old.

Nnemuruora's twelve-day restriction against newborns can be explained by the fact that in this Nsukka culture, a child is not named until she or he is twelve days old. And it is the performance of naming that essentially breathes a life sustaining force into the said child.[55] Eze continued:

> If you commit manslaughter and Nnemuruora gets hold of you, the deity will kill you, but before she kills you, she will give you notice. She will first make you sick and you may or may not recover. However, if you have committed many heinous crimes, Nnemuruora will kill you instantly. She might even go as far as killing all your relatives until sacrifices are performed for her.
>
> Anything that is evil, Nnemuruora abhors. A person that poisons you, or maltreats you, hasn't that person killed you? If someone has destroyed the yams you cultivated on your farm through medicine or witchcraft, hasn't that person killed you? Anything that is evil Nnemuruora detests. But what Nnemuruora wants is for you [points to me] to have your own and this person [points to Erobuike Eze] to have his own. Do you understand?

Anthony Eze then explained the process of becoming Nnemuruora's *male* priestess:

> What happens is that Nnemuruora chooses the person she wishes will become her priestess. She may choose a little child to become her priestess, but sometimes she chooses an older person. The community finds out by consulting a diviner. . . . I was a Christian before I became Nnemuruora's priestess. I have been her priestess since 1984 and I am 36 years old.[56]
>
> When I want to offer sacrifices to Nnemuruora, I tie white cloth around my waist like a woman because I am a woman. The reason that I am regarded as a woman is that it is her that I worship and I represent her as *nne*

> ["mother"]. I represented her as mother, so if I want to offer sacrifice to her, I will tie cloth as mothers do. Do you understand?

In Anthony's present position, he is both male *eze*[57] ("traditional leader") and *male* priestess of Nnemuruora, revealing the flexibility of the Igbo gender construct, which allows individuals to occupy positions as men and women simultaneously:

> I am the Eze of Adani. As Eze I am male, but as Attama, I am a woman. It is in our lineage. . . . I am called *eze-nwanyi* ["queen"] even though I am a man. . . . [I]t is my job to look after Nnemuruora.

Nnemuruora also has a number of female functionaries, who see to it that her shrine runs smoothly. Attama Anthony Eze described, in the next passage, the duties of some of the women who worship Nnemuruora:

> Yes, there are certain duties performed by women. . . . It is a woman who does the cooking meant for the deity. It is done by my wife. She is called Oboloko. Oboloko does the cooking and at the end of the cooking she has her own share. The women get a special part of any animal slaughtered for Nnemuruora. . . . If a person offering a sacrifice committed a crime, Nnemuruora might demand that clothing or something else be purchased for her Oboloko, as part of that person's punishment. She might also instruct you to work for her, her male priestess, and her Oboloko.[58]

In Augustine Ntehe and Anthony Eze, we witness men in Nsukka Division transforming themselves into women in order to occupy positions of influence in the most powerful realm of politicking in society. They both firmly insisted they neither had *become* a woman but they *were* women. They dressed as women and abided by feminine norms. Their positionality was, however, merely a social construction. They were both married to women and engaged in heterosexual sex. Moreover, society did not belabor the fact that they were biological males. They were born male but their gender was female.

In this chapter, I have sought, through a number of case studies, to advance the thesis that the female principle in Igbo religion pervaded all aspects of society—politics, economics, culture—and sat in judgment of its members therein. It was this female principle that discerned the forces that caused social disintegration (e.g., violence, murder, adultery) and worked toward societal cohesiveness, thus breathing life into Meek's assertion that the real rulers of Nsukka towns were indeed the spirits and that human beings were merely there to interpret the will of the gods and, as I have argued throughout this chapter, the goddesses.

NOTES

1. *Oge gbo* means "a long time ago."

2. In another telling, Nimu Kwome was believed to be a woman who had migrated from Igalaland to Obukpa. Igwebueze Ugwuoke, interview with author, tape recording, Obukpa, Enugu State, Nigeria, November 6, 1996.

3. An *afa* is a diviner.

4. Paulinus I. Eze, "Numu Kwome, Mother of Obukpa People" (Diploma, Department of Religion, University of Nigeria, Nsukka, June 1984), 3.

5. For more on Igbo religion, see Francis Arinze, *Sacrifice in Igbo Religion* (Ibadan, Nigeria: Ibadan University Press, 1970); Jude C. U. Aguwa, *The Agwu Deity in Igbo Religion: A Study of the Patron Spirit of Divination and Medicine in an African Society* (Enugu, Nigeria: Fourth Dimension, 1995); J. Awolalu and P. Dopamu, *West African Traditional Religion* (Ibadan, Nigeria: Onibonoje Press, 1979); G. T. Basden, *Among the Ibos of Nigeria: An Account of the Curious and Interesting Habits, Customs and Beliefs of a Little Known African People by One who Has for Many Years Lived Amongst then on Close and Intimate Terms* (London: Nonsuch, 1921); G. T. Basden, *Niger Ibos: A Description of the Primitive Life, Customs and Animistic Beliefs, &c., of the Ibo Peoples of Nigeria by One Who, for Thirty-five Years, Enjoyed the Privilege of their Intimate*

Confidence and Friendship (London: Frank Cass, 1966); Edmund Ilogu, *Christianity and Ibo Culture* (Leiden, The Netherlands: Brill, 1974); Emefie Ikenga Metuh, *God and Man in African Religion* (London: Geoffrey Chapman, 1981); Emefie Ikenga Metuh, *Comparative Studies of African Traditional Religions* (Onitsha, Nigeria: IMICO, 1987).

6. The female principle as used in this chapter refers to all supernatural forces that are considered female by practitioners of Igbo religion. These include goddesses, female medicines, female masked spirits, priestesses, *male* priestesses, and female diviners. For more on this, see Nwando Achebe, *Farmers, Traders, Warriors, and Kings: Female Power and Authority in Northern Igboland, 1900–1960* (Portsmouth, NH: Heinemann, 2005), 27.

7. For more on this, see Nwando Achebe, "*Igo Mma Ogo*: The Adoro Goddess, Her Wives, and Challengers—Influences on the Reconstruction of Alor-Uno, Northern Igboland, 1890–1994," in "Revising the Experiences of Colonized Women," special issue, *Journal of Women's History* 14, no. 4 (2003): 83–104.

8. The term "interwar period" refers to the period of fighting between Nsukka communities to secure more land for themselves. This occurred primarily during the seventeenth century and intensified during and after the abolition of the Atlantic slave trade.

9. Nwando Achebe, "When Deities Marry: Indigenous 'Slave' Systems Expanding and Metamorphosing in the Igbo Hinterland," in *African Systems of Slavery*, ed. Jay Spaulding and Stephanie Beswick (Trenton, NJ: Africa World Press, 2010), 105–33; A. E. Afigbo, "The Nsukka Communities from Earliest Times to 1951," in *The Nsukka Environment*, ed. G. E. K. Ofomata (Enugu, Nigeria: Fourth Dimension, 1978), 32.

10. See Achebe, "When Deities Marry," 105–33; Achebe, "*Igo Mma Ogo*," 83–104; Achebe, *Farmers, Traders, Warriors, and Kings*, 54–80.

11. Afigbo, "Nsukka Communities from Earliest Times to 1951," 33; J. O. N. Eze, "Population and Settlement," in *Nsukka Division: A Geographical Appraisal*, ed. P. K. Sircar (Nsukka: University of Nigeria, Annual Conference of the Nigerian Geographical Association Proceedings, 1965), 78.

12. I put the word "slave" in quotes because the indigenous institution of slavery in Igboland was extremely benign, especially when compared to its chattel-type counterpart of New World slavery. Indeed, I have argued elsewhere that the Igbo "slave" institution had the ability to enhance one's station in society as was the case with the wives of deities. See Achebe, *Farmers, Traders, Warriors, and Kings*, 72–73; and Achebe, "When Deities Marry," 105–33.

13. For more on this, see Achebe, "When Deities Marry," 105–33.

14. Again, see Achebe, "*Igo Mma Ogo*," 83–104.

15. Unugwu, interview by author, tape recording, Okpara Nrobo, Enugu State, Nigeria, November 1, 1998.

16. Bridget Echena, interview by author, tape recording, Okpara Nrobo, Enugu State, Nigeria, October 3, 1998.

17. See Achebe, *Farmers, Traders, Warriors, and Kings*, 109–10.

18. In Eha-Ndiagu, potting is only restricted to a certain slave caste, and the people have also constructed traditions to explain why this is so. See case study of Mary Odo of Eha-Ndiagu presented in Achebe, *Farmers, Traders, Warriors, and Kings*, 133–38.

19. See Nsukka Division geoeconomic workzone map in Achebe, *Farmers, Traders, Warriors, and Kings*, 110.

20. In fact, Nrobo and Edem claim a blood relationship. See Roswell C. Blount and Efiong Ben Attah, *A Brief History of the Nsukka Area* (Nsukka: University of Nigeria, 1963), 3; Samuel Francisco Ezema, "A History of Edem, Nsukka from the Earliest Times to 1910" (BA thesis, Department of History, University of Nigeria, Nsukka, June 1977), 15; Unugwu, interview by author, tape recording, Okpara Nrobo, Enugu State, Nigeria, November 1, 1998.

21. We know that the previously friendly towns of Edem and Alor-Uno would break out into war over the latter's support of Nsukka during the Edem-Nsukka-Asadu war. Because of this betrayal, Edem declared war on Alor-Uno town, which she defeated on the second day. Ezema, "A History of Edem," 22; Edi Nwa Enete, interview with Samuel Francisco Ezema, Umuko, Edem, December 29, 1976, in Ezema, "A History of Edem," 92.

22. *Attama* Obeta Ogbali was actually able to place the emergence of Iye-Ojah to have happened in 1929.

23. The Igbo week, called *izu*, has four days: *Eke, Oye, Afo*, and *Nkwo*. *Nkwo* is the fourth day of the Igbo week.

24. *Attama* Obeta Ogbali was later able to pin down this occurrence to November 1929.

25. This statement means that he would have many descendants.

26. Obeta Ogbali, Attama of Iye-Ojah, interview by author, tape recording, Ogurugu, Enugu State, Nigeria, September 16, 1998.

27. C. K. Meek, *Law and Authority in a Nigeria Tribe: A Study of Indirect Rule* (London: Oxford University Press, 1937), 159.

28. Roseline Ezeugwu, "Shrines in Igboland and Its Significances [*sic*] to African Traditionalist [*sic*]: A Case Study of Nsukka Area" (Diploma, Department of Religion, University of Nigeria, Nsukka, June 1994), 8.

29. Emmanuel Francis Ezema, "The Traditional Beliefs and Practices in Ibagwa-Ani Town in Nsukka Local Government Area of Enugu State" (Diploma, Department of Religion, University of Nigeria, Nsukka, June 1995), 14. See also Nwando Achebe, "Balancing Male and Female Principles: Teaching About Gender in Chinua Achebe's *Things Fall Apart*," *Ufahamu: A Journal of the African Studies—A Tribute Issue to Dr. Boniface Obichere* 29, no. 1 (2002): 121–43.

30. Anthony O. Ugwu, "A Pre-Colonial History of Obukpa" (BA thesis, Department of History, University of Nigeria, Nsukka, June 1980), 6.

31. Aniemeka Michael Ugwu, "Some Aspects of the History of Obukpa Town Before 1960" (BA thesis, Department of History, University of Nigeria, Nsukka, June 1984), 11; Ngwu Nwomeke, interview by Aniemeka Michael Ugwu, Obige, Obukpa, Anambra [now Enugu] State, Nigeria, October 23, 1983, in "Some Aspects of the History of Obukpa Town Before 1960," 6; Ugwokeja Ozioko, interview by Aniemeka Michael Ugwu, Uzo Anyinya, Obukpa, Anambra [now Enugu] State, Nigeria, October 26, 1983, in "Some Aspects of the History of Obukpa Town Before 1960," 21.

32. Ngwu Nwa Omeke, interview by Anthony O. Ugwu, Umuora, Obukpa, Anambra State, Nigeria, December 9, 1979, in "A Pre-Colonial History of Obukpa," 51.

33. Alekeja Agare, interview by Anthony O. Ugwu, Uwani, Obukpa, Anambra State, Nigeria, December 11, 1979, in "A Pre-Colonial History of Obukpa," 63; Ugwuoke Okwo, interview by Anthony O. Ugwu, Umuobo, Obukpa, Anambra State, Nigeria, November 29, 1979, in "A Pre-Colonial History of Obukpa," 70; Omeje Otti, interview by Anthony O. Ugwu, Obukpa, Anambra State, Nigeria, December 12, 1979, in "A Pre-Colonial History of Obukpa," 73; Odo Nwa Alumona, interview by Anthony O. Ugwu, Uwani, Nkalagu, Obukpa, Anambra State, Nigeria, December 9, 1979, in "A Pre-Colonial History of Obukpa," 76.

34. Ikeja Nwa Ike, interview by Anthony O. Ugwu, Uwani, Obukpa, Anambra State, Nigeria, December 7, 1979, in "A Pre-Colonial History of Obukpa," 81.

35. Ugwu, "A Pre-Colonial History of Obukpa," 27; Alekeja Agare, interview by Anthony O. Ugwu, Uwani, Obukpa, Anambra State, Nigeria, December 11, 1979, in "A Pre-Colonial History of Obukpa," 63.

36. Attah Nwa Ugwuanyi, interview by Anthony O. Ugwu, Umuojo, Obukpa, Anambra State, Nigeria, November 29, 1979, in "A Pre-Colonial History of Obukpa," 88.

37. Peter Donatus Ezeh, "Igbo Traditional Religion in the Life of the People of Obukpa, Nsukka Local Government Area" (BA thesis, Department of Religion, University of Nigeria, Nsukka, June 1984), 32.

38. A "full man" is a man who has undergone *ikpo ani*, a masquerade initiation. This was the symbol of manhood in Igboland.

39. See A. O. Onyeneke, *The Dead Among the Living: Masquerades in Igbo Society* (Nimo, Nigeria: Holy Ghost Congregation, Province of Nigeria and Asele Institute, 1987) for more about this.

40. Eze, which means "king," was one of the highest titles in Obukpa.

41. Igwebueze Ugwuoke, interview, 1996.

42. Ugwu, "A Pre-Colonial History of Obukpa," 4–10.

43. See Nwando Achebe, *The Female King of Colonial Nigeria: Ahebi Ugbabe* (Bloomington: Indiana University Press, 2011), 22, 25, 42, 57–61; Achebe, "When Deities Marry."

44. Attama literally means "high priest."

45. Onyishi means the oldest man in the community.

46. Innocent Chiturugo Uwadiegwu, "Sister Ngozi of Alor-Uno and the Removal of the Dreaded Adoro Deity" (BA thesis, University of Nigeria, Nsukka, February 2003), 22.

47. Ọfọ is the Igbo symbol of truth.

48. Augustine was in Hausaland during World War II.

49. Yellow chalk was used in the worship of Anunje.

50. See Alma Gottlieb, "Menstrual Cosmology Among the Beng of Ivory Coast," in *Blood Magic: The Anthropology of Menstruation*, ed. Thomas Buckley and Alma Gottlieb (Los Angeles: University of California Press, 1988), 55–74.

51. All excepts taken from interview with Augustine Ntehe, *male* priestess of Anunje. Augustine Ntehe, interview by author, tape recording, Adani, Enugu State, Nigeria, November 20, 1998.

52. Ejike Omowo Anthony Eze, interview by author, tape recording, Adani, Enugu State, Nigeria, November 20, 1998; John Utazi, interview by author, tape recording, Ajuona, Adani, Enugu State, Nigeria, November 20, 1998.

53. Nnemuruora literally means "the mother that gave birth to the people."

54. The Igbo believe in the existence of special children called *ogbanje*. The Yoruba also acknowledge the existence of such children, whom they call *abiku*. *Ogbanje* children are believed to be children of the spirit world who are allowed to visit the human world but do not stay unless the tie (*iyi uwa*) that binds them to the spiritual world is broken. For more on this, see Christie Chinwe Achebe, *The World of Ogbanje* (Enugu, Nigeria: Fourth Dimension, 1986), 1–68.

55. Achebe, *The Female King of Colonial Nigeria*, 36.

56. He was thirty-six years old in 1998 (when the interview took place).

57. A previously noted, *eze* means "king." However, Anthony uses the term to refer to the fact that he is the traditional ruler of the area.

58. Excerpts above taken from Ejike Omowo, interview by author, tape recording, Adani, Enugu State, Nigeria, November 20, 1998.

4 GENDER RELATIONS IN NINETEENTH- AND EARLY TWENTIETH-CENTURY IGBO SOCIETY

Gloria Chuku

For many centuries Igbo society has demonstrated a capacity to shape the direction of change within its boundaries. The people's creativity, shared experiences, and collective memories were products of internal dynamisms and external elements, which they either voluntarily adapted or were imposed on them. The Igbo have demonstrated ingenuity in their creative adaptability to their environment and in the exploitation of their natural resources, the development of complex sociocultural and political institutions, the proliferation of trading networks, intra- and intergroup relations and exchanges, and in their interaction with the outside world. Unlike passive or docile social groups, the Igbo gave agency to the sociocultural changes and transformations in their society. Similar sociocultural and political dynamics have shaped gender relations in Igbo society. The main thrust of this chapter is that the interactions between internal and external processes as historical agencies underpinned gender relations and transformations in Igbo society during the nineteenth and early twentieth centuries.

On the surface, Igbo society could be seen as highly stratified along gender lines. Gender differentiation was perceived as a vital feature of social organization. This perception has presented a picture of superior masculinity vis-à-vis inferior or subordinate femininity. However, a critical evaluation of the various institutions of Igbo cultural groups reveals a society in which gender complementarity was the norm; men and women, boys and girls played diverse but important roles for the sustenance of their families, lineages, and society. Certain roles might be performed more by men than women and vice versa, but the flexibility and dynamism of gender constructs ensured that roles were not rigidly masculinized or feminized. Such roles were valued not because they were performed more by men than women but because of their significance in the sustenance, maintenance, and reproduction of Igbo institutions and society. Moreover, Igbo gender construct has demonstrated a society that was made up of social hierarchies in which certain categories of men and women were superior to others and in which higher regard was placed on ability and achievement than on biological sex. Further, in Igbo society, females were not defined in antithesis to males. Rather, men and women, boys and girls were all valued according to their contributions to their families and the larger society.

The Igbo were predominantly a patrilineal group. There were also dual-descent subgroups such as the Ohafia and Afikpo.[1] In these dual-descent subgroups, matrilineal principles dictated rights over agricultural land, while patrilineal laws governed the control of residential property. In both patrilineal and dual-descent groups, gender flexibility had created avenues for both male and female to excel in society. Instructively, gender mobility (for both men and women) and individual accumulation of wealth were rarely constrained by patriarchal and other cultural forces. It was an achievement-oriented society, which engendered the spirits of competition and hard work among its people. While emphasizing individual achievements and personally acquired social status, the Igbo maintained a strong sense of community, especially in the areas of social responsibility and collective well-being.

In this chapter, effort is made to analytically examine those internal and external processes and historical agencies that were instrumental to social change and structural transformation, as well as specific kinds of transformation that took place, and how they affected gender roles in nineteenth- and early twentieth-century Igbo society. To ascertain the degree of transformation that had occurred during the period under review and place it within proper contexts, an examination of conditions and institutions in Igbo society before the nineteenth century will suffice.

PRE-NINETEENTH-CENTURY IGBO CULTURE AND SOCIETY

The Igbo are the third largest ethnic group in Nigeria. They share borders with the Efik, Ibibio, and the Ijo on the southeast; the Edo on the west; and the Igala, Idoma, and Ogoja on the north. The origins of the Igbo are shrouded in myth and legend. Oral traditions and archaeological evidence suggest that they have lived in their present home in southeastern Nigeria for several millennia.[2] The Igbo were a culturally heterogeneous people, whose cultures and history have been marked by regional and geographical variations—diversity in political institutions, social organization, kinship structures, economic activities, and intergroup relations and exchanges with their neighbors. However, the people were marked by such common cultural elements as the Igbo language (with dialectical variations), familiar religious and cosmological worldview and lifestyle, institutionalized republicanism devoid of individual authoritarianism, common calendar through institutionalized market days, and ritualized crops—yams and kolanuts—features that had developed over the past centuries.

SOCIAL AND POLITICAL ORGANIZATION

Igbo people's social and political organizations were not uniform. Even within the institutionalized republican political structures where political organization was highly diversified and decentralized, there were variations from one polity to the other.[3] While there were a few states with monarchical features, referred to as constitutional village monarchies, many of the communities were mini-states or what some have called democratic village republics. In monarchical states, usually associated with such West Niger Igbo polities as Aboh, Osomari, Asaba, Onitsha, Oguta, Nri, and Arochukwu on the east, power and authority were vested in a body composed of the king and titled chiefs. These polities had features of well-established chiefdoms with titles and chieftaincy paraphernalia, where the king (Eze or Obi) was the overall head of government. In the democratic republican mini-states, it was a council of elders in alliance with titled chiefs and senior age-grades that managed the political affairs of their polities. However, the decentralized nature of Igbo political organization, the small size of the political units, and the fluidity of the executive, judicial, and legislative functions contributed to the wide dispersal of political authority among the sexes, age-grades, secret and title societies, and such religious practitioners as diviners, priests, and priestesses.

In monarchical states and democratic republican mini-states, both men and women wielded political power and authority, though with differing degrees. This is because in Igbo society, gender equality was measured in comparative worth, and social roles and responsibilities were the channels through which power diffused. Individuals earned power, authority, and respect not necessarily because of their gender but as a result of their moral probity, leadership charisma, persuasive oratory, heroic military service, and intellectual and business acumen. These attributes were not the sole possession of one gender or social group. While generally Igbo political system was male dominated and kinship based, it was flexible enough to accord certain women complex political opportunities. For instance, while the governments in Aboh and Onitsha were each headed by the Obi (a male monarch), that in Arochukwu was provided over by the Eze Aro (a male monarch), and each with its *ndichie* (male council of elders). Certain women such as the *Isi Ada* (oldest daughter of the family or lineage), royal wives, and heads of women's organizations in these polities wielded important political power and authority as well.

While in some polities the *Isi Ada* could participate in decision-making processes, in others she was only an observer of lineage proceedings, with occasional invitations to report to the all-male state or village assembly of women's concerns and would receive on behalf of women the assembly's decisions that affected them. Her reports and advice to women could form the basis for their collective actions against male authority. She also played religious and judicial roles, serving as the venerator of all female deities in her lineage and performing cleansing and propitiatory functions. In most cases, women's organizations, of which the *Isi Ada* was the head, acted as parallel authority structures to those of men in order to promote harmony and the well-being of the society. Collectively, women as members of these organizations wielded political power and influence. One of the important female political positions was the Ọmu (Nneọmumu—mother of the society) associated with the west Niger and Onitsha Igbo. The Ọmu was usually a woman of outstanding conduct, character, and ability (measured in terms of wealth) who did not derive her status from her relationship to either the king or any other man. She was regarded as a female monarch with her own female councils, palace (which served as female court), and insignia of office. She presided over women's affairs and was in charge of the marketplace. She did not wield as much political power and authority as the male monarchs, nor did her councilors enjoy as much political power and privileges as the king's *ndichie* (council of elders). But the Ọmu and her councilors often acted as a pressure group in political matters and reserved the right to impose fines on men and women who disturbed the peace of the marketplace as well as those who broke certain traditional taboos such as incest and adultery. Other powerful women's organizations with similar political clout and influence were the Inyamba society of Arochukwu, Otu Ogene in Oguta, and the Ekwe title society in Nnobi.[4] *Otu Umuada* or *Otu Umuọkpu* (society of daughters of the lineage, who might be married, unmarried, divorced, or widowed), *Otu Alutaradi/Inyemedi* (association of lineage wives), and *Ọha Ndiyom* or *Ndiome* (women's assembly) were also female organizations that wielded political power and authority and served as checks and balances to male political structures.

Igbo people had hierarchical social organizations that conferred certain privileges and obligations on their members. One such social organization was the age-grade system. It was a mechanism where special social duties and responsibilities were assigned to the different segments of the society's population based on the principle of seniority. Persons within certain age brackets usually belonged to an age-grade. Age-grade members acquired power and authority as they advanced in age. Thus, while the most junior age-grades performed the most menial jobs, the most senior ones engaged in decision making, judicial process, and diplomacy. There were both male and female age-grades in Igbo society. Both male and female age-grades, depending on their seniority, performed executive and judicial functions that affected the entire population. There were also achievement-based titled and secret organizations that conferred political power and social status on the initiates. Some male titles in Igbo society included Ọzọ, Ekpe, Ogbuefi/Ogbuehi (cow-killer), and Otigbu or Ogbu Inyinya (horse-killer). While in some communities the Ọzọ title was the highest male status, in others, such as Arochukwu and Ohafia, it was the Ekpe or Ọkọnkọ in Ngwa area.[5] In Oguta, the highest men's title was Ikwa-Muọ.

Women's titled societies, which served similar functions as the men's, included Otu Ọdu (ivory society) in Onitsha; Ogbuefi society in Oguta; Lọlọanyi, Ọgbaidi, and Ogbunobodo in Nsukka area; Iyamba in Arochukwu; Ekwe in Nnobi; and Onwene in Onicha-Ugbo, to name but a few. While Lọlọanyi was the highest and most important women's title, the equivalent of male Ọzọ title among the Nsukka, Ogbuefi was the highest female title in Oguta. Because initiation into these titles was largely based on one's ability to finance the expenses, they served as a motivation for hard work. Elaborate ritual ceremonies during membership initiation provided avenues for men and women initiates to exercise important religious power in their communities. In the case of titled women, some of them enjoyed certain privileges such as admittance into exclusive men's societies,[6] immunity from the menace of masked spirits,[7] and participation in the breaking and sharing of kolanuts.[8]

RELIGION AND WORLDVIEW

Igbo people were deeply religious. Their religious beliefs and worldview were intertwined with the people's lives and daily activities. The Igbo believed in the existence of a pantheon of supernatural powers and forces, which operated within the human and spiritual realms. The highest deity in Igbo society was *Chi-ukwu* (Chukwu—the Supreme Being) or *Chineke* (the Creator of universe) or *Obasi di elu* (the Almighty who resides above). But in usefulness and direct interaction with the people, the Igbo regarded the *Ala/Ana/Ani* (Earth Goddess) as the most valuable deity. While the Igbo regarded *Chukwu/Chineke* as the all-powerful male deity, they feared and respected the Earth Goddess as a female deity responsible for their economic survival and reproduction of their society. They also believed in the existence of lesser gods and goddesses whose abodes were shrines and oracles. Oracles performed religious, judicial, and political functions. The most important oracles in the Igbo region were the Ubiniupkabi of Arochukwu, Agbala of Awka, Igwekala of Umunneoha, and Kamalu of the Ngwa. These were regarded as male oracles and could be attended by male priests or female priests. There were equal female deities and shrines such as the Alusi Onishe in Asaba; Ogwugwu, Agwazi, and Omaku of Aguata area; Ohamiri of Oguta; and Nimo Kwome of Obukpa. Ritual experts such as diviners, *dibia* (native doctors), seers, priests, and priestesses served as mediums through which the Igbo effectively navigated and communicated with the spirit world. They therefore commanded high respect and status as a result of their spiritual powers and the important roles they performed in the Igbo cosmological world.

The Igbo also believed in reincarnation, or what Olaudah Equiano referred to as the "transmigration of souls."[9] This was a process through which, after death, an individual, in agreement with his or her *chi* (guardian angel), could decide in what form and when to return to the human world. The Igbo-inherited principles, values, and practices were articulated in the concept of *omenani/omenala. Omenani/omenala* encapsulated the people's code of conduct—the ideas of right or wrong, appropriate and inappropriate behaviors, morality and immorality, good and evil, aesthetic and ugly—and also served as a means to enforce conformity to acceptable social behaviors and norms as well as reproduce such social ethos and values from generation to generation. Thus, the ideologies and sensibilities guiding sociopolitical organization, economic activities, and gender relations were rooted in Igbo *omenani/omenala. Omenani/omenala* also encompassed the *iwu* (laws), *nsọ ala* (taboos), and *aru* (abominations) that guided the people's conduct. Such abominable acts and taboos included homicide, suicide, poisoning, kidnapping, incest, adultery, stealing of farm crops, desecration of the land, and twin or multiple births. They carried severe punishments. As deterrent to future offenders, punishments included protracted and expensive ritual cleansing, fines, banishment, enslavement, ostracism, and death penalty.

THE ECONOMY

Igbo people displayed uncanny skills and dynamism in the experimentation and mastery of their environment. They demonstrated ingenuity in their application of technological skills to exploit their environment and improve their lives. Their knowledge and skill in ironworking was instrumental in their ability to overcome the difficulties of the forest environment. The mainstay of the Igbo economy was agriculture, which involved farming, food processing, small-scale animal husbandry, fishing, hunting, and gathering. Farming was central to Igbo economy. Both men and women were involved in farming but their work was to certain degree gendered. For instance, while men engaged in tilling the ground, planting and stemming yam (an Igbo king crop), and climbing trees, women were preoccupied with a wide range of tasks including weeding and planting vegetables and crops such as three-leaved yams (ọna), cocoyam (Colocassia), pumpkins, beans, maize, okra, melons, and peppers. Both men and women took part in clearing the bush or forest for farming but the activity was predominantly carried out by men. There were also valuable trees such as the kolanut, breadfruit, cowpea, benniseed, oil palms (Elaeis guineensis), raffia palms, castor oil beans, native pear, starapple, and oil bean. One can only speculate on the antiquity of these crops and trees in the Igbo area but the sophistication of their cultivation and processing into food and the high population density of the Igbo suggest a long history of their presence in the region. The introduction and adoption of certain American and Southeast Asian species of yam, cocoyam, and rice as well as cassava, bananas, plantain, mangoes, and corn offered new varieties of food, which further led to the transformation of Igbo economy and the people's dietary system. They also supported the growth in Igbo population.[10]

Farming and certain indigenous crops were highly ritualized. The Igbo performed certain rituals and festivals to mark the beginning of the farming season and the harvesting of crops (the Ahiajọku or Ifejiọku—new yam festivals). Yams and cocoyams, which constituted the major staples of the Igbo, were ritualized, and it was believed that each of them had a spirit force. To the Igbo, the yam's spirit force (Njọku or Ifejiọku) and that of the cocoyam (Njọku Ede) were responsible for the code of conduct for cultivating, harvesting, cooking, and eating these crops. Cultural rather than biological factors were important in the allocation of crops and crop tasks in most of Igbo society. The yam was cultivated exclusively by men. It was the favorite food of the people and a key measure of a man's wealth and social status. However, cocoyam and cassava, regarded as female crops and subsidiary to the yam, were cultivated by women. Many Igbo people, especially titleholders, never ate cassava because of its inferior status.

For the Igbo, being an agrarian people, land was critical for their existence and for the reproduction of their society. The people's relationship to the land constituted the basic principle of economic organization. It was not only the most important economic asset of the people but also the active spirit force, which played a central role in their religious beliefs and cosmological worldview. The land was the abode of the Earth Goddess, a burial place for the dead, and the sustainer of the living. It was worshipped and constantly appeased through sacrifice and ritual performances. Because it was the most important resource of the people, a source of security and sustenance, land was protected from alienation. Land was ultimately owned by the lineage and held in sacred trust by the elders and heads of the families, who were usually men, on behalf of their people. It was the responsibility of the male head of the family and male elders of the lineage to ensure equitable distribution of lineage or communal land. Thus, every member of a family or lineage (male or female) had usufructuary rights over delineated lands. Over time, individual males began to own land through permanent claims to certain land, inheritance, and other ways. Although transmission of land rights by inheritance was usually from father to son or female son, Igbo land tenure was so flexible that all the members of society were accommodated. This explains the emphasis on use rights rather than on ownership.[11]

Every household provided labor for its farming activities, usually comprising a man, his wife or wives, unmarried children, dependent relatives, and servile dependents. The man could also solicit the aid of other relatives, in-laws, friends, and such social organizations as the age-grades. The need to increase the household labor force encouraged polygyny among the Igbo. The question of who dominated in farming activities depends on a number of factors, including the economic/cultural zones in question—craft industrial or trading or farming zones, the period, and the status of the individual men and women. In the economic zones where women engaged in such other economic activities as cotton weaving (in Akwete) and trading (in Oguta and Onitsha), men dominated in farming activities. But where the main economic activity was farming (Abakaliki), women played a more dominant role than men did based on the amount of time they invested in farming—from clearing the bush to planting seeds, weeding and maintaining the farm, harvesting, and transporting home the farm produce.[12] They also planted more crops and vegetables than did the men, who in most cases concentrated all their efforts on yams. It was the women's farm produce that sustained the household more than the men's throughout the lean periods, largely because of lack of adequate storage technology. Food processing and preparation were solely the responsibilities of Igbo women with their children's assistance.

The Igbo engaged in such other economic activities as blacksmithing, salt manufacturing, pottery, cloth weaving, carving, mat making, basket weaving, soap making, and palm oil and palm kernel processing. Most of these crafts and industries were governed by guilds, which exercised control over methods and standards of production, prices, and entry into the industry. Iron technology, an important industry, was associated with the Awka, Udi, Nkwerre, Abiriba, Afikpo, and Nsukka Igbo who had rich deposits of iron ore. The industry was the preserve of men. Smiths produced a range of agricultural and other tools, war implements, household utensils, and monetary objects as well as objects used for social ceremonies and religious rituals. The art forms of fine quality, including copper alloy castings, bronze, and pottery objects discovered at Igbo-Ukwu demonstrate the people's artistic, cultural, and technological sophistication dating back to the tenth century.[13] Notable cloth-weaving areas were Nsukka, Abakaliki, Akwete, and the Aniocha and Oshimili areas in the western Igbo region. Apart from in Abakaliki, where men wove, weaving in the Igbo region was done by women.

Salt production was associated with women in Igbo society and was limited to the Okposi, Uburu, and Abakaliki areas endowed with brine lakes. Salt served as food, medicine, and currency. Carving was a very lucrative occupation among the Northern Igbo of Umudioka near Awka. It was a men's occupation. Carving products included tools, doors, panels, wooden utensils, and other domestic property as well as products used for ritual purposes and as insignia. Leather and ivory works were important in Abakaliki, Nsukka, and the areas along the Anambra River. They were the preserves of men. Pottery was another local industrial craft associated with women. The Inyi, Nsukka, Ishiagu, Unwana, Isuochi, Okigwe, Udi, and Umuahia achieved regional recognition as pottery specialists. The sizes, designs, and shapes of the earthenware depended on the purposes for which they were intended. These included household utensils, musical instruments, and ritual objects.

The Igbo were also engaged in local and regional trades. Markets were usually held during the cycle of a four-day week (the days were named Eke, Orie, Afor, and Nkwo). Some markets were held every eight days. These were usually big fairs attended by traders from different Igbo polities and their non-Igbo neighbors. Some village markets were held daily, usually in the evenings. Generally, Igbo markets were temporally and spatially organized in order to reduce clashes and the cost of collecting and distributing trade goods. The marketplace was not only a place for exchange of goods; it also served other important functions to the Igbo. It was a place for socialization, for exchange of information and ideas, and for holding group meetings. It was also a venue for pre-marriage outing ceremonies for maidens, and where persons who committed certain offences and abominations were paraded to shame them. The maintenance of the village marketplace was the responsibility of women. While more men than women were engaged in long-distance and regional trade, traders at the local village markets were predominantly women. Since long-distance trade interfered with the basic traditional roles of Igbo women—child rearing and care, household chores, food processing and preparation, and tending the farms—men tended to dominate it. Women from areas with networks of rivers, (Onitsha, Osomari, Aboh, and Oguta, for instance) took advantage of the water transportation by canoe to fairly compete with men in long-distance trade.

Two types of long-distance trade developed in the Igbo region: one involving Igbo people within the region and another between them and their neighbors—Edo/Bini, Igala, Idoma, Efik, Ibibio, and Ijo. The Aro, Awka, Nkwerre, and the Abiriba were professionals, who dominated Igbo hinterland trade. Other Igbo professional traders of fame were the Aboh, Umunneoha, Nike, Aku, and Isuochi. While the Awka, Nkwerre, and Abiriba, in addition to trading were famous blacksmiths, the Aro and Umunneoha were also oracular agents, and the Nri were ritual and medical specialists. The activities of these professional traders have been well documented.[14]

The origin of the long-distance trade between the Igbo and their neighbors is uncertain. The more than 165,000 pieces of glass and stone beads excavated at Igbo-Ukwu, assigned to the Egyptian, Venetian, and Indian provenance and dating back to the ninth century, suggest a long history of commercial relations between the Igbo and their neighbors.[15] The archaeological evidence has been reinforced by accounts of early European visitors to the Niger Delta region, oral traditions of the people, and studies on the subject.[16] The Igbo obtained mostly salt and fish (and later, European goods) from their Niger Delta neighbors, and horses, ivory, coral beads, and other articles from the Igala and other northern non-Igbo traders in exchange for farm produce—yams and palm oil—and small animals and slaves (some of which they obtained from the Igala traders).

By the eighteenth century, slaves had become the most important article of Igbo trade with their neighbors, following the development of the trans-Atlantic slave trade in the sixteenth century. Scholarship on slavery and the slave trade in the Igbo region and on the Atlantic slave trade has attributed the emergence of the Aro to the increased number of the Igbo slaves exported across the Atlantic Ocean, even though the Aro never acted alone. There were other Igbo groups such as the Aboh, Osomari, Onitsha, Awka, Mgbowo, Oguta, Nike, Nkwerre, Abiriba, and Ohafia who were actively engaged in the trade. But the Aro played a more dominant role than the other Igbo professional traders because they were able to develop a network of trading diaspora throughout the Niger Delta and its hinterland.

The Aro oracle, the Ibiniukpabi, enjoyed regional prominence and provided Aro traders with traveling immunity. To guarantee free flow of trade, they used judicious marriage relationships and also entered into covenants (*igbandu*) with the leaders of the communities they traded with or passed through or settled in. These activities helped the Aro cement bonds of friendship and trust with influential non-Aro people. They also took advantage of such regional institutions as the Ekpe secret society, called Ọkọnkọ by the Ngwa, Uzuakoli, Umuahia, Nkwerre, and other southern Igbo and Niger Delta people, where the Aro exported it.[17] Members of the Ekpe and Ọkọnkọ societies enjoyed certain privileges that were not available to noninitiates—trade monopolization, traveling immunity, credit facilities, and access to important goods and commercial information through their monopolization of the unique Ekpe script—*Nsibidi*/*Nsibiri*.[18] They also served as brokers, law enforcement agents, and mediators among other roles. Aro traders increased their respectability and immunity because they supplied rare, important, and novel commodities to both the Igbo and non-Igbo people. One of the issues discussed in the next section is how the trans-Atlantic slave trade transformed Igbo society, engendered class differentiation, and intensified gender imbalance following the exportation of more men than women from the region.

EUROPEAN PENETRATION OF THE IGBO REGION IN THE NINETEENTH AND EARLY TWENTIETH CENTURIES AND IMPACT ON GENDER RELATIONS

Igbo society in the nineteenth and early twentieth centuries was shaped by the abolition of the Atlantic slave trade and the emancipation of the enslaved; the emergence of trade in palm produce; European penetration of the Igbo region, and the activities of the foreign trading firms, missionaries, and the colonizers. It was a period marked by aggression and resistance, which involved the Igbo, British consuls and colonial officers, foreign traders, and missionaries. Increased European activities generated tension and open conflicts in the region. There were wars of subjugation and the eventual conquest of the people. In addition to colonial military campaigns, the Igbo fought most of their intragroup wars during this period as a result of their increased access to firearms and frequent land disputes. These activities made the nineteenth and early twentieth centuries the most violent period in Igbo history prior to the Biafra-Nigeria war of 1967–1970. The following discussion focuses on the above external forces, how the Igbo responded to them, and the consequences of such encounters, especially on gender relations in Igbo society.

THE ABOLITION AND EMANCIPATION

At the beginning of the nineteenth century in 1800, the slave trade remained a major economic base of the Igbo and the most important aspect of their relations with their neighbors. The abolition of the slave trade by the British in 1807 and subsequent passage of the emancipation act in 1833 gave the British the impetus to end the slave trade in the Niger Delta, its hinterland, and other areas, and to replace trade in human beings with that in nonhuman commodities such as agricultural products and mineral resources—the so-called legitimate commerce. By the end of the 1850s, the activities of the British abolitionists and the British Naval Squadron, which plied the Atlantic Ocean, had paid off in ending the shipment of slaves from the Delta ports. Export of captives ceased at most Delta ports in the 1830s; the last slave ship left Brass in 1854. Even though there was noticeable decline in the trans-Atlantic slave trade by the mid-nineteenth century, slave dealings persisted in the Igbo region for over a century. Adiele Afigbo's work on the abolition and emancipation demonstrates that "slave dealing was real for almost the entire duration of the colonial period, even though it kept changing in character and technique."[19] Despite the fact that the Niger Delta people were forced to turn their attention away from the export of slaves across the Atlantic after 1860, they continued to engage in the slave trade for their domestic needs until the mid-twentieth century.

Ironically, as the internal slave dealers had become more efficient in their means of procuring slaves for sale, the British naval patrols intensified, leading to the closure of overseas markets. The Islamic reform movement launched from Sokoto in 1804 led to many wars and generated many captives in the region. These captives made their way to the markets in northern Nigeria and the Lower Niger. Aboh and Osomari were the leading slave dealers on the Lower Niger in the nineteenth century when the Niger route saw the transportation of an increasing number of slaves. Aboh, for instance, evolved a canoe-house system that was similar to that of the Niger Delta city-states. The king of the town and his leading chiefs recruited slaves to man the canoe-houses equipped with firearms. In 1831 the Lander brothers, who were captured at Asaba, were sent to the Aboh king, Obi Ossai, who released them after a ransom was paid. Obi Ossai owned more than 300 slaves; his sons Chukwuma and Aje owned, respectively, more than 200 and 100.[20] The Aro, Nike, Bende, and Uzoakoli got most of their captives from communities that engaged in wars and kidnapping during this period. The nineteenth century was also the period when the coastal states of the Bight of Biafra and the Cross River communities served as bases for launching military campaigns against the interior communities.

The continued internal trade in slaves and the decline in external trade had profound implications for the Igbo and their society. One outcome of the end of the trans-Atlantic slave trade was an increased number of slaves domestically, which resulted in their relative cheap price. For instance, at Aboh, a sixteen-year-old in 1832 cost sixty shillings, and an adult female slave sold for more.[21] In 1854, at Aboh, a pair of ivory tusks was worth three to four slaves, a stout male slave was exchanged for ten to twelve bags of salt or 60,000–70,000 cowries, and a good-looking young female eight to ten bags of salt or 45,000–50,000 cowries.[22] In the hinterland market of Uburu in the 1880s, four to six adult slaves exchanged for a horse, and a bull exchanged for one slave. At the Itu market on the Cross River in 1901, Aro traders sold a healthy male slave for ten pounds, a female between fourteen and twenty years old sold for twelve to fourteen pounds, and children about seven years old sold higher.[23] At Uzuakoli, an adult male sold for forty *mkpona* (a brass rod or three pounds), *apapa* five to ten pounds, and *asamiri* (young female) four hundred *mkpona* or thirty pounds.[24]

The dramatic drop in the price of slaves in the region resulted in an unprecedented increase in the incidence of human sacrifice. Because slaves were cheaper than during the trans-Atlantic trade, relatives of the dead could afford to buy them for burial rites. Slaves were also sacrificed to appease the gods and goddesses.[25] Depending on the seriousness of the matter and for more efficacious results, oftentimes young female virgins were the most sought after for sacrifices to the gods and goddesses. The dehumanizing treatments meted to slaves resulted in series of slave resistance in the Igbo region. Examples include the mid-nineteenth-century mass exodus of slaves from the West Niger town of Abara-Uno to a new settlement called Abara-Ugada; from Isele-Uku to a settlement founded by one of its chiefs; and emigration from Osomari, which left the town a ghost of its former self.[26] Slaves who organized the Nkanu slave uprisings of the 1920s included in their grievances a high incidence of kidnapping and selling of their children and ritual sacrifice of their women.[27] Abo, Asaba, and other areas of large concentration of slave populations also witnessed series of slave migrations during this period.[28]

Another feature of this era was a tremendous influx of Igbo slaves into the Delta region, resulting in increased numbers of the Igbo in such places as Bonny, Calabar, and Brass as well as in the Bight of Biafra region of Fernando Po. The Delta became increasingly Igbo in terms of population and language. For instance, Opobo, a town that was founded by Jaja, an Igbo slave, saw an increase in its population from 1,500 in 1869 to about 20,000 in 1911, due to the influx of Igbo slaves.[29] While male slaves were primarily sought after for military and protection purposes, female slaves were procured for their productive and reproductive capabilities. On the whole, it is believed that women dominated the Igbo population in the coastal areas. While some of them were sent there as child-commodities, others were married away to coastal men. One important implication of the demography of Igbo immigrants in the Niger Delta is that a considerable percentage of the population could trace its ancestry to Igbo women.

Abundance of cheap slaves also led to the establishment of large farms and plantations, cultivated and managed by slaves. Those who could afford more slaves were able to deploy them in farming, food production, and other productive activities. During the trans-Atlantic slave trade, when able-bodied men were required as slave raiders, escorts, and porters, farming activities and food production fell on the shoulders of older men, their wives, and young children. On the average, women did most of the work. But with the closure of the external trade in slaves, some wealthy slave dealers diverted their wealth to large farms and plantations. Pockets of farming communities such as Amuro and Amankwu near Okigwe, Ijomanta, and Okoroji on the banks of the Enyong River and Cross River, and in Isele-Uku and many others in the western Igbo region developed. On the average, each of these farms had a population of more than a thousand persons. Each had a headman, a number of slave families, and a market and was occasionally visited by the owner. In these communities, both male and female slaves were engaged in cultivation but women dominated in food processing. While women were responsible for the marketing of the more perishable of the foodstuffs in the local markets where the communities were located, men were responsible for transporting and selling the more durable foods in faraway regional markets. In most cases, men owned these farms and farming communities. Almost all the large farms were owned by wealthy Aro, Aboh, Isele-Uku, Oguta, and Osomari men. However, a few wealthy women had large farms cultivated by their slaves. For example, in 1841, Macgregor Laird reported visiting the plantation of an Aboh woman who owned over

200 slaves whom she kept to cultivate yams and collect palm oil.[30]

The labor needed for food production also resulted in increased incidence of polygyny. In many Igbo communities, men who bought female slaves usually absorbed them into their households as wives, especially if such women had children for them and were also hardworking and obedient. So, acquiring female captives became a means of enlarging one's household and labor force. With incidents of runaway slaves, which rose to an unprecedented proportion following the emancipation efforts of the British colonial government and the Christian missionaries, men resorted to marrying more wives and having more children. It was more valuable to invest in women (whether free or slave), who would eventually become wives and have children, than to buy male slaves. The general belief is that, whereas one's slaves could run away, one's wives seek for divorce; his children would always stay with him. This belief is captured in two Igbo names: *Nwagbọsọ* (one's child never runs away or escapes) and *Ohuabunwa* (a slave was never one's child). Further, the Igbo name, *Nwabuaku* (a child is wealth) underscores the value Igbo people placed on their children. Susan Martin's studies on the Ngwa Igbo during this period show that it was more valuable to invest in wives and have more children than to accumulate male slaves.[31]

There were a number of laws enacted by the British colonial government to end the slave trade and slavery in the Igbo region and the Niger Delta. One of such laws was the 1901 Slave Dealing Proclamation, which made it an offense, punishable under the law, to engage in slave dealing within the protectorate. It declared that any enslaved persons within the protectorate should become free, and rendered void any contracts of slave dealing. Violation of this law carried a seven-year prison term or a fine or both. There was also the ambivalent Native House Rule Ordinance of 1901 that granted freedom to the enslaved population of the Niger Delta city-states while tightening the authority and control of the heads of houses over them. The law imposed punishments on slave resistance—up to a fine of £50 for an insubordinate slave, and the same amount plus a one-year prison term for anyone who employed a slave without the consent of the house head. It stipulated that every house member was free and immune from resale.[32] The passage of the Master-Servant Proclamation of 1903 allowed Niger Delta coastal middlemen to recruit apprentices from the interior for trade and other occupations with some monetary compensation to their parents/guardians for the twelve-year period of apprenticeship.[33] This proclamation was primarily directed to address the problem of the high incidence of child stealing and enslavement in the Igbo area. Rather than selling or pawning their children to strangers, it was reasoned that parents would prefer to send them to the Niger Delta cities where they would be trained in certain occupational skills that will bring them some financial rewards. The 1916 Emancipation Decree provided that no court should enforce slavery.[34] The British government also used military campaigns. For instance, according to official record, the Aro Expedition of 1901–1902 was directed against "the last stronghold of slavery," and its successful execution had "freed [the protectorate] forever from the evils of slave raiding and slave dealing on an organized scale."[35]

Antislavery campaigns by the British colonial administration peaked in the 1930s, a period with a high incidence of child stealing and dealing. It is important to note that child stealing and trade in children increased during this period because children, more than adults, were easily controlled, transported from place to place, and absorbed within the households of their captors or buyers. Their vulnerability and malleability to enslavement posed a much more complicated problem to the British officers during the emancipation than did adult slaves. The high demand for children may explain why they were more expensive than adult slaves as indicated in the figures above. While some of the children were victims of kidnapping, others were given away or pawned by their parents and relatives. Economic and cosmological imperatives led parents to pawn or sell their children. S. P. George, an assistant commissioner of police in Owerri Province, listed the characteristic features of victims as children who cut an upper tooth first; twins; those born as bastards or were physically and mentally defective; and those who committed incest, failed to cry at birth, or were boys born with one testicle.[36] For example, one Udorie, a nine-year-old girl, was put up for sale by her people because she committed an abomination by pushing a little boy into a pond or stream, causing his death.[37] In order to deter parents or kidnappers and slave dealers, the government increased the maximum punishment for child stealing and slave raiding from seven years (or a fine) to up to fourteen years of imprisonment in 1931.[38] On the whole, economic imperatives more than any other reasons motivated parents to sell or pawn their children during this period.

It is equally instructive to note that the people who engaged in child-dealing—kidnapping, selling, and buying—were the powerful persons in society. They were the ones who had the means to organize the business of child-dealing even under the nose of the British officials. Often both the victims and government officials were deceived into believing that such children were sent away either as apprentices to acquire a trade or, in the case of girls, were married away. While in most cases, men more than women made the decision on who was to be sold or pawned, recipients of those children were both wealthy men and women. Some of the children were adopted by childless women. Others were used as domestic servants and in different productive activities. Beautiful girls among them were married away or placed in special social relationships with prominent men in society to advance their owners' personal interests. Examples of such prominent Igbo women include Omu Okwei of Osomari, Ahebi Ugbabe of Umuida, Enugu-Ezike, Ikpeaku Ifeobu of Oguta, Aboh women mentioned in the accounts of early European visitors, and the fictional Ma Palagada in Buchi Emecheta's *The Slave Girl*.[39]

Frederick Lugard had criminalized the bridewealth, which legalizes any marriage in Igbo society, for the increased cases of female child-dealing during this period. But, it is important to differentiate actual marriage, which is an alliance of kin groups through ritual and material exchanges (including the bridewealth), from "wife purchase" or female child-dealing, which was often done secretly and without any ritual performances. While the victims of female child-dealing were kinless persons who lived at the mercy of their owners, wives had kinship relations with their relatives and could seek for divorce. It has been suggested that the institutionalization of woman-to-woman marriage and the status of female husband (a practice where certain women married others because they provided the bridewealth and where it was taboo for a female husband to have any sexual relationship with her wife) is a twentieth-century phenomenon linked to the emancipation of the enslaved women in Igbo society.[40] I have argued elsewhere that the institution of female husband—either surrogate or autonomous—predates slave emancipation in the Igbo region that began in the nineteenth century.[41]

THE OIL PALM INDUSTRY AND THE "LEGITIMATE" EXPORT TRADE: TRANSITIONS AND ADAPTATIONS

Palm oil had been for centuries a staple food product of the Igbo due to its nutritional value and appealing taste. It was part of the provisioning trade that went hand in hand with the trans-Atlantic slave trade because European slave merchants fed it to their slaves during the Middle Passage. The Igbo also ate palm kernels, a by-product, and used its oil for various purposes. Other than climbing the trees to cut down bunches of palm fruits and at times pounding the nuts, everything involved in palm oil and kernel processing was carried out by Igbo women and their children.[42] While the external slave trade declined with emphasis on "legitimate" commerce, export in palm oil and kernels witnessed a vast increase partly because of demands in the United Kingdom where the products were used in making soap, pomade, candles, and industrial lubricants. The growth of the palm oil trade, which existed simultaneously with internal slave trade and accumulation, saw at least to a certain point a great deal of transition, adaptation, and transformation in social organization and the new export production and trade.[43] It also led to the emergence of a new class of export producers and traders, especially those within the palm-belt of southeastern Nigeria, who had access or control over land in which the oil palm trees grew. While in some areas the new class displaced the old middlemen, in other communities members of the latter group used their acquired wealth in the slave trade to maintain control over the shifting economic markets by investing in land and more labor. Yet others had struggled to create new avenues and strategies to take advantage of the new economic order.

The rise in palm oil trade in the mid-nineteenth century witnessed the devotion of food-producing groups to production of palm oil and kernels. Palm oil and kernel production was labor intensive and was performed mostly by women and children.[44] Processing palm oil required harvesting the fruit bunches (which was done by men), separation of individual fruits from spiky bunches, carrying the fruits to the production center, boiling, pounding, separating nuts from fibers, and squeezing oil out of the fibers (activities that were performed by women and their children). To obtain kernels, the nuts had to be cracked between stones to remove the hard cover. These were laborious and time-consuming tasks. It has been estimated that it would require 300 pounds of palm nuts to produce 36 pounds of oil, a process that would take a person three to five days to produce.[45]

From the 1830s and throughout the colonial period, palm produce (palm oil initially and palm kernel later) became the chief export of the Igbo region. The region as a result became an economic satellite of the European industrial economy, a dependent monoculture that, while supplying raw materials, also provided a market for European industrial products. In the 1870s, when the demand for palm oil declined, palm kernels were in high demand for making soap, margarine, and residue for animal feeds. Women's labor was vital in the new export production and in food production, which was required for both domestic consumption and for the market. Thus, the labor needs for these economic activities contributed to the expansion of the domestic slave market and slavery and to the increase in polygyny, as many senior men strove to strengthen the labor force of their households for maximum exploitation of the new economic order.

The demand for industrial raw materials in place of human cargoes in the United Kingdom led to the establishment of large oil palm farms and plantations by wealthy merchants for large-scale production and the expansion of smallholder producers. While the large-scale production relied more on slaves than any other source of labor, the small-scale individual production depended primarily on household labor. In both systems, women, whether slave or free, did most of the work in the production process. In their 1832 expedition report, Macgregor Laird and R. A. K. Oldfield reported seeing women and children in Aboh collecting palm oil (processing) as men were trading with Brass traders, kidnapping their neighbors, and drinking spirits (alcohol).[46] The continued reliance on female labor in the palm oil industry must have prompted John Whitford, a British trading agent on the Niger in about 1875, to urge an Aboh prince to use his slaves in collecting palm oil in exchange for "desirable things"—European products.[47]

Generally, male slave labor was involved more in cultivation, harvesting palm fruits, and in marketing of large-scale palm oil than in the extraction process. In some areas such as the Ngwa and Ndoki, women carried the produce to depots where it was sold, but they were usually escorted by men. Palm produce, a bulky commodity, could only be transported by canoe or human porterage in the nineteenth-century Igbo society. Thus, its trade was confined to areas of production and those along navigable waters with links to the Niger Delta. Trading factories were opened up along the Niger at Aboh in 1843, Onitsha in 1857, Asaba in 1863, Osomari in 1877, and Oguta, Atani, and Aguleri in 1884.[48] Even though women dominated small-scale marketing of palm oil in local markets, the establishment of *pax Britannica* and trading stations by foreign companies along nearby waterways and railway lines (such as Ohambele, Akwete, Azumiri, Obegu, Umuoba,

Mbawsi, Owerrinta, Umuahia, Ovim, Nomeh, Agbani, Ogrugu, and Eha-Amufu) expanded their marketing avenues but also brought more men into the distribution sector.

Improvement in the transportation system gave more men than women access to such innovations as bicycles, motorized vehicles, and locomotives, which carried more produce than human porterage. Individual producers carried their palm oil in calabashes (and later, in metal containers) to these collecting centers where they were sold. Overall, Igbo women played such a dominant role in the oil palm industry that the Kalabari and other coastal middlemen began advancing credit to the wives of prominent men in the Ngwa, Akwete, Owerrinta, and Oguta areas to guarantee regular supplies of palm oil. As heads of household who also controlled the land where the oil palm trees grew, men asserted their power over the control of the revenue from the industry even though women did most of the work. However, many women for the first time began to acquire some income from the sale of their husbands' oil and from kernel, which was solely theirs. Because smallholders dominated the palm oil industry in the Igbo region, the new economic order offered an unprecedented opportunity for upward mobility of women, slaves, and other marginalized persons, as many of them began to participate in export production and trade on their own rights.

Following a fall in oil prices and foreign firms' attempts to retain their profit margins by cutting prices, a chronic conflict of interest ensued between them and the Igbo producers, who resorted to the collective action of trade stoppage. The firms responded through the collective action of forming amalgamations in the name of the Royal Niger Company (RNC). With full monopoly and authority to administer the region, the RNC became more ruthless and formed the worst government in the history of the Igbo (1886–1899). It engaged in exploitative, oppressive, and monopolistic activities. Igbo producers and local traders were underpaid for their palm produce. The company was also involved in land-grabbing intrigues and periodic bombardments of Igbo communities. Its attempt to establish botanical gardens to increase the range of products for export failed. Thus, the 1870s witnessed sporadic outbreaks of violence, deep-seated and endemic hostility, and even wars between the trading firms and the local people. Trading factories at Aboh, Oko, Alenso, and Osomari were attacked by the local people. The British naval force silenced these states and communities including Aboh, which was bombarded twice in 1862 and 1893, Onitsha in 1879, Atani in 1880, Asaba in 1888, and Aguleri in 1892. The Ekumeku rebellion of the Anioma Igbo in 1898–1910 was primarily against the RNC and the Roman Catholic missionaries of the Society of African Missions stationed at Asaba.[49]

CHRISTIAN MISSIONARY ACTIVITIES

The Christianization of Igbo society, which has had fundamental impact on gender ideology and roles, began in 1841 with the work of Simon Jonas, a Sierra Leonean of Igbo parentage, at Aboh. The first Christian mission in the Igbo region was established at Onitsha in 1857 by the Church Missionary Society (CMS), under the leadership of Rev. John C. Taylor, another Sierra Leonean of Igbo origin. In 1885 the Roman Catholic Mission followed. The Presbyterians built their first station in 1888 at Unwana. The Niger Delta Pastorate and the Garrick Braide Charismatic Movement were very active in southern Igbo, including the Akwete, Ndoki, Ngwa, and Umuahia areas.[50] The majority of early converts came from the marginalized and underprivileged population in Igbo society such as people of servile origins, outcasts (shrine/cult dedicatees), women, children, the sick, the poor, and the needy. These people saw the missions as their shelter and source of protection. Missions' schools and health centers became instruments of conversion to Christianity as the Igbo came to realize the power of Western education in securing employment opportunities and the efficacy of modern medicine in curing certain illnesses and diseases. Thus, the early twentieth century witnessed an increase in the population of Igbo Christian converts following the hardships engendered by World War I, the 1918–1919 influenza epidemics, and the 1920–1921 outbreak of smallpox.

This period also saw the emergence of Igbo missionaries who helped spread Christianity throughout the region. Some of them were trained at the CMS training school for catechism at Lokoja, which was later moved to Asaba, then to Inyienu, and finally to Awka in 1904. These pioneer Igbo missionaries and church workers were mostly men of little education—mostly former employees of the Royal Niger Company and ex-slaves—but were known for their piety and devotion.[51] In fact, all the missions depended heavily on these pioneer Igbo mission workers for the spread of the gospel. At this early stage, there were no Igbo female missionaries or church workers because training opportunities were focused on men and boys.

The missions established schools. By the early 1900s, there were a number of primary schools scattered in different parts of the Igbo region and a few postprimary ones located in major towns. These schools were primarily focused on the education of boys and young men. As a result, more boys and men than girls and women graduated from the schools during this period. Western education prepared them to become interpreters, clerical staff, warrant chiefs, court messengers and clerks, stenographers, typists, bookkeepers, teachers, artisans, and missionaries. They formed a new class of privileged Igbo. With their perceived views on marriage and the role of women at home and in society, white women missionaries established girls' schools and adult education centers for women in such Igbo areas as Egbu (Owerri), Bende, Asaba, Iyienu, and Onitsha, where they were offered instruction in bible study, domestic science, character formation, marriage life, hygiene, cookery, sewing, needlework, and drawing—just to prepare them to become Christian wives to the emerging male elite and also as mothers capable of raising future leaders and public servants. The CMS was the first mission to provide any form of postprimary education for girls in an Igbo region. In 1895 it established the Onitsha Girls School. A Girls' Training Institute was established at Iyienu, near Onitsha, in 1905, where girls were taught laundry, cookery, baking, tailoring, and the care and training of infants. Edith Warner, after a long missionary career, was able to establish a boarding school for girls at Onitsha, which was largely financed by what the students produced.

Western education and Christianity engendered rapid social transformations and class and gender differentiations in Igbo society. While training girls and women for domestic services that aimed to confine them at home, they trained boys and young men in English language, science, and new technologies that equipped them to take up leadership and other positions in the growing bureaucracies. However, certain percentages of Igbo women who acquired modern skills and knowledge were able to take advantage of new economic opportunities introduced during this period. Persons of servile origin enthusiastically embraced these two forces that provided them avenues to attend significant measures of social mobility. Western education as a social equalizer might have offered the descendants of slave populations an unprecedented opportunity to rise in the Igbo sociopolitical ladder, but the freeborn population was not left behind. A review of the list of early prominent Western-educated Igbo who descended from the freeborn class reinforces this observation: Nnamdi Azikiwe of Onitsha, Nwafor Orizu of Nnewi, Akanu Ibiam of Uwana, Kenneth Dike of Awka, Denis Osadebey of Asaba, and Mbonu Ojike and Kingsley Mbadiwe of Arondizuogu to mention but a few.

Backed by the force of colonial power, the missionaries fought to suppress inhuman practices in Igbo society—human sacrifice, slavery, twin infanticide, banishment of people accused of committing certain crimes such as witchcraft (usually old and childless women), and those suffering from certain illnesses. Often the victims were women and girls. Many Igbo lives were saved from these obnoxious cultural practices. Before mission intervention against twin infanticide, more boys were saved than girls. When a mother secretly delivered twins of a boy and a girl, she would kill or discard the girl and take home the boy. The decision to spare the boy was due to Igbo preference for sons as family heirs. The woman also escaped from being ostracized.[52] Mission stations became a refuge for slaves, women, and others who were escaping from what they saw as the tyranny of the Igbo social system. Another benefit of the missions was the provision of modern health services. While at school, girls and young women were taught certain aspects of health education, the Christian missions provided health services that improved the health of the Igbo, especially pregnant women, nursing mothers, and infants.

As a result of the activities of the Christian missionaries, the Igbo region witnessed a decline in the influence of the oracles—Ibiniupkabi, Agbala, Igwekala, and Kamalu. The passage of the Native Ordinances Act of 1901, which declared all judicial institutions but the native courts as illegitimate, was a major blow to oracular consultation in Igbo society.[53] Despite of the decline in the practice, the services of indigenous healers—*dibias*, diviners, priests and priestesses, herbalists, bonesetters, and midwives—were still sought after. Christian missionary activities also led to the violation of native laws and customs, misguided assaults, and desecration of sacred religious sites (shrines and temples, places of ritual and worship) and objects by converts, especially the overzealous ones. They also led to disobedience and disrespect of indigenous authorities—such as elders and parents—by the youths. Thus, the missionaries and their overzealous converts were regarded as cultural polluters and dangerous innovators.

THE BRITISH COLONIAL CONQUEST AND EARLY COLONIAL RULE

Although the process of colonial conquest began in the Igbo region in the mid-1880s, it took the British up to the 1920s to finally subjugate all the states and mini-states of the Igbo. The conquest of the Igbo region took more than three decades of constant military action, making the Igbo resistance to colonial conquest the most tenacious in Nigeria. There were, for instance, military campaigns against Aguleri (1892), Akwete, Obohia, and Ohuhu (1896), Anioma/western Igbo (the Ekumeku, 1898–1910), the 1901–1902 Aro Expedition, and the Bende-Onitsha Expedition (1905–1906), regarded as the largest military operation undertaken by the Protectorate government under Walter Egerton as the governor of the Colony and Protectorate of Southern Nigeria. Others included the Ezza and Ahiara Mbaise (1905–1916), Isuikwuato and Ishiagu (1907), the Udi-Okigwe area (1914), and the Ikwo (1918).[54] At the end, the Igbo lost for a number of reasons, including the fact that whereas they fought with cap guns, dane guns, machetes, and occasionally rifles, and suffered from a chronic shortage of ammunition, the British colonizers enjoyed an unlimited supply of sophisticated weaponry. The defeat cleared the way for the colonizers, the traders, and the missionaries.

The colonial project introduced a new political system that was dominated by men, taxation, a new monetary system, land alienation and commercialization, improved transportation systems, urbanization, and new technologies. It also brought about increased foreign capital and goods, increased presence of foreign trading companies and Christian missionaries, Western education, health services, and the erosion of Igbo culture and religion. These innovations had serious implications on gender relations in Igbo society. While some of them created opportunities that women exploited to enhance their status in society, others undermined their economic, political, and religious powers and entrenched men's dominance of the new order. As the discussion below shows, colonialism imposed Western concepts of the state, family, and gender roles on the Igbo, notions that privileged men over women.

The British colonial government apparatus in the region started with the establishment in 1891 of the Oil Rivers Protectorate (renamed the Niger Coast Protectorate in 1893) in the Niger Delta. In 1896 the officials of this government incorporated parts of southern and western Igbo (including Aboh, Obohia, and Ohuhu) into the protectorate. In 1900, following the revocation of the charter given to the Royal Niger Company, the 1900 Native Courts Proclamation No. 9 was passed, which authorized colonial officials to establish Native Administrations through the creation of native courts and the appointment of indigenous administrative personnel. Subsequently, a warrant chief system of native administration was introduced in southeastern provinces, a predominantly Igbo region. Under this system, certain male figures were selected and issued a warrant of authority by the British colonial officials, who had limited knowledge of the indigenous sociopolitical organization. In some cases, warrant holders were not selected based on the indigenous norms and practices but instead were men who collaborated with the British, could speak English, and were also enterprising. The appointment of Samuel Okosi of Onitsha (r. 1900–1931), and Kanu Okoro of Arochukwu are just two examples. Others were persons of questionable backgrounds, who used their new office for personal aggrandizement.

The warrant gave the holders the authority to sit in the Native courts, where they exercised both executive and judicial powers.[55] Those who could speak English—court clerks, court messengers, interpreters, policemen, and others—found themselves in the corridors of the new power structure. These were almost exclusively men. In fact, the British "indirect rule" governed through male authorities, and while formalizing male institutions, it ignored and undermined female equivalents. Many of the indigenous sociopolitical structures and institutions—kinship ties, Ọmu-ship, title societies, age-grades, the marketplace, and others—through which women exercised their power and acted as checks and balances to male authority, were weakened and rendered inactive. There were, however, a small number of women who were offered positions in the new system of government: Ọmu Okwei Ezeiwene (nèe Afubeho) of Osomari, who served in the Onitsha Native Court (1912–1930s); Eze Ahebi Ugbabe, who served in the Enugu-Ezike Native Court in the 1920s and was later appointed a warrant chief, the only woman to occupy such a coveted political position in the entire colonial Nigeria; and a couple of Ngwa, Owerrinta, and Mbaise women, who as a result of the Women's War of 1929, which resulted in the reformation of the local government in the region, were appointed in the 1930s as members of the local councils in their respective communities.[56] This new system of government was a radical departure from the indigenous forms of government described in the first section of this chapter.

Another colonial policy that led to social transformation in Igbo society was labor recruitment. Under the 1903 Roads and Creeks Proclamation, colonial officers were authorized to conscript from the indigenous population unpaid labor to perform public work and services. Both free and slave persons were conscripted and used as carriers, in road construction, and in the construction of the railway line between Port Harcourt and Enugu. The colonial government relied on this type of labor between 1903 and 1926. It became a social leveler or equalizer, where both titleholders and commoners, slaves and their masters, and ex-slaves and their former owners were subjected to the same type of work and under the same harsh labor conditions. This labor system was very unpopular and notorious because of its arbitrariness and excessiveness. The laborers were subjected to long hours of work and under the vagaries of weather. Some were forced to carry heavy loads on their heads and walk long distances, at times without any meals. There was, for example, the case of a man forced to carry a fifty-six-pound bag of coal on his head on a 100-mile walk from Udi to the Niger.[57] Igbo women were not as involved as their male counterparts in colonial forced labor.

Similarly, the new colonial economic order favored men more than women. Men and boys were trained in skill acquisitions to manage newly introduced technologies. They were employed in the Native courts, the transport industry, the mines, the Christian missions, and expatriate trading companies. Women's access to Western education, the gateway to modern employment, was limited by its dual-gender structure that emphasized domestic science training for girls and leadership and technical instructions for boys. Access to the newly introduced British money also favored men more than women through the male-dominated cash crop economy and the colonial gendered employment policy that discriminated against women. Colonial economic policy favored men more than women in access to land, extension services, high-yielding palm seedlings, fertilizer, demonstration farms, oil presses, kernel crackers, pioneer oil mills, cassava graters, loans, and other innovations and new technologies that gave men an enviable position to dominate the export and local economies of the region. With the above advantages, men penetrated and controlled hitherto female economic spheres. As a result, most Igbo women were pushed to an informal and petty sector of the colonial economy.[58]

IGBO RESISTANCE TO EUROPEAN PRESENCE AND ACTIVITIES

Igbo resistance involved both violent and nonviolent responses to threatening and unacceptable sociocultural, religious, political, and economic conditions and interferences. While violent resistance involved protest-demonstrations and military confrontations, nonviolent responses included adulteration of trade goods and withholding of produce, insulting and demeaning verbal utterances, songs and dances, provocative gestures and performances, peaceful demonstrations, flight, work stoppage and strikes, boycotts, and other forms of civil disobedience.[59] As shown above, the mid-nineteenth century saw the beginning of European penetration of the hinterland and, subsequently, extensive European activities. The granting of a royal charter in 1886 to the National African Company (subsequently, the Royal Niger Company) engendered an atmosphere of hostility between it and the Igbo. The company's ruthlessness escalated conflicts into open wars fought between its constabulary forces and various Igbo groups between 1892 and 1899. The royal charter, which gave the company the right to administer the Niger from Aboh northward to Nupe, was revoked in 1900, and subsequently the British Protectorates of Northern and Southern Nigeria were established.

The takeover by the British colonial government did not help matters. From the 1890s through the 1920s, various Igbo states and mini-states mounted violent resistance movements against the British encroachments into their territories. For instance, the Aro defiantly fought back British efforts to penetrate into the hinterland and resorted to anti-British intrigues with other local communities such as the Ikwo, Izzi, and Ezza, and against local groups friendly to the British. Between 1898 and 1910 the Ekumeku mounted ruthless reprisals against the Europeans and their local agents in the western Igbo region. As Don Ohadike demonstrated in his study of the west Niger Igbo resistance movement, "the Ekumeku uprising was a revolt of slave owners against the British emancipation ideals, together with the unwelcome involvement of the Christian missionaries with local customs and politics."[60] It was against the people's loss of their authority and independence. Although women contributed in a number of ways in these military campaigns, they were masterminded and executed by Igbo men. Comparatively, while Igbo men generally employed more violent means of resistance, women resorted more to nonviolent strategies.

In terms of punishments meted to the Igbo during this period, men suffered more than women. Men were the ones who were executed and were the sector of the indigenous population subjected most to long periods of imprisonment. For instance, chiefs were singled out as the organizers of the Ekumeku uprising—many were shot to death, others were imprisoned. In 1906, following the forced labor protest-demonstrations by men from the Agbor District, several hundreds of them were shot to death by the colonial troops.[61] Even where women deployed acts of violence, as in the case of the Women's War of 1929, for example, the highest punishments meted to them were short-term detention and fines. Women referred to themselves as the "untouchable vultures," and were therefore emboldened by the belief that they would not be subjected to capital punishments as the men were. They therefore launched the stiffest resistance against the British colonial government and its agents between the 1920s and 1950s.

CONCLUSION

There is little doubt that the trans-Atlantic slave trade, its abolition and the emancipation of the enslaved, the transition to the export agricultural commodity production, and the imposition of British colonialism on the Igbo unleashed forces that altered existing gender ideologies and relations. This chapter has demonstrated how colonialism, Christianity, Western education, foreign capital, and new technologies imposed Western gender ideologies and class differentiations in Igbo society. Different segments of the Igbo population—freeborn, slaves and ex-slaves, outcasts, men and women, boys and girls—were forced by the above external elements and internal dynamics to engage in power negotiations and contestations for resource control, social mobility, and economic survival. Igbo people responded in various ways—receptivity, adaptability, collaboration, and violent and nonviolent resistance—to increased European presence and activities in their territories. While striving to make sense of the new order of society imposed on them, the Igbo became an agency of change. They became as creative and innovative as possible in their efforts to contribute to the shaping of their society despite the powerful winds of change coming from outside.

Igbo women in particular had managed to engage in constant negotiations and contestations of power to advance their interests in the face of entrenched patriarchal ideologies. They had demonstrated that they were a productive and reproductive force to reckon with. Overall, the forces unleashed by Christianity and colonialism may have resulted in social transformations and class differentiations in Igbo society, but such changes were not engraved in stone—that is, they were not permanent and final. Instead, the transformations demonstrated certain degrees of change and continuity in Igbo life—in terms of the acceptance of Christianity and the survival of certain aspects of indigenous religious practices, acceptance of both monogamous and polygynous marriages, reliance on modern and indigenous medicines, and others. The dynamics of gender relations, capital accumulation, and class differentiations would remain constant features of Igbo society as the people continued to engage in selective appropriations of new ideas and innovations.

NOTES

1. Three important works on dual-descent groups of the Igbo are John McCall, *Dancing Histories: Heuristic Ethnography with the Ohafia Igbo* (Ann Arbor: University of Michigan Press, 2000); Philip O. Nsugbe, *Ohafia: A Matrilineal Ibo People* (Oxford: Clarendon Press, 1974); Simon Ottenberg, *Double-Descent in an African Society: The Afikpo Village-Group* (Seattle: University of Washington Press, 1968).

2. For sources on Igbo origins, see John Oriji, *Traditions of Igbo Origin: A Study of Pre-Colonial Population Movements in Africa* (New York: Peter Lang, 1990); Philip Oguagha and Alex Okpoko, *History and Ethnoarchaeology in Eastern Nigeria: A Study of Igbo-Igala Relations with Special Reference to the Anambra Valley* (Oxford: B.A.R., 1984); Adiele Afigbo, *Ropes of Sand: Studies in Igbo History and Culture* (Oxford: Oxford University Press, 1981); Thurstan Shaw, *Unearthing Igbo-Ukwu* (Oxford: Oxford University Press, 1977); Shaw, *Igbo Ukwu: An Account of Archaeological Discoveries in Eastern Nigeria* (London: Faber and Faber, 1970).

3. Gloria Chuku, "Igbo Women and Political Participation in Nigeria, 1800s–2005," *International Journal of African Historical Studies* 42, no. 1 (2009): 81–103; Don C. Ohadike, *Anioma: A Social History of the Western Igbo People* (Athens: Ohio University Press, 1994); Elechukwu N. Njaka, *Igbo Political Culture* (Evanston, IL: Northwestern University Press, 1974); Ikenna Nzimiro, *Studies in Ibo Political Systems: Chieftaincy and Politics in Four Niger States* (Berkeley: University of California Press, 1972); Adiele E. Afigbo, *The Warrant Chiefs: Indirect Rule in Southeastern Nigeria, 1891–1929* (London: Longman, 1972).

4. Chuku, "Igbo Women and Political Participation;" Chuku, *Igbo Women and Economic Transformation in Southeastern Nigeria, 1900–1960* (New York: Routledge, 2005); Kamene

Okonjo, "Nigerian Women's Participation in National Politics: Legitimacy and Stability in an Era of Transition," (Working Paper no. 221, Michigan State University, July 1991); Okonjo, "The Dual-Sex Political System in Operation: Igbo Women and Community Politics in Midwestern Nigeria," in *Women in Africa: Studies in Social and Economic Change*, ed. Nancy Hafkin and Edna G. Bay (Stanford, CA: Stanford University Press, 1976), 45–58.

5. Ekpe was a secret male cult, which flourished among the Efik, the Ibibio and their Igbo neighbors as well as the Banyang of Mamfe in Cameroon. It was an important agency of social control through which the male initiates exercised power over noninitiates, particularly women and slaves.

6. For women admitted into all-male exclusive Ekpe society, see John McCall, "Portrait of a Brave Woman," *American Anthropologist* 98, no. 1 (1996): 127–36. See also Gloria Chuku, "From Petty Traders to International Merchants: A Historical Account of Three Igbo Women of Nigeria in Trade and Commerce, 1886 to 1970," *African Economic History* 27 (1999): 8 for Oguta women admitted into the exclusively men's Ikwa Muo society.

7. Generally, women and girls were excluded from participation in masquerading in Igbo society. In fact, there were certain masked spirits that women and girls were not supposed to see. To prevent women and girls from committing an abomination by *itikwo isi muọ* ("unmasking" the masquerades by the mere sight of them), certain masquerades could only operate at night. Women and girls were required to announce that they were passing by as novices who were uninterested in men's affairs. But menopausal titled women were regarded as males and therefore could see masked spirits or engage in masked performances. There were also a few female masking cults especially in northern Igbo. See Chinyere Okafor, "From the Heart of Masculinity: Ogbodo-Uke Women's Masking," *Research in African Literatures* 25, no. 3 (1994): 7–17.

8. Because kolanut was a social and ritual symbol in Igbo society, breaking and sharing it involved certain rites that invoked the *ndichie* (ancestors). It was always presented with prayers at the beginning of such important events as festivals, marriage ceremonies, contracts, covenant, rites of passage and adjudication of cases. It was the first thing an Igbo presented to his or her guest as a symbol of welcome, Igbo hospitality and friendship. Women were not allowed to break kolanuts whenever a male figure was around. But in Oguta and Onitsha, titled women could break and share kolanuts with men. See Victor Uchendu, "'Kola Hospitality' and Igbo Lineage Structure," *Man* 64, no. 53 (1964): 47–50.

9. Olaudah Equiano, *The Interesting Narrative and Other Writings*, ed. with an Introduction and Notes by Vincent Carretta (New York: Penguin Books, 1995), 40.

10. Chuku, *Igbo Women*; Linus C. Okere, *The Anthropology of Igbo Food in Rural Igboland, Nigeria* (Lanham, MD: University Press of America, 1983); Bede Okigbo, *Plants and Food in Igbo Culture and Civilization*, Ahiajoku Lecture (Owerri, Nigeria: Ministry of Information and Culture, 1980); W. B. Morgan, "Farming Practice, Settlement Pattern and Population Density in Southeastern Nigeria," *Geographical Journal* 121, no. 3 (1955): 320–33.

11. Chuku, *Igbo Women*, 36–37; Victor Uchendu, *The Igbo of Southeast Nigeria* (New York: Holt, 1965), 22–23; L. T. Chubb, *Ibo Land Tenure* (Ibadan, Nigeria: Ibadan University Press, 1961).

12. See Chuku, *Igbo Women*, for the delineation of Igbo economic zones and gender activities.

13. Shaw, *Unearthing Igbo-Ukwu*; Shaw, *Igbo Ukwu*.

14. Chuku, *Igbo Women*; Kenneth O. Dike and Felicia Ekejiuba, *The Aro of South-eastern Nigeria, 1650–1980: A Study of Socio-economic Formation and Transformation in Nigeria* (Ibadan, Nigeria: Ibadan University Press, 1990); Afigbo, *Ropes of Sand*; David Northrup, *Trade Without Rulers: Pre-Colonial Economic Development in South-Eastern Nigeria* (Oxford: Clarendon Press, 1978); Northrup, "The Growth of Trade among the Igbo before 1800," *Journal of African History* 13, no. 2 (1972): 217–36; Kenneth O. Dike, *Trade and Politics in the Niger Delta, 1830–1850* (London: Oxford University Press, 1956).

15. Shaw, *Igbo Ukwu*; Shaw, *Unearthing Igbo-Ukwu*; J. E. G. Sutton, "Igbo-Ukwu and the Nile," *African Archaeological Review* 18, no. 1 (2001): 49–62; Arnold Rubin's review of Frank Willet, *Ife in the History of West African Sculpture*, in *African Notes* 6, no. 2 (1971): 113–23.

16. Northrup, *Trade Without Rulers*; Dike, *Trade and Politics*; Duarte Pacheco Pereira, *Esmeraldo de Situ Orbis*, trans. and ed. George H. T. Kimble (London: The Hakluyt Society, 1937); John Adams, *Sketches Taken during Ten Voyages to Africa, between the Years 1786 and 1800; including Observation on the Country between Cape Palmas and the River Congo; and Cursory Remarks on the Physical and Moral Character of the Inhabitants* (London: G. and W. B. Whittaker, 1822); John Barbot, *A Description of the Coasts of North and South-Guinea; and of Ethiopia Interior, Vulgarly Angola; Being a New and Accurate Account of the Western Maritime Countries of Africa* (London: Churchill, 1732); Olfert Dapper, *Description de l'Afrique*, French trans. (Amsterdam: Wolfgang, Waesberge, Boom, and van Someren, 1686).

17. For more information on the Aro and the slave trade, see G. Ugo Nwokeji, *The Slave Trade and Culture in the Bight of Biafra: An African Society in the Atlantic World* (Cambridge: Cambridge University Press, 2010); Dike and Ekejiuba, *The Aro of South-eastern Nigeria*; Afigbo, *Ropes of Sand*; Gloria Chuku, "The Rise and Fall of Aro Business Oligarchy from 15th Century to 20th Century" (MA thesis, Department of History, University of Port Harcourt, Nigeria, 1989); John Oriji, "The Slave Trade, Warfare and Aro Expansion in the Igbo Hinterland," *Transafrican Journal of History* 16 (1987): 151–66; Dike, *Trade and Politics*. On the Ekpe and Ọkọnkọ societies, see John Oriji, "A Re-Assessment of the Organization and Benefits of the Slave and Palm Produce Trade amongst the Ngwa-Igbo," *Canadian Journal of African Studies* 16, no. 3 (1982): 523–48; John Oriji, "Oracular Trade, Okonko Secret Society and the Evolution of Decentralized Authority among the Ngwa-Igbo of Southeastern Nigeria," *Ikenga* 5, no. 1 (1981): 35–52.

18. *Nsibidi* script has ideograph symbols as in Chinese, and each symbol represents a concept. For example, semicircles represent wealth, and they may depict copper currency. Over 500 symbols of *Nsibidi* were recorded in southeastern Nigeria. See J. K. Macgregor, "Some Notes on Nsibidi," *The Journal of the Royal Anthropological Institute of Great Britain and Ireland* 39 (1909): 209–19; Elphinstone Dayrell, "Some 'Nsibidi' Signs," *Man* 10 (1910): 113–14; E. Dayrell, "Further Notes on 'Nsibidi Signs' with their Meanings from the Ikom District, Southern Nigeria," *The Journal of the Royal Anthropological Institute of Great Britain and Ireland* 41 (1911): 521–40.

19. A. E. Afigbo, *The Abolition of the Slave Trade in Southeastern Nigeria, 1885–1950* (Rochester, NY: University of Rochester Press, 2006), xiii.

20. Richard Lander and John Lander, *Journal of an Expedition to Explore the Course and Termination of the Niger with a Narrative of a Voyage Down that River to its Termination*, vol. 2 (New York: J. and J. Harper, 1832). William Baikie, who visited Aboh in 1854, indicated that while Aje had 4 large war canoes and about 250 slaves, his brother Tshukuma [Chukwuma] had 50–60 slaves. See William B. Baikie, *Narrative of an Exploring Voyage up the Rivers Kwora and Binue, Commonly known as the Niger and Tsadda in 1854* (London: Frank Cass, 1856, reprint 1966), 303.

21. Macgregor Laird and R. A. K. Oldfield, *Narrative of an Expedition into the Interior of Africa by the River Niger*, vol. 2 (London: R. Bentley, 1837), 103, 106.

22. Baikie, *Narrative of an Exploring Voyage*, 49, 302, 317.

23. F. Ifeoma Ekejiuba, "The Aro System of Trade in the Nineteenth Century," *Ikenga* 1, no. 1 (1972): 21, 24, quoting Richard Morisey, Acting Divisional Commissioner of the Cross River Division.

24. A. J. Fox, *A Short History of Uzuakoli by Students of the Methodist College, Uzuakoli, under the Direction of A. J. Fox* (London: Oxford University Press, 1964), 23.

25. Afigbo, *The Abolition of the Slave Trade*, 38–39; Elizabeth Isichei, "Historical Change in Ibo Polity: Asaba to 1885," *Journal of African History* 10, no. 3 (1969): 421–38. Dike and Ekejiuba, *The Aro of South-eastern Nigeria*, 253, gave accounts of an Aro chief whose burial in 1898 led to the killing of 700 slaves, and another 80 slaves slaughtered when one Chief Okoroji died

in 1900; Baikie, *Narrative of an Exploring Voyage*, 315, reported the killing of 40 slaves during the burial of an Aboh king.

26. Elizabeth Isichei, *A History of the Igbo People* (London: Macmillan, 1976), 102.

27. Carolyn A. Brown, "Testing the Boundaries of Marginality: Twentieth-Century Slavery and Emancipation Struggles in Nkanu, Northern Igboland, 1920–29," *Journal of African History* 37, no. 1 (1996): 51–80; W. R. G. Horton, "The Ohu System of Slavery in a Northern Ibo Village-Group," *Africa* 24, no. 4 (1954): 311–35.

28. Don C. Ohadike, "'When Slaves Left, Owners Wept': Entrepreneurs and Emancipation among the Igbo People," *Slavery and Abolition* 19, no. 2 (1998): 189–207.

29. Dike and Ekejiuba, *The Aro of Southeastern Nigeria*, 252.

30. Don Ohadike, *The Ekumeku Movement: Western Igbo Resistance to the British Conquest of Nigeria, 1883–1914* (Athens: Ohio University Press, 1991), 33–34, quoting Macgregor Laird.

31. Susan Martin, "Slaves, Igbo Women and Palm Oil in the Nineteenth Century," in *From Slave Trade to 'Legitimate' Commerce: The Commercial Transition in Nineteenth-Century West Africa*, ed. Robin Law (Cambridge: Cambridge University Press, 1995), 183–85.

32. Afigbo, *The Abolition of the Slave Trade*, 43–44.

33. PRO, CO 520/12, Southern Nigeria Dispatches to the Colonial Office, July 7, 1901.

34. F. D. Lugard, *Political Memoranda*, [1919] 3rd ed. (London: Frank Cass, 1966), 216–46.

35. NNAI, CSO 1/3, Southern Nigeria Dispatches to the Colonial Office, No. 361, July 29, 1903.

36. NNAE, RIVPROF 2/1/24, C.136, No. 217/Vol.3/210/09 by S. P. George on February 4, 1935.

37. NNAE, AW 546, AWDIST 2/1/363, Udorie (Girl) of Aro-Nanka—Whereabout of, 1932; NNAE, RIVPROF 8/5/47, Rex vs. Ebube Dike of Nkwerre Charged with Kidnapping.

38. NNAE, C.P. 2039-CALPROF 3/1/1928, File No. M.P. no. P.C. 1/1/1931 of June 15,1931.

39. Afigbo, *The Warrant Chiefs*, 193, shows the case of a warrant chief who had 130 wives by the time he was convicted of slave dealing and child stealing. The bridewealth on each of them was less than fifteen shillings. For accounts of prominent Igbo women who owned slaves during this period, see Nwando Achebe, *Farmers, Traders, Warriors, and Kings: Female Power and Authority in Northern Igboland, 1900–1960* (Portsmouth, NH: Heinemann, 2005), 197–224; Gloria Chuku, "Women and the Complexity of Gender Relations," in *Nigeria in the Twentieth Century*, ed. Toyin Falola (Durham, NC: Carolina Academic Press, 2002), 86; Buchi Emecheta, *The Slave Girl* (New York: George Braziller, 1977), 50, 58, 60–61; Felicia Ekejiuba, "Omu Okwei, the Merchant Queen of Ossomari: A Biographical Sketch," *Journal of the Historical Society of Nigeria* 3, no. 4 (1967): 633–46; Macgregor Laird, quoted in Ohadike, *The Ekumeku Movement*, 33–34.

40. Nwokeji, *The Slave Trade*, 158; Nwokeji, "The Slave Emancipation Problematic: Igbo Society and the Colonial Equation," *Comparative Studies in Society and History* 40, no. 2 (1998): 337.

41. Chuku, "Women and the Complexity of Gender Relations," 79–100.

42. Chuku, *Igbo Women*; Susan Martin, *Palm Oil and Protest: An Economic History of the Ngwa, South-Eastern Nigeria, 1800–1980* (New York: Cambridge University Press, 1988).

43. Law, *From Slave Trade to 'Legitimate' Commerce*; Martin Lynn, "The West African Palm Oil Trade in the Nineteenth Century and the 'Crisis of Adaptation,'" in *From Slave Trade to 'Legitimate' Commerce*, 57–77; Martin, "Slaves, Igbo Women and Palm Oil," 172–94; Oriji, "A Re-Assessment of the Organization."

44. Chuku, *Igbo Women*; Martin, *Palm Oil and Protest*; Susan Martin, "Gender and Innovation: Farming, Cooking, and Palm Processing in the Ngwa Region, South-Eastern Nigeria, 1900–1930," *Journal of African History* 25, no. 4 (1984): 411–27; Eno J. Usoro, *The Nigerian Oil Palm Industry: Government Policy and Export Production, 1906–1965* (Ibadan, Nigeria: Ibadan University Press, 1974).

45. Northrup, *Trade Without Rulers*, 186, quoting a 1938 report on oil palm survey in the Igbo, Ibibio, and Cross River areas by A. F. B. Bridges.

46. Laird and Oldfield, *Narrative of an Expedition*, vol. 1, 105.

47. John Whitford, *Trading Life in Western and Central Africa*, 2nd ed. (London: Frank Cass, 1877, reprint 1967), 163.

48. Gloria Chuku, "Women in the Mid-19th and Early 20th-Century Palm Oil Trade in Igboland, Nigeria" (paper presented at the 43rd Annual Conference of the African Studies Association, Nashville, TN, November 16–19, 2000).

49. Ohadike, *The Ekumeku Movement*; Philip Igbafe, "Western Igbo Society and Its Resistance to British Rule: The Ekumeku Movement, 1898–1911," *Journal of African History* 12, no. 3 (1971): 441–59.

50. For more information on the introduction and spread of Christianity in the Igbo region, see Ogbu Kalu, *The Embattled Gods: Christianization of Igboland, 1841–1991* (Lagos, NG: Minaj Publishers, 1996); G. O. M. Tasie, *Christian Missionary Enterprise in the Niger Delta, 1864–1918* (Leiden, NL: Brill, 1978); Edmund C. Ilogu, *Christian Ethics in an African Background: A Study of the Interaction of Christianity and Ibo Culture* (Leiden, NL: Brill, 1974); Felix Ekechi, *Missionary Enterprise and Rivalry in Igboland, 1857–1914* (London: Frank Cass, 1972); Elizabeth Isichei, "Seven Varieties of Ambiguity: Some Patterns of Igbo Response to Christian Missions," *Journal of Religion in Africa* 3, no. 2 (1970): 209–27; Elizabeth Isichei, "Ibo and Christian Beliefs: Some Aspects of a Theological Encounter," *African Affairs* 68, no. 271 (1969): 121–34; E. A. Ayandele, *The Missionary Impact on Nigeria, 1842–1914* (London: Longman, 1966); Samuel Crowther and John C. Taylor, *The Gospel on the Banks of the Niger: Journals and Notices of the Native Missionaries Accompanying the Niger Expedition of 1857–1859* [1859] (London: Dawsons of Pall Mall, 1968).

51. The Igbo acceptance of Christianity was a gradual process. While Christian teachings resonated with the lowly in Igbo society, the traditional elite and titleholders reluctantly embraced the new religion. The missionary condemnation of Igbo religious beliefs and cultural practices such as polygyny made their religion unattractive to the people. However, there were prominent Igbo men, such as Kings Idigo of Aguleri and Nzedegwu of Osomari, who were instrumental to the establishment of Christian missions in their respective communities. There was also Alexander Ubuechi of Issele, who converted to Catholicism when he was already a diviner, a titleholder, and a skilled craftsman; his commitment to the mission earned him the missionary acclamation of a saint when he died in 1903. Another example was Nwafor Ogwuma of Arochukwu, a successful slave dealer and polygamist, who later assisted Rev. Rankin and J. A. T. Beattie to establish a Presbyterian mission at the town in 1907. He was among the people who helped Archdeacon Dennis in the translation of the Igbo Union Bible.

52. Anene Ejikeme, "Subterfuge and Resistance: A History of Infanticide in Onitsha," in *Power and Nationalism in Modern Africa*, ed. Toyin Falola and Salah M. Hassan (Durham, NC: Carolina Academic Press, 2008), 155–68; Misty L. Bastian, "'The Demon Superstition': Abominable Twins and Mission Culture in Onitsha History," *Ethnology* 40, no. 1 (2001): 13–27.

53. Uzodinma Nwala, "Some Reflections on British Conquest of Igbo Traditional Oracles, 1900–1924," *Nigeria Magazine* 142 (1982): 25–35; Simon Ottenberg, "Ibo Oracles and Intergroup Relations," *Southwestern Journal of Anthropology* 14, no. 3 (1958): 295–317.

54. For more information on some of these military campaigns and wars, see Ohadike, *The Ekumeku Movement*; Igbafe, "Western Igbo Society;" Elizabeth Isichei, *The Ibo People and the Europeans: The Genesis of a Relationship—To 1906* (New York: St. Martin's Press, 1973), chap. 10; Isichei, *A History of the Igbo People*, chap. 9; Dike and Ekejiuba, *The Aro of South-eastern Nigeria*; Felix Ekechi, "Merchants, Missionaries and the Bombardment of Onitsha, 1879–89: Aspects of Anglo-Igbo Encounter," *The Conch* 5, nos. 1–2 (1973): 61–81.

55. Afigbo, *The Warrant Chiefs*.

56. Chuku, "Igbo Women and Political Participation"; Achebe, *Farmers, Traders, Warriors, and Kings*; Ekejiuba, "Omu Okwei."

57. Isichei, *The Ibo People and the Europeans*, 164.

58. For a meticulous analysis of the colonial economic policy and its impact on Igbo women, see Chuku, *Igbo Women*.

59. For detailed studies of forms and examples of Igbo resistance to increased European presence in their society, see Chuku, *Igbo*

Women; Felix Ekechi, "The Culture of Resistance to Western Imperialism among the Igbo," in Falola and Hassan, *Power and Nationalism*, 135–53; Felix Ekechi, "The British Assault on Ogbunorie Oracle in Eastern Nigeria," *Journal of African Studies* 14, no. 2 (1981): 69–77; Felix Ekechi, "Igbo Response to British Imperialism: The Episode of Dr. Stewart and the Ahiara Expedition, 1905–1916," *Journal of African Studies* 1, no. 2 (1974): 145–57; Adiele Afigbo, "Revolution and Reaction in Eastern Nigeria: 1900–1929," *Journal of the Historical Society of Nigeria* 3, no. 3 (1966): 539–51; Ohadike, *The Ekumeku Movement*. Toyin Falola, *Colonialism and Violence in Nigeria* (Bloomington: Indiana University Press, 2009) covers most part of Nigeria and shows how the British colonialism engendered a circle of violence in the region.

60. Ohadike, *The Ekumeku Movement*, 39–40.

61. Don Ohadike, "The Decline of Slavery among the Igbo People," in *The End of Slavery in Africa*, ed. S. Miers and R. Roberts (Madison: University of Wisconsin Press, 1988), 448–49.

PART II

THE IGBO IN THE AFRICAN DIASPORA

The Mechanics and Patterns of Migrations, Settlements, and Demographics

5 THE ARO AND THE TRADE OF THE BIGHT

A. E. Afigbo

Relative to other themes in the history of this area, much has been written on the Aro and the trade of the Bight of Biafra from about 1650 on. But a close and critical examination of this literature will show that many specific aspects of the topic remain to be taken up and studied in detail. A case in point is the subject of this chapter, which remains vague. Often the Aro are portrayed as having dominated that trade with no details given. In the first place, there was more than one trade of the Bight—the slave trade, which was mainly an external trade although also an internal one, and the indigenous trade in local products (agricultural and crafts), which preceded the slave trade by hundreds of years. How far the much-touted Aro dominance affected this latter and earlier trade is not usually discussed, nor is the total context of the trade of the region discussed in order to show the role of the Aro in full perspective. Similarly, the role of the Aro in the trade of the zone is often discussed as if that role ceased with the so-called successful abolition of the external slave trade by about 1860, when in fact after that magic date the Aro continued to try to maintain their old role as if not much had changed. This anachronistic Aro rearguard action continued for about a century, fizzling out only in the 1950s.

To correct some of these wrong or unintended impressions, this chapter sets out specifically to examine the actual role of the Aro in the trade of the Bight. In doing so, it considers the total context (geographical, ethnocultural, and economic) of the trade of the zone. It looks at the mechanics and infrastructure of Aro activity, the generally neglected story of the Aro, and the trade of the Bight after the ending of the external slave trade. The hope is that the trend started here will overflow to other aspects of Aro studies, which, in spite of Dike and Ekejiuba,[1] who have devoted a whole book to the Aro, still remain for the most part at the general level.

The much-written-about Aro are mainly an Igbo ethnocultural group with a substantial admixture of Benue-Congo elements demographically, culturally, and linguistically. That immediately defines the Aro as a people living in the frontier zone between the Kwa and Benue-Congo-speaking peoples of Africa. Specifically, especially if we follow the cultural demarcation of the Igbo by Daryll Forde and G. I. Jones,[2] they are located in the Cross River subcultural group of the Igbo. In that area, the Benue-Congo peoples with whom they came into contact and interaction, and who therefore modified their ethnic composition demographically and culturally, were the Ibibio of the middle Cross River, the Efik of the Cross River Delta, and the Ekoi of the upper Cross River. Their evolution as an ethnic group parallels that of their other Igbo kinsmen and goes back for millennia into the past. Their ancestors were part of the Igbo, generically known as Isu Ama (the Isu who had gone abroad), who left the Orlu uplands and went in the eastern direction in search of living space. The force that powered their migration was the same force behind the rise and making of the Nri civilization in the millennium and a half after about 600 BC—the impact of the agricultural and iron revolutions. In the general area of today's boundary between the Kwa and the Benue-Congo, the migration was deflected northeastward. It was from the melee of the ensuing clash between the two peoples that ethnocultural groups like the Aro, the Afikpo, the Ohafia, the Abam, the Edda, and other kindred border Igbo peoples with recognizable evidence of Benue-Congo impact emerged,[3] perhaps centuries before the first European set foot on the soil of the Bight.

During the colonial period and the immediate postcolonial years, scholars who were unfamiliar with this story said the Aro emerged as an ethnocultural group around 1650. In our view, this is mistaking the emergence of the Aro as a force in the trade of the Bight for their origin as an ethnic group. This mistake arose from the then-reprehensible habit of explaining every important development in early West African history in terms of the European factor. Dike and Ekejiuba repeated the same mistake in their book, *The Aro of Southeastern Nigeria*, but this was probably because Dike was unable to depart from his fundamental thesis in his earlier work, *Trade and Politics in the Niger Delta* (which was and still is much celebrated), that the important developments in the Bight started with European advent.[4]

A sketch of the broad context of the trade of the Bight will help us understand more fully the range and depth of this topic. Here we are concerned with the geographical patch of Nigeria bounded in the south by the deltas of the River Niger and the Cross River, in the west by the lower Niger from the entry of that river into the Atlantic to its confluence with the Benue River, in the north by the Benue Valley, and in the east by the Cross River. This river system is now known to have served the zone well in the matter of communication among the groups that were situated along the riverbanks, thanks to the emergence of the canoe as a vital means of communication early in West African history. The writings of Professor E. J. Alagoa on the Delta, of David Northrup on the lower Niger, of Femi J. Kolapo on the lower Niger and the Delta, and of S. F. Nadel on the Niger-Benue confluence people of Kede, for instance, confirm this statement beyond doubt.[5]

Still pursuing the geographic context, we are dealing here with the eastern corner of the primary and secondary tropical forest lands of West Africa, which are, *par excellence*, an agricultural zone that offered and still offers scope for the cultivation of a wide range of crops as well as being the home of many economically important trees, such as the oil palm and raffia palm, which are said to have been domesticated early in the history of the region. There were also countless other trees that supplied raw materials for the many crafts that were practiced there. The vegetation of the area ran more or less west to east—the mangrove forest of the coastal swamps, followed by the evergreen forest and then the secondary forest or derived savanna, which kept thinning out as it ran north until it merged with the savanna belt proper in Kasar Hausa. Another prominent feature of the zone is the range of hills running north to south with a southeasterly extension to Arochukwu, which geographers refer to as the Nsukka-Okigwe cuesta. It is rich in iron ore deposits, which were mined and smelted for use by many communities of smiths situated in different parts of it. Situated in the secondary forest or derived savanna zone of the region, it offered no obstacles to communication. Indeed, it was crisscrossed by trade routes that were in use over the centuries.

Also important is the ethnocultural context. The delta of the Niger is the home of the Ijo-speaking peoples, whose language is said to be at least 5,000 years old and to constitute something of a transition or bridge between the Kwa and Benue-Congo languages. An ancient people indeed, it is believed they penetrated the Niger Delta by about the first century AD, many centuries before Europe contemplated setting foot in West Africa. On this matter of Ijo settlement of the Delta, the archaeologist Dr. Nzewunwa wrote as follows:

> The evidence from dated sites so far only extends to late in the first millennium A.D. This shows that Ke is at present the oldest settlement, beginning about the 9th century A.D. The evidence from Okochiri also suggests that at about the time the mangrove swamp sheltered site of Ke was bring occupied, the mainland coastal fringe zone of Okochiri was settled.[6]

Like their neighbors—the Igbo, the Ibibio, the Efik, and the Ogoja peoples—the Ijo began with a segmented lineage and fragmented political system, but as many of them made the transition to a mainly salt-boiling, fishing, and trading economy, they also made the transition to a political system of centralized city-states. This was before the coming of the Europeans, but the latter event, which occurred in the fifteenth century, tended to strengthen this trend in the Ijo's sociopolitical evolution.[7]

Coming after the Ijo are the Benue-Congo-speaking Efik of the Cross River Delta who, like the Ijo, were involved in salt-boiling, fishing, and trading, and similarly made the political transition from segmentary lineage communities to centralized city-states that came to specialize in trading. To the north of the Efik are the Ibibio, also Benue-Congo speaking, with a much larger population than the Efik. They too were characterized socially and politically by the segmented system. Economically, unlike the Efik, their strength lay in agriculture and handicrafts. To the north of the Ibibio are the multifarious Benue-Congo-speaking peoples of Ogoja, among whom the most prominent are the Ekoi. These peoples were also predominantly agricultural. They were also great hunters and thus marketed agricultural products and smoked meat. North of the Ijo and west of the Ibibio are the Igbo-speaking peoples, who dominate the zone demographically, followed in this matter of numbers by the Ibibio. Territorially they occupy the land from the right bank of the Niger to the west, to the right bank of the Cross River to the east, and the dry land immediately to the north of the coastal Ijo, to the southern borders of such Kwa-speaking peoples of the Benue basin as the Igala and the Idoma and of the Benue-Congo-speaking Tiv. Like their neighbors, the Igbo were largely an agricultural people but were also keenly involved in craft work and short- and long-range trade. Their fragmented political organization gave this region its dominant (unfavorable) political image during the colonial era.

North of the Igbo, as already mentioned, are the Kwa-speaking Igala and Idoma and the Benue-Congo-speaking Tiv. They were great agriculturists who were also engaged in crafts and trade. In addition, the Idoma and the Tiv occupy an area of salt-bearing lakes and thus produced and marketed salt. The Igala evolved a centralized state that exerted much influence culturally on the northern borders of Igboland at the same time as they dominated the trade of the lower Niger down to the city-state of Abo to the south. To the west of the Igbo are the Edo-speaking peoples, whose dominant polity was the celebrated Benin Empire, which on its own exerted great political and cultural influence on the western marches of Igboland up to Onitsha east of the Niger.

In sum, the context of the trade we are concerned to discuss could be said to present the following picture ethnoculturally. At the center is what we may designate the Igbo Cultural Area (ICA). To the south of it is the Niger Delta Cultural Area (NDCA). Then we have the Lower Niger Cultural area (LNCA), the Cross River Cultural Area (CRCA), and finally the Benue Basin Cultural Area (BBCA). Each was a cultural and economic area with its own peculiar internal economy and dynamics, at the same time being linked to its neighboring cultural areas by trade and other means of cultural interaction—marriage, religion, and ritual, secret, and more-or-less open societies like titles and age-grades. They were also linked by war and diplomacy. Of this network of relationships we shall have more to say when we come to examine what impact, if any, Aro dominance of the external trade of the hinterland of the Bight left on the region. It should equally be mentioned that this was an area of ancient human settlement. In sections of it, the Nsukka area, for instance, settlement of Neolithic communities has been reported for as far back as the third millennium BC.[8]

And now we come to the trade of the region proper and the role of the Aro in it, which is the main focus of this chapter. However, let it be restated that there were two trades or trading systems in the zone during our period, not one—that in which the Aro came to play the main part, and another that preceded it by thousands of years, which operated outside their dominance. But this point has not always been as emphasized as it should be. The first trade may be described as the primordial trade of the Bight of Biafra. It had two major features. It distributed the products of the people themselves—what they produced in their farms and in their craft workshops as well as their indigenous healing herbs, roots, parts of animals believed to be endowed with psychic qualities, and so on. Its second main feature was that it came into existence for no other reason than for the basic sustenance of the populations of the zone and, maybe in course of time, for the benefit of peoples of neighboring zones with whom our region was in some kind of regular contact.

It is our belief that this trade originated very early in the history of our zone, in any case, as soon as the Neolithic Revolution took roots among the Aro. It is also our belief that trade originated in a kind of relay fashion in which surplus goods and services moved from one community to the one immediately adjoining it and so on to the remotest parts imaginable. As time went on this exchange gathered momentum, leading first to the emergence of what we may call real local trade and then to long-distance trade. By Igbo Ukwu times (ninth century) this latter stage had long emerged, judging by evidence presented by the research of Thurstan Shaw and M. A. Onwuejeogwu.[9] The energy derived from the economy helped the peoples of our region build up the political and socioeconomic system by which they came to be known in historic times. By the late fourteenth and early fifteenth centuries, the Ijo of the Niger Delta began building their centralized village states on the same economy and their long-range trade connecting them to the far interior, as shown by the research of their most famous historian, E. J. Alagoa.[10]

This trade continued side by side with the slave trade throughout the three centuries of the latter's existence and in fact outlasted the slave trade (or better-named, the foreign trade). In the course of the nineteenth century, what was left of the foreign trade, after the abolition of the external slave trade, merged with it to give rise to the trade with which our zone entered the twentieth century and negotiated with it. It is our view that the slave trade was largely the business of the elite members of the communities of the zone. But the internal (indigenous) trade was—for every class—at the village or local level, mainly for women, and at the long-distance level, mainly for men. While the ordinary Aro man and woman participated in this internal trade, we do not think the Aro elite of businessmen and their rivals who ran the slave trade among the Igbo, the Ibibio, the Ogoja, and among the Idoma and the Tiv would have paid much attention to the distribution of local goods and services for local use, which, as we have said, was the business of the internal trade.

By more-or-less general consensus, this foreign trade or the slave trade started along the coast in the course of the fifteenth century, but no one has been able to say for certain when it reached the Igbo and the Ibibio of the interior or registered the kind of impact that stimulated the desire of groups from there to begin taking part in it. But perhaps there is no doubt that by the end of the sixteenth century the impact of the trade was already being felt in many parts of the interior through the activities of the delta peoples along the Niger and up the creeks and rivers between the Nun estuary of the Niger and the Cross River. Under European pressure, promptings, and cajoling they must have started asking for human beings in addition to the natural produce that had constituted the items of the first trade. They must have also made occasional forays inland during which they captured or kidnapped those unfortunate enough to be in their way.

We are inclined to believe that it would not have been too difficult or taken too long to stimulate trade along this line. From earliest times communities here, like communities in other parts of Africa and the world, had had pools or potential pools of people who had destined themselves or been destined for removal by death or some other measures from the company of their fellow villagers. Some of these had broken primordial taboos by the way they were born or by the way they behaved as they grew up. Some had transgressed laws and customs that qualified them for death by execution or suicide or for lifelong exile. These would have been the first victims of the trade. The taste of the gain made from the disposal of these unfortunates would then lead to many other developments. For instance, there would soon arise in various communities persons who would make it their business to dispose of such human rejects. Then also certain persons who were used to traveling beyond their communities for business—such as smiths, medicine men, and oracle agents—and who therefore were used to receiving and supplying orders, would soon have added to their list the supply of such unfortunates.[11]

We have traced this development that no one has traced before for two reasons. One is to make more obvious a point that should be obvious—that the Aro cannot take the credit or the blame for originating the internal or the external slave trade. The second is to make a point we believe no one has made before—that the Aro probably entered the slave trade through practicing first as agents of their oracle, the Ibini Ukpabi. From their own account, the oracle was captured from their Benue-Congo opponents in the process of forming the Aro clan. What we are suggesting is that in those dim days when these developments were taking place, the Aro would have been like any other group of traveling Igbo professionals and would have quietly added the removal of unwanted men and women to their business list.

The picture painted above might suggest also that, in those days when the business of participation in the trade by individual hinterland entrepreneurs and groups was in its early stages, there would have been different centers, individuals, and groups making the bid to participate. In other words, there would have been rivalry and competition. In such a situation it would have been anybody's guess who would succeed or emerge dominant in the trade. The Awka as smiths and oracle agents, the Nkwerre as smiths, the Abiriba as smiths, and the Umunoha as oracle agents, for example, would have been among the group competitors for participation and for supremacy. As individuals, there would have been thousands. We do not know when or how the struggle was resolved, but we do know that by the time it was resolved it was the Aro agents of the oracle of Ibini Ukpabi who emerged as the dominant party or group. It is from hindsight that we now have to adduce reasons for their emergence.

Conjectures established on emerging historical facts can generate useful insights. Even a casual study of the Aro trading system at maximum maturity shows that it was based on social, political, and economic practices and usages that must have been from the earlier times essential ingredients of the Igbo social, economic, and political system and life. These institutions and usages must have also been available to other rivals and competitors of the Aro in the trade. Therefore, the ultimate explanation we might be seeking may be lie in the ability of the Aro to perceive the usefulness of these institutions and practices as aids in the business and in their ability to actually harness and use them. Perhaps first among these institutions and usages was the exploitation of occult arts and institutions—fortune-telling, practice of herbal and other medicines, oracles, and so on—for material ends. These offered opportunities for external travel, for settling in strange communities to promote and practice one's business, and thus to worm oneself into the confidence of his customers whom he could then serve and exploit as much as possible.

Two other pillars on which Aro success and ascendancy rested offered the same advantages. These were the establishment of settlement colonies of their own people all over their area of operation and the zoning of their business area among the different segments of their community to avoid internal rivalry and friction, which could lead to revealing whatever business secrets they may have to their competitors. Only the third pillar of Aro economic dominance operated in a different fashion to achieve the same purpose—the promotion of Aro economic interest. This was the working understanding between the Aro and the professional merchants of bloody violence in the interior of the Bight—the headhunters of Ohafia, Abam, Edda, and related peoples—which the Aro used to teach business associates who turned coat that such action did not pay. The fourth pillar was the blood-oath (*igbandu*—the joining of lives), which created fictitious blood links, and thus confidence and trust, between the Aro and their trade associates. Perhaps a fifth pillar is what Professor Elizabeth Isichei has described as the Aro "brilliant talent for diplomacy"—what their Igbo neighbors call Aro double-tongue or sweet-tongue—the fact that an Aro never gives the same account or story of an event to two different persons, or at two different times or in two different places. Each gets a different version.[12] We do not need to give details of how each of these pillars functioned in practice, for such accounts have been given often enough in the history of the Bight, the slave trade, and the Aro. There have also been unsuccessful attempts to rank them in order of importance, which we do not intend to pursue here, as the hard evidence for such ranking does not exist.[13]

With the aid of these pillars, the Aro emerged dominant in the trade of the Bight some time in the eighteenth century. Now what did that dominance mean? To remind ourselves, there were by this time two parallel trades in the region—the primordial trade in agricultural produce and craft work, which was for the basic sustenance of the teeming millions of the population, and the trade in slaves, which came much later, was foreign, and catered mainly to the needs of the elite members of the population. Each of these trades at its own level linked into one economic community the five sociocultural and economic zones that we described above as jointly constituting the context of economic, cultural, and social relations in the area. It was this top and adventitious level of trade and marketing in the interior of the Bight that the Aro dominated. This must be emphasized again and again and borne steadily in mind so that we do not perpetuate K. O. Dike's exaggerated statement that the Aro built themselves up as the economic dictators of the hinterland of the Bight of Biafra. This earlier trade went its unhindered way to serve its original purpose without the slightest control by the Aro.

This independence of the Aro of the internal local trade was not only at the local market but also at the regional market, even though the Aro were active in the regional market. Furthermore, the production, movement, and distribution of the items that the trade dealt with were beyond Aro control. Furthermore, we should remember that even with the slave trade, which the Aro dominated, there were other participants, such as the Nkwerre and the Awka, who helped collect slaves from local producers and supply them to local demanders like the Aro did. The main difference was that the Aro controlled the supply of slaves to the coastal middlemen and the collection and distribution of the manufactured and other goods that the white slave dealers gave in return for slaves. Aro dominance in the context of this and similar discussions also meant that the Aro dominated the trade routes that crisscrossed our zone, including the very major ones that ran from the Benue basin in the north to the coast in the south. However, they did not control the north-south route on the River Niger or that on the Cross River since they were not water travelers.

How the Aro came to control these routes, which emerged probably centuries before the slave trade, has never been explained. But it is our view that the situation arose in the following manner. Because they were widely spread out in the zone in pursuit of their principal, oracular, business, the Aro came in time to master every twist and turn in these bush paths in which every wrong turning made by a traveler could mean instant death or capture and sale by marauders. As a result of this, successful travel beyond one's immediate community for business or for pleasure came to depend on the good will and cooperation of the Aro, and thus on their preparedness to act as guides or escorts.

Aro dominance also meant Aro control of the important markets of the region, not by way of dictating whether or when they should be held or what should be bought and sold in them, but in the sense that regular Aro attendance at a market raised the status of such a market and extended its hinterland because traders, knowing that slaves could be bought and sold there and that European wares could also be obtained from there, visited from far and near. This Aro control of the important markets was more apparent with the two or three markets that scholars of this subject have described as fairs; these are the markets that during this period were held at Bende and at Uburu in the Ohaozara area. There was a third, so to speak, Uzuakoli, but this came to transform from an ordinary regional market to a fair only after the British captured Bende and made it an administrative headquarters following the expedition against the Long Juju or Ibini Ukpabi, the Aro oracle. With this development

Bende lost to Uzuakoli its premier position as a slave market. Each of these fairs held for eight days at a stretch, and the Aro were preeminently visible in and around them. In fact, the markets were hedged round with their settlements or colonies.

However, it must be clearly stated that even though the Aro had contact with the Ijo and the Efik of the coast and may have had some influence through their oracle, they never contested the trade of the coast or the direct contact with the visiting Europeans with these opulent and powerful men. Their direct economic and trading reach in the south stopped at such coastal headwaters as Itu on the Cross River, Azumiri on the Imo River, and Oguta on the Urashi River. The coastal middlemen came up in their canoes to those points for the exchange of imported wares for slaves. Finally, Aro dominance was dominance by an oligarchy. It was an oligarchy because it was a closed circle. No one person or single group that was non-Aro was admitted into it except after going through a change in personality or what we may describe as intense "Aronization" by means of prolonged emersion in Aro culture.[14] The circle also exercised power, although in this case it was economic rather than political.[15]

This is the previously untold story of the Aro and the trade of the Bight during the period of the Atlantic slave trade. To complete the picture we still have to tell the previously untold story of the Aro and the trade of the hinterland of the Bight after the Atlantic abolition. It is to this that we now turn our attention. As far as West Africa was concerned, there were three critical steps in the abolition. The first was taken in 1807 when the British Parliament passed the act abolishing trading in slaves for her nationals. The second was taken when the British Government set up the West African naval squadron to enforce the abolition initially against British ships. The third was when the same government decided to make the abolition "universal" to, among other things, ensure that her rivals did not continue to grow rich from a trade that she had unilaterally excluded its nationals from.

We do not know when and in what garbled form news of these great happenings got to the Bight from where it penetrate the interior, which was the operational field of the Aro. We do not know how the Aro received the news at first, but we do know that they went on with their ancient business as if the slave trade was going to continue as usual. In adopting this posture they must have been encouraged by a number of factors. First, the Europeans and Americans, individuals, groups, and nations who opposed Britain's unilateral action continued to bust the blockade of the British naval squadron and thus to come to the Bight to buy slaves for the New World. Thus some export in slaves continued for decades after 1807. Second, the coastal middlemen who would have taken the news of abolition to the Aro did not themselves immediately bow to the will of the British but continued to take from the interior, and therefore from the Aro slaves, to meet their own internal needs and the needs of the white blockade busters. Third, the internal market for slaves remained largely unaffected by the developments taking place in the Atlantic and in the chanceries of Europe. Indeed the period of transition from the days of unrestricted slave trade to the days of the so-called legitimate trade, and for some time after the transition, witnessed an expansion in the internal slave trade. This was because the new trade added extra labor demands to the demand that existed in the old regime. The production of the palm oil and palm kernel was labor intensive, as was the movement of these items to the old trading frontier between hinterland businessmen and the coastal traders, from where the latter picked them up in their canoes to the coast, where they exchanged the products with the Europeans. But there is no doubt that from this period there was a pileup of slaves in the interior both in the hands of the Aro and in the hands of their suppliers. This led to a fall in prices and to a situation in which not-so-well-off individuals and families became able to purchase slaves for their varied needs—for labor in the household and the farm, for burying their dead, and for meeting the demands of their gods for both human sacrifice and individuals dedicated to the services of the gods.[16]

However, the period after the final cessation of the external slave trade was one of worsening economic conditions for all old-time hinterland businessmen, especially the Aro. This was because the coastal middlemen began heeding the promptings and pressures from the European legitimate traders along the coast to penetrate farther and farther into the interior, to spread the doctrine and practice of the new trade, requiring the increased production of trade items and thus the expansion of the abilities of these hinterland peoples to absorb more European goods. With this development. whatever love and goodwill existed between the Aro and the coastal middlemen withered away as the Aro adopted the new policy of obstructing every attempt at hinterland penetration beyond the old trading frontier. To a large extent the Aro were able to do this effectively, with their wide-ranging alliances and blood-oath with many communities along this trading line, their widespread colonies and settlements, and the spiritual thunders of their oracle, the Ibini Ukpabi. The result was an evenly matched and intensely waged battle that lasted until the 1890s when the situation changed dramatically. The situation changed because in the meantime the British had declared the Bight and its hinterland part of its protectorate and with that the area came under Her Majesty's imperial control. With this, the British found it difficult to continue to tolerate Aro obstruction of the roads into the interior and decided to throw the sword into the scale. Unfortunately for the Aro, they had no military might to speak of. In the Christmas season of 1901–1902 the British launched the historically famous Aro Expedition, which simply marched through the territory believed to be under baleful Aro influence and captured and occupied Arochukwu, the home base of the Aro.[17]

It was the hope of the British that with their defeat the Aro would become their ally and use their previous influence in the interior to promote the new trade. But this turned out to be a miscalculation. The Aro stuck doggedly to the slave trade, conducting it underground. They continued to use the pillars that had supported their dominance during the halcyon days of the slave trade: their oracle (which they ran underground and tried to move from place to place to avoid detection), their colonies, and their blood pact with various communities, which made the latter unwilling to inform against the Aro and against other slave traders. Furthermore, the Aro were helped in this matter by the refusal of the colonial administration to mount an open and sustained campaign against the internal slave trade, instead depending on the corrosive effect of time and *pax Britannica* to complete the elimination of the evil. As the impact of these two phenomena grew with time, the internal slave trade metamorphosed for the most part into a trade in women and children, especially female children, whose sale could easily be camouflaged as marriage or apprenticeship.[18]

However, it must be mentioned that some of the Aro, like other slave dealers, moved fully into the oil trade. Some did so only in part, pursuing the produce trade and the slave trade at the same time.[19] But the overall impression is that the majority clung to the slave trade until it ended with a whimper about 1950. This apparent indestructibility of the internal slave was due in part to the fact that the social structure and mores of the coastal and Ogoja communities made them bottomless pits for the absorption of slaves and strangers. In sum, the Aro were unable to adjust the means that had sustained their oligarchic dominance in the slave trade to give them the same advantage in the new trade. In fact the oligarchy collapsed and fizzled out, as individual Aro men made good in the new trade and the new era. The result was that the glamor, awe, and mystery that characterized the Aro in the era of the slave trade as *umu Chukwu, umu Chineke*—the children or the chosen of their high god—vanished. Today one still comes across that title in the region but it refers to Pentecostal Christians who have appropriated the name for themselves.

Perhaps we should conclude by asking, what was the effect of Aro dominance for three centuries or so of the hinterland trade of the Bight? For those who see the slave trade as an unmitigated disaster, the answer is futility. The trade brought misery to individuals and groups. It caused overall depopulation. It brought about a general and forced redistribution of population, the greater majority to the New World (where they experienced hell on earth) and the lesser part throughout the region. Nor did the Aro derive a significantly great deal of lasting benefit from their dominance. When the twentieth century opened with everyone in the region under British *imperium*, the Aro were not ahead of the rest of the people and communities in the zone in any aspect of what is called modern development. Thus their dominance can be described as blind and sterile.

Such a damning assessment would gladden the hearts of Ibibio scholars like Monday Noah. Reacting to Philip Curtin's suggestion that the use of the Aro oracle as a slave-recruiting agency must have in some way moderated the incidence of violence in the Cross River region, Noah wrote:

> It has been variously argued that since the Aro dominated the slave trade in the region and that since slaves sold by the Aro were human beings converted from being objects of sacrifice to the famous Arochuku oracle into slaves, this would have had the effect of reducing social violence in the region. If anything the Aro factor as it affected the society during the period of the slave trade can only be seen as having exacerbated the degree of social violence in the area. . . . Therefore the Aro factor could not have mitigated against violence.[20]

No one can argue that the Aro enterprise in the hinterland of the Bight was not to some extent socially disruptive. Similarly, no objective scholar can deny that this was only one aspect of a many-sided story, because there is enough evidence to suggest an ironic socially and politically integrative side to Aro activity. No one can successfully sweep under the carpet of ethnic prejudice the Aro contributions to intergroup relations and travel, to the establishment and development of markets, to the relieving of families and communities of socially and morally disruptive members, to transforming of what would have been death sentences to sentences of transportation to the New World, and to the handling of complex religious and psychological problems by means of oracular pronouncements and counseling.[21] Many other scholars have drawn attention to different aspects of these services rendered by Aro. Thus Aro dominance of the trade of the hinterland of the Bight had both positive and negative sides. Professor Daryll Forde postulated for the peoples of southeastern Nigeria a substratum of common heritage of culture.[22] There can be no doubt that Aro dominance during the period of the slave trade contributed to this common heritage along with other influences and factors, some of which preceded the Aro, some of which emerged and operated contemporaneously with the Aro.

The history of southeastern Nigeria or of the Bight and its hinterland is by and large the history of four sociocultural peoples or communities who could be seen and heard from afar. These were the Nri, whose emergence into the limelight of history goes back to the first millennium AD or even earlier; the Ijo of the Niger Delta, whose emergence probably goes back to the late fifteenth century; the Efik of the Cross River Delta, whose emergence came a little after that of the Ijo; and then the Aro, whose emergence goes back to about the middle of the seventeenth century. Thus, by their dominance of the trade of the hinterland of the Bight, the Aro became one of the four peoples or communities who made contributions to the history and historiography of the zone. Without the achievements of these four peoples, the history of the Bight and its hinterland would have been almost a lacuna and thus more difficult to trace and write about. But, as it is, these four peoples provide pegs around which such an effort can be made with some hope of positive reward.

The fact that the Igbo language survived as one language in spite of the enormous numbers of the people and their sociopolitical fragmentation can be attributed in part to the Aro. The coming and going that Aro businesses entailed for themselves and their associates—the frequent gatherings at the regional markets and fairs—helped ensure that the elite of the race and the carriers of Igbo culture kept speaking the same language, no matter what happened. Another impact that the Aro left on the Igbo is in the general area of ethnography. A division of the Igbo into cultural subareas, using easily identifiable cultural criteria, shows that we are dealing with four or five Igbo subareas. One of these, which also happens to come second in territorial and demographic size, has been named Igbo *abamaba*. It incorporates the so-called Cross River Igbo or Eastern Igbo of Forde and Jones, the Ohuhu-Ngwa, and the Isu-Item. Their most outstanding social characteristic is the possession of such Benue-Congo secret societies as *Ekpe*, *Akang*, *Obong*, and *Okonko*. It is the opinion of scholars that it must have been the Aro who first adopted these societies from among the Benue-Congo peoples, especially from among the Efik and the Ibibio and then planted them in the communities in question in the course of their business travels.[23] Thus Aro dominance of the slave trade of the hinterland of the Bight was not entirely negative and sterile. It also left behind positive impacts, some of which can still be identified today.

NOTES

1. K. O. Dike and Felicia Ekejiuba, *The Aro of South-eastern Nigeria 1650–1980* (Ibadan, Nigeria: Ibadan University Press, 1990).

2. D. Forde and G. I. Jones, *The Ibo- and Ibibio-speaking Peoples of South-Eastern Nigeria* (London: International African Institute, 1950).

3. A. E. Afigbo, *Ropes of Sand: Studies in Igbo History and Culture* (Ibadan, Nigeria: Ibadan University Press, 1981).

4. A. J. H. Latham, *Old Calabar 1500–1891* (Oxford: Clarendon Press, 1973), 26–27.

Elizabeth Isichei, *A History of the Igbo People* (London: Macmillan, 1976), 58–59. Dike and Ekejiuba, *The Aro of South-eastern Nigeria*, chap. 2. The man who initiated this error was H. F. Matthews, Government Anthropologist, in his Reports on the Aro, see the file A.D. 635 on Aro Subtribes in the National Archives, Enugu, Nigeria. See also Afigbo, *Ropes of Sand*, chap. 6; and David Northrup, *Trade without Rulers: Pre-Colonial Economic Development in South Eastern Nigeria* (Oxford: Clarendon Press, 1978), 34–36.

5. E. J. Alagoa, "Long-Distance Trade and States in the Niger Delta," *Journal of African History* 11 (1970): 319–29; and E. J. Alagoa, *A History of the Niger Delta* (Ibadan, Nigeria: Ibadan University Press, 1972). David Northrup, "The Growth Trade Among the Igbo before 1800," *Journal of African History* 13 (1972): 217–36; Northrup, *Trade without Rulers*, chap. 1; S. F. Nadel, "The Kede: A Riverain State in Northern Nigeria," in *African Political Systems*, ed. M. Fortes and E. E. Evans-Pritchard (London: Oxford University Press, 1940): Femi J. Kolapo, "The Canoe in Nineteenth Century Lower Niger and the Delta," in *The Aftermath of Slavery*, ed. Chima Korieh and Femi J. Kolapo (Trenton, NJ: Africa World Press, 2007).

6. N. Nzewunwa, *The Niger Delta: Prehistoric Economy and Culture* (Oxford: Cambridge Monographs in African Archaeology 1, B.A.R. International Series 75, 1982), 239.

7. E. J. Alagoa, "The Development of Institutions in the States of the Eastern Niger Delta," *Journal of African History* 12 (1971): 269–78.

8. D. D. Hartle, "Archaeology in Eastern Nigeria," *Nigeria Magazine* 93 (1967): 134–43.

9. T. Shaw, Igbo-Ukwu, *An Account of Archaeological Discoveries in Eastern Nigeria*, 2 vols. (Evanston, IL: Northwestern University Press, 1970); M. A. Onwuejeogwu, *An Igbo Civilization: Nri Kingdom and Hegemony* (Benin: Ethiope, 1981).

10. Alagoa, "Long-Distance Trade and States in the Niger Delta," 319–29. Alagoa, "The Development of Institutions in the States of the Eastern Niger Delta," 269–78.

11. For more details, see A. E. Afigbo, *The Abolition of the Slave Trade in Southeastern Nigeria* 1885–1950 (Rochester: University of Rochester Press, 2006), 128.

12. Elizabeth Isichei, *A History of the Igbo People* (London: Macmillan, 1976), 62.

13. On theories of Aro success, see *Northrup*, *Trade without Rulers*, 114.

14. For more on cultural emersion, see Afigbo, *The Abolition of the Slave Trade*, 111–12.

15. The description of the Aro trading interest and group in some of our earlier publications as a "slaving oligarchy" has not gone down well with the educated Aro elite to the extent that they sought to use a popular resolution at a centenary celebration to counter it. "The Communiqué, The Centennary Celebration of Anglo-Aro War, 1901–1902" (unpublished),

November 2002, especially No. 2, says, "The colloquium debunked as baseless the allegation that the Aro Chukwu Kingdom was a slaving oligarchy." The publications in question are: A. E. Afigbo, "The Nineteenth Century Crisis of the Aro Slaving Oligarchy," *Nigeria Magazine* 110–12 (1974): 66–73; and A. E. Afigbo, "The Eclipse of the Aro Slaving Oligarchy 1901–1927," *Journal of the Historical Society of Nigeria* 6, no. 1 (1971): 3–23. They never mentioned an Aro Chukwu Kingdom, which actually is a recent idea nor did they suggest that Aro Chukwu was involved in the slave trade as a business corporation.

16. Afigbo, "The Nineteenth Century Crisis of the Aro Slaving Oligarchy," 66–73; Don Ohadike, "The Decline of Slavery Among the Igbo People," in *The End of Slavery in Africa*, ed. S. Miers and R. Roberts (Madison: University of Wisconsin Press, 1988), 437–61.

17. Afigbo, "The Nineteenth Century Crisis of the Aro Slaving Oligarchy," 66–73; Afigbo, "Eclipse of the Aro Slaving Oligarchy," 3–23; A. E. Afigbo, "The Aro Expedition of 1901–1902: An Episode in the British Occupation of Igboland," *Odu, A Journal of West African Studies* 7 (1972): 3–27; Afigbo, *Ropes Of Sand*, chap. 8.

18. Afigbo, *Abolition of the Slave Trade in Southeastern Nigeria 1885–1950*. The whole book is about this story.

19. Afigbo, *Abolition of the Slave Trade in Southeastern Nigeria 1885–1950*, 124. Dike and Ekejiuba, *Aro of South-eastern Nigeria*. See the last chapter on Aro attempt to toe the new order as a result of worsening conditions in their traditional business.

20. M. E. Noah, "Social and Political Developments: The Lower Cross Region," in *A History of the Cross River Region*, ed. M. B. Abasiattai (Enugu: University of Calabar Press, 1990), 96. See also A. E. Afigbo, "The Igbo in Efik-Ibibio and Related Studies," in *The Image of the Igbo*, ed. A. E. Afigbo (Lagos, Nigeria: Vista Books, 1991).

21. A. E. Afigbo, "Igbo-Efik Relations in Historical Perspective," in *The Efiks and Their Neighbours: Historical Perspectives*, ed. Okon E. Uya et al. (Calabar, Nigeria: CATS Publishers, 2005), 140–66.

22. D. Forde, *Yako Studies* (London: Oxford University Press, 1964), 213.

23. A. E. Afigbo, "Igbo Cultural Sub-Areas: Their Rise and Development," in *Groundwork of Igbo History*, ed. A. E. Afigbo (Lagos: Vista Books, 1992), chap. 7.

THE TRANS-ATLANTIC SLAVE TRADE FROM THE BIGHT OF BIAFRA

AN OVERVIEW

Kenneth Morgan

The Igbo diaspora in the trans-Atlantic slave trade emanated from the Lower Guinea region of the Bight of Biafra, stretching from the River Nun on the Niger Delta in the west to Cape Lopez in the south. This was one of seven regional coastal areas in West Africa from which slaves were gathered.[1] This sector of the trans-Atlantic slave trade was important for the extent of the Igbo contribution, for its magnitude over time, and for its significance to British trans-Atlantic slaving in particular.[2] Historians disagree over the relationship of the ethnic label "Igbo" to changing social identities; over whether the Igbo were a cohesive people in terms of manners and customs; and over the proportion of Igbo-speaking people among slave exports from the Bight of Biafra.[3] But there is no dispute that Igbo society kept slaves and that a large proportion of captives in the eastern Niger Delta came from Igbo areas.[4] There is also no doubt that Igbo speakers composed the majority of the captives dispatched into the Middle Passage from the Bight of Biafra.[5] A contemporary source from the 1780s reckoned that 80 percent of the slaves exported from Bonny were Igbo.[6] A modern appraisal argues for the same share of Igbos among slave exports from the Bight of Biafra as a whole.[7] After the end of the British slave trade in 1807, Sierra Leone registers of slaves captured by the British Navy show that Igbos composed 60 percent of the captives on ships bound from the Bight of Biafra.[8] The high proportion of Igbos exported as slaves meant that non-Igbos would have picked up some of the linguistic baggage of the majority. This would have increased the Igbo influence over slave cargoes from this West African coastal region. The Igbo themselves had numerous dialects but they were broadly understood among all people in that group.[9]

During the era of the trans-Atlantic slave trade (1519–1867), West Central Africa was the leading departure region for captives, accounting for nearly 5.7 million slave embarkations (approx. 48 percent share). In second place came the Bight of Benin, which dispatched 2 million Africans (17 percent). The Bight of Biafra assumed third place, with 1.6 million slave embarkations (13 percent).[10] The contribution of the Bight of Biafra to the "Guinea" traffic was achieved despite the area having mixed potential for slave trading. On the one hand, the Bight of Biafra was the most densely populated region along the West African coast in the eighteenth and nineteenth centuries. High population densities in the Igbo heartland, sustained by a balance between the sexes and good reproductive capacity, meant that large numbers of slaves could be supplied to ships without depleting the demographic stock. This appears to have remained the case for most of the two centuries (1650–1850) when the slave trade was conducted from the Bight of Biafra.[11] On the other hand, the Biafran coast had many creeks and mangrove swamps, where it was difficult to moor ships; reefs posed problems for navigation; malaria was rife; and local rulers forbade European settlements there. The Bight of Biafra had a higher mean loss rate for slaves exported than any other West African region, even though, as with those regions, there was a significant decline in slave mortality on the Middle Passage between 1650 and 1850. Contemporaries realized the propensity to loss of life on voyages from the main Biafran ports, Bonny, Old Calabar, and New Calabar. In the late seventeenth century, for example, it was noted that, "whosoever carries slaves from New Calabar River to the West-Indies, had need pray for a quick passage, that they may arrive there alive and in health."[12] Old Calabar was the West African port of departure with the highest overall mean loss rate of slaves on the Middle Passage between 1597 and 1864, and Bonny was in second place.[13]

Britain dominated the slave trade from the Bight of Biafra, which was, by a considerable margin, the most important West African region for slave departures on British ships. Between 1525 and 1859, Britain accounted for more than two-thirds of the slave trade from the Bight of Biafra. Portugal, mainly via the Luso-African trade from Bahia, lagged a long way behind in second place. France and Spain/Uruguay were the flags in third and fourth place.[14] During the eighteenth century, when the British slave trade peaked, more than four out of every five Africans exported from the Bight of Biafra were carried in British ships. Two out of every three of these migrants ended up in the British Caribbean.[15] The dominance of British trading in the Bight of Biafra made the area less cosmopolitan before 1807 in attracting different Europeans than other parts of coastal West Africa, such as the Bight of Benin, the Gold Coast, and West Central Africa. The Bight of Biafra was an important trading region for British slave merchants because they did not establish such an ascendancy consistently elsewhere in Atlantic Africa.[16]

To provide a broad context for the other contributions to this volume on the Igbo experience in the Atlantic world, this chapter offers an overview of the volume, distribution, and organization of the slave trade from the Bight of Biafra during its entire existence. British domination in this branch of the trade determines that most of the analysis falls upon that national sector of trans-Atlantic slaving.[17] The chapter is divided into three chronological phases to emphasize changing features of this sector of the slave trade over time. The first phase covers the long period before 1730 when the slave trade from the Bight of Biafra experienced slow beginnings for well over a century, followed by a marked rise after the mid-seventeenth century. The second period, from 1730 to 1810, deals with the peak years of the Biafran slave trade. This was the era when the Bight of Biafra was closely tied to the fortunes of the British slave trade as a whole until that national sector of the trade was abolished. The eighty years after 1730 was also the period when the commercial organization of the trade in the Niger Delta became highly coordinated. The third phase considers the slave trade from the Bight of Biafra between 1810 and the trade's demise in the 1850s. During this period, Spanish, Portuguese, and French traders increased their slave trade at the Bight of Biafra, and British naval and diplomatic activity impinged significantly on the shipment of enslaved Africans from that region.

1500–1730

During the sixteenth century, the trans-Atlantic slave trade was overwhelmingly in the hands of the Iberian powers, who dispatched enslaved Africans to their possessions in South America and the Caribbean. During that period West Central Africa and Senegambia, the two main slave provenance regions before 1600, far exceeded the Bight of Biafra in terms of slave exports: only 8,458 slaves were dispatched from the Biafran coast in the sixteenth century.[18] The early slave trade of the Bight of Biafra was more frequently conducted from the Gulf of Guinea islands than from the mainland. The Portuguese island possessions of São Tomé and Principé, situated north of the equator about 170 miles from the African mainland, took some slaves from the Bight of Biafra in exchange for gold, notably from the Rio Real and the Cameroon River, but much fewer than came from West Central Africa. This trade was often conducted in ships under Spanish auspices.[19]

British traders shipped more than 90 percent of the enslaved from the Bight of Biafra between 1662 and 1713. The Dutch, Portuguese, and French, by contrast, had a much smaller interest in this branch of the slave trade, embarking less than 8 percent of the African captives supplied to ships in the same period.[20] These continental European powers already had established commercial arrangements with other parts of West Africa—the Dutch in the Bight of Benin, the Gold Coast, and West

Central Africa, the Portuguese in Senegambia and Angola, and the French in Senegambia and the Bight of Benin.[21] Britain also had a considerable slave trade with various regions of West Africa in the late seventeenth century, notably the Gold Coast and the Bight of Benin.[22] British traders had a commercial advantage over other European trading powers in the Bight of Biafra, however, because 80 percent of the merchandise carried by British-chartered companies to that region comprised metal goods, notably copper and iron products. The supply of semiprocessed metals became an essential continuing part of trade transactions between the British and African suppliers of Biafran slaves.[23] Apart from supplying enslaved Africans, British ships also took produce from the Bight of Biafra, including ivory, palm oil, redwood, and pepper.[24]

Slave exports from the Bight of Biafra never exceeded 2,500 people in any decade before the 1640s but increased significantly thereafter. Between 1641 and 1650, some 31,442 Africans embarked on vessels at the Bight of Biafra, which placed the region second after West Central Africa for slave exports. The slave trade from the Bight of Biafra increased in the three decades after 1650, when it provided 96,853 (16.5 percent) of the enslaved West Africans dispatched to the New World. This was closely connected to the emergence of an British slave trade on a significant scale and to the demand for Africans as plantation workers in the Americas, notably in Barbados, the Leeward Islands, and Jamaica.[25] A deceleration then followed in the relative level of slave exports from the Bight of Biafra. In the period 1680–1730 slave embarkations from that region totaled 151,432, only 7.7 percent of the 1,970,345 slaves dispatched from West Africa.

Several possible reasons account for this relative decline. First, the period 1680–1730 witnessed substantial growth in slave exports from the Gold Coast and the Bight of Benin, the continued rise of slave exports from West Central Africa, and the entry of Sierra Leone and the Windward Coast into slave exportation on a modest but rising trajectory. The Gold Coast and the Bight of Benin had forts and factories maintained by European trading companies, including the Royal African Company, based in London, and this boosted slave trading activity in those regions.[26] Thus the slave trade from the Bight of Biafra in the half century after 1680 declined partly because of competition in slave deliveries from other West African regions. Second, high mortality among slaves exported from the Bight of Biafra was a factor, and thus European slave traders found it unattractive to trade there. Nearly one-third of the slaves embarked from the Bight of Biafra between 1663 and 1713 died on the Middle Passage, whereas in no other region did as many as 20 percent die.[27] Third, the Bight of Biafra was the only region of slave provenance where women outnumbered men at a time when most planters in the New World preferred males for their plantation labor force.[28] Fourth, slaves from the Bight of Biafra were held in low esteem by many settlers in the Americas. "Old and New Calabar yields plenty of slaves," it was claimed in 1714, "but they are not much esteemed by the English." The alleged reasons for the low esteem included lethargic behavior and unwillingness to work among Biafran slaves.[29] These problems may have influenced some traders against full-scale slaving from the Bight of Biafra in the later seventeenth century, but the weight one should attach to each of these factors needs further research.

Disembarkation points for slaves taken across the Atlantic from the Bight of Biafra before 1650 are known in only a relatively small number of cases, but they were mainly in the English Caribbean, Spanish America, and Brazil. In the second half of the seventeenth century Barbados was the main destination for slaves from the Bight of Biafra taken on British vessels, followed by Jamaica and the British Leeward islands. Barbados took the lead because it was the first British colony in the West Indies to undergo a transition to sugar cultivation on a significant scale. After the English capture of Jamaica in 1655 and the subsequent decade when the island became a society based mainly on sugar production, Biafran slaves were dispatched to the western Caribbean. The number of slaves disembarked from the Bight of Biafra in Jamaica increased between 1661 and 1690 but then declined: more "saltwater" slaves arrived in Jamaica from the Gold Coast and the Bight of Benin than from the Bight of Biafra between 1695 and 1725.[30] The supply of slaves to the British Leewards experienced a surge in the 1670s before declining to a more modest level. Slave imports from the Bight of Biafra to the Chesapeake increased after the transition from the use of indentured servants to the deployment of slaves on tobacco plantations at the turn of the eighteenth century.

In the second half of the seventeenth century, the number of slaves disembarked from the Bight of Biafra at non-British territories included 5,508 in the Dutch Guianas and Dutch Caribbean, 2,961 in Spanish Mainland America, and 7,537 in Brazil (mainly Bahia but also in Pernambuco).[31] The Dutch West India Company's slave trade with the Bight of Biafra declined from the 1680s, however, because Surinam planters cut back slave purchasing in that region; within thirty years, this branch of the Dutch slave trade was virtually extinct.[32] The number of Africans ending up in Dutch and, especially, Spanish America was probably higher than surviving statistics indicate because contemporary reports point to a considerable Dutch presence in the Bight of Biafra in the 1660s and holders of the *asiento* (contract) to ship slaves to Spanish America were buying slaves from Jamaica and Barbados.[33]

London merchants began to trade with the Bight of Biafra in the 1640s and dominated the slave trade with that region before 1730. The merchants involved included members of the Company of Adventurers of London Trading to the Parts of Africa (usually known as the "Guinea Company"), which held a monopoly of trade in Africa.[34] From 1662 until 1671 the Company of Royal Adventurers into Africa, with headquarters in London, was active in the trade, though it was mainly concerned with acquiring gold. The Royal African Company dominated the British slave trade from 1672 to 1698—the years when it held, in theory, a monopoly over British slave trading. Some of its vessels acquired slaves from the Bight of Biafra, though most of its trade concentrated on the coast from Senegambia to the Bight of Benin, where fortified establishments were the norm.[35] Between 1645 and 1730, London ships embarked 47,695 slaves at the Bight of Biafra—two-thirds of the British slave traffic there in that period.[36]

The slave trade in the Bight of Biafra was partly determined by the geography of the region. All along the coast, trade was conducted on rivers and creeks, with ship captains and crew liaising with black middlemen and canoe men. The inland rivers could be navigated safely on canoes. Coastal towns became firmly established as the conduits through which slaves were exported. As with the rest of West Africa, slaves were embarked at a limited number of ports in the region.[37] The Cross River people resident near Old Calabar forbade European trading factors from living on shore. There were no European forts or fixed factories anywhere in the Cross River region until 1846—a marked contrast to other parts of coastal West Africa, where such establishments flourished.[38]

Most slaves from the Bight of Biafra were drawn from outlets that became major supply centers for the entire Atlantic slave trade: Bonny and Old Calabar, both in the central portion of the Niger Delta, and New Calabar (Efem Kalabari) on the eastern edge of the delta. These relatively small ports were located within 100 miles of each other.[39] They were easily accessible from the ocean and their river channels were deep. Old Calabar was the generic name for a collective group of settlements situated five miles upstream from the Calabar River's entrance into the Cross River estuary, which was forty miles from the Gulf of Guinea. Settled in the early seventeenth century by an Efik branch of the Ibibio people, it was originally a fishing community before it became involved in the slave traffic after 1650.[40] Bonny was located on the Bonny River, an eastern distributary of the Niger River, six miles upstream from the Atlantic coast and to the west of Old Calabar. New Calabar, which had no connection with Old Calabar, lay to the west of Bonny.

In the second half of the seventeenth century Old Calabar was the main point of departure for slaves in the Bight of Biafra, with New Calabar in second place. Bonny, by contrast, appears to have been a relatively small port for slave embarkation: between 1601 and

1700, seventeen times as many slaves were embarked at Old Calabar and eleven times as many at New Calabar as were dispatched from Bonny. Jean Barbot, drawing on observations made on voyages to Africa in the late 1670s and early 1680s, noted that the British conducted their main slave trade in the Bight of Biafra at Old and New Calabar, "and they do more there than do any other Europeans."[41] In 1672, Royal African Company traders found that slaves and ivory were available at Old and New Calabar "in great plenty."[42] In the period 1701–1730, Old Calabar remained the chief port for embarking slaves in the Bight of Biafra, New Calabar's contribution declined significantly, and Bonny began to increase its share of slaves exported. In these ports, black traders took European goods to upland blacks and brought back from the hinterland slaves for British and European vessels. The Calabar blacks carried out these transactions in two or three days, whereas Bonny traders, lying near the coast, took between eight and ten days to gather slaves.[43] Slave trading on the southeastern fringes of the Bight of Biafra was limited in extent before the mid-eighteenth century. The Gabon estuary, for instance, had a low volume of external trade in the seventeenth century, when it had a minuscule slave trade. This was partly because of the prevalence of violence in the region, with examples of European vessels being subject to panyarring (i.e., forcible seizure of persons as temporary slaves) in the 1680s.[44]

1730–1810

Britain continued to dominate the slave trade from the Bight of Biafra from about 1730 until the British abolition of the slave trade. Between 1730 and 1810 the national contribution to slave departures at the Bight of Biafra was as follows. Britain shipped 663,833 (87 percent) of the 759,512 embarked slaves. Other flags lagged well behind. France was the next European power in rank order, with 51,928 embarked slaves (7 percent). Luso-Brazilian traders, mainly based in Bahia, were the only other group to take numerous Biafrans; they dispatched 39,832 slaves (5 percent) to the Americas. In the second half of the eighteenth century, Luso-Brazilian traders curtailed their trade in the Bight of Biafra and concentrated more on slave shipments from the Bight of Benin and West Central Africa, which were major supply areas for slave exports. American and Dutch slave traders each took less than 0.5 percent of the slaves embarked from the Bight of Biafra between 1730 and 1810.[45]

After 1730 the Bight of Biafra substantially increased its volume of slave exports from Africa. In each decade between 1730 and 1790 the volume of slaves embarked there rose, apart from the 1770s when slave voyages were reduced during the American War of Independence. A threefold growth in slaves exported from the Bight of Biafra occurred between 1731 and 1740, when 56,583 Africans embarked there on slave voyages, and 1791–1800, when slave departures amounted to 154,642. The slave trade at the Bight of Biafra continued to flourish through to the end of the British slave trade: in the first decade of the nineteenth century, some 140,385 captives were loaded on board British ships in that region.

The growth of slave exports from the Bight of Biafra reflected the increased volume and intensity of trans-Atlantic slaving during the eighteenth century. This was based on a growing international demand for slaves as plantation economies expanded in the Caribbean and South America. A distinctive feature of the eighteenth-century Biafran slave trade was the higher proportion of women who entered that traffic compared with other African regions. This reflected different gender conceptions of work in Igboland, with men there having an important laboring and cultural role in agriculture and therefore being retained to a considerable degree rather than made available for export.[46] As in other periods of trans-Atlantic slaving, Biafran captives experienced relatively high levels of mortality during the Middle Passage. The average slave mortality rate on British vessels leaving the Bight of Biafra between 1791 and 1797, for instance, was 10.6 percent, more than twice that of any other West African coastal region of embarkation.[47] But this potential disadvantage was outweighed by positive factors that suited British merchants and American planters. Well-coordinated trade connections between British captains and African intermediaries and swift turnaround times for vessels—both discussed below—facilitated the relatively quick and efficient loading of slaves on board ship at Bonny and the Calabars. Planters also bought slaves from the Bight of Biafra for cheaper nominal prices than Africans from other provenance regions.[48]

Between 1730 and 1810, Jamaica, the largest British sugar island in the Caribbean, was easily the most important delivery area for Biafran slaves. Jamaica took 218,404 (almost 35 percent) of the 629,200 disembarked slaves from the Bight of Biafra in that period.[49] The Jamaican market for slaves was sufficiently large to absorb Africans from various West African supply zones. Therefore slaves arriving in Jamaica were heterogeneous in their ethnic origins in most decades when the British slave trade was under way.[50] Virginia, the Carolinas, and various British Caribbean islands also imported Igbo slaves during the eighteenth century but on a much smaller scale than Jamaica.[51] Barbados and the British Leeward Islands together imported 70,657 slaves from the Bight of Biafra in 1751–1780 but declined as importers thereafter as their plantation sectors experienced relatively good demographic growth: in the thirty years after 1781 they collectively imported 9,254 slaves from the Bight of Biafra.[52]

Other Caribbean territories imported Biafran slaves. Three Windward or "Ceded" Islands acquired by Britain at the Peace of Paris (1763)—Grenada, Dominica, and St. Vincent—emerged as significant import centers for slaves from the Bight of Biafra. These islands were populated rapidly by British settlers in the era of the American Revolution, and sugar cultivation spread rapidly.[53] Between 1751 and 1800—but effectively after 1763—the Bight of Biafra shipped nearly two-thirds of the slaves for these relatively small Windward Islands that the region sent to the much larger and longer established slave market in Jamaica. New destinations for Igbo slaves appeared during the French revolutionary and Napoleonic wars. Trinidad (captured from Spain in 1797 and ceded to Britain in 1802) and Demerara, Berbice, and Essequibo (taken from Spain in 1796 and formally acquired by Britain in 1814) together absorbed 25,063 Biafran slaves between 1776 and 1810.[54] The French Caribbean received 53,282 slaves from the Bight of Biafra between 1730 and 1810; over half arrived at the largest French sugar colony, Saint-Domingue.[55] Some 27,012 Biafran slaves disembarked in Bahia between 1730 and 1810. Nearly half arrived there in the first decade of the nineteenth century, when planters bought large numbers of Africans in response to rising sugar production and sugar exports from that region.[56]

Bristol and, more particularly, Liverpool merchants dominated the slave trade from the Bight of Biafra between 1730 and 1810. London merchants, by contrast, gradually whittled down their trading interest in this region, especially in the late eighteenth century. They concentrated instead on the slave trade with the Gold Coast where they had patronage and commercial connections stemming originally from the Royal African Company's presence there in the late seventeenth century.[57] Bristol merchants found a ready market for locally produced copper and brass goods in Bonny and the two Calabars.[58] Bristol dominated the shipments of slaves from the Bight of Biafra to Virginia between 1716 and 1755, accounting for over 60 percent of the slave deliveries from that region to the Old Dominion, especially to the Rappahannock and York rivers.[59] The contribution of Liverpudlians to the slave trade from the Bight of Biafra was even more impressive. From 1730 to 1810 Liverpool slavers gathered 476,880 (72 percent) of the 662,396 Africans sent from the Bight of Biafra from British ports. In the same period Bristol slave ships picked up 149,842 (23 percent) and London vessels 32,146 (5 percent) of the remaining Biafran slaves taken on British-based ships. Liverpool gained the ascendancy over Bristol in this branch of the slave trade in the 1750s. Until the British abolition of the slave trade, it remained the leading port involved in slaving with the Bight of Biafra and, in fact, it extended its lead over Bristol and London in each subsequent decade. In 1791–1800, Liverpool accounted for 85 percent of the slaves loaded on British vessels in the Bight of Biafra; in 1801–1808, the proportion was 94 percent.[60]

From the 1740s onward, Bonny superseded Old Calabar as the leading port for slave exports in the Bight of Biafra. Bonny had a more central location in that region and benefited from the growth and consolidation of royal authority and a sophisticated credit system between Africans and Europeans.[61] During the subsequent extensive growth in the Biafran slave trade, the export of captives was mainly concentrated at Bonny, Old Calabar, and New Calabar: between 1730 and 1810 these three ports embarked over 600,000 enslaved Africans. Other ports in the Bight of Biafra handled far fewer slaves. Before 1750, the Gabon estuary, at the southern limits of the region, mainly traded in wood, water, and provisions. It was not until the 1760s that Gabon's slave exports reached decadal figures of thousands rather than hundreds. More French slavers called at Gabon between 1763 and 1792 than at any other point on the West African coast south of Calabar, but British merchants surpassed those from the French ports thereafter.[62] The Cameroon rivers were even smaller suppliers of slaves than the Gabon River but attracted Liverpool merchants after 1750.[63] Most of the slave trade on the Cameroon rivers occurred in the period in and after the 1760s, but the number exported was a fraction of those emanating from Bonny and the two Calabars.[64]

The growth of the slave trade from the Bight of Biafra was connected to the political reorganization of that region from the 1730s onward. Stronger political communities emerged around this time among the states of Bonny and Kalabari and among the Efik traders of the lower Cross River, who began to dominate trade there by 1720.[65] The rise of strong leaders such as King Amakiri in New Calabar, King Pepple in Bonny, and Duke Ephraim of Old Calabar enabled different Biafran communities to focus their energies on the movement of goods and slaves into and out of their areas. The size, wealth, and power of African communities trading with Europeans expanded considerably during the eighteenth century. Economic rents were common in the Bight of Biafra, where slaves were acquired from near the coast.[66] These rents reflected the wealth and status of Africans who traded in slaves. In the 1780s, Captain John Adams reported that some local traders at Bonny and Calabar had become "extremely opulent in consequence of the great extent to which the trade in slaves has been carried on by them, and are in possession of European articles to a considerable amount."[67] European ships paid "comey" to the Efik traders. Toward the end of the eighteenth century, this customs duty based on the ship's tonnage amounted to about £400 per ship in Bonny and £250 at Old Calabar.[68]

Efik traders devised effective ways of supplying slaves to the coast without necessarily relying on violence or warfare. Wealthy merchants making use of trade canoes, which could transport up to 120 people and provisions on a single voyage, dominated the business of supplying slaves to coastal areas. The introduction of the secret male-only Ekpe society at Calabar enforced commercial laws and oversaw debt payments, thereby aiding the supply of slaves from the interior to the shore. This society determined who could be enslaved and who could not. It imposed strict sanctions against those who failed to meet commercial obligations. British traders were particularly successful in forging links with Efik traders, who could often read and write English, which helped them communicate effectively. The one surviving diary of an Efik trader on the coast, Antera Duke, who was active in the 1780s, illustrates the ability to write in English.[69] The traders of the Bight of Biafra maintained close relations with known British merchants through letters and through accommodation of British customs and conventions to facilitate trade. They were expert at talking in the languages of their own countries and those of the Europeans.[70] Effective credit relations were forged to facilitate trade between British merchants and traders in the Bight of Biafra.[71]

Itinerant Aro traders and their allies had well-established interior trading routes in the Bight of Biafra by the 1720s at the latest.[72] The Aro, an Igbo clan, used their position of leadership to coordinate slave trading from all parts of Igbo country and to supply them to the Cross River Delta and to ports of the Niger Delta. With their armed porters they marched captives over distances of 100–150 miles to coastal towns for export. The Aro commercial fair at Bende, about three days' march north of Bonny and held at twenty-four-day intervals, was one of the main market towns where they acquired slaves. By the middle of the eighteenth century, large inland fairs at Bende and Uburu were handling many slaves destined for the Middle Passage at the Bight of Biafra. The Aro were protected in slave gathering throughout the Igbo hinterland by the divine sanction of a supreme deity (Chukwa). They called themselves Umuchukwu (children of God), hailing from the oracle of Arochukwu. These sanctions were universally respected throughout Igboland, and they enabled the Aro to move without interference through the hinterland of the Cross River and Cameroon.[73] Near the coast, competition between merchant communities existed over the supply of slaves. Occasionally the competition had violent results, the most notable example being the massacre in 1767 when Duke Town warriors, aided by British ship captains, killed around 300–400 notables at Old Town and thereby emerged as the most prominent traders in Old Calabar.[74]

The supply of slaves in the Bight of Biafra was both regular and quickly obtained. The abolitionist Thomas Clarkson noted that "the regularity . . . of the trade and the small space of time in which a cargo may be completed, are considerations, which have made these places more resorted to than any other upon the coast."[75] This emphasis on the speed at which slave cargoes were loaded at the Bight of Biafra is confirmed by modern research showing that this was the region, along with West Central Africa, where coastal loading of slaves was fastest.[76] In the second half of the eighteenth century, the loading rates of Liverpool ships at Bonny, which dominated slaving there, were double those of ships at Old Calabar and usually higher than for Liverpool vessels visiting other places. Quick loading was possible because Africans were supplied to a few locations to supply a full complement of slaves, whereas in Sierra Leone and the Windward Coast, delays occurred in slaving because cargoes were gathered from several coastal locations.[77]

Successful conduct of the trade at Bonny and Old Calabar relied on restrictive trade practices. Credit was tightly controlled and granted by British merchants to the heads of the canoe organizations that fetched the slaves from the interior. In Old Calabar, credit involved the use of pawns for debt bondage. The earliest known instance of pawning at Old Calabar dates from 1702, but evidence about its practice before 1750 is limited.[78] Pawns were black people lodged with British ship captains as pledges against the delivery of slaves: they were not in themselves slaves. This was a mechanism for ensuring that European commodities were bartered for slaves and that both the vending of goods and gathering of slaves were carried out effectively. Efik people and European traders became familiar with this mode of trade. The system continued in the nineteenth-century palm oil trade.[79] Pawning as an institutional mechanism has been seen as a crucial "way of securing credit until Britain abolished its slave trade in 1807." Between 1770 and 1800 there were around thirty local traders in Old Calabar with whom British ship captains conducted business in this way.[80]

Bonny did not make much use of pawns as a mechanism for securing credit. Royal authority, based on lineage, was much stronger there than at Old Calabar. In particular, the Pepple dynasty had assumed leadership in Bonny by the late seventeenth century and regulated trade with Europeans on the coast, working out exchange rates and customs dues in negotiations with ship captains. Royal authority served to enforce local people to carry out their contracts to supply slaves to ships. Kings at Bonny had fiscal and political authority, commercial acumen in dealing with Europeans, strong connections with local Aro traders and their inland networks, and military power. The death of a king in Bonny, such as happened in 1792, could bring trade relations between Europeans and Africans to a halt. Therefore royal authority was essential for ensuring trust in trade relations between ship captains and local traders in Bonny. This was achieved more successfully than through the pawnship found at Old Calabar: the institutions associated with the monarch's authority were impersonal rather than reliant on personal connections and therefore compliance was better guaranteed.[81]

1810–1860

The British and American abolition of their respective slave trades in 1807 and 1808 largely decimated the Anglophone involvement in the slave trade at the Bight of Biafra. But this did not stop slave trafficking in that region by other flags to supply the sugar and coffee plantations of Brazil, Cuba, Puerto Rico, and the French Caribbean. Between 1810 and 1860, the contribution of various flags to slave exports at the Bight of Biafra was as follows: Portugal/Brazil accounted for 65,688 embarked slaves out of a total of 186,276 shipped from the region (35 percent); Spain/Uruguay accounted for 62,215 (33 percent); and France shipped 55,306 (30 percent).[82] During the nineteenth century, the commercial organization of the slave trade at the Bight of Biafra extended the methods used in earlier periods. Aro traders continued their role as intermediaries and undertook wars and raids in central and northern Igbo areas to procure slaves. They hired mercenaries as warriors and plundered villages for slaves both for internal use and for the trans-Atlantic slave trade. They retained links with canoemen and connections with traders near the coast who liaised with European slave ship captains.[83]

In the nineteenth century, the Bight of Biafra supplied fewer women slaves than had been the case previously. This was partly the result of the growth of the palm oil trade (see below) in which women played an important role and were therefore retained in the Niger Delta and Cross River areas.[84] The proportion of children among enslaved Africans from the Bight of Biafra rose significantly in the first half of the nineteenth century. Merchants were willing to take more children on trans-Atlantic slaving voyages when preferred adult slaves were unavailable, and planters in countries such as Brazil employed them as cheap laborers in coffee production.[85]

Between 1811 and 1830, some 229,395 slaves were dispatched from the Bight of Biafra, 17 percent of the African captives embarked in West Africa in those twenty years. Slave prices collapsed in the Bight of Biafra after 1807–1808, but coastal middlemen could gather a plentiful supply of slaves from Igbo hinterland regions. The Americas still demanded slaves, and the Niger Delta could supply them.[86] By contrast, other areas of the West African coast, notably Senegambia and the Gold Coast, declined significantly as slave supply centers after the British abolition of the trade.[87] The nineteenth-century slave trade from the Bight of Biafra was accompanied by growth in the trade in African products, notably vegetable oils cultivated and processed by slaves. These products were intended primarily for the British market and used for lubricating machinery and manufacturing candles and soap. Biafran ports were prominent in the expansion of palm oil exports after 1807. Liverpool merchants who had been slave traders transferred their African trading interests to the palm oil trade.[88] African traders carried on the slave and palm oil trades simultaneously, although the land-based Aro were not involved in the bulky transportation of palm oil by water. Exporters shifted partly toward palm oil from slave trading because of lower earnings in supplying slaves than before 1807. Bonny and New Calabar became significant exporting ports for palm oil, accounting for about half of West Africa's exports in that commodity between the 1830s and the early 1850s.[89]

Between 1831 and 1867 the Bight of Biafra dispatched 125,385 slaves but its relative share of slave exports among West African regions declined to 10 percent. After 1840 the slave trade from the Bight of Biafra plummeted to levels from which it never recovered. The most dramatic fall occurred in the 1840s, when slave exports from the Bight of Biafra were just over one-quarter of the volume achieved in the 1830s. The decline continued, and numbers never recovered. The last known slave vessel to depart from the region with slaves was the brig *Juliet*, registered in the United States, which left Havana, embarked 673 Africans in the River Brass in 1859, delivered 558 to Cuba, and was then shipwrecked or destroyed.[90]

After 1807 the slave trade from the Bight of Biafra became more cosmopolitan as the gap left by the British was filled by Spanish, Portuguese, Brazilian, and French traders. The markets for delivery of Igbo slaves shifted to the non-Anglophone world, especially to Brazil, between 1811 and 1820, with the French Caribbean as a secondary market. But the Brazilian market for slaves from the Bight of Biafra declined significantly in the 1820s and only recovered modestly thereafter, and disembarkations of slaves in the French Caribbean collapsed in the 1830s. During the 1820s and 1830s, nearly 26,000 Igbo slaves ended up in Sierra Leone—over twice the number reaching the French Caribbean.[91] These were slaves carried on vessels intercepted by Britain's West Africa Squadron, which patrolled the West African coast in search of illegal slave shipments. The squadron escorted captured vessels from Bonny and the Calabars to Freetown in the British Crown Colony of Sierra Leone, where the multinational Courts of Mixed Commission were established in 1819. There were three courts: Anglo-Dutch, Anglo-Spanish, and Anglo-Portuguese. There the slaves were registered, freed, and resettled.

Havana, Nantes, and Rio de Janeiro, in descending order, were the three leading ports of origin for slaves loaded at the Bight of Biafra after 1810, when Cuban-based Spanish slave traders emerged as the largest merchants trading with Biafran ports.[92] Often these were engaged in clandestine trading, using São Tomé as a collection point for slaves. Between 1791 and 1865, just over one-quarter of the slaves arriving in Cuba came from the Bight of Biafra. The fact that Biafran ports continued as effective suppliers of Africans to Cuba until about 1840 resulted partly from the difficulties faced by the West Africa Squadron while intercepting slave ships. Helped by shallow creeks and lagoons near the coast of the Bight of Biafra, and by the length of the Cuban coast and the still legal interisland slave trade in the Spanish Caribbean, slavers taking captives from the Biafran coast to Cuba stood a reasonably good chance of landing and selling their cargoes without British naval interference. After the Anglo-Spanish treaty of 1835, it was more feasible for the British to intercept slavers from the Bight of Biafra through setting up a blockade to cut off ships from the African coast. This contributed to the decline of Igbo slave exports to Cuba after 1840.[93]

Bonny continued its prominence as the major port for slave embarkations from the Bight of Biafra between 1810 and 1860. During that final half-century of the slave trade from the eastern Niger Delta, Bonny accounted for 55,272 slave exports whereas Old Calabar shipped 27,435 slaves and New Calabar only 1,826. Other Biafran ports, such as the Cameroon Rivers and Gabon, played a more minor role in the slave trade, just as they had done in the eighteenth century.[94] Bonny was the leading Biafran port supplying slaves to the Cuban market between 1810 and 1840.[95] Its continuing importance as a supplier of slaves to trans-Atlantic destinations in the nineteenth century was such that it can be considered "the most successful slave port in sub-Saharan Africa." Bonny's flexible mechanisms for credit protection helped it maintain its role as a supplier of slaves by transferring the practices to non-British traders after 1807.[96]

Political and naval policies played a major part in the decline of the nineteenth-century slave trade from the Bight of Biafra. British foreign policy opposed the continuation of slavery and the slave trade in Portuguese Brazil and Spanish Caribbean territories such as Puerto Rico and Cuba. The British navy stopped Spanish and Portuguese ships whether or not they were carrying slaves. Slaving vessels avoided Old Calabar and the Cameroon estuary between 1829 and 1832 because British naval activities in those years were based at the nearby island of Fernando Po (occupied after gaining permission from Spain).[97] The Portuguese and Latin American slave trade then shifted its center of operations in the Bight of Biafra to the Brass River, which was hidden in the recesses of the Niger Valley and approached by creeks with no outlet into the Atlantic Ocean. These geographical features made it easier for illegal slave trading in that area to escape the attentions of the naval blockade.[98] Throughout the 1840s and into the 1850s, Spanish factors continued to take slaves from the Brass River, which was less open to inspection than were Old Calabar and Bonny.[99] New Calabar also avoided this impediment to shipping but its slave exports were small by 1840.[100]

British treaties with France (in 1833) and Spain (in 1835) allowed the naval squadron to seize violators by allowing them to capture ships with equipment for slaving. This appears to have been effective, for the Royal Navy freed 17,622 slaves from the Bight of Biafra in the 1830s. Britain followed up this strategy for ending illegal slave trading by signing several suppression treaties with kings and chiefs in the Bight of Biafra. Subsidies (effectively bribes) were given as a reward for cessation in slave trading. The first suppression treaty was signed in May 1841 with the Cameroons. Treaties were signed with the kingdom of Bonny in 1839, 1841, and 1848. Further treaties were agreed with New Calabar in 1851, which entitled the king there to compensation of $1,000 for three years, and with Brass in 1856. These policies drove the external slave trade away from the Bight of Biafra to the Bight of Benin.[101] In 1840 the capture of two ships with slaves from Old Calabar and the wreck of two more in the mouth of the Calabar River brought the slave trade there to an end. The two kings of Old Calabar signed treaties with Britain on December 6, 1841, against selling slaves in exchange for five annual payments of 2,000 Spanish dollars.[102] The last slaving venture from Old Calabar was the illegal voyage of the French ship *Luis d'Albuquerque*, which disembarked 277 slaves in 1843.[103] The major Biafran slave ports did not pursue further slave trading at this time because palm oil exports were thriving.[104]

By 1860 the Bight of Biafra had been involved in slave trading on a significant scale for over two centuries. The early slave trade at the Bight of Biafra was dominated by British slave merchants. This dominance continued between 1730 and 1810 as British slave merchants consolidated connections with suppliers in the hinterland of Bonny and the Calabars. After 1810, the Bight of Biafra's slave trade continued through the contribution of Spanish, Luso-Brazilian, and French traders gathering slave supplies for their colonies in the Americas. But this trade gradually declined in the first half of the nineteenth century, partly because Africans in the Bight of Biafra transferred some of their commercial activities to palm oil rather than slaves and partly because naval and diplomatic pressure was brought to bear to curtail its slave trade. The decline of the external slave trade and the growth of the palm oil trade did not mean, however, that slavery vanished from the Bight of Biafra. Slavery has always been an adaptive institution, resurrected in new forms just as its old forms declined. This was the case in the Bight of Biafra, for slaves were used there to cultivate and process agricultural products for internal consumption and external sale well into the twentieth century. In the second half of the nineteenth century the Biafran hinterland absorbed thousands of slaves into the domestic economy. It was not until the 1930s that slavery disappeared in the Bight of Biafra, now absorbed into Nigeria, where an internal slave trade continued until after the Second World War.[105]

NOTES

1. The areas were Senegambia, Sierra Leone, the Windward Coast, the Gold Coast, the Bight of Benin, the Bight of Biafra, and West Central Africa. This follows Philip D. Curtin, *The Atlantic Slave Trade: A Census* (Madison: University of Wisconsin Press, 1969), 127–30; and The Trans-Atlantic Slave Trade Database, http://www.slavevoyages.org.

2. For a summary of the Igbo hinterland in the Bight of Biafra, see Douglas B. Chambers, *Murder at Montpelier: Igbo Africans in Virginia* (Jackson: University Press of Mississippi, 2005), 22–37.

3. For a range of views, see Douglas B. Chambers, "'He Gwine Sing He Country': Africans, Afro-Virginians, and the Development of Slave Culture in Virginia, 1690–1810" (PhD dissertation, University of Virginia, 1996), chap. 2; Lorena S. Walsh, *From Calabar to Carter's Grove: The History of a Virginia Slave Community* (Charlottesville: University Press of Virginia, 1997), 53–80; David Northrup, "Igbo

and Myth Igbo: Culture and Ethnicity in the Atlantic World, 1600–1850," *Slavery and Abolition* 21, no. 3 (2000), 1–20; Femi J. Kolapo, "The Igbo and their Neighbours during the Era of the Atlantic Slave Trade," *Slavery and Abolition* 25, no. 1 (2004), 114–33; Gwendolyn Midlo Hall, *Slavery and African Ethnicities in the Americas: Restoring the Links* (Chapel Hill: University of North Carolina Press, 2005), 126–43; and Alexander X. Byrd, "Eboe, Country, Nation, and Gustavus Vassa's *Interesting Narrative*," *William and Mary Quarterly* 63, no. 1 (2006), 123–48.

4. Victor C. Uchendu, "Slaves and Slavery in Igboland, Nigeria," in *Slavery in Africa: Historical and Anthropological Perspectives*, ed. Suzanne Miers and Igor Kopytoff (Madison: University of Wisconsin Press, 1977), 131.

5. Kenneth Onwuka Dike, *Trade and Politics in the Niger Delta, 1830–1885: An Introduction to the Economic and Political History of Nigeria* (Oxford: Clarendon Press, 1956), 30, 38; Hall, *Slavery and African Ethnicities*, 127–32.

6. John Adams, *Remarks on the Country Extending from Cape Palmas to the River Congo: Including Observations on the Customs and Manners of the Inhabitants. With an Appendix Containing an Account of the European Trade with the West Coast of Africa* (London: G. and W. B. Whittaker, 1823), 116, 129.

7. Douglas B. Chambers, "'My own nation': Igbo Exiles in the Diaspora," *Slavery and Abolition* 18, no. 1 (1997), 73–77.

8. David Northrup, *Trade without Rulers: Pre-Colonial Economic Development in South Eastern Nigeria* (Oxford: Clarendon Press, 1978), 58–65, 231.

9. Walsh, *From Calabar to Carter's Grove*, 71.

10. David Eltis and David Richardson, "A New Assessment of the Transatlantic Slave Trade," in *Extending the Frontiers: Essays on the New Transatlantic Slave Trade Database*, ed. David Eltis and David Richardson (New Haven, CT: Yale University Press, 2008), 46–47. For the impact of the slave trade at the Bight of Biafra, see Carolyn A. Brown and Paul E. Lovejoy, eds., *Repercussions of the Atlantic Slave Trade: The Interior of the Bight of Biafra and the African Diaspora* (Trenton, NJ: Africa World Press, 2011).

11. David Eltis, *Economic Growth and the Ending of the Transatlantic Slave Trade* (Oxford: Oxford University Press, 1987), 71; Ebiegberi Joe Alagoa, *A History of the Niger Delta: An Historical Interpretation of Ijo Oral Tradition* (Ibadan, Nigeria: Ibadan University Press, 1972); G. Ugo Nwokeji, "The Atlantic Slave Trade and Population Density: A Historical Demography of the Biafran Hinterland," *Canadian Journal of African Studies* 34 (2000), 618, 640.

12. P. E. H. Hair, Adam Jones, and Robin Law, eds., *Barbot on Guinea: The Writings of Jean Barbot on West Africa 1678–1712*, Hakluyt Society, 2 vols. (London: Hakluyt Society, 1992), ii, 700.

13. Herbert S. Klein, Stanley L. Engerman, Robin Haines, and Ralph Shlomowitz, "Transoceanic Mortality: The Slave Trade in Comparative Perspective," *William and Mary Quarterly* 58, no. 1 (2001), 114–15. See also Alexander X. Byrd, *Captives and Voyagers: Black Migrants across the Eighteenth-Century British Atlantic World* (Baton Rouge: Louisiana State University Press, 2008), 51–52.

14. For estimates of each national carrier of slaves from the Bight of Biafra, see http://www.slavevoyages.org.

15. See http://www.slavevoyages.org; Philip D. Morgan, "The Cultural Implications of the Atlantic Slave Trade: African Regional Origins, American Destinations and New World Developments," *Slavery and Abolition* 18, no. 1 (1997), 125.

16. David Eltis and David Richardson, "West Africa and the Transatlantic Slave Trade: New Evidence of Long-Run Trends," *Slavery and Abolition* 18, no. 1 (1997), 19, 22–23.

17. Unless otherwise referenced, all data cited derive from the tables at the end of the chapter. These are based on the expanded and online database of the trans-Atlantic slave trade available at http://www.slavevoyages.org.

18. Eltis and Richardson, "A New Assessment of the Transatlantic Slave Trade," 40, 46.

19. Curtin, *The Atlantic Slave Trade*, 100; Northrup, *Trade without Rulers*, 50–51.

20. For statistics, see David Eltis, *The Rise of African Slavery in the Americas* (Cambridge: Cambridge University Press, 2000), 166.

21. Herbert S. Klein, *The Atlantic Slave Trade* (Cambridge: Cambridge University Press, 1999), 58–59, 61, 66.

22. K. G. Davies, *The Royal African Company* (London: Longmans, 1957), 224–30.

23. Eltis, *The Rise of African Slavery in the Americas*, 166, 187–88.

24. This produce trade is analyzed in Stephen D. Behrendt, A. J. H. Latham, and David Northrup, eds., *The Diary of Antera Duke, an Eighteenth-Century African Slave Trader* (Oxford: Oxford University Press, 2010), 82–101.

25. The emergence of slave labor in the British sugar islands is analyzed in Richard S. Dunn, *Sugar and Slaves: The Rise of the Planter Class in the English West Indies, 1624–1713* (Chapel Hill: University of North Carolina Press, 1972).

26. Eltis and Richardson, "A New Assessment of the Transatlantic Slave Trade," 46–47.

27. Eltis, *The Rise of African Slavery in the Americas*, 184–85.

28. David Eltis and Stanley L. Engerman, "Fluctuations in Sex and Age Ratios in the Transatlantic Slave Trade, 1663–1864," *Economic History Review* 46, no. 2 (1993), 308–23. For data on the share of men and women leaving the Bight of Biafra compared with other African slaving regions, see G. Ugo Nwokeji, "African Conceptions of Gender and the Slave Traffic," *William and Mary Quarterly*, 58, no. 1 (2001), 67.

29. Huntington Library, San Marino, CA, "Observations on the Trade to Africa and Angola by the Reverend Mr Gordon" (1714), f. 49 (quotation), Stowe MSS, ST 9. See also Elizabeth Donnan, ed., *Documents Illustrative of the History of the Slave Trade to America*, 4 vols. (Washington, D.C: Carnegie Institute, 1930–35), i, 205; and Johannes Menne Postma, *The Dutch in the Atlantic Slave Trade, 1600–1815* (Cambridge: Cambridge University Press, 2008), 106–7, 241–42. For aversion to slaves from the Bight of Biafra in South Carolina and the Caribbean, see Darold D. Wax, "Preferences for Slaves in Colonial America," *Journal of Negro History* 58 (1973), 371–401; and Philip D. Morgan, *Slave Counterpoint: Black Culture in the Eighteenth-Century Chesapeake and Lowcountry* (Chapel Hill: University of North Carolina Press, 1998), 62.

30. Data are tabulated in Trevor Burnard, "The Atlantic Slave Trade and African Ethnicities in Seventeenth-Century Jamaica," in *Liverpool and Transatlantic Slavery*, ed. David Richardson, Suzanne Schwarz, and Anthony Tibbles (Liverpool: Liverpool University Press, 2007), 143. For slaves dispatched from Old Calabar to Jamaica in 1685–1692, see David Buisseret, "Slaves arriving in Jamaica, 1684–92," *Revue Française d'Histoire d'Outre-Mer* 64 (1977), 85–88.

31. For the Dutch trade from Calabar to Brazil in the 1630s, see Ernst van den Boogart and Pieter C. Emmer, "The Dutch Participation in the Atlantic Slave Trade, 1596–1650," in *The Uncommon Market: Essays on the Atlantic Slave Trade*, ed. Henry A. Gemery and Jan S. Hogendorn (New York: Academic Press, 1979), 359–60. For data on slaves dispatched from the Bight of Biafra to mainland South America, see Daniel Barros Domingues da Silva and David Eltis, "The Slave Trade to Pernambuco, 1561–1851"; Alexandre Vieira Ribeiro, "The Transatlantic Slave Trade to Bahia, 1582–1851"; and Jelmer Vos, David Eltis, and David Richardson, "The Dutch in the Atlantic World: New Perspectives from the Slave Trade with Particular Reference to the African Origins of the Traffic," in *Extending the Frontiers*, ed. Eltis and Richardson, 119, 141, 244.

32. Postma, *The Dutch in the Atlantic Slave Trade*, 106–7, 112–14.

33. Northrup, *Trade without Rulers*, 52; David Eltis, "The British Transatlantic Slave Trade before 1714: Annual Estimates of Volume and Direction," in *The Lesser Antilles in the Age of European Expansion*, ed. Robert L. Paquette and Stanley L. Engerman (Gainesville: University Press of Florida, 1996), 194.

34. P. E. H. Hair and Robin Law, "The English in Western Africa to 1700," in *The Oxford History of the British Empire*. Vol. 1, *The Origins of Empire*, ed. Nicholas Canny (Oxford: Oxford University Press, 1998), 255.

35. Davies, *The Royal African Company*, 225, 233, 361–63. Based on this source, Philip D. Curtin calculated that only 6.7 percent of the slaves loaded on Royal African Company vessels in 1673–1689 came from Benin and the Calabars (*The Atlantic Slave Trade*, 122). For contemporary evidence on the Company's slave trade at New Calabar, see Donnan, *Documents*, i, 226–34.

36. Calculated from http://www.slavevoyages.org.

37. David Eltis, Paul E. Lovejoy, and David Richardson, "Slave-Trading Ports: Towards an Atlantic-Wide Perspective," in *Ports of the Slave Trade (Bights of Benin and Biafra): Papers from a Conference of the Centre of Commonwealth Stud-*

ies, University of Stirling, June 1998, ed. Robin Law and Silke Strickrodt (Stirling: Centre for Commonwealth Studies, 1999), 12–34.

38. Behrendt et al., *The Diary of Antera Duke*, 50.

39. For detailed commentary on Biafran ports and trans-Atlantic slaving, see Paul E. Lovejoy and David Richardson, "The Slave Ports of the Bight of Biafra in the Eighteenth Century" in *Repercussions of the Atlantic Slave Trade*, ed. Brown and Lovejoy, 19–56.

40. Behrendt et al., *The Diary of Antera Duke*, 48–49; A. J. H. Latham, *Old Calabar 1600–1891: The Impact of the International Economy upon a Traditional Society* (Oxford: Clarendon Press, 1973), 17–18.

41. Hair et al., *Barbot on Guinea*, ii, 672, 691.

42. Donnan, *Documents*, i, 193.

43. Donnan, *Documents*, ii, 775.

44. Eltis, *The Rise of African Slavery in the Americas*, 186 n. 70, 188; Henry Bucer, "The Atlantic Slave Trade and the Gabon Estuary: The Mpongwe to 1860," *Africans in Bondage: Studies in Slavery and the Slave Trade*, ed. Paul E. Lovejoy (Madison: University of Wisconsin Press, 1986), 137–38.

45. Calculations from http://www.slavevoyages.org. See also David Richardson, "Slave Exports from West and West-Central Africa, 1700–1810: New Estimates of Volume and Distribution," *Journal of African History* 30 (1989), 13, 14, 17; Roger Anstey, "The Slave Trade of the Continental Powers, 1760–1810," *Economic History Review* 30, no. 2 (1977), 265. The minor Dutch trade to peripheral ports in the Bight of Biafra is outlined in Ralph A. Austen and K. Jacobs, "Dutch Trading Voyages to Cameroon, 1721–1759: European Documents and African History," *Annales de la Faculté des Lettres et Sciences Humaines*, Université fédérale du Camerones/de Yaounde 2 (1974), 47–83.

46. Nwokeji, "African Conceptions of Gender and the Slave Traffic," 53–60.

47. Herbert S. Klein and Stanley L. Engerman, "Slave Mortality on British Ships 1791–1797," in *Liverpool, the African Slave Trade, and Abolition*, ed. Roger Anstey and P. E. H. Hair (Liverpool: Historical Society of Lancashire and Cheshire, 1976), 117–18.

48. David Eltis and David Richardson, "Prices of African Slaves Newly Arrived in the Americas, 1673–1865: New Evidence on Long-Run Trends and Regional Differentials," in *Slavery in the Development of the Americas*, ed. David Eltis, Frank D. Lewis, and Kenneth L. Sokoloff (Cambridge: Cambridge University Press, 2004), 198–99.

49. See also Audra A. Diptee, *From Africa to Jamaica: The Making of an Atlantic Slave Society, 1775–1807* (Gainesville: University Press of Florida, 2010), 47.

50. Trevor Burnard, "E Pluribus Plures: African Ethnicities in Seventeenth and Eighteenth Century Jamaica," *Jamaican Historical Review* 21 (2001), 15. The experience of Biafrans and other Africans in Jamaica is explored in Byrd, *Captives and Voyagers*, 57–64.

51. For the supply of slaves from the Bight of Biafra to the Chesapeake, see Allan Kulikoff, "The Origins of Afro-American Society in Tidewater Maryland and Virginia, 1700 to 1790," *William and Mary Quarterly* 35, no. 2 (1978), 232; and Lorena S. Walsh, "The Chesapeake Slave Trade: Regional Patterns, African Origins, and Some Implications," *William and Mary Quarterly* 58, no. 1 (2001), 148.

52. Cf. Stanley L. Engerman and B. W. Higman, "The Demographic Structure of the Caribbean Slave Societies in the Eighteenth and Nineteenth Centuries," in *General History of the Caribbean*. Vol. III, *The Slave Societies of the Caribbean*, ed. Franklin W. Knight (London and Basingstoke: UNESCO/Macmillan, 1997), 61; and Selwyn H. H. Carrington, *The Sugar Industry and the Abolition of the Slave Trade, 1775–1810* (Gainesville: University Press of Florida, 2002), 76–77.

53. Richard B. Sheridan, *Sugar and Slavery: An Economic History of the British West Indies, 1623–1775* (Baltimore: Johns Hopkins University Press, 1974), 457–59.

54. Calculations from http://www.slavevoyages.org.

55. See http://www.slavevoyages.org. For further material on the shipment of slaves from the Bight of Biafra to the French Caribbean, see David Geggus, "The French Slave Trade: An Overview," *William and Mary Quarterly* 58, no. 1 (2001), 135, 137–38.

56. http://www.slavevoyages.org; Ribeiro, "The Transatlantic Slave Trade to Bahia," 138.

57. Stephen D. Behrendt, "Human Capital in the British Slave Trade," in *Liverpool and Transatlantic Slavery*, ed. Richardson, Schwarz, and Tibbles, 82–83.

58. David Richardson, "Slavery and Bristol's 'Golden Age,'" *Slavery Abolition* 26 (2005), 43–45.

59. Douglas B. Chambers, "The Murder of Old Master Madison in 1732: A Local Event in Atlantic Perspective," *The Maryland Historian* 28 (2003), 10–19. See also David Richardson, ed., *Bristol, Africa and the Eighteenth-Century Slave Trade to America.* Vol. 1, *The Years of Expansion 1698–1729*, Bristol Record Society's Publications, xxxviii (Gloucester: Bristol Record Society, 1986), xxiv.

60. Calculations from http://www.slavevoyages.org. See also Kenneth Morgan, "Liverpool's Dominance in the British Slave Trade, 1740–1807," in *Liverpool and Transatlantic Slavery*, ed. Richardson, Schwarz, and Tibbles, 24–25. Liverpool's important role in the slave trade at the Bight of Biafra was noted in R. M. Jackson, *Journal of a Residence in Bonny River on Board the Ship Kingston during the Months of January, February and March 1826* (Letchworth: Garden City Press, 1934), 133.

61. Paul E. Lovejoy and David Richardson, "'This Horrid Hole': Royal Authority, Commerce and Credit at Bonny, 1690–1840," *Journal of African History* 45 (2004): 363–92.

62. Honfleur merchants particularly favored slave trading at Gabon because of lack of commercial competition from other slave traders there. See Robert Louis Stein, *The French Slave Trade in the Eighteenth Century: An Old Regime Business* (Madison: University of Wisconsin Press, 1979), 76, 79.

63. David Richardson, "Profits in the Liverpool Slave Trade: The Accounts of William Davenport, 1757–1784," in *Liverpool, the African Slave Trade, and Abolition*, ed. Anstey and Hair, 66–67; Bucher, "The Atlantic Slave Trade and the Gabon Estuary," 138.

64. Ralph A. Austen and Jonathan Derrick, *Middlemen of the Cameroons Rivers: The Duala and their Hinterland, c. 1600–c. 1960* (Cambridge: Cambridge University Press, 1999), 25–28.

65. Stephen D. Behrendt and Eric J. Graham, "African Merchants, Notables and the Slave Trade at Old Calabar, 1720: Evidence from the National Archives of Scotland," *History in Africa: A Journal of Method* 30 (2003), 56; Behrendt et al., *The Diary of Antera Duke*, 52–53.

66. Patrick Manning, *Slavery and African Life: Occidental, Oriental, and African Slave Trades* (Cambridge: Cambridge University Press, 1990), 95.

67. Adams, *Remarks on the Country Extending from Cape Palmas to the River Congo*, 140.

68. Hugh Crow, *Memoirs of the Late Captain Hugh Crow of Liverpool* (London: *Longman*, Rees, Orme, Brown, and Green, 1830), 43; David Northrup, "West Africans and the Atlantic, 1550–1800," in *The Oxford History of the British Empire Companion Series: Black Experience and the Empire*, ed. Philip D. Morgan and Sean Hawkins (Oxford: Oxford University Press, 2004), 44.

69. Paul E. Lovejoy and David Richardson, "Letters of the Old Calabar Slave Trade, 1760–1789," in *Genius in Bondage: Literature of the Early Black Atlantic*, ed. Vincent Carretta and Philip Gould (Lexington: University Press of Kentucky, 2001), 91, 95–96; C. Daryll Forde, ed., *Efik Traders of Old Calabar, Containing the Diary of Antera Duke 1785–88* (Oxford: Oxford University Press, 1956); Behrendt et al., *The Diary of Antera Duke*, 32–36.

70. Donnan, *Documents*, ii, 598; Randy Sparks, "The Two Princes of Calabar: An Atlantic Odyssey from Slavery to Freedom," *William and Mary Quarterly* 59, no. 3 (2002), 7–8.

71. David Richardson, "Background to Annexation: Anglo-African Credit Relations in the Bight of Biafra, 1700–1891," in *From Slave Trade to Empire: Europe and the Colonisation of Black Africa 1780s–1880s*, ed. Olivier Pétré-Grenouilleau (London: Routledge, 2004), 47–66.

72. Paul E. Lovejoy and David Richardson, "Anglo-Efik Relations and Protection against Illegal Enslavement at Old Calabar, 1740–1807," in *Fighting the Slave Trade: West African Strategies*, ed. Sylvane Diouf (Athens: Ohio University Press, 2003), 104–6. Interior trading networks

from Old Calabar are outlined in Behrendt et al., *The Diary of Antera Duke*, 102–19.

73. Northrup, *Trade without Rulers*, 105, 151; Paul E. Lovejoy and Jan S. Hogendorn, "Slave Marketing in West Africa," in *The Uncommon Market*, ed. Gemery and Hogendorn, 225–31; Chambers, *Murder at Montpelier*, 25–26, 28–29; G. Ugo Nwokeji, *The Slave Trade and Culture in the Bight of Biafra: An African Society in the Atlantic World* (Cambridge: Cambridge University Press, 2010).

74. Northrup, *Trade without Rulers*, 68, 89–90, 104; Randy J. Sparks, *The Two Princes of Calabar: An Eighteenth-Century Atlantic Odyssey* (Cambridge, MA: Harvard University Press, 2004); Behrendt et al, *The Diary of Antera Duke*, 23. For a contemporary account of this massacre, see Thomas Clarkson, "The Substance of the Evidence of Sundry Persons on the Slave-Trade, Collected in the Course of a Tour Made in the Autumn of the Year 1788," in *The British Transatlantic Slave Trade*. Vol. 3, *The Abolitionist Struggle: Opponents of the Slave Trade*, ed. John Oldfield (London: Pickering and Chatto, 2003), 185–86, 188–92.

75. Thomas Clarkson, *An Essay on the Slavery and Commerce of the Human Species, Particularly the African: in Three Parts* (London: J. Phillips, 1786), 31.

76. David Eltis and David Richardson, "Productivity in the Transatlantic Slave Trade," *Explorations in Economic History* 32 (1995), 465–84.

77. Paul E. Lovejoy and David Richardson, "African Agency and the Liverpool Slave Trade," in *Liverpool and Transatlantic Slavery*, ed. Richardson, Schwarz, and Tibbles, 53, 57–58.

78. Lovejoy and Richardson, "'This Horrid Hole,'" 377.

79. A. J. H. Latham, "Currency, Credit and Capitalism on the Cross River in the Pre-Colonial Era," *Journal of African History* 12 (1971), 603; Latham, *Old Calabar*, 27; Lovejoy and Richardson, "Anglo-Efik Relations," 109–13.

80. Lovejoy and Hogendorn, "Slave Marketing in West Africa," 225–27; Paul E. Lovejoy and David Richardson, "Trust, Pawnship, and Atlantic History: The Institutional Foundations of the Old Calabar Slave Trade," *American Historical Review* 104 (1999), 333–55 (quotation on 335).

81. Lovejoy and Richardson, "'This Horrid Hole,'" 377–78, 383–91.

82. Calculated from http://www.slavevoyages.org.

83. Paul E. Lovejoy, *Transformations in Slavery: A History of Slavery in Africa*, 2nd ed. (Cambridge: Cambridge University Press, 2000), 148; Northrup, *Trade without Rulers*, 177–223; David Northrup, "The Ideological Context of Slavery in Southeastern Nigeria in the 19th Century," *Asian and African Systems of Slavery*, ed. James L. Watson (Berkeley: University of California Press, 1980), 101–8.

84. Nwokeji, "African Conceptions of Gender and the Slave Traffic," 65–66.

85. Paul E. Lovejoy, "The Children of Slavery—The Transatlantic Phase," *Slavery and Abolition*, 27, no. 2 (2006), 199, 201–2, 207.

86. Paul E. Lovejoy and David Richardson, "The Initial 'Crisis of Adaptation': The Impact of British Abolition on the Atlantic Slave Trade in West Africa, 1808–1820," in *From Slave Trade to 'Legitimate' Commerce: The Commercial Transition in Nineteenth-Century West Africa*, ed. Robin Law (Cambridge: Cambridge University Press, 1995), 38; David Eltis, "The Slave Trade in Nineteenth-Century Nigeria," in *Studies in the Nineteenth-Century Economic History of Nigeria*, ed. Toyin Falola and Ann O'Hear (Madison: University of Wisconsin Press, 1998), 93.

87. See the data in Eltis and Richardson, "A New Assessment of the Transatlantic Slave Trade," 47.

88. Austen and Derrick, *Middlemen of the Cameroons Rivers*, 49, 55; Martin Lynn, *Commerce and Economic Change in West Africa: The Palm Oil Trade in the Nineteenth Century* (Cambridge: Cambridge University Press, 1998), 12, 17, 26.

89. David Northrup, "The Compatibility of the Slave and Palm Oil Trades in the Bight of Biafra," *Journal of African History* 17 (1976), 353–84; Lovejoy and Richardson, "The Initial 'Crisis of Adaptation,'" 43, 47; G. I. Jones, *From Slaves to Palm Oil: Slave Trade and Palm Oil Trade in the Bight of Biafra* (Cambridge: Cambridge University Press, 1989), 43.

90. http://www.slavevoyages.org/voyage/4975/variables.

91. Based on data in http://www.slavevoyages.org.

92. See http://www.slavevoyages.org; Eltis and Richardson, "West Africa and the Transatlantic Slave Trade," 20.

93. Oscar Grandío Moráguez, "The African Origins of Slaves Arriving in Cuba, 1789–1865," in *Extending the Frontiers*, ed. Eltis and Richardson, 184–87.

94. For the Cameroons, see G. Ugo Nwokeji and David Eltis, "Characteristics of Captives Leaving the Cameroons for the Americas, 1822–37," *Journal of African History* 43 (2002), 191–210.

95. Moráguez, "The African Origins of Slaves Arriving in Cuba, 1789–1865," 188, 191.

96. David Eltis, "African and European Relations in the Last Century of the Transatlantic Slave Trade," in *From Slave Trade to Empire*, ed. Pétré-Grenouilleau, 31–32, 38 (quotation); Paul E. Lovejoy and David Richardson, "From Slaves to Palm Oil: Afro-European Commercial Relations in the Bight of Biafra, 1741–1841," in *Maritime Empires: British Imperial Maritime Trade in the Nineteenth Century*, ed. David Killingray, Margarette Lincoln, and Nigel Rigby (New York: Boydell, 2004), 13, 29.

97. Latham, *Old Calabar*, 21.

98. Dike, *Trade and Politics in the Niger Delta*, 52.

99. Northrup, *Trade without Rulers*, 55, 57–65, 231.

100. Waibinte E. Wariboko, "New Calabar: The Transition from Slave- to Produce-Trading and the Political Problems in the Eastern Delta, 1848–1891," in *Ports of the Slave Trade*, ed. Law and Strickrodt, 155.

101. Dike, *Trade and Politics in the Niger Delta*, 81–88; Northrup, "The Compatibility of the Slave and Palm Oil Trades," 357; Eltis, *Economic Growth and the Ending of the Transatlantic Slave Trade*, 172–73, 250–51; E. J. Alagoa, "The Slave Trade in Niger Delta: Oral Tradition and History," in *Africans in Bondage: Studies in Slavery and the Slave Trade*, ed. Paul E. Lovejoy (Madison: University of Wisconsin Press, 1986), 126.

102. Latham, *Old Calabar*, 22.

103. Behrendt et al., *The Diary of Antera Duke*, 253.

104. Eltis, *Economic Growth and the Ending of the Transatlantic Slave Trade*, 173.

105. Jones, *From Slaves to Palm Oil*, 44; David Northrup, "Nineteenth-Century Patterns of Slavery and Economic Growth in south-eastern Nigeria," *International Journal of Historical Studies* 12 (1979), 1–16; Paul E. Lovejoy and Jan S. Hogendorn, *Slow Death for Slavery: The Course of Abolition in Northern Nigeria, 1897–1936* (Cambridge: Cambridge University Press, 1993).

7 THE IGBO AND AFRICAN BACKGROUNDS OF THE SLAVE CARGO OF THE *HENRIETTA MARIE*

John Thornton

The *Henrietta Marie* was an ill-fated slave ship that foundered off Key West in a storm in 1700 and sank after delivering its cargo of slaves to Jamaica. The wreck was uncovered by divers associated with the famous treasure hunter Mel Fisher while seeking Spanish treasure ships in 1972. Beginning in 1983, the wreck was carefully researched by underwater archaeologist David Moore at the Mel Fisher Maritime Heritage Museum.[1] An exhibition of finds (including items such as child-sized leg irons) that began touring the United States in 1995 strongly evokes the slave trade, especially that originating from the Niger Delta.[2]

Most of the evidence from the cargo of the *Henrietta Marie* points to its African port of origin as being New Calabar in the delta of the Niger River in modern Nigeria.[3] New Calabar was one of the most important ports of the region in the era of the slave trade and one especially frequented by the "Ten Percenters" whose ships were not always welcomed at the posts that the Royal African Company controlled on the Gambia River, Gold, and Slave Coasts, or where similar control was exercised by French, Dutch, or Danish African Companies. There was never a permanent European presence in the river and its surrounding areas, since the environment saturated with malaria was considered fatal to Europeans, including the Portuguese, who were the first to visit the area. This point is of critical importance for historians, for it means that written documentation supplies very few details of New Calabar or its neighbors and sources of supply. Consequently, unlike the Gold and Slave Coasts farther west, the records of commercial contacts are sketchy and the people writing the notes are poorly informed about the region.

New Calabar and the complex of towns that were sometimes under its authority along the river was one of three points of call along the Niger Delta and related river systems of southeastern Nigeria. The other regular points of call were at Benin (or its port town of Ughoton) and Warri on the west and, later, Old Calabar on the east. Even though many other rivers and creeks emptied out into the Atlantic between these points, no regular commerce developed from those areas. But although these three zones were separate from each other when viewed from the Atlantic trade, they were connected by considerable lateral trade, through a maze of creeks, estuaries, and coastal waterways. While Benin, its port of Ughoton, and the nearby kingdom of Warri served a different hinterland in their Atlantic trade, the Ijo boatmen of this area often traded as far to the east as New Calabar.

New Calabar's connections with the Atlantic trade were old indeed. The first Portuguese to visit the coast dubbed a branch of the Niger the Rio Real (Royal River), and an early Portuguese navigator, Duarte Pacheco Pereira, noted around 1506 that some distance up the river was "a very large village which had some two thousand inhabitants," where they made salt and had great boats, all made from a single log, which went far and wide trading the salt of this village. The river was bordered on the east by the "Jos" or Ijos, whose boats connected the river to points farther west.[4] In fact the language of New Calabar today and probably in the past was Ijo. This town was certainly the town of New Calabar, for Alessandro Zorzi, an Italian cartographer and geographer with close ties to Portuguese sailors, described the coast in 1517, noting that there was the "Rio Regal, which is the largest river that comes down from the land of the blacks . . . and there is found another [place] called a village, but like a city, Calabar."[5]

Archaeologists have uncovered some of the material remains of the culture of the region, confirming, at least on the documentation available now, that a complex interregional trade that gave rise to fairly large nucleated towns such as New Calabar dated back as far as the tenth century. Furthermore, many of these sites show the continuity of trade through the "Atlantic period," when remains of European or non-African origin are found in the same places. The importance of the area as a trading center is attested by very large hordes of manilas, omega-shaped brass ingots used to trade metal, and often a currency of international dimensions.[6]

Calabar's trade with Europe was varied but included slaves from an early time. When the king of Portugal made a grant of exclusive rights for the inhabitants of São Tomé to the trade from "the Rio Real to Manicongo" in 1493, it specified that slaves would be among the exports and manilas among the imports, although not necessarily from the Rio Real.[7] In 1516 authorities from São Tomé intercepted a slave ship making an illegal voyage to this river.[8] These slaves found their way to America fairly soon, for an inventory made in Hispaniola in 1547 already includes "Calabars" among its slaves, although only a handful of the total slaves in the listing.[9]

The Portuguese traded regularly with New Calabar throughout the following period, from their bases on the islands of São Tomé and Príncipe, which lay just off the coast. They sent ships to the area, and when other Europeans began visiting the area they usually stopped at other points along the coast where there were permanent settlements before braving the mosquitos of the Rio Real. Portugal sought diplomatic ties with the rulers of the states of the region, including New Calabar. A survey of Portugal's African trade made in 1620 noted that they sent one large ship a year to the king of New Calabar, whose people were "very warlike, our friends." Three ships were sent to the two other kings in the area, the "King of the Rio Real, and another king who is called [king of] Oere [Warri], who are almost united with each other."[10] Alonso de Sandoval, a near-contemporary priest who collected information about Africa from Portuguese ship captains as well as from the many slaves he knew in Cartagena (modern Colombia), noted that there was another kingdom, called Zarabu, near to Warri, which might be a reference to the same state.[11] A tradition collected in modern times suggests that the state of Nembe (known in post-seventeenth-century documents as Brass) in that area was founded by dissident members of Warri's elite,[12] although it is not clear whether de Sandoval's name of Zarabu relates to this.[13] At that time, slaves were most important among the exports of the area.[14]

Many of these slaves were sent to America on Portuguese ships, as it was Portugal that dominated the trade of the region until well into the seventeenth century. A study of inventories of estates and sales records in Spanish Peru, which was provisioned largely by Portuguese shippers, from 1560–1650 shows that "Calabars" were fairly rare before about 1610 but that between 1610 and 1640 they became quite numerous, making a sizable proportion of the overall trade.[15] Although they drop off subsequently in Spanish records, ships from other parts of Europe continued visiting and bringing out slaves in the post-1650 period.

The Portuguese hoped to maintain their monopoly over this part of the African trade through diplomatic measures, as it would be impossible to maintain it by force in this section of the African coast. Part of Portuguese diplomacy was an attempt to get African rulers to convert to Christianity, and to that end, there was considerable ecclesiastical diplomacy in the area. Their efforts, which began at Benin in the early sixteenth century, were crowned with its first success when the ruler of Warri was baptized in the 1590s. Warri became a Christian state, regularly supporting the church in the centuries that followed.[16] In 1620 de Sandoval paid it the considerable compliment of saying, "this king and kingdom, I am told in all seriousness, is Catholic, without any error against our Holy Faith, priests come from Santo Tomé to preserve the purity of the True Faith among them."[17] Though priests had little luck in making formal conversions among the neighboring peoples, there were frequent missions, and hopes were often raised that a Christian alliance between Portugal and another African state might ensue.

However, even without formal conversion, Christian ideas and artifacts did find their way into New Calabar. When Juan de Santiago, a Spanish priest, was forced to spend seventeen months in New Calabar in 1647, he was surprised to see a large watercraft carrying the image of Saint Anthony on its prow and a lesser statue on other craft. He supposed that the statues were salvaged from a shipwreck but noted that the people called them "Great Jesus" and "Lesser Jesus" and paid them religious, if not exactly Christian, respect.[18] Nearly half a century later, the people of Calabar wrote the Capuchin prefect in São Tomé to ask which was the true God, "Jesus Mary of Calabar or Joseph Mary of São Tomé," which was, according to the priest, "what they call their idols."[19]

New Calabar was still experimenting with Christianity and with missionaries on the eve of the visit of the *Henrietta Marie*, for in 1691, the king of New Calabar wrote a letter to Francesco da Monteleone, the Capuchin prefect of São Tomé, announcing that he was prepared to allow missionaries to come and build a hospice.[20] When Jean Barbot visited New Calabar in 1699 he noted that the King of Ibani, William, spoke Portuguese and "seems to have been instructed by Romish priests,"[21] perhaps a fruit of this mission.

From the Portuguese point of view, they hoped that these diplomatic alliances would allow them to claim a monopoly of the external trade of the region. But without shore bases such a monopoly was impossible, and ships from other European countries began visiting the Niger Delta shortly after the first Dutch visits in the late sixteenth century. Neither the Dutch nor the English participated in the slave trade of the coast at first—a Dutch description of the coast in 1636 mentioned a prominent export of Rio Real as "Negros who were captured in war in the interior" but did not list slaves among any of the exports that the West India Company took from Africa in the 1623–1636 period.[22] Dutch merchants began buying slaves in Africa only in 1638, and the first known slaving voyage to Calabar was in 1641.[23] The English opened a slave trade to Calabar in the same year when the *Star* brought slaves to Barbados.[24] The northern European intrusion into areas the Portuguese had been monopolizing for years was resented. Portuguese reported in frustration in 1645 that an English ship, the *Pristor*, was dealing with slaves at Calabar and bound for Barbados, while another captained by Robert Adam had taken on 250 slaves, and was headed for "Virginia."[25]

Sailors' guides noted customs to be paid and trading practices in the early 1650 by regular Dutch visitors.[26] In the mid-seventeenth century they describe a cluster of towns and villages under a fairly rough authority of the king of New Calabar. Separate dues had to be paid at all the towns, so that one should not imagine that New Calabar was a centralized state subject to a single ruler.[27]

Much the same picture is presented by English sources of around 1700, the year of the *Henrietta Marie*'s voyage to New Calabar. Although the earlier Dutch practice had been to approach New Calabar from the west, past the town of Ifoko (Fokké, Focke, Foko),[28] in the early eighteenth century English ships approached from the east, past the town of Ibani (Bandy, Bonny). Large ships rode at anchor near Ibani; smaller craft went up river to New Calabar.[29] New Calabar was favored as a trading site because it was much closer to the inland supplies of slaves than was Ibani.[30] At that time English ships were also regularly calling on the port of Odoni (Dony) still farther to the east.[31] All these ports, Ifoko, Obani, and Odoni were part of a single trading system, although in 1700, as earlier, they were only loosely connected to each other politically.

Each town was ruled by a leader, which European sources routinely called a king. Jean Barbot, author of an important account on the area, thought that "king" was an exaggeration of their power and the extent of their authority, "but are at best such kings as the two and thirty that Joshua defeated at once, mention'd in holy writ," and informally he thought they were best called captains.[32]

The power of the kings of New Calabar and related towns was limited for two reasons.

First, their jurisdiction did not extend over a very large area or very many people. New Calabar probably did not exceed the two thousand citizens that Pacheco Pereira attributed to it at the dawn of the sixteenth century; Barbot thought that Ibani and New Calabar each contained three hundred houses, or perhaps fifteen hundred people, in his day.[33] Although these towns possessed tributary villages scattered thickly along the riverbanks between them, total population was unlikely to have exceeded ten thousand.[34] An Italian account of early-eighteenth-century Warri, a state somewhat larger than New Calabar, gave its total inhabitants as some thirty thousand, "including the free people and slaves," though it was perhaps somewhat of an exaggeration.[35]

The king's power was limited in a second crucial way, in that he was by no means an autocratic or absolute monarch. Other powerful people exercised authority in the kingdom and clearly checked royal authority. The Dutch accounts of the 1650s suggest that these "great men" [*grooten*] had to agree collectively on the prices to be paid for imports and exports.[36] The English ship *Arthur* could only trade after meeting with the king and "his gentlemen" in 1678.[37] The King of Calabar, who wrote for missionaries in 1691, noted that in addition to his support, "my great chiefs [caboceiros]" were present when the request for a hospice was read, and it was presumably these who signed the letter: "Amaral + Captain of Ship, Petri + Clâs, Agoa + diero [water bearer?], Captain Bollo, + Comal +, Little Pitri +, Ca+brito [goat]."

The trading voyages recorded in Jean Barbot's collection for the period around 1700 more or less confirm this collective leadership. John Barbot noted in 1699 that at Ibani, the king, known to Europeans as William, and his brother Pepprell acted as a royal group, but presents were given not only to the king but also to his principal officers: Captain Forty, the king's general, captain Boileau, alderman Bougsby, my lord Willyby, duke of Monmouth, drunken Henry and some others.[38] At the same time, John Grazilhizier traveled from Ibani to Calabar, where he gave presents to the king, Robert, as well as the "Duke of Monmouth, the duke of York," captain Jan Alkmaers, these four being "the principal Blacks, who claim presents."[39]

Modern historians recognize these other great men with their mixture of Portuguese, Dutch, English, and Kalabari names as being the heads of "canoe houses," that is, corporate associations organized to conduct trade and eventually parlaying their success into demographic expansion through the incorporation of slaves and eventually the attaining of political influence. No doubt Amaral, signing as "Captain of Ship" [Captiam de Navio] in the 1691 letter of the king of New Calabar, was leader of what was to be called a "canoe house." The "Duke of Monmouth" mentioned in Barbot's collection is still known to tradition as a house created by one of the early Calabar kings, and the Dukes of Monmouth found at both Calabar and Ibani clearly represent branches of this important association.[40] The government, in fact, was fairly loosely structured by cooperation between kings and house leaders, who ate and drank together in rotation.[41] Indeed, if modern Ibani traditions are to be believed, the Pebble family, represented in Barbot's day by the "king's brother" (probably a title rather than a real biological relationship) Pepprell, who himself noted that his relationships with Europeans had "much inriched him by trade,"[42] were originally heads of a house that took power when the king was unable to finance a war from his own resources.[43]

Somewhat later, in the 1760s, a Moravian missionary named Christian Georg Andreas Oldendorp interviewed some Calabaris in the Danish West Indies, and from them he learned that in his day, which probably reflected conditions in the mid-eighteenth century, Calabar was ruled by a king he understood to be called "Drelemongo, a word which means great man." The country was divided into quarters, each under the control of a "captain." The king's authority was not great, however, as there could be civil wars resulting from disputes between subjects of the captains, which the king allowed, but "which, however, the king has under observation and makes an end when it has become too widespread and harmful."[44]

When Europeans traded with Calabar, they were purchasing people who had been enslaved over a fairly wide area and brought to the port for sail. Some of the slaves probably came from the region around Benin. In the last years of the seventeenth century, Benin underwent a violent civil war. In consequence of the war, a portion of the government withdrew from the city of Benin to an area east of the city.[45] From there a number of wars and raids between the two parties ensued into the early 1720s at least. While slaves captured in these wars by the rulers in Benin were undoubtedly exported to Dutch merchants based at the port of Ughoton, the rebels, adherents of the so-called Street Kings, probably sold the captives they took through the river network east of Benin and along the Niger River, especially perhaps to Ijo boatmen and pirates, and in their hands they may well have passed out of Africa through New Calabar.

Likewise, a number of other slaves may have come from the immediate vicinity of New Calabar itself: even though the sources of 1700 do not mention any wars waged by New Calabar or its immediate neighbors, and indeed specifically mention the dispatch of canoes to fill the ships, reports of the 1690s do mention wars in the area between Warri and Benin in which armed men were everywhere and travel was difficult.[46] But documentary sources are scanty enough that we cannot say much about the frequency of warfare. The situation in the mid-eighteenth century, described by enslaved Calabaris interviewed by Oldendorp, included a variety of processes of enslavement of people from New Calabar itself, including the civil wars that wracked the region from time to time, and involved significant armed forces, and "those they take as prisoners they sell to Negroes . . . [who] sell them again to others . . . and so it goes until they come to the sea and are sold to whites."[47] But people were enslaved in ways other than warfare. One of Oldendorp's informants described being taken in an ambush, and another was enslaved while on a commercial voyage to the north, yet another was enslaved by his own friends, while a woman was enslaved and deported as a result of a marital dispute involving a husband she divorced and another she subsequently married.[48]

It is most likely, however, that most of the slaves that the *Henrietta Marie* took in were not from the immediate coast but from areas in the interior and brought down by boat, as indeed the Dutch had already noted in 1636.[49] When the Barbot brothers were in Ibani and New Calabar, they noted that as soon as trading agreements were made with the king, boats were dispatched into the interior to obtain slaves from markets there.[50] The markets were closer to New Calabar than to Ibani, for one of the advantages of dealing in New Calabar, which somewhat offset its difficulty of access to ocean-going ships, was that it was several days closer to the best markets of the area.[51] These interior regions were the great Igbo-speaking area that lay directly north of the town along the Niger River and its tributaries, and also areas lying to its east along the Cross River, whose people, who spoke Ibibio, were often called Mokkos (or variants) in earlier times. New Calabar had an intimate relationship with the "Hackbous" (Igbo) country, which, according to Barbot, supplied most of the city's food supplies, and a good many other items, such as metal goods, which could hardly be produced in the marshy environment of the lower Niger Delta.[52]

The earliest description of the Niger Delta region, by Alonso de Sandoval in the early seventeenth century, begins by differentiating the people known in the Indies as "Caravalies" (Calabaris) into two groups: "Pure Caravalies" and "Particular Caravalies." Of these, the "pure" ones represent the people of New Calabar and its environs, while the "particular" ones were what would today be called Igbos and Ibibios. The Particular Caravalies were divided into forty or fifty villages of "different castes and nations." He went on to note, "here [in America] we call them Particular Caravalies, even though in reality they are not [Caravalies]. Because they come and trade with the Caravalies, we take them for such." De Sandoval noted their loose political organization: "They do not recognize a king, they give many justifications for their wars and trade, to be certain they injure each other."[53]

De Sandoval thought the Particular Caravalies were innumerable and spoke various languages, as indeed even the Pure Caravalies could not always understand each other (presumably the various Niger Delta languages are meant here). He then provided a list of the various Particular groups: "Abalomo, Bila, Cubai, Coco, Cola, Dembe, Done, Evo, Ibo, Mana, Moco, Oquema, Ormapri, Quereca, Tebo, and Teguo"; some spoke the same language, but others were differentiated from one other.[54] The appearance of "Ibo" and "Moco" in the group more or less confirms that the Igbos and Ibibios were intended as well as Ijo-speaking people near New Calabar, and his comment about linguistic variation is also consistent with the rather larger area. Later in the seventeenth century, Dapper would call the interior neighbors of New Calabar "Mokos,"[55] and this term was often also used as a "national name" in the New World, along with "Eboe" and "Ibo" the term already in use in English-speaking America by the early eighteenth century, even though their home languages were different. Igbo is a wide-ranging term, even today, for a group that was hardly homogenous, as one would expect from the political description and the extent of the country. In fact there are significant linguistic and dialectical differences between the residents of the region from which even "Ibos" and "Eboes" were drawn, and in many cases their apparent unity was created as much in America as in Africa.[56]

De Sandoval's list of names were not national names in the ethnolinguistic sense of the word but rather represented subgroups organized on quasi-kinship units, into which presumably the forty to fifty independent villages were grouped under no form of royal rule—all of which sounds strongly reminiscent of Igbo and Ibibio social organization described in the mid-eighteenth century. Unfortunately, no other seventeenth-century source gives us anything resembling the detail of de Sandoval's account, and we must wait for mid-eighteenth-century documentation to explore the region that probably exported most of the slaves through New Calabar.

The first of these sources was written by Oldendorp, who, like de Sandoval, collected information about their homeland from slaves. He interviewed three male and two female Karabaris, four Igbo men, and two male and one female Mokko (and also recognized "Bibi" as a special group as well).[57] In addition Oldendorp interviewed another Igbo, whose name we can determine was Ofodobendo Wooma, during his stay in Bethlehem, Pennsylvania, in 1769.[58] Since his informants had probably been in the Americas for some time (Wooma came in 1741) and could thus speak local creole, his report reflects conditions of roughly the mid-eighteenth century. Much of his writing confirms that of de Sandoval, including giving the local names of Ibo, Mokko, and Ero (probably Edo, the language of Benin), to which he adds Igan and Bebumde, who bordered the Calabaris.[59] Wooma, who had his own separate account within Oldendorp's narrative, was more explicit about his geography, not mentioning the Mokko but noting that the Bibi were a "separate realm" within what he considered the Igbo country. He also knew of Akwa (perhaps Awka) as a place some distance from his home where the people were reputed to be cannibals (a claim mostly that they were culturally different).[60]

Another valuable source of this sort is the account of Gustavus Vassa, a noted abolitionist who claimed in a celebrated biography published in 1789 that he was originally named Olaudah Equiano, an Igbo born in the town of "Essaka" around 1745 and enslaved and transported to America at age eleven around 1756. Recently, Vincent Carretta, after discovering documents in which Gustavus Vassa declared that his birthplace was South Carolina, has argued that he invented both the name Olaudah Equiano and an Igbo identity to increase his credibility as a witness to the slave trade.[61] This assertion has been strongly challenged, however, and it is just as likely that at another time he invented a South Carolina identity for other purposes, a position I am inclined to support and thus use Olaudah Equiano as his name.[62] However that may be, his account was at least partially based on information he collected from other Igbos in England and perhaps elsewhere. It was probably still at least secondhand from the experience of African-born Igbos and, if not his own story, then one whose story must have been similar to his. As such, it is as reliable as those of Oldendorp, also collected directly from people of the Niger Delta region. In any case, the information he presents about Africa is both singularly detailed and not derived from any published sources and holds up when tested against other sources or ethnography.[63] On the basis of an analysis of ethnographic literature and ecology, the anthropologist G. I. Jones concluded that Equiano came from east of the Niger River and continued to live in the general area as a slave for some years before being sent first to Warri and the eventually to the New Calabar region, where he was sold to Europeans for export to America.[64]

Common geography, linguistic similarities, and similar cultural patterns did not, however, create much political unity in the region or perhaps even a sense of an Igbo or Mokko identity—such unities were more common in the Diaspora to America. Instead, people, while conscious of distant neighbors distinguished themselves from nearer neighbors. For example, all the people of the area bore various ethnic marks, noted in passing first by de Sandoval, who did not provide a detailed description as they were "innumerable."[65] Oldendorp also saw markings on his informants; some Igbos and the Mokkos were marked with vertical cuts on the face, which were of various length, number, and spacing according to their specific group. Calabaris and other Igbos had horizontal marks on the foreheads; others of the Igbo nation had ray like marks around the eyes. Yet others, especially the Mokkos, had additional marks on their bodies, and Mokkos were elaborately designed.[66]

Equiano's Essaka was a small self-contained town, like the "independent villages" of de Sandoval's description, ruled not by a king but by an association of "elders or chiefs . . . styled Embrenché [Mbreechi]," of which his father was a member. Their symbol was a deeply cut horizontal facial mark on the forehead, such as Oldendorp had also seen on Igbo slaves in Saint John about the time Equiano arrived in America. These chief men decided cases, punished crimes, and met frequently to discuss matters of significance to the community.[67] This group of chiefs and elders was a titled association, for the majority of the people were organized in four simple age-grades, composed of married men, married women, unmarried young men, and unmarried young women.[68] Although Equiano does not mention it, if modern analogy is correct, one became an Mbreechi by paying a large initiation fee, thus making the association essentially a plutocracy.[69] But we need not accept that Equiano's Essaka was the only pattern of government in the broader Igbo region. The Igbos that Oldendorp interviewed described a position of "governor" [*Gouverneur*] in their lands, whom they said was "always called Oba."[70] Perhaps in keeping with this somewhat more hierarchical structure, a Moravian convert of Igbo origin living in Pennsylvania in 1761 known to us only as Joshua, gave his birthplace as "the Ybo Kingdom, in the province of Schomma, in the village of Umoque."[71]

Wooma also made note of a special class of people, almost certainly the social group known as *uso* in modern Igbo society: "There are various people under him, which can be called living sacrifices. No shears come to them, no hair of theirs can be cut. They do not marry, do not have their own house, rather they are always with others, they eat and drink by themselves, take what they will and no one prevents them. The priests are named from among these people."[72]

The clearest indication of this rule by the wealthy was the complex distribution of wealth that Equiano described in his own town. A wealthy man built a simple but sturdy house within "a large square piece of land" to accommodate "his family and slaves; which, if numerous, frequently present the appearance of a village," the whole was "surrounded with a moat or fence, or inclosed with a wall made of red earth tempered," which was "hard as brick." He continued to note that the "principle building," the house of the master, stood in the middle of this, a two-room apartment with one room being a private assembly area for the family and a second one a reception room for guests. The master and his sons also kept a separate sleeping area, while the simpler houses of other wives and slaves were scattered around in the compound.[73] Accumulating dependents, whether they were slaves, servants, or wives was crucial to the development of wealth, and Oldendorp, whose religious interests spurred his concern about marriage, noted the widespread presence of polygamy by his witnesses.[74] His Mokko informants told him that a governor in their land had so many wives that he did not even know who they were, and such hypergamy was not just restricted to the governors.[75]

Although Equiano, no doubt interested in presenting the best face to a European audience, does not mention it, Oldendorp's Igbo informants, including Wooma, noted that "servants and slaves" were sacrificed upon the death of the more powerful people.[76] In the case of Mokko, people from that area told him that the death of a "governor" was kept secret and then his first wife, all his servants, and as many people as could be caught "for many miles around" were rounded up for the sacrifice.[77] In both cases, the presence of human sacrifice on such occasions reflects on the scope of such people's power over their slaves and dependents, while their slaughter, like the destruction of valuable property, was a testimony to their value.

Wealth was mostly displayed in the size of the compound and numbers of dependents, rather than in elaborately separate lifestyles, for Equiano noted a general equality in dress and food.[78] Likewise, as elsewhere in Africa, wealth was founded on dependents, especially slaves, and not in land ownership. "Our tillage is exercised in a large plain or common," Equiano wrote, "and all the neighbors resort there in a body."[79] The slaves whose product must be shared with a master accompanied this group of neighbors, though as Equiano argued, "their food, clothing, and lodging, were nearly the same" as those of their masters, and their biggest disability was in that the master exercised the same authority over them as he did "over every part of his household." Some of the slaves, he continued, "have even slaves under them, as their own property, and for their own use."[80]

Eighteenth-century Igbo slaves in America often noted that they moved many times within the Niger Delta before ending up in the slave trade. For several months, Equiano moved around within the Igbo-speaking area as a temporary slave, spending a few months here, a few more there.[81] His experience as a recently enslaved but not yet settled slave was common; Oldendorp's informants often described this peripatetic existence—claiming to have, they reported with some exaggeration, a hundred masters.[82] Wooma, who was made a slave as a child, was also sold many times before finally arriving at the coast; Joshua stated in his biography that he was sold many times before reaching the sea as well.[83] These experiences point to an important domestic slave trade, connecting one master to another, and no doubt there were a good number of Igbos whose slave itinerary never included a trip to America but instead were part of the burgeoning populations of wealthy men.[84]

However, it was surely this domestic use of slaves that helped promote and continue the external slave trade. According to Equiano, slaves were obtained in two ways: by interstate war and by illegal kidnapping. He believed that many wars were caused by the actions of merchants, "mahogany coloured men from the south-west, called Oye-Eboe" or "red men living at a distance," whose wares included such imported manufactures as hats, guns, and gunpowder.[85] Wooma also knew of a country, which he called "Egypt" or "Alo," where such imported wares as "Turkish sabers, knives, powder, lead and linen" could be purchased, and he also noted that when "they have reason to think that something has been stolen, or a cow has gone astray or the like, so they go to Egypt to a brown man [*einem braunen Mann*], who discovers its location."[86] This combination of information points to a critical rule played by the famous Aro Chukwu diaspora (Wooma's "Alo"), who were involved both in commerce and dispute mediation and also took in slaves. Whether the Aro Chukwu trading system was in place in 1700 and helped supply the captives who boarded the *Henrietta Marie* is problematic, although Wooma, who left Africa in 1741 but lived only two days' journey from Alo, said nothing to imply that it was a recent development.[87]

As Equiano understood it, these merchants "always carry slaves through our land,"

and because kidnapping was common, they were required to demonstrate that no local people were among their slaves. Nevertheless, Equiano recorded that "sometimes indeed we sold slaves to them." These slaves were prisoners of war or those convicted of crimes "we esteemed heinous."[88] The battles were the "irruptions of one little state or district on the other, to obtain prisoners or booty" incited, perhaps, by the merchants who applied to a chief and "tempts him with his wares," and the chief in turn "yields to his temptations" and resolves to "fall on his neighbours." If this leader "prevails, and takes prisoners, he gratifies his avarice by selling them; but, if his party be vanquished, and he falls into the hands of the enemy, he is put to death."[89] Perhaps Equiano, now a spokesperson for abolitionist interests, oversimplified the causes of wars, but his picture is probably not without reason.[90]

Equiano had reason to know about kidnapping, what he thought was the second most important cause of enslavement, for he was himself a victim of it. His capture happened when the adults were working in the fields in common, leaving the smaller children in a single location to play. Kidnapping was clearly common, for the group took precautions against surprise attacks as a routine matter. On the day of Equiano's capture he was alone in the house when he was surprised by two men and a woman who broke into the house after climbing the compound wall. He was bound and quickly carried far enough away where the protection of his home country would not help him.[91]

Oldendorp's informants described a number of other modes of enslavement. One was sold in "a neighboring country" where he owed a debt and was seized when visiting it. Another was taken in by his father's stepbrother following his father's death, served him for two years, and then was sold away. Under a new master he was traveling into a neighboring country where "they had enmity" against his nation (they being uncircumcised and his group being circumcised); they seized him and sold him into slavery. One of the Mokkos was sold by his own father for being arrogant while yet another was sent by the "regents" [*Regenten*] of the country (presumably a title association) to recapture runaway slaves but was in fact captured and sold by them. Finally, a Mokko woman was set to be sacrificed upon the death of her husband but ended up being sold as a slave instead.[92] In addition to these personal stories, they told him of judicial enslavements; for example, he learned that "whoever among them commits adultery, whether it is man or wife, is sold along with their family."[93]

It was from this varied background that the 188 slaves who boarded the *Henrietta Marie*, bound for Jamaica in 1699, came. While we cannot know precisely how they came to be slaves or exactly where they came from, we can reconstruct something of the lives they lived in Africa, and this would form a background for African American history.

NOTES

1. David Moore, "Anatomy of a 17th Century Slave Ship: Historical and Archaeological Investigations of 'The Henrietta Marie'" (PhD dissertation, East Carolina University, Greenville, NC, 1989); Michael Cottman, *The Wreck of the Henrietta Marie: An African American Journey to Uncover a Sunken Slave Ship's Past* (New York: Crown, 1999). See also Madeleine Burnside, ed., *Spirits of the Passage* (New York: Simon and Schuster, 1997).

2. The exhibition is called "A Slave Ship Speaks: The Wreck of the *Henrietta Marie*." See the exhibition home page at http://www.melfisher.org/henriettamarie.htm.

3. New Calabar in the sixteenth century through the nineteenth century was simply called "Calabar" though sometimes also called New Calabar. It is known today as Elem Kalabari, while the modern Nigerian town of Calabar corresponds to the town first called Old Calabar by the Dutch in the mid-seventeenth century, a designation that stuck in English sources as well. Old Calabar, located near the mouth of the Oil River on the extreme eastern side of Nigeria, fit into a different trading pattern than New Calabar did.

4. Duarte Pacheco Pereira, *Esmeraldo De Situ Orbis* (MS of ca. 1506), bk. 2, chap. 9,

modern ed. from two eighteenth-century MSS, Augusto Epifânio da Silva Dias (Lisbon: Typographia Universal, 1905, reprint, Lisbon: Sociedade de Geografia de Lisboa, 1975). Other editions in modernized Portuguese have been made as well as French and English translations.

5. Alessandro Zorzi, "Informatiõ hauuto jo Alexandro da Portogalese. 1517. Venecia," fol. 140. Edited and published by Francisco Leite de Faria and Avelino Teixeira da Mota in "Novidades Náuticas e ultramarinas numa informação dada em Venezia em 1517," *Memórias da Academia das Ciéncias de Lisboa. Classe de Ciéncas* 20 (1977): 7–75, Separata by Centro de Estudos de História e Cartografia Antiga 99 (1977), also found with original foliation of MS in, *Monumenta Missionaria Africana*, ed. António Brásio (Lisbon: Agência Geral do Ultramar, 1952–1988), 8:35–41.

6. E. J. Alagoa, "Oral Tradition and Archaeology: The Case of Onyoma," *Oduma* 1 (1974): 10–12; E. J. Alagoa, "Ke, the History of an Old Delta Community," *Oduma* 2 (1974): 4–10; F. N. Anozie, "Onyoma and Ke: A Preliminary Report on Archaeological Excavations in the Niger Delta," *West African Journal of Archaeology* 6 (1976): 89–99; Nwanna Nzewunwa, *The Niger Delta: Aspects of its Prehistoric Economy and Culture* (Cambridge: Cambridge University Press, 1980).

7. License to the Moradores of São Tomé, 11 December 1493, in Brásio, *Monumenta*, 15:15–16.

8. "Imquiriçam que se tyrou nesta Ilha de SantÃtonjo sobre a nao dos armadores da Ilha de Santomé, que foy a Benj este ano de bcxbj (19 November 1516)" in Brásio, *Monumenta*, 1:494–95 (the editor has misdated the document in the introduction).

9. J. Marino Incháustegui Cabral, *Reales Cedulas y Correspondencia de Gobernadores de Santo Domingo. De la Regencia del Cardenal Cisneros en adelante* (Madrid: Graficas Reunidas, 1958), 1:236–39.

10. Garcia Mendez Casteloblanco, "Relação da Costa de Africa, començando da Mina atee o Cabo Negro (1620)," Brásio, *Monumentai*, 6:471. The actual text is in Spanish.

11. Alonso de Sandoval, *Naturaleza, policia sagrada i profana, costumbres i ritos, disciplina i catechismo Evangelico de todos Etiopes* (Seville: Francisco de Lira, 1627); modern ed., Angel Valtierra, *De Instauranda aethiopum salute. El Mundo de la esclavitud negra en América* (Bogotá: Imprensa Nacional de Publicaciones, 1956), 17.

12. E. J. Alagoa, *The Small Brave City-State* (Ibadan, Nigeria: Ibadan University Press, 1964), 52. Alagoa's traditions record an early period of coalition of settlements in the area prior to the founding of the state and the arrival of the Itsekeri immigrants from Warri. He also dates the events on the basis of genealogical reckoning to 1460. While not impossible, this may be too early a date. In any case, the event seems to have occurred before 1620, and the documentation is too sketchy for us to be able to comment further on it from available materials.

13. Later seventeenth-century sources refer to a king of Farahu, perhaps a later references to this state—they include a letter to the Prefect of the Capuchin mission in São Tomé asking for missionaries. Some of this documentation seems to refer to the Calabar area, but in a fairly specific note, the Prefect placed Farahu north of Arda (Allada). However, this location seems unlikely, for the nature of the captains listed on the document and the fact that no such state is known north of Allada in other sources make the possibility that this is a late reference to Zarabu not impossible. See documents published in Brásio, *Monumenta*, 14.

14. Mendez de Castelblanco, "Relaçao," Brásio, *Monumenta*, 6:471.

15. Frederick Bowser, *The African Slave in Colonial Peru, 1560–1650* (Stanford, CA: Stanford University Press, 1974), 44–46.

16. On the history of the missions in Warri, see Alan F. C. Ryder, "Missionary Activity in the Kingdom of Warri to the Early Nineteenth Century," *Journal of the Historical Society of Nigeria* 2 (1960): 1–24.

17. De Sandoval, *Naturaleza*, 17.

18. Biblioteca del Palacio (Madrid) MS 722, Juan de Santiago, "Brebe relacion delo sucedide a doce Religiosos Cappuchinos . . ." (MS of 1648), fols. 143–45; a published summary in Giovanni Antonio Cavazzi da Montecuccolo, *Istorica Descrizione de' tre regni Congo, Matamba ed Angola* (Bologna: Giacomo Monti, 1687), bk.

V, para. 121 (modern ed. and Portuguese trans., Graziano Maria [Saccardo] da Leguzzano, *Descrição Histórica dos três reinos, Congo, Matamba e Angola*, 2 vols. [Lisbon: Junta de Investigaçôes do Ultramar, 1965], which marks the original paragraphing).

19. Francesco da Leone to Secretary of Propaganda Fide, 29 September 1691, Brásio, *Monumenta*, 14:271.

20. Rey de Calabar to Francesco da Monteleone (22 September 1692), Brásio, *Monumenta*, 14:224; Francesco da Monteleone to Giuseppe Maria da Busseto (10 July 1692), Brásio, *Monumenta*, 14:252; Archivio "De Propaganda Fide" (Rome), Scritture riferite nelli Congressi, Africa, Congo, etc., vol. 2, fol. 553, Francesco da Monteleone to Propaganda Fide, 19 March 1692. However, the superior of the mission, Giuseppe Maria da Busseto, said definitely that the "Prince of Calabar (his domain as also smaller than that of Ouueri [Warri]) is heathen, and has never asked to be Christian up to the time when I left São Tomé." Da Busseto to Propaganda Fide, 12 January 1692, in, *Le missioni a Benin e Warri nel XVII secolo. La relazione di Bonaventura da Firenze*, ed. Vittorio Salvadorini (Milan: Giuffré Editore, 1972), 289.

21. Jean Barbot was a "Ten Percent" trader with English connections. P. E. H. Hair, Adam Jones, and Robin Law, *Barbot on Guinea: The Writings of Jean Barbot on West Africa, 1678–1712* (London: Ashgate, 1992), 2:695.

22. Universitetsbiblioteket Uppsala, L 123, fol. 62, "Handel op alle de kuste van Africa van Cap: Spartell tott Cab: Bona Esperanca," the trading list is on fols. 63v–65. The export must have been to Portuguese shippers, as it was elsewhere on the coast when mentioned in this report.

23. Nationaal Archief Nederland (formerly Algemeen Rijksarchief), *Oude West Indische Compagnie* 56, no. 3 (n.p.) description of African trade to Brazil in 1641. As recently as 1639, the Calabar lodge reported only non-slave exports from Calabar, *id.* 8, fol. 245, Jan Maurtis to Herren XIX, 22 October 1639.

24. National Archives of Barbados, Recopied Deed Books, RB 3/1, 202. Contract of Nicholas Crispe of London Samuel Chrispe and John Wood of London merchants, last day of February 1642, assuming here that the English yacht bound for Barbados that the Dutch factor on São Tomé observed passing the island sometime in 1641, *Oude West Indische Compagnie* 57, Journal of Jan Claesz Cock, 8 May 1642. (Journal runs from 2 December 1641.)

25. Auto of António Malhorquim (24 July 1645), Brásio, *Monumenta*, 9:328 (the destination was probably not Virginia, but simply English America, in all likelihood, Barbados). The English government protested the practice of seizing English ships with regards to the *St. John* bound for Calabar about 1661. Elizabeth Donnan, ed., *Documents Illustrative of the Slave Trade to America* (Washington, DC: Carnegie Institute, 1930, reprint, William S. Hein, 2002, 1:165n6.

26. "Aenwijsingese van diverssche Beschrijvingen van de Noort-Cust van Africa," fol. 10v, journal of a voyage to the Rio Reale, February 1652; fol. 11v, notes on customs at the "Calbary River or River Reale"; in *West Africa in the Mid-Seventeenth Century: An Anonymous Dutch Manuscript*, ed. and trans. Adam Jones (Madison, WI: African Studies Association, 1995), marking original foliation in transcription and translation; Arnout Leers, *Pertinente Beschryvinge van Africa . . . getrokken en vergadert uyt Reys-boeken van Johannes Leo Africanus* (Rotterdam: Arnout Leers, 1655), 312–13.

27. Olifert Dapper, *Naukeurige Beschrijvinge van Africa gewesten* (Amsterdam: Jacob van Meurs, 1668/1676), 135–38; Leers, *Pertinent Beschryvinge*, 312–13; "Aenweijsinge," fols. 10v, 11v.

28. Dapper, *Naukeurige Beschrijvinge*; Leers, *Pertinent Beschryvinge*; "Aenweijsinge," fols. 10v, 11v.

29. Much of our information on New Calabar and its surroundings in the late seventeenth and early eighteenth century is owed to materials collected by Jean Barbot. See Hair et al., *Barbot on Guinea* 2:673–75.

30. Ibid., 2:691.

31. Ibid., 2:676.

32. Ibid., 2:701n1.

33. Ibid., 2:675, 693.

34. Ibid., 2:673.

35. Francesco da Morro and Francesco da Monte Cassiano, "Relazione sulla missione de San Tome," ca. 1707, in Salvadorini, *Missioni*, 294; Archivio "De Propangada Fide," Acta, vol.

81, fol. 277, Francesco da Collevecchio to Propaganda Fide, 12 May 1711. This section is quoted in extenso in Salvadorini, *Missioni*, 219n25.

36. Leers, *Pertinent Beschryvinge*, 312–13; "Aenweijsinge," fols. 10v, 11v.

37. Journal of the *Arthur*, 5 December 1677–25 May 1678, in Donnan, *Documents*, 1:226.

38. Hair et al., *Barbot on Guinea*, 2:689.

39. Ibid., 2:691.

40. Ibid., 2:709–10n57 (editor's note). See also G. I. Jones, *The Trading States of the Oil Rivers* (London: International African Institute, 1963), 134, 218–19.

41. Hair et al., *Barbot on Guinea*, 2:693.

42. Ibid., 2:688.

43. Ibid., 2:708n48. The editors' critical statement made in Jones, *Trading States*, 105–7, suggest that this Pepprell was the original Pebble in the process of taking power, because later accounts suggest that the son of the first King Pebble died only in 1830. Clearly the process of changing power would take place more slowly than a single generation.

44. Christian Georg Andreas Oldendorp, *Historie der caribischen Inseln Sanct Thomas, Sanct Crux und Sanct Jan, inbesondere der dasigen Neger und der Mission der evangelischen Brüder under denselben*, ed. Gudrun Meier, Stephan Palmié, Peter Stein, and Horst Ulbricht (Berlin: Verlag für Wissenschaft und Bildung, 2000–2002), 1:427.

45. The civil war is described in Willem Bosman, *Naukeurige Beschryving van de Guinese Goud-, Tand-, en Slave Kust* (Utrecht: Anthony Schouten, 1704), 255–56. Secondary literature is found in A. F. C. Ryder, *Benin and the Europeans, 1472–1891* (New York: Humanities Press, 1969); and Paula Ben-Amos and John Thornton, "Civil War in the Kingdom of Benin: Continuity or Social Change, 1689–1732," *Journal of African History* 42 (2001): 353–76.

46. Archivio "De Propaganda Fide," Scritture riferite nel Congressi, Africa, Congo, etc., vol. 2, fol. 480v, Francesco da Monteleone to Propaganda Fide, 25 April 1691.

47. Oldendorp, *Historie*, 1:427.

48. Ibid., 1:487.

49. Universitetsbiblioteket Uppsala, L 123, fol. 62, "Handel."

50. Hair et al., *Barbot on Guinea*, 2:689.

51. Ibid., 2:691.

52. Ibid., 2:693, and plate 54, illustrating weapons made by the Hackbous.

53. De Sandoval, *Naturaleza*, 17.

54. Ibid., 94.

55. Dapper, *Naukeurige Beschrijvinge*, 509–10.

56. For a good overview of the linguistic situation and nomenclature in Sandoval and Oldendorp, see David Northrup, "Igbo and Myth Igbo: Culture and Identity in the Atlantic World, 1600–1850," *Slavery and Abolition* 21 (2000): 1–20, and for a corrective to my earlier views on these questions.

57. Oldendorp, *Historie*, 1:426, 430, 434.

58. Ibid., 1:431–32. His story in the account in Oldendorp leads us to "Andrew the Moor" who had a biography that seems to match that of Oldendorp's Pennsylvania informant, especially since there were very few Igbos in Pennsylvania, as given in Andrew's life story (*Lebenslauf*) in the Moravian Archives, Bethlehem, Pennsylvania, dated 13 March 1779.

59. Oldendorp, *Historie*, 1:430.

60. Ibid., 1:432.

61. Vincent Carretta, "Olaudah Equiano or Gustavus Vassa? New Light on an Eighteenth-Century Question of Identity," *Slavery and Abolition* 20 (1999): 96–105; and more fully in Vincent Carretta, *Equiano, The African: Biography of a Self-Made Man* (Athens: University of Georgia Press, 2005).

62. For an excellent rebuttal, among others and citing earlier literature as well is Paul Lovejoy, "Autobiography and Memory: Gustavus Vassa, alias Olaudah Equiano, the African," *Slavery and Abolition* 27 (2006): 317–47.

63. Olaudah Equiano, *The Interesting Narrative of the Life of Olaudah Equiano or Gustavus Vassa, the African*, 2 vols. (London: Gustuvas Vassa, 1789). See modern critical edition by Vincent Carretta (New York: Penguin, 2003). For our purposes the most useful edition is the extract annotated by G. I. Jones, "Olaudah Equiano of the Niger Ibo," in *Africa Remembered: Narratives of Africans from the Era of the Slave Trade*, ed. Philip Curtin (Madison: University of Wisconsin Press, 1968), 60–98. See his reference to "numbers of the natives of Eboe, now in London" could be brought to confirm some

statements, which suggests that he had communication with his fellow countrymen concerning customs of his country, p. 76.

64. G. I. Jones, "Introduction to Olaudah Equiano" in Curtin, *Africa Remembered*, 64–69; and Equiano, *Interesting Narrative*, 90–93.

65. De Sandoval, *Naturaleza*, 94. For other nations from Africa, however, de Sandoval describes detailed descriptions of ethnic marks.

66. Oldendorp, *Historie*, 1:426, 430.

67. Equiano, *Interesting Narrative*, 70–71.

68. Ibid., *Interesting Narrative*, 72.

69. Jones, "Introduction to Olaudah Equiano," 63.

70. Oldendorp, *Historie*, 1:430.

71. Moravian Archives, Bethlehem, Biography of Joshua, 1761.

72. Oldendorp, *Historie*, 1:432.

73. Equiano, *Interesting Narrative*, 74.

74. Oldendorp, *Historie*, 1:431.

75. Ibid., 1:436.

76. Oldendorp, *Historie*, 1:431 (but excludes wives from the sacrifice), 433 (Wooma's testimony which includes wives).

77. Ibid., 1:435 (basic sacrifice), 487 (a Mokko woman who was scheduled for sacrifice in this way, but spared and exported may well have been his primary informant).

78. Equiano, 72–73.

79. Ibid., 76.

80. Ibid., 78.

81. Ibid., 85–92.

82. Oldendorp, *Historie*, 1:427 (while this section relates to Kalabaris in the text, he must have meant the more interior people as well).

83. Moravian Archives, Bethlehem, biography of Andrew the Moor; biography of Joshua, 1761.

84. On the logic of internal slavery and its connections to the export trade, see G. Ugo Nwokeji, "The Biafran Frontier: Trade, Slaves and Aro Society, 1750–1905" (PhD dissertation, University of Toronto, 1999), 102–28.

85. Equiano, *Interesting Narrative*, 83.

86. Oldendorp, *Historie*, 1:432, 433–34.

87. On Aro Chukwu, which has a large bibliography, see K. O. Dike and F. I. Ekejiuba, *The Aro of South-Eastern Nigeria, 1650–1980: A Study of Socio-Economic Formation and Transformation in Nigeria* (Ibadan, Nigeria: Ibadan University Press, 1990); also Nwokeji, "The Biafran Frontier," esp. chaps. 2 and 3. Chronological issues are crucial in determining when the Arochukwu extended its network into areas where it might have linked to New Calabar, as opposed to Old Calabar (on the Cross River) closer to its home area.

88. Equiano, *Interesting Narrative*, 75.

89. Ibid., 77.

90. For a carefully considered interpretation of this statement in light of the Aro-Chukwu expansion and the slave trade, see Nwokeji, "The Biafran Frontier," 84–85.

91. Equiano, *Interesting Narrative*, 84–85.

92. Oldendorp, *Historie*, 1:487. For a consideration of various modes of enslavement, though using largely oral traditions and more recent ethnographic data, see Nwokeji, "The Biafran Frontier," 128–45.

93. Oldendorp, *Historie*, 1:431.

8 "A GREAT MANY BOYS AND GIRLS"

IGBO YOUTH IN THE BRITISH SLAVE TRADE, 1700–1808

Audra A. Diptee

In mid-June 1793, the slave ship *Jupiter* arrived at Martha Brae, Jamaica, with 359 African men, women, and children held captive on board. It was a long voyage. The ship had left the port of Bonny thirty-seven days earlier, but for the Africans on board this was merely one part of a long journey. Many of the captives had trekked through the Biafran hinterland for weeks, perhaps even months, and were passed from one African slave trader to another until they arrived at the coast and were sold to the captain of the *Jupiter*, John Goodrich. One month before the ship set sail, Goodrich reported that he had "130 young and Healthy negroes" on board. By the time the ship left the Biafran coast, some of those held captive had been on board for as long as four months. Some of them, however, did not even last that long. Nine died while the ship was on the coast and another twenty-two during the Atlantic crossing. Quite probably, another seventeen died after the ship arrived at Jamaica.[1] When the *Jupiter* arrived at Jamaica it held eighty-three children, sixty-one adolescents, and one infant. Approximately 42 percent of the *Jupiter*'s "cargo" transported from Bonny was composed of youths. In all probability, most of them were Igbo.[2]

As the case of the *Jupiter* suggests, children were forcibly transported from the Biafran ports in sizable numbers. It is now well established in scholarship that in the eighteenth century, larger proportions of women and children entered the trans-Atlantic slave trade from the Bight of Biafra than from other coastal regions of Africa.[3] This is consistent with the reporting of the Bristol merchant James Jones, who noted that "More Females are had [in Bonny] and better than on any other part of the Coast: they are in general small, more than one third Females and a great many Boys and Girls."[4] Expressing a similar sentiment, slave trader Captain Forsyth apologetically explained to his employer that the reason he was unable to get more male captives at Old Calabar was because they were being marched "through the cuntry [*sic*] for the Camaroo [*sic*] where they receive a greater price for them."[5]

This chapter looks at the experiences of Igbo youth in the Atlantic slave trade. Between 1700 and 1808, Igbo children were transported on British ships in larger numbers than children of other ethnic groups, and the vast majority of them ended up in the Caribbean. As will be suggested below, during this period, both ship captains on the African coast and purchasers in the Caribbean were more amenable to purchasing Igbo children than the current scholarship suggests. Furthermore, the numerical dominance of Igbo in the British slave trade made it likely that Igbo youth held captive in the Caribbean, compared to other young captives, had more opportunities to interact with persons from their ethnic community. Yet enslaved Igbo children had a range of experiences. When they were inserted into Caribbean slave society, they were put into a world in which there were diverse living and labor conditions and an increasing number of Caribbean-born slave children. How these young captives responded to their enslavement was not only influenced by their circumstances in the Caribbean but also by their personal histories in Igboland.

THE TRADE IN CHILDREN

Statistics on children in the Atlantic slave trade rely very heavily on documentation left by European (in this case British) slave traders. Because the price of a captive African was determined by, among other things, the perceived age of that captive, slave traders needed a reliable and consistent way to determine who was to be considered a child. They were creative. In the absence of birth certificates, they deemed that measuring the height of individual captives was the most practical way to decide which captives were children. Those persons "below 4 feet 4 inches" were bought and sold at the going rate for captive Africans listed as "boys" or "girls."[6] This group did not include adolescents, who were generally categorized as "men boys" and "women girls." Infants were also recorded separately and sometimes listed as being "at the Breast."[7]

Between 1701 and 1808, children accounted for 20.5 percent of all African captives forcibly transported out of the Bight of Biafra by British slave traders. Although the *proportion* of enslaved children sold from this region was generally comparable to (and sometimes even less than) other African regions involved in the Atlantic slave trade, the numbers of children from the Biafran region are particularly significant.[8] Quite simply, during the eighteenth and early nineteenth centuries, British slave traders purchased more captive Africans from this area than any other slave-trading region, and so, in absolute numbers, children left in far greater excess than elsewhere. Between 1701 and 1808, approximately 182,500 captive children left the Bight of Biafra on British slave ships.[9] The sex ratio among children fluctuated over time. The boys outnumbered the girls in significant numbers, perhaps until the mid-eighteenth century, after which the sex ratio came closer to parity though generally still favoring boys. It was not until 1780 that girls came in marginally greater numbers.[10] It should be noted that these statistics do not include adolescents. The *Trans-Atlantic Slave Trade Database*, which provides data on just fewer than thirty-five thousand slave voyages, gives no statistics on adolescent captive youth and seems to include their numbers under the categories for adults. Individual records, however, suggest that Igbo "men boys" and "women girls" did arrive in fair numbers, though their numbers are more difficult to ascertain.[11]

Of course not all children sold from the Biafran region were Igbo. People of various African ethnicities, most notably the Ibibio and Ijaw, also crossed the Atlantic from Biafran ports. However, it is worth noting that these very labels are problematic. As Brown and Lovejoy point out, these groups were in contact for centuries and had "porous conceptual boundaries." These ethnolinguistic categories, although seen by anthropologists as distinct, have not been universally accepted and are considered subgroups by some. That said, those men, women, and children who left the Bight of Biafra were part of a "cultural amalgamation that was heavily Igbo."[12]

Most specialists agree that it is impossible to determine the actual number of Igbo sent across the Atlantic with any precision, given the paucity of records and, of course, the problematic ways in which captive Africans were ethnically labeled.[13] What is clear, however, is that during the eighteenth century the slave port Bonny, enabled by its strong credit system, rose to prominence with British traders and that the majority of captives transported from that port were Igbo. Using information on population densities and slaving patterns, David Northrup estimates that the percentage of people from Igboland leaving that port could have been as high as 60 percent over the course of a century starting in 1730.[14] It may have very well been higher.

As might be expected, there were fluctuations in the proportion of children forcibly transported from the region. For most of the eighteenth century, the percentage of children sold into the Atlantic slave trade was slightly less than 20 percent (see table 8.1). The notable exception being the period 1751–1775, when children accounted for as much as 30.4 percent of all enslaved Africans, although the causes for this increase do not seem to be specific to the Biafran region. For reasons that are unclear, during this twenty-five-year period, children were sent across the Atlantic in unusually high numbers from all regions involved in the Atlantic slave trade.[15] What can be said with certainty, however, is that for most of the eighteenth century, it was by no means unusual to see children on slave vessels in the

TABLE 8.1 Percentage of captive children sold to British slave traders at the Bight of Biafra

Years	*Children from Bight of Biafra (%)*
1701–1725	18.5
1726–1750	19.8
1751–1775	30.4
1776–1800	18.4
1801–1808	14.0

Biafran region. In fact, between 1701 and 1808, on about one-quarter of all British slave ships, children accounted for more than 30 percent of the captives put on board, and although small in number, there are records for at least six slave ships in which children made up more than 50 percent.[16]

Not surprisingly, very few of those children sold into the slave trade were infants. In fact, the Igbo (and Ibibio) custom of killing twin infants continued throughout the era of the Atlantic slave trade, even though potentially they could have been sold. Ugo Nwokeji sees this as evidence that cultural forces sometimes trumped economic ones when shaping the demographic contours of enslavement. He argues that it is unlikely that economics can "explain why the Igbo and Ibibio killed twins, when selling two or more children fetched more money than selling one." Yet there is much evidence to suggest that there was virtually no market for infants in the slave trade.[17] In fact, there were even times when infants were killed by African slave traders for no other reason than there was no one willing to buy them. Such was the case when Captain Joseph Williams of the *Little Pearl* refused to purchase a mother and child put up for sale at one of the Biafran ports, as he believed the latter would be a burden during the Atlantic crossing. From all indications, no one else was willing to buy both the mother and child, and there was little point in trying to sell them separately, as "sucking children" could rarely be sold without their mothers. As a result, the child was killed and the mother was made available for sale—albeit in a distressed state—the next day. Although Williams may have been reluctant to purchase infants, he certainly was willing to purchase children. Of the 102 captives who lived long enough to be sold in Grenada, 32 were boys and 24 were girls.[18]

Even if the difficulty of selling infants sometimes led to their murder, it was not unknown for very young children to make it on board slave vessels. Reporting on trading activities at the Biafran coast, Alex Falconbridge, who had been employed as a surgeon on various slave ships, observed captive women who were in the final weeks or days of their pregnancy and so delivered their babies on the long trek to the coast or even during the Middle Passage.[19] From an economic standpoint, ship captains had good reasons to be reluctant about taking infants on board. The horrid conditions of the Middle Passage made it unlikely that they would survive the voyage across the Atlantic. Those infants who did survive could only be sold at a very low price or were sometimes given away to buyers, as a sort of bonus, if their mothers were purchased. Such was the case of the Jamaican-based merchant Allan White who, in 1792, made no hesitation in expressing his frustration at having to include in the calculation of his average sale price "two mere infants who must have been given [away] with their mothers."[20] As a result, regardless of whether an infant lived or died during the Middle Passage, their very purchase by a ship captain had the effect of reducing the overall sale average for his "cargo." This is no minor point, as ship captains and commissioned merchants were always concerned about sale expectations when making a report on the final "sale average."

Although there was little demand for infants, it is clear that ship captains were less reluctant to purchase children than current scholarly thinking suggests. This, of course, contradicts the notion that purchasers in the Americas had an unwavering preference for adult male captives that was far in excess of their demand for women and children.[21] All things being equal, on a theoretical level, this may have been the case. In reality, however, things were quite different. Ship captains knew and understood that, on the other side of the Atlantic, the greatest demand was for *healthy* captives and that concerns about the age and sex of captives were a secondary matter. There can be little doubt about this. Even the most cursory examination of sales records show that children considered relatively "healthy" were sold at higher prices than captive men who were considered "refuse."[22] That said, there was still some concern about purchasing too many children or those that were considered too young. It is difficult to determine what was considered an acceptable age when purchasing captive children, though one Jamaican merchant expressed some dissatisfaction at having to sell children who were "not more than 8 or 9 years of age."[23]

The availability of captive youth on the Biafran coast and the general willingness to purchase healthy children and adolescents by ship captains ensured that Igbo youth were sold into the Atlantic slave trade in significant numbers. The vast majority of Biafran youth sold into the British slave trade (93 percent) ended up in the Caribbean. Jamaica received captives far in excess of any other island (39 percent), but other significant areas of disembarkation include Dominica (10 percent), Barbados (8 percent), Grenada (6.5 percent), and St. Kitts (6 percent).[24]

At least by the late eighteenth century, Caribbean planters were not only amenable to purchasing African youths in general but also Igbo youths in particular. When offering a description of the African captives he hoped to sell, the Antiguan merchant James Maud advised that "Windw[ard] Coast Negroes" were preferred, but "should they be Eboes, avoid grown men . . . let the majority be young Women, with girls and boys in proportion . . ."[25] Igbo captives may not have been the first choice for Caribbean purchasers, but they were certainly one of the preferred groups. In August 1789, Jamaican merchant Francis Grant made it clear that his first choice was for captives from the Gold Coast, but if that was not possible he asked his contact in Bristol to send one of his "best Ebo Cargoes." By October, however, he changed his request and made it clear that he preferred "an Eboe Cargo to a Gold Coast one," noting that those captives from Bonny "are the sort most run upon among us."[26]

Of course, it is reasonable to question the accuracy with which Caribbean merchants and planters could distinguish between captives of different ethnic backgrounds. At times, captives were labeled only by the port from which they were exported and buyers' preferences for African captives were quite often described in those terms. Writing from Dominica, for example, merchants Francis and Robert Smyth advised that a captive from Old Calabar "does not answer so well, as those from new C[alabar] & Bonny . . ."[27] Yet, there is evidence that whites in the Caribbean did have a mechanism for determining the ethnic background of captives. Quite simply, they relied on the knowledge of "seasoned" Africans to help them distinguish between the various ethnic groups of the newly arrived.[28]

IGBO YOUTH MADE CARIBBEAN SLAVES

In recent years, there has been an increasing body of scholarship looking at the experiences of enslaved children in the Caribbean. In her pioneering work in this area, Colleen Vasconcellos argues that definitions of childhood were a point of contestation, and that planters' attitudes toward enslaved children in Jamaica changed significantly after the abolition of the British slave trade. More recently, Cecily Jones has explored the ways in which enslaved youth often exercised agency and found ways to resist their enslavement. Other studies focusing on children look at a range of issues including health, labor conditions, and child socialization under slavery.[29] As this author has argued elsewhere, however, the historical experiences of captive African children must be situated within the broader context of childhood.[30]

Africans brought their own ideas about childhood and child labor to the Caribbean, and given that most children transported to the Caribbean on British ships were in fact Igbo children, this raises important questions about the ways in which Igbo perceptions shaped childhood experiences under slavery. Although largely discredited in the scholarship, the reports of contemporary observers often suggest that African attitudes toward enslavement varied, depending on where in Africa the individuals were from and their cultural predisposition. According to the Jamaican plantation owner Bryan Edwards, for example, "Eboes," had a "timid and desponding temper." As he saw it, an act of punishment that would lead the "Kormantyn" of the Gold Coast to rebel would drive the "Ebo" to commit suicide. Edwards reportedly once witnessed the branding of twenty young boys, ten of whom he identified as Igbo, the other ten were from the Gold Coast. By Edwards's estimation, the oldest of the Igbo was no more than thirteen years of age. In his description, the first Igbo boy that was branded "screamed dreadfully" and the other Igbo boys "manifested strong emotions of sympathetic terror." However, the boys from the Gold Coast, according to Edwards, laughed aloud, "offered their bosoms undauntedly" when they were to be branded, and received the mark without so much as flinching.[31]

Fortunately historians have long seen past such ethnic stereotyping. Instead, they have looked to historical specificities in Africa to explain the behavior of captives on the other side of the Atlantic. Paul Lovejoy and David Trotman, in particular, argue that Africans must be seen as individuals with "peculiar histories." In other words, *individual* Africans crossed the Atlantic with their "own attitudes, ideas, beliefs and expectations," and they used their previous experiences to interpret and make sense of their situation in Americas.[32] This is no less the case for children. Take the case, for example, of the young Igbo (re)named Esther, once she arrived in Jamaica. Esther's age at the moment of capture is uncertain, but it is clear that she was young enough to still be under the influence of her father. She was reportedly the daughter of a man who "possessed many slaves" and had "a plantation of corn, yams, and tobacco." According to Esther, her grandmother's village, which was "one day's journey" from the coast, was attacked while she was there on a visit. She and all the women (and conceivably the other youth too young to fight) were sent into "the woods" as the warring party descended on the community. Unfortunately, they were discovered. Those who resisted and the elderly, which included her grandmother, were put to death. Within three days she was sold and put on a ship headed for Jamaica. Despite her slave status in Jamaica, as Esther saw it, her many "marks about the chest" were proof of her free birth.[33]

Given Esther's background, how did she contextualize her enslavement in the Caribbean? Just as importantly, how did her personal history shape her response to her enslavement? Although other details may be in doubt, it is certain that the realities of Caribbean slavery and the racist ideology that was used to give it legitimacy made little sense to Esther or other newly arrived Igbo youth. As with all captive Africans, children transported across the Atlantic came with little more than their memories of life in Africa. Most Igbo children made the transition to slavery in the Caribbean without parents or other relatives, and so they had to draw on their Igbo-oriented child's view of the world to make sense of slavery systems in the Americas. Some Igbo children, if they were old enough to remember them and fully comprehend them, would rely heavily on proverbs and stories they were told by parents, relatives, and community elders. Oral traditions were, after all, an important mechanism used in child socialization among the Igbo (as with other ethnic groups).[34]

It is important to note, of course, that the very context into which Igbo youth were inserted also shaped their experiences under slavery. Kristen Mann has rightly called on scholars to move beyond analyses that only take into account "who the slaves were and what they brought with them." Instead she urges historians to explore the ways in which specific circumstances encountered in the Americas "helped or hindered" captive Africans in their efforts to reconstruct a world that drew on African cultural beliefs and practices.[35]

In general, from at least 1750, Igbo youth transported to the Caribbean entered a world in which children were a common feature in the local landscape. Although it is often overlooked in the scholarship, captive youth were not only transported directly from Africa; a growing number of enslaved children were born in the Caribbean. This oversight is caused, in part, by the fact that historians continue to assume that the heavy importation of captive Africans into the Caribbean was caused chiefly by the inability of the enslaved population to increase its numbers through natural reproduction.[36] This interpretation ignores "facts so obvious" that at best it can only be described as an exaggeration of the circumstances. Historian Michael Craton has long argued that the importation of captive Africans should *not* be seen solely as a function of natural increase or decrease among the enslaved. As he points out, the slave trade to British West Indies served "to 'top up' the numbers depleted through natural decrease . . . *and* to allow for expansion towards socio-economic 'saturation' in each island."[37] In other words, the issue of reproduction aside, the importation of captive African men, women, and children was also linked to the expanding frontier and the subsequent increased agricultural production. This explains why Barbados, which had no space for further expansion by the early eighteenth century, was the only sugar colony to have a self-reproducing enslaved population in 1807.[38] It also explains why, on islands such as Jamaica, which did not reach its "saturation point" for enslaved laborers even by the end of slavery in 1838, there were many established plantations for which generalizations about high mortality and low fertility are not applicable. On some of these plantations there was a "trend towards self-sufficiency," and newly arrived Africans were needed only for "topping up" when there were labor deficiencies.[39] Hence, in Jamaica, the key destination of captive Igbo youth, and arguably other Caribbean islands, a growing number of children were being born into slavery. Clearly then, many Igbo youth held captive in the Caribbean entered a world in which they had to interact with children who were born locally: other Igbo children as well as African youth of other ethnicities.

Given the sheer numerical dominance of the Igbo among those captive Africans brought to the Caribbean, even among captive adults, it seems possible that Igbo children and adolescents may have had more opportunities in the West for continued exposure to Igbo traditions than other youth born in Africa. According to the above-mentioned Bryan Edwards, it was common, at least among the slaves he owned, for "old-established Negroes" to request permission to take in newly arrived "young people" who were "from their own nation and kindred." Granted, Edwards was a slavery apologist, and so he would be inclined to emphasize or exaggerate those aspects of slavery that he believed gave the perception that the institution was a humane one. Nonetheless, it certainly is plausible, or even very likely, that seasoned captives were more drawn to those newly arrived Africans who were part of their ethnic community. By Edwards's estimation, this allowed for the "revival and continuance of the ancient system" and was a sort of compensation for children left behind in Africa or lost by death. Thereafter, these adopted children were, to use Edwards's words, "protected" in their newly established relationships.[40] Perhaps it is more accurate to say that they were, in effect, mentored on how to survive the Caribbean slave system. Those newly arrived Igbo youth in this situation, then, found themselves getting advice from older Igbo with long experience of the realities and peculiarities of slavery in the Caribbean. Whether they chose to resist, rebel, or accept their life under slavery in the Caribbean, Igbo wisdom would be their guide.

But this was not the reality for all Igbo youth. Some, for example, may have been purchased to work outside the agricultural sector. In 1775, upon the arrival of a slave vessel to Jamaica, one female purchaser hoped to get "an Ebo girl, about 12 years of age" so that she could be trained as a "sempstress." Her ambition was to get a young Igbo "with small feet, not bow-legged, nor teeth filed, small hands & long, small taper fingers, &c."[41] In the case of this young girl, circumstances might have been different. She was purchased for domestic labor, which suggests that she would have fewer opportunities to interact with members of the enslaved community. It is uncertain who was going to be responsible to train her as a seamstress, but it could have been another, no doubt older, enslaved female who was skilled in this area. The person may not have been Igbo or even born in Africa. If this was the case, this young girl's experience would have been quite different from those Igbo youth who labored on large plantations and so had greater opportunities for exposure to other Igbo.

IGBO YOUTH AND THE TRANSITION TO ADULTHOOD

Considering the range of Igbo childhood experiences under slavery, it is difficult to make generalizations about the ways in which their experiences in youth influenced their behavior in adulthood. What is clear, however, is that although some planters deliberately purchased young Africans because they were perceived as less troublesome, this did not always work out as planned.[42] In fact, some young Igbo brought to the Caribbean were persistent runaways well into adulthood. Case in point is that of Coobah, who was brought to Jamaica in 1761 when she was approximately fifteen years of age. Unfortunately, there is no record representing Coobah's perspective, but if her actions are to be interpreted, it is clear that she was not only rebellious and openly defiant, but at times her behavior might even be described as reckless. Coobah was relentless in her efforts to escape. Between January 1770 and May 1774, she ran away no fewer than fourteen times. Nor did harsh punishments deter her. In June 1770, Coobah escaped for just over a month. It was reported that, during this period, she was guilty of "robbing a Negro wench." Apparently, under the pretense of wanting to help the woman, Coobah offered to carry her load and instead "marched away" with her rice and pigeons. When Coobah was found she was put in a device of restraint, known as "the bilboes," which was used to lock the victim's hands and/or feet. The very next day, she was "collared and chained" before being sent out to work. Within a few days she had escaped again, and stole "rice, beads, calabashes, &c" from another captive called Nancy. Unfortunately, she was caught before the day was over. This time, she was flogged and branded on her forehead. But not even this was enough to stop her, as within five days she made yet another attempt to escape.[43]

There is little known about Coobah before she was transported to Jamaica, and so we have little insight about how her early years in Africa may have shaped her behavior in Jamaica. What is clear, however, is that she went to great lengths to antagonize her owner with little concern for her own well-being. There is no other way to describe her decision to "shit" in the punch strainer one night as she slept in the cookroom. This was something that was bound to be discovered. Yet, when she received her punishment, which was to have the fecal matter put all over her face and mouth, she maintained her face of defiance. At least she certainly left her owner Thomas Thistlewood with the impression that "she minds it not." Despite his continued efforts to keep her in line, Thistlewood was never able to break her rebellious spirit. Coobah continued to steal and escape at every opportunity. Instead, it seems Coobah broke Thistlewood's will. In May of 1774, Thistlewood gave up on trying to tame Coobah's defiant tendencies. In that month she was sold and transported to Savanna, Georgia. She was a full-fledged adult, about twenty-eight years old.[44]

It is easy to see Coobah as a defiant and rebellious Igbo woman who never learned to accept her life under slavery in Jamaica. Although few would argue with this interpretation, it is tempting to contemplate a wider range of complexities in her life story: her actions were often reckless; she routinely betrayed the trust of other captives and targeted them during her acts of theft; and she deliberately made efforts to antagonize those with power and authority, often having little regard for the repercussions she was bound to face. In what ways did Coobah's life as a young Igbo child and adolescent shape her behavior in adulthood? Was she so affected by her enslavement during her adolescence that her actions were in fact those of a person severely traumatized? Or was she born into slavery in Africa? Did she demonstrate these defiant and reckless tendencies even before she was brought to Jamaica? Could she have been sold into the Atlantic slave trade precisely because she was so difficult to control? Or perhaps she was born with the status of a free Igbo child but found life under slavery in Jamaica unbearable. Perhaps she could relate only too well to the words of Jimmy, an adolescent who, while throwing a tantrum, shouted to his master Thistlewood, that "if this be living he did not care whether he lived or died."[45]

CONCLUSION

For most of the eighteenth century, up until the end of the British slave trade, Igbo youth were brought to the Caribbean in larger numbers than those from other ethnic groups. Because of the numerical dominance of Igbo transported to the Caribbean during this period, these children were more likely to have continued exposure to the various forms of the Igbo cultural complex. Initially, upon their arrival in the Caribbean, they used their youth-oriented Igbo worldview to make sense of their new life. With time, and perhaps even with help from adult Igbo, these children began to develop a better understanding of the racially hierarchical slave system into which they were inserted. Of course, not all Igbo children had ready access to Igbo adults and the consequent cultural reinforcements that such interactions engender. Youth, in such situations, no doubt relied more heavily on the Igbo proverbs and stories they were told before their capture, as they tried to maneuver the Caribbean slave system. Regardless of their situation, however, as the case of the above-mentioned Coobah makes clear, some of these enslaved youth rejected their life under slavery well into adulthood.

NOTES

1. The record of sale for the captives on the *Jupiter* accounts for only 342 captives not including "a male infant at the breast," which leaves seventeen captives unaccounted for.

2. Details on the voyage were taken from six letters, the record of sale and the *Trans-Atlantic Slave Trade Database* (2008), http://www.slavevoyages.org/. See John Goodrich to James Rogers, December 30, 1792; John Goodrich to James Rogers, January 11, 1793; John Goodrich to James Rogers, January 24, 1793; John Goodrich to James Rogers, March 5, 1793, John Goodrich to James Rogers, April 9, 1793; John Goodrich to James Rogers, June 15, 1793; "Sales of 342 Slaves Imported in the Ship Jupiter . . . July 3rd 1793." All letters are in the C107/59 series, National Archives, Kew Gardens (London, UK). Hereafter, please note that all records cited from the C107 series (Chancery Records) were located at the National Archives and the *Trans-Atlantic Slave Trade Database* will be referred to as the TSTD.

3. See, for example, David Eltis and Stanley L. Engerman, "Was the Slave Trade Dominated by Men?," *Journal of Interdisciplinary History* 23, no. 2 (1992): 237–57.

4. James Jones to Lord Hawkesbury, July 26, 1788, Elizabeth Donnan, *Documents Illustrative of the History of the Slave Trade to America*, vol. II (New York: Octagon Books, 1965), 590.

5. Captain Forsyth to James Rogers, July 9, 1792, C107/13. There may be some merit to this as, according to the TSTD, between 1750 and 1808, approximately 71 percent of all captives leaving the Cameroons were males. See http://slavevoyages.org/tast/database/search.faces?yearFrom=1750&yearTo=1808&mjbyptimp=60609.

6. See Audra Diptee, "African Children in the British Slave Trade During the Late Eighteenth Century," *Slavery and Abolition* 27, no. 2 (2006): 183–96. The editors of the TSTD estimate that children of four feet four inches tall were about thirteen or fourteen years of age. There may have been other physical indicators of age. I have found no specific mention of this in the historical record, but conceivably when slave traders were in doubt about a person's age they used other markers of maturity. For example, regardless of height, "fallen breasts" on women, wrinkled skin, grey hair, and the condition of teeth can all give some indication about age.

7. "Account Sales of 45 Slaves Including an Infant at the Breast," July 28, 1789, C107/6.

8. According to the TSTD, the average percentage of children put on British ships between 1701 and 1808 from other regions are as follows: Senegambia, 12.2 percent; Sierra Leone, 24.0 percent; Windward Coast, 26.3 percent; Gold Coast, 16.5 percent; Bight of Benin, 16.9 percent; West Central Africa, 16.9 percent. For data from the TSTD, see http://slavevoyages.org/tast/database/search.faces?yearFrom=1701&yearTo=1808&natinimp=7.

9. This number represents 20.5 percent of the 890,261 captives estimated by the TSTD to have left the region on British ships. See http://

slavevoyages.org/tast/assessment/estimates.faces?yearFrom=1701&yearTo=1808&flag=3. The other two regions that exported African children in significant numbers were the Gold Coast (106,280) and West Central Africa (82,180).

10. See http://slavevoyages.org/tast/database/search.faces?yearFrom=1701&yearTo=1808&natinimp=7&mjbyptimp=60600&chilrat7From=0&chilrat7To=100.

11. With reference to the absence of statistics on adolescents in the TSTD, compare, for example, statistics in the database with "Sales of 342 Slaves Imported in the ship Jupiter . . ." July 3, 1793, C107/59.

12. See the introduction of Carolyn Brown and Paul Lovejoy, eds., *Repercussions of the Atlantic Slave Trade: the Interior of the Bight of Biafra and the African Diaspora* (Trenton, NJ: Africa World Press, 2009).

13. For a discussion of African ethnicities in the Biafran region, see Gwendolyn Midlo Hall, *Slavery and African Ethnicities in the Americas: Restoring the Links* (Chapel Hill: University of North Carolina Press, 2005), 126–43. For a debate on methodological problems of determining the number of Igbo sold into the Atlantic slave trade, see Femi J. Kolapo, "The Igbo and their Neighbours during the Era of the Atlantic Slave-Trade," *Slavery and Abolition* 25, no. 1 (2004): 114–33; Douglas B. Chambers, "'My own Nation': Igbo Exiles in the Diaspora," *Slavery and Abolition* 18, no. 1 (1997): 72–97; David Northrup, "Igbo and Myth Igbo: Culture and Ethnicity in the Atlantic World, 1600–1850," *Slavery and Abolition* 21, no. 3 (2000): 1–20; Douglas B. Chambers, "The Significance of Igbo in the Bight of Biafra Slave-Trade: A Rejoinder to Northrup's 'Myth Igbo,'" *Slavery and Abolition* 23, no. 1 (2002): 101–20. See also Ugo Nwokeji, "The Atlantic Slave Trade and Population Density: A Historical Demography of the Biafran Hinterland," *Canadian Journal of African Studies* 34, no. 3 (2000): 616–55.

14. Northrup, "Igbo and Myth Igbo," 1–20. For a discussion of Bonny, see Paul E. Lovejoy and David Richardson, "'This Horrid Hole': Royal Authority, Commerce and Credit at Bonny, 1690–1840," *Journal of African History* 45, no. 3 (2004): 363–92.

15. It is uncertain why there was a spike in the number of children for all slave-trading regions. It could have been caused by a variety of factors. Typically, for example, during periods of drought children were often sold into slavery in greater numbers. See Joseph Miller, "The Significance of Drought, Disease and Famine in the Agriculturally Marginal Zones of West-Central Africa," *Journal of African History* 23, no. 1 (1982): 17–61. See also Philip Curtin, "Nutrition in African History," *Journal of Interdisciplinary History* 14, no. 2 (1983): 371–82. All data from table 8.1 were taken from the TSTD. See http://slavevoyages.org/tast/database/search.faces?yearFrom=1701&yearTo=1808&natinimp=7&mjbyptimp=60600. The database also provides the following statistics for children between 1751 and 1775: Senegambia, 30.5 percent; Sierra Leone, 33.6 percent; Windward Coast, 37.2 percent; Gold Coast, 37.3 percent; Bight of Benin, 28.1 percent; West Central Africa, 43.3 percent. See http://slavevoyages.org/tast/database/search.faces?YearFrom=1701&yearTo=1808&natinimp=7.

16. In total, the TSTD has records for 254 British ships that documented the number of children leaving the Biafran coast between 1701 and 1808. For sixty-one of these, children accounted for greater than 30 percent. See http://slavevoyages.org/tast/database/search.faces?yearFrom=1701&yearTo=1808&mjbyptimp=60600&natinimp=7&chilrat7From=30&chilrat7To=100.

17. See Ugo Nwokeji, "African Conceptions of Gender and the Slave Traffic," *William and Mary Quarterly* 58, no. 1 (2001): 47–68. I first made this argument in Diptee, "African Children in the British Slave Trade," 183–96.

18. Records indicate that 169 captives embarked at the ports Andony and Old Calabar and 67 died during the Middle Passage. For further data on the voyage also see the TSTD. For the reference to the murder of the infant, see *Account of a Voyage to the Coast of Africa by James Arnold*, March 24, 1789, BT 6/11 (no folio number). For the reference to "sucking children" see Isaac Parker, *Minutes of the Evidence Taken before the Select Committee*, Public Records Office, Publications of the House of Commons, 1/84, 125.

19. Alexander Falconbridge, *An Account of the Slave Trade on the Coast of Africa* (New York: AMS Press, 1973), 14.

20. Allan White to James Rogers & Co., January 27, 1793, C107/6.

21. According to Barry Higman, for example, "All of the masters favoured adult male slaves, and hence Africans." James Walvin also writes, "Women slaves were not thought as valuable as men." See B. W. Higman, *Slave Population and Economy in Jamaica, 1807–1834* (Cambridge: Cambridge University Press, 1976), 80. See also James Walvin, *Black Ivory: A History of British Slavery* (London: Harper Collins, 1992), 119.

22. See, for example, a case where "refuse" captives—including adult males—were sold in Jamaica at forty-two pounds while captive boys and girls were sold at sixty-six pounds each. The captives were transported from *Bonny*. For the record of sale see "Sales of 342 Slaves Imported in the ship Jupiter . . ." July 3, 1793, C107/59. For another case, see "Sales of Two Hundred and Two Slaves Imported in the Ship African Queen," March 10, 1793, C107/59. The captives were transported from Old Calabar and sold in Jamaica.

23. This comment was made in reference to captives purchased at Sierra Leone but there seems little reason that it could not also be applied to Igbo children. John Cunningham to James Rogers, April 20, 1792, C107/6.

24. Approximately 10 percent of Biafran captives on British ships ended up in Martinique; Guadeloupe; and the Spanish, Dutch, and Danish Caribbean. For the statistics, see http://slavevoyages.org/tast/database/search.faces?yearFrom=1701&yearTo=1808&natinimp=7&mjbyptimp=60600.

25. James Maud to James Rogers, July 30, 1786 (Antigua). Though not referring specifically to Igbo children, the merchant Samuel Richards advised that, in Barbados, remittances for "young slaves, say Men Boys and Women Girls have been here, the best in all the Islands." See Samuel Richards to James Rogers, June 21, 1788, C107/9.

26. Francis Grant to James Rogers, August 4, 1789; Francis Grant to James Rogers, October 10, 1789. Both letters were found in C107/9.

27. Francis & Robert Smyth to James Rogers, February 22, 1788, C107/8. Reporting on Jamaica, Francis Grant also advised that "Negroes from Old Calabar are not nearly in so much estimation with the generality of people amongst us here as from Gold Coast. . . ." Francis Grant to James Rogers, December 1788, C107/7, Box 2. For another reference to Jamaica, see a note by John Taylor when he noted that "Angola slaves are not so much liked in Jamaica as Eboe or Gold Coast . . ." John Taylor Letter to Simon Taylor, August 7, 1793, Taylor/14, Letterbook A. Writing from Grenada, one merchant asked to be sent "one or two of your good Bonny or Windward Ships." See Munro MacFarlane to James Rogers, September 4, 1792, C107/5.

28. Neither of these two cases deal specifically with Igbo captives, but it does not undermine the argument in any way. According to a notice in the Jamaican *Royal Gazette*, a runaway slave "of the Nago country" was found. Initially, the escapee "pretend[ed]" not to understand English, but he provided more information after "negroes of his own country . . . were put to interrogate him." Similarly, another report was put in the same paper announcing that a runaway "stout new negro" who was "quite naked" had been found. His ethnic background remained unknown as "no negro [could] be found that understands him." See the *Royal Gazette*, June 23–30, 1781, and November 10–17, 1781.

29. Colleen Vasconcellos, "And a Child Shall Lead Them?: Slavery, Childhood, and African Cultural Identity in Jamaica, 1750–1838" (PhD dissertation, Florida International University, 2004); Sheila Aird, "'The Forgotten Ones: Enslaved Children and the Formation of a Labor Force in the British West Indies" (PhD dissertation, Howard University, 2006); Tara Inniss, "From Slavery to Freedom: Children's Health in Barbados, 1823–1838," *Slavery and Abolition* 27, no. 2 (2006): 251–60; Jerome Teelucksingh, "The 'Invisible Child' in British West Indian Slavery," *Slavery and Abolition* 27, no. 2 (2006): 237–50; Cecily Jones, "'Suffer the Little Children': Setting a Research Agenda for the Study of Enslaved Children in the Caribbean Colonial World," *Wadabagei* 9, no. 3 (2006): 7–25; Cecily Jones, "'If this be living I'd rather be dead': Enslaved Youth, Agency and Resistance on an Eighteenth Century Jamaican Estate," *The History of the Family* 12 (2007): 92–103; Audra Diptee, "Imperial Ideas, Colonial Realities: Enslaved Children in Jamaica, 1775–1834," in *Children in Colonial*

America, ed. James Marten (New York: New York University Press, 2007), 48–60.

30. Diptee, "Imperial Ideas, Colonial Realities."

31. Bryan Edwards, *The History, Civil and Commercial, of the British West Indies* (New York: AMS Press, 1966), 2:83–84, 88.

32. Paul Lovejoy and David V. Trotman, "Enslaved Africans and Their Expectations of Slave Life in the Americas: Towards a Reconsideration of Models of 'Creolisation,'" in *Questioning Creole: Creolisation Discourses in Caribbean Culture*, ed. Verene A. Shepherd and Glen A. Richards (Kingston, JM: Ian Randle, 2002), 67–91.

33. This story was recorded by Brian Edwards. According to Edwards, it was initially recorded "without any view to publication." Edwards, *The History, Civil and Commercial*, 126–27.

34. Asonye Uba-Mgbemena, "The Role of Ífò in Training the Igbo Child," *Folklore* 96, no. 1 (1985): 57–61; Jack Daniel, Geneva Smitherman-Donaldson, and Milford A. Jeremiah, "Makin' a Way Outa No Way: The Proverb Tradition in the Black Experience," *Journal of Black Studies* 17, no. 4 (1987): 482–508.

35. Kristin Mann, "Shifting Paradigms in the Study of the African Diaspora and of Atlantic History and Culture," *Slavery and Abolition* 22, no. 1 (2001): 10.

36. For example, Trevor Burnard argues that "Jamaicans had an insatiable appetite for acquiring slaves, few of whom survived long enough to establish a naturally reproducing slave population." See also Cecily Jones, who argues that "most enslaved populations throughout the Caribbean failed to reproduce themselves by natural increase. As a result planters were forced to rely on the importation of enslaved Africans well into the years before slavery was finally abolished in 1807." Trevor Burnard, *Mastery, Tyranny & Desire* (Chapel Hill: University of North Carolina Press, 2004): 15; Jones, "'Suffer the Little Children,'" 19.

37. Emphasis mine. Michael Craton, "Jamaican Slave Mortality: Fresh Light from Worthy Park, Longville and the Tharp Estates," *Journal of Caribbean History* 3 (1971): 3. Higman also sees a link between "small islands capable of only limited expansion" and the growth of the enslaved population. See B. W. Higman, *Slave Populations of the British Caribbean, 1807–1834* (Baltimore, MD: Johns Hopkins University Press, 1984), 78.

38. According to Higman, the enslaved population of Barbados "leveled off" after about 1710. See Higman, *Slave Populations of the British Caribbean*, 43.

39. According to Craton, in Jamaica the rate of natural decrease had fallen from 4 percent in the early eighteenth century to 1 percent in 1808. Craton, "Jamaican Slave Mortality," 5.

40. Edwards, *The History, Civil and Commercial*, 155.

41. Douglas Hall, *In Miserable Slavery: Thomas Thistlewood in Jamaica, 1750–1786* (Kingston, JM: University of the West Indies Press, 1998), 178.

42. For example, in his well-known diaries, Thomas Thistlewood documented that when purchasing captives he would choose "men boys and girls, none exceeding 16 or 18 years old, as full grown men or women seldom turn[ed] out well." Hall, *In Miserable Slavery*, 119.

43. Ibid., 191–92.

44. Ibid., 192, 195.

45. Jimmy was reportedly from the Gold Coast. Hall, *In Miserable Slavery*, 204.

9 BECOMING AFRICAN

IGBO SLAVES AND SOCIAL REORDERING IN NINETEENTH-CENTURY NIGER DELTA

Raphael Chijioke Njoku

The existing studies of Igbo participation in the trans-Atlantic slave trade have so far given cursory attention to the impact of Igbo slaves on social transformation of their non-Igbo African host communities. Rather, related studies on the Igbo have paid extensive attention on the role of the Aro middlemen in the slave trade along with the extraordinary entrepreneurial successes of such ex-slaves as Jaja of Opobo, Oko Jumbo, Madu, and Alali of the Anna Pepple House.[1] Other studies have analyzed the challenges associated with slave trade manumission in the Igbo area while covering the emergence and organization of the unique "House System" as a sociopolitical unit in the new delta society of eighteenth and nineteenth centuries.[2] This chapter adds to the existing literature on slavery and emancipation with focus on the impact of Igbo slaves on sociocultural and economic alteration of the delta communities. It is a study of the dynamics of adjustment for enslaved Igbo diaspora within an African social setting. Given that socioeconomic statuses and cultural practices converge on identity, this study is also an exploration of how the Igbo slaves and their offshoots defined and redefined themselves as their social ranks changed over time in the Niger Delta.

NINETEENTH-CENTURY NIGER DELTA

The Niger Delta city-states of southeastern Nigeria, like other coastal communities of West Africa in the nineteenth century, were in a state of rapid flux. The key forces of social and economic alteration included the decline of the Atlantic slave trade and the shift to trade in palm produce.[3] Coming on the heels of the commercial revolutions vis-à-vis rise of the supposed "legitimate" trade were Christian missionary incursions, the introduction of early mission schools, and, soon after, European imperial claims in Africa. While the Niger Delta area embraces the entire communities on the Bights of Benin and Biafra (a curve on the western coast of Africa extending eastward for about four hundred miles), the major focus of this study is on the Ijo, Efik, and Ibibio-speaking clusters.[4] These are the earliest known groups that occupied this part of modern Nigeria. Their main centers were Bonny, Andoni, Elem Kalabari (or New Calabar), Nembe (or Brass), Okirika, and Opobo.

Along with the communities on the Cross River estuary, the city-states of the delta constituted one of the leading West African entrepôts in the Atlantic slave trade that began in the fifteenth century.[5] In the first three decades of the nineteenth century, when the trade in palm oil had begun to surpass the slave trade, the delta entrepôt exported more oil than the total volume originating from the rest of West Africa. Usually commercial interchanges always go with exchange of cultures, ideas, peoples, and social transformation. Likewise, with the expanding commercial exchange that connected the Europeans, the delta, and their Obolo, Ogoni, Ndoki, Ogbia, and Igbo neighbors; the development of cash economy; increasing tastes for foreign goods; and the gradual intrusion of Christian religion and Western ideas—all combined in initiating an extensive social reordering in the various local delta communities.

Reminiscent of the anxieties raised about the American post-abolition society, the overwhelming number of Igbo slaves in the Niger Delta over this period created what the local

Niger Delta elite had perceived as "an Igbo peril"—the threat of the indigenous ways of life being polluted by the culture of servile Igbo elements scorned as alien to the people. While slave trade (not slavery) was abolished by Britain in 1807 and the final slave cargo left the delta coast in the 1830s, internal slavery continued in many parts of eastern Nigeria even as late as 1912.[6] The slaves previously meant for the export market were now deployed to inland plantations to facilitate the development of the palm oil trade. In most delta communities, the slaves outnumbered the freemen. Unlike the practice in the Western world where slaves were treated as personal property and permanently consigned to the lowest rung of social strata, slaves in the delta society could easily purchase their freedom through outstanding demonstration of industry. Opportunities also existed for them to ascended the social ladder and occupy positions of influence and power in their new society. In light of this, the delta was on the path to revolutionary changes, even as the indigenous elite struggled to safeguard their strategic interests and privileges.

In his "Kalabari Ekine Society: A Borderland of Religion and Art" and "Igbo: An Ordeal for Aristocrats," Robin Horton, an expert historian of Niger Delta, has analyzed one of the elaborate methods by which the Kalabari people fought the so-called peril of Igbo cultural intrusion and distortion in some detail.[7] The fight for the preservation of the indigenous ways of life, as will be elaborated upon, did not, however, halt the wheel of change. By the 1830s when the export of slaves had ceased at most delta ports, Igbo presence there had produced "a very marked effect on society."[8] At this time, the "generation of Africans who had grown up with the new trade in oil was coming of age . . . new men, and new ideas were making powerful inroads into the Niger Delta."[9] The social transformations that began in the 1500s and spanned the more than four hundred (1500s–1900s) years that the trans-Atlantic slave trade lasted drew on both internal and external dynamics. The marked alterations emerged in gradual and cumulative order rather than in spontaneous and sudden manner.

Starting in the sixteenth century, for instance, Aro oracular influence had begun to manifest in the Niger Delta. In their separate studies, E. J. Alagoa and G. I. Jones have noted "several nineteenth century accounts of trips to the [famous Igbo] oracle at Arochukwu, known as *Ibiniukpabi* (or Long Juju for the British) from several delta states."[10] The Aro of southeastern Nigeria exploited the judicial, political powers, and privileges associated with the oracle to procure the Igbo victims of the slave trade. Being the single most powerful force behind the mass movement of slaves that sustained the trans-Atlantic exchange, the Aro oracular influence traveled far and wide, to the point that the delta indigenes began to make trips to the famous Ibiniukpabi oracle for solutions to varied personal and community problems. In other words, such ritual consultations may have begun at an earlier date.[11] Before delving into the history of sociocultural influences brought about by the Igbo influx to the delta society of the nineteenth century, it is crucial to briefly highlight some aspects of the economic history from which these changes emanated.

TRADE, SLAVERY, AND SOCIETY

The history of the nineteenth-century post-abolition era (1807–1900) goes back to the several centuries of slavery, which drew the Niger Delta communities into a more vigorous contact with their other neighbors, including the Igbo. Separate studies remind us that there was a preexisting trade between the landlocked Igbo and other neighboring groups before the rise of the overseas commerce. Although on a less dramatic scale, the internal long-distance trade had involved with typical delta products like salt, crayfish, fish, periwinkles, vegetables, snail, crabs, and other riverine products that were exchanged for such Igbo hinterland products as yams, vegetables, palm oil, art works, beads, brass, and iron tools. Both the older regional trade and the later development of the Atlantic slave traffic brought the Igbo in a closer contact with neighboring peoples of the coastal area of the delta.[12] The delta ports, particularly Bonny, served as the clearinghouses for the Atlantic trade, providing a large proportion of the slaves received by European slavers from the West African Coast.[13]

To what extent the delta inhabitants depend on their Igbo partners for their supply of slaves is still to be fully ascertained by scholarly investigation. But different estimates show that at the end of the eighteenth century, Igbo slaves accounted for about three-quarters of the annual slaves exported at Bonny.[14] The Aro merchants sold the Igbo captives to the delta middlemen at markets on the borders of the delta country. Over the period between 1600 and 1800, the delta peoples developed their internal institutions in fluid and dynamic relationships with influences coming from their European and African contacts, including the Igbo. In response to the pressures coming from the anti-slavery movement, however, the delta states responded by reorganizing the mainstay of their economies from a base on slavery to palm oil trade.[15] This is despite the fact that slave hunting was more fun and more profitable for the poachers and dealers than the arduous task of squeezing palm oil by hand and cracking palm kernels in commercial quantity. But the shrinking and dangerous export market for slaves—thanks to the vigilance of the British naval squadrons—left no option but to switch to "legitimate" trade. This in turn brought the need to absorb the slaves either in the plantations located in the delta, or in Igboland. Consequently, slaves became cheaper, and their availability for the local labor markets increased immensely. Their rising number in the delta exacerbated "the social distortions which the slave trade had created."[16]

As many Igbos and elements of their culture were absorbed into the Niger Delta society, the social distortions the delta elite worried about became more pronounced. Some of the significant impacts that resulted included radical changes in notions of kinship system as the universal institution transformed from its traditional agnatic ties to fictional ties. Other changes included the opening up of new frontiers of opportunities in trade, which were duly exploited by the diligent slaves to improve upon their social class—a development that transformed the preexisting class system. Yet, other effects mirrored an expansion in the use of Igbo language as a medium of communication and the adoption of some Igbo names for children, including those born of non-Igbo parents. Also, as society became more heterogeneous, there was a purported sexual laxity blamed on the presence of these slaves.

Cultural interchange always involves a multidimensional and complex traffic. The Igbo in general, including those in the hinterlands, also adopted some elements of cultural practices from the delta like new vocabularies and dressing habits. For instance, in the late nineteenth century, some Onitsha-Igbo local chiefs adopted the Ijo hombre hat as part of their "traditional" regalia.[17] In essence, the semblance of cultural transformations taking place in the delta society of the nineteenth century was a complex mix of the various indigenous cultures of the delta peoples with Igbo, European, and later the *Saro*—freed slaves who migrated from Sierra Leone.[18] Understanding this complex hybridity is crucial to appreciating the history of the Niger Delta peoples and the nature of the social relationships with their Igbo neighbors today.

IGBO SLAVES AND SOCIAL CHANGE

One of the most prominent areas of social transformation in the new delta society was seen in the emergence and expansion of the "House" or "Canoe" system as a unit of social organization. This competitive socioeconomic and political system, described by J. B. Webster and A. A. Boahen as "trading corporations," replaced the older and more conservative type of lineage or kinship group based on blood ties.[19] There is no reliable account of how this system sprouted, but it must be stressed that "the new Houses of the city-states were developed out of the old lineage institutions of the Eastern Delta fishing village, and ultimately the old Ijo prototype of the Central Delta."[20] Similar to the role played by the Duala middlemen in the development of Atlantic slave trade on the Cameroonian coast, one can only affirm that the stimulus for change started with the establishment of contacts between European merchants and some business speculators from the delta.[21]

The "black brokers," as referred to them by Consul Livingston in 1872, had received some incentives from their European partners in forms of trade goods with the bargain for them to search for slaves from the markets in the interior. Loaded up with European goods such as mirrors, umbrellas, and guns, the African opportunists ventured into the hinterlands, procuring slaves at a huge profit margin.[22] As profits from the trade flowed, the demand for slaves increased—not only for export but also for incorporation into the delta dealers' own households. Like in most preindustrial societies, the precolonial Africans explored ways to increase the size of their households because members served as a crucial source of labor and defense against external attacks. In the nineteenth century, an average House comprised about three hundred to one thousand members, including the master's family. According to Rev. Hope Waddell, the legendary Scottish missionary and pioneer educationist on the Cross River Estuary, the House of King Eyo of Creek Town, Old Calabar, for example, could boast of thousands of members, and four hundred canoes—each with a captain and crew.[23]

As the Canoe Houses expanded, their heads assisted the very industrious and capable slaves with setting up their own businesses by granting them credits in form of goods, servants, and transport facilities. The small traders' business was subject to taxation by their heads.[24] Usually, the practice of slavery comes with a degree of militarization of society.[25] Besides the typical violence that accompanies the procurement and handling of slaves, rival Houses engaged one another in heated competition for power and control over the lucrative overseas commerce. Thus, the Canoe House also served as a military unit in protection of convoys of slave cargoes against pirates and ambush from members of rival trading communities. In the period under survey, Bonny enjoyed both military and commercial supremacy. P. A Talbot, a British colonial anthropologist, reported that in 1790 the King of Bonny "destroyed the town of New Calabar [Kalabari] twice," preventing them from engaging in any shipping business.[26] For both the merchants and people of the delta, the capability to manage a war canoe became a sign of success, power, and responsibility. To ensure a progressive standard, succession to the headship of the Houses were based on proven entrepreneurship and drive. Although it was naturally desirable for a man to be succeeded by his son, a gifted and hardworking "slave-born person" often took over the headship of a Canoe House.[27]

Heads of Canoe Houses enjoyed enormous power quite uncommon to the heads of the village descent group—*ekpuk* (in Efik) or *wari* or *polo* (in Ijo) or *umunna* (in Igbo). European merchants usually negotiated business directly with the Canoe head, although the latter reserved the option of appointing agents who could trade on his account. The head served as the sole financial controller of the House and received taxes from those that he had extended trade permission. Canoe heads not only had control over means of production, they also controlled means of reproduction. They procured female slaves for distribution to members as wives.[28] Often, the House head aimed to protect his investments by giving the hands of his own daughters in marriage to his most favorite and trusted traders. Through this way, the heads built networks of loyalties that consolidated their power, authority, and wealth. While indolent slaves were expelled from the Household, the intelligent and enterprising ones were propelled to the top of the social system. As aptly noted by K. O. Dike, "it was this incentive [for social mobility], ever present in the House system, that made it in the nineteenth century an institution full of vitality, flexible, and in a large measure beneficial to all."[29]

John Pape's study of "Black and White: The 'Perils of Sex' in Colonial Zimbabwe" reveals that "sexual relations rarely earn a mention in history books." Indeed, while Pape and Van Olsen, in their different studies, have detailed how "black" scares embittered race relations in South Africa during the years before the World War I, the encounter between Igbo and delta peoples has received inadequate attention.[30]

Expectedly, the high proportion of males of Igbo extraction in the Niger Delta resulted in interethnic sexual relations with the local women. Oral sources claimed that for the Efik, Ibibio, Andoni, and Degema women, the thousands of successful Igbo entrepreneurs of slave descent became their target for both short- and long-term relationships. Therefore frustrated and angered, the male indigenes of delta society came to perceive the Igbo slaves as indulging in acts of sexual laxity. From oral sources, it is also deduced that some Efik, Ibibio, and Kalabari men favored Igbo women as spouses because the delta men were obsessed with "fairer and more beautiful women from the hinterland Igbo area."[31] The Andoni people in particular were said to be "fond of marrying Igbo women from Umuahia area."[32] This complex mix of ethnicity and sexuality is often inadequately situated in the popular accounts alluding to Igbo "impulsive" and "mischievous" nature as encountered in a Kalabari song invoked during its annual *ekine* festival:

> His mother sent him to buy red dye; He went and bought yellow. O, Igbo, son of a chief! O, Igbo, son of a chief! His mother sent him to buy red dye; He went and bought a woman's vagina. O, Igbo, son of a chief! O, Igbo, son of a chief![33]

In this song, Igbo is portrayed as a willful, lustful young man, whose crave for women has reached to a point of obsession if not madness.

In his *Ibibio Profile* published in 1982, A. J. A. Esen, an Efik polemic, attributed sexual laxity among the Ibibio on the Igbo. "Ibibio women," he claimed, "get so easily attracted to strangers—that is to non-Ibibio men."[34] More than anything, this allusion reechoes the familiar hysteria from the nineteenth-century Niger Delta freeborn elite. Although it remains a begrudging admission of Igbo success with delta women, Esen's views need to be considered in light of the wider context of African culture in which material success, rather than mere affection, has largely influenced the disposition of parents to reject or accept a potential suitor. In other words, delta women were simply responding to a widely practiced African pattern of courtship and marriage value. In modern Nigeria, Igbo business successes and exuberance have been the target of unbridled jealously and, at the same time, a point of admiration among the wider non-Igbo Nigerian neighbors, including the peoples of Niger Delta. In the present day the *ekine* festival in Kalabari still represents an ordeal loaded with symbols of values largely associated with Igbo flamboyant life of the nineteenth-century era.[35]

As more children were born in the delta with varying degrees of Igbo blood in their veins, Igbo language and names naturally gained a wider popularity. Language is one of the strong markers of identity. Therefore, for the thousands of slaves in the new delta environment, Igbo remained a unifying factor. Although linguistics emphasize differences in dialects, "they have also stressed that living together as neighbors has woven a web of common cultural vocabularies that link the various peoples together."[36] This perspective explains the complex development of languages in the Niger Delta of which far-reaching trade contacts with outsiders played a significant part.

In the delta, especially among the Degema, Bonny, Ubani, Ndoki, Diobu, Efik, and Ibibio societies, the Igbo language started to infiltrate popular vocabularies as early as the fifteenth century and even supplanted the indigenous languages in some places like Bonny and Creek Town in Old Calabar. According to Elizabeth Isichei, an authority on Igbo history, by the mid-nineteenth century, many Ijo families had Igbo blood in their veins, and in the Degema (New Calabar) area, many of them spoke Igbo as a second language. "In Bonny, Ubani was almost replaced by Igbo, and most foreign observers assumed the state was Igbo in origin."[37] In Andoni, Ogoni, and Bonny, in the nineteenth and early twentieth centuries, the Igbo language served as a lingua franca.[38] It is striking that late in the nineteenth and early twentieth centuries, when the European missionaries were seeking to develop a common form of Igbo language out of the many dialects, the Bonny dialect of Igbo was one of the five favored for the project, notwithstanding that Bonny is not originally Igbo.[39]

In Calabar, Esen has further noted that "when the Igbo cloth traders and oil merchants arrived in the scene the Ibibio did not hesitate to adopt such names as Ngozi, Mbafor, Mbodi, Adalakwu, Okoro, and Chukwuma, for their own children. Esen has wondered the likelihood for Igbo parents to adopt non-Igbo names like Akpan, and Ekpo."[40] The reality, as the study by Innocent Uzoechi demonstrates, is that new words originating from the delta like *ikporo* or *iporo* (money), *palaver* (disagreement), *dash* (Portuguese for gift), *epele* (game of drought), and *odoguma* (duck) were picked by the Igbo.[41] Similarly, Igbo parents did not hesitate to adopt for their children some names of Kalabari, Efik, and Ibibio origins such as "Eno," "Duku-ugbo," "Kamalu," "Bassey," and "Udo."[42] Indeed, Kay Williamson was right in her assertion that "speakers from different communities meet a great deal, in markets, through intermarriage, and so on, and therefore have many opportunities for becoming familiar with other people's forms of speech without making a conscious effort to learn them."[43] In the delta area, this theoretical postulation has been vindicated.

Overall, the most outstanding impact of the Canoe House in the delta was its successful supplanting of the descent groups and assumption of most of the duties and social expectations of the institution—among them physical and economic protection to members. For a smooth and successful incorporation, young slaves were procured for integration into the Household. They were given ascriptive or fictional kinship ties to the master as "father," his wive(s) as "mother(s)," and the master's children were the slaves' brothers or sisters. A dramatic rite of passage was designed to psychologically strip the slave from all previous kinship ties. In the Ijo societies (Bonny, Elem Kalabari, Nembe, and Okirika), this initiation process involved having the slave's hair shaved off as a symbol of dropping his old kinship loyalties. The adopting parents were supposed to live up to that "title to the fullest possible sense."[44]

Among the Efik and Ibibio of Old Calabar, this pattern of incorporation led to the formation of a complex and heterogeneous family structure. Unlike in the Ijo society where incorporation involved mainly people of slave origin, those who sought membership in the Efik Houses were mostly strangers who had voluntarily settled in Calabar and desired personal security through attachment to one of the powerful Efik nobles. This scenario in the Old Calabar society brought together Igbo elements, freed slaves from other ethnic groups, individuals running away from the cruel hands of their community sanctions, and other classes of oppressed people into common households.

Originally, the traditional Efik household consisted only of the immediate family dependents of the headmen and their kinsmen. But with the transition to palm oil trade, the Houses became increasingly heterogeneous and sophisticated in nature. The term *ekpuk* (or lineage), which was applied to those tied to a common ancestor, gradually vanished among the Efik and was replaced by the term *ufok*—which literally means a house with a collection of families under *ete ubom* or *etubom* ("father of the canoe"). Because a considerable part of the members no longer shared common blood ties, the Efik began to consider themselves as citizens and members of a Household based on residence.[45]

In this fictional notion of kin relations, slaves in reality remained outside the traditional rank system, preserved for the *idip ete* or members of agnate lineage. As also obtained everywhere in the delta, the master of the Efik House was referred to as "father" and his wives as "mothers," and new members usually adopted the names of their masters. According to an eyewitness account by Rev. Hope Waddell, in the mission schools in Calabar, there was no discrimination between children of masters and slaves. "They [the children] sat side by side, read in the same classes, and were treated as they deserved, without reference to their relations . . . masters sprang from slaves and slaves became masters."[46] Although the kinship affiliations were fictional, the slaves remarkably demonstrated a sense of patriotism toward their respective House.

Another significant effect of the trading Houses in the nineteenth century was the emergence of rich and influential slave and stranger elements in the delta society. These successful slaves shouldered the welfare of other members of their Houses. They recruited other slaves, who were subject to the *etubom* or the figure father of the House. In her *West African Studies*, Mary Kingsley observed in 1861 that the best thing about the House system was that it gave "to the poorest boy who paddles an oil canoe a chance to become a king."[47] According to an estimate by Hugh Goldie, her Majesty's overseer of trading interests in the Niger area, in 1853, Igbos formed more than half of the population of Creek Town of Old Calabar.[48] Thus, by virtue of their population strength over the freeborn of the Houses to which they belonged, the slaves exerted an enormous influence. Kannan Nair notes that the "free members of the House not only constituted a minority, but were often also poorer section of the total [House] membership."[49]

By implication, the new men of servile and predominantly Igbo origin began to rise in influence and power. A careful examination of the context of the transition will reveal that the switch from slave to palm oil trade played a crucial role in the improvement of the fortunes of Igbo slaves. Slavery was in many ways the prerogative of the aristocracy, and while it lasted, the various rulers of the delta city-states maintained a firm hold on the trade. Traditionally, only royal princes could found or head Houses, and before the eighteenth century, there was a royal family in each city-state. When the king died, royal princes played the role of kingmakers, choosing the wealthiest among their members as successor. The royal princes occupied top position in the social hierarchy. Freemen and slaves born in the land and forbidden by tradition to be sold into slavery occupied the middle position. At the bottom were ordinary slaves.[50] This social class system held as long as the slave trade lasted.

But the trade in palm produce was different because success required physical presence and face-to-face contacts with the hinterland producers. Bound by ritual and symbolic traditionalism not to travel outside their home communities for days unbroken, it became unavoidable for the traditional rulers of the delta city-states to rely heavily on the same slaves that came from the hinterland as their favored trading agents in the hinterland. The Igbo slaves, while trading for their masters, also transacted their own businesses. As their fortunes brightened, the slaves were elected House heads and participated in electing kings. Thus, as the slaves and commoners rapidly acquired social influence, they also began to desire all the privileges associated with their new success.

Theoretically, the liberty and rights enjoyed by the people of slave descent were considered gifts from the king and from the freemen that could be withdrawn at the latter's discretion. This is in spite of the fact that from the ranks of the slaves "were derived the richest traders, the bravest soldiers, and the ablest commanders, and all their labors entirely depended the economic welfare of city-states."[51] What emerged was a complex form of class struggle with multiple opposites: the old versus the new elite of slave origin; the old elite versus the poor slaves; the freemen versus all peoples of slave descent—whether rich or poor, and even between wealthy and poor slaves.

The question could be raised as to whether delta society could have prevented these wealthy and therefore powerful slaves from seeking to wield political authority commensurate with their economic growth. Or whether the delta society could have successfully resisted the wave of forces of change—new trade and cash economy, Igbo influx, Christianity, and new ideas, precipitated by the trans-Atlantic commercial contacts—thereby preserved their customs from the so-called Igbo peril. The evidence shows that there were diverse patterns of responses taken by the various Niger Delta host societies to reconcile Igbo cultural influence on society. These belated responses differed from community to community and ranged from a combination of exclusion and accommodation as in the Old Calabar, to either pragmatic accommodation or outright exclusion as demonstrated by the cultural elite in Kalabari and Bonny, respectively. It will be appropriate to discuss a number of them and their results.

The response of the Efik and Ibibio aristocracy of Old Calabar represents an apt example of exclusion and accommodation. Niar's erudite study on the Efik and Ibibio indicates that while the Calabar aristocrats tried to accept the wealthy town slaves as part and parcel of their new society, they also attempted to contain the poorer ones on the plantation. This strategy met with initial success but was soon confronted with slave revolts because those left on the plantations suffered serious deprivations and oppressions unknown to their cohorts who stayed in the towns to organize the trade of their masters. Also, sacrificial victims were selected from among their ranks when important personalities died. In response, the slaves banded themselves into the "Order of Bloodmen" to fight against their oppression. With the support of leading Efik rulers like Eyamba V and King Eyo Honesty II, the early Presbyterian missionaries eventually concluded an agreement banning human sacrifice in Calabar. This meant that by mid-nineteenth century various "developments attendant on the suppression of the overseas slave trade and the switch to palm oil trade were beginning to affect the powers and authority of the rulers of the coastal states" of the delta.[52]

Meanwhile, the town slaves exploited their access to trade, missionary service, and mission education to amass wealth and influence for themselves. In time, these wealthy slaves were recognized and absorbed as part of the new aristocracy. Like their counterparts elsewhere, the Igbo ex-slaves among them also craved for an aristocratic ideal of life; they used their money to connect influential friendships, including buying memberships in the prestigious Efik and Ibibio *ekpe* (or leopard) society. In the past, the ekpe fraternity was exclusively reserved for the freemen who had attained outstanding material achievements. Members of the fraternity were supposed to acquire progressive strength and the prowess of the leopard. They were bound together by an oath of secrecy, obedience, and absolute loyalty to their leaders.[53] This forum originally provided slave masters grounds for discussion on how to control their slaves and their offspring. As an arm of social administration and control, the ekpe, which was divided into different grades, held real power, although this was not strict in its decisions and operations. The ekpe, in executing their legislative and judicial functions, often overstepped their bounds. They could visit any offender to levy a fine, confiscate property, or even to kill.[54] The ekpe mode of operation helped the Efik manage slave revolts and confiscate the assets of their opponents along with those of their slaves.[55]

While the ekpe in the nineteenth-century post-abolition era remained the elitist club with some of the accoutrements of its old powers intact, the big difference was that wealthy people of slave descent were now allowed to buy membership in the fraternity. Some of the members achieved success through the new avenues and opportunities opened by the presence of the Europeans—trade, cash economy, mission schools, and new ideas. The ekpe institution also found its way into Arochukwu part of Igboland.[56] By and large, the transformations of the nineteenth century in Calabar ensured that the ekpe could no longer exercise acts of oppression without the knowledge of the new members of slave descent who had, by the 1840s, become some of the wealthiest elements in society.[57]

The Ijo society adopted a more pragmatic approach in response to the social changes. Through the mask-dancing secret society *ekine* or *sekiapu* (or dancers—also known as *opoma* in Bonny), the Kalabari cultural elite attempted to preserve elements of their culture while also incorporating some new developments. As an agency of acculturation, the ekine masquerades believed to be representing the water spirits (*owu*), demanded upon members "to speak Kalabari language or be killed."[58] In Bonny, Nembe, and Igbani the strangers were allowed freedom of language. In Kalabari, a "recruit to the community who became a member of the ekine and publicly performed in its dances was a socially accepted individual." Also the *Koronogbo* or "the association of the strong," a militant vigilante group, while patrolling the streets at night also derided and penalized the poorly acculturated. As Horton asserts, the adoption of such an aggressive culture-consciousness was aimed to avoid being overwhelmed by the culture brought to it by its slaves.[59]

However, Kalabari still retained a prominent place for the Igbo in its value system embodied in the notion of aristocratic ideal. For Kalabari, the notion of nobility implied notions of "youthfulness" and "flamboyance" (*asa*), preparedness, and dignity (*bu bimi*). Although the Kalabari had a high admiration for wealth and power, the culture insisted that the qualities embodied in *asa*—that is, youthfulness and flamboyance—should never be lost in the hunt for wealth. The society scorned at misers and individuals who eschewed the chasing and courtship of women, fine clothes, good food, dancing, conviviality, and other luxuries for the pursuit of money and power. In other words, there was a social expectation that a man should always live with a certain style of affluence, grace, and decorum (or *bu nimi*).[60] It is in this context of expectations that the Igbo was despised and admired at the same time.

Bonny's exclusionist response to the revolutionary developments of the nineteenth century amounted to a failure. The reasons for this are not far-fetched. Besides its predominant Igbo population, the greater part of wealth of Bonny was in the hands of its people of slave origin. This situation demanded for new social and political order that the reactionary elite of freemen failed to consider. As wealth of members of the royal house diminished, so did their authority. Early on, Opubu the Great (r. 1792–1830) of Bonny had led his kingdom to the apogee of its greatness. His death in 1830 brought Madu, one of his most trusted Igbo slaves, to power as Regent. The King's son prince Dappa Pepple was still a minor then. Madu's own son, Alali, succeeded him as Regent at his death in 1833. Finally, William Dappa Pepple, son of Opubu the Great, came of age and assumed kingship in 1835.[61] The new king resented the prominent position occupied by individuals of slave ancestry and was anxious to secure full power for himself. Thus, between 1853 and 1866, when Dappa Pepple died, there were series of conflicts involving the new king, the former members of his father's House, and their European counterparts.[62] Dappa Pepple was neither as wealthy as Alali (who had, at the assumption of power by Dappa Pepple, broken off to found the "Anna Pepple House") nor as popular as another prominent Igbo ex-slave, Oko Jumbo, whose Manilla Pepple House continued to grow in power and influence.[63] Meanwhile, the king's powers declined considerably as he struggled to rebuild his House and compete with the more powerful Houses of his rivals and ex-slaves of his father.

Some of the slave revolts witnessed in Bonny in the nineteenth century were not aimed directly at the existing political order. Rather, the slaves aspired to secure a place in that system and to protect their interests within the society.[64] Therefore, if King Dappa Pepple had applied a bit more cautionary and accommodative relationship with the "new men," he could have delayed the eventual collapse of his kingdom. In 1855 and 1869 there were two violent revolts carried out by the liberated slaves, most of them influential and rich "merchant princes" who were excluded from enjoying political positions proportionate with their economic strength.[65] George Pepple, who was under the influence of Oko Jumbo, succeeded King Dappa Pepple in 1866.[66] In 1868, the new king gave his support to Oko Jumbo to attack the Anna Pepple House under Alali's successor Jubo Jubogha (a.k.a. Jaja). To avoid a total civil war, Jaja moved his trading empire to Opobo, located closer to the mouth of the Imo River. There, Jaja established his business in palm oil as the wealthiest and most popular of all the emergent class of new men. According to Webster and Boahen,

> Jaja represented the triumph of the new men of servile and common origin; these men had risen with the palm-oil trade at the expense of the nobility who had declined as the trade in slaves came to an end.[67]

This chapter focused on the impact of Igbo slaves on the Niger Delta society of the post-abolition period. While the huge influx of Igbos brought to the delta through the slave trade transformed the host society, the local culture also affected the newcomers' overall habits and values systems. Some of the new habits and practices developed in the delta also filtered into the Igbo hinterland as the slave dealers and merchants moved to and fro between the interior and the delta city-states. Today, some of the attitudes developed over the centuries have survived in new contexts; the fully cultivated Kalabari or Bonny, or Efik, or Igbo, or Ijo man or woman has become hard to find due to the continuing intermingling of peoples and fluidity of cultural identities heightened by the introduction of Western education, Christianity, the revolution in modes of transportation, and the rapid growth of urbanization.

Meanwhile, the postcolonial Nigerian state has seen a considerable resurgence of ethnic consciousness among the Niger Delta minorities of the federation due to what they have perceived as exploitation of the natural resources located in their area by the national government. This is despite the rise of one of their own in the person of President Goodluck Jonathan, who served as civilian President of Nigeria from 2010 to 2015. Thus, conflicts now exist between loyalty to the federation and such primordial identities as Niger Delta, Kalabari or Ogoniland or Ibibioland. In this context it is easy for the aggrieved to find himself in the same situation as the ambitious slave of the past centuries. Today, the descendants of the ex-slaves in the delta area of modern Nigeria have continued to nurse a disturbing sense of bitterness toward their fellow Igbo born in the interior. This is despite the fact that Niger Delta Igbo have continued to honor and dramatize their Igbo cultural heritage. A perceptive observer may underscore a similar problem in the relationship between recent African immigrants in the United States and their Afro-American counterparts who are descendants of African slaves. For the observer, the situation calls for a thoughtful approach to ameliorate the continuing circle of ordeal the four hundred years of the Atlantic slave trade has left with mankind.[68]

NOTES

1. See Adiele Afigbo, "The Eclipse of the Aro Slaving Oligarchy of Southeastern Nigeria, 1901–1927," *Journal of Historical Society of Nigeria* 6, no. 1 (1971): 3–24; E. J. Alagoa, *Jaja of Opobo: The Slave Who Became a King* (London: Longman, 1970).

2. G. Ugo Nwokeji, "The Slave Emancipation Problematic: Igbo Society and the Colonial Equation," *Comparative Study in Society and History* 40, no. 2 (1998): 318–55; Kenneth O. Dike, *Trade and Politics in the Niger Delta 1830–1885* (1956; reprint, Oxford: Clarendon Press, 1966); Gwilym Iwan Jones, *From Slaves to Palm Oil: Slave Trade and Palm Oil Trade in the Bight of Biafra* (Cambridge, UK: Centre of African Studies, 1989); E. J. Alagoa, "The Development of Institutions in the States of the Eastern Niger Delta," *Journal of African History* 12, no. 2 (1971): 269–78.

3. Palm oil was not the only commodity of trade originating from this area. It was however, by a far margin, the most important. Other items of trade originating from the delta included ivory, dyewoods, camwood, and timber. See Public Records Office (PRO) Kew, Parliamentary Papers (Parl. Pa). 1842, XI. Memorandum on British Trade with Africa, appendix and index No. 7, 574–84.

4. The Bight of Benin is a curve on the western coast of Africa extending eastward for about four hundred miles from Cape St. Paul to the Nun outlet of the River Niger. It is extended by Bight of Biafra (now Bight of Bonny). The bight is part of the Gulf of Guinea frequented by early European visitors and merchants.

5. PRO Kew, Parliamentary Papers (Parl. Pa). 1842, XI.

6. Nigerian National Archives Enugu (hereafter NNAE), ARODIV/20/1/15. Anthropological Papers on Aro Origin: Discussion and the Basis of the Widespread of Aro Influence, 1927.

7. Robin Horton, "Kalabari Ekine Society: A Borderland of Religion and Art," *Africa* 33, no. 2 (1963): 33–47; Robin Horton, "Igbo: An Ordeal for Aristocrats," *Nigeria Magazine* 90 (1966): 169–83.

8. Elizabeth Isichei, *A History of the Igbo People* (New York: St. Martin's Press, 1976), 94–95. While the trans-Atlantic slave trade ceased substantially in most parts of the delta, "the last slave ship finally sailed from Brass in 1854."

9. Dike, *Trade and Politics*, 111.

10. E. J. Alagoa, "The Niger Delta States and their Neighbors, 1600–1800," in *History of West Africa*, ed. J. F. Ade Ajayi and Michael Crowder

(New York: Columbia University Press, 1972), 1:300; Gwilym Iwan Jones, *The Trading States of the Oil Rivers, a Study of Political Development in Eastern Nigeria* (London: Oxford University Press, 1963), 69. See also NNAE, ARODIV/3/1/55. Anthropological Report on the Aro Confederation by H. F. Mathews and T. M. Shankland.

11. NNAE, ARODIV/20/1/15. Anthropological Papers on Aro Origin: Discussion and the Basis of Widespread of Aro Influence, 1927.

12. Ukwu I. Ukwu, "Markets in Iboland" (PhD thesis, University of Cambridge, 1965) [microform]; From the perspective of the Riverine peoples, E. J. Alagoa's "Long-Distance Trade and States in the Niger Delta," *Journal of African History* 11, no. 3 (1970): 319–29, remains a useful source of information on the trade that preceded the development of Euro-African commercial exchange.

13. See Robin Hallet, ed., *The Niger Journal of Richard and John Lander* (London: Routledge, 1965), 253.

14. See John Adams (Captain), *Sketches taken During Ten Years Voyages to Africa Between 1786–1800* (London, 1822). Adams' eyewitness account remains one of the most authoritative on the slave trade and the rise of the oil palm trade in the nineteenth century.

15. NNAE, C665/17-5/7/539. Oil Palm Report on Tapping of, 1917. See also Felix K. Ekechi, "The Development of the Palm Oil Trade at Oguta (Nigeria) with Special Reference to Kalabari Traders, 1900–1930," *Nigeria Magazine* 134–35 (1981): 51–70.

16. Isichei, *Igbo People*, 95.

17. I owe this information to professor Ikem Stanley Okoye.

18. The *Saro* or *Amaro* were recaptives who immigrated to Lagos, Abeokuta, the Niger Delta, and other West African locations including the Gold Coast (Ghana) from their initial resettlement in Sierra Leone. For details on the Niger Delta group, see studies by Mac Dixon-Fyle, "The Saro in the Political Life of Early Port Harcourt, 1913–49," *Journal of African History* 30 (1989): 125–38.

19. James B. Webster, Adu A. Boahen, and H. O. Idowu, *History of West Africa: The Revolutionary Years—1815 to Independence* (New York: Praeger, 1967), 184.

20. Alagoa, "The Development of Institutions," 274.

21. For a good read on the development of Duala trading houses, see Ralph Austin, "The Metamorphoses of Middlemen: The Duala, Europeans and the Cameroon Hinterland, ca. 1800–ca. 1960," *International Journal of African Historical Studies* 16, no. 1 (1983): 3.

22. Foreign Office (hereafter F.O.) 84/816. Bonny Supercargoes to Beecroft, October 1, 1850.

23. Hope Masterton Waddell, *Twenty-nine Years in the West Indies and Central Africa: A Review of Missionary Work and Adventure, 1829–1858* (London: T. Nelson, 1863), 320.

24. Robin Horton, "From Fishing Village to City-State: A Social History of New Calabar," in *Man in Africa*, ed. M. Douglas and P. M. Kabbery (London: Travistock Publications, 1969), 46.

25. F.O. 2/1 End. 1 in No. 1. HMS Thalia at Sea, Campbell to Craige, March 11, 1837. Reports created by Europeans on the ground contain details of violent challenges even among the various European merchants on the African coasts.

26. P. Amaury Talbot, *Peoples of Southern Nigeria: A Sketch of their History, Ethnology, and Languages, with an Abstract of the 1921 Census*, vol. 1 (London: Oxford University Press, 1926), 250–51, 289.

27. NNAE, Cons. 2. King Pepple's Correspondences 1847–1848; NNAE, Cons. 14. Manumission Papers 1856–1878.

28. Horton, "Fishing Village," 47; Alagoa, "The Development of Institutions," 271, 274.

29. Dike, *Trade and Politics*, 37.

30. See John Pape, "Black and White: The 'Perils of Sex' in Colonial Zimbabwe," *Journal of South African Studies* 16, no. 4 (1990): 700.

31. Ufor Akpabio, 62, farmer, Oral Interview with, Calabar, July 23, 2000.

32. Uwem Nsidibe, 69, retired teacher, Oral Interview, Calabar, June 3, 2004. I owe the information on Umuahia to a private discussion with N. C. Ejituwu, an Andoni indigene and university history professor during the conference on "Nineteenth-century Post-Abolition Commerce and the Communities of the Niger River Basin (Nigeria)," Imo State University, Owerri, Nigeria, June 11–12, 2004.

33. Horton, "Igbo: An Ordeal for Aristocrats," 169–70.

34. A. J. A. Esen, *Ibibio Profile* (Lagos, Nigeria: Paico Press, 1982), 179.

35. Horton, "Igbo: An Ordeal for Aristocrats," 171.

36. See Kay Williamson, "Languages of the Niger Delta," *Nigeria Magazine* 97 (1968): 130.

37. Isichei, *Igbo People*, 95; Dike, *Trade and Politics*, 29–30.

38. N. C. Ejituwu provided this information about the Andoni people at the conference: "Nineteenth-century Post-Abolition Commerce and the Communities of the Lower Niger River Basin (Nigeria)," Imo State University, Owerri, Nigeria, June 11–12, 2004.

39. See James Johnson, "An African Clergyman's Visit to Bonny," *Church Missionary Intelligencer* 22 (Jan, 1897): 27–28. Parliamentary Papers 1842, XI part I, appendix, and index, No. 7 contains information on Bonny indicating that "The King of New Calabar . . . and King Pepple of Bonny, were both of Ibo descent, of which also are the mass of the natives."

40. Esen, *Ibibio Profile*, 179.

41. Innocent F. A. Uzoechi, "The Vocabulary of the Niger Delta Historiography," in *Aftermath of Slavery: Transitions and Transformations in Southeastern Nigeria*, ed. Chima Korieh and Femi Kolapo (Trenton, NJ: Africa World Press, 2007), 197–208.

42. The successful ex-slaves such as Jaja and his successors in the delta did not hesitate to give their children "foreign" names too. See Sir Harry Huntley, *Seven Years Service on the Slave Coast of Western Africa* (London, 1850), 158–60.

43. Williamson, "Languages of the Niger Delta," 124.

44. Horton, "Fishing Village," 48.

45. Jones, *Trading States*, 54–55; Kannan K. Nair, *Politics and Society in Southeastern Nigeria 1841–1906* (London: Frank Cass, 1972), 38; Esen, *Ibibio Profile*, 9, 117.

46. Waddell, *Twenty-nine Years*, 315; Esen, *Ibibio Profile*, 10; See also Nair, *Politics and Society*, 38.

47. Mary Henrietta Kingsley, *West African Studies* (London: Macmillan, 1899), 427.

48. Hugh Goldie, *Old Calabar and Its Mission* (Edinburgh: Oliphant Anderson and Ferrier, 1890), 18.

49. Nair, *Politics and Society*, 40; Goldie, *Old Calabar*, 18. Dike, *Trade and Politics*, 29.

50. Webster and Boahen, *West Africa*, 185.

51. Dike, *Trade and Politics*, 153.

52. Obaro Ikime, *The Fall of Nigeria: The British Conquest* (London: Heinemann, 1977), 19; Nair, *Politics and Society*, 37.

53. NNAE, CALPROF. CP2061/2/2/1/1952. Efik, Egbo (Ekpe) Secret Society, Calabar 1918–41.

54. Ibid.

55. Ibid.

56. Ibid.

57. Ikime, *The Fall of Nigeria*, 18. See also Webster and Boahen, *West Africa*, 189–92.

58. See Alagoa, "The Development of Institutions," 272; Jones, *Trading States*, 67–68.

59. See Horton, "Kalabari Ekine Society," 33–34; Horton, "Fishing Village," 54; Alagoa, "The Development of Institutions," 276.

60. Horton, "Igbo: An Ordeal for Aristocrats," 180.

61. F.O.3/1. Huntley to Craig, March 27, 1837.

62. Details of these conflicts over trade and power are documented in the NNAE, Cons. 2. King Pepple's Correspondences 1847–1848; NNAE, Cons. 14. Manumission Papers 1856–1878.

63. Church Missionary Society (hereafter CMS) CA3/04. W. E. Carew to S. A. Crowther, Sept. 27, 1860.

64. See Command Paper C 5165, "Papers Relating to King Jaja of Opobo and the Opening of the West African Market to British Trade," 1888.

65. CMS CA3/04. W. E. Carew to S. A. Crowther, Sept. 27, 1860.

66. CMS CA3/04. George Pepple to Crowther, Nov. 3, 1866.

67. Webster and Boahen, *West Africa*, 190–91. See also Isichei, *Igbo People*, 98–99.

68. This message is at the center of Dieudonne Mayi's *The Selling of Joseph: A Healing Message from History* (Philadelphia: Xlibris, 2003).

10 THE CLUSTERING OF IGBO IN THE AMERICAS

WHERE, WHEN, HOW, AND WHY?

Gwendolyn Midlo Hall

> The newly arrived [Igbo] find help, care, and example from those who have come before them.
>
> —MOREAU DE ST.-MÉRY, DESCRIPTION TOPOGRAPHIQUE, PHYSIQUE, CIVILE, POLITIQUE, ET HISTORIQUE DE LA PARTIE FRANÇAISE DE L'ISLE DE ST. DOMINGUE, 1797

There are several persistent myths about Igbos in the Americas that this chapter addresses, including the changes over time of proportions of Igbo sent from the Bight of Biafra, where they were distributed throughout the Americas, and why. These questions are quite complex. Aside from variations in spelling of Igbo, they were listed under distinct and sometimes unclear designations in documents housed in the Americas. The Igbo were shipped from the Bight of Biafra, the most eastern section of the Lower Guinea Coast. The *Trans-Atlantic Slave Trade Database 2* has no field that could enlighten us about Igbo as opposed to other ethnicities sent from the Bight of Biafra.[1] The Names Database mounted on that website contains many hyphenated places of origin for slaves recaptured from illegal slave trade voyages during the nineteenth century. Many of them begin with Calabar using various spellings linked perhaps with place names.

The Bight of Biafra region is located in the Niger Delta and the Cross River Valley. It is now southeastern Nigeria. Its geography, economy, and politics as well as the patterns of its trans-Atlantic slave trade were distinct. Extensive mangrove swamps made access by oceangoing vessels difficult. Europeans did not get access to the interior until the mid-nineteenth century. Enslaved Africans were brought down to the Atlantic Coast in boats operating along its creeks and lagoons. Well over 90 percent of the slaves from the Bight of Biafra were exported from three ports: Elem Kalabar (New Calabar), Calabar (Old Calabar) on the Cross River, and Bonny, which arose as the leading port during the eighteenth century. *The Trans-Atlantic Slave Trade Database 1* indicates that 85 percent of these voyages sailed under the British flag. Most slave trade ships left England from Bristol and later from Liverpool. Despite the escalation of the British slave trade from the Bight of Biafra after 1740, only 7.7 percent (n = 43) of these voyages arrived in South Carolina.

The Atlantic slave trade from the Bight of Biafra began early but got off to a slow start. It rose during the late 1670s and 1680s and escalated rapidly during the eighteenth century. Slave trade voyages rose from about 1,000 a year during the first decade of the 1700s to 3,800 during the 1730s, 10,000 during the 1740s, 15,200 during the 1760s, and reached its peak of 17,500 during the 1780s. It continued well into the nineteenth century. Significant numbers of Igbo were brought to Cuba and to the United States in trans-Atlantic slave trade voyages long after the maritime slave trade was outlawed in 1808 by both Great Britain and the United States. Pirates raided slave trade ships heading for Cuba and brought them to ports along the northwest coast of the Gulf of Mexico and the lower Mississippi Valley to Texas and Louisiana as well as to Florida.[2] Other patterns in the trans-Atlantic slave trade involving Igbos were unique as well. An unusually high proportion of Igbo females were sent to the Americas in contrast to the high proportions of males sent from the Ibibio/Moko ethnicity, all of whom left Africa from the Bight of Biafra.

There appears to be a consensus among scholars that the Igbo occupation of the Niger Delta was quite ancient. There was no oral tradition of migration from another region. Their creation myths state that they came from the earth.[3] Archaeological evidence indicates more ancient human occupation and productive activities in Igboland than scholars had previously believed. A rock shelter at Afikpo revealed Stone Age tools and pottery some five thousand years old. Yams were grown at least three thousand years ago. Iron working is ancient, and bronze art is of the highest quality.[4]

The pioneer Nigerian historian Kenneth Dike convincingly argues that the Igbo were very heavily represented among slaves shipped across the Atlantic from the Bight of Biafra. He cites "scientific research" carried out by Captain John Adams between 1786 and 1800 and published in 1822. Adams wrote:

> This place [Bonny] is the wholesale market for slaves, as not fewer than 20,000 are annually sold here; 16,000 of whom are members of one nation, called Heebo [Igbo], so that this single nation . . . during the last 20 years [exported no less] than 320,000; and those of the same nation sold at New Calabar [a delta port], probably amounted, in the same period of time, to 50,000 more, making an aggregate amount of 370,000 Heebos. The remaining part of the above 20,000 is composed of the natives of the Brass country . . . and also of Ibbibbys [Ibibios] or Quaws.[5]

Dike points out an ongoing process of creolization among the peoples living near the Atlantic Coast encompassing diverse peoples speaking various languages. He comments:

> It is broadly true to say that owing to their numerical superiority and consequent land hunger the Ebo migrants (enforced or voluntary) formed the bulk of the Delta population during the nineteenth century. They bequeathed their language to most of the city-states—to Bonny, Okrika, Opobo, and to a certain extent influenced the language and institutions of Old and New Calabar. But the population, which evolved out of this mingling of peoples, was neither Benin, nor Efik, Ibo nor Ibibio. They were a people apart, the product of the clashing cultures of the tribal hinterland and of the Atlantic community to both of which they belonged.[6]

In the Americas, the Igbo were the least endogamous among African peoples. The proportion of women as well as the proportion of their surviving children born in the Americas were among the highest, and they mated with or married men from a variety of other ethnicities. This pattern of exogamous marriage among Igbo women seems to be true throughout the Americas. Igbo, then, were least likely to remain as a separate enclave culture among Africans in the Americas.[7]

In several other respects, the Bight of Biafra contrasts sharply with other African coasts. In the Bight of Biafra, Muslim influence arrived very late and was of minor importance. Highly centralized states were absent. The political structure was strong but segmented. Loose confederations maintained commercial and religious ties. The prestige of powerful oracles and some armed mercenaries enforced conformity and played an important role in obtaining slaves to ship across the Atlantic. Although large-scale warfare connected with state building was weak, slaves were "produced" through raids among villages, some kidnapping, legal proceedings, and religious rites.[8]

Which ethnicities were shipped out of the Bight of Biafra, when, and in what proportions? This is a hotly debated question. Some historians, mainly Americanists, believe that they were heavily Igbo, especially during the eighteenth century. Other historians, mainly Africanists, challenge this conclusion. In southern Nigeria, the denomination "Igbo" came to be associated with slave. The Aro, major slave traders in Igboland,

> distinguished themselves from the more traditional Igbo groups. In addition, they strive to maintain ancient kinship, cul-

tural and ethnic relationships with the Efik, Ibibio and Ekoi on the basis of trade, *ekpe*, inter-marriage and the original ethnic composition ties with various Aro settlements which are still found in these parts of non-Igbo areas.[9]

But it is possible that some of these patterns have been read too far backward in time. Joseph Inikori wrote:

> It should be noted . . . that a pan-Igbo identity as we know it today did not exist during the Atlantic slave trade era. As Dike and Ekejiuba correctly observe, Igbo as an ethnic category is a twentieth-century development reluctantly accepted by several of the constituent groups on political and administrative grounds. As they put it, "during the period covered by our study (18th and 19th centuries), the now twelve million or more 'Igbo,' distributed over 30,000 square miles of territory east and west of the Niger, were variously referred to either as cultural groups . . . or by the ecological zone in which they were found. . . . Since Igbo was used at this time pejoratively to refer to the densely populated uplands, the major source of slaves and by extension to slaves, it is not surprising that many of these groups have been reluctant to accept the Igbo identity. The Aro were among the groups that did not consider themselves Igbo at the time. These facts of identity and socio-political organization are important in understanding the politico-military conditions in Igboland that facilitated the procurement of captives for sale at the coastal ports."[10]

Americans, however, cannot help but be impressed by the large numbers of Africans identified or self-identified as Igbo recorded in American documents. We will see that in some times and places Igbo were clearly differentiated from Ibibio, Moko, Calabar, and Bioko, all ethnic designations from the Bight of Biafra. The Igbo "nation," or "casta," appears among several other ethnicities in Alonso de Sandoval's book dating from 1627.[11] The Igbo were very significant in both numbers and proportions in slave lists created in eight different colonies in North America between 1770 and 1827. One could perhaps argue that "Igbo" was a name imposed by Europeans on Africans. But Africans often identified their own ethnicities recorded in American documents. C. G. A. Oldendorp, a Moravian missionary who worked in the Danish West Indies in 1767 and 1768, interviewed an African in Pennsylvania who described himself as Igbo.[12] Deminster, a forty-year-old slave, identified his nation as Igbo when he testified about runaway slaves in Louisiana in 1766. L'Eveille, a blacksmith, identified his nation as Igbo when he testified during the trial of the Pointe Coupee Post Louisiana conspirators seeking to abolish slavery in 1795. There were self-identifications of other ethnicities from the Bight of Biafra in Louisiana. Guela ran away from his master and was recaptured in 1737. He identified his nation as Bioko (native of the island of Fernando Po in the Gulf of Guinea). He explained that he had run away because his master beat him often and did not give him enough to eat. He had run away once before and came back voluntarily. His ears were cut off, and he was branded on the shoulder. The man in this case and other Africans from the Bight of Biafra were not simply lumped together as Igbo.[13] Some were identified as Ibibio, Moko, Ekoi, Esan/Edoid, Bioko, and Calabar (Karabali in Cuba). The well-populated Bamenda grasslands northwest of the slave-trading ports of the Bight of Biafra supplied some enslaved Africans who were shipped out directly from the Cameroon River. Estimating the slave trade from the Cameroons poses many difficulties. It appears to have peaked between 1760 and 1776 and was always a tiny fraction of the slave trade from the Bight of Biafra ports. I have not found ethnicities from the Cameroons or the Bamenda grasslands recorded in American documents.[14]

It is clear that the vast majority of Africans from southeastern Nigeria and the Bight of Biafra found in American documents were recorded as Igbo. They were a heavy majority during the eighteenth century and a smaller majority during the nineteenth century. If we discuss the Igbo in the United Suites, the focus of the works of Douglas B. Chambers, Michael A. Gomez, and Lorena Walsh, we can affirm the assumption made by those scholars that the Igbo represented a high percentage of Africans from the Bight of Biafra.[15] They were reasonably likely to have identified their own ethnicities. They were clustered in the Caribbean as well as in the Chesapeake. Some of the Africans exported from the Bight of Biafra were recorded in American documents as Ijo, Ibibio, Moko, Ekoi, and Bioko, but they were a very small minority before the nineteenth century.

It is not possible to determine the approximate percentage of Igbo exported from the Bight of Biafra by studying trans-Atlantic slave trade voyages or by studying ethnicities recorded in any one colony in the Americas. Since some ethnicities were shipped from more than one coast, descriptions of Africans in American documents can tell us about the proportions of ethnicities recorded among enslaved Africans in particular times and places in the Americas, but they cannot always (or perhaps even often) tell us which coasts they were shipped from. Sex ratios among Africans shipped from various coasts cannot be extrapolated to ethnicities presumably shipped from a particular coast.[16] But information about ethnicities listed in a significant number of colonies during the same period is more enlightening. Various ethnicities were exported from the same ports, and their proportions changed over time. Enslaved Africans exported from Bonny were evidently most likely to be Igbo. During the early eighteenth century, Bonny emerged as the major slave trading port on the Bight of Biafra. Paul E. Lovejoy and David Richardson indicate that by about 1730 Bonny already outpaced Old Calabar as a port in the Atlantic slave trade, at least forty years earlier than historians previously believed. The early predominance of Bonny resulted from its superior financial structures, including the important role of pawnship. There is a consensus that Bonny shipped mainly Igbo, indicating that Igbo were indeed prominent in the Atlantic slave trade to the Chesapeake as well as elsewhere after the 1720s. Lovejoy and Richardson's calculations on *The Trans-Atlantic Slave Trade Database 1* reveal that for the entire trans-Atlantic slave trade, 40.5 percent (n = 1,046) of voyages leaving the Bight of Biafra came from Bonny; 27.0 percent (n = 697) from Old Calabar; and 9.2 percent (n = 238) from Elem Kalabar (New Calabar). These data are likely to be reasonably complete and accurate since they were mainly British voyages. The documents are centrally located in large archives and studied by David Richardson. Lovejoy and Richardson wrote that voyages from Bonny were most heavily clustered between 1726 and 1820.[17]

"Calabar" sometimes appears as an ethnic designation in American documents but its meaning is uncertain. It might refer to Africans shipped from two different slave trade ports in the Bight of Biafra: Old Calabar or New Calabar. Or it could mean the Calabar Coast, which would include Bonny and other ports. "Calabar" could also have been an ethnic designation. Dike referred to the "Kalahari" during the early nineteenth century as "a Delta people."[18] Oldendorp interviewed five slaves who described themselves as members of the Kalahari nation. They reported that they lived far up the Calabar River and that the Igbo were a very populous people who were their "neighbors and friends who share the same language with them."[19] In Cuba, Calabar (usually written as "Karabali") was certainly a broad, coastal designation, not an ethnic one. Among slaves from the Bight of Biafra sold there between 1790 and 1880, 93.2 percent (n = 2,943) were listed as Karabali, 5.8 percent (n = 183) as Bibi (meaning Ibibio), and one percent (n = 32) as Ibo. These few references to specific ethnicities from the Bight of Biafra in Cuban sales documents were almost all from documents found among French-language documents in Santiago de Cuba, where St. Domingue/Haitian slave owners predominated.[20] "Calabar" was not found in documents in St. Domingue.[21] Among Africans from the Bight of Biafra listed on probated estate documents dating from 1721 to 1797, 90.7 percent (n = 1,129) were listed as Igbo, 6.6 percent (n = 83) as Ibibio/Bibi, and 2.7 percent (n = 33) as Moko and others.[22] But aside from Cuba, where broad, regional designations predominated and Karabali encompassed Igbo, there are many listings of Igbo in American documents dating from the eighteenth century. In Louisiana and elsewhere as well, Ibibio/Moko numbers were heavily male in contrast to the

Igbo, whose numbers were about half female during the eighteenth century.

Some historians are questioning whether an Igbo identity existed at all before the twentieth century. They cite the work of Sigismund W. Koelle, a minister and linguist who interviewed recaptives from illegal slave trade voyages in Freetown, Sierra Leone, around 1850. They had been landed by British anti-slave trade patrols during the 1820s and 1830s. Although Koelle designated them as Ibo, he did so with a caveat:

> Certain natives who have come from the Bight are called Ibos. In speaking to some of them respecting this name, I learned that they never had heard it till they came to Sierra Leone. In their own country they seem to have lost their general national name, like the Akus [Nago/Lucumi/Yoruba], and know only the names of their respective districts or countries. I have retained this name for the language, of which I produce specimens, as it is spoken in five of the said districts or countries.[23]

Historians of Africa have effectively used Koelle's remarkable work. He was a careful scholar. He expressed his reservations about the reliability of his informants, pointing out that he interviewed them in English during the early 1850s. Most of them had been recaptured by British anti-slave trade ships and brought to Sierra Leone several decades before. Among the six Igbo he interviewed, four had been in Sierra Leone for thirty years, one for twenty-four years, and one for eleven years after he was kidnapped from his home when he was three years old. When Koelle wrote that the Igbo he interviewed had "lost their general national name," he implied that they previously had one.[24]

From this single ambiguous statement made late in the slave-trading era, transcendent conclusions have been drawn about all Africans throughout the Americas, for example, that all Africans were so isolated and immobilized that they were unaware that there were other Africans who were different from themselves. Therefore, terms for African ethnicities appearing in American documents arose not in Africa but rather in the Americas after slaves were first exposed to Africans unlike themselves. Maybe they called themselves something else. Maybe they did not fully understand their interrogators or their interrogators did not fully understand them. Perhaps they could not remember too well. A word is an imperfect representation of reality. Regardless of which word they did or did not use to identify themselves in the past, it did not prevent them from considering themselves an internally related group different from others. In any case, Koelle's statement should not be extrapolated backward in time and to all African ethnicities. David Northrup wrote:

> Some other "nations" in Sierra Leone shared a common language. Speakers of the various dialects of Efik ("Calabar" in Sierra Leone), Hausa, Fulbe, Akan ("Kronmantee") of the Gold Coast, or Wolof came to use language as a way of distinguishing themselves from other Africans in Sierra Leone, even though no such national consciousness or political unity existed in their homelands.[25]

This is a very broad generalization indeed. For example, the Wolof lived in developed, hierarchical states for many centuries before the Atlantic slave trade began and certainly identified themselves through common descent, history, law, politics, culture, religion, and language.

By the mid-nineteenth century, the designation "Igbo" might have had more shame attached to it than in earlier times when it was less clearly identified with "slave." The designation "Igbo" was recognized by Africans as well as by Europeans long before the mid-nineteenth century, including Alonso de Sandoval in 1627. Sandoval did not discuss either numbers or percentages of African ethnicities arriving in Cartagena de Indias. Some of Sandoval's information about Africa and African ethnicities was obtained from reports and studies, mainly by Portuguese and Spanish missionaries stationed in Africa. He does not always make it clear which Africans he encountered in Cartagena de Indias and which he obtained information about from other sources. Although the vast majority of ethnicities he discussed were probably brought to the Americas, some of them may never have been brought at all. Nor can we assume that each ethnicity he mentioned was brought over in the same proportions. In any case, Sandoval obviously was writing well before any significant number of African slaves arrived anywhere in the British colonies.[26]

Nevertheless, some historians have concluded that the Igbo identified only with their regions or villages and had no broader identity before they were brought to the Americas, where the Igbo ethnic identity arose. This shaky conclusion is then extrapolated to all Africans throughout the Americas at all times and places. The Igbo were not as isolated as many historians claim. Their "state" system and social organization did not conform to what Western scholars steeped in broad sociological constructions and delusions of progress have looked for. It was not a weak, fragmented system. "Segmented" would be a better word.[27] Interviews of Igbo at Freetown during the nineteenth century indicate that the "production" of slaves there involved a high level of kidnapping of individuals, condemnation of "criminals" to slavery, and raiding among villages.[28] Large-scale warfare in the course of empire building was less common than in some other regions of Africa. But the likelihood that Africans were isolated and immobilized in regions where the trans-Atlantic slave trade was active is slim. Ancient trade routes proliferated throughout Africa long before the Atlantic slave trade began.[29] Extensive trade networks over land, sea, lagoons, and rivers; mutual conquest and empire building; and a normal process of creolization in Africa had long exposed Africans to many peoples besides their own. It is reasonable to generalize Boubacar Barry's description of the peaceful interactions and interpenetrations among African ethnicities in Greater Senegambia long before the trans-Atlantic slave trade began. After it began, warfare, capture, and displacement of populations through flights and famine were endemic to the process of "producing" slaves.

Documents generated in the Americas containing ethnicity listings point toward an overwhelming Igbo majority among enslaved Africans from the Bight of Biafra and a diminishing majority during the nineteenth century. Chambers, Gomez, and Walsh, writing about the African population in the British North American mainland during the eighteenth century, assumed that the vast majority of Africans arriving from the Bight of Biafra were Igbo. The highest estimate of Igbo or Igbo-speaking slaves was published by Chambers, who claimed that it was "likely or at least possible" that they were 80 percent of the Africans arriving from the Bight of Biafra, although he subsequently revised this estimate slightly downward.[30]

Notarial documents created and housed in the Americas can provide us with less speculative information. Unlike eighteenth- and early nineteenth-century evidence from the African side or trans-Atlantic slave trade voyages, databases constructed from documents housed in the Americas allow for calculations of ethnic designations recorded over time and place by gender as well as much other important information about individual slaves.[31] For eighteenth-century St. Domingue/Haiti, David Geggus studied nearly four hundred probate inventory documents dating between 1791 and 1797, which listed over thirteen thousand enslaved Africans. He found that the Igbo were 90.7 percent of Africans coming from the Bight of Biafra (n = 1,129). There were very few if any Calabar listed in this sample.[32] For Guadeloupe, Nicole Vanony Frisch studied and databased all extant, legible probate inventories listing slaves between 1770 and 1789. She found that fully 37 percent of *all* African-born slaves listed were Igbo (n = 248). There were no Calabar listed in her sample.[33]

We do not have valid, direct evidence from the British Atlantic mainland colonies because of the scant attention paid to African ethnicities in English-language documents. If we restrict ourselves to the eighteenth century, the most important time period for the United States, Chambers, Gomez, and Walsh's assumption of large numbers of Igbo in Virginia is supported by documents created on the American side of the Atlantic but with some caveats. *The Trans-Atlantic Slave Trade Database* shows that voyages from the Bight of Biafra to Chesapeake took place early: 84 percent (n = 89) before 1750, 16 percent (n = 17) between 1750 and 1775, and none recorded after 1775. But voyages from Bonny from which a high proportion of Igbo were exported began earlier than scholars have previously believed.

We do not know the coastal origins or ethnicities of new Africans brought to the Chesapeake or the Carolinas via the transshipment trade from the Caribbean when enslaved Africans were first landed in Caribbean ports and then placed on another, normally smaller ship and sent to the colonial or national US Atlantic coast. If this trade followed the pattern for Louisiana, these voyages would have been organized by Chesapeake and Carolina ship owner/slave owners or aspirant slave owners to buy slaves for their own use, normally leaving no sales documents in archives or maritime documents in ports.[34] Other undocumented slave trade voyages were carried out by freebooters and pirates.

Evidence from the American side of the Atlantic indicates that the proportion of Igbo exported from the Bight of Biafra during the eighteenth century was very high—probably as high as what Chambers, Gomez, and Walsh stated or assumed, even if we draw the very unlikely conclusion that none of the Africans recorded as Calabar in American documents with the exception of Cuba (Karabali) were identified or self-identified as Igbo. Unlike evidence from the African side during the eighteenth and early nineteenth centuries, we have rich African ethnicity information coming from eight different colonies on the North American continent. The most detailed and reliable information dates between 1770 and 1827. Notarial documents in French-speaking colonies (Louisiana, Guadeloupe, and Martinique) are especially rich and detailed about African ethnicities. The other five lists are from registration lists in British West Indies in preparation for general emancipation. Among these five British West Indies islands having African ethnicity information in these lists, four were former French colonies and the other was Trinidad, largely settled by French Creole-speaking masters and slaves from Martinique. Africans described in these British West Indies lists were later arrivals than Africans recorded in the probate documents studied in the other three colonies, but sale documents from Louisiana go through 1820 and were likely to have been recent arrivals.

There were varying percentages of Igbo in British West Indies islands, ranging from 51.8 percent for Trinidad and to high of 72.4 percent for St. Kitts. On all of these lists, the Igbo were a total of 57.9 percent (n = 4,312; T = 7,566) of Africans from the Bight of Biafra. Unlike in Cuba, documents from these eight colonies do not lump Igbo with other ethnic designations from the Bight of Biafra, designating all of them Karabali. They list the Northwest Bantu speakers, Ibibio/Moko in some detail over time as well. The Ibibio and Moko, the only other numerically significant Africans from the Bight of Biafra found thus far in American documents, were overwhelmingly male. Louisiana documents show that the Igbo had a slight majority of females until 1790 and thereafter a slight majority of males. Data in both Africa and the Americas indicate a substantially higher proportion of Northwest Bantu language-group speakers sent to the Americas during the nineteenth century. Nevertheless, the Igbo remained a majority.

In Louisiana, ethnicities were abundantly listed in notarial documents. In probate inventories in Louisiana between 1770 and 1789, Africans listed as Igbo were 78.6 percent (n = 81) of all identified Africans from the Bight of Biafra. Louisiana probate documents show that the Northwest Bantu language speakers, Ibibio and Moko, had a very high percentage of males: 88.9 percent. Africans listed as Calabar on Louisiana estate inventories between 1770 and 1789 were 84.6 percent male. There was one male listed as Ekoi and another listed as Bioko, both runaways. Numbers for all non-Igbo were very small, only eleven. Those listed as Calabar were probably unlikely to be Igbo at this place and time. Data from sales documents recording Africans sold during a period approximately the same time of arrival in the Americas (1790–1820) are higher than in

Trinidad but close to the data from St. Kitts. The proportion of Igbo in these Louisiana sales documents dropped slightly from the earlier probate lists: from 78.6 percent to 75 percent. The "Calabar" sold after 1789 had a lower percentage of males (48.8 percent) than the Igbo (54.6 percent) while the Ibibio/Moko continued to have a very high percentage of males (81.5 percent). It is very likely that at least some of these Africans sold as Calabar in Louisiana were indeed Igbo. If we add some of the Calabar to the Igbo, it brings the Igbo to nearly 80 percent of Africans from the Bight of Biafra sold in Louisiana between 1790 and 1820. The sex ratio among slaves listed as Calabar closely tracked the sex ratio among Igbo, which might make this slight drop more apparent than real.

Looking at the African side, the 1848 census of Freetown, Sierra Leone, reflects the African ethnicities of recaptives brought in by the British anti-slave-trade patrols. Among those who arrived from the Bight of Biafra (excluding the 657 Hausa from the totals in order to compare Igbo with their non-Igbo neighbors), we find 60.9 percent (n = 1,231) Igbo, 15.8 percent (n = 319) Efik, and 23.3 percent (n = 470) Moko.[35] This census shows a substantial majority of Igbo. In sum, the evidence presented here indicates a drop in the proportion of Igbo exported during the nineteenth century and a rise in the proportion of males among them. Nevertheless, the Igbo continued to be a substantial majority.

It is a truism in the historical literature that Igbo, especially Igbo males, were not at all appreciated in the Americas, mainly because of their propensity to run away and/or commit suicide. Igbo were, indeed, sometimes described as "refuse slaves" who were purchased in high percentages in Virginia because the poverty of the slave owners left them no alternative.[36] Female Igbo were valued as more emotionally stable than the men, physically attractive, and hard workers. If we look closer at marketing patterns and other data, we see a strikingly different image of the Igbo in various regions of the Americas. In some places, they were especially prized. Colin Palmer's study of the British *asiento* slave trade to Spanish America (1700–1739) makes it clear that Spanish purchasers, having the advantage of easy access to Mexican silver coins, bought only prime Africans, for whom they paid the highest prices. According to Palmer, "The Ibo were considered tractable and hence were highly sought after by some of the slaveholders in America."[37] When Igbo could not be bought to settle a new upland plantation in Jamaica, the manager explained that he did not buy other slaves because the Ibo "will answer best there."[38] In 1730, a Barbados merchant complained, "There has not [been] a Cargo of Ebbo slaves sold here [for] a long time and many people are Enquirering [*sic*] for them." Daniel C. Littlefield presents convincing evidence that Igbo women were uniquely valued by British slave traders along the African coast.[39] Evidence from Cuba does not demonstrate that Igbo, either female nor male, were compliant to slavery but they were listed under the broad category Karabali and could have included Ibibio/Moko. Manuel Barcia wrote that the slaves who revolted in Puerto Principe in 1798, and on sugar estates in 1817 and 1822, were Calabar. Federico Calabar was one of three leaders of a slave revolt in 1825 in Guamacaro in East Matanzas. He was described as a respected leader and sorcerer, and his fellow slaves believed in his supernatural powers. A large majority of the slaves who revolted there were Carabali and included some from the coffee plantation La Hermita. Gertrudis Carabalí, the companion of a Congo leader of a Congo revolt in Cayajabos in 1812, had her own clothing for the day she would be proclaimed queen. Her costume was composed of a "white muslin dress with short sleeves and a decorated silk bonnet with some holes, probably made by the mice."[40]

We must be cautious about relying heavily on anecdotal evidence disparaging the Igbo. Most evidence comes from surviving documents written by large planters. Planters operating small units might have been more positive about the Igbo, but they rarely left documentation of their activities and opinions. We need more systematic evidence. Documents in Louisiana, for example, demonstrate a lack of enthusiasm for Igbo slaves. They were underrepresented in Louisiana before 1790, although a high proportion of voyages from the Bight of

Biafra arrived in Jamaica and Cuba, both major Caribbean transshipment points for Africans brought to Louisiana during the Spanish period (1770–1803). A slave sale document in Louisiana explained that the seller did not know the nation of the newly arrived African figuring in the transaction, but he guaranteed he was not an Igbo.[41]

It is evident that after the United States took over Louisiana in late 1803, Africans from the Bight of Biafra were being smuggled into Louisiana in large numbers. Between 1804 and 1820, Igbo began to appear in growing proportions among all Africans and became one of the five most frequent ethnicities encountered in documents. Their mean age did not advance significantly over time, although the foreign slave trade to Louisiana was illegal after 1803. Those sold were slightly more male than female. An insignificant number of Igbo (a total of nine) were listed as children. Some of these Igbo could have been legally transshipped to Louisiana from Charleston before 1808, when the foreign slave trade to the United States was outlawed, but few trans-Atlantic slave trade voyages arrived in Charleston from the Bight of Biafra after 1803. Igbo were obviously among ethnicities actively smuggled into Louisiana as well as into Cuba long after the foreign slave trade was outlawed.[42]

Was this relative and absolute growth of the Igbo population in Louisiana because those who purchased them had no choice? The *Louisiana Slave Database* allows us to compare the prices paid for Africans of various ethnicities, male and female, and a mixed picture emerges.[43]

Results for the Igbo are both surprising and anomalous. If Igbo men were despised and Igbo women prized, this is not reflected in prices during the Spanish period in Louisiana, when the mean price of Igbo men was highest among the most numerous ethnicities. The price of Igbo women was only 64 percent of the price of Igbo men, by far the greatest gap between male and female prices for any of these five ethnicities. Curiously, the pattern was entirely reversed during the early US period (1804–1820) as Louisiana quickly shifted from a "society with slaves" to a "slave plantation society," as Ira Berlin phrases it.[44] The mean price of Igbo men fell to last place. The mean price of Igbo women rose to 97.5 percent of that of Igbo men, by far the smallest gap between male and female prices within the same ethnicity during the early US period. This reversal of the price gap between male and female Igbo slave is even more surprising because the gender price gap increased sharply among all other slaves sold.

The anomalous price trend among enslaved Igbo has several possible explanations. Igbo did not adjust to working in large slave gangs growing sugar or cotton. According to Michael Mullin, South Carolina slave owners considered Igbo unsuitable for rice production.[45] This could explain why Igbo were not appreciated in South Carolina, where rice was the major export crop, but were more appreciated in Virginia, where tobacco was the major export crop. During the early US period in Louisiana (1804–1820), sugar and cotton plantations displaced the varied indigo, rice, garden crop, tobacco, corn, cattle, meat, leather, naval stores, cypress, and other timber and wood production of the Spanish period. These products had usually been produced on small farms with relatively few slaves. The dramatic narrowing of the gap between male and female prices of Igbo in Louisiana might also have stemmed from the slave owners' growing acquaintance with their strengths and weaknesses, at least from the point of view of the masters. Igbo women were among the two African ethnicities whose women had the highest proportion of surviving children. They mated widely outside the Igbo group. By the early US period, Igbo women without children might have been recent arrivals who had been separated from their children in Africa. Some of them might not have given birth to children in Louisiana as yet. Their buyers might have held out hope for their reproductive future. The other ethnicity with high reproductive results was the Wolof. During the Spanish period, the mean price of Wolof women was higher than that of Wolof men. Wolof women were sought out as mates in colonial Louisiana, where they were considered especially beautiful, intelligent, and elegant. But their relative mean price dropped during the early US period along with that of almost all slave women, except for the Igbo. Mandingo women demonstrated relatively low reproductive results. Between the Spanish and the early US periods, Mandingo women dropped from third place to last place in the mean price of women among the most frequent ethnicities. Kongo women were numerous despite high male ratios, but their reproductive results were substantially lower than that calculated for women of any other African ethnicity, possibly because of a high abortion rate among them and/or the impact on their health and reproductive powers of the long trek from interior regions of Africa followed by a long trans-Atlantic crossing. The price gap between Kongo men and women diminished slightly from the Spanish to the early US periods.

These price differentials point toward a substantial value placed on the reproductive powers of enslaved women. The price of women plummeted after age thirty-four, while the price of men remained stable until age forty. In regions like the Chesapeake, where natural reproduction of the slave population was a high priority, the Igbo were probably not "refuse" slaves but were actually preferred. Because of the independent position and stance of Igbo women in Africa, their willingness to mate outside their ethnicity and to bear and raise children, their identification with small, local places, and their attachment to the land where their first child was born, they were well equipped to establish new communities on small estates where clear hierarchical structures were weak or absent. African Americans are likely to be descended directly from African women via the female line because they have greater number of white male than white female ancestors. In the United States, African mothers were reasonably likely to be Igbo or Wolof, a thesis that can eventually be tested through DNA studies.

The Igbo and their neighbors have been neglected and unjustifiably depreciated in the historical literature about Africans in the Americas. There is no better way to conclude this chapter than by quoting from Dike:

> Perhaps the overriding genius of the Ibos, Ibibios, Ijaws, Ekoi, and Efiks and their political institutions lay in their extraordinary powers of adaptability—powers which they displayed time and again in the nineteenth century and throughout the period of the Atlantic slave trade in the face of the constantly changing economic needs of Europe. No less was their genius for trade. Dr. Talbot, a well-informed nineteenth-century observer living there, declared, "They are a people of great interest and intelligence, hard-headed, keen-witted, and born traders. Indeed, one of the principal agents here, a [European] of world-wide experience, stated that, in his opinion, the Kalabar [a delta people] could compete on equal terms with Jew or Christian or Chinaman."[46]

NOTES

1. Gwendolyn Midlo Hall, "Africa and Africans in the African Diaspora: The Uses of Relational Databases," *American Historical Review* 115, no. 1 (2010): 136–50.

2. Ernest Obadele-Starks, *Freebooters and Smugglers: The Foreign Slave Trade in the United States after 1808* (Fayetteville: University of Arkansas Press, 2007); Jane G. Landers, *Black Society in Spanish Florida* (Urbana: University of Illinois Press, 1999), 101, 175–76.

3. A. A. Boahen, "The States and Cultures of the Lower Guinean Coast," in *UNESCO General History of Africa*, ed. B. A. Ogot (Berkeley: University of California Press, 1992), 5:399–433.

4. C. Wondji, "The States and Cultures of the Upper Guinea Coast," in *UNESCO General History of Africa*, ed. B. A. Ogot, 5:368–98, 377.

5. Adams, Captain John, *Sketches Taken During Ten Years Voyages to Africa Between the Years 1786 and 1800* (London: Hurst, Robinson and Co., 1822), 38; cited in Kenneth Onwuka Dike, *Trade and Politics in the Niger Delta, 1830–1885: An Introduction to the Economic and Political History of Nigeria* (Oxford: Clarendon Press, 1956), 29.

6. Dike, *Trade and Politics in the Niger Delta*, 30.

7. Gwendolyn Midlo Hall, "African Women in Colonial Louisiana," in *The Devil's Lane: Sex*

and Race in the Early South, ed. Catherine Clinton and Michele Gillespie (New York: Oxford University Press, 1997), 247–62, 253.

8. Dike, *Trade and Politics in the Niger Delta*, 19–46; Paul E. Lovejoy, *Transformations in Slavery: A History of Slavery in Africa*, rev. ed. (Cambridge: Cambridge University Press, 2000), 59–60.

9. G. Ugo Nwokeji, *The Slave Trade and Culture in the Bight of Biafra: An African Society in the Atlantic World* (Cambridge: Cambridge University Press, 2010).

10. Joseph E. Inikori, "The Development of Entrepreneurship in Africa: Southeastern Nigeria during the Era of the Trans-Atlantic Slave Trade," in *Black Business and Economic Power*, ed. Alusine Jalloh and Toyin Falola (Rochester, NY: University of Rochester Press, 2002), 78n44.

11. Alonso de Sandoval, *De Instauranda Aethiopum Salute: El mundo de la esclavitud negra en America*, facsimili of 1627 edition (Bogotá: Empresa Nacional de Publicaciones, 1956).

12. Soi-Daniel W. Brown, "From the Tongues of Africa: A Partial Translation of Oldendorp's Interviews," *Plantation Society in the Americas* 2, no. 1 (1983): 37–61, 49–50.

13. Gwendolyn Midlo Hall, *Africans in Colonial Louisiana: the Development of Afro-Creole Culture in the Eighteenth Century* (Baton Rouge: Louisiana State University Press, 1992), 358; Gwendolyn Midlo Hall, *Louisiana Slave Database: 1719–1820*, http://www.ibiblio.org/laslave.

14. Ralph A. Austen and Jonathan Derrick, *Middlemen of the Cameroons River: The Duala and their Hinterland, c. 1600–c. 1960* (Cambridge: Cambridge University Press, 1999), 5–47.

15. Douglas B. Chambers, "The Significance of Igbo in the Bight of Biafra Slave Trade: A Rejoinder to Northrup's 'Myth Igbo,'" *Slavery and Abolition* 23, no. 1 (2002): 101–20; Michael A. Gomez, *Exchanging our Country Marks Transformation of Identities in the Colonial and Antebellum South* (Chapel Hill: University of North Carolina Press, 1998); Lorena Walsh, *From Calabar to Carter's Grove: The History of a Virginia Slave Community* (Charlottesville: University Press of Virginia, 1997).

16. Joseph E. Inikori, "The Sources of Supply for the Atlantic Slave Exports from the Bight of Benin and the Bight of Bonny (Biafra)," in *De la traite a l'esclavage: Actes du Colloque international sur la traite des Noirs, Nantes*, ed. Serge Daget (Paris: Société française d'histoire d'outre-mer: Diffusion, L'Harmattan, 1988), 2:26–43.

17. Paul E. Lovejoy and David Richardson, "'This Horrid Hole': Royal Authority, Commerce and Credit at Bonny, 1690–1840," *Journal of African History* 45, no. 3 (2004): 363–92.

18. Dike, *Trade and Politics in the Niger Delta*, 46.

19. *C. G. A. Oldendorp's History of the Mission of the Evangelical Brethren on the Caribbean Islands of St. Thomas, St. Croix, and St. John*, ed. John Jakob Bossard (Bossart), trans. Arnold R. Highfield and Vladimir Barac (Ann Arbor, MI: Karoma, 1987).

20. These calculations were made from a database constructed for Laird W. Bergad, Fé Iglesias García, and María del Carmen Barcía, *The Cuban Slave Market, 1790–1880* (Cambridge: Cambridge University Press, 1995). I am grateful to Fé Iglesias for giving me a copy of this database.

21. Email communication from David Geggus, September 2002.

22. Calculated from David Geggus, "Sex Ratio, Age and Ethnicity in the Atlantic Slave Trade: Data from French Shipping and Plantation Records," *Journal of African History* 30 (1989): 23–44.

23. Reverend Sigismund Koelle, *Polyglotta Africana*, ed. P. E. H. Hair (Graz, Austria: Akademische Druck- u. Verlagsanstalt, 1963), 7–8.

24. Koelle, *Polyglotta Africana*, 7–8.

25. David Northrup, *Africa's Discovery of Europe 1450–1850* (New York: Oxford University Press, 2002), 131.

26. De Sandoval, *De Instauranda Aethiopum Salute*.

27. Dike, *Trade and Politics in the Niger Delta*, 19–46.

28. David Northrup, *Trade without Rulers: Pre-Colonial Development of South-Eastern Nigeria* (Oxford: Clarendon Press, 1978), 79–80.

29. D. T. Niane, "Relationships and Exchanges among the Different Regions," in *UNESCO General History of Africa*, ed. D. T. Niane (Berkeley: University of California Press, 1984), 4:614–34.

30. Chambers, "The Significance of Igbo in the Bight of Biafra Slave Trade," 101–20.

31. Gwendolyn Midlo Hall, *Louisiana Slave Database 1719–1820*, in *Databases for the Study of Afro-Louisiana History and Genealogy, 1719–1860. Computerized Information from Original Manuscript Sources. A Compact Disk Publication*, ed. Gwendolyn Midlo Hall (Baton Rouge: University Press of Louisiana, 2000). The entire database can be downloaded free of charge in several formats with a search engine for many fields; see http://www.ibiblio.org/laslave. For a discussion of the origin of the *Louisiana Slave Database* and possibilities of others created from various types of original manuscript documents housed throughout the Americas, see http://afropop.org/multi/interview/ ID/76 /Gwendolyn+Midlo+Hall-2005.

32. David Geggus, "Sex Ratio, Age and Ethnicity in the Atlantic Slave Trade: Data from French Shipping and Plantation Records," *Journal of African History* 30 (1989): 23–44; email communication to writer from David Geggus, September 2002.

33. Nicole Vanony-Frisch, "Les esclaves de la Guadeloupe a la fin de l'ancien régime," *Bulletin de la Société d'Histoire de la Guadeloupe* 63–64 (1985).

34. Gwendolyn Midlo Hall, *Slavery and African Ethnicities in the Americas: Restoring the Links* (Chapel Hill: University of North Carolina Press, 2005), 69–76.

35. Philip D. Curtin, *The Atlantic Slave Trade: A Census* (Madison: University of Wisconsin Press, 1969), table 71, p. 245.

36. For a review of the literature citing negative perceptions about the Igbo, see Michael A. Gomez, "A Quality of Anguish: The Igbo Response to Enslavement in America," in *Trans-Atlantic Dimensions of Ethnicity in the American Diaspora*, ed. Paul Lovejoy and David Trotman (London: Continuum, 2003), 82–95.

37. Colin Palmer, *Human Cargoes: the English Slave Trade to Spanish America, 1700–1739* (Urbana: University of Illinois Press, 1981), 29.

38. Michael Mullin, *Africa in America: Slave Acculturation and Resistance in the American South and the English Caribbean 1736–1831* (Urbana: University of Illinois Press, 1992), 26.

39. Daniel C. Littlefield, *Rice and Slaves: Ethnicity and the Slave Trade in Colonial South Carolina* (Baton Rouge: Louisiana State University Press, 1981), 20, 26, 72–73.

40. Manuel Barcia *Seeds of Insurrection: Domination and Resistance on Western Cuban Plantations, 1808–1848* (Baton Rouge: Louisiana State University Press, 2008), 34, 45, 46.

41. Original Acts, Pointe Coupée Parish, May 1787, document no. 1571, Vente d'esclave, Monsanto to LeDoux.

42. Gwendolyn Midlo Hall, "In Search of the Invisible Senegambians: The Louisiana Slave Database (1723–1820)," in *Saint-Louis et l'esclavage: Actes du Symposium international sur "La traite négrière à Saint-Louis du Sénégal et dans son arrière-pays,"* ed. Djibril Samb (Saint-Louis, 18, 19 et 20 décembre 1998) (Dakar: Institut Fondamental d'Afrique Noir [IFAN], 2001), 237–64.

43. Hall, *Slavery and African Ethnicities in the Americas*, appendix A, 173–79, compares slave prices by ethnicity and gender in Louisiana and discusses the comparative reliability of the price date, including the complexities of inflation and the changing value of currencies.

44. Ira Berlin, *Many Thousands Gone: The First Two Centuries of Slavery in North America* (Cambridge, MA: Harvard University Press, 1998).

45. Mullin, *Africa in America*, 23.

46. Dike, *Trade and Politics in the Niger Delta*, 45–46.

11 THE DEMOGRAPHY OF THE BIGHT OF BIAFRA SLAVE TRADE, CA. 1650–1850

Paul E. Lovejoy

A key issue in understanding the history of the Igbo people is the relationship of the Bight of Biafra to the trans-Atlantic slave trade.[1] The traffic in human beings for slavery in the Americas sent a significant number of people from the Bight of Biafra to the Americas, estimated at 1,550,000. Among them, 1,284,000 either arrived in the Americas or were rescued off slave ships and sent to Sierra Leone, so they did not actually reach the Americas. They were especially prominent in British colonies and North America, and they were a sizable and active community in Cuba in the nineteenth century, as reflected in the importance of *abakua*, which is a secret society related to *ekpe* of Calabar and the interior of the Bight of Biafra.[2] There was also a community in Sierra Leone because of British naval patrols off the West African coast after 1807. This migration represented 13.7 percent of the total number of Africans (11,350,000) who crossed the Atlantic or who went to Sierra Leone during the course of the trans-Atlantic slave trade.

The slave trade from the Bight of Biafra was heavily concentrated in the eighteenth century and the first decades of the nineteenth century. The number of people leaving for the Americas, mostly through the ports of Bonny and Calabar, was at its height at the time of the British debate over the abolition of the slave trade, and subsequently the Bight of Biafra became a target of British anti-slave trade suppression.[3] This chapter examines the demographics of the slave trade and attempts to establish context for what we know about the origins and destinations of people from the Bight of Biafra who were destined for the Americas. Not everyone made it to the Americas; many died at sea because of illness, mistreatment, and accidents, while others ended up in Freetown, Sierra Leone, as "recaptives" taken off slave ships by the British Navy.

Estimates of the slave trade allow an assessment of how this area was able to supply a significant number of enslaved people for the Americas. The trade represented just fewer than 14 percent of total departures from Africa between 1651 and 1850 (table 11.1). Departures increased dramatically in the early eighteenth century; while approximately 67,000 people left the Bight of Biafra in the first quarter of the century, 182,000 left in the second quarter, and then rose to 320,000 in the third quarter and 336,000 in the last quarter. The number was about 265,000 in the first quarter of the nineteenth century and then about 230,000 in the period 1826–1850, thus making the Bight of Biafra a leading region of departure for a little more than a century from 1725 to 1840. The trade in the Bight of Biafra was heavily concentrated at two ports, Calabar on the Cross River and Bonny in the Niger Delta, with Elem Kalabari, Gabon, Bimbia, and Cameroon providing some slaves in specific periods but never in numbers that questioned the dominance of the two principal ports. Calabar commanded the route along the Cross River into the interior, while Bonny was located at the main entrance to the myriad rivers of the Niger Delta that also connected via the Imo River into the densely populated Igbo interior, with easy river traffic via the delta. Merchants at both ports sent commercial expeditions inland to markets where Aro merchants operated. The Aro were from Arochukwu but increasingly by the middle of the eighteenth century operated from satellite communities scattered in many parts of Igbo and Ibibio country.[4] The Aro monopolized the slave trade through a network of markets, the twenty-four-day fairs at Bende

TABLE 11.1 Africa departures by region

Years	Senegambia	Sierra Leone	Windward Coast	Gold Coast	Bight of Benin	Bight of Biafra	West Central Africa	SE Africa	Total
1651–1675	27,741	906	351	30,806	52,768	80,780	278,079	16,633	488,064
1676–1700	54,141	4,565	999	75,377	207,436	69,080	293,340	14,737	719,674
1701–1725	55,944	6,585	8,878	229,239	378,101	66,833	331,183	12,146	1,088,909
1726–1750	87,028	16,637	37,672	231,418	356,760	182,066	556,981	3,162	1,471,725
1751–1775	135,294	84,069	169,094	268,228	288,587	319,709	654,984	5,348	1,925,314
1776–1800	84,920	94,694	73,938	285,643	261,137	336,008	822,056	50,274	2,008,670
1801–1825	91,225	89,326	37,322	80,895	201,054	264,834	929,999	182,338	1,876,993
1826–1850	17,717	84,416	6,131	5,219	209,742	230,328	989,908	227,518	1,770,979
Total	554,010	381,199	334,386	1,206,824	1,955,585	1,549,638	4,856,528	512,157	11,350,328
Percentage	4.9	3.4	2.9	10.6	17.2	13.7	42.8	4.5	

Source: Voyages: *The Trans-Atlantic Slave Trade Database* (http://www.slavevoyages.org/).

and Uburu, and the influence of their oracle, Ibini Ukpabi, at Arochukwu. The rise of the Aro corresponds with the great expansion in the number of people departing from Calabar and Bonny in the early eighteenth century and continuing for another century.

British merchants dominated the trade to the Bight of Biafra before 1807, where after Cuba and Brazil took over the trade until it ended in the 1830s. British merchants, particularly from Bristol and increasingly Liverpool, developed the trade as a mainstay of achieving British supremacy in the slave trade in the eighteenth century.[5] As can be seen in table 11.2, Britain commanded 65.0 percent of total trade from the Bight of Biafra between 1651 and 1850, despite the fact that it was not involved after 1807.

For the period 1651–1807 and abolition in 1807, British ships carried just over one million people, while all other countries took only 185,000. In other words, the British share represented almost 85 percent of the total trade of the Bight of Biafra before 1808. In the nineteenth century, Cuban and Brazilian ships, sometimes sporting US flags, and France virtually monopolized the trade. The figures here carefully distinguish between departures from Africa and arrivals in the Americas, the second being lower because of deaths during the Middle Passage. As can be seen in table 11.3, it is possible to estimate the number of both departures and arrivals. While approximately 1,550,000 people left the Bight of Biafra, only 1,284,000 are estimated to have survived, a loss of 266,000 at sea (17 percent) (table 11.3).

The destinations of the enslaved leaving the Bight of Biafra can be determined in relation to the various colonies of European countries and then the independent United States and Brazil. It can be seen in table 11.4 that between 1651 and 1850, 60 percent of all people went to British colonies, including North America. Cuba was the second principal destination and almost entirely confined to the nineteenth century; for the period as a whole, the Hispanic America portion represented 15.8 percent, while Brazil and the French Caribbean accounted for 9.4 percent and 8.7 percent, respectively. The preponderance of British merchants in the trade before 1808 and the heavy concentration of people in British territory indicate that an overwhelming proportion of Igbo and Ibibio and other people from the Bight of Biafra went to Jamaica, Barbados, other British possessions in the Caribbean, and North America.

Departures for Jamaica, Barbados, and North America indicate that 357,000 people went to Jamaica, 152,000 to Barbados, and 83,000 to North America in a total migration of 1,548,000 (table 11.5). This does not mean that all arrivals remained in Jamaica and Barbados, because many people were sent to Central America, the Hispanic mainland, and North America. Hence the North America figure for arrivals does not include transfers made in Barbados, Jamaica, and elsewhere. Gustavus Vassa (sometimes known as Olaudah Equiano) first went to Barbados and then to Virginia. Hence his arrival is recorded for Barbados, not North America.[6]

TABLE 11.2 National carrier, Bight of Biafra, 1651–1850

Years	*Spain/Cuba*	*Portugal/ Brazil*	*Great Britain*	*North America*	*Netherlands*	*France*	*Denmark/ Baltic*	*Total*
1651–1675	434	54	62,334	—	17,178	780	—	80,780
1676–1700	—	12,050	53,935	—	3,096	—	—	69,080
1701–1725	—	20,793	37,906	264	524	6,900	445	66,833
1726–1750	—	9,901	166,288	2,813	—	3,065	—	182,066
1751–1775	3,569	2,261	293,541	689	974	18,674	—	319,709
1776–1800	2,033	7,537	287,969	—	—	38,293	176	336,008
1801–1825	29,721	65,630	104,556	2,818	—	62,108	—	264,834
1826–1850	136,933	31,772	—	—	53	51,570	—	230,328
Total	182,690	149,998	1,006,530	6,584	21,825	181,389	622	1,549,638
Percentage	11.8	9.7	65.0	0.4	1.4	11.7	—	

Source: Voyages: *The Trans-Atlantic Slave Trade Database* (http://www.slavevoyages.org/).

TABLE 11.3 Departure and arrival estimates, Bight of Biafra

Years	*Embarked*	*Disembarked*
1651–1675	80,780	59,248
1676–1700	69,080	48,976
1701–1725	66,833	51,811
1726–1750	182,066	145,939
1751–1775	319,709	253,687
1776–1800	336,008	293,461
1801–1825	264,834	230,979
1826–1850	230,328	199,601
Total	1,549,638	1,283,702

Source: Voyages: *The Trans-Atlantic Slave Trade Database* (http://www.slavevoyages.org/).

The enslaved population was heavily concentrated in North America in two areas, the low country of the Carolinas and Georgia and the Tidewater region of Virginia and Maryland (table 11.6). Together these regions accounted for over 90 percent of African immigration. The Carolinas and Georgia received 249,000 people (of 298,000 who were sent), 56.1 percent of the total number of people who actually arrived, while the Chesapeake region accounted for more than 153,000 people (of 191,000 who were dispatched), 34.6 percent of all arrivals. By contrast, the area north of the Chesapeake received less than 20,000 people (4.1 percent) of a total 23,000 who were sent, and the areas south and west of Georgia, including Florida and Louisiana, received about 21,000 people (4.7 percent) of 24,000 who left Africa. The overwhelming proportion of Biafrans in the Chesapeake suggests that Igbo in particular were prominent, although Vassa, himself Igbo, claimed he did not meet anyone who spoke his language, although he was only in Virginia for a couple of months. Otherwise, at Carter Grove and many other plantations in the Tidewater, Igbo formed almost half the population.[7]

The immigration of Africans occurred in several stages, which affected each receiving area in North America (table 11.6). The earliest immigration was centered on the Chesapeake, and by 1700, almost ten thousand Africans had arrived in the region, and thereafter the numbers of Africans increased rapidly; more than nine thousand came in the first decade of the eighteenth century, with seventeen thousand five hundred arriving in the second decade, almost thirty-five thousand arriving in the third decade, and peaking at more than thirty-seven thousand in 1731–1740. Thereafter there was a significant decline in immigration through 1775, when immigration ended. By contrast, few Africans were taken to the Carolinas and Georgia before the 1720s. Immigration increased rapidly, rising from only twelve hundred in the 1710s to six thousand in the 1720s, and then increasing enormously to almost forty thousand in the 1730s.

Despite a dramatic decrease in the following decade to less than four thousand, as a reaction to the Stono Rebellion, the number of newly arrived Africans rebounded,

TABLE 11.4 Destinations—Bight of Biafra, 1651–1850

Years	*North America*	*British Caribbean*	*French Caribbean*	*Dutch America*	*Danish colonies*	*Spanish America*	*Brazil*	*Africa*	*Total*
1651–1660	911	15,798	2,854	1,189	0	2,986	374	679	24,791
1661–1670	0	28,493	1,768	6,041	0	588	0	293	37,183
1671–1680	1,390	26,834	508	1,450	0	615	3,284	259	34,340
1681–1690	892	17,666	0	2,513	0	0	638	0	21,709
1691–1700	3,954	17,759	458	0	0	2,227	6,901	0	31,299
1701–1710	6,870	8,483	1,258	0	557	902	3,910	0	21,979
1711–1720	5,815	9,298	5,672	0	0	684	13,147	0	34,615
1721–1730	12,604	23,307	0	10	0	0	5,909	0	41,830
1731–1740	17,811	32,523	864	0	0	60	4,641	0	55,899
1741–1750	10,440	76,431	3,119	0	0	770	3,131	0	93,891
1751–1760	11,554	69,435	10,309	0	0	244	1,752	0	93,294
1761–1770	3,520	110,435	19,600	83	0	12,279	625	0	146,542
1771–1780	954	94,959	10,307	891	533	0	2,321	32	109,997
1781–1790	395	116,791	19,982	0	936	11,482	1,656	0	151,242
1791–1800	0	118,369	20,668	2,286	3,551	6,254	3,337	176	154,642
1801–1810	4,332	74,963	3,367	8,479	4,675	15,449	28,259	860	140,385
1811–1820	1,181	3,379	12,428	0	0	13,726	30,153	5,003	65,870
1821–1830	105	0	32,656	2,550	9,079	94,634	3,656	20,845	163,525
1831–1840	0	522	465	0	0	69,730	7,131	19,982	97,829
1841–1850	0	0	0	0	0	12,399	14,194	961	27,554
Total	82,727	845,444	146,282	25,493	19,331	245,029	135,020	49,090	1,548,414
Percentage	5.4	54.6	9.4	1.6	1.2	15.8	8.7	3.2	

Source: Voyages: *The Trans-Atlantic Slave Trade Database* (http://www.slavevoyages.org/).

TABLE 11.5 Departures for Jamaica and Barbados

Years	*Number*
JAMAICA	
1659–1675	9,706
1676–1700	21,802
1701–1725	3,005
1726–1750	65,417
1751–1775	85,647
1776–1800	134,413
1801–1808	36,799
Total	356,789
BARBADOS	
1651–1675	45,689
1676–1700	14,352
1701–1725	7,235
1726–1750	30,785
1751–1775	47,066
1776–1800	4,954
1801–1808	2,011
Total	152,091

Source: Voyages: *The Trans-Atlantic Slave Trade Database* (http://www.slavevoyages.org/).

accounting for more than twenty-four thousand in the 1750s, almost twenty-nine thousand in the 1760s, more than twenty-five thousand in the 1770s, and despite war, totaling almost seventeen thousand in the 1780s and about twenty-two thousand in the 1790s. In the final seven years of the legal trade, more than eighty-one thousand enslaved Africans arrived, a figure that was more than double the earlier peak in the 1730s. Hence, in contrast to the Tidewater region, enslaved Africans came later and in much larger numbers to the Carolinas and Georgia, and there was a final influx of substantial proportions at the very end of the slave trade from Africa, which is the only time that substantial numbers of Igbo and Ibibio could have arrived.

In the northern colonies, most of the enslaved population arrived in the period after 1730, averaging over three thousand five hundred per decade until the American Revolution and accounting for almost 80 percent of total arrivals in the northern colonies. By contrast, the Gulf region, including Florida and Loui-

TABLE 11.6 Africans sent to North America, 1626–1822

Years	*Northern Region*	*Chesapeake*	*Carolinas & Georgia*	*Gulf states*	*Unspecified*	*Total*
1626–1650	114	239	0	0	0	353
1651–1675	1,177	3,355	0	0	0	4,532
1676–1700	1,246	8,436	21	0	174	9,876
1701–1725	1,245	55,552	3,220	4,076	0	64,093
1726–1750	8,817	87,619	58,118	5,804	537	160,895
1751–1775	9,100	35,362	93,733	1,490	0	139,686
1776–1800	312	0	44,946	2,827	0	48,085
1801–1822	515	0	97,588	9,989	1,278	109,370
Total	22,527	190,564	297,625	24,186	1,989	536,891
Percentage	4.3	35.6	55.5	4.5	0.4	

Source: Voyages: *The Trans-Atlantic Slave Trade Database* (http://www.slavevoyages.org/).

siana, received a large number of Africans in two waves, first in 1718–1730, when more than eight thousand Africans arrived, and during a second influx in 1801–1808, when almost nine thousand Africans arrived. These two periods accounted for over 80 percent of all Africans arriving in the Gulf region, and while the numbers were not large by comparison with the Carolinas and Georgia or even the Chesapeake, there were still concentrations of population because of the patterns of the slave trade but relatively few from the Bight of Biafra.

The enslaved population that reached North America came from specific parts of Africa, most notably Senegambia and the upper Guinea coast, the Gold Coast, the Bight of Biafra, and west-central Africa, these regions accounting for more than 90 percent of migrants (table 11.7). Approximately one-fifth (19.8 percent) came from Senegambia and another tenth (11.6 percent) from the upper Guinea coast, representing almost one-third of all arrivals. This population included two large components; people from the Muslim interior and people from the rice-producing coast. Another one-quarter of the enslaved population was from west-central Africa, specifically from the Kingdom of Kongo, Angola, and the region north of the Congo River, a region of similar languages and cultures and many people long exposed to Christianity. Those from the Bight of Biafra accounted for more than one-fifth (22 percent), and the people from this region were heavily Igbo and to a lesser extent Ibibio. As noted above, they mostly left through Bonny or Calabar. Another 12–15 percent of the slaves left from the Gold Coast and neighboring parts of the Windward Coast and were mostly Akan in ethnic identity.

As can be seen from the demographic data, there was considerable concentration of trade on the African coast that was reflected in the ethnic configuration of migration, with corresponding settlement in specific parts of North America. The patterns of enslavement in Africa resulted in a considerable degree of ethnic homogeneity among the enslaved population in North America. Moreover, the timing of settlement in North America and the extent of concentration in the Tidewater region of the Chesapeake and the low country of South Carolina and Georgia enable an examination of the background of the African population in some detail (tables 11.8 and 11.9). The largest number of enslaved Africans (112,000), perhaps one-quarter of all Africans who came to North America, came from west-central Africa, where languages and cultures were closely related. About 70 percent ended up in the lowlands of Carolina and Georgia, almost three times the number who went to the Tidewater region. Immigrants from west-central Africa accounted for almost one-third of all Africans who arrived in Georgia and South Carolina, while people from west-central Africa accounted for about one-sixth of the immigrants in the Tidewater region (17.5 percent).

TABLE 11.7 Regional origins of Africans arriving in North America

Years	Senegambia	Sierra Leone	Windward Coast	Gold Coast	Bight of Benin	Bight of Biafra	West Central Africa	SE Africa	Total	Percentage
1621–1630	0	0	0	0	0	0	100	0	100	—
1631–1640	0	0	0	0	0	0	78	0	78	—
1641–1650	0	0	0	0	0	0	0	97	97	—
1651–1660	498	0	0	0	0	203	523	0	1,224	0.3
1661–1670	627	0	0	0	0	366	624	0	1,617	0.4
1671–1680	842	0	0	902	326	715	0	104	2,890	0.7
1681–1690	1,314	0	0	83	0	718	0	210	2,325	0.5
1691–1700	60	65	52	32	0	2,280	64	922	3,475	0.8
1701–1710	2,383	0	0	1,186	484	5,076	247	30	9,406	2.1
1711–1720	2,597	274	0	3,551	1,108	9,155	938	2,769	20,392	4.6
1721–1730	9,420	1,440	1,087	3,287	1,811	26,855	3,824	1,214	48,940	11.0
1731–1740	15,496	1,142	580	2,524	921	17,622	42,750	0	81,035	18.3
1741–1750	4,296	1,940	0	2,467	0	10,756	4,403	0	23,862	5.4
1751–1760	12,372	4,466	2,575	4,358	980	8,078	6,755	434	40,019	9.0
1761–1770	12,779	7,043	6,005	8,402	1,138	2,884	8,265	0	46,517	10.5
1771–1780	11,493	4,725	3,481	5,556	1,476	389	3,140	0	30,259	6.8
1781–1790	3,027	1,882	1,666	6,448	0	606	3,291	0	16,921	3.9
1791–1800	2,618	11,563	1,103	6,216	78	0	1,168	0	22,746	5.1
1801–1810	8,846	17,391	5,436	11,679	1,433	4,846	36,337	1,755	87,722	19.8
1811–1820	887	406	0	0	700	2,234	0	0	4,228	1.0
1821–1822	15	0	0	0	0	0	0	0	15	—
Total	89,570	52,338	21,984	56,692	10,456	92,785	112,507	7,535	443,867	
Percentage	20.2	11.8	5.0	12.8	2.4	20.9	25.3	1.7		

Source: Voyages: The Trans-Atlantic Slave Trade Database (http://www.slavevoyages.org/).

TABLE 11.8 Chesapeake Tidewater region

Years	Senegambia	Sierra Leone	Windward Coast	Gold Coast	Bight of Benin	Bight of Biafra	West Central Africa	SE Africa	Total	Percentage
1621–1630	0	0	0	0	0	0	100	0	100	0.1
1631–1640	0	0	0	0	0	0	78	0	78	—
1641–1650	0	0	0	0	0	0	0	0	0	0
1651–1660	498	0	0	0	0	203	0	0	701	0.5
1661–1670	627	0	0	0	0	366	144	0	1,136	0.7
1671–1680	842	0	0	902	326	715	0	0	2,786	1.8
1681–1690	1,314	0	0	83	0	597	0	180	2,174	1.4
1691–1700	60	65	52	0	0	2,280	64	0	2,521	1.6
1701–1710	2,383	0	0	1,071	484	5,076	247	0	9,262	6.0
1711–1720	2,061	274	0	2,316	333	8,958	938	2,624	17,504	11.4
1721–1730	1,442	874	1,087	2,749	41	24,953	2,548	1,135	34,829	22.7
1731–1740	9,410	1,020	580	1,533	921	10,433	13,371	0	37,267	24.2
1741–1750	2,511	1,443	0	451	0	9,394	2,944	0	16,742	10.9
1751–1760	2,863	1,008	747	572	82	3,737	3,605	0	12,614	8.2
1761–1770	3,958	634	1,697	2,583	578	1,363	2,358	0	13,172	8.6
1771–1775	918	288	112	664	0	288	579	0	2,848	1.9
Total	28,885	5,605	4,275	12,924	2,765	68,364	26,976	3,939	153,735	
Percentage	18.8	3.9	2.6	8.4	1.9	44.2	17.5	2.6		

Source: Voyages: *The Trans-Atlantic Slave Trade Database* (http://www.slavevoyages.org/).

TABLE 11.9 Carolinas and Georgia, 1698–1820

Years	*Senegambia*	*Sierra Leone*	*Windward Coast*	*Gold Coast*	*Bight of Benin*	*Bight of Biafra*	*West Central Africa*	*SE Africa*	*Total*	*Percentage*
1698–1700	0	0	0	18	0	0	0	0	18	—
1701–1710	0	0	0	48	0	0	0	0	48	—
1711–1720	366	0	0	718	0	198	0	0	1,282	0.5
1721–1730	2,641	555	0	476	0	1,902	535	0	6,109	2.5
1731–1740	4,513	0	0	0	0	7,189	28,157	0	39,859	16.0
1741–1750	840	0	0	434	0	1,363	922	0	3,558	1.4
1751–1760	8,311	3,076	1,700	2,662	573	4,340	2,971	434	24,068	9.7
1761–1770	7,834	5,133	3,843	4,093	488	1,521	5,907	0	28,819	11.6
1771–1780	9,096	3,872	3,369	4,826	1,476	101	2,560	0	25,301	10.2
1781–1790	3,027	1,882	1,666	6,448	0	606	3,104	0	16,733	11.2
1791–1800	2,403	11,461	1,103	5,961	0	0	686	0	21,613	8.7
1801–1810	7,461	16,910	5,436	10,688	1,063	4,846	33,911	1,141	81,454	32.7
1811–1820	**160**	**0**	**0**	**0**	**0**	**0**	**0**	**0**	**160**	**0.1**
Total	46,651	42,890	17,117	36,373	3,599	22,065	78,752	1,576	249,022	
Percentage	18.7	17.2	6.9	14.6	1.4	8.9	31.6	0.6		

Source: Voyages: *The Trans-Atlantic Slave Trade Database* (http://www.slavevoyages.org/).

Approximately one in five Africans (21 percent) came from the Bight of Biafra, and these people were mostly Igbo and Ibibio in origin or, in the course of the Atlantic crossing, became associated with these dominant groups. About three-quarters of these people went to the Tidewater region, so that close to half of all African immigrants who went to the Chesapeake were from the Bight of Biafra (44.5 percent). Moreover, the Biafran population in the Tidewater arrived early and was the largest group of immigrants from the 1690s through the 1750s. By contrast, less than 10 percent of the Africans who went to the Carolinas and Georgia were from the Bight of Biafra. The number of people was about twenty-two thousand, with arrivals concentrated in the 1730s (more than seven thousand), the 1750s (more than four thousand) and the years before 1808 (almost five thousand). The implications of these patterns indicate that Gustavus Vassa could have been born in South Carolina, as Vincent Carretta wants to believe, but it is highly unlikely on the basis of demography alone.[8]

In the early decades of African immigration in the Chesapeake region, there were many immigrants from Senegambia, initially as many as from the Bight of Biafra. During the period of importation through 1775, almost twenty-nine thousand people came from Senegambia, about 18.8 percent of all arrivals in the Chesapeake. The upper South had a considerable concentration of people from the Bight of Biafra, apparently enough to evolve a distinct subculture among the enslaved population. The Bight of Biafra stands out in the demography of the eighteenth-century slave trade because of the relatively high numbers of women in comparison with all other parts of the African coast. Women from the Bight of Biafra were particularly important in giving birth to a new generation in the Americas, in sharp contrast with the virtual lack of women from Muslim areas.

Issues relating to age and gender are discussed in this volume by Audra Diptee. There is ample evidence on the mode of enslavements in the proceedings of earlier conferences and published in Brown and Lovejoy, *Repercussions of the Slave Trade*.[9] There is considerable evidence of the routes that extended inland from Bonny and Calabar. There seems to have been relatively little Niger River trade until the nineteenth century for reasons that are not known, at least in terms of slaves that could have come from farther north than Igbo country but apparently did not. There is some evidence that Calabar drew on trade as far inland as the Bamenda grass fields plateau. The trade southward of Calabar, such as at Bimbia, was much smaller than at Calabar and Bonny and was mostly confined to the nineteenth century. Many details of this trade are recorded in the Sessional Papers of the House of Commons enquiry into the slave trade between 1788 and 1893 and continuing through other hearings in the House of Lords.[10]

NOTES

1. See, for example, Carolyn A. Brown and Paul E. Lovejoy, eds., *Repercussions of the Atlantic Slave Trade: The Interior of the Bight of Biafra and the African Diaspora* (Trenton, NJ: Africa World Press, 2010).

2. Ute Röschenthaler, *Purchasing Culture in the Cross River Region of Cameroon and Nigeria* (Trenton, NJ: Africa World Press, 2011); Paul E. Lovejoy, "Transformation of the Ékpè Masquerade in the African Diaspora," in *Carnival: Theory and Practice*, ed. Christopher Innes, Annabel Rutherford, and Brigitte Bogar (Trenton, NJ: Africa World Press, 2013); Ivor Miller, "Cuban Abakuá Chants: Examining New Linguistic and Historical Evidence for the African Diaspora," *African Studies Review* 48 (2005): 23–58; Ivor Miller, *Voice of the Leopard: African Secret Societies and Cuba* (Jackson: University Press of Mississippi, 2009); Joseph Miller, "A Secret Society Goes Public: The Relationship Between Abakuá and Cuban Popular Culture," *African Studies Review* 43, no. 1 (2000): 161–88; Shubi L. Ishemo, "From Africa to Cuba: an Historical Analysis of the *Sociedad Secreta Abakuá (Ñañiguismo)*," *Review of African Political Economy* 92 (2002): 253–72.

3. Paul E. Lovejoy and David Richardson, "The Slave Ports of the Bight of Biafra in the Eighteenth Century," in *Repercussion of the Atlantic Slave Trade*, ed. Brown and Lovejoy; David Northrup, "The Growth of Trade Among the Igbo Before 1800," *Journal of African History* 13 (1972): 217–36; David Northrup, *Trade without Rulers: Pre-Colonial Economic Development in South-Eastern Nigeria* (Oxford: Oxford University Press, 1978).

4. For the Aro, see G. Ugo Nwokeji, *The Slave Trade and Culture in the Bight of Biafra: An African Society in the Atlantic World* (Cambridge: Cambridge University Press, 2010); John Nwachimereze Oriji, "The Slave Trade, Warfare and Aro Expansion in the Igbo Heartland," *Transafrican Journal of History* 16 (1987): 151–66; Kenneth Onwuka Dike and Felicia Ekejiuba, *The Aro of South-eastern Nigeria, 1650–1980: A Study of Socio-economic Formation and Transformation in Nigeria* (Ibadan, Nigeria: Ibadan University Press, 1990).

5. Paul E. Lovejoy and David Richardson, "Trust, Pawnship and Atlantic History: The Institutional Foundations of the Old Calabar Slave Trade," *American Historical Review* 104, no. 2 (1999): 332–55; Paul E. Lovejoy and David Richardson, "'This Horrid Hole': Royal Authority, Commerce and Credit at Bonny, 1690–1840," *Journal of African History* 45 (2004): 363–92; Paul E. Lovejoy and David Richardson, "Letters of the Old Calabar Slave Trade, 1760–89," in *Genius in Bondage: Literatures of the Early Black Atlantic*, ed. Vincent Carretta and Philip Gould (Lexington: University of Kentucky Press, 2001), 89–115; and Stephen D. Behrendt, "The Captains in the British Slave Trade from 1785 to 1807," *Transactions of the Historic Society of Lancashire and Cheshire* 140 (1991): 79–140.

6. For the inconsistency in reading the documents on Vassa's birth, see Vincent Carretta, *Equiano, the African: Biography of a Self-Made Man* (Athens: University of Georgia Press, 2005); Paul E. Lovejoy, "Autobiography and Memory: Gustavus Vassa, alias Olaudah Equiano, the African," *Slavery and Abolition* 27, no. 3 (2006): 317–47; and Paul E. Lovejoy, "Olaudah Equiano or Gustavus Vassa—What's in a Name?," *Atlantic Studies* 9, no. 2 (2012): 165–84, reproduced in this volume in slightly expanded form.

7. Lorena S. Walsh, *From Calabar to Carter's Grove: The History of a Virginia Slave Community* (Charlottesville: University Press of Virginia, 1997); Lorena S. Walsh, "The Chesapeake Slave Trade: Regional Patterns, African Origins, and Some Implications," *William and Mary Quarterly* 58 (2001): 139–70; Douglas B. Chambers,

Murder at Montpelier: Igbo Africans in Virginia (Jackson: University Press of Mississippi, 2005); Douglas B. Chambers, "Tracing Igbo into the African Diaspora," in *Identity in the Shadow of Slavery*, ed. Paul E. Lovejoy (London: Continuum, 2000), 55–71.

8. Carretta, in this volume, refers to the significance of baptismal and naval records that purport to show Vassa was born in South Carolina. It is important for readers to also see Lovejoy's contribution in this volume that provides convincing evidence of an African birth.

9. Brown and Lovejoy, *Repercussions of the Atlantic Slave Trade*.

10. See the many references to Sheila Lambert, ed., *House of Commons Sessional Papers of the Eighteenth Century* (Wilmington, DE : Scholarly Resource, 1975), vols. 67–72, and 82, in Paul E. Lovejoy and Vanessa S. Oliveira, "An Index to the Slavery and Slave Trade Enquiry: The British Parliamentary House of Commons Sessional Papers, 1788–1792," *History in Africa* 40 (2013): 1–63.

12 THE IGBO DIASPORA IN THE ERA OF THE SLAVE TRADE

Douglas B. Chambers

In 1816, nearly a decade after the British abolished their slave trade, a runaway enslaved woman in Jamaica named Bessy turned herself in to the St. George parish workhouse, on the eastern end of the island. Apparently she had a rather complicated story to tell the workhouse jailor. Initially she said that she was "an Eboe" (Igbo) and that she had belonged to a master living at Black River, in western Jamaica but that he had died. The jailor noted that Bessy was branded with the letters *W B* on her left shoulder and that she had come in "of her own accord." A week later, the jailor revised his description of Bessy, apparently based on new information she provided. She was not in fact born in Africa but either on a slave ship during the Middle Passage or shortly after her enslaved mother landed in Jamaica:

> BESSY, formerly said she was an Eboe, but now found out to be a salt-water creole, and that she belonged to a Gentleman at Black River, since dead, but does not know his name, marked with *W B* on left shoulder; she came in of her own accord, and has no owner.[1]

This desperate slave, Bessy, after making her way literally from one end of Jamaica to the other as a runaway, claimed not to know her owner's name or, rather, claimed that she had no master. She did claim, however, a personal ethnic identity as "an Eboe." One presumes that Bessy had found her personal claim useful in her journey across Jamaica as a fugitive slave.

Of the estimated 1.7 million enslaved people taken from the Bight of Biafra into the trans-Atlantic diaspora, some three-quarters or about 1.3 million were Igbo. As the British dominated the Biafran ocean-borne trade, especially before 1810, the great majority of these Igbo slaves wound up in the British Americas. The single most important destination in this massive forced migration was Jamaica, the "Pearl of the Antilles," England's richest and most important American colony.[2] Enslaved Igbo were also taken in large numbers to other British Caribbean islands as well as to what became the United States, to the French sugar island of Saint-Domingue (Haiti), and, in the nineteenth century, to Cuba.

The historical geography of the Igbo diaspora in the era of the slave trade connected particular African and American histories, as the Atlantic was as much a bridge as a barrier. Igbo contributed in many ways to slave resistance and to the historical development of early Afro-American cultures in the New World. The extensive social violence of this vast slave trade also had major consequences for Igboland itself, most notably the rise of the slave-trading warlordism of the Aro, with their network of settlements and powerful *agawhu* (warlords) who controlled the major trade routes to the coast, and the consequent decline and near-collapse of the ancient pacifistic civilization centered at Nri.[3]

HISTORICAL GEOGRAPHY OF THE IGBO DIASPORA

The most reliable estimates of the numbers of the trans-Atlantic slave trade suggest that, over the course of four centuries, some twelve million enslaved Africans were loaded onto ships (90 percent after 1700), with about ten million surviving the Middle Passage. The slave trade was a highly organized, regulated, and capital-intensive international business, and therefore was anything but random.[4] Over all, some 40 percent of enslaved Africans were taken from just one Atlantic region, west-central Africa (Kongo and Angola). In the Americas, 40 percent of all African slaves were taken to Brazil, 35 percent to the West Indies (Caribbean islands and Suriname), 15 percent to the Spanish Mainland (including Mexico, Venezuela, Peru, and Colombia), 5 percent directly to Europe (largely before 1700), and finally, 5 percent to what became the United States, mostly in the eighteenth century.

One in six of all enslaved Africans originated from the Bight of Biafra. Data on some 3,000 voyages that embarked nearly 950,000 enslaved people (of whom 760,000 survived the crossing) show how important Jamaica was to the trade from the Bight of Biafra (one-third of the total) as well as how widely distributed enslaved Igbo and other Biafran Africans were throughout the Americas (about 30 other colonies, half of them British).[5] Other West Indies islands that were particularly important in the Bight of Biafra trade were, in order, Dominica, Barbados, Grenada, and St. Kitts.[6]

Compared to the Caribbean, the slave trade to what became the United States was relatively small. The Bight of Biafra, however, was particularly important in the slave trade to Virginia, where Biafran Africans made up about half of all Africans taken to that colony before the prohibition of further importations in 1778. Enslaved Igbo certainly were the most numerous group of African slaves in the colony and deeply influenced the development of early Afro-Virginia culture.[7] In the two other major plantation regions of the American South—coastal South Carolina and Louisiana along the lower Mississippi River—the Bight of Biafra trade was tiny (less than 10 percent), although Igbo and Ibibio ("Moco") are clearly visible in the historical records, including runaway slave advertisements.[8] Before the British and American abolition of their slave trades in 1808, hundreds of thousands of Igbo and Ibibio (and others) had been transported as slaves to the British West Indies and tens of thousands to North America.

The French slave trade to the sugar island of Saint-Domingue (Haiti) was so huge before the Haitian revolution erupted in 1791 that Biafran Africans were also taken there in some numbers. Though only a small percentage of the Saint-Domingue slave trade (less than 10 percent), about thirty thousand or so Biafran Africans—mostly Igbo—were transported in just one generation (c. 1770–1790), where they influenced the development of Haitian *vodun* (voodoo), originally the religion of the African slaves from Dahomey and the coastal kingdoms of the Bight of Benin. Identifiably Igbo *lwa* (gods/spirits) in Haitian vodun include Ibo Foula, Ibo Mariané, Ibo Héquoiké, Ibo Lazile, Ibo Lélé, Un Pied Un Main Un Jé (One Hand, One Foot, One Eye), and Takwa (who was said to speak an "unknown language"), and Ibo Ianman.[9] In the twentieth century there were a number of vodun chants that called out Igbo spirits and Igbo as a diasporic nation in Haiti:

> Nanchon Ibo m'ta mangé gros coq oh
> nanchon Ibo!
> Nanchon Ibo m'ta mangé gros coq!
> Nanchon Ibo m'ta mangé gros coq oh
> nanchon Ibo!
>
> Ibo nation, I am going to eat a large cock
> [rooster], oh, Ibo nation!
> Ibo nation, I am going to eat a large cock!
> Ibo nation, I am going to eat a large cock,
> oh, Ibo nation![10]
>
> Ibo lélé!
> Ibo lélé!
> Nanchon Ibo ça ou gainyain con ça Ibo lélé!
> Ianman, con ça, con ça!
> Ianman con ça'm dansé Ibo!
>
> Ibo *lélé*!
> Ibo *lélé*!
> Ibo Nation, what are you doing there, Ibo
> *lélé*!
> Ianman, like that, like that!
> Ianman, like that I dance the Ibo![11]

Though officially prohibited in 1818, the French slave trade actually flourished in the 1820s, particularly to the Caribbean islands of Martinique and Guadeloupe, and the Bight of Biafra was significant in this latter trade (perhaps half of all slaves taken by the French in the 1820s). Thus we should also look to Guadeloupe and Martinique for evidence of Igbo cultural influences in the French Caribbean.[12]

The least documented part of the Biafra slave trade was to Cuba. Between about 1780 and 1850, some 250,000 Africans from the Calabar Coast region wound up in Cuba, or perhaps a quarter of total importations in the massive Cuban slave trade. Especially after 1820 many of these slaves were from the lower Cross River and Ibibioland and eastward (Ekoi, Ejagham), and in Cuba they were generally called Carabalí. In Cuba enslaved Carabalí reinvented or redeveloped the men's masquerade (leopard) societies of their home communities (Ejagham *ngbe*, Efik *ekpe*, Igbo *egbo* and *okonko*) into Afro-Cuban Abakuá, including the drums and dances and masques and the secret writing system, called in Efik *nsibidi* and in Cuba *anaforuana*.[13]

In general, Igbo made up about 75 percent of slaves taken from the Bight of Biafra. In some places, like Virginia, the Biafran trade was far more important to the colony—again, about half and in some decades fully two-thirds of all enslaved Africans taken to Virginia were brought from the Bight of Biafra—than the colony's commerce ever was to that African regional slave trade (less than 3 percent).[14] Recent archaeological excavations on eighteenth-century Virginia sites, recovering those "small things forgotten" that slaves left behind in the domestic spaces where they once lived, shows that Igbo Africans had a profound influence in the formation of early slave material culture there, notably so on the level of everyday life.[15] There is now the beginning of a sustained scholarly recognition of the historical presence of Igbo in North American cultural history, including studies in archaeology, literature, folklore, and sociocultural history.[16]

Based on the known trans-Atlantic slave trade evidence for North America and the patterns of the nineteenth-century US interstate trade (some one million forcibly migrated from the old Atlantic states to the new Deep South from 1830 to 1860), I estimate that today some 60 percent of all black Americans (about thirty-five million people) have at least one genealogical ancestor who was in fact Igbo. And yet, because of the tragedy of slavery (compounded by institutionalized white supremacy in the twentieth century, which also stigmatized Africans), practically no one remembers this historical connection.[17] Hence the importance of "sites of memory" and of historical museums and other forms of public history, which are the only guard against complete social amnesia and historical erasure; for example, the newly established "Igbo Farm Village" living-history exhibition at the Frontier Culture Museum of Virginia.[18] As another kind of "site of memory," see the website of one black American family that has traced its genealogy (in part) to enslaved Igbo taken to coastal Georgia in 1803.[19] Or, as a further example, the physical place called Ibos Landing (St. Simons Island, Georgia), which marks a site of violent resistance from an event that happened in May 1803 and which local black people have considered a "sacred place" ever since.

Throughout the Igbo diaspora, however, Jamaica was the single most important destination in this massive and violent forced migration. For example, more than 300,000 enslaved Biafran Africans, or ten times the number of those taken to Virginia, were landed in this one island.[20] In fact Jamaican records, in particular runaway slave advertisements published in local newspapers, provide invaluable information not just on enslaved Igbo in the diaspora but also important evidence for how slaving and the slave trade changed historical experience in Igboland.

For example, in the last quarter of the eighteenth century, Jamaican advertisements document a kind of "country mark" (facial tattoo) that was unique to a particular kind of Igbo, the "Breechee" or "Bruchee" cut.[21] I have documented seven such Igbo *mgburichi* in Jamaica from 1777 to 1793, and the descriptions are entirely consistent with those of historical Igbo *ichi* from the 1750s to the 1850s.[22] In historical Igboland the ennobling *ichi* cut was the outward sign of being *mgburichi* [mbree-chi]—literally "cut-face," figuratively spiritual royalty—within the ancient and pacifist Nri civilization (founded c. 1000 CE).[23]

Ichi marks were a core sign of the ancient civilization of Nri, and specifically of the highest titles of the *ọzọ* society, whose initiates represented (and enacted) the sacred power of the *Eze Nri* (Priest-King of Nri) through ritual cleansing (*ikpu alu*) and peacemaking, wielding the *ọfọ*, staff of ancestral authority, and the *otonsi*, spear of peace. At Nri, a traditional song during the cutting ceremony evoked the symbolic associations of *ichi* with peacemaking and spiritual royalty:

> Nwaichi nyem ma aguu egbunem
> Ichi Eze, ichi Nwadiokpala.
>
> Ichi child give me food so I will not die of hunger
> Facial scar for kings, facial scar for first sons.[24]

According to one of the last surviving *Mgburichi* of Nri, Ichie Okoye Mmefu (b. c. 1914), Nri distinguished between two grades of *ichi*: the *Mgburichi* with full ritual powers represented by the *otonsi* (spear of peace), and the *Azunri* ("at the back of Nri") without *otonsi* but sharing the same exalted status among the outlying settlement areas, that is, among communities descended from Nri or culturally allied with the Nri civilization.[25] At Nri itself, the people traditionally recognized two kinds of *Ichi* marks: the full-face form (*Mgbuzu ichi*, "facial marks for the rulers of Nri"), which was agonizing to endure and traditionally performed only on those from royal lineages; and *Ntuche* (*ichi Nwadiokpala*), consisting of a few lines of marks on the forehead and radiating across each temple.[26] These historical distinctions, between *mgburichi/azunri* or *Mgburichi/Ntuche* may be the roots of the Breechee/Bruchee difference in eighteenth-century Jamaica, or alternatively, "Bruchee" in Jamaica may simply have been a homonym of "Breechee," itself the Anglicization of Igbo *Mgburichi*.

In any case, the historical connection was with the ancient Nri civilization, for whom the shedding of human blood in anger was the greatest abomination. *Mgburichi* are remembered as universally respected because they "were regarded as Nri men."

> They were respected throughout Igboland. We have facial marks (*ichi*) that distinguish us from other Igbo people, and this served as a passport, enabling us to travel unharmed at a time when human beings were essential commodities. People with *ichi* marks were regarded as Nri men, and were not enslaved. It was probably because of this that some parts of Igboland started to wear *ichi*.[27]

The fact that Igbo "Breechee" show up in Jamaica among runaways from 1777–1793 is significant. It is a concrete sign that the trans-Atlantic slave trade had reached all the way to the Nri heartland in the Anambra valley of northern Igboland, and that by the 1770s (if not earlier) the social violence wrought by slaving and the *agawhu* (merchant-warlords) was violating even the ancient sacred authority—and the personal safety—of titled "Nri men," who no longer were preserved from capture or kidnapping and enslavement.[28] The orature of the reigns of *Eze Nri* in the eighteenth century evoke a larger narrative of crisis and calamity, of social violence and slaving, of drought and famine, from the murder of *Eze Nri* Ezimilo (official r. 1701–1723) to the long-term famine and drought under his successor *Eze Nri* Ewenetem (official r. 1724–1794), when slave trading was ubiquitous and the first Aro settlements were established in the Nri heartland. Toward the close of the century, the situation around Nri itself had become dire. In the 1790s, a newly consecrated but aged *Eze Nri*, Nri Añua, agreed to abdicate in favor of a young firebrand, Enweleana of Ezekammadu, who upon becoming *Eze Nri* was driven by his desperate times to the ultimate abomination of organizing a war, the *Amakom* ("defense of the land"), against the Aro *agawhu* Okolie Ijoma (d. 1820s) of Ndikelionwu.[29] The oldest remembered age-grade at Nri is from Obeagu, the village of both Nri Añua, and Nri Enwelani I—that is, Ochi Ogu [Ochogu] [Who Wants War]—which can be dated to the 1790s.[30]

Advertisements for Biafran runaways in eighteenth-century Jamaica, then, underscore the significance of Igbo among captives from the Bight of Biafra hinterland. And the rather sudden appearance of "Breechee" Igbo in the 1770s–1790s suggest that by the last quarter of the century, if not earlier, even *mgburichi*—the famed "Nri men" of Igboland—were no longer safe.

CULTURES OF RESISTANCE

Wherever enslaved Igbo found themselves in the Americas, whether on small tobacco farms in marginal colonies like Virginia or on the teeming sugar plantations of Jamaica, they forged cultures of resistance. In fact, throughout the Atlantic world Igbo gained a well-deserved reputation as "bad slaves."

Stereotyped as lazy and despondent, ornery and obstreperous, and tending to bolt (and even commit suicide) rather than to revolt outright, enslaved Igbo resisted their bondage in ways that confounded their masters.[31] As a German traveler to Bonny on the Calabar coast in 1840 learned, even after generations of slaving the Ibani still spoke of Igbo "as they would speak of sharks, *Iboman wawa too much*, 'Ibo people are very wicked.'" In other parts of the Atlantic littoral like coastal Carolina in the 1770s, other Africans berated Igbo as rogues and rascals. As a visitor to a late-colonial South Carolina rice plantation in the 1770s noted, slaves would tease each others' African nationalities, especially "Gulli" (Gullah, i.e., Angola) and "Iba" (Igbo). James Barclay wrote that, "The one will say to the other, 'You be Gulli Niga, what be the use of you, you be good for nothing.' The other will reply, 'You be Iba Niga; Iba Niga great 'askal' [rascal]."[32] The core message of Igbo as "bad" slaves, of course, is in their refusal to be slavelike. One can enslave my body, these stories seem to say, but not my mind, not my soul.

Igbo slaves also participated in violent revolts and conspiracies, including Monday Gell's "Ibo Company" of about forty slaves in Denmark Vesey's famous 1822 rebellion in South Carolina.[33] At roughly the same time, in March of 1816 in the Black River region of western Jamaica, as many as one thousand slaves (all Africans, and likely Igbo) plotted a general insurrection, and elected a "King of the Eboes" and two Captains.[34] Over three hundred African slaves swore blood oaths to join the rebellion, but the plot was discovered. The "King of the Eboes" and one of the Captains were captured and at their trial "were perfectly cool and unconcerned, and did not even profess to deny the facts with which they were charged."[35] At his execution, this "King of the Eboes" in western Jamaica declared that "he left enough of his countrymen to prosecute the design in hand, and revenge his death upon the whites." The condemned Captain escaped from the jail "by burning down the prison door," but was later recaptured, and, notably, he was found "concealed in the hut of a notorious Obeah-man."[36]

Another such site of direct resistance is called Ibos Landing on St. Simons Island, Georgia.[37] Here on the banks of Dunbar Creek, on one of the "sea islands" just offshore, local tradition says that a group of enslaved Igbo who had just arrived and were landed in chains, began to sing a song in their language. Then, following their chief and all singing together, they marched into the water to go back to Africa, and they all drowned.

The historical fact that throughout the Atlantic Diaspora, from Bonny to colonial North America to Jamaica to the antebellum US South, masters generally saw Igbo as "bad" slaves should, today, be a point of pride. Who in their right mind would wish to be remembered as a "good" slave?

SOCIAL MEMORIES

I will close with three examples of social memories of Igbo as "bad slaves," all from North America with the following points. The first is a general folk memory. In some parts of the South, people used the term "very eboe" (or in the southern vernacular, "plumb eboe") as a metaphor for that peculiar kind of resistance to authority known as giving the master—and white people in general—the runaround. The dissembling slave is a classic American stereotype of passive-aggression. And in parts of the South like Virginia, to do so was to be "plumb eboe."

For example, in his historical novel *The Fathers* (1938) about the coming of the Civil War in central Virginia, the Kentucky-born writer Allen Tate set up a scene in which an aged slave man confronts a group of ornery slaves who were being sold South. The house-slave Uncle Coriolanus gave them some food and questioned them, and when the slaves gave him the runaround, refusing to answer his questions as if they were "puttin' on ol' master himself," Coriolanus turned to his own master and called the slaves "plumb eboe." One of those dissembling slaves, Yellow Jim, had known Coriolanus and spoke to him "with an assurance that had in it no trace of servility or insolence":

> "I reckon you mought know me. I reckon you mought because I knows you. You Marster Major Buchan's keeriage driver, I knowed you all along." He glanced at the other negroes. "I was sold by myself. I didn't come with there yere niggers." He looked about him. "I ain't no Virginia nigger."
>
> Coriolanus looked at him contemptuously. "What kind of nigger is you?"[38]

The implied answer to Coriolanus's last question is precisely what he had already told his own master: "plumb eboe."

The second example is a specific folk memory of violent resistance, Ibos Landing. The story identifies the site of a confrontation in 1803 with the catastrophe of enslavement, and which is still today an undeveloped "sacred place" on private property, without even an official historical marker, on one of the remote Georgia sea islands. Initially largely forgotten by whites (the earliest documentary reference dates to 1857), the story resurfaced in the twentieth century.[39] The first published account, in 1926, is presented as a romanticized legend of local lore:

> **Ebo's Landing**
> Tradition says that many, many years ago a slave ship that came to St. Simons brought a young African chieftain, by the name of Ebo, who was purchased by one of the planters on St. Simons. Ebo never became reconciled to his new life. One day he gathered a band of countrymen and led them through the woods, singing as they went, to the banks of the Frederica River, where they plunged into the stream and were drowned, preferring death to a life of servitude. This site is known as Ebo's Landing.[40]

This "white" version of the story focuses on the individual supposedly named Ebo and speaks to his failure to adjust to slavery, as he "never became reconciled to his new life," thus "preferring death to a life of servitude" and then leading others on to their suicidal ruin.

At about the same time, however, there also was a "black" version, rooted directly in local folk culture and oral history. The narrator, Floyd White, was telling his WPA interviewers about how back in slavery times they had drums and would sing in procession for funerals and how they all baptized in the river; this was the segue to his story of Ibo's Landing.[41] Here is Floyd White's telling:

> "Heahd bout duh Ibo's Landing? Das duh place weah dey bring duh Ibos obuh in a slabe ship an wen dey git yuh, dey ain lak it an so dey all staht singin an dey mahch right down in duh ribbuh tuh mahch back tuh Africa, but dey ain able tuh get deah. Dey gits drown."
>
> [In standard English: "Heard about the Ibo's Landing? That's the place where they bring the Ibos over in a slave ship and when they got here, they ain't like it and so they all started singing and they marched right down in the river to march back to Africa, but they ain't able to get there. They got drowned."][42]

This vernacular version evokes a collective response by "the Ibos"—who indeed had a well-deserved reputation throughout the Atlantic world for escaping slavery by suicide—who sought to "march back to Africa."[43] Having survived the Middle Passage, these Igbo slaves—no doubt still in chains—started singing together and turned and all marched into the river that had brought them from Africa. And, of course, they all drowned.[44]

In the 1980s and 1990s, "Ibo Landing" was appropriated in fictional works, including Paule Marshall's *Praisesong for the Widow* (1983) and Julie Dash's film, *Daughters of the Dust* (1991) and subsequent novelization (1999) under the same title. Since the 1990s, historians have tended to mistakenly conflate the regional "flying Africans" tale and the local story of Ibos Landing.[45]

The core event, however, which occurred in early or mid-May in 1803, at Dunbar Creek on St. Simons Island, Georgia, was historically real. Having survived in the folk memory of the descendant black communities, then standardized as a "colorful local legend" in the mid-twentieth century and later appropriated as a regional Lowcountry myth, the subject was transformed from the possessive to the plural, that is, from "Ebo's Landing" (the possessive) to "Ibos Landing" (the plural).

As a folk phenomenon the story of Ibos Landing survives in local oral traditions and thus continues to evolve in the retelling, though the essential meaning remains the same. For example, a recent narration by a descendant of St. Simons slaves, who was born in 1924 and has lived in the area all her life, maintains the essential truth of the historical event by Christianizing it:

> When they brought the slaves over, they landed at Dunbar Creek on St. Simons Island. All the black people chained themselves together. They were singing the song about, "Before I be a slave, I'll be buried in my grave. Go home to my Lord and be at rest." Every time I go down to St. Clair subdivision, I think about [how] those slaves chained themselves together, and all of them drowned. That's right. Right there in Dunbar Creek. There's not a day I go onto St. Simons I don't think about how they did them people, did us. It's a very sacred place.[46]

The third, and final, example is the covert or coded or signified testimony of the slaves themselves, through their trickster (animal) tales. Though the most famous character in the American corpus is Brother (Bruh) Rabbit, perhaps the most important is Bruh Tarrypin (Terrapin) (that is, Tortoise (*Mbe*)), who directly evokes Igbo Africans in the briar patch of American slavery.[47] The very first Terrapin tale in the most important collection of such stories, that of Joel Chandler Harris of Georgia, published in 1880, is entitled "Mr. Terrapin Appears Upon the Scene."[48] In this story, Bruh Tarrypin actually rescues the slave community in a moment of crisis but then Bruh Rabbit takes all the credit. The actual truth of what happened, however, and the importance of Bruh Tarrypin, remains a mystery. Here is the tale,[49] in the telling:

> One day Bruh Rabbit allowed as he was going to go and see Miss Meadows and de Gals, and set out on de road. Gwine canterin' 'long de road, he was, an' who should he see but old Bruh Tarrypin—de same ole one-en-sixpence.[50] Bruh Rabbit stopped, he did, and rapped on de roof of Bruh Tarrypin's house.
>
> Yes, indeed, Bruh Tarrypin always carry his house with him. Rain or shine, hot or col', strike up with ol' Bruh Tarrypin when you will an' whilst you may, an' where you find 'im, there you'll find his shanty. It's jus' like I tell you.[51]
>
> So Bruh Tarrypin he decides to go on with Bruh Rabbit to see Miss Meadows and de Gals, and do some dancin' his own self too. When they got in, Bruh Tarrypin was so flat-footed that he was too low on de flo', and he weren't high enough in a chair, and so Bruh Rabbit, he pick him up an' put 'im on de shelf [—literally shelving him for the duration of the party]. And they all set to gossiping and especially so about Bruh Fox who always brought them trouble, and Bruh Rabbit, chewin' his cud of tobacco, boasted that he ought to sell Bruh Fox, and Bruh Tarrypin he tease that if he did, well, they ought to sell him somewheres out'n this neighborhood, 'cause he done been here too long now.[52] Why just the other day, says Bruh Tarrypin, Bruh Fox done cursed at me, hailing me on de road and callin' me "Stinkin Jim!"[53]
>
> Bye and bye Bruh Fox he came by and stuck his head in, heard 'em all gossiping against him—trouble indeed!—and he made a wild dash to strike Bruh Rabbit, and every-

one holler and squall, they did, holler and squall and scatter, and Bruh Tarrypin got to scramblin' aroun' up on he shelf there, and off he came, and blip! he tuck Bruh Fox on de back o' de head! This sorta stunned Bruh Fox, and after he gedder his 'membrance [regained consciousness] the most he seen was a pot of greens turned over in the fireplace: Bruh Rabbit was gone, en Bruh Tarrypin was gone, en Miss Meadows an' de Gals was all gone.

So Bruh Fox sorta looked aroun' here and looked aroun' there, an' he didn't see no sign of anyone, didn't see Bruh Tarrypin who croped under the bed, didn't see Miss Meadows an' de Gals who run out in de yard, didn't see Bruh Rabbit up in the chimnee, and the smoke and the ashes goin' up in there too, an' bye and bye Bruh Fox he heard a sneeze—*huckychow!* Aha! says Bruh Fox, there you are, is you, and Well I'm gwine to smoke you out, if it takes a month. You are mine this time, says he. Bruh Rabbit he ain't sayin' nothin'. Ain't you comin' down? says Bruh Fox, says he. Bruh Rabbit ain't sayin' nothin'. Then Bruh Fox, he went after some wood, did he, and when he come back he hear Bruh Rabbit laughin'.

"What you laughin' at, Bruh Rabbit," says Bruh Fox, says he.

"Can't tell ya, Bruh Fox," says Bruh Rabbit, says he.

"Better tell, Bruh Rabbit," says Bruh Fox, says he.

"Tain't nothin' but a box of money somebody done gone and left up here in de chink of de chimnee," says Bruh Rabbit, says he.

"Don't believe ya," says Bruh Fox, says he.

"Look up an' see for yourself," says Bruh Rabbit, says he, and when Bruh Fox look up, Bruh Rabbit spit his eyes full o' that tobacco juice, he did, right in his eyes, an' Bruh Fox, he make a break for de creek, an' Bruh Rabbit he come down out de chimnee and tol' de ladies goodbye.

"How you git 'im off, Bruh Rabbit?" says Miss Meadows, says she.

"Who? me?" says Bruh Rabbit, says he. "Why I just tuck an' tol' 'im that if he didn't go along home and stop playing his pranks on 'spectable people, that I'd take 'im out and thrash 'im," says he. Ol' Bruh Rabbit done forgot all 'bout Bruh Tarrypin an' how he done tuck Bruh Fox on de head, blip!, and knock 'im out.

And what became of Bruh Tarrypin?

Oh, well then, now, chilluns can't 'spec to know all about everything! ['fo' dey git some rest].

CONCLUSION

It is now clear that Igbo, and indeed others from Biafran Africa, were part and parcel of the African diaspora in the Americas. Though we know that they were "there," and sometimes in huge numbers, American scholars still tend to overlook them as major actors in particular diasporic histories. It is as if the slave descendants themselves anticipated this historical purblindness, this social amnesia ("And what became of Bruh Tarrypin?"). Our task today is to tell these tales anew, starting in Igboland.

NOTES

1. *Cornwall Chronicle*, St. George Workhouse (1816), incarcerated Feb. 2, 1816. For further discussion of Bessy, see Douglas B. Chambers, "The Black Atlantic: Theory, Method, and Practice," in *The Atlantic World, 1450–2000*, ed. Toyin Falola and Kevin D. Roberts (Bloomington: Indiana University Press, 2008), 151–52. For a compilation of some 371 Biafran African runaways (including 209 Igbo) from newspaper advertisements in eighteenth-century Jamaica (1718–1795), see also Douglas B. Chambers, ed., *Enslaved Igbo & Ibibio in America: Runaway Slaves and Historical Descriptions* (Enugu, Nigeria: Jemezie Associates, 2013), chap. 2.

2. Douglas B. Chambers, "The Links of a Legacy: Figuring the Slave Trade to Jamaica," in *Caribbean Culture: Soundings on Kamau Brathwaite*, ed. Annie Paul (Kingston, JM: University of the West Indies Press, 2007), 287–312.

3. For Aro warlordism and the collapse of the region's moral economy from slaving, which I would suggest was not limited to the nineteenth century, see G. Ugo Nwokeji, *The Slave Trade and Culture in the Bight of Biafra: An African Society in the Atlantic World* (Cambridge: Cambridge University Press, 2010).

4. The starting point for modern evidence on the volume of the trade is Philip Curtin, *The Atlantic Slave Trade: A Census* (Madison: University of Wisconsin Press, 1969). However, it has been superseded, especially for the better documented British and French trades as well as for the Cuban and Brazilian trades, by David Eltis, Stephen D. Behrendt, David Richardson, and Herbert S. Klein, eds., *The Trans-Atlantic Slave Trade: A Database on CD-ROM* (Cambridge: Cambridge University Press, 1999) [hereafter *TAST* (1999)]; and Eltis et al., eds., *The Transatlantic Slave Trade Voyages Database* (2010), available online at http://www.slavevoyages.org.

5. In order of numbers: British: Jamaica, Dominica, Barbados, Grenada, St. Kitts, Virginia, Antigua, St. Vincent, Guianas, Virgin Islands, Carolinas, Trinidad, Nevis, Tobago, Bahamas, Maryland; French: St. Domingue [Haiti], Martinique, Guadeloupe, St. Lucia, Montserrat; Spanish: Cuba, Rio de la Plata, Puerto Rico, Spanish Main; Brazilian: Southeast Brazil, Bahia, Northeast Brazil, Pernambuco; Dutch: Dutch Caribbean (Suriname, Curacao). Biafrans were also taken as slaves to other parts of Atlantic Africa including Sierra Leone, Gold Coast, and Senegambia. See *TAST* (1999), Query: Full time period and Where slaves embarked: Bight of Biafra.

6. The most comprehensive slave trade database contains records on 2,944 voyages from the Bight of Biafra, on which 941,463 captives were transported, with 760,242 surviving the Middle Passage. In this large sample, some 218,007 are recorded as landing in Jamaica, followed by 57,353 in Dominica, 51,982 in Barbados, 38,254 in Grenada, and 35,923 in St. Kitts; *TAST* (1999), Query: Full time period and Where slaves embarked: Bight of Biafra.

7. Douglas B. Chambers, "The Transatlantic Slave Trade to Virginia in Comparative Historical Perspective, 1698–1778," in *Afro-Virginian History and Culture*, ed. John Saillant (1999), 3–28; Douglas B. Chambers, *Murder at Montpelier: Igbo Africans in Virginia* (Jackson: University Press of Mississippi, 2005).

8. For Louisiana, a database of slaves (mostly from wills and inventories, and local sales) contains records for some 8,910 Africans with a specific ethnicity noted, including 517 Igbo, 144 Calabar, and 83 Ibibio/Moko. Gwendolyn Midlo Hall, *Afro-Louisiana History and Genealogy, 1719–1820* [CD-ROM] (Baton Rouge: Louisiana State University Press, 2000), available online at http://www.ibiblio.org/laslave.

9. Harold Courlander, *The Drum and the Hoe: Life and Lore of the Haitian People* (Berkeley: University of California Press, 1960), 328, and see also pp. 48, 84–87.

10. Courlander, *The Drum and the Hoe*, 84–85.

11. Courlander, *The Drum and the Hoe*, 86–87, emphasis in the original.

12. See for example, François Thesée, *Les Ibos De L'Amelie: Destinée d'une Cargaison de Traite Clandestine á la Martinique (1822–1838)* (Paris: Editions Caribeénnes, 1986), based largely on the 1822 voyage of the slave ship *l'Amelie*, and the list of 214 Igbo slaves by their "African names" (noms africains), pp. 137–38. For the voyage of the *l'Amélie* (1822), see *TAST* (1999), ID#34281, the *Amélie*, Capt. André-Joseph Anglade, departed Martinique July 21, 1821, via Bonny where 245 slaves were purchased, losing 18 to death during the Middle Passage, and arrived at Martinique with 227 slaves on February 6, 1822.

13. The best study of Abakuá is Ivor L. Miller, *Voice of the Leopard: African Secret Societies and Cuba* (Jackson: University Press of Mississippi, 2009). For a study of the "cabildos de nación" that nurtured early Abakuá in Cuba, see Philip A. Howard, *Changing History: Afro-Cuban Cabildos and Societies of Color in the Nineteenth Century* (Baton Rouge: Louisiana State University Press, 1998). The starting point for understanding Abakuá, as for all else in Afro-Cuban cultural history, is the work of Fernando Ortiz, especially *Hampa afro-cubana: Los negros esclavos; Estudio sociológico y de derecho público* (La Habana, Cuba: Revista Bimestre Cubana, 1916); *Los Bailes y El Teatro De Los Negros En*

El Folklore De Cuba, 2nd ed. (1951; La Habana, Cuba: Editorial Letras Cubanas, 1981); *Los Instrumentos de la Musica Afrocubana*. Vol. V, *Los pulsativos, los fricativos, los insuflativos, y los aeritivos* (Habana, Cuba: Cardenas y Cia, 1955). See also the following by Lydia Cabrera, *La Sociedad Secreta Abakuá: Narrada Por Viejos Adeptos*, rev. ed. (Miami, FL: Collección del Chicherekú, 1970); *Anaforuana: Ritual y símbolos de la iniciación en la sociedad secreta Abakuá* (Madrid, Spain: Ediciones R., 1975). Also useful is Robert Farris Thompson, *Flash of the Spirit: African and Afro-American Art and Philosophy* (New York: Vintage Books, 1983), chap. 5.

14. The *TAST* (1999) documents 435 voyages to Virginia, which carried nearly 102,000 African slaves of whom nearly 63,000 have a known coastal African provenance; these include 28,159 from the Bight of Biafra (or 45 percent of those with known regional origins), who were more than twice as numerous as the next largest group (Senegambians, with 11,294 documented).

15. Patricia M. Samford, *Subfloor Pits and the Archaeology of Slavery in Colonial Virginia* (Tuscaloosa: University of Alabama Press, 2007).

16. See for example, Lorena S. Walsh, *From Calabar to Carter's Grove: The History of a Virginia Slave Community* (Charlottesville: University Press of Virginia, 1997); Michael A. Gomez, *Exchanging Our Country Marks: The Transformation of African Identities in the Colonial and Antebellum South* (Chapel Hill: University of North Carolina, 1998), chap. 6; Douglas B. Chambers, "Tracing Igbo into the African Diaspora," in *Identifying Enslaved Africans: The "Nigerian" Hinterland and the African Diaspora*, ed. Paul Lovejoy (London: Continuum, 2000), 55–71; Hall, *Databases for the Study of Afro-Louisiana History and Genealogy* (2000); Lorena S. Walsh, "The Chesapeake Slave Trade: Regional Patterns, African Origins, and Some Implications," *William and Mary Quarterly* 58, no. 1 (2001): 139–70; Chambers, *Murder at Montpelier*, 159–87; Gwendolyn Midlo Hall, *Slavery and African Ethnicities in the Americas: Restoring the Links* (Chapel Hill: University of North Carolina Press, 2005), chap. 6; Jennifer Hildebrand, "'Dere Were No Place in Heaven for Him, An' He Were Not Desired in Hell': Igbo Cultural Beliefs in African American Folk Expressions," *Journal of African American History* 91, no. 2 (2006): 127–52; Douglas B. Chambers, "Igbo Women in the Early Modern Atlantic World: The Burden of Beauty," in *Olaudah Equiano and the Igbo World: History, Society, and Atlantic Diaspora Connections*, ed. Chima J. Korieh (Trenton, NJ: Africa World Press, 2008), 311–29; J. Akuma-Kalu Njoku, "'There's got to be a tortoise in it': Lore as the Conceptual Focus of Igbo Folklore," *Southern Quarterly* 46, no. 4 (2009): 159–72; Barbara Heath, "Space and Place within Plantation Quarters in Virginia, 1700–1825," in *Cabin, Quarter, Plantation: Architecture and Landscapes of North American Slavery*, ed. Clifton Ellis and Rebecca Ginsburg (New Haven, CT: Yale University Press, 2010), 156–76; Michael Gomez, "The Anguished Igbo Response to Enslavement in the Americas," in *Repercussions of the Atlantic Slave Trade: The Interior of the Bight of Biafra and the African Diaspora*, ed. Carolyn A. Brown and Paul E. Lovejoy (Trenton, NJ: Africa World Press, 2011), 103–18; Chambers, *Enslaved Igbo & Ibibio in America*, 12–14.

17. Compare the modernist African-American poet Countee Cullen (1903–1946) and his iconic poem "Heritage" (1925) with its ambivalence toward Africa and Africans, as in this excerpt (emphasis in the original):

> What is Africa to me:
> Copper sun or scarlet sea,
> Jungle star or jungle track,
> Strong bronzed men, or regal black
> Women from whose loins I sprang
> When the birds of Eden sang? . . .
>
> Africa? A book one thumbs
> Listlessly, till slumber comes. . . .
>
> *Not yet has my heart or head*
> *In the least way realized*
> *They and I are civilized.*

18. See E. C. Ejiogu, "Igbo Farm Village (IFV) at the Frontier Culture Museum of Virginia (USA). A Site of Memory for the Modern Igbo Diaspora" (paper presented at the 11th Annual Igbo Studies Association, June 27–29, 2013, Modotel, Enugu, Nigeria). The FCMV (founded in 1986) is an official state museum located in Staunton, Virginia, in the central Shenandoah

Valley. Currently the museum consists of eight historically authentic "living-history" farms to interpret early Virginia history, including the one African farmstead, with a ninth (Native American encampment) under planning; the official title is "1700s West African Farm," which opened in 2010.

19. The Thomas family, whose American paternal ancestry begins with Benjamin Thomas (b. 1810), whose enslaved mother and father were both Africans "from Nigeria" taken to one of the sea islands south of Savannah, Georgia, in mid-May 1803. See http://thomasfamilyhistory.com (accessed February 7, 2011). Note the chronological parallel with the historical events that resulted in Ibos Landing (St. Simons Island).

20. For a biographical study of one such enslaved Igbo, Aneaso (c. 1790–1864), who in Jamaica was known as Archibald Monteath, see Maureen Warner-Lewis, *Archibald Monteath: Igbo, Jamaican, Moravian* (Kingston, JM: University of the West Indies, 2007). See also Angelo Costanzo, "The Narrative of Archibald Monteith, a Jamaican Slave," *Callaloo* 13, no. 1 (1990): 115–30.

21. See Douglas B. Chambers, "Biafran African Runaways in 18th-Century Jamaica and Saint-Domingue: Evidence for an African Ecumene," Igbo Studies Review, no. 2 (2014): 1–20.

22. For citations, see Chambers, "Biafran African Runaways," 11–12.

23. Quotation from William Balfour Baikie, *Narrative of an Exploring Voyage up the rivers Kwora and Binue, Commonly known as the Niger and Tsadda, in 1854* (London: John Murray, 1856; repr., London: Frank Cass, 1966), 310. See A. E. Afigbo, *Ropes of Sand: Studies in Igbo History and Culture* (Ibadan, Nigeria: Ibadan University Press, 1981), 151–52; M. Angulu Onwuejeogwu, *An Igbo Civilization: Nri Kingdom & Hegemony* (London: Ethnographica, 1981), 11, 14–15; Chambers, *Murder at Montpelier*, 31–32.

24. In the following discussion, special thanks to Prince Paschal Mebuge-Obaa II for his invaluable research assistance. Ichie Anago Okoye (1912–2002), Onwanetilora of Nri & Isinze of Obeagu, initiated into Ozo in 1944: interview by Mebuge-Obaa, Nri, April 2002. *Ichi* was discontinued at Nri in the 1940s, and by 2003 there were only three surviving *mgburichi* at Nri (two in Agukwu and one in Akampkisi). See Prince P. N. Mebuge-Obaa II, "An Oral History Research Project: History of Scarification (Tattoo) in Nri" (TS., May 1, 2002).

25. Ichie Okoye Mmefu, interview by author, Nri, December 2003, Chambers Field Notes (II). Technically, Ichie Mmefu is "ichi Nwadiokpala" (Ntuche), having lines of marks on the forehead and corners of each eye, which historically was a lesser form of ichi, though he is Mgburichi. In his account, the Azunri cut "extended down the cheek and down the neck" whereas his Mgburichi one fanned out around the eyes (like extensive and deep laugh marks) and included horizontal lines across the forehead (but not a classic massive weal).

26. Ichie Anago Okoye, interview by author, April 2002, in Mebuge-Obaa II, "An Oral History Research Project."

27. Nkwonto Nwuduaku (b. c. 1914) oral history, Enugwu-Ukwu, in *Igbo Worlds: An Anthology of Oral Histories and Historical Descriptions*, ed. Elizabeth Isichei (London: Macmillan Education, 1977), 30–34, quotation p. 34.

28. For *agawhu* (bandit, outlaw, crook, hero) and the collapse of the region's moral economy from slaving, which I would suggest was not limited to the nineteenth century, see Nwokeji, *Slave Trade and Culture in the Bight of Biafra*, 192–94.

29. *Eze Nri* Nri Añua is not included in official king-lists and therefore has been officially forgotten but is memorialized by the Añua minimal lineage within UmuNri major lineage of Obeagu by maintaining an "Eze Nri Añua Royal Band" (sponsored by Mr. "Acrobatic" Onuigbo) (interviews by author, Nri, March 2005, Chambers Field Notes (III)). The family tradition of *Eze Nri* Nri Añua was related to me by his great-grandson (b. 1946) in March 2005. Compare the accounts in Onwuejeogwu, *An Igbo Civilization* (1981), esp. pp. 26–28. Ijoma was the fifth son of Ikelionwu (fl. 1750), the founder of Ndikelionwu (the central settlement of the seven confederated Aro colonies in the Awka area, known as Ndieni), an *mgburichi* in the Nri-Awka region, who was enslaved by the Aro merchant-warlord, Ufere Mgbokwu Aka, as early as the 1730s; Kenneth Onwuka Dike and Felicia Ekejiuba, *The Aro of South-eastern Nigeria, 1650–1980: A Study of Socio-economic Formation and Transformation in*

Nigeria (Ibadan: Ibadan University Press, 1990), 176–81; Nwokeji, *Slave Trade and Culture in the Bight of Biafra*, 20n32, 58, 66, 106, 190–91.

30. The oldest official age-grade is Oli Okuku (1846–1854): *Tradition and Modernisation in Nri*, vol. II (pamphlet, Eze Nri Enweleana II, n.d., c. 1989), 9. Interviews in 2003 with eleven respondents aged sixty-seven to ninety-nine years old in Obeagu village of Nri, however, yielded the names of nine age-grades that predate Oli Okuku, the earliest of which was Ochogu: Prince P. N. Mebuge-Obaa II, "Age Grade/Group (Oral History Project Report)" (TS., December 7, 2003).

31. For classic summaries of these stereotypes in the secondary literature, see Ulrich Bonnell Phillips, *American Negro Slavery: A Survey of the Supply, Employment and Control of Negro Slavery* (1918; repr., Baton Rouge: Louisiana State University Press, 1966), 43–44; Darold D. Wax, "Preferences for Slaves in Colonial America," *Journal of Negro History*, 54, no. 4 (1973), 391–98; Daniel C. Littlefield, *Rice and Slaves: Ethnicity and the Slave Trade in Colonial South Carolina* (Baton Rouge: Louisiana State University Press, 1981), 10, 72, 127, 150–51; Michael Mullin, *Africa in America: Slave Acculturation and Resistance in the American South and the British Caribbean, 1736–1831* (Urbana: University of Illinois Press, 1992), 27; Gomez, *Exchanging Our Country Marks*, 116–17. For primary source texts, see Chambers, *Enslaved Igbo & Ibibio in America*, chaps. 5 and 6.

32. First quotation (emphasis in the original), Hermann Koler (1840), quoted in Isichei, *Igbo Worlds* (1977), 15; second quotation, James Barclay, *The Voyages and Travels of James Barclay, Containing Many Surprising Adventures and Interesting Narratives* (Dublin, IE: n.p., 1777), 26.

33. The basic contemporary source for Vesey's conspiracy is James Hamilton, *Negro Plot: An Account of the Late Intended Insurrection among a Portion of the Blacks of the City of Charleston, South Carolina* (Boston, MA: Joseph W. Ingraham, 1822), available at http://docsouth.unc.edu/church/hamilton/hamilton.html. For a recent popular study, see David Robertson, *Denmark Vesey* (New York: Knopf, 1999). For the Igbo role in Vesey's conspiracy, see Walter C. Rucker, *The River Flows On: Black Resistance, Culture, and Identity Formation in Early America* (Baton Rouge: Louisiana State University Press, 2006), chap. 5.

34. For primary source texts on this Eboe conspiracy, see Chambers, *Enslaved Igbo & Ibibio in America*, chap. 6.

35. Matthew Lewis, *Journal of a West India Proprietor, Kept during a Residence in the Island of Jamaica*, ed. with an introduction and Notes by Judith Terry (1834; Oxford: Oxford University Press, 1999), 137–44; the four quotations are from, respectively, pp. 139, 143, 144.

36. Afro-Caribbean *obeah* was the diasporic derivation of ancestral Igbo *ôbia*, practitioners of which are called *dibia* (obia-experts).

37. For primary source texts on Ibos Landing, see Chambers, *Enslaved Igbo & Ibibio in America*, chap. 7, below. Ibos Landing is one of the few public sites in the US South that calls out particular historical African groups in American history. Another example is "Congo Square" in New Orleans, Louisiana. On the latter, see Jerah Johnson, *Congo Square in New Orleans* (New Orleans: Louisiana Landmarks Society, 1995); Freddi Williams Evans, *Congo Square: African Roots in New Orleans* (Lafayette: University of Louisiana Press, 2011). Currently I am completing a historical study of Ibos Landing as a "site of memory": *Ibos Landing: History, Myth, and Memory* (forthcoming in 2017).

38. The racist vernacular, of course, is in the original; Tate, *The Fathers* (New York: G. P. Putnam's Sons, 1938), 53–54. Tate (1899–1979) was a major poet and essayist in mid-twentieth-century US southern literature, and a member of the apologist "Fugitives" literary movement, including as a contributor to their iconic volume of essays; John Crowe Ransom, ed., *I'll Take My Stand: The South and the Agrarian Tradition by Twelve Southerners* (New York: Harper, 1930). *The Fathers* was Tate's only published novel. For a general discussion of the American literary tradition of southern "plantation novels" such as Tate's, see Donald R. Noble Jr., Introduction to *The Valley of Shenandoah: Or, Memoirs of the Graysons*, ed. George Tucker (Chapel Hill: University of North Carolina Press, 1970), xx–xxxi.

39. The earliest known reference is in a letter dated March 5, 1857; see *Anna: The Letters of a*

St. Simons Island Plantation Mistress, 1817–1859, ed. Anna Matilda Page King and Melanie Pavich-Lindsay (Athens: University of Georgia Press, 2002), 326–27.

40. Margaret Davis Cate, *Our Todays and Yesterdays: A Story of Brunswick and the Coastal Islands* (Brunswick, GA: Glover Bros., 1926), 62–63. She did not include the site on her map of St. Simons in the book.

41. Georgia Writers' Project, Work Projects Administration (WPA), *Drums and Shadows: Survival Studies Among the Georgia Coastal Negroes* (1940; repr. Athens: University of Georgia Press, 1986), 184–85. Earlier the WPA writers had interviewed Wallace Quarterman (1844–1938), of Darien, and when they asked him had he known any Africans, he replied, "Sho I membuhs lots ub um." When they asked if he was referring to "the Ibos on St. Simons who walked into the water," Quarterman said, "No, ma'am, I ain mean dem," and then proceeded to tell a story about how African slaves "tun hesef intuh buzzuds an fly right back tuh Africa," pp. 150–51. The editors, however, inserted a note in reference to Ibos: "*A group of slaves from the Ibo tribe refused to submit to slavery. Led by their chief and singing tribal songs, they walked into the water and were drowned at a point on Dunbar Creek later named Ebo (Ibo) Landing*" (emphasis in original), p. 150. Floyd White, of St. Simons Island, informed the WPA interviewers that "Uncle Quawt" (Quarterman) was a conjure-man/root-doctor, which they did not know (Quarterman had not told them himself), p. 184.

42. WPA, *Drums and Shadows*, 185.

43. The key to understanding "suicide" by enslaved Igbo is in the significance of reincarnation and the transmigration of souls in pre-Christian Igbo religion.

44. Subsequent iterations (1946, 1955, and 1956) elaborated on this basic scenario and included "Ebo Landing" on maps, while adding narrative details and statements about how local blacks avoided fishing in that spot and that the place was haunted. See WPA, *Georgia: A Guide to Its Towns and Countryside* (Athens: University of Georgia Press, 1946), 295, 298; Orrin Sage Wightman and Margaret Davis Cate, *Early Days of Coastal Georgia* (St. Simons Island, GA: Fort Frederica Association, 1955), frontispiece, p. 67; Burnette Vanstory, *Georgia's Land of the Golden Isles* (Athens: University of Georgia Press, 1956), 152.

45. See Gomez, *Exchanging Our Country Marks* (1998), 118–19; and especially Timothy Powell, "Summoning the Ancestors: The Flying Africans' Story and Its Enduring Legacy," in *African American Life in the Georgia Lowcountry: The Atlantic World and the Gullah Geechee*, ed. Philip Morgan (Athens: University of Georgia Press, 2010), 253–80. These interpretive errors are, unfortunately compounded by the literary scholar Abena P. A. Busia, "'Those Ibos! Jus' Upped and Walked Away': Story of the Slaves at Ibo Landing," 329–40.

46. The reference is to the American "Negro" spiritual called "Oh Freedom." Sadie Marie Jackson Ryals (b. 1924 in Darien, Georgia) was descended from slaves owned by Pierce Butler, the largest slaveholder on St. Simons Island, who in 1793 had 441 slaves on his main plantation, "Hampton," and hundreds of others on his other plantations; Stephen Doster, ed., *Voices from St. Simons: Personal Narratives of an Island's Past* (Winston-Salem, NC: John F. Blair, 2008), 2–15, quotation p. 6. For Butler, see Malcolm Bell Jr., *Major Butler's Legacy: Five Generations of a Slaveholding Family* (Athens: University of Georgia Press, 1987).

47. See, for example, Njoku, "'There's got to be a tortoise in it,'" 159–72.

48. Joel Chandler Harris, *Uncle Remus: His Songs and His Sayings* (New York: D. Appleton and Co., 1880), repr. in *The Complete Tales of Uncle Remus*, comp. Richard Chase (Boston: Houghton Mifflin, 1955), 32–36.

49. I have adapted this excerpt from the antiquated "Negro dialect" of the original into southern-inflected standard English.

50. This reference to colonial English money (a shilling and a half) rhetorically situates the story in the eighteenth century. "Tarrypin" (Terrapin) was a large turtle; the diasporic analog of Tortoise (*Mbe*), the Igbo trickster figure.

51. Not only does this passage show the wordplay characteristic of these stories, it is a rhetorical statement of the authenticity of these

stories, these accounts, about the self-contained Tarrypin/Tortoise.

52. This signifies that the events of this story occurred in the era of slavery as well as another form of satire, as Fox signifies the slave master.

53. Following alliteration, pronounced "Steenkin Jeem"; an interesting wordplay, as *ji'm* [Jee'm] means "My yam" in Igbo. In a pidginized *Englibo*, this phrase could mean "My Stinking Yam."

PART III

CULTURAL CROSSCURRENTS

Dimensions of the Igbo Experience
in the Atlantic World

13 THE IGBO DIASPORA IN THE ATLANTIC WORLD

AFRICAN ORIGINS AND NEW WORLD FORMATIONS

Chima J. Korieh

> It is beyond credulity that the Igbo, a group with such profound impact upon African American society, has received so little recognition in the scholarly literature on North American slavery. In numerable studies on the continuity of African culture in the New World, much is made of the contributions of the Yoruba, the Akan, the Fon and the Ewe, the Bakongo, and so on. Although richly deserved, the attention afforded these groups has tended to minimize the signal contribution of the Igbo, who for reasons better explored elsewhere, have not enjoyed similar prominence and popularity.
>
> —MICHAEL GOMEZ, *EXCHANGING OUR COUNTRY MARKS*, 114

Malcom Laing in a letter to William Philip Perrin on January 10, 1773, wrote: "the new negroes that have been imported lately are what we call Windward Negros . . . the worst kind . . . to buy such negros for sugar works is throwing away money . . . will try to buy Gold Coast men and Ibo women."[1] Like Laing, planters had a fairly good idea of the ethnic origins of enslaved Africans and their reputation as good or bad slaves. The reputation of the Igbo of the Bight of Biafra hinterland as bad slaves was legendry and repeated in several accounts. Indeed certain planters, according to Michael Gomez were "particularly loath to accept captives from the bight, associated as they were with tendencies inimical to the enterprise of slavery."[2] This chapter explains Igbo identity in the Atlantic diaspora in terms of their old world cultures and identity, while sorting through many misconceptions and stereotypes associated with them, and explores Igbo influences on the Americas. The chapter emphasizes the fruitfulness of understanding what Paul Lovejoy and David Trotman have identified as the "interconnectedness of the histories of Africa and the colonial sites where Africans and their descendants lived on the other side of the Atlantic."[3]

The Igbo region of the Bight of Biafra hinterland is rightfully considered to be a major contributor to the enslaved African populations during the era of the Atlantic slave trade.[4] During the four centuries of the slave trade, it has been estimated that the Bight of Biafra exported one for every seven Africans shipped to the Americas.[5] The data from the Eltis et al. *The Trans-Atlantic Slave Trade* database shows that an estimated 11.9 percent of the total number exported between 1601 and 1800 came from the Bight of Biafra.[6] Douglas Chambers suggests that of the 11.6 million people estimated to have been shipped to the New World between 1470 and 1860, some 1.7 million were transported from the Bight of Biafra.[7] According to Chambers, "of the estimated 1.7 million enslaved people taken from the Bight of Biafra into the transatlantic diaspora, some three-quarters or about 1.3 million were Igbo."[8] Ugo Nwokeji suggests that between 1551 and 1850 about 13 percent of slaves in the trans-Atlantic slave trade came from the Bight of Biafra regions of West Africa.[9]

TABLE 13.1 The trans-Atlantic slave trade

Region	Number	Percentage of total	Percentage (less unspecified)
Africa unspecified	2,281,660	28.70	—
West Central Africa	20,645,00	26.00	36.50
Bight of Biafra	941,463	11.90	16.60
Gold Coast	617,674	7.78	10.90
Southeast Africa	291,060	3.66	5.14
Senegambia	24,350	3.07	4.30
Sierra Leone	208,316	2.62	3.68
Windward Coast	16,529	2.03	2.85

Source: Eltis et al., *The Trans-Atlantic Slave Trade.*

Very high proportions of the people shipped from the Bight of Biafra were Igbo-speaking and reached the Americas in British ships.[10] Consequently, a vast majority of enslaved Africans from the Bight of Biafra disembarked in British Caribbean and North American mainland, thus accounting for perhaps a third of all slave arrivals in these colonies between 1700 and 1807.[11]

Indeed, questions have been raised about the ethnic identity of enslaved Africans from the Bight. For example, G. W. Koelle's *Polyglota Africana*, published in 1857, asserted that Igbo received in Sierra Leone had never heard of the name Igbo until they were sent away. Olaudah Equiano is often given as an example of the absence of an Igbo nation or an Igbo identity until recent times—for Equiano's "Igboness" only emerged during the Middle Passage and in the diaspora.[12] That was not unusual. Even in contemporary terms, notions of identity and territory are ongoing processes in every society. For many Africans in the pre-European contact era, the most important mark of identity was perhaps language, and Equiano, like many other slaves in the Middle Passage, was importantly quick to recognize it. Cultural life, economics, and social practices were equally more important markers of identity than territory. Indeed, Equiano's use of the term "our people" in describing the economic and social life of his village in the eighteenth century spoke beyond his immediate environment. "Our people" was recognition of a group of people who had certain things in common and embraced certain worldviews, even if his knowledge of a pan-Igbo ethnic or cultural group was limited.

Even though the point at which Igbo consciousness and identification with the Igbo nation began cannot be pinned down easily, an early European visitor to the Bight of Biafra, John Grazilhier, writing in 1699 on Kalabari/Igbo relations, noted about the people living north of Kalabari called "the Hackbous [Igbo] Blacks. . . . In their territories there are two market-days every week, for slaves and provisions, which Calabar Blacks keep very regularly, to supply themselves both with provisions and slaves, palm-oil, palm-wine, etc. there being great plenty of the last."[13] William Baikie made reference to the Igbo in the 1850s. Both Grazilhier and Baikie's references to the Igbo were not generic but were in terms of a particular ethnic group in the Biafra hinterland. According to Baikie, "In I'gbo each person hails . . . from the particular district where he was born, but when away from home all are I'gbos."[14] Enslaved Africans from the Bight of Biafra hinterland shared common languages and other cultural traits that would come to mark them as distinct in the New World.

The impact of Africans in the making of the early history and cultures of the New World has been a matter of academic debate since the late 1930s. Some scholars have minimized the influence of Africans in the making of the new societies in the Americas. Sociologist Franklin Frazier argues that the African background of enslaved Africans could not have influenced the United States in any meaningful way. In his view, the isolated nature of the plantation system meant that significant numbers of Africans from the same African background did not have opportunities to interact with one another. Thus, their African memories did not always find "a congenial milieu in which to perpetuate the old way of life."[15] He later extended this argument, stating that "because of the manner in which the Negroes were captured in Africa and enslaved, they were practically stripped of their social heritage."[16] Similarly, Sidney Mintz and Richard Price stressed the numerous differences that emerged describing slaves on the Middle Passage as a "crowd of disparate cultures rather than a grouping in any cultural sense."[17] The key elements in African-American culture according to this school of thought were forged in the New World and contained components that were not originally African. Indeed, John Thornton maintains that the cultural disorganization of slave society made slaves much more dependent upon the culture of the Europeans or Euro-American rather than the transmission of their African heritage.[18] For this group of scholars, enslaved Africans arrived in the New World without a common identifiable ethnicity or clearly defined identity reflecting the many differences among the cultures of the Atlantic coast of Africa. Thus the African identities that emerged in the New World evolved out of their experience of slavery.

The publication of Melville Herskovits's *The Myth of the Negro Past* in 1941 brought significant impetus to the debate. Herskovits argues that it is possible to identify many broad similarities among the disparate cultures of Atlantic Africa. Since enslaved Africans did not arrive in the New World as *tabular rasa*, they were able to transmit African cultures sufficiently to influence Afro-Atlantic culture.[19] As Herbert Klein argues, although the slaves who arrived in the Americas "spoke a multitude of different languages, and had a few if any common ties," their color and status, "soon bound them together, so they were able slowly to create a community and culture in the New World."[20] Philip Morgan concurred, emphasizing that the "diverse and heterogeneous" parts of the Atlantic world "became one—a unitary whole, a single system."[21]

One must agree with Peter Manuel that diasporic identities are "inherently unstable and complex entities"[22] yet are regionally and ethnically informed approaches in which African backgrounds are compared, analyzed, and contrasted with New World identities. This suggest that African cultures survived in identifiable patterns that mirror their African origins.[23] And although the experiences of enslaved Africans bonded them together, their differing African backgrounds elicited different responses to slavery, the emerging identities in the Americas, and the perception of American slavers to different African groups. It is important, therefore, to move beyond the homogenized and at times anachronistic characterization of Africans in the Atlantic world to consider specific regional, cultural, and historical experiences of the enslaved African brought to the Americas. That is, what do we know of their African background in relation to their identity as redefined in the Atlantic world? According to Paul Lovejoy, "sufficient information exists about individuals [and groups] taken as captives in the slave trade to allow historians to dispense with a generalized notion of a 'traditional' African background for New World blacks and, accordingly, to articulate the Africanness of the black diaspora with ethnic and historical specificity."[24] Such a regional approach is critical to transcend the narrow conceptualization of African continuities in the New World and help appreciate a much more fluid process of identity and ethnic formation in the Atlantic World focusing on the role of particular individuals/ethnic groups.[25]

New data provides opportunities to map out the system of enslavement and their possible cultural implications for the Americas. The historical geography, according to Chambers shows that the slave trade "was a highly organized and regulated and capital intensive international business in the era of merchant-capitalism and Europeans mercantilism, and therefore was anything but random."[26] Similarly, Gwendolyn Hall illustrates that "Atlantic slave ships did not meander along several African coasts collecting enslaved Africans and bringing them to many different places in the America."[27] Recent data from shipping records support a more harmonized sequence of movements between African coasts and different parts of the Americas.[28] The Eltis et al. *The Trans-Atlantic Slave Trade* database, containing over 27,000 slave voyages and other data, shows that slave ships confirmed their ports of call, the pattern of ship movements, and ports of disembarkation in the New World.[29] For example, the French ship, *The Diligent* obtained its slave cargo from a single port in the Guinea Coast and disembarked in Martinique during its maiden slave voyage of 1731–1732.[30] Records of several other voyages follow similar patterns. The English ship *William* that sailed from London in December 1662 collected its cargo of 154 enslaved Africans from two ports, Rio Num and C. Lopez, and disembarked the 126 slaves except for 1 that survived the journey in Barbados. Another English ship, *Hope*, which sailed in 1663, called only at Calabar, where it began its journey to the Caribbean with 196 slaves. Of the surviving 159 slaves, 138 disembarked in Jamaica while the remaining 21 disembarked in Barbados. The *Blackmore* discharged all but 1 of its 330 slaves in Jamaica in a voyage from Calabar in 1665. *Two Friends*, a Royal African Company slaver discharged all but 1 of 103 slaves from Gambia in Virginia in 1686.[31] Because slave ships operated in a fairly identifiable pattern and picked their cargoes of enslaved Africans in specific regions of Africa meant that they also collected what can be speculated as fairly homogenous ethnic groups. The pattern of disembarkation in the New World followed similar patterns. A significant consequence of the pattern of trade would have been the resettlement of Africans of identifiable "ethnic" and cultural origins in specific regions of the New World.[32] As John Thornton argues, "although the process of enslavement, sale, transfer, shipment, and relocation on a plantation was certainly disruptive to the personal and family lives of those people who endured it, its effect on culture may have been less than many suggest."[33] While the slaves did not arrive into a cultural vacuum, they certainly were not *tabular rasa* on arrival in the New World. The struggle for survival in their new environment undoubtedly required adjustment and radical changes, but slaves, Lovejoy argues, also sought "connections with the past through language, religion, and cultural practices."[34] Thornton supports the notion that language and shared common norms brought people who shared these characteristic together especially where they were together in significant numbers.[35]

According to Kenneth Stampp, "when the slaves left Africa, they carried with them knowledge of their own complex culture. Some elements of their cultures—or at least some adaptations or variations of them—they planted somewhat insecurely in America."[36] These surviving "Africans" were evident in their speech, dances, music, folklore, and religion. In other words, Africans brought a cultural heritage in language, aesthetics, and philosophy that helped to form the cultures of the Atlantic world.[37] The role of individuals of African origins in shaping a much more heterogeneous sociocultural and political life in the New World offers a window into a neglected aspect of these cultural encounters.[38] Overall, the discourse on the influence of enslaved Africans in the formation of New World cultures and new identities has not merely added to our understanding of the genesis of contemporary American cultures but also has added to the rich historical tapestry of African identities both in Africa and across the Atlantic.

The manner in which the "slaves were captured and sold on the slave markets and confined in the slave pens in African ports had a more important effect upon the integrity of their cultural heritage." There and elsewhere, Frazier argues that such experiences and the ordeal of the "Middle Passage," did not entirely destroy their African heritage. They were retained as memories of their homeland, certain patterns of behavior and attitude toward their fellow men, and the physical world.[39] Many scholars are agreed, however, on the notion of what Lovejoy referred to as an Atlantic world that continued to be "fragmented, politically, economically, and culturally throughout the period of slavery."[40] Hence one can argue for continuity as much as adjustment for enslaved Africans in the new environment since the subsequent transfer of African to the New World was not a very randomizing process.

IGBO: AFRICAN BACKGROUND AND NEW WORLD FORMATIONS

The Igbo have been described in historical and anthropological literature as a "stateless" or "segmentary" society consisting of autonomous village groups. The most important feature of their political organization is the perceived lack of a formalized leadership that Victor Uchendu described as "an exercise in direct democracy" and "representative assembly."[41] In Igbo traditional system, most communities were not subjected to the powers of chiefs. As such their representative political structure gave every man and woman an opportunity to participate in public matters and "nobody enjoyed any special privilege because of ancestry."[42] As G. I. Jones notes, "The usual pattern here is for public matters to be discussed at a general meeting at which every able bodied male who is a full member of the community has a right to attend and to speak if he so wishes . . . the community particularly in the I[g]bo area is not prepared to surrender its legislative authority to any chiefs, elders or other traditional office holders."[43] Obafemi Awolowo spoke of the Igbo and Ibibio as people who "cannot tolerate anyone assuming the authority of a chieftain over them."[44]

The Igbo political and social structure is then distinguished by its preservation of individual liberty and assertion of individual rights. This basic premise of Igbo political system was ignored when the British imposed colonial rule in the early years of the twentieth century. Indirect rule had sought to create chiefs and chieftaincy institutions that were alien to the culture of the Igbo. The failure to appreciate the structure of the Igbo political system accounted for the failure of the British indirect rule system during the colonial period. S. Cronje argues in *The World and Nigeria* that indirect ruled failed altogether among the Igbo because "there were no big chiefs, emirates or empires which could be adapted to the needs of British administrators. The Eastern people lived in village groups administered by councils which were presided over by senior men who held office by virtue of their personal ability as much as by age or lineage."[45]

The individualism of the Igbo was shared by Jack Shepherd, senior editor of *Look*, who said of the Igbo during the Biafra war: "Ibo aggressiveness and ambition in commerce, public utilities, and the civil service made them a hated people." They were called the "Jews of Black Africa."[46] Describing the different qualities and identities of the major ethnic groups in Nigeria during the civil war, *Time* characterized the Igbo as

> Ambitious and clever . . . Within their tribal culture lay unique seeds for Western-style self-improvement. Unlike many other tribes, they had no autocratic village chiefs. Instead, they were ruled by open councils of what sociologists called high achievers . . . successful yam farmers, warriors, public speakers. The titles a man earned were buried with him and his sons were forced unlike most Africans to make their own reputations.[47]

Edward C. Schwarzenbach, writing in the *Swiss Review of World Affairs*, portrayed the Igbo society as an egalitarian society "free of hierarchical structures."[48] Michael Mok quoting a Reverend Father in Biafra during the Nigeria-Biafra war notes, "The Igbo man never begs. He is much too proud. He wants to pay for what he gets."[49] Their individuality and resourcefulness when compared with other ethnic groups in Southern Nigeria was praised by Major Darwin et al. in their 1913 study of the region.[50]

Similarly, Igbo egalitarian gender ideology was praised by early European writers and administrators in the region. Emphasizing the pragmatic social structure of the Igbo, Frederick Lugard, first colonial governor of Nigeria, described Igbo women as "ambitious, self-reliant, hardworking, and independent [and claims] full equality with the opposite sex and would seem indeed to be the dominant partner."[51]

Yet, the absence of a formalized political structure did not mean the absence of traditional intellectuals or stable political institutions and culture.[52] Traditional intellectuals derived their power and authority through an elaborate status-conferring mechanism—age, lineage headships, powerful titled and secret societies, and possession of certain spiritual powers. Others are based on individually achieved status and purchasing power.[53] Thus, traditional intellectuals included the native doctors, the *ọzọ* and other titleholders, oracular priests and priestesses, ritualists, diviners, custodians of sacred shrines, men and women elders, griots, women leaders, and fortunetellers and interpreters of dreams, who had the knowledge and power to read and interpret sociopolitical and economic phenomenon and to advance practical or spiritual solutions to perceived notions of wrongs affecting their society. The African background and sociopolitical structures of the Igbo would come to play very important roles in their responses to slavery and the imprint they left on the Americas.

STEREOTYPES AS MARKERS OF IGBO IDENTITY

The contributions and impacts of specific groups of African origin to the transformation of New World societies have received significant attention in recent times. Toyin Falola and Matt Childs, in *The Yoruba Diaspora in the Atlantic World*, reveal the usefulness of the ethnically focused perspective. *The African Diaspora: Origins and New World Identities*, edited by Isidore Okpewho, Carole Boyce Davies, and Ali A. Mazrui, revisits the classic debate in Afro-American studies concerning the relative importance of African origins versus and New World formations in the making of black society and culture in the Atlantic diaspora.[54] Yet, far less explored are the connections between the people the Bight of Biafra and the emergence of the cultural patterns of the New World despite the proportionally high number of enslaved African from the region. When compared with the cultural continuities and ethnic identities of other African groups, the Igbo have received relatively little attention.[55] Why is the Igbo case a neglected area in diaspora studies, considering the sheer size of Igbo contingent to the New World? Did the Igbo assimilate into their new environment more than other ethnic groups? Answers to these questions are difficult to provide because they involve the interrogation of the whole issue of a pan-Igbo identity and to what extent this identity was created outside Igboland.

It is evident that many myths and stereotypes were associated with people from the Bight of Biafra in general and the Igbo in particular. Although the Igbo contribution to British trade in slaves was disproportionately high, Gomez and others have shown that planters were reluctant to accept slaves of Igbo origin.[56] The attitudes of American slavers toward Igbo slaves have helped define their identity in the Americas. Gwendolyn Midlo Hall agrees that "it is a truism in the historical literature that Igbo, especially Igbo males, were not at all appreciated in the America, mainly because of their propensity to run away and/or commit suicide."[57] South Carolina planters "expressed an abiding preference for Senegambia and Gold Coast captives but were 'disdainful' of the Igbo/Biafra and 'short people' in general."[58] Daniel Littlefield explains that Africans who were "small, slender, weak and tended towards a yellowish colour, were less desirable. Calabar people or Ibo [*sic*] slaves, with whatever justice, seemed to epitomize these qualities."[59]

Slaves of Igbo origin were loathed in North America primarily for what Gomez and others have identified as the frequency by which they committed suicide. The myth about Igbo suicidal tendencies proved remarkably resilient—and the identity of Igbos as troublemakers crystallized on a wider scale and were inspired by racist stereotypes, even among slaves. Like other slaves, the Igbo employed old strategies, including revolts and escape, but they also devised new strategies in their struggle, including suicide. But how did a practice of suicide so despised in Igboland become very much associated with them in the diaspora? The Igbo abhorred suicide in their traditional society. Victims were not given normal burial but were thrown into the "evil forest." Special rituals are often performed by the priest of *Amadiọha* (the god of thunder) before victims of suicidal death were buried.

To explain their propensity for suicide as groups and as individuals, one has also to understand the cosmology of the Igbo and their attachment to the land of their birth. The Igbo

TABLE 13.2 Summary of slaves embarked from the Bight of Biafra and principal port of disembarkation, 1601–1800

Region	*Number*	*Percentage of total*	*Percentage (less unspecified)*
Jamaica	218,007	28.70	32.00
Not specified	79,158	10.40	—
Dominica	57,353	7.54	8.42
Barbados	51,982	6.84	7.63
Grenada	38,254	5.03	5.62
St. Kitts	35,923	4.73	5.62
Cuba	35,552	4.73	5.22
St. Dominique	30,436	4.00	4.47
Sierra Leone	29,937	3.94	4.40
Virginia	22,520	2.94	3.31
Antigua	21,569	2.84	3.17
Martinique	19,556	2.57	2.87
St. Vincent	18,692	2.46	2.74
Guianas	17,300	2.28	2.54
Virgin Islands	13,167	1.73	1.93
Carolinas	10,766	1.42	1.58
Trinidad	10,408	1.37	1.53
Guadeloupe	10,399	1.37	1.54
Southeast Brazil	9,189	1.21	1.35
Bahia	6,485	0.85	0.95
Nevis	4,288	0.56	0.63
St. Lucia	3,670	0.48	0.54
Rio de la Plata	3,010	0.40	0.44
Tobago	2,994	0.39	0.44
Puerto Rico	2,865	0.38	0.42
Spanish America (main)	1,717	0.23	0.25
Bahamas	1,199	0.16	0.18
Dutch Caribbean	1,061	0.14	0.16
Northeast Brazil	816	0.11	0.12
Pernambuco	676	0.09	0.10
Montserrat	528	0.07	0.08
Maryland	310	0.04	0.05
Off-shore Atlantic	232	0.03	0.03
Gold Coast	144	0.02	0.02
Senegambia	81	0.01	0.01

Source: Calculated from Eltis et al., *The Trans-Atlantic Slave Trade.*

have a real attachment to the land (*ala*) literarily and symbolically. The unit of production was the family, consisting of a man, his wife or wives, and their unmarried children. The production unit had access to land for production, rituals, burials, and so forth. Land was not just a factor of production; it remained a link with the ancestors. For instance, the umbilical cord of a newborn child is buried in ancestral land—that way, the Igbo can make the connection between the living and the land and between the land and the ancestors. Uprooted from the connection with the land and the ancestors, which was vital to their identity, the Igbo responded emphatically by committing what may be described as "acceptable abomination." In the context of slavery, suicide was perhaps a justifiable evil and one that the ancestors would be willing to accommodate. This rationality was, of course, lost to New World scholars, a fact that scholars have failed to link to Igbo cosmology, attitude toward death, and the fundamental belief in life after death. Amid the inhumanity of slavery, the Igbo, like many other slaves, responded in unique ways, sometimes taking their own lives—the ultimate form of resistance.

Yet the abiding preference for other ethnic groups in relation to the Igbo was by no means consistent. Indeed, Holloway argues that "it is quite possible South Carolina merchants sent their male Igbo cargo to North Carolina because of the refusal by local planters to purchase Igbo men and Africans from the Bight of Biafra."[60] Elizabeth Donnan has shown, however, that it was because Virginian planters were uninterested in the ethnic origins of the Africans that they imported a large number from the Bight of Biafra, a reflection of their dominant representation in the British slave pool as a whole.[61] In fact, James Rawley argues that the divergence between Virginia and South Carolina in their receptivity to the Igbo was such that the former importation of the Igbo between 1710 and 1760 constituted some 38 percent of its total importation of Africans, a figure that mirrors precisely the British export trade from Africa. In contrast to Virginia, it has been estimated that South Carolina may have imported only 2 percent of its African captive population from the Bight of Biafra from 1733 to 1807.[62] The Igbo were purchased in high percentages in Virginia, Hall argues, "because the poverty of slave owners left them no alternative."[63]

Ironically, some deeply rooted qualities in the Igbo slaves that some planters found attractive were the same qualities that drove them toward suicidal tendencies. Colin Palmer noted that the Igbo as a group were "considered tractable and hence were highly sought after by some of the slaveholders in the Americas."[64] And Moreau de St.-Méry noted that while some St. Domingue planters hesitated to buy Igbo slaves because of their suicidal tendencies, "others preferred them because they were very attached to each other and 'the newly arrived find help, care, and example from those who have come before them.'"[65] This ethos is deeply rooted in Igbo traditional system of what Chieka Ifemisia characterizes as "traditional humane living" among the Igbo.[66]

This body of mythology surrounding enslaved Igbo did not have universal application in the diaspora. Igbo women seem to have been a preferred group among planters. Joseph Holloway argues that "Igbo women were highly desired as concubines," accounting for a high level of retention in South Carolina, unlike their male counterparts.[67] Littlefield confirms that "it is remarkable that Ibos as a group and the Bight as an area had a greater proportional representation of women among runaways that were produced by the native populace of South Carolina. In this they differed from all other African entities."[68] Douglas Chambers recently noted in "Igbo Women in the Early Modern Atlantic: The Burden of Beauty" that although the Igbo had a reputation as "bad" slaves, their female counterparts "had a surprisingly 'good' reputation" and were "generally thought to be hard workers, industrious and diligent."[69]

Anthony de Verteuil suggests that the Igbo, the largest group in Trinidad, adjusted well to slavery in Trinidad when compared to Jamaica, where Igbo rate of suicide and rebellion were high.[70] Why, for example, did the Igbo respond differently to slavery in Jamaica and Trinidad? It has been suggested that this was because of the relatively benign system of slavery in Trinidad. The conditions of slavery and victimization explain their prominence in suicide accounts despite their small number in South Carolina. In contrast to South Carolina, Virginia and Maryland planters, according to Gomez, lacked comparable traditions concerning Igbo reputation as bad slaves.[71]

The Igbo responded to slavery in unique ways. Their response to the institution of slavery was shaped by their African background. The sense of inequality that characterized slave societies was at odds with the libertarian tendencies of their African political system. The republican ideals of the Igbo was obviously at odds with the institution of slavery; their attitude toward slave masters and the institution itself drew heavily from an identity formed and derived from the African background. Gomez attributed the high proportion of Igbo women in the runaway population to the various freedoms that women expressed in several areas of Igbo society, including politics, agriculture, commence, and trade.[72] Similarly, Daniel Kloza associates "the existence and prevalence of male Igbo runaways to the freedoms, democratic institutions, and social mobility enjoyed in their indigenous African culture."[73] What emerges from these descriptions and stigmatization of the Igbo in some parts of the Atlantic world is a picture of individuals whose native culture emphasizes the dignity of liberty and as such responded to their victimization in very emphatic, decisive, and irreversible ways.

CONTINUITY AND CHANGE IN THE ATLANTIC DIASPORA

The scholarship and general commentaries on the Igbo is instructive about the influence of the Igbo cosmology in shaping their identity and suggests that certain elements and stereotypes associated with the Igbo were New World developments that emerged from the specific ways the Igbo responded to enslavement. Indeed, contrary to common assumptions, the lack of a pan-Igbo identity did not derive from unswerving loyalty based on sentimental attachment to a local community. Indeed, a cursory examination of their African origin explains Igbo uniqueness. Igbo self-identification among contemporary societies is not markedly different from how those in the Igbo diaspora identified themselves during the era of slavery. While the Igbo language was a force that defined a pan-Igbo identity, many other forces upon which their African identities were built have often lacked homogeneity among the Igbo. In many African societies, name and common identity was sometimes forged by the creation of a new powerful state.

Let us consider the case of the Yoruba. The Igbo lacked centralized political and religious institutions that brought large populations together and created a universal identity for groups such as the Yoruba. Unlike in the Yoruba society, where religious deities have a pan-Yoruba influence, Igbo communities worshiped several deities that often lacked any influence beyond their immediate locale, although the reputation of a select few, such as Kamalu of Ozuzu and Ibini Ukpabi of Arochukwu, spread beyond the immediate communities that were custodians of these deities. Also there is no common myth of origin or a legendary progenitor of the Igbo, such as the Oduduwa myth, which represents the greatest symbol of pan-Yoruba identity. Thus religion and political institutions provided the consciousness of a common Yoruba identity before the arrival of the Europeans in the nineteenth century. Even though the Igbo may have shared a common language, a common sense of origin and identity developed much later because locality that formed the basis of religious, political, and social interaction was destroyed by the pattern of slavery. Like their kin in the Atlantic diaspora, the Igbo forged, in the wake of slavery (for those in the diaspora) and European encounters (for those in Africa), a new sense of identity based on a common language and new historical experience.

The way Igbo exiles related to their new environment and enslavement was influenced by their African experience. Unlike the Igbo, the legacies of the various ethnic cultures from where slavers were drawn remained ingrained in their consciousness as they are moved across the Atlantic. From the West African coast, most other groups had traditions of centralized authorities, kingship, and aristocratic tendencies, most of which wielded political and religious power over subject peoples. Thus slaves from Benin, Huasaland, and Yorubaland had traditions of overseers, conformity to authority, and control. The Igbo are very individualistic. This is very important in understanding the attachment to locality rather than to a pan-Igbo identity within Igboland. Once outside Igboland, however, this individual identity and strong loyalty to the locality transformed to make the new and unfamiliar environment meaningful. That Equiano, for example, continued to use a generic name "country" to designate his homeland did not necessarily mean that there was not an Igbo nation. Although generalizations are dangerous at this stage, until further research is completed, one can trace Igbo identity from their distinct set of behaviors (social and ideological) that marked them as a peculiar group to slave owners and from the special ways they adapted to their New World environment.

Largely, the perceived cohesion and Igbo identity that developed in the diaspora can be traced to the strong identification with the local community. In other words, the Igbo were not creating a new identity but rather rebuilding a community to reinforce the identity of their old world. Within the structure of the slave society, which largely reduced individual autonomy, the Igbo must have attempted to strike a balance between individual autonomy and servitude with community identity. Writing on the Igbo susceptibility to change in another context, John C. Merriam notes that the achievement-based norms of the Igbo compelled them to adapt quickly to Westernization.[74] The Igbo of the eighteenth century were primarily loyal to their respective village and village groups, but they were very much aware of their shared qualities and identities as Igbo. This "latent potential of Igbo ethnicity," according to Gomez, "matured very rapidly under the pressure of North American slavery."[75] To a great extent, therefore, the distinct political institutions, religious, and ideological perspective of the Igbo informed the behavior of those enslaved in the Americas and must have left their mark on the New World cultures.

The discriminatory tendencies of planters throughout the Americas resulted in distinct patterns of ethnic distribution and concentration of enslaved Africans in particular locations. Such patterns, Gomez contends, assist immensely in any analysis of subsequent sociocultural development, operating under the premise that black life and culture in a given area evolved out of, and in creative tension with, norms associated with specific ethnic groups imported via the slave trade.[76] Gomez argues, for example, that Virginia and Maryland developed a servile population largely out of Igbo (in majority) and Akan antecedents. Both groups were largely rural, their diet equally dependent on root crops. Despite the fragmentary nature of information on enslaved Africans of Igbo origin, some tentative conclusions can be made on their contributions to early American culture.

Evidently, enslaved Africans of Igbo origin were important in shaping the larger history of slavery, patterns of slavery, and new identity formations in the Americas. Douglas Chambers also identifies evidence of what he calls "Igboisms" in Anglophone American slave societies, which includes Igbo dietary habits.[77] Igbo practices such as "one-pot" cooking and use of such vegetables as okoro have been widely practiced among enslaved people in the Americas. Chambers has further argued that the "vegetal part of the basket of African-American 'soul food'" has been strongly influenced by Igbo food ways in Anglophone parts of the African diaspora in the New World.[78] Igbo staples such as yams, black-eyed peas, and greens are very prominent.[79] These were the basic food crops in nineteenth- and early twentieth-century Igbo society. In the diaspora, the Igbo continued to grow yams and maintained nearly all the secondary subsistence crops of their ancestral village agriculture.[80]

Igbo attitude toward power and authority was transmitted to the New World. The African background and identity of the Igbo, like many other African ethnicities, was fundamental in their response and recreation of such world in the Americas. There is clear evidence of Igbo influence in "power ways," which Fischer has defined as "attitudes towards authority and power" and "patterns of political participation."[81] Igbo slaves in the Americas drew on their African background, particularly their abhorrence for centralized authority, to order their individual and collective lives. There were no major slave rebellions in areas such as the Chesapeake and Western Jamaica; in regions that hosted strong Igbo slave presence, enslaved Igbo employed subtle and less bustle forms of resistance to the institution of slavery, resorting more to resistance: suicide, escape, or getting some concession. Such political consciousness was also important in understanding why Igbo women featured prominently among runaway slaves in America.[82] Their sense of independence can be traced to Igboland itself, where they were prominent in the political, economic, and social arrangements of society. Igbo society had established a high regard for women, reflected by such evidence as the veneration and popularity of the earth mother (Ala), the perfection of gender balance, and the independent spirit exhibited by Igbo women in their new environment.[83]

At the cosmological level, the Igbo, like other African groups, seemed to have retained a lot of their spiritual worldview. The Igbo slaves drew on their African institution to recreate the world familiar to them and to maintain contact with the spirit world and their personal gods (chi). Two institutions in Igboland that were recreated in the diaspora include the Ahiajọku, yam-spirit cult and Ọkọnkọ society. It is likely, Chambers argues, that diasporic Igbo combined these essentially shared traditions into a Creole institution in the *jonkonu* masquerade.[84] Chambers has also drawn attention to other evidence of Igbo continuities as can be found in the system of "doctoring" called *obeah*. According to Chambers, Igbo slaves drew on ancestral ideological resources to make sense of their new environment and, in the process, "Igboized" slave religious tradition throughout British America. Chambers identifies a strong link between the function of *obeah* men and women in the diaspora to the functions of *dibia* (medicine men) in Igboland.[85]

Igbo Africanisms survived in other forms. Burial rituals in the Sea islands have strong Igbo roots. The ritual of birthing and dressing the dead and the notions that the spirit of the dead will not rest until it is properly buried was a strong African carryover. The Gullahs retained these African traditions of pacifying the spirit of the dead by "placing their things on the grave." Among the Onitsha Igbo, "all the implements of the dead are placed before the corpse: tools, gun, and bag, as well as other implements in accordance with his profession. . . . They represent the equipment that the man will need in the underworld; the tools to enable him to prosecute his occupation."[86]

African culture of Igbo origin has survived in the language, music, and oral literary traditions in the Caribbean. While Caribbean culture has undergone some "recreativity and hybridity," Hannah Chukwu has shown evidence of a strong connection between some oral features and language use in earlier poetry to its ancestral root among the Igbo in Africa.[87] Work songs chanted according to the rhythmic movement of work (aimed to lighten the burden and monotony of work as well as to offer some pleasure to the workers), which abound in Caribbean oral poetry, have African or Igbo antecedents.[88] Caribbean poetry, including work songs and music, embody Igbo sense of community, prevalent feature of Igbo oral tradition such as call-and-response.[89]

NOTES

1. Derbyshire Record Office, D239 M/E 16753–16754, "West Indian Papers," Plantations of William Perrin and William Philip Perrin, Correspondence of the Jamaican Attorneys, January 10, 1773.

2. See Michael A. Gomez, *Exchanging Our Country Marks: The Transformation of African Identities in the Colonial and Antebellum South* (Chapel Hill: The University of North Carolina Press, 1998), 114. See also David Brion Davis, *The Problem of Slavery in the Age of Revolution 1770–1823* (Ithaca: Cornell University Press, 1975). The Igbo reputation as "bad" slaves who tended to run away, shrink work, or commit suicide rather than face perpetual servitude must have contributed to the social relation of slavery in the areas where there were substantial numbers of Igbo. See Douglas B. Chambers, "'My own nation': Igbo Exiles in the Diaspora," *Slavery and Abolition* 18, no. 1 (1997): 72–97.

3. Paul E. Lovejoy and David V. Trotman, "Introduction: Ethnicity and the African Diaspora," in *Trans-Atlantic Dimensions of Ethnicity in the African Diaspora*, ed. Paul E. Lovejoy and David V. Trotman (London: Continuum, 2003).

4. The most recent works on this region include G. Ugo Nwokeji, *The Slave Trade and Culture in the Bight of Biafra: An African Society in the Atlantic World* (New York: Cambridge University Press, 2010); and Douglas Chambers, *The Igbo Diaspora in the Era of the Slave Trade: An Introductory History* (Glassboro, NJ: Goldline and Jacobs, 2014).

5. See David Eltis and David Richardson, "West Africa and the Transatlantic Slave Trade: New Evidence on Long-Run Trends," *Slavery and Abolition* 18, no. 1 (1997): 18–21.

6. David Eltis, Stephen D. Behrendt, David Richardson, and Herbert S. Klein, eds., *The Trans-Atlantic Slave Trade: A Database on CD-ROM*

(New York: Cambridge University Press, 1999); and Chambers, *The Igbo Diaspora*, 6.

7. See Chambers, "'My own nation,'" 72–97. For African export figure for 1470s–1699, see Paul E. Lovejoy, "The Volume of the Atlantic Slave Trade: A Synthesis," *Journal of African History* 23 (1982): 478–81; for 1700–1809, see Richardson, "Slave Exports from West and West-Central Africa, 1700–1810: New Estimates of Volume and Distribution," *Journal of African History* 30 (1989): 3, 6–17; and for 1811–1870, see David Eltis, *Economic Growth and the Ending of the Transatlantic Slave Trade* (New York: Oxford University Press, 1987), 249, 250–52. Chambers based his estimate for Igbo numbers on these sources. See note 17.

8. Chambers, *The Igbo Diaspora*, 3.

9. Nwokeji, *The Slave Trade.*

10. Chambers, "'My own nation,'" 75–77.

11. Ibid., 77.

12. Olaudah Equiano, *The Interesting Narrative of Olaudah Equiano, Written by Himself*, ed. Robert J. Allison (1789; Boston, MA: Macmillan, 1995).

13. John Barbot, "Mr. John Grazilhier's Voyage from Bandy to New Calabar," in *A Collection of Voyages and Travels*, ed. Awnsham Churchill (London: Churchills, 1746), 5:380–81. Cited in Elizabeth Isichei, *Igbo Worlds: An Anthology of Oral Histories and Historical Descriptions* (Philadelphia: Institute for the Study of Human Issues, 1978), 10.

14. William Balfour Baikie, *Narrative of an Exploring Voyage up the River Kwora and Binue* (London: J. Murray, 1856), 307.

15. E. Franklin Frazier, *The Negro Family in the United States*, rev. and abridged ed. (1939; New York: Dryden Press, 1948).

16. E. Franklin Frazier, *The Negro Church in America* (New York: Schocken, 1963).

17. Sidney Mintz and Richard Price, *An Anthropological Approach to Afro-American Past: A Caribbean Perspective* (Philadelphia: Institute for the Study of Human Issues, 1976), 3–26.

18. John Thornton, *Africa and Africans in the Making of the Atlantic World, 1400–1680* (Cambridge: Cambridge University Press, 1982), 183.

19. Melville J. Herskovits, *The Myth of the Negro Past* (Boston: Beacon Press, 1941). On the debate between Herskovits and Frazier, see the introduction in Joseph E. Holloway, ed., *Africanisms in American Culture* (Bloomington: Indiana University Press, 2005), 1–17.

20. Herbert S. Klein, *African Slavery in Latin America and the Caribbean* (New York: Oxford University Press, 1986), 163.

21. Philip D. Morgan, "The Cultural Implications of the Atlantic Slave Trade: African Regional Origins, American Destinations and New World Development," *Slavery and Abolition* 18, no. 1 (1997): 122.

22. Peter Manuel, "Music, Identity, and Images of India in the Indo-Caribbean Diaspora," *Asian Music* 29, no. 1 (1997): 18–35.

23. David Eltis, "Ethnicity in the Early Modern Atlantic World" (paper presented at the Harriet Tubman Seminar, York University, January 26, 1999).

24. Paul E. Lovejoy, "The African Diaspora: Revisionist Interpretations of Ethnicity, Culture and Religion under Slavery," *Studies in the World History of Slavery, Abolition and Emancipation* 2, no. 1 (1997): 1–23. http://www2.hnet.msu.edu/~slavery/essays/esy9701love.html.

25. For more recent work, see, for example, Toyin Falola and Matt D. Childs, *The Yoruba Diaspora in the Atlantic World* (Bloomington: Indiana University Press, 2005); Lovejoy and Trotman, *Trans-Atlantic Dimensions.*

26. Chambers, *The Igbo Diaspora*, 6.

27. Gwendolyn M. Hall, *Slavery and African Ethnicities in the America: Restoring the Links* (Chapel Hill: University of North Carolina Press, 2005), 56.

28. See Eltis et al., *The Trans-Atlantic Slave Trade.*

29. For some analysis, see Paul E. Lovejoy, "Identifying Enslaved Africans: Methodological and Conceptual Considerations in Studying the African Diaspora," in *Identifying Enslaved Africans: the "Nigerian Hinterland" and the African Diaspora*, ed. Paul E. Lovejoy (Proceedings of the UNESCO/SSHRCC Summer Institute, York University, Toronto, 1997), 17–46; Thornton, *Africa and Africans*, esp. 192–205; David Eltis and Stanley L. Engerman, "The 'Numbers Game' and Routes to Slavery," *Slavery and Abolition* 18, no. 1 (1997): 1–15; David Richardson, "Slave Exports from West and West-Central." See also more recent data from Eltis et al., *The Trans-*

Atlantic Slave Trade, and Eltis, "Ethnicity in Early Modern Atlantic World."

30. Robert Harms, *The Diligent: A Voyage through the Worlds of the Slave Trade* (New York: Basic Books, 2001).

31. See Eltis et al., *The Trans-Atlantic Slave Trade*. See also Public Record Office/CO 388/10 for information on the slave ship *Two Friends*.

32. New data provided by Eltis, *Economic Growth and the Ending of the Transatlantic Slave Trade*, has been significant in this direction.

33. Thornton, *Africa and Africans*, 204–5.

34. Lovejoy, "The African Diaspora."

35. See also Thornton, *Africa and Africans*, 205.

36. Kenneth M. Stampp, "Between Two Cultures," in *Americans from Africa: Slavery and Its Aftermath*, ed. Peter I. Rose (New York: Atherton Press, 1970), 56.

37. Thornton, *African and Africans*, 129.

38. For more recent works focusing on individuals, including Igbo Africans, see, for example, Maureen Warner-Lewis, *Archibald Monteath: Igbo, Jamaican, Monrovian* (Kingston, JM: University of the West Indies Press, 2007). See also the much better known account of another Igbo whose autobiography and activities contributed significantly to the abolition discourse and the ending of the Atlantic slave trade.

39. Unlike many other parts of the New World, conditions in what became the United States destroyed the significance of their African heritage and caused new habits and attitudes to develop to meet new situations. See E. Franklin Frazier, "The Significance of the African background," in *Americans from Africa: Slavery and Its Aftermath*, ed. Peter I. Rose (New York: Atherton, 1970), 37–38.

40. Lovejoy, "Situating Identities."

41. Victor Uchendu, *The Igbo of Southeastern Nigeria* (New York: Harcourt College, 1965), 41–46. There were exceptions. Some Igbo communities like Onitsha, Oguta, and Nri had chieftaincy institutions in precolonial times.

42. Cyril Agodi Onwumechili, "Igbo Enwe Eze: The Igbo Have No Kings," 2000 Ahiajoku Lecture (Owerri, Nigeria: Ministry of Information, 2000).

43. G. I. Jones, *Report on the Position, Status and Influence of Chiefs and Natural Rulers in the Eastern Region of Nigeria* (Enugu, Nigeria: Government Printer, 1957).

44. Obafemi Awolowo, *Path to Nigerian Freedom* (London: Faber and Faber, 1947), cited in Ekwe Nche Organization, "Leadership in Igbo Society: Analysis, Challenges and Solutions," December 12, 2004, http://www.biafraland.com/leadership_Igbo%20Identity.rtf.

45. S. Cronje, *The World and Nigeria* (London: Sidgwick and Jackson, 1972), cited in Ekwe Nche Organization, "Leadership in Igbo Society: Analysis, Challenges and Solutions," December 12, 2004, http://www.biafraland.com/leadership_Igbo%20Identity.rtf.

46. *Look*, November 26, 1968.

47. *Time*, August 23, 1968.

48. Ekwe Nche Organization, "Leadership in Igbo Society," December 12, 2004, http://www.biafraland.com/leadership_Igbo%20Identity.rtf.

49. Ibid.

50. Major Darwin, Walter Egerton, Dr. Falconer, and A. E. Kitson, "Southern Nigeria: Some Considerations of its Structure, People, and Natural History: Discussion," *The Geographical Journal* 41, no. 1 (1913): 34–38.

51. Ekwe Nche Organization, "Leadership in Igbo Society."

52. Translated literally, the term "intellectual" (*inwe ọgọgọ isi*) or "to possess brain power or be knowledgeable" defined traditional intellectuals among the Igbo and other Eastern Nigerian societies.

53. Traditional titles in Igbo society can be grouped into four main categories: (1) symbolic titles or those emanating from acquisition of wealth; (2) those awarded due to heroic achievement, (3) honorary awards and (4) ascribed or titles of institutionalized social force origin. The *Duru* and *Ọzọ* titles are example of status symbols among the Igbo. Its legitimacy was enhanced if conferred by the Nri since they are the direct descendants of Eri (a legendary figure regarded as the creator of the earth). An *ọzọ* titleholder was revered and possessed a kind of diplomatic immunity that is respected throughout Igboland.

54. Isidore Okpewho, Carole Boyce Davies, and Ali A. Mazrui, eds., *The African Diaspora: Origins and New World Identities* (Bloomington: Indiana University Press, 1999).

55. A modest attempt has been made to call attention to the Igbo diaspora in the Atlantic world, See, for example, Chambers, "Murder at Montpelier"; Chambers, "'My own nation,'" 72–97; Gomez, *Exchanging our Country Marks*, chap. 6; Gwendolyn M. Hall, *Slavery and African Ethnicities in the America: Restoring the Links* (Chapel Hill: University of North Carolina Press, 2005); Chima J. Korieh, ed., *Olaudah Equiano and the Igbo World: History, Society and Atlantic Diaspora Connections* (Trenton, NJ: Africa World Press, 2009).

56. Gomez, *Exchanging our Country Marks*, 115.

57. Hall, *Slavery and African Ethnicities*, 139.

58. Donnan, in Gomez, *Exchanging our Country Marks*, 115.

59. See Daniel C. Littlefield, *Rice and Slaves: Ethnicity and the Slave Trade in Colonial South Carolina* (Baton Rouge: Louisiana State University Press, 1981), 10. While these stereotypes may not indicate Igbo origin, Jamaican folklore also refers to people with a yellowish skin as "Red Ibo."

60. Joseph E. Holloway, "'What Africa Has Given America': African Continuities in the North American Diaspora," in *Africanisms in American Culture*, ed. Joseph E. Holloway (Bloomington: Indiana University Press, 2005), 41.

61. Elizabeth Donnan, "The Slave Trade into South Carolina before the Revolution," *American Historical Review* 33 (1927–1928): 816–17. See also Philip D. Curtin, *The Atlantic Slave Trade: A Census* (Madison: University of Wisconsin Press, 1969), 156–57; Douglas Chambers, "Eboe, Kongo, Mandingo: African Ethnic Groups and the Development of Regional Slave Societies in Mainland North America," International Seminar, "The History of the Atlantic World," Harvard University, September 3–11, 1996.

62. See Gomez, *Exchanging our Country Marks*, 115.

63. Hall, *Slavery and African Ethnicities*, 139.

64. Colin Palmer, *Human Cargoes: The British Slave Trade to Spanish America, 1700–1939* (Urbana: University of Illinois Press, 1981), 29.

65. Cited in Hall, *Slavery and African Ethnicities*, 126.

66. See Chieka Ifemisia, *Traditional Humane Living among the Igbo: An Historical Perspective* (Enugu, Nigeria: Fourth Dimension, 1979).

67. Holloway, "What Africa Has Given," 41.

68. Littlefield, *Rice and Slaves*, 143–55.

69. Douglas B. Chambers, "Igbo Women in the Early Modern Atlantic: The Burden of Beauty," in *Olaudah Equiano and the Igbo World: History, Society and Atlantic Diaspora Connections*, ed. Chima J. Korieh (Trenton, NJ: Africa World Press, 2009), 315–31.

70. Anthony de Verteuil, *Seven Slaves and Slavery: Trinidad, 1777–1838* (Port of Spain, Trinidad: Scrip-J, 1992).

71. Gomez, *Exchanging our Country Marks*, 124.

72. Ibid., 126–27.

73. Daniel Kloza, "African Origins of Igbo Slave Resistance in the Americas," in *Olaudah Equiano and the Igbo World: History, Society, and Atlantic Diaspora Connections*, ed. Chima J. Korieh (Trenton, NJ: Africa World Press, 2009), 349–68.

74. John C. Merriman, "The Lagacy of the Biafran War," *The Harvard Crimson*, November 12, 1968.

75. Gomez, *Exchanging our Country Marks*, 126.

76. Ibid., 146.

77. Chima J. Korieh, "African Ethnicity as Mirage? Historicizing the Essence of the Igbo in Africa and the Atlantic Diaspora," *Dialectical Anthropology* 30, no. 1–2 (March 2006): 116.

78. Chambers, "'My own nation,'" 85.

79. Ibid.

80. Ibid.

81. David Hackett Fischer, *Albion's Seed: Four British Folkways in America* (New York: Oxford University Press, 1989), 9. Cited in Chambers, "'My own nation,'" 85.

82. Gomez, *Exchanging our Country Marks*, 126.

83. Cf. the 1929 Women's revolt in Eastern Nigeria during the colonial period and the part played by women in the post-emancipation slave revolts in Trinidad.

84. Chambers, "'My own nation,'" 87.

85. Ibid. See P. Amury Talbot, *Tribes of the Niger Delta: Their Religions and Customs* (London: Sheldon Press, 1932); M. M. Green, *Ibo Village Affairs* (New York: Frank Cass, 1964), 54, for the functions for *dibia* in Igboland. See also Jane C. Beck, "The West Indian Supernatural World:

Belief Integration in a Pluralistic Society," *Journal of American Folklore* 88, no. 349 (1975): 235–44. Compare also with Equiano, *The Interesting Narrative*, 12.

86. Joseph E. Holloway, "The Sacred World of the Gullahs," in *Africanisms in American Culture*, ed. Joseph E. Holloway (Bloomington: Indiana University Press, 2005), 187–223.

87. Hannah N. Eby Chukwu, "African Cultural Values: The Significance of Igbo Oral Forms in Selected Carinnean Poetry," in *Olaudah Equiano and the Igbo World: History, Society and Atlantic Diaspora Connections*, ed. Chima J. Korieh (Trenton, NJ: Africa World Press, 2009), 334.

88. Chukwu, "African Cultural Values," 335.

89. Ibid.

14 OLAUDAH EQUIANO AND THE FORGING OF AN IGBO IDENTITY

Vincent Carretta

Of the surviving eighteenth-century descriptions of Igboland in the kingdom of Benin, *The Interesting Narrative of the Life of Olaudah Equiano, or Gustavus Vassa, the African. Written by Himself* (London, 1789) is by far the most fully developed.[1] Equiano's description is certainly the most complete eighteenth-century ethnography of "Eboe" we have from a person of African descent and the only one not mediated by a white translator or transcriber. Consequently, ethnographers and historians rely heavily on it as a primary source on eighteenth-century Igboland.[2] The evidence in Equiano's description of Africa alone, however, does not prove that he was born and raised there. Recent documentary discoveries regarding Equiano's possible birthplace, as well as the problematic eighteenth-century definition of *Igbo*, require us to reconsider the ethnic and national identities of Olaudah Equiano, or Gustavus Vassa. Did the man who was arguably a pioneer in forging (or creating) an Igbo ethnic and national identity forge (or counterfeit) his personal identity to do so? And if he did so, why? Because the troublesome records existed, he risked being called an imposter, whether or not he invented an African birth. But the financial and rhetorical success of his book demonstrated that it was a risk well worth taking.

In one of the earliest and most judicious treatments of Equiano's claim to be an African-born Igbo, A. E. Afigbo concludes that the description of Africa in Equiano's *Narrative* was based on his personal recollections and thus, "though limited in scope and depth could be said to provide a base line for the study of traditional Igbo society."[3] Afigbo comes to his somewhat qualified conclusion even though he acknowledges that "[a]fter reading *The Interesting Narrative*, one of the first things that strikes the critical scholar is how scanty and muddled Equiano's 'recollection' of Igbo society is."[4] Afigbo was one of the first commentators to recognize that much of Equiano's account of Igboland came from information he received from other enslaved Africans; Equiano's youth would have limited his knowledge of Igbo customs and society. Much of the information about the Igbo that he gives us can also be found in contemporaneous published sources, many of which we know he was familiar with, and that the data unique to his account are often either false (such as the spontaneous growth of cotton and the use of women warriors) or unverifiable precisely because of their uniqueness. Afigbo attributes many of Equiano's mistakes and omissions to rhetorical choices he made as "a skilful propagandist" in service of the movement to abolish the trans-Atlantic slave trade.[5] Evidence unavailable to Afigbo suggests that Equiano's skills as a propagandist served personal and ethnic causes as well.

The revelation in 1995 that Equiano's baptismal and naval records contradict his own account of his birth and upbringing by saying that he was actually born in South Carolina raises the very strong possibility that nothing in Equiano's account of Africa was based on firsthand experience.[6] Scholars and critics have increasingly come to recognize that the apparent uniqueness of his account does not guarantee its authenticity.[7] We will probably never know the truth about Equiano's birth and upbringing. Nonetheless, whether or not Equiano's account is authentic, Afigbo's conclusion that it is the most reliable description of eighteenth-century Igboland we have may still be correct.

We must keep in mind, however, that in many ways, the notion of an eighteenth-century

Igboland is an anachronism. As Chinua Achebe has observed, the consciousness of the Igbo identity that Equiano asserts is a quite recent phenomenon: before the 1960s, "the Igbo people . . . did not see themselves as Igbo. They saw themselves as people from this village or that village. In fact in some places 'Igbo' was a word of abuse; they were the 'other' people, down in the bush."[8] During the much later colonial period, the peoples in Africa who were earlier called Igbo by others and who shared a common language increasingly came to identify themselves as Igbo. As Joseph Inikori reminds us, modern commentators may be retrojecting a post-eighteenth-century conception of Igbo identity into the earlier period: "It should be noted . . . that a pan-Igbo identity as we know it today did not exist during the Atlantic slave trade era. . . . Igbo as an ethnic category is a twentieth-century development reluctantly accepted by several of the constituent groups on political and administrative grounds. Since Igbo was used pejoratively [during the eighteenth century] to refer to the densely populated uplands, the major source of slaves and by extension to slaves, it is not surprising that many of these groups have been reluctant to accept the Igbo identity."[9]

Contemporary scholars value Equiano's "unique first-hand account of eighteenth-century Igboland" so highly because so little other direct information about the mid-eighteenth-century Igbo exists.[10] Compared to the publicly available information about some other West African ethnic groups and political states in the eighteenth century, very little was known in Britain about either Igbo culture or Benin, even though almost one-quarter of the enslaved Africans sent to North America came from the Bight of Benin and Biafra during the last decades of the period. And what little other information existed came through white intermediaries or observers. For example, in 1788, James Penny, a merchant who had spent eighteen years in the slave trade until 1784, testified before the House of Commons that he could speak only indirectly about "the interior Part of the Country from whence the Bulk of the Slaves are received, and which is of vast Extent, called Ebo. . . ."[11]

To be sure, an argument has been made that an Igbo national identity was developing during the eighteenth century, but even if such an identity had been established by the time Equiano was writing, it was not the primary identity a native West African would likely have claimed, except possibly to outsiders.[12] During the eighteenth century the now more familiar national sense of Igbo was the result of the involuntary African diaspora: "A sense of pan-Igbo identity came only when its people left Igboland—an experience first imposed by the slave trade."[13] Whites used the term *Eboe*, or *Igbo*, in the diasporan sense throughout the eighteenth century. Like the terms Guinea and Koromantyn, "Eboe" was a geographical and supraethnic concept Europeans created that elided the significant cultural differences among various ethnic groups in West Africa. "No sense of pan-Igbo identity" existed before the nineteenth century.[14] In the era of the slave trade, Africans living in the area of present-day Nigeria distinguished between Olu and Igbo, riverain and inland: "olu meant riverain or riverain-derived, slave-dealing, kingdom-associated peoples; igbo meant upland, slave-providing, kingship-lacking populations."[15] Claiming or reclaiming an Igbo identity in the eighteenth century was by definition an act of invention because Igbo, roughly translated as "outsider," was a term Europeans and coastal Africans often used pejoratively to cover a range of peoples living farther inland in West Africa.

Equiano's representation of Igboland challenged images of Africa as a land of savagery, idolatry, cannibalism, indolence, and social disorder. Proponents of the transatlantic slave trade argued that enslavement by Europeans saved Africans from such evils and introduced them to civilization, culture, industry, and Christianity. However, David Northrup (an eminent African historian) has shown that to talk of Igbo nationalism in the eighteenth century is anachronistic because "populations like those in the hinterland of the Bight of Biafra . . . neither possessed centralized political institutions nor were in the process of developing them."[16] Equiano must have known that most earlier and contemporaneous commentators disagreed with his positive assessment of the peoples that Europeans called Igbos, the slaves least desired by planters in the British colonies.[17] As one historian points out, "No Chesapeake planter is known to have expressed a preference for laborers originating in the Bight of Biafra, and indeed Ibo . . . slaves were held in particularly low esteem in much of the Caribbean and in South Carolina."[18] No doubt aware that if he could rehabilitate the reputation of the Igbo in particular, he would rehabilitate the reputation of Africans in general, Equiano speaks with the voice of an Igbo proto-nationalist proud of his homeland. He was a pioneer in the forging of an Igbo national identity.

The lack of information about the Igbo gave Equiano the opportunity for invention he needed if he was born in South Carolina rather than Africa. Equiano uses his autobiography to practice nation-formation as well as self-creation. His British readers were more sympathetic to the familiar idea of a state centrally organized by nationality, culture, economics, and religion than they would have been to the eighteenth-century reality of autonomous villages in Igboland. Equiano indicates his own uneasiness, or at least uncertainty, about the term "Eboe" in several ways. Only the first edition of *The Interesting Narrative* includes the words "called Eboe" in the sentence, "This kingdom is divided into many provinces or districts: in one of the most fertile of which, called Eboe, I was born, in the year 1745, in a charming fruitful vale, named Essaka" (32). Perhaps on second thought, Equiano acknowledged that no such place actually existed. Similarly, attempts by modern scholars to locate "Essaka" have been unsuccessful, though of course the name may have changed.[19] Scholars also disagree about which side of the Niger River his native village was located on.[20] Equiano oddly seems to see Benin and Eboe as separate places, even though elsewhere he tells us that the latter is in the former. The fact that Benin was located west of the Niger River and Igboland largely east may explain the inconsistency. He uses Eboe once to mean outsider: "Oye-Eboe, which term signifies red men living at a distance" (37).

The eighteenth-century account of Igbo culture closest in length to Equiano's is the very brief Moravian *Lebenslauf* (spiritual autobiography) dictated in German by Ofodobendo Wooma to an amanuensis in 1746. Born in "Ibo land" around 1729, Wooma was kidnapped into slavery about eight years later and renamed Andrew the Moor. Significantly, Andrew the Moor locates "Ibo land, in the unknown part of Africa." Unfortunately, the accounts of Igboland by Equiano and Andrew the Moor have so little in common that one cannot be used to corroborate the other. We have no evidence that Equiano knew of Andrew, whose German *Lebenslauf* was completed after his death in 1779. It was not translated into English and published until 1988.[21]

Nor was Equiano likely to have read the references to Igbos in the text radically abridged from the manuscript of the Moravian missionary Christian Georg Andreas Oldendorp, *Geschichte der Mission der Evangelischen Brüder auf den Caraibischen Inseln S. Thomas, S. Croix und S. Jan* (1777). With the exception of the scarification "reserved for notables," there appears to be no significant overlap between Equiano's account and that published under Oldendorp's name. Oldendorp's references to African cannibalism and the Igbo practice of human sacrifice are notably absent from Equiano's story, though not surprisingly so, given his abolitionist agenda.[22]

Further complicating the lack of information about the Igbo in Africa was the assumption that the behavior of enslaved people of African descent in the West Indies represented native African culture. At midcentury, James Grainger noted in "The Sugar-Cane. A Poem" that the "teeth-fil'd Ibbos or Ebboes, as they are more commonly called, are a numerous nation. Many of them have their teeth filed, and blackened in an extraordinary manner. They make good slaves when bought young; but are, in general, foul feeders, many of them greedily devouring the raw guts of fowls: They also feed on dead mules and horses; whose carcases, therefore, should be buried deep, that the Negroes may not come at them. But the surest way is to burn them; otherwise they will be apt, privily, to kill those useful animals, in order to feast on them."[23] In *An Essay on the More Common West-India Diseases*, Grainger remarks, "In the Ibbo country, the women chiefly work; they, therefore, are to be preferred to the men of the same country at a negroe sale. . . ."[24] Similarly, Edward Long gives us in *The History of Jamaica* a very negative picture of the Igbo in Africa based on his observations in the West Indies: "The Ebo men are lazy, and averse to every laborious employment; the women performing almost all the work in their own country; these men are sullen, and often make away with themselves, rather than submit to any drudgery: the Ebo women labour well, but are subject to obstructions of the *menstrua*, often attended with sterility, and incurable."[25] Equiano's praise of Igbo women and his emphasis on the sanctity of marriage contrast sharply with pro-slavery assertions of African sexual promiscuity. Such promiscuity allegedly accounted for the low birthrate among slaves that necessitated the slave trade. Grainger, for example, claims that "Black women are not so prolific as the white inhabitants, because they are less chaste. . . ."[26]

Bryan Edwards, in *The History, Civil and Commercial, of the British Colonies in the West Indies*, also offers an image of the Igbo that helps account for why planters often refused to buy them as slaves: "all the Negroes imported from these vast and unexplored regions [the Bight of Benin and Biafra] . . . are called in the West Indies Eboes; and in general they appear to be the lowest and most wretched of all the nations of Africa. . . . I cannot help observing too, that the conformation of the face, in a great majority of them, very much resembles that of the baboon . . ." Edwards reports that the Africans called "Eboes" in the West Indies are less desirable as slaves than other Africans because they require more care due to their alleged "constitutional timidity, and despondency of mind; which are so great as to occasion them very frequently to seek, in a voluntary death, a refuge from their own melancholy reflections." Apparently aware of such accusations, Equiano represents his own occasional death wishes while enslaved as demonstrating that he is a man of feeling, not as expressing cowardice. And he responds to the accusation by Edwards and others that "Eboes" practiced cannibalism by turning it back on them. From Equiano's perspective, the roles of civilized and savages as Europeans saw them are reversed. Thus, he tells us that when he first entered the slave ship and saw the large cooking pots he feared that he had fallen into the hands of cannibals. The widely reported African belief that the slave traders ate the people they took away is a plausible explanation for why the enslaved were almost never seen again.[27]

Scholars who overemphasize the few times Equiano uses the term *Eboe* often ignore the way he organizes his account of Africa. He moves from recollections about "Eboe" specifically to comments about Africans in general, and he closes his first chapter with a series of rhetorical questions that force his readers to draw uniformitarian conclusions from the evidence he has presented. Despite claiming to describe distinctively Igbo manners, he conflates accounts of various African ethnic groups to construct a kind of pan-African identity, a sort of essential African. For example, he cites John Matthews's pro-slavery *A Voyage to the River Sierra-Leone* in support of his own story.[28] If we see Equiano as intentionally moving outward in chapter one from an Igbo identity to the African identity announced on his title page, we should not be surprised to find that his apparently unique account of a particular African people often echoes earlier works. Equiano's own footnotes citing works by James Field Stanfield, Anthony Benezet, and John Matthews, among others, indicate that he depended on secondary sources for at least some of his information about Africa to supplement "the imperfect sketch my memory has furnished me with" (43). Certainly, he is more fastidious than many eighteenth-century writers about citing sources, as one would expect from a history writer, though he is understandably not as careful as current scholarly standards would require. Later readers have assumed that Equiano's footnotes serve to verify the accounts he cites, and he certainly uses his notes to demonstrate his familiarity with the debate over the slave trade and his intention to participate in that debate.

A closer look at some of the details of African life Equiano mentions (but does not footnote) reveals that very similar information was available elsewhere. For example, in the opening sentence of his description of Africa—"That part of Africa, known by the name of Guinea, to which the trade for slaves is carried on, extends along the coast above 3400 miles . . ." (32)—Equiano paraphrases without acknowledgment a passage in Benezet's *Some Historical Account of Guinea*: "That part of Africa from which the Negroes are sold to be carried into slavery, commonly known by the name of Guinea, extends along the coast three or four thousand miles."[29] In other places, Equiano cites Benezet as his authority for general comments beyond his own personal experience about the punishments for adultery and the means for procuring slaves in Africa. William Smith, Thomas Astley, and Michel Adanson anticipated much of Equiano's African story, as did John Wesley in *Thoughts upon Slavery* (London, 1774). Smith and Astley, for example, had earlier described similar African religious beliefs and customs, and both had also likened them to the faith and practices of Judaism.

Many of Equiano's predecessors were themselves heavily dependent on the accounts of others. Benezet's books were essentially digests of earlier writings, many of which were themselves redactions of even earlier accounts of Africa. Benezet's digests differed significantly from earlier such compilations because he very selectively included only examples and evidence favorable to the anti-slavery cause. Equiano found in earlier works accounts of African, albeit not always specifically Igbo, social and military practices much like the ones he ascribes to the homeland he claims. He tells us, for example, that if a chief who starts a war is "vanquished, and he falls into the hands of the enemy, he is put to death: for, as he has been known to foment their quarrels, it is thought dangerous to let him survive, and no ransom can save him, though all other prisoners may be redeemed" (39). Equiano had read the description of a very similar practice reported earlier by William Bosman and quoted by Benezet: "If the person who occasioned the beginning of the war be taken, they will not easily admit him to ransom, though his weight in gold be offered, for fear he should in future form some new design against their repose."[30] When Equiano could, he used positive accounts of Africa by others to support his own argument. In the last two editions of his autobiography, both published in 1794, Equiano underscores his rather idyllic depiction of his homeland by quoting from Letter 4 of James Field Stanfield's *Observations on a Voyage to the Coast of Africa*: "I never saw a happier race of people than those of the kingdom of Benin, seated in ease and plenty, the Slave Trade, and its unavoidable bad effects excepted; every thing bore the appearance of friendship, tranquillity, and primitive independence."[31]

Like Benezet, Equiano often carefully chose his evidence from earlier ambivalent and even hostile descriptions of Africa and Africans. His description of "Eboe" architecture and the enclosed groups of masters' houses and slave quarters that "frequently present the appearance of a village" (36) is quite similar to Matthews's description of the dwelling arrangements in Sierra Leone.[32] Equiano elsewhere cites Matthews as a corroborating authority, even though he and Matthews were writing about quite different and geographically widely separated ethnic groups: "I recollect an instance or two, which I hope it will not be deemed impertinent here to insert, as it may serve as a kind of specimen of the rest, and is still used by the negroes in the West Indies. A young woman had been poisoned, but it was not known by whom; the doctors ordered the corpse to be taken up by some persons, and carried to the grave. As soon as the bearers had raised it on their shoulders, they seemed seized with some[33] sudden impulse, and ran to and fro', unable to stop themselves. At last, after having passed through a number of thorns and prickly bushes unhurt, the corpse fell from them close to a house, and defaced it in the fall; and the owner being taken up, he immediately confessed the poisoning" (42–43). A lieutenant in the royal navy, Matthews had been one of the principal witnesses testifying in Parliament in 1788 in favor of the African slave trade, and his *Voyage* argued for the continuation of the trade as well. By citing him, Equiano in effect cleverly compels him to testify for the opposition.

Sources for even some of the erroneous or dubious information Equiano includes about his homeland can be found in contemporaneous writings. For example, his erroneous claim that cotton grows wild in Africa is one that Carl Bernhard Wadstrom, an original subscriber to Equiano's *Narrative*, also makes in *Observations on the Slave Trade and a Description of Some Part of the Coast of Guinea during a Voyage Made in 1787, and 1788, in Company with Doctor A. Sparrman and Captain Arrehenius* (London, 1789). And Thomas Astley may have influenced Equiano's improbable statement that "Even our women are warriors, and march boldly out to fight along with the men" (39).[34] Later in his autobiography, Equiano says that he encountered warrior women everywhere he went in Africa: "both the males and females, as with us, were . . . trained in the arts of war" (55).[35]

Equiano's eclectic comments about Benin may also have been indebted to information found in William Smith's *A New Voyage to Guinea*, either directly or through Benezet. Benin, Smith says, "is the most potent Kingdom of Guinea, and more nearly resembles an European Monarchy than any other, and [a]s to Religion, they believe there is a God, the efficient Cause of all Things." "The Inhabitants are generally very good-natur'd and exceedingly civil and courteous." "Pregnant and menstruous Women," Smith writes, "they abstain from, and circumcise both Male and Female."[36] Smith, as well as Bosman and Benezet, all mention the absence of beggars and idleness that Equiano notes.[37] Smith, too, likens social customs in Benin to those "practised by the Patriarchs of the Old Testament."[38]

Smith and Equiano both use comparative cultural anthropology in part to render unfamiliar African practices comprehensible to their European audiences. Equiano renders the alien familiar through the analogy he draws between eighteenth-century Africans and ancient Hebrews. The practice of circumcision is a good example. The rhetorical effect of Equiano's references to the African custom is clear. They underscore his contention that the eighteenth-century Igbo are at a cultural and religious stage of development comparable to that of Hebrews before the Christian era. Equiano's Igbo, like the ancient Hebrews, are pre-Christian. He uses circumcision as a marker of innocence. Neither group, he implies, should be faulted for not having embraced Christianity because the Igbo, like the Hebrews before them, have not yet been introduced to Christianity. Equiano does not associate the Igbo practice of circumcision with that of contemporaneous Jews, who have chosen not to become Christians, because to do so would imply to his readers that the pre-Christian Igbo deserve condemnation for practicing a custom considered barbaric in the eighteenth century.

The Bible serves as more than simply a standard of cultural comparison for Equiano. For him it was a mnemonic device so powerful that we should question the extent to which it may have affected his memory through the power of suggestion. He tells us that just before he was sold into West Indian slavery at the end of 1762 a fellow seaman taught him "to read in the Bible, explaining many passages . . . which I did not comprehend." He was "wonderfully surprised to see the laws and rules of my country written almost exactly there: a circumstance which I believe tended to impress our manners and customs more deeply on my memory" (92).

Equiano's story of his life in Africa differs from the rest of his autobiography in the amount and specificity of detail it contains and in the way it is told. For example, he recalls the names of neither his parents nor any of his siblings, not even his beloved sister. Such an erasure of specific identities is more appropriate for a diasporan author of African descent than for one of African birth. Equiano's post-Africa account of his life, on the other hand, is extremely specific in providing contextual details. There he gives dates, places, and names almost without fail, as one would expect a diasporan writer to do. Much of the lack of specificity in his first chapter may derive from the calculated innocence he uses to represent a past that can now be reconstructed only with the help of others. In recalling "Eboe" he alternates between using the first-person "we" and the third-person "they." The effect of doing so gives readers the impression of someone who has neither quite lost his identification with a former African culture nor fully embraced the European one in which he now finds himself. Similarly, his alternating use of present and past tenses to describe life in "Eboe" demonstrates just how present the past remains in his memory. He generally uses the first-person voice and past tense to refer to events that he says he experienced or observed and the third-person and present tense to refer to Igbo practices that he has learned about from others. Equiano gives us the point of view of both the innocent boy who lived in Africa and of the experienced man who tells his story.

In the face of the small but increasingly influential number of polygenicists, who argued that God created various types of humans at different times, Equiano uses his description of "Eboe" to support the orthodox Christian monogenetic belief that all humans descended directly from Adam and Eve.[39] By elaborating his analogy between Africans and Old Testament Jews he both makes his monogenetic point and implies that Africans are fully prepared for Christian Revelation. Not even the most fervent eighteenth-century opponent of slavery contended that Africans were the cultural equals of Europeans, of whom the most advanced, in the eyes of the English, were of course themselves. But like the ancient Hebrews, Equiano implies, Africans are as fully human as Europeans, although at different stages of social and economic development.

Why might Equiano have created an African nativity and disguised an American birth? Before 1789 the abundant evidence and many arguments against the trans-Atlantic slave trade came from white voices alone. Both opponents and defenders of the trade recognized the rhetorical power an authentic African voice could wield in the struggle. In *An Essay on the Slavery and Commerce of the Human Species*, Equiano's future subscriber Thomas Clarkson acknowledged the desirability of hearing the victim's point of view. Clarkson dramatized the trans-Atlantic slave trade by placing the trade in "the clearest, and most conspicuous point of view." Employing the virtual reality of fiction to convey factual experience, he imagined himself interviewing a "melancholy African." "We shall," he wrote, "throw a considerable part of our information on this head into the form of a narrative: we shall suppose ourselves, in short, on the continent of Africa, and relate a scene, which, from its agreement with unquestionable facts, might not unreasonably be presumed to have been presented to our view, had we really been there."[40] Gilbert Francklyn, an apologist for the slave trade and slavery, responded to Clarkson in *An Answer to the Reverend Mr. Clarkson's Essay* (London, 1789) with a letter dated November 30, 1788: "Horrid picture of West India tyranny and brutality! And this is drawn upon the authority of people whose names Mr. Clarkson ventures not to produce. . . . I challenge Mr. Clarkson to produce a single man of decent character who ever gave him such an account. I do not mean a gentleman—I do not mean even a white man: I defy him to produce a Negro of character who would not turn pale in fabricating such assertions. I call upon Mr. Clarkson to produce any book he ever perused . . . in which he found such stories related."[41]

Equiano knew that to continue its increasing momentum the anti-slave trade movement needed precisely the kind of account of Africa and the Middle Passage he could supply. An African, not an African-American, voice was what the abolitionist cause required. He gave a voice to the millions of people forcibly taken from Africa and brought to the Americas as slaves. Equiano recognized a way to do very well financially by doing a great deal of good in supplying that much-needed voice. He may have forged a part of his personal identity and created an Igbo national identity *avant la lettre* to enable himself to become an effective spokesman for his fellow diasporan Africans.

Personal as well as political motives lay behind Equiano's claim to an African identity. Equiano wishes us to believe that he is not an egocentric social climber. He is, he suggests, returning socially to the status denied him but never rejected by him, the status lost in Africa of Embrenché equivalent to that of gentleman in Europe.[42] By the time of the *Narrative*'s publication, a claim of high-born African status had long been a convention in fictional and factual narratives recounted by and about former slaves, such as Aphra Behn's *Oroonoko*.[43] The social significance to an English-speaking audience of Equiano's placing himself in the category of Embrenché was clear. Several decades later John Adams noted, "[Em]Breeché, in the Heebo [Ibo] language, signifies *gentleman*. . . ."[44] In the cultures of both Equiano's Iboland and Britain, a *gentleman* was ideally someone who did not have to work for a living, someone who had the leisure and disinterest required of a judge and legislator, someone who lived by codes of honor, propriety, and decorum.

A confused memory of childhood events recounted some forty years later may explain the discrepancy between the ages Equiano records in his *Narrative* and the external documentary evidence, the problematic nature of his account of Africa, and his uncertainty about the name and location of his native village. This explanation, however, seems unlikely given the extraordinary accuracy of his memory for details when it can be checked against the historical record. The discrepancy was more likely rhetorically motivated: Equiano no doubt recognized that the younger he was thought to have been when he left Africa, the less credible his memories of his homeland would be. External evidence suggests that he was significantly younger than he says he was when he first entered exclusively English-speaking environments. He was too young to have experienced or observed many of the events and customs in Africa he describes and probably too young to have recalled others.

Acts of appropriation and the combination of sources, imagination, and memory characterize the account Gustavus Vassa gives us of Olaudah Equiano's Africa. The evidence that Gustavus Vassa invented the African birth of Olaudah Equiano is indecisive, but a compelling circumstantial case for self-invention can be made based on what we now know about the evolution of his claim to an African identity, the timing and context of the publication of his autobiography, his manipulation of dates, his reliance on secondary sources, and his rhetorical shaping of an African past. The opening chapters of *The Interesting Narrative* remain a classic example of cultural memory if not history.[45] Whether or not he was born an Igbo in Africa, Gustavus Vassa recreated himself as the spokesman for a nation not yet born on a continent still largely unknown during the eighteenth century. He anticipated by more than a century the Igbo nationalist and pan-African movements of the twentieth century. He did so to supply the abolitionist cause with the much-needed African voice that Thomas Clarkson wanted of someone who had apparently "really been there." As the father of the Igbo national identity, Equiano may have earned Afigbo's description of him as "an Igbo man to the marrow." He may just never have actually been in Africa.

NOTES

I am very grateful to Queen Mary College, University of London, for the Distinguished Visiting Fellowship that enabled me to research and write this essay.

1. All quotations, cited parenthetically in the text below, are taken from Vincent Carretta, ed., *The Interesting Narrative and Other Writings*, rev. ed. (New York: Penguin, 2003).

2. The most recent argument that Equiano was born an Igbo in Africa is made by Paul Lovejoy, "Autobiography and Memory: Gustavus Vassa, alias Olaudah Equiano, the African," *Slavery and Abolition* 27, no. 3 (2006): 317–47. For what I see as significant flaws in Lovejoy's argument and methodology, and Lovejoy's reaction, see my "Response" and his "Rejoinder," Vincent Carretta, "Response to Paul Lovejoy's 'Autobiography and Memory: Gustavus Vassa, alias Olaudah Equiano, the African,'" *Slavery and Abolition* 28, no. 1 (2007): 115–19; Paul Lovejoy, "Issues of Motivation—Vassa/Equiano and Carretta's Critique of the Evidence," *Slavery and Abolition* 28, no. 1 (2007): 121–25. A fuller and more balanced treatment than Lovejoy's of the question of Equiano's birthplace is Alexander Byrd, "Eboe, Country, Nation and Gustavus Vassa's *Interesting Narrative*," *William and Mary Quarterly* 63, no. 1 (2006): 123–48.

3. Adiele E. Afigbo, *Ropes of Sand: Studies in Igbo History and Culture* (London: University Press Limited, 1981), 183.

4. Ibid., 151.

5. Ibid., 155.

6. I first revealed the documentary evidence in endnotes to my edition of Olaudah Equiano's *The Interesting Narrative and Other Writings* in 1995, and subsequently in a series of elaborations of the evidence and its possible implications: "Olaudah Equiano or Gustavus Vassa?: New Light on an Eighteenth-Century Question of Identity," *Slavery and Abolition* 20, no. 3 (1999): 96–105; "More New Light on the Identity of Olaudah Equiano or Gustavus Vassa," in *The Global Eighteenth Century*, ed. Felicity Nussbaum (Baltimore: Johns Hopkins University Press, 2003), 226–35; *Equiano, the African: Biography of a Self-Made Man* (Athens: University of Georgia Press, 2005; paperback edition, New York: Penguin, 2007).

7. Steve E. Ogude, "Facts into Fiction: Equiano's *Narrative* Reconsidered," *Research in African Literatures* 13 (1982): 30–43, argues that because an eleven-year-old was very unlikely to have the almost total recall that Equiano claims: "Equiano relied less on the memory of his experience and more on other sources" (32) in his account of Africa. And in "No Roots Here: On the Igbo Roots of Olaudah Equiano," *Review of English and Literary Studies* 5 (1989): 1–16, Ogude denies that linguistic evidence supports Equiano's account. Despite Ogude's skepticism about Equiano's veracity, he does not question Vassa/Equiano's fundamental identity as an African. Gwilym I. Jones, "Olaudah Equiano of the Niger Ibo," in *Africa Remembered: Narratives by West Africans from the Era of the Slave Trade*, ed. Philip D. Curtin (Madison: University of Wisconsin Press, 1967), 60–69, finds Equiano's account of his "home and travels in Nigeria . . . disappointingly brief and confused" (61). He believes that "the little he can remember of his travels is naturally muddled and incoherent" because Equiano "was only eleven years old when he was kidnapped" (69). In her review of Paul Edwards, *The Life of Olaudah Equiano*, and Catherine Acholonu, *The Igbo Roots of Olaudah Equiano*, *Journal of African History* 33 (1992): 164–65, Elizabeth Isichei remarks of Equiano's description of Africa, "I have come to believe that it is a palimpsest, and that though he was indeed an Igbo (though even this has been questioned) he fused his own recollections with details obtained from other Igbo into a single version" (165). Katherine Faull Eze, "Self-Encounters: Two Eighteenth-Century African Memoirs from Moravian Bethlehem," in *Crosscurrents: African Americans, Africa, and Germany in the Modern* World, ed. David McBride, LeRoy Hopkins, and C. Aisha Blackshire-Belay (Columbia, SC: Camden House, 1998), 29–52, considers "Equiano's Igbo past [to be] mostly a reconstruction of European or Colonial American travel narratives, most obviously" (50n22).

8. Chinua Achebe, *Morning Yet on Creation Day: Essays* (London: Heinemann, 1975), 177.

9. Joseph Inikori, "The Development of Entrepreneurship in Africa: Southeastern Nigeria during the Era of the Transatlantic Slave Trade," in *Black Business and Economic Power*, ed. Alusine Jalloh and Toyin Falola (Rochester, NY: University of Rochester Press, 2002), 41–79; quotation 78n44. Quoted in Gwendolyn Midlo Hall, *Slavery and African Ethnicities in the Americas: Restoring the Links* (Chapel Hill: University of North Carolina Press, 2005), 129–30.

10. Elizabeth Isichei, *A History of the Igbo People* (New York: St. Martin's Press, 1976), 21. John Thornton, *Africa and Africans in the Making of the Atlantic World, 1400–1800*, 2nd ed. (Cambridge: Cambridge University Press, 1998), 310, notes that "almost all we know about the [Igbo] region in the eighteenth century comes from the testimony of Olaudah Equiano, an Igbo who was enslaved as a youth around 1755."

11. Sheila Lambert, ed., *House of Commons Sessional Papers of the Eighteenth Century* (Wilmington, DE: Scholarly Resources, 1975), 69:19. Penny had made five voyages to Bonny, on the Bight of Biafra.

12. The most thorough treatment of the effects the trans-Atlantic slave trade had on the conception and development of African identities during the early modern period is Thornton, *Africa and Africans*. On the absence of a pan-Igbo identity in Africa during the eighteenth century, see Sigismund W. Koelle, *Polyglotta Africana* (London: Church Missionary House, 1854), 7–8; Douglas B. Chambers,

"'My Own Nation': Igbo Exiles in the Diaspora," *Slavery and Abolition* 18, no. 1 (1997): 72–97; Michael Gomez, *Exchanging Our Country Marks: The Transformation of African Identities in the Colonial and Antebellum South* (Chapel Hill: University of North Carolina Press, 1998), 125–26; David Northrup, "Igbo and Myth Igbo: Culture and Ethnicity in the Atlantic World, 1600–1815," *Slavery and Abolition* 21, no. 3 (2000): 1–20; Douglas B. Chambers, "Ethnicity in the Diaspora: The Slave-Trade and the Creation of African 'Nations' in the Americas," *Slavery and Abolition* 22, no. 3 (2001): 25–39; Douglas B. Chambers, "The Significance of the Igbo in the Bight of Biafra Slave-Trade: A Rejoinder to Northrup's 'Myth Igbo,'" *Slavery and Abolition* 23, no. 1 (2002): 101–20; Chima J. Korieh, "African Ethnicity as Mirage? Historicising the Essence of the Igbo in Africa and the Atlantic Diaspora," *Dialectical Anthropology* 30 (2006): 91–118.

13. Isichei, *A History of the Igbo People*, 20.

14. Ibid., 19.

15. Richard N. Henderson, *The King in Every Man: Evolutionary Trends in Onitsha Society and Culture* (New Haven: Yale University Press, 1972), 41.

16. Northrup, "Igbo and Myth Igbo," 15.

17. Philip D. Morgan, *Slave Counterpoint: Black Culture in the Eighteenth-Century Chesapeake and Lowcountry* (Chapel Hill: University of North Carolina Press, 1998), 62–67. Stephen D. Behrendt, "Markets, Transaction Cycles, and Profits: Merchant Decision Making in the British Slave Trade," *William and Mary Quarterly* 58 (2001): 196.

18. Lorena S. Walsh, "The Chesapeake Slave Trade: Regional Patterns, African Origins, and Some Implications," *William and Mary Quarterly* 58 (2001): 139–70, 153.

19. Achebe, *Morning Yet on Creation Day*, says, "Equiano was an Ibo, I believe from the village of Iseke in the Orlu division of Eastern Nigeria" (59). Arguments supporting the accuracy of Equiano's memory of Africa appear in Catherine Obianju Acholonu, "The Home of Olaudah Equiano—A Linguistic and Anthropological Search," *Journal of Commonwealth Literature* 22 (1987): 5–16; and Paul Edwards and Rosalind Shaw, "The Invisible *Chi* in Equiano's *Interesting Narrative*," *Journal of Religion in Africa* 19 (1989): 146–56; Acholonu, *The Igbo Roots of Olaudah Equiano* (Owerri, Nigeria: Ata Publications, 1989), identifies "Essaka" as modern-day Isseke, near Ihiala, Nigeria, and claims she has found Equiano's direct descendants. But since her argument requires us to believe that her sources lived to be more than one hundred fifty years old, her methodology is suspect.

20. Paul Edwards, "Introduction," *The Life of Olaudah Equiano. Or Gustavus Vassa, the African* (London: Dawsons of Pall Mall, 1969), xix–xx, suggests east of the Niger; G. I. Jones, "Olaudah Equiano of the Niger Ibo," 61, suggests west.

21. Daniel B. Thorp, "Chattel with a Soul: The Autobiography of a Moravian Slave," *The Pennsylvania Magazine of History & Biography* 112 (1988): 433–51. Thorp notes that "the phrase 'the unknown part of' seems to be a marginal addition" (447).

22. A translation into English of Christian Georg Andreas Oldendorp's abridged manuscript published in 1777 is Oldendorp, *History of the Mission of the Evangelical Brethren on the Caribbean Islands of St. Thomas, St. Croix, and St. John*, ed. Johann Jakob Bossard, trans. Arnold R. Highfield and Vladimir Barac (Ann Arbor, MI: Karoma, 1987). The complete German manuscript of Oldendorp's text has been published as *Historie der caribischen Inseln Sanct Thomas, Sanct Crux und Sanct Jan, insbesondere der dasigen Neger und der Mission der evangelischen Brüder unter denselben*, ed. Gudrun Meier, Stephan Palmié, and Horst Ulbricht (Dresden, DE: Staatliches Museum für Völkerkunde, 2000). I thank John Thornton for providing me with an English translation of the section on Igbos in the German manuscript.

23. James Grainger, "The Sugar-Cane. A Poem" (London, 1764), 2:75. Like many other eighteenth-century commentators, Grainger confuses the Ibibio people and Igbo.

24. James Grainger, *An Essay on the More Common West-India Diseases* (London, 1764), 7.

25. Edward Long, *The History of Jamaica* (London, 1774), 2:403–4.

26. Grainger, *An Essay*, 14.

27. Bryan Edwards, *The History, Civil and Commercial, of the British Colonies in the West*

Indies (London, 1793), 2:74. Other negative eighteenth-century characterizations of the Igbo include Bernard Romans, *A Concise Natural History of East and West Florida* (New York, 1775), 105; William Beckford, jun., *Remarks upon the Situation of Negroes in Jamaica, Impartially Made from a local Experience of nearly thirteen Years in that Island, by William Beckford, jun.* (London, 1788), 23; and Hector McNeill, *Observations on the Treatment of the Negroes, in the Island of Jamaica, Including some Account of their Temper and Character, with Remarks on the Importation of Slaves from the Coast of Africa. In a letter to a Physician in England, from Hector McNeill* (London, 1788), 24–25.

28. John Matthews, *A Voyage to the River Sierra-Leone, on the Coast of Africa; Containing an Account of the Trade and Productions of the Country, and of the Civil and Religious Customs and Manners of the People; in a Series of Letters to a Friend in England. By John Matthews, Lieutenant in the Royal Navy; During his Residence in that Country in the Years 1785, 1786, and 1787* (London, 1788).

29. Anthony Benezet, *Some Historical Account of Guinea*, 2nd ed. (London, 1788), 5.

30. Ibid., 92.

31. James Field Stanfield, *Observations on a Voyage to the Coast of Africa, in a Series of Letters to Thomas Clarkson, by James Field Stanfield, Formerly a Mariner in the African Trade* (London, 1788), 241.

32. Matthews, *A Voyage*, 113.

33. Equiano's note in editions 1–9 reads, "See also Lieut. Matthew's Voyage, 123."

34. Thomas Astley, *A New General Collection of Voyages and Travels* (London, 1745), 2:502.

35. G. I. Jones, "Olaudah Equiano of the Niger Ibo," remarks on the improbability of Equiano's having seen women warriors, p. 66.

36. William Smith, *A New Voyage to Guinea*, 2nd ed. (London, 1745), 233–34, 237, 228, 233.

37. Ibid., 230; William Bosman, *A New and Accurate Description of the Coast of Guinea* (London, 1705), 409; Benezet, *Some Historical Account*, 33, 50n22.

38. Smith, *A New Voyage to Guinea*, 244.

39. The most significant polygenicist at the time was Edward Long, whose atypical eighteenth-century arguments in his *History of Jamaica* anticipate dominant nineteenth-century pseudoscientific racism.

40. Thomas Clarkson, *An Essay on the Slavery and Commerce of the Human Species* (London, 1786), 117–18.

41. Gilbert Francklyn, *An Answer An Answer to the Reverend Mr. Clarkson's Essay* (London, 1789), 191–92.

42. Equiano's proper place in literary history has not yet been widely recognized. For example, even the Equiano scholar Angelo Costanzo wrongly "places [Vassa's] work in the secular autobiographical tradition established by Benjamin Franklin" (1019). Michael Mascuch, *Origins of the Individualist Self: Autobiography and Self-Identity in England, 1591–1791* (Cambridge: Polity, 1997) overlooks Equiano as a contender for status as the first self-published autobiographer who advertized and distributed the story of his life. Mascuch bestows that recognition on James Lackington, one of the booksellers through whom Equiano sold his *Interesting Narrative* two years before Lackington published his own autobiography in 1791.

43. Other examples are Thomas Bluett, *Some Memoirs of the Life of Job, the Son of Solomon the High Priest of Boonda in Africa* (London, 1734); James Albert Ukawsaw Gronniosaw, *A Narrative of the Remarkable Particulars in the Life of James Albert Ukawsaw Gronniosaw, an African Prince, as Related by Himself* (Bath, 1772); and the brief autobiographical comments by Equiano's binomial friend and sometime collaborator Quobna Ottobah Cugoano (John Stuart), *Thoughts and Sentiments on the Evil and Wicked Traffic of the Slavery and Commerce of the Human Species* (London, 1787).

44. John Adams, *Sketches Taken during Ten Voyages to Africa, Between the Years 1786 and 1800* (London, 1822), 41 (emphasis added).

45. Pierre Nora, "Between Memory and History: *Les Lieux de Mémoire*," *Representations* 26 (1989): 7–25; Ralph A. Austen, "The Slave Trade as History and Memory: Confrontations of Slaving Voyage Documents and Communal Traditions," *William and Mary Quarterly* 58, no. 1 (2001): 229–44.

15 OLAUDAH EQUIANO OR GUSTAVUS VASSA

WHAT'S IN A NAME?

Paul E. Lovejoy

The person portrayed in *The Interesting Narrative of the Life of Olaudah Equiano; or, Gustavus Vassa, the African* (London, 1789) was known in his own day as Gustavus Vassa, and sometimes the African, although today he is known as Olaudah Equiano and most often simply as Equiano, as if that was his last name.[1] The man was clearly of ethnic origin that today we would call Igbo, and on his own testimony was born in a place he called Essaka but also referred to as Elese. The evidence is overwhelming; moreover, his African origins were certainly not in doubt to German ethnographer, Johann Friedrich Blumenbach, when he met Vassa in London in 1792. Blumenbach had reviewed *The Interesting Narrative* in Berlin in 1790.[2] The question raised here is whether we should refer to the literary *persona* as Olaudah Equiano, which has become fashionable in scholarly circles and more generally in the public, or to the name that he consciously called himself, which was Gustavus Vassa? There is some confusion in what the author of *The Interesting Narrative* meant by his reference to being "Eboe," "African," and sometimes even calling himself "Ethiopian" and "Libyan." This might suggest that he wanted to be known by his African name, but he did not ever use his African name alone and only used his birth name rarely, most notably on the cover of his autobiography, where he also identified himself as Gustavus Vassa, the African. Therefore, one is forced to ask: what name should literary scholars and historians now use in identifying the man and his story, and why does it matter where he was born or what his name was?

Determining the man behind the biography in part relates to where he was born and how he identified with his place of birth, which is a much contested subject. G. I. Jones early postulated that Vassa's "Essaka" was to be found on the west bank of the Niger River, in part because of Vassa's reference to the Kingdom of Benin.[3] Subsequently, it has been thought that he came from Isieke in central Igboland from near Orlu, most forcefully by Catherine Obianuju Acholonu.[4] To the best of my knowledge, Acholonu is the only scholar who has attempted to explain the two names that Vassa used to describe his birthplace—Essaka and Elese.[5] Carretta and other scholars have chosen to ignore her contribution. Subsequently, it has been suggested that Vassa's "Essaka" may have been Usaka, near Umuohia, which makes considerable sense in terms of Vassa's description of his trip to the coast, which would have been along the Cross River to Calabar, if he came from Usaka.[6] If he came from Isieke, he would have more likely gone to Bonny, in the Niger Delta.

Vincent Carretta has raised the possibility, and sometimes he is thought to claim, that Vassa was born in South Carolina instead of Africa and specifically that he was not born in Igboland.[7] Carretta even thinks that Vassa's description of his supposed Igbo homeland, which Carretta thinks is fabricated, was "in the kingdom of Benin," which is clearly a misreading of Vassa's autobiography and which overlooks a considerable amount of scholarship on Igbo history.[8] The details that Vassa provides are unique and specific and are not found in any of the sources that he cites as references in his *Narrative*. This unique information, which includes details on facial scarification, circumcision, the terminology for elders, and the conception of Igbo as "the other," is why historians of the Bight of Biafra and its interior consider Vassa's descriptions and the details of his childhood important. Vassa not only fought against slavery but he chronicled the story of his people, even coming to realize that he, too, was "Egbo," that is one of the "others" who in fact had a shared identity.

Certainly, literary names are common, especially for women authors, such as the Bronte sisters. But was Vassa's use of Olaudah Equiano on the cover of his autobiography intended to be a literary name? I would suggest not. A few other examples of the literary name versus the legal name come to mind, including George Eliot (legal name Mary Anne Evans), Isak Dinesen (Karen Blixen), Lewis Carroll (Charles Dodgson), Mark Twain (Samuel Clemens), H. D. (Hilda Doolittle), O. Henry (William Sydney Porter), and George Orwell (Eric Arthur Blair), or perhaps more appropriate for comparison, Linda Brent (Harriet Jacobs). Authors chose *noms de plume* for various reasons, as Carmela Ciuraru has noted.[9] Sometimes authors wanted to disguise their gender; other times writers feared or sought to avoid recognition. Occasionally, names were shortened for marketing purposes. Usually, authors were subsequently known by their pen names, though not so in the case of Harriet Jacobs, who initially wrote under a pseudonym to avoid possible reenslavement but has always been known by her given name otherwise.[10] Although Ciuraru considers the various motivations for "pseudonymity," none of the reasons explaining these other cases seems to apply to Vassa. Gustavus Vassa was not trying to disguise his identity but rather used both names on the cover of his autobiography. Nor did he fancy the use of his birth name, which subsequently has become his *nom de plume*. The birth name has become the signifier of the man but in fact—and as this chapter indicates—this identity has been assigned to him by later generations, not by himself in his own lifetime or even in the minds of others who knew him while he was alive, including his wife and children.

Unlike the common patterns in which *noms de plume* were promoted by individuals themselves, Vassa received the *nom de plume* Olaudah Equiano through attribution after he was dead for more than one hundred and fifty years. At least since 1960, when Thomas Hodgkin first published excerpts from *The Interesting Narrative*, virtually all scholars have referred to the author as Equiano, not Vassa.[11] Most recently, Brycchan Carey has even claimed that the man should be referred to as Olaudah Equiano, "since this is the name by which he appears to have wanted posterity to remember him."[12] But this assertion is not accurate; indeed, available evidence suggests that he actually wanted to be—and was—called Gustavus Vassa. On at least one occasion, the man himself appears to have protested passionately at the use of his birth name. In information on the back of a letter written by Vassa to Granville Sharp on May 6, 1780, there is a note, certainly written some time after Vassa's death in 1797, which claims Vassa "fell into fits if any One pronounced his Real name, which was Olaudah Equiano."[13] According to the note, the source of information was J. Phillips of Middle Hill, Cornwall, whose father, James Phillips, was the Quaker printer who published many of the major abolitionist works of the 1780s, including Clarkson's Cambridge thesis. He knew Vassa personally.[14] Phillips' note on the Vassa letter introduces the interesting idea of a "Real name," which it seems Phillips equated with birth name and an African identity. Not only does the comment suggest that Vassa did not use the name Equiano, except for purposes of establishing his African birth, but actually preferred not to use his African name in personal settings. He used his birth name as part of the proof that he had been born in Africa and that his enslavement and transport were crucial aspects of his identity, but it seems that he was not reclaiming the name for purposes of being called by that name.

Like Vassa, those who were sent from Africa as slaves certainly remembered the names of their birth but they did not always use them. Birth names had special symbolism for enslaved Africans, as for most people, and sometimes these names survived, as in the use of Akan names in Jamaica and elsewhere. In Jamaica, Muhammad Kaba Saghanughu was known as Dick when he first arrived at Spice Grove estate from West Africa in 1777 but he took the name of his deceased master, Robert Peart, when he became a Moravian in 1813, fifteen years after his master's death. Nonetheless,

Kaba always retained his Muslim name and asked other Muslims to call him by that name.[15] Mahommah Gardo Baquaqua was called José as a slave in Brazil from 1845 to 1847 but reclaimed his name upon his escape in New York City and his residency in Haiti, despite the fact that it was a Muslim name and he had become a Baptist.[16] Although individuals sometimes reasserted the use of childhood names, slave names often stuck when people achieved emancipation. They were the names individuals had come to be known by, as with Venture Smith, who was named Venture because his purchase price constituted the full capital of the young man, Robinson Mumford, who bought him at Anomabu on the Gold Coast in 1739. He was called Smith after his last master who allowed him to buy his freedom and that of his wife and children.[17] Yet he appears never to have used his birth name, which he records in his autobiography as Broteer, the eldest son of Saungm Furro.

Vassa was thus not unique in remembering his childhood name, but he only used the name given to him as a slave, except on the cover of his autobiography and in some letters to newspapers at that time and after, which Carretta and other scholars have clearly recognized. Vassa always used the name Gustavus Vassa, even after publication of *The Interesting Narrative* in which he included his birth name as Equiano, which appears to be derived from Ekwuno, Ekweano, Ekwoanya, or Ekwealuo, all common Igbo names, but in no case was it a surname, which Igbo did not use at the time.[18] In the first edition, Vassa stated that when he was a slave he "was obliged to bear the present name [Vassa], by which I have been known ever since."[19] In the ninth edition in 1794, he revised this statement, admitting only that it was the "name I have been known ever since." Apparently, he no longer felt an obligation to use his slave name because he had become widely known under the name, Gustavus Vassa, but the birth name had meaning in terms of his establishing his Africanity.

Hence what is in the name Vassa/Equiano raises the concept of the literary name, or "pen name," and the politics of such a distinction enable a better understanding of the man and his times and indeed his continuing relevance and influence on the abolition movement and as a literary persona. Theories of naming in a literary context additionally provide useful coordinates for what can be said about the use of "Equiano" as a surname and the politics of his naming or misnaming.[20] By coincidence, it should be noted that one of his possible birthplaces, Usaka, is located in a district that is called Ikwuano, but lest the similarity between Equiano and Ikwuano be thought significant, a word of caution about historicizing names. The term "Ikwuano" was adopted by the four clans that inhabit an area south of Bende that originally was called, pejoratively, Ala Ala, "for many centuries." Ala Ala means "going down, down, down," and in the late 1940s, the elders of the four clans decided to adopt a term that literally means "four clans."[21] To examine Vassa's terminology more closely, therefore, it will be worthwhile to distinguish among a few categories that are operative throughout this essay: the names by which others called him; the name by which he called himself; the name by which he was legally recognized in Britain; and the ways in which he referred to Africans, Ethiopians, Libyans, and people of his own "nation," who were "Eboe," that is, Igbo.[22]

That the autobiography was a political tract, it is argued here, reveals the answer to the question of what's in a name. His birth name was useful in establishing his credentials as African because his authority rested on his African birth, his kidnapping, his endurance of the Middle Passage, and his subsequent slavery and emancipation. Nonetheless, from when he was about twelve years old in 1754 until his death in 1797, he was known in public and in private as Gustavus Vassa. After 1786, he usually identified himself in print as Gustavus Vassa, the African, but rarely by his birth name, which he never did by that name alone. As author and abolitionist he identified by the name that he was known, that is, Gustavus Vassa, not Olaudah Equiano. "Vassa" was the name legally assigned to him by the British Empire (this was his name on his baptismal record and manumission papers as well). And as a British citizen, now free with the papers to prove it, he was willing, for protection, convenience, and consistency, to go by the name Vassa, but this may have had something to do with the restraints in which he had to live and survive in a country in which slavery was still legal. Vassa was additionally assigned other names; during the Middle Passage, he was known as Michael, while in Virginia he was called Jacob, before finally being named Gustavus Vassa, the name he received when he was being taken to England.[23] In his home country, Igboland, he noted that:

> our children were named from some event, some circumstance, or fancied foreboding at the time of their birth. I was named Olaudah, which, in our language, signifies vicissitude, or fortunate also; one favoured, and having a loud voice and well spoken.[24]

He did not explain the meaning of "Equiano," but he did preface chapter 1 in his autobiography, "The Life of Gustavus Vassa" without reference to the name Equiano.

His master, Captain Michael Henry Pascal, was responsible for giving him the name Gustavus Vassa, which is recorded in *The Interesting Narrative* as an unwelcome imposition. According to Vassa's account,

> Some of the people of the ship used to tell me they were going to carry me back to my own country, and this made me very happy. I was quite rejoiced at the idea of going back; and thought if I should get home what wonders I should have to tell. But I was reserved for another fate, and was soon undeceived when we came within sight of the English coast. While I was on board this ship, my captain and master named me Gustavus Vasa. I at that time began to understand him a little, and refused to be called so, and told him as well as I could that I would be called Jacob; but he said I should not, and still called me Gustavus; and when I refused to answer to my new name, which at first I did, it gained me many a cuff so at length I submitted, and by which I have been known ever since.[25]

One has to ask if the apparent reluctance, recounted in hindsight, was a literary device of its own, which emphasized Vassa's understanding of fate, as Paul Edwards and Rosiland Shaw have argued in relation to the Igbo conception, "*chi*,"[26] which holds that each individual has a personal deity and hence an individual fate. It is perhaps possible that Vassa's Methodism through the Huntingdon Connexion was a retention or adaption of the Igbo worldview, which was not incompatible with respect to ideas of predestination, with which the Countess of Huntingdon and her followers were particularly associated.

The idea that he was literally beaten into acceptance of this name is worth pausing over. How are we to explain his reluctance to accept the name given to him by his master? He could not have understood the significance of the biblical name, Jacob, until much later, although the name is consistent with the many "Hebrewisms" in *The Interesting Narrative*. Nor would he have known that King Gustavus Vasa of Sweden (1496–1560) was the liberator of his people and the national hero of the Swedish nation at the time he was named. Therefore, I assume that he did not actually protest his new name in the way he describes but said he did so later for effect, for a reason. It makes no sense that he objected at the time, but in 1788–1789 when he wrote *The Interesting Narrative*, he understood the significance of his namesake, as his readers would have also. It was an immodest way by which he informed his readers that he had only reluctantly accepted his fate, determined by his *chi*, which was thrust upon him, as reflected in his name. Vassa was obviously giving himself agency, even if his alleged resistance was suppressed, but surely he projected his later knowledge of his namesake as an implicit recognition of his own preordained authority. Vassa appears to have attached significance to his assigned name because it drew on public knowledge of the Swedish monarchy, although in 1755 at the time he was allegedly protesting, he could not possibly have known this, any more than he would have known that Jacob climbed a ladder and confronted God.

The choice of name seems to have been prophetic, although it is still unclear why Captain Pascal selected that name of all names in 1754. Known as Gustavus Eriksson before his coronation, King Gustavus I was the son of Erik Johansson, Swedish senator and nationalist, who was killed in the massacre at Stockholm in 1520, under the orders of King Christian II of Denmark.[27] Gustavus was imprisoned but escaped to lead the peasants of Dalarna to victory over the Danes, being elected Protector of Sweden in 1521. In 1523 the Riksdag at Strangnas elected him king, ending the Kalmar Union that King Christian II of Denmark was attempting to enforce. Two centuries later, English playwright Henry Brooke recorded these heroic deeds in his play, *Gustavus Vasa, The Deliverer of his Country*, published in 1739. The play was banned for political reasons and was not actually staged in London until 1805. However, it was performed in Dublin in 1742 as *The Patriot*, and it was republished in London in 1761, 1778, 1796, and 1797. According to Vincent Carretta, "republication . . . kept the play and its discourse of political slavery before the British public."[28] Moreover, the example was also kept before the public because the reigning king of Sweden from 1771 until his tragic death in 1792 was the popular Gustavus Vasa III, who was murdered by Count Ankarstrom at a masked ball, dying of wounds on March 29, 1792. The tragedy became the inspiration for Giuseppe Verdi's *Un Ballo in Maschera*. The significance of the name Gustavus Vassa (particularly for an African) figured into the London imagination as an image of an African Moses comparable to the Swedish model, and the public was reminded of that image through assassination. How did Vassa react to these events? Were his own tribulations in 1792 when he was falsely being accused of being born in the Caribbean somehow related to the killing of the Swedish king? The timing of these events is important, as discussed below, and it is useful to consider how the constellation of events might have had an impact on Vassa.

As a child, Vassa would have learned that the relationship of an individual with the supernatural was special, depending on a personal *chi*. As he stated in *The Interesting Narrative*, "I regard myself as a particular favourite of Heaven, and acknowledge the mercies of Providence in every occurrence of my life."[29] His apparent reluctance when named Vassa seems to have been related to the necessity of accepting his fate. Indeed his comments on his personal destiny are consistent with this interpretation. On board ship to England with his new master, Pascal, he noted that he was "still at a loss to conjecture my destiny." He wanted to return to Africa, but he came to accept the fact that he "was reserved for another fate."[30] His recognition of this Igbo philosophical construct must have become more coherent to Vassa as he grew older and reflected on his life. The suggestion is that by the time of his enslavement at age eleven or twelve, he was already imbued with this cosmological framework, which is confirmed by his closeness to his mother, who most certainly would have espoused such ideas.

Gustavus Vassa only used the name Olaudah Equiano in relation to the story of his life to attest to his African birth. This literary purpose related to the political importance of identification as an African in the abolition movement. Why today's scholars and student public that read his autobiography have adopted his "African" name, which in fact was part of his political statement, rather than the name he actually used, is a subject worthy of reflection. It says more about those who identify with a literary "Equiano" and the contemporary need to adopt African names as a form of political activism than with the identity of the author in his everyday life and his commitment to the abolition movement of his day.

Historian Thomas Hodgkin was apparently the first scholar to use the name Olaudah Equiano, when he published excerpts of Vassa's autobiography in *Nigerian Perspectives* (1960).[31] Hodgkin appears to have referred to the man as Olaudah Equiano because his focus was on Vassa's account of his Nigerian homeland and at a time when that was his name. However, in 1962, Christopher Fyfe referred to the man as Gustavus Vassa in his monumental *A History of Sierra Leone*, because it was "the name he went by."[32] Paul Edwards, a literary critic, was already following Hodgkin's lead in calling Vassa by his birth name, Olaudah Equiano, and the future of the name was virtually sealed.[33] In 1967, anthropologist G. I. Jones attempted to reconstruct where Vassa might have come from in Nigeria, although he settled on using only the first name,

Olaudah, perhaps because he was aware that Igbo did not use surnames until modern times. Nonetheless, Jones's chapter, "Olaudah Equiano of the Niger Ibo," appears to have helped further set the name among scholars.[34] In the same year, Edwards published his edition of *The Interesting Narrative*, which he attributed to Olaudah Equiano[35] and which subsequently has been the almost universally used name.[36] In the case of Vincent Carretta's biography, moreover, it is clear that the title, *Equiano, the African: Biography of a Self-Made Man*, refers both to the biography of Vassa as "a self-made man" and to the creation of the literary figure, Equiano, the African. Carretta considers that Vassa, the author, probably fabricated his African birth in the course of creating the literary figure, Equiano's African birth being part of a campaign of self-promotion. The problems with Carretta's interpretation, however, expose the slippery slope between autobiographical invention and biographical reconstruction.[37]

Vincent Carretta once claimed that "except for its appearance on the title page, the name Olaudah Equiano was never used by the author of *The Interesting Narrative* in either public or private written communication," although Carretta later realized that Vassa did call himself Equiano elsewhere. As Carretta acknowledges, it is still safe to say that "Whether in print, unpublished correspondence, or in his will, he always identified himself as Gustavus Vassa."[38] When he did refer to himself by his birth name, he never used it alone. He identified himself with both names in cosigning a letter to William Dickson, who subscribed to the first edition of *The Interesting Narrative*, which was published April 25, 1789, where Vassa writes as one of the "Sons of Africa," and in a letter dated May 14, 1792, Grosvenor Street, to "the Lords Spiritual and Temporal, and the Commons of the Parliament of Great Britain."[39] Otherwise, his marriage certificate, his will, and the rental agreement for his flat in Plaisterers' Hall, near the London City Wall, are all in the name of Vassa, without reference to his birth name, as is the case with all other known documentation. Those documents that were registered with the British courts establish his legally recognized name.

Hence the entry for his baptism in the parish register for St. Margaret's Church for February 9, 1759, reads: "Gustavus Vassa a Black born in Carolina 12 years old."[40] The muster book for the Arctic expedition of 1773 lists a Gustavus Weston, identified as a seaman, age twenty-eight, born in South Carolina, and who Carretta concludes is Vassa, although as John Bugg has observed, there is some reason to doubt this. If he was twenty-eight in 1773, he would not have been twelve in 1759 but fourteen, and he would have been twenty-one when he received his freedom in 1766. As I have argued, however, he was probably born in about 1742 and hence would have been sixteen or seventeen when he was baptized and twenty-three to twenty-four when he obtained his freedom. We are certain that Vassa was on board the Arctic expedition, which we know from *The Interesting Narrative*.[41] Nonetheless, the entry proves little else, especially in terms of his age. Even if Vassa is to be equated with Weston, as a former slave, he would have carried documentation that he was free, and in most cases such proof came from baptismal records and letters of emancipation. Vassa had both, which he may well have carried with him most of the time. As a freeman on the Arctic expedition, he was unlikely to contradict what was on his baptismal record and his emancipation documentation, although he apparently did, if he claimed he was an age not compatible with what was on his baptismal record. It is clear from *The Interesting Narrative* that he had personal papers with him that would establish his identity. Although he may have been listed in the muster roll of the Arctic-bound *Race Horse*, if Weston is Vassa, Vassa was not an ordinary seaman. He served as Dr. Charles Irving's assistant in the distillation of sea water and in conducting various other scientific experiments.[42] Whether his Swedish name was or was not transcribed accurately, the proof that he was free depended on his baptismal identification stating his birth in South Carolina and his manumission from Robert King, which is reproduced in *The Interesting Narrative*. Vassa was unlikely to have changed his baptismal testimony, whether true or not. Hence the records for the *Race Horse* only attest to his freed status and do not independently verify a birth in South Carolina.[43] Moreover, it should be noted that shortly after his baptism in 1759, he claims that he "had frequently told several people . . . the story of my being kidnapped with my sister, and of our being separated, as I have related before; and I had as often expressed my anxiety for her fate, and my sorrow at having never met her again."[44]

Indeed Vassa gives the impression that he longed to return to Africa. He claims that as early as 1754, he was pining for such a homecoming. On his way to England, Vassa remembered that "Some of the people of the ship used to tell me they were going to carry me back to my own country, and this made me very happy."[45] Either these memories are fabricated because they directly contradict the Carolina baptismal record or they prove that the baptismal documentation is wrong for some reason. Despite the possibility that he made up the story of an African birth, there is a consistent and steady reference in *The Interesting Narrative* to telling people of his ordeal and his identification as someone from Africa, from 1754 to 1759, and from 1775 to 1779, well before Vassa might have envisioned writing a political autobiography dedicated to Queen Charlotte, the *malata* queen. Vassa's African origins were further demonstrated in 1775–1776 when Dr. Charles Irving employed him on an expedition and plantation scheme on the Mosquito Shore of Central America because he assumed that Vassa would be able to recruit his own "countrymen," which he appears to have done.[46] In 1779, in a request to the Lord Bishop of London that he was "desirous of returning to Africa as a missionary," Vassa additionally described himself as "a native of Africa, and has a knowledge of the manners and customs of the inhabitants of the country."[47] Similarly, he said he was "from Guinea" in the *Morning Herald* of London on December 29, 1786.[48] In all cases, whether or not he mentioned his name, he was only using the name Vassa as far as can be seen. Not only is Gustavus Vassa the name on baptismal and naval records and in letters to newspapers and his private correspondence but also on his marriage certificate with Susannah Cullen (whom he married at St. Andrew's Church, Soham, Cambridgeshire, on April 7, 1792) and in his "Will and Codicil."[49] When his wife died in February 1796, the *Cambridge Chronicle and Journal* reported: "On Tuesday died at Soham, after a long illness, which she supported with Christian fortitude, Mrs. Susannah Vassa, the wife of Gustavus Vassa the African."[50] Again, these include legal documents, so there is considerable logic to his use of his legal name here.

Vassa's two children were also called by his name; Anna Maria was born October 16, 1793, and baptized in St. Andrew's Church, Soham, January 30, 1794. Joanna was born April 11, 1795, and also baptized in Soham, on April 29, 1795. Anna Maria died July 21, 1797, aged four years and was buried in St. Andrew's Church, Chesterton, Cambridge, where her commemorative stone notes that she was the daughter of "GUSTAVUS VASSA, the African."[51] Her sister, Joanna, married the Rev. Henry Bromley; the couple appears to have had no children. Joanna died on March 10, 1857, at the age of sixty-one and was buried at Abney Park Cemetery in Stoke Newington on March 16, 1857. Rev. Bromley lived another twenty years and was buried alongside her on February 12, 1878. The inscription on Joanna's gravestone reads "Memory of Joanna beloved wife of Henry Bromley, daughter of Gustavus Vassa, the African. Born April 11, 1795 and died March 1857." *The Ipswich Journal* reported her death as follows: "DIED. 10th inst., at Benyon-terrace, Beckingham Road, London, in her 62nd year, Joanna, wife of the Rev. Henry Bromley, daughter of Gustavus Vasa, the African, and ward of the late John Audley, Esq.: some years since a well known and highly-respected resident in Cambridge."[52]

In his letters to newspapers and his private correspondence, Vassa also used the name given to him as a slave, although he was already identifying himself as "African" according to stories he related as early as 1759, at the time of his baptism, and from "Guinea" since at least 1779.[53] By 1788, he also identified with Ethiopia, according to a letter in *The Public Advertiser*, January 28, 1788, addressed "To J. T. [James Tobin] Esq; Author of the BOOKS called CURSORY REMARKS & REJOINDER," he signed "Your fervent Servant, GUSTAVUS

VASSA, the Ethiopian and the King's late Commissary for the African settlement." And again on February 5, 1788, he identified himself in *The Public Advertiser* as "GUSTAVUS VASSA, the Ethiopian, and late Commissary for the African Settlement, Baldwin's Gardens," in Holborn. Obviously, Ethiopian and indeed Libyan were synonymous with African in his effort to communicate the fact that he had come from the continent.[54]

By July 5, 1788, Vassa was only identifying as "African." In the *Morning Post and Daily Advertiser* he signed himself "GUTAVUS [*sic*] VASA, *the African*." By the following April he was also using the name Equiano but never alone, as he did in a letter in *The Diary; or Woodfall's Register*, April 25, 1789, "To Mr. William Dickson, formerly Private Secretary to the Hon. Edward Hay, Governor of the Island of Barbadoes.[55] We are, Sir, Your most obedient humble servants, OLAUDAH EQUIANO, or GUSTAVUS VASSA [and many others]." It was noted on May 9, 1789, in *The Gazeteer and New Daily Advertiser* of London that "the celebrated Oluadah Equiano, or Gustavus Vassa, who has lately published his Memoirs, will speak." Thereafter, however, he usually referred to himself and was referred to by others as Gustavus Vassa (Vasa), the African, as inscribed in various letters from 1789 to 1794.[56]

In 1794, for example, Vassa subscribed to Carl Bernhard Wadstrom's *An Essay on Colonization*, and he listed himself as "Gustavus Vassa, a native of Africa." Similarly, on May 19, 1795, The *Morning Post and Fashionable World* reported that "At a Meeting of the COMMITTEE of the SUBSCRIBERS for defraying the Expence of Defendants in the late Trials for HIGH TREASON, held at the house of Messrs. Clarkson, Essex-street, Strand, London, on Thursday the 7th May, 1795," it was noted that "Gustavus Vassa" was one of thirty-seven subscribers, although he was only one of two whose subscription was less than one pound. His political involvement continued thereafter, at least until his final illness in 1797. On November 7, 1796, *The Telegraph* reported that

> Saturday being the Anniversary of the memorable acquittal of THOMAS HARDY, a numerous meeting of the Friends of Freedom was held at the Crown and anchor Tavern, in the Strand, to celebrate that triumph of Liberty so propitious for the Rights of the People—so honourable to English Juries . . . Gustavus Vasa, the celebrated African, made some observations respecting the Slave Trade.

Granville Sharp, who attended him on his deathbed, again referred to him as Gustavus Vassa in his account of the visit.[57] Hence the discovery of the gloss on the letter from Vassa to Sharp in 1780 that purports to recount Vassa's displeasure at being called by his "real name" is particularly significant.[58]

As Edwards and Shaw have argued, Vassa sustained a sense of destiny, but we can only imagine how he learned about Danish abolition and the death of the Swedish king on March 29, both of which happened at the time he was in Edinburgh in 1792. At the time, Vassa's public image was at its zenith. His marriage had been reported in the press, and his lengthy and successful book tours promoting abolition were well known. These events coincided with revolutionary events in France and the French Caribbean. Wilberforce's decision to reintroduce a motion to abolish the British slave trade at this time electrified the situation once the radical implications of abolition confronted the radicalism of the French Revolution. This was the context in which two London newspapers, the *Oracle* and the *Star*, published stories that Vassa was not born in Africa but in the Danish West Indies on the island of St. Croix. The accusation was a direct assault on Vassa's integrity and the use of his African birth name in his autobiography and in letters to newspapers, since the implication of being born in the Caribbean was that the African birth was a fabrication. In accusing Vassa of deceiving the public, the editor of the *Oracle* (April 25, 1792) charged:

> It is a fact that the Public may depend on, that Gustavus Vasa, who has publicly asserted that he was kidnapped in Africa, never was upon that Continent, but was born and bred up in the Danish Island of Santa Cruz

> [St. Croix], in the West Indies . . . What, we will ask any man of plain understanding, must that cause be, which can lean for support on falsehoods as audaciously propagated as they are easily detected?[59]

These claims were spurious, with malicious intent, but to some extent anticipated recent interpretations that Vassa may have been born in South Carolina. Vassa's response to his contemporary critics is noteworthy and informs the apparent contradiction between the existence of documents claiming a birth in America and Vassa's account. Clearly the editors of the London newspapers did not know of the baptismal certificate in St. Margaret's Church or the enlistment records for the Arctic expedition of 1773. The question remains, however, whether the adoption of his birth name was intended to confirm that he had been born in Africa and whether through his autobiography he was able to express his lost identity. His claim that he resisted Pascal's assignment of name to him attests to the social death incumbent with slavery, in which African identity was denied but which Vassa was able to reclaim in his writings.

Vassa protested the efforts to strip him of his identity and clearly was upset by the implications of the *Oracle*'s editorial. In a letter to Thomas Hardy, the founder of the London Corresponding Society, with whom Vassa and his wife lived in 1792, Vassa wrote, "Sir, I am sorry to tell you that some Rascal or Rascals have asserted in the news papers viz. Oracle of the 25th. of april, & the Star. 27th.—that I am a native of a Danish Island, Santa Cruz, in the Wt. Indias." He wanted Hardy to get a copy of the *Star* "& take care of it till you see or hear from me," signed "Gustavus Vassa The African."[60] It is clear that there was considerable gossip about his origins, and Vassa feared that it would affect the sale of his book and thereby inhibit the abolition movement. Indeed, if his kidnapping, sale to the coast, and his rendition of the Middle Passage were fictional, then Vassa's credibility would have been completely undermined, as his critics in the *Oracle* and the *Star* tried to do. But surely there was more to his reactions than just his resentment toward defamatory editorials. Vassa had to have been aware of Danish abolition on March 16, the death of King Gustavus Vasa III on March 29, and the approval of Wilberforce's motion before the House of Commons on April 22. Moreover, the interplay of these events and his recent marriage, and the presence of his new wife, must have had an impact on his reactions. His names, moreover, reflected his reputation. His childhood name established his African birth and his Swedish name established his prophetic mission; together, these were vital to his sense of identity.

Publicly, Vassa responded to the charges that he was born a Danish slave in the preface to the ninth edition of *The Interesting Narrative*, which appeared in 1794:

> An invidious falsehood having appeared in the Oracle of the 25th, and the Star of the 27th of April 1792, with a view to hurt my character, and to discredit and prevent the sale of my Narrative, asserting, that I was born in the Danish island of Santa Cruz, in the West Indies, it is necessary that, in this edition, I should take notice thereof, and it is only needful of me to appeal to those numerous and respectable persons of character who knew me when I first arrived in England, and could speak no language but that of Africa.[61]

Vassa did not claim that his description of the interior of the Bight of Biafra was entirely based on his own experiences. He did note that his account was an "imperfect sketch my memory has furnished me with the manners and customs of a people among whom I first drew my breath," and acknowledged that he had gained information from some of the "numbers of the natives of Eboe" he encountered in London.[62] His discussions in London influenced what he wrote, just as his quotations from Anthony Benezet and other sources did, but the weight of evidence still indicates that Vassa had firsthand knowledge of Africa.[63] Nonetheless, his critics in the *Oracle* taunted Vassa about his place of birth, "*Ex hoc unodisce omens*—this one fact tells all."[64] Vassa was accused of being a fraud, not the namesake of a Swedish king but a Danish slave, as the Swedes once were.

The attack on Vassa's credibility as a witness to slavery, the form it took, and the timing on April 25, 1792, were a commentary on the abolition movement. The Danish edict had been enacted on March 16, and while it did not end Danish involvement in the slave trade for another decade, it inspired Wilberforce's renewed motion to abolish the slave trade. According to Erik Gøbel,

> news of the sensational Danish edict of 16th March 1792 reached London just a couple of weeks later, and the full text was soon translated into English, and was published in the *Times*. This was the immediate reason why the subject of abolition was once again taken up by William Wilberforce, who raised the question anew in the House of Commons on 2nd April 1792.[65]

The biting satire in the *Oracle* and the *Star* was a response to the passage of the motion to abolish the slave trade in the House of Commons on April 22. Although it is difficult to document, it has to be assumed that Danish abolition was widely discussed in abolition circles and in Parliament. That the motion was controversial was revealed when it was subsequently defeated in the House of Lords on May 8.[66]

The full effect of the public attack on Vassa is difficult to assess, but Vassa took the charges against him seriously enough to respond in the preface of the next edition of his autobiography. The timing of the satire suggests that considerable derision circulated in May, both before and after the House of Lords rejected abolition. Implicitly, the public ridicule projected a reversal of roles for Danes, who had just instituted abolition, and Swedes, who had suddenly lost the popular descendant of their "liberator" through assassination. The attack explicitly mocked the ineffectual Danish edict and the leading "African" proponent of abolition by insinuating assassination, as had proved the fate of King Gustavus Vasa III. The defeat of the motion to abolish the slave trade in the House of Lords perhaps foreshadowed the political repression of 1794 in Britain and subsequent treason trials in London. The abolition of the slave trade and parliamentary reform were beginning to be associated with the perceived terror of the French Revolution and the uprising currently underway in St. Domingue.[67] Vassa experienced the threat of this repression, as reported in a letter from Colchester on June 20, 1794, when he had to return to London to enquire whether or not he was under investigation and wanted for questioning:

> I make no doubt but you have heard of the false report which the Sons of Belial have raised of Late in saying that the Kings messengers were in quest of me, & my friends here persuaded me to go to London—so I did & inquired of Gentlemen in Power—my friends—& they went to the Privy Council & were told that there was not any messengers after me. So I went to Soham to see my family which is well.[68]

John Bugg speculates on who these "friends" might have been, probably including William Wilberforce, but given Vassa's relationship with Hardy, who was tried for treason, and other reformers, it is not surprising that Vassa and his associates were concerned.

Equiano's lifelong voyage was providential or so it appeared to Vassa when he wrote his autobiography. Many contemporaries, including leading abolitionists, seem to have thought that Vassa had been chosen to lead his people out of bondage, a mission that was reflected in the significance of his name, Gustavus Vassa. The slave boy Olaudah Equiano was the Moses of his people, not only "his countrymen" but all Africans, whom at times he came to include in his definition of his people, as Libyans, Ethiopians, and Africans, as well as his own "Eboe" "countrymen." His identification with "Africa" implied that he recognized a common destiny with all of his enslaved sisters and brothers. As his Swedish namesake led his people out of subjugation under Danish oppression, he would do the same. The parallel with Moses and the exodus was immediately brought to mind in the irony of naming a slave after such a hero. Accepting his fate, his *chi*, Vassa therefore played a major role in the abolition movement. He was a friend of the British abolitionist, the Rev. James Ramsay, possibly meeting him first in the West Indies and then again in London when Ramsay became a publicist in the fight against slavery.[69] He told Granville Sharp of the *Zong* affair in 1783, in which 132 enslaved Africans from the Bight of Biafra were thrown overboard alive in order to collect insurance from the underwriters.[70] The scandal helped mobilize support for the abolitionist movement. By the late 1780s, he was an acknowledged advocate and one of the principal leaders of the "black poor" of London.[71] From November 1786 until May 1787, he was working on the Sierra Leone project (where London blacks would be resettled in West Africa) but then withdrew, in the end becoming the spokesman for the grievances and failures of the project.[72] His image at this time was that of an African, signing his name with others as one of the "sons of Africa" in various letters to newspapers.[73]

The baptismal and naval documents raise important issues, especially since some scholars have claimed "Equiano" as an "American," even though he called himself "African." His autobiography became the archetypal "slave narrative" in North America, but at the time, Vassa, the "African," was fighting the British slave trade, in Britain.[74] In fact, Vassa spent only a few months in Virginia in 1754; later on ships trading to South Carolina, Georgia, and Philadelphia as a slave; and then as a freeman sailing to Georgia and South Carolina. After he visited Wales in 1783, he went to New York in 1784 and Philadelphia in 1785 and 1786 in conditions that were quite different from his earlier experiences.[75] Not only was he a freeman, he was also well known, residing with prominent members of abolitionist circles in both cities. As a Briton, he displayed a keen interest in science through his friendship with Dr. Irving; expressed himself musically through his mastery of the French horn; participated in debating societies, most notably the London Corresponding Society, as one of its first members; and demonstrated his commitment to interracial marriage through his liaison with Susannah Cullen.

Do Vassa and Equiano represent two *personas*, one created for ambitious self-gain and self-interest and the other representative of the abolitionist cause? I think not. Vassa's autobiography is only part of what we know about the man. Certainly, *The Interesting Narrative* is a key document in reconstructing Vassa's life and his political influence in the late eighteenth-century Atlantic world, but it is far from the only source on his life. The issue is not the validity of autobiography, whether something is being remembered accurately or being distorted for some purpose of obfuscation or political intent, but whether or not subsequent generations and scholarship choose to interpret ambiguities in a particular fashion. Vassa was a prominent historical figure, and it matters whether or not he was telling the truth about his birth, which is the reason that he used his birth name in the title of his autobiography and occasionally double signed his name on letters to newspapers, always identifying as African. The literary name adopted by modern scholarship to identify Vassa taps into current historical interpretations of the abolition movement that require a voice that can represent the enslaved, whether or not the individual was born in Africa or the Americas.

While he probably will continue to be called Olaudah Equiano because of the importance of his autobiography, the use of his birth name has complicated an understanding of the man who people in his own day knew as Gustavus Vassa, the African, not Olaudah Equiano. Current scholarship may be confused, but his wife was almost certainly not. Whether she called him "Gus" or "Ola" we do not know, but she certainly could not have doubted his African birth because she would have known that he was circumcised. Circumcision was not practiced in eighteenth-century Anglo-America; Vassa's own circumcision is thus revealing of his African origins, especially in reference to his discussion of scarification, both of which were important in Igbo society. The significance of his birth name can give the impression of a dual identity in the authorship of *The Interesting Narrative*,[76] but I would suggest that the logic of using his birth name was directed at establishing his place of birth. His description of *ichi* scarification, which he was too young to receive because he had not reached puberty, informs his references to circumcision, another ritualized practice of scarification that was performed in his homeland. As *The Interesting Narrative* records, as a young boy newly enslaved, Vassa passed through places where the people did not circumcise, which he considered surprising, and in contrast to his own "country." The ritualized context of circumcision was one of the reasons he compared his own culture with both Jews and Muslims. How does this relate to his name? At that time in Britain, by contrast, circumcision was considered barbaric, far from being ritualized, in complete contradiction with Vassa's cultural experience.[77] Circumcision was not even practiced in British hospitals until one century later. As a child, Vassa could not have been and would not have been circumcised in South Carolina, if he had been born there. There was no ritual context, and it is doubtful that masters would have tolerated the practice in any event. Vassa's several references to circumcision demonstrate his African authenticity; he mentions and discusses circumcision at least five times in a book aimed at a public that abhorred the practice. He does not say that circumcision is barbaric—far from it—nor is he trying to sell the idea. The references have no obvious purpose of justification or explanation. Why did he mention circumcision so much if the memory of the ritual and the context were not important to him? Could he have acquired this sensitivity from someone else or by reading about it? The rituals involved in circumcision, as with the significance of *ichi* scarification, were in Vassa's memory of his homeland and were important in the evolution of his identity as Igbo and African.

Nonetheless, his birth name was a reflection of where he came from even while he continued to identify as Gustavus Vassa. What's in a name for the author of *The Interesting Narrative* has more to do with the politics of representation and political correctness of a later generation of scholarship, not with the intention of the man, in contradiction to the interpretation of Brycchan Carey and Vincent Carretta. As Julia Watson has argued, "Naming, unnaming, renaming, misnaming, being called out of one's name—these tropes indicated stages in the formation or divestiture of autobiographical identity."[78] Vassa conforms with Watson's conception that "the autobiographer may return to a given African name as a sign of origin that precedes and defies oppression,"[79] but in Vassa's case he chose to identify with his slave name, which was also prophetic, and instead used his birth name to confirm his African birth and as "a sign of origin that precedes and defies oppression." Vassa's birth name signified his African birth, the significance of which was established by Henry Louis Gates, Jr.[80] The imposition of the birth name as the signifier long after he died, however, has allowed the postulation of a series of dichotomies that need to be questioned, such as place of birth being in Africa and/or Carolina and whether or not the man was self made, meaning creating his identity and benefitting from that creation, as opposed to a committed activist motivated by principles and sacrifice. The veneer of this kind of interpretation melts away if it is recognized that Vassa consciously operated in a different mode of expression and implementation than subsequent literary scholars and historians have fancifully projected. The dichotomy between evangelical man and crass entrepreneur evaporates. The reason for the debate over his birth has more to do with the present clash between literary scholarship and historical interpretation. The danger in confusing names can lead to misinterpretations and misrepresentations of the past.

NOTES

The research for this paper was carried out with the assistance of a grant from the Social Sciences and Humanities Research Council of Canada and under the auspices of the Canada Research Chair on African Diaspora History. I wish to thank Mark Duffill, John Bugg, James Sidbury, Karlee Sapoznik, Peitra Arana, Sydney Kanya-Forstner, Laura Murphy, Henry Louis Gates, Jr., David Imbua, and Arthur Torrington for their comments, suggestions, and assistance. I am particularly grateful to Neil Marshall for research support and ongoing interest in this project.
I wish to thank Erik Gøbel for his tolerant explanation of Scandinavian nationalities, which

provided the inspiration for this paper. This is an expanded and revised version of an article published in *Atlantic Studies* 9, no. 2 (2012): 165–84, and is reprinted here in expanded form with permission of the publisher, Taylor and Francis.

1. The edition used here is Vincent Carretta, ed., *The Interesting Narrative and Other Writings* (New York: Penguin, 2003), referred to as Vassa, *The Interesting Narrative*, when citing the text itself, and otherwise cited as Carretta, *The Interesting Narrative and Other Writings*, when referring to other materials in Carretta's edition.

2. For Blumenbach's opinion of Vassa, see *The Anthropological Treatises of Johann Friedrich Blumenbach*, trans. Thomas Bendyshe (London: Longman, Green, Longman, Roberts, and Green, 1865), 310. Blumenbach's review was apparently written in London, which suggests that he was there in that year as well as in 1792, when he actually met Vassa. In 1790, Blumenbach discussed Vassa's life in his "Contributions to Natural History," published as *Beytraege zur Naturgeschichte* (Göttingen, DE: Johann Christian Dieterich, 1790), in the chapter "Ueber die Negern insbesondere" ("About the negroes in particular"), 1:84–118; he gives a favorable account, among others, about the lives and writings of Amo (98–99), Sancho (102–7), and Vassa (107–18), telling his readers that Sancho's letters (3rd ed., 1784) as well as Vassa's autobiography (2nd ed.) were given to him by a D. Crichton, London. Blumenbach specifically refers to "Vassa" and not "Equiano." Arthur Torrington has been very helpful in reference to Blumenbach's connection with Vassa.

3. G. I. Jones, "Olaudah Equiano of the Niger Ibo," in *Africa Remembered: Narratives by West Africans from the Era of the Slave Trade*, ed. Philip D. Curtin (Madison: University of Wisconsin Press, 1967), 60–98.

4. Catherine Obianuju Acholonu, *The Igbo Roots of Olaudah Equiano—An Anthropological Research* (Owerri, NG: Afa Publications, 1989).

5. According to Acholonu (*Igbo Roots*, 54), Elese is a short form for Ala-Isse, "land of Isee," formed by joining the two words, "Ala" and "Isse." Isieke is short form of "Isi-Eke-Ise," which means "Head of Five Eke," there being five Eke deities in Isieke, with the leading deity of the five named Ogwugwu. Accordingly, the Isieke market is held daily, one of the few daily markets in traditional Igboland but does not function on Eke day, "which is regarded as the day spirits and powerful wizards and god-men from all over Igboland buy and sell at the market. Ala-Ise, Land of Five, is Equiano's 'Elese' and is the local name for Isieke." Isieke is located in Orlu in Imo State.

6. I. B. Onyema, *Hail Usaka: Olaudah Equiano's Igbo Village* (Owerri, NG: Ihem Davis Press, 1991). Based on interviews with Ben Emele, who is from Ikwuano where Usaka is located, conducted by David Imbua in Calabar on October 14, 2014; and with the Traditional Rulers Council at Usaka on January 9, 2015, including Eze P. U. Ngwankwe, Chief Oby Oguama (Secretary), and Dr. Joe Ushie Dickson, also conducted by David Imbua.

7. Vincent Carretta has received considerable currency for arguing that the author of *The Interesting Narrative* was not born in Africa (in what is now Nigeria) but in South Carolina; see Vincent Carretta, "Olaudah Equiano or Gustavus Vassa? New Light on an Eighteenth-Century Question of Identity," *Slavery and Abolition* 20, no. 3 (1999): 96–105; Vincent Carretta, "More New Light on the Identity of Olaudah Equiano or Gustavus Vassa," in *The Global Eighteenth Century*, ed. Felicity Nussbaum (Baltimore, MD: Johns Hopkins University Press, 2003), 226–35; and Vincent Carretta, *Equiano, the African: Biography of a Self-Made Man* (Athens: University of Georgia Press, 2005), 1–16. Carretta has attempted to explain his approach in "Methodology in the Making and Reception of Equiano," in *Biography and the Black Atlantic*, ed. Lisa A. Lindsay and John Wood Sweet (Philadelphia: University of Pennsylvania Press, 2013), 172–91, and repeats the argument in this volume, ignoring the evidence that clearly establishes that Vassa was born in Igboland, whether or not Essaka is to be identified with Isieke or Usaka or indeed some other place. Trevor Burnard is certainly premature in entitling his otherwise serious scholarly reflection on the debate over where Vassa was born, "Goodbye, Equiano the African," apparently being swayed by partial evidence and without acquaintance with the details on Vassa's African birth; see Trevor Burnard, "Goodbye, Equiano, the African," *Historically*

Speaking: The Bulletin of the Historical Society 7, no. 3 (2006): 10–11.

8. Carretta, in this volume, colors the way he presents Vassa's reference to published accounts of Africa, particularly to Anthony Benezet, John Matthews, et al., as if he is accusing Vassa of plagiarism rather than scholarly referencing, with footnotes, to substantiate his argument or to report where he obtained information. This pattern of referencing was the same tradition as Thomas Clarkson employed in his investigation of the slave trade, without plagiarism ever being implied. As argued elsewhere, Vassa tagged Igboland on to the Kingdom of Benin, because in his reading of Benezet, there was a gap between Benin and Angola, and he knew his homeland was in there somewhere. Benezet made no observations on Igboland or the interior of the Bight of Biafra, a fact that Carretta and others suspicious of the extent of Vassa's personal, firsthand knowledge fail to acknowledge or explain. Of course Vassa learned a lot from a great number of people. Why wouldn't he? Africa was what he was most interested in; he wanted to return home; he wanted to go as a missionary; he almost went on the disastrous Sierra Leone expedition of 1787. He learned a lot about Africa from Matthias MacNamara, the former governor of the Province of Senegambia, who recommended Vassa to the Archbishop of London as someone to be appointed as a missionary to his homeland in Africa. Vassa clearly knew other "Igbo" because that identity already existed, despite doubts among some scholars, including Carretta and David Northrup. Vassa provides proof that an Igbo (Egbo) identity was recognized, and he explained how this identity came about. Vassa's insight that becoming Igbo was a diaspora experience subsequently has been virtually stolen by those who think they have "discovered" that Igbo identity was created in diaspora. Vassa should be acknowledged for this insight.

9. Carmela Ciuraru, *Nom de Plume: A (Secret) History of Pseudonyms* (New York: Harper Collins, 2011), xiv–xxiv.

10. Jean Fagan Yellin, *Harriet Jacobs: A Life* (New York: Basic Civitas, 2004).

11. Thomas Hodgkin, ed., *Nigerian Perspectives: An Historical Anthology* (London: Oxford University Press, 1960), 155–66.

12. Brycchan Carey, "Olaudah Equiano: African or American?," *1650–1850: Ideas, Aesthetics, and Inquiries in the Early Modern Era* 17 (2010): 231.

13. Gustavus Vassa to Granville Sharp, May 6, 1780, in Anti-slave trade movement—Great Britain—Collection, Series VI, Supplement 1, Box 1, Folder 1, University of Illinois at Chicago. I am grateful to Neil Marshall for obtaining a copy of this letter. The full note is as follows, in reference to the identification of the signature, Gustavus Vassa: "a Black & an African, who wrote his own life[.] He fell into fits if any One pronounced his Real name, which was Olaudah Equiano[.] My Father knew him—J. Phillipps of Middle Hill."

14. Carretta, *Equiano the African*, 241, 249, 251, 253.

15. Yacine Daddi Addoun and Paul E. Lovejoy, "Muhammad Kaba Saghanughu and the Muslim Community of Jamaica," in *Slavery on the Frontiers of Islam*, ed. Paul E. Lovejoy (Princeton, NJ: Markus Wiener, 2004), 201–20; Yacine Daddi Addoun and Paul E. Lovejoy, "The Arabic Manuscript of Muhammad Kaba Saghanughu of Jamaica, c. 1820," in *Caribbean Culture: Soundings on Kamau Brathwaite*, ed. Annie Paul (Kingston, JM: University of the West Indies Press, 2007), 313–41; and Maureen Warner-Lewis, "Religious Constancy and Compromise among Nineteenth-Century Caribbean-based African Muslims," in *Islam, Slavery and Diaspora*, ed. Behnaz Mirzai, Ismael Musah Montana, and Paul E. Lovejoy (Trenton, NJ: Africa World Press, 2009), 237–68.

16. Robin Law and Paul E. Lovejoy, eds., *The Biography of Mahommah Gardo Baquaqua: His Passage from Slavery to Freedom in Africa and America*, 2nd ed. (Princeton, NJ: Markus Wiener, 2007). Also see Lovejoy, "Identity and the Mirage of Ethnicity: Mahommah Gardo Baquaqua's Journey in the Americas," in *African Re-Genesis: Confronting Social Issues in the Diaspora*, ed. Jay B. Haviser and Kevin C. MacDonald (London: Cavendish, 2006), 90–105; and Lovejoy, "Narratives of Trans-Atlantic Slavery: The Lives of Two Muslims, Muhammad Kaba Saghanaghu and Mahommah Gardo Baquaqua," in *Africa and Trans-Atlantic Memories: Literary and Aesthetic Manifestations of Diaspora and History*, ed. Naana Opoku-Agyemang, Paul E.

Lovejoy, and David V. Trotman (Trenton, NJ: Africa World Press, 2008), 7–22.

17. Venture Smith, *A Narrative of the Life and Adventures of Venture Smith, A Native of Africa: but Resident about Sixty Years in the United States of America. Related by Himself* (New London: C. Holt, 1798); and James B. Stewart, ed., *Venture Smith and the Business of Slavery and Freedom* (Amherst: University of Massachusetts Press, 2009).

18. Acholonu, *Igbo Roots of Olaudah Equiano*; and Adiele E. Afigbo, *Ropes of Sand: Studies in Igbo History and Culture* (Ibadan, NG: Ibadan University Press, 1981), 154.

19. Carretta, *Interesting Narrative and Other Writings*, 253.

20. Julia Watson, "What's in a Name? Heteroglossic Naming as Multicultural Practice in American Autobiography," *Prose Studies* 17, no. 1 (1994): 95–119; Ciuraru, *Nom de Plume*; and Yellin, *Harriet Jacobs: A Life*.

21. Usaka elders, interview with author, January 9, 2015.

22. Alexander X. Byrd, "Eboe, Country, Nation, and Gustavus Vassa's "Interesting Narrative," *William and Mary Quarterly* 63, no. 1 (2006): 123–48; and James Sidbury, "From Igbo Israeli to African Christian: The Emergence of Racial Identity in Olaudah Equiano's Interesting Narrative," *Africans of the Americas* 33 (2008): 79–106.

23. Vassa, *Interesting Narrative*, 63.

24. Ibid., 41.

25. Ibid., 64. Emphasis in the original.

26. Paul Edwards and Rosiland Shaw, "Invisible Chi in Equiano's *Interesting Narrative*," *Journal of Religion in Africa* 19 (1989): 146–56.

27. Michael Roberts, *Gustavus Adolphus: A History of Sweden, 1611–1632*, 2 vols. (London: Longmans, 1953–1958).

28. Carretta, *Interesting Narrative and Other Writings*, 252.

29. Vassa, *Interesting Narrative*, 31. Emphasis in the original.

30. Ibid., 64.

31. Hodgkin, *Nigerian Perspectives*, 155–66. Earlier, Eric Williams had referred to him as Gustavus Vasa; see *Capitalism and Slavery* (Chapel Hill: University of North Carolina Press, 1944), 158. I wish to thank Arthur Torrington for drawing this to my attention.

32. Christopher Fyfe, *A History of Sierra Leone* (London: Oxford University Press, 1962), 13, 15, 18–19, 25, 26.

33. Paul Edwards, "Embrenche′ and Ndichie," *Journal of the Historical Society of Nigeria* 2, no. 3 (1962): 401–2.

34. Jones, "Olaudah Equiano of the Niger Ibo," 60–98. Curtin adopted the name Equiano in "General Introduction," *Africa Remembered*, 7.

35. Paul Edwards, ed., *Equiano's Travels: His Autobiography; The Interesting Narrative of the Life of Olaudah Equiano or Gustavus Vassa the African* (London: Heinemann, 1967); Paul Edwards and James Walvin, *Black Personalities in the Era of the Slave Trade* (London: Macmillan, 1983); and Paul Edwards and David Dabydeen, eds., *Black Writers in Britain, 1760–1890* (Edinburgh, UK: Edinburgh University Press, 1991).

36. For example, Walvin uses the name Equiano, as in *An African's Life: The Life and Times of Olaudah Equiano, 1745–1797* (London: Cassell, 1998), as does Henry Louis Gates, Jr., "The Interesting Narrative of the Life of Olaudah Equiano," in *The Classic Slave Narratives*, rev. ed. (New York: Mentor, 2011). Also see Folarin Shyllon, "Olaudah Equiano: Nigerian Abolitionist and First National Leader of Africans in Britain," *Journal of African Studies* 4, no. 4 (1977): 433–51; Peter Fryer, *Staying Power: The History of Black People in Britain* (London: Pluto Press, 1984); S. E. Ogude, "No Roots Here: On the Igbo Roots of Olaudah Equiano," *Review of English and Literary Studies* 5 (1989): 1–16; Acholonu, *Igbo Roots of Olaudah Equiano*; Angelo Costanzo, *Surprizing Narrative: Olaudah Equiano and the Beginnings of Black Autobiography* (New York: Greenwood Press, 1987); Akiyo Ito, "Olaudah Equiano and the New York Artisans: The First American Edition of the *Interesting Narrative of the Life of Olaudah Equiano, or Gustavus Vassa*," *Early American Literature* 32, no. 1 (1997): 82; Nini Rodgers, "Equiano in Belfast: A Study of the Anti-Slavery Ethos in a Northern Town," *Slavery and Abolition* 18, no. 2 (1997): 73–89; Adam Hochschild, *Bury the Chains: The British Struggle to Abolish Slavery* (New York: Houghton Mifflin, 2005); and Arthur Torrington (President of the Equiano Society), "Biography and History: The Debate over Olaudah Equiano's Interesting Narrative" (unpublished paper, American Historical

Association, Annual Meeting, New York, January 2, 2009). Also see William L. Anderson, *To Tell a Free Story: The First Century of Afro-American Autobiography, 1760–1865* (Urbana: University of Illinois Press, 1986); and Louise Rolingher, "A Metaphor of Freedom: Olaudah Equiano and Slavery in Africa," *Canadian Journal of African Studies* 38, no. 1 (2004): 88–122.

37. For a discussion, see Paul E. Lovejoy, "Autobiography and Memory: Gustavus Vassa, alias Olaudah Equiano, the African," *Slavery and Abolition* 27, no. 3 (2006): 317–47; and Vincent Carretta, "Response to Paul Lovejoy's 'Autobiography and Memory: Gustavus Vassa, alias Olaudah Equiano, the African," *Slavery and Abolition* 28, no. 1 (2007): 115–19; and Carretta, *Equiano the African*, 1–16. Also see John Bugg, "The Other Interesting Narrative: Olaudah Equiano's Public Book Tour," *PMLA* 121 (2006): 1422–42, who reconsiders the debate over where Vassa was born. Carretta's interpretation is also presented in this volume.

38. Usually he signed himself as Gustavus Vassa or Vasa, the African, sometimes "an African"; see Carretta, *Interesting Narrative and Other Writings*, 253.

39. *The Diary; or Woodfall's Register*, April 25, 1789, cited in Folarin Shyllon, *Black People in Britain, 1555–1833* (New York: Oxford University Press, 1977), 271–72. The letter to "Lords Spiritual and Temporal," cited in Shyllon, *Black People in Britain*, 261, as March 1789, has different dates, depending on the edition of *The Interesting Narrative*.

40. Cited in Carretta, *Interesting Narrative and Other Writings*, 261n198.

41. See Carretta, *Interesting Narrative and Other Writings*, 286n486, citing the surviving musters for the *Race Horse* (National Archives, London, ADM 36/7490). Carretta thinks Vassa was born in 1747, which means that Vassa would have been only nineteen when he acquired his freedom in 1766, which seems highly unlikely.

42. Dr. Charles Irving was a naval surgeon and inventor. He was credited with the development of an apparatus for distilling seawater and turning it into drinking water. The Royal Navy began using his desalination process in 1770, and in 1772 Parliament granted Irving five thousand pounds for the invention, although in fact a similar apparatus had been demonstrated in 1764 by Dr. James Lind (1716–1794), and there were at least two other similar devices in operation before Irving developed his. Lind's distillation apparatus was already in use on several ships of the Royal Navy, most notably in HMS *Dolphin*, while circumnavigating the world, and also in ships of the merchant service. Irving's invention was entirely derivative and owed practically everything to Lind's earlier work, the founding father of naval and maritime medicine, a self-effacing and modest "man of science," who never courted the limelight. See Paul E. Lovejoy, "Gustavus Vassa and the Scottish Enlightenment" (paper presented at the annual meeting of the American Historical Association, New York, January 2, 2009). *Gentleman's Magazine*, vol. 42, May 1772 incorrectly identified Charles Irving as "the same who invented the marine chair some years ago." However, as Ann Savours has shown, the Board of Longitude papers identify the inventor as Christopher Irving; see "'A Very Interesting Point of Geography': The 1773 Phipps Expedition towards the North Pole," in Louis Rey, ed., *Unveiling the Arctic* (Calgary, CA: The Arctic Institute of North America, 1984), 402–28. Carretta mistakenly accepted the error of the *Gentleman's Magazine* in identifying Dr. Charles Irving with Christopher Irving; see *Equiano the African*, 137.

43. As Bugg observes, "Might 'Gustavus Weston' have been Charles Gustavus Weston, of Brompton, whose son of the same name would ascend to the rank of captain? Or might Gustavus Weston have been the Gustavus Westman who was later prosecuted in Lancashire? Could Gustavus Weston/Feston have been the soldier Gustavus Denniston?" See Bugg, "The Other Interesting Narrative," 1425. We know Vassa was on board, but we do not know if he was in the musters, without making certain assumptions.

44. Vassa, *Interesting Narrative*, 79.

45. Ibid., 64.

46. James Sweet suggests that Vassa's reference to Libya in describing people of his own "nation" disproves the contention that Equiano was purchasing slaves from the Bight of Biafra; see "Mistaken Identities? Olaudah Equiano, Domingos Alvares, and the Methodological Challenges of Studying the African Diaspora,"

American Historical Review 114 (2009): 279–306. However, Vassa clearly uses the term "Libya" as a substitute for Africa and Ethiopia and not as a point of embarkation. In fact, many ships arriving in Jamaica at the time in question came from the Bight of Biafra.

47. Vassa, *Interesting Narrative*, 221–22.

48. Cited in Carretta, *Equiano, the African*, 3.

49. National Archives, London, PROB/10/3372 CF/2236.

50. *Cambridge Chronicle and Journal*, February 20, 1796, and cited in Carretta, *Equiano, the African*, 363.

51. Angelina Osborne, *Equiano's Daughter: The Life of & Times of Joanna Vassa* (London: KrikKrak, 2007), 11.

52. *The Ipswich Journal*, March 21, 1857.

53. The various letters are widely scattered, many published in Carretta, *Interesting Narrative and Other Writings*. Also see Shyllon, *Black People in Britain*, 244–71. Arthur Torrington, Vincent Carretta, and John Bugg have discovered further correspondence, which has been conveniently combined in Karlee Sapoznik, ed., *The Letters and Other Writings of Gustavus Vassa (Olaudah Equiano, the African): Documenting Abolition of the Slave Trade* (Princeton, NJ: Marcus Wiener, 2013).

54. For a discussion of when recognition of "Africa" became important in the discourse of people of African descent in the Anglophone diaspora, see James Sidbury, *Becoming African in America: Race and Nation in the Early Black Atlantic* (New York: Oxford University Press, 2007), 38–40. Sidbury notes that identification with Africa became a common element in the formation of self-help associations and institutions, but also the use of the term "Africa" was used in recognition of birth in Africa.

55. William Dickson, *Letters on Slavery: To Which Are Added, Addresses to the Whites, and to the Free Negroes of Barbadoes; and Accounts of Some Negroes Eminent for their Virtues and Abilities* (London: J. Phillips, 1789). Dickson was a subscriber to Vassa's *Narrative*.

56. See *The Cambridge Chronicle and Journal; and General Advertiser for The Counties of Cambridge, Huntingdon, Lincoln, Rutland, Bedford, Herts, Isle of Ely, &c.*, August 1, 1789, "Your humble Servant, GUSTAVUS VASSA, The African. CAMBRIDGE, 30 July 1789"; *Sheffield Register, Yorkshire, Derbyshire, & Nottinghamshire Universal Advertiser*, August 27, 1790, "GUSTAVUS VASA, the free African, now in Sheffield—his manners polished, his mind enlightened, and in every respect on a par with Europeans"; *The Manchester Mercury, & Harrop's General Advertiser*, August 31, 1790, "I am, Gentlemen, Your obedient humble Servant, GUSTAVUS VASA, THE AFRICAN, Manchester, August 18, 1790"; while the *Newcastle Chronicle* and *Newcastle Courant*, October 6, 1792, both print "GUSTAVUS VASSA; the AFRICAN, Newcastle, 4 October 1792." On March 15, 1794, the *Norfolk Chronicle* published a letter from "GUSTAVUS VASSA, the AFRICAN. To the Inhabitants of this City and Its Environs, And also of Bury St. Edmund."

57. Prince Hoare, *Memoirs of Granville Sharp, Esq. Composed from his Own Manuscripts and Other Authentic Documents in the Possession of his Family and of the African Institution* (London: Henry Colburn, 1820).

58. Vassa to Sharp, May 6, 1780.

59. The article also charged that William Wilberforce, Henry Thornton, and William Thornton were "concerned in settling the island of Bulam in Sugar Plantations; of course their interests clash with those of the present Planters and hence their clamour against the Slave Trade." See *The Oracle*, April 25, 1792, and the discussion in Carretta, *Interesting Narrative and Other Writings* (237) and for the attack in the *Star* (238). Bulom was not an island but the shore north of the Sierra Leone River and is now the site of the Freetown airport.

60. Vassa to Thomas Hardy, Edinburgh, May 28, 1792, National Archives, London, TS 24/12/2, and reprinted in Carretta, *Interesting Narrative and Other Writings*, 361–62.

61. The passage was addressed "To the Reader"; see Carretta, *Interesting Narrative and Other Writings*, 5.

62. Vassa, *The Interesting Narrative*, 38. It should be noted that Carey reaches the astonishing conclusion that Vassa could have learned such details of Igbo culture and society from anyone from Africa, as if Africa was one country. According to Carey, the few details in the African sequences that could not be found

in published accounts are vague and generalized and could easily have been supplied by Vassa's African friends and acquaintances. We should remember that there were thousands of people of African birth or descent living in London in the 1780s, and there is no reason why Vassa could not have simply asked one of them for some information on the African interior. See Carey, "Olaudah Equiano: African or American?," 241. There is no evidence that he learned the meaning of his own name, the name of his hometown, or the practice of *ichi* scarification and ritual circumcision from anything he had read or from anyone he had met. This conclusive evidence is ignored by Carretta and other scholars who question his African birth.

63. Anthony Benezet, *Some Historical Account of Guinea, Its Situation, Produce and the General Disposition of Its Inhabitants with an Inquiry into the Rise and Progress of the Slave Trade, Its Nature and Lamentable Effects* (1771; repr., London: Frank Cass, 1968). Benezet quoted at length various European observations of western Africa, but nothing on the interior of the Bight of Biafra, skipping from the Kingdom of Benin to Kongo and Angola in his descriptions and reports. He quotes some information on Barbados that presumably Vassa could have used but not on his homeland. Of course, Vassa incorporated generalized and romanticized visions of Africa that he acquired in reading Benezet and other sources. While these descriptions may have influenced Vassa's in what he wrote, the geographical descriptions are in fact reasonably accurate and reflect what Vassa could have remembered. In paraphrasing "authorities," it seems to me that Vassa was only reinforcing what he had seen and experienced.

64. *The Oracle*, April 25, 1792.

65. Erik Gøbel, "Foreign Influence upon the Danish Edict of 1792 to Abolish the Slave Trade" (paper presented at the Conference L'Impact de l'Abolition de la Traite par la Grande-Bretagne sur les discours nationaux en France, aux Etats-Unis, au Danemark, en Espagne, au Portugal et aux Pays-Bas (me´tropole et colonies), Paris, June 11–12, 2009). John Bugg also notes the influence of Danish abolition on the timing of Wilberforce's motion; see "The Other Interesting Narrative," 1434.

66. Erik Gøbel, "The Danish Edict of 16th March 1792 to Abolish the Slave Trade," in *Orbis in Orbem Liber Amicorum*, ed. John Everaer, Jan Parmentier, and Sander Spanoghe (Ghent, BE: Academia Press, 2001), 262.

67. See the discussion in Peter Linebaugh and Marcus Rediker, *The Many-Headed Hydra: Sailors, Slaves, Commoners, and the Hidden History of the Revolutionary Atlantic* (Boston: Beacon Press, 2000), 334–41.

68. Reprinted in John Bugg, "'The Sons of Belial': Olaudah Equiano in 1794," *Times Literary Supplement* (August 1, 2008), 1315.

69. James Ramsay, *An Inquiry into the Effects of Putting a Stop to the African Slave Trade and of Granting Liberty to the Slaves in the British Sugar Colonies* (London: James Phillips, 1784). For a discussion, see Folarin Shyllon, *James Ramsay, the Unknown Abolitionist* (Edinburgh, UK: Cannongate, 1977).

70. For the *Zong* affair, see James Walvin, *The Zong* (New Haven, CT: Yale University Press, 2011). According to Granville Sharp, "An Account of the Murder of 132 Negro Slaves on board the Ship Zong, or Zung, with some Remarks on the argument of an eminent Lawyer in defence of that inhuman Transaction" (British Library, Ms. 1783), on March 19, 1783, "Gustavus Vasa, a Negro, called on me, with an account of one hundred and thirty Negroes being thrown alive into the sea, from on board and English slave ship"; see Hoare, *Memoirs of Granville Sharp*, 236–41. The murders had been committed in December 1781. According to Arthur Torrington, it may be that ten people deliberately jumped overboard, rather than being thrown.

71. See Stephen J. Black Braidwood, *Black Poor and White Philanthropists: London's Blacks and the Foundation of the Sierra Leone Settlement, 1786–1791* (Liverpool, UK: Liverpool University Press, 1994); Shyllon, *Black People in Britain*; Gretchen Gerzina, *Black London: Life before Emancipation* (New Brunswick, NJ: Rutgers University Press, 1995), 133–64; and Fryer, *Staying Power*, 191–214.

72. Braidwood, *Black Poor and White Philanthropists*; Shyllon, *Black People in Britain*, 150–58; Ellen Gibson Wilson, *John Clarkson and the African Adventure* (London: Macmillan, 1980); and Yellin, *Harriet Jacobs: A Life*.

73. For the importance of identification as "African" in the British Atlantic world in this period, see Sidbury, *Becoming African in America*.

74. See Henry Louis Gates, Jr., *The Signifying Monkey: A Theory of African-American Literary Criticism* (New York: Oxford University Press, 1988); Gates, *Classic Slave Narratives*; Gates, *Signifying Monkey*; and William L. Andrews, *To Tell a Free Story: The First Century of Afro-American Autobiography, 1760–1865* (Urbana: University of Illinois Press, 1986). For contrast, see Edwards and Walvin, *Black Personalities in the Era of the Slave Trade*; and Shyllon, *Black People in Britain*. Elsewhere, I have argued that Vassa's account should be considered a "freedom narrative" rather than a "slave narrative"; see Paul E. Lovejoy, "Freedom Narratives of Trans-Atlantic Slavery," *Slavery and Abolition* 32, no. 1 (2011): 91–107.

75. See Walvin, *An African's Life*; and Shyllon, *Black People in Britain*, chapter on Equiano.

76. The importance of circumcision in Vassa's *Interesting Narrative* has been drawn to my attention by Karl Magnuson, who has undertaken a history of circumcision and British attitudes toward the practice. I am indebted to Rodrigo Barahona, whose first-year essay, "Equiano's Early Life: True or False?" (History 101/English 262, October 13, 2010, University of Wisconsin-Marinette), is based on a discussion of how Vassa portrays circumcision in *The Interesting Narrative*.

77. Karl Magnuson, *Circumcised Mind: the Dark Side of the Anglo-American Myth* (forthcoming). I wish to thank Dr. Magnuson for allowing me to read his manuscript and for our discussions of Vassa and circumcision. Also see Robert Darby, *A Surgical Temptation: The Demonization of the Foreskin and the Rise of Circumcision in Britain* (Chicago, IL: University of Chicago Press, 2005), 22–43.

78. Watson, "What's in a Name?," 96, 102.

79. Ibid., 99.

80. Gates, *Signifying Monkey*, 87.

16 ARCHIBALD MONTEATH

IMPERIAL PAWN AND INDIVIDUAL AGENT

Maureen Warner-Lewis

A life is shaped both by environmental conjunctures and by individual agency. This interplay manifests itself tellingly in the life story of Archibald Monteath. He was born in Igboland most probably in the 1790s and was kidnapped from his home in Nri territory around 1800–1802 and forcibly transported to the island of Jamaica in the Caribbean.[1] The boy's name, Aniaso, indicates that he was dedicated to the service of the Earth Mother, Ani, as an upholder of the ideals for which she stood: spiritual cleanliness and pacificism, in contradistinction to "what the Earth forbids," such as the breaking of ritual taboos and murder.[2] My own interpretation of his adult life choices is that he attempted, even while in a foreign land and under the ownership of others, to make his life an example of those values for which Ani stood. In other words, his commitment to abhorring and avoiding "what the Earth forbids" was made congruent with his dedication to a life of Christian virtue.

In fact, his life story forms the content of a conversion narrative compiled from interviews and conversations and composed by two Moravian missionaries for use as an *exemplum* in the Moravian Church's mission enterprises in the late nineteenth century and also as the basis of a memorial to be read at the subject's funeral.[3] The Church not only organized his memoir; it designed his burial place to lie alongside a row of burial spots dedicated to European missionaries and bearing a similar engraving to theirs. It reads: "Archibald Monteith, born in Africa 1800, died July 3 1864."[4] It is perhaps the only identifiable grave spot in Jamaica of a named enslaved African.

By the time he left Igboland, Aniaso would have been conversant with enough Igbo to have understood the meaning of his name, and if even he were not cognizant of the responsibilities of adult male Nri culture, he would have imbibed some knowledge of this from adopted Igbo kinsmen in Jamaica.[5] As various chapters in this volume indicate, one of the main features of slave importations into Jamaica at the turn of the nineteenth century was precisely the increased number of Igbo as well as the noticeable demographic representation of women and children among them.[6] After all, there were other Igbo who were his friends on the estate on which he worked and on neighboring plantations, and he acted as interpreter for adult Igbo whose understanding of English was poor.[7]

It is not therefore totally coincidental that the attractiveness of Christian participation made its appeal to him in full adulthood, between thirty and thirty-two years of age. Already by this time he had struck up several sexual partnerships, fathered a child with the daughter of an Igbo woman,[8] and worked as a domestic and children's companion in the home of his first owner. He was now a "driver" or type of overseer on the plantation of his original owner's son—what next was there to do to exercise his talents, to grab his interest? Already in 1821 he had "followed fashion" by having himself baptized as an Anglican:[9] "fashion" because he had submitted to the rite having seen it performed for his first master's children. This was at a time when there was agitation in Britain for the amelioration of the slave regime in British colonies and even advocacy for the abolition of slavery itself. In response to this "wind of change," the Established Church (the Church of England or the Anglicans) had begun to see that it might have a mission not only to minister to Britons living in the colonies but also to the mass of enslaved workers who were the backbone of Britain's very economy. On the invitation of landowners, Anglican clergy went to estates to perform mass baptisms of the enslaved, in addition to individual baptisms of whites, coloreds, and blacks in the church. Prior to the early nineteenth century, the Church of England had shown no spiritual interest in the enslaved, thus leaving this niche to be filled by the Moravians, the Wesleyans, and the Baptists. But at this historical juncture, the Anglicans were willing to carry out single and mass baptisms of slaves, even though this was unaccompanied by any catechization. As a result, Monteath was nominally an Anglican as of 1821, the ritual having entitled him to the name Archibald John Monteath. Spiritually, however, he was disengaged.

But his exercise of agency is obvious in the choice of his Christian names. The Anglican minister conducting the rite would not have had the time or inclination to have worked out slaves' names with such care and symmetry. John Monteath was the name of Archibald's first owner in Jamaica, a Scotsman from Glasgow who had come to Jamaica to build his fortune, apparently in the early 1790s. He had worked as an overseer on two or three estates in southwestern Jamaica before he began investing in land as of 1800, clearly with an eye to establishing himself not only as a slave owner but more so as a gentlemanly "planter" in his own right.[10] By 1802, John Monteath purchased the freedom of a quadroon (three-quarters-white) slave with whom he had three children. It is therefore likely that, although no purchase documents for Aniaso have been found, it was in this (1800–1802) period that John Monteath would have purchased a group of eleven young people to help establish his "pen" or cattle- and horse-breeding farm and to help look after his nuclear family. As a child of ten or less, Aniaso, now renamed Toby, would have been a useful playmate and servant for the young Monteath children. But by his early teens, he would have been sent out into the fields to do work to sustain the animal husbandry enterprise of his owner. So there were years enough when Toby would have been sufficiently close to the master's family to have overheard the names of John Monteath's relatives, and the name "Archibald" was one of this slate of Monteath family names—a brother's name and an uncle's name—that apparently appealed to him. In fact, even nearer home, one of John's sons born in 1807 was named Archibald John Monteath. The fact that an older Igbo boy who was a friend of Archibald was baptized on the same day as Archibald and took the name James Monteath, the name of John Monteath's first son, seems to me suggestive of the fashioning of a parallel family relationship between the two boys to that which obtained between John's first and second sons. Archibald himself states that John Monteath acted toward him as a father. This mirroring of the master's family structure and names was ironically part of the trajectory of building one's new identity and bolstering one's self-esteem and is a pattern of behavior exhibited in other cases of slave naming as well. Archibald's wife relinquished her slave name, Anne, for Rebecca. Both were names of her owner's children, so it would appear that the choice of "Rebecca" signalled a closer psychological affinity between slave Anne and free-born Rebecca Hart than between slave Anne and Anne Hart.[11]

Returning to his estate one evening in 1824, Archibald encountered a worker from a neighboring plantation who told him about the prayer meetings that were held at her master's and mistress's home. She further indicated that her owners were prepared to welcome enslaved persons from adjoining properties. Archibald later recounted that something pierced his heart at her words. No doubt it was fear: fear of going to a white person's home, fear of an activity that he did not understand, fear of facing choice. After much soul-searching and no little timidity, he went, and although Archibald did not understand much of what he heard at first, it is clear that he was moved by the gentleness of the message and the kindliness with which he was received by the Christian white landowners he met there.

Archibald was now caught in the contradictory currents of Christianity and a new cosmopolitanism: though bought by other human beings, he was to learn of the brotherhood of mankind and himself preach the need to relate to the Eskimos of the Arctic; he was to come to see Africa, his homeland, as in need of spiritual salvation; he was to pray for the freedom of those enslaved in Cuba and Jamaica; he was to receive help toward Western literacy from the same landowners in his vicinity who kept people like himself in subjugation. His own master at the time scolded him for what he must have perceived as Archibald's now divided loyalties: even while still subject to the dictates of the plantation regime, he was putting his time and energy at the service of a parallel "order"—the Christian brotherhood to which "pious" planters and some of their slaves belonged; clearly, his "master," James Monteath, was not the "pious" sort. In addition, Archibald's female partner in 1824 as well as his coworkers railed against him for immersing himself in "white people's business," by attending their prayer meetings and learning to read and write. Was Archibald not already a pawn in their wretched system of culling people from Africa and transporting them for weeks and months across the "sally water" [salt water] to be put to work in the boiling sun on sugarcane estates, on coffee fields, on cattle pens, on ships—wherever the Europeans had devised work projects? These slaves were made to supply free labor; but they had to be minimally fed and clothed; the projects required capital; the enslaved, whether African or Caribbean-born, had to be bought off entrepreneurs who had bought them in turn from captors and owners. An analysis of John Monteath's finances and the business interests of the eighteenth-century Glasgow merchant class exposes the network of imperial economic concerns in which Archibald was already wedged before he allowed himself to be further enmeshed in European religious networks.[12]

John Monteath's paternal grandfather had been feudal laird of lands at Kep in Stirlingshire and at Arnmore and Pow in the Perthshire county of Scotland. But by the young adulthood of John's father, Walter, the profits of merchandising appeared more appealing and the family seems to have moved to Glasgow, a business center near to shipbuilding ports on the Atlantic side of Scotland. One assumes that the rural lands still brought in rents, but Kep and Arnmore were comparatively speaking modest acreages.[13] Meanwhile, Britain owned lands on the North American mainland where, with slave labor, tobacco, maize, and other crops were bringing good incomes to investors. Walter became a minor player in the exploitation of tobacco in the Chesapeake, but the outbreak of the secessionist war in 1775 brought massive losses to Scots and other British investors in these agricultural and trading enterprises. Some of these investors also financed the building of ships to bring agricultural produce to Europe from across the Atlantic, just as they financed the construction and equipping of ships that went out from British ports to Africa to procure slaves in the first place. These ships had to be provisioned with crews, water, food, guns, alcohol, iron bars, cowrie shells, and cloth with which the crew bartered for African men, women, and children.

John appears to have been the eldest son of Walter Monteath and was born in the 1770s. Had things gone well with his father's American business, John may well have traveled to that Mecca, but the presence of paternal uncles as overseers, import-based merchants, and real estate dealers in the Caribbean, both in St. Vincent and Jamaica, no doubt persuaded him to make his fortunes in Jamaica, which by the late eighteenth century was the major source of sugar for Britain. John's capital for his later land and slave acquisitions came from several sources. A paternal great-aunt had come into great wealth from a short but influential marriage with Archibald, Duke of Douglas. She lent or gave handsome sums of money to her several nephews, including John's father, she herself being widowed and childless. Even if John received some largess from his cousins and uncles, he is not likely to have succeeded to such generosity through his father, as Walter had been declared bankrupt after his losses in America. But John had a brother who had joined the nineteenth-century Light Dragoons and had gone out to southern India to clear the way for the East India Company's trading enterprises. Officers in the colonial army in India could earn lucrative bonuses when the palaces of Moslem princes were sacked. This brother had loaned John moneys before his death in 1799, in addition to which John had secured posthumous loans from this brother's Scots investments in 1801 and 1804. His security for these loans was the value of several of his then small stock of slaves. John had also been able in 1806 to forge a copartnership of Glaswegians like himself to purchase additional land in Jamaica. Apart from these lump sums, John worked as an overseer and by 1800 became an attorney or superintendent to two or three very large properties, which should have earned him good money from the absentee estate owners whose representative he legally was.[14] He thus began his investments by buying up land and slaves from property on which another overseer had defaulted and subsequently buying land that his absentee clients wanted to sell. Perhaps his uncles in real estate in Jamaica were of help to him in matters like these; indeed, the first evidence of slave purchase by John concerned a mature male from one of his uncles' business connections.[15]

Monteath's own enterprises had just begun to flourish when he died in 1815. He had been able to buy several swathes of land for himself and his principal concubine, Nancy, and he had acquired a wharf for his coffee exports. Obviously anticipating his demise, Monteath deeded eleven slaves to Nancy in 1814, among them Toby/Archibald. This legal act, however, seems unknown to Archibald and any removal that may have been involved seems to have been minimal, given that Nancy's property adjoined that of John's. But Nancy, a free "brown" woman since 1802, had been herself a slave, and she was illiterate, so it appears that as her elder son matured he became her man-of-business, and the language of Archibald's story suggests that some years after John's passing, he considered the son, James, his new master. At this juncture, although appointed driver or overseer of Nancy's 431-acre property, the relationship between James the free mestize (seven-eighths' white) and Archibald the slave became strained.[16] This development was not unexpected given the caste hierarchy of plantation society where freedom and enslavement were two polarizing factors, on top of which color differentiation was marked: James almost white, Archibald black. Furthermore, the two had been playmates as children; now one held the other's life in his hands. Again, not surprisingly, James was profligate, drunk with the power of his (or rather his mother's) modest wealth in slaves and land; puffed up by his Scots connections whom he had known firsthand since he had traveled to Scotland in the first decade of the century; psychologically confused by his near, but not quite, status to a European in a culture profoundly shaped by skin color and hair minutiae and gradations; and son to a mother who had once been enslaved. Before she began to sell parcels of her land after slave emancipation in 1838, Nancy had been legally harassed regarding her rights to own certain slaves. Although Archibald seemed unaware of this court case, he knew that there was a period in which the financial affairs of the property were at a low ebb.[17] This meant that Nancy's slaves were in fear of being kidnapped by the property's creditors and claimants, and they had had to exercise great care on the open roads and tracks lest they be seized as compensation.

So there were occasional constraints on the slaves' capacity to move around. True, they were sent on job-work at other estates; they took messages to other plantations on behalf of their masters; they were sent to fetch water from ponds and streams; they walked to marketplaces to buy and sell food items, clothing, and other necessaries; and they moved from estate to estate to participate in birth and funerary rites of their enslaved brethren. But they were at the beck and call of their owners and had to show documentation to justify their presence in strange places. In addition to movement constraints, objection could be taken to their choice of marriage partners. This was Archibald's experience when he wished to marry a Christian woman from a nearby estate. But her owner was not Archibald's owner, and the latter had much to lose financially since the progeny of a woman was the property of the owner of the female slave. It would therefore have been to Nancy's advantage if Archibald had married a woman from her own estate. This was why cross-plantation marriages were discouraged. Eventually, Archibald's owners relented when they witnessed the marriage of two of Archibald's friends from neighboring estates. Archibald and Rebecca Hart were married in 1826.[18]

One could well imagine, though, that Archibald had shown some petulance over this obstruction to his proposed marriage. His own narrative reveals that he had thrown tantrums as a child when the captain of the ship on which he had sailed to Jamaica had decided not to part with the boy but instead to take him to England where he could be sold as a young servant to the monied classes there. Archibald had obviously made such a nuisance of himself that the captain had relented and let him be sold with some of the other boys with whom he had traveled. Clearly, having lost his parents, Aniaso did not want to lose the new companions he had made. Even earlier, in Igboland, he had also struggled to free himself when he realized, too belatedly, that he was being sold by someone who had enticed him from his father's compound. His captor was a young man who had been visiting the family compound under the pretense of wanting to marry Aniaso's sister. Had he wanted to hurt the family when he felt his suit was not being well received? Was he a covert agent of the Aro[19] traders who had infiltrated the Nri culture belt and subverted Nri's idealistic ethos with the enticement of monetary gain? Whatever the teasing cause of this betrayal of trust was, Aniaso's captor tempted him with the sights of a great market, the likes of which he had never before seen. The place to which they walked for a day and a half is likely to have been the lake port of Oguta, which sits on the Orashi or Engenni River, some miles before it joins the New Calabar River, itself a tributary of the Niger. Oguta was therefore a trading post for exports of yams, kola nuts, rice, goats, fowls, palm oil, horses, and ivory, and imports of guns, gunpowder, cottons, rum, and looking glasses.[20] There, negotiations to sell the boy were covertly made and Aniaso was seized and thrown into a canoe and bound, then paddled out to a large ship with a European captain aboard. He had become another statistic in Europe's insatiable hunger for manpower to work its trans-Atlantic plantations and build up its colonial public works and infrastructure. The Aro and other slave-capturing and slave-trading peoples like them were part of the African response to this overseas demand for the physical energy, positive disposition toward a work culture, and mental agility and technical skills that African populations could provide. As Archibald described for his father's and grandfather's Igbo culture, Africans were experienced agriculturalists, specializing in tuber, legume, gourd, and grain cultivation. In savanna areas they were additionally pastoralists, and as their arts illustrate, there were among them skilled metal craftsmen, fabric weavers and dyers, and woodworkers.

Archibald would again display petulant behavior in 1837 when he wished to buy his own freedom. James Monteath's initial response was to attempt to talk him out of the proposal. At this point in time, slavery was to have come to a complete end in 1840, just three years later. Archibald was not pacified. His counter was to fall ill and abstain from work. James then came to Archibald's hut to propose ninety pounds sterling to relieve him of his obligations to them. This amounted to one hundred twenty-six Jamaican pounds—far in excess of what he had saved. Archibald gave no answer and continued to be "sick." The Monteaths accurately interpreted his unspoken message. Next morning James came to Archibald's hut to announce that they had lowered their demand to fifty pounds. Archibald immediately rose from his bed, took out the forty pounds he had ready, and went to James to pay him. The remaining ten pounds Archibald obtained from a source he does not divulge, but it seems likely that he may have received some help from his Moravian minister. Perhaps it was from one of his good friends. Having paid off James in full, he was given his receipt, his "free paper"; he then dressed in his best suit and rode on his mule to the church compound where he took off his hat, waved his paper about his head, and "cried out with a loud voice: THANK GOD! I AM FREE." In these negotiations, then, Archibald showed himself to be as much a man of guile as a man of planning and forward thinking.[21]

Archibald's wiliness and quick intelligence are evident as well in his argumentation with a big landowner who challenged him as to why he had dissuaded the landowner's slaves from drinking alcohol and dancing on a particular occasion. Archibald did not initially answer his query but in riposte posed him another query instead. Having then gotten the landowner to acknowledge the distinction between an old regime and a new, Archibald then drew a parallel distinction between the moral practices of the Old Testament (which allowed polygamy, feasting, and alcoholic indulgence) and the self-denial enjoined by the New Testament teachings.

Some amount of guile may also be read into his decision in late 1831 to avoid involvement in a large anti-slavery revolt. It had been engineered by some Baptist church elders and members in the Montego Bay area north of Archibald's estate. But Archibald had had no foreknowledge of the plan, which was initially to refuse to work but which escalated into the arson of several estate houses and outbuildings to the value of over a million pounds. Rioters were moving from estate to estate recruiting members from among the enslaved, but it may have been from estate owners themselves that word of the movement reached James Monteath, Archibald's "owner." He then relayed the information to Archibald, a key actor on his estate, given that he was the driver and was responsible for the management and performance of the field staff. Had he joined the revolutionaries, there was the potential for defection of other workers under him. But Archibald chose to remain loyal to his work assignments. He clearly felt a personal loyalty to the colored Monteath family with whom he had worked for about thirty years by that time; he was also mindful of the conservative nature of Moravian teachings advocating obedience of servants to their masters. Although the uprising spread into the parishes of Westmoreland and St. Elizabeth across whose boundaries Archibald's estate lay, the plantations in his immediate vicinity did not join the action. This may have reflected the conciliatory influence on their slaves of the Moravian and evangelical landowners in the area. In addition, not having had contact with the organizers of the scheme, Archibald doubtless felt on shaky ground in ceding to any temptation to join the agitation. He had been enslaved long enough to know the price that was paid when such schemes failed. Plotters were executed in short shrift, either by being shot forthwith or being hanged after trial. Their bodies were left on display as a deterrent. According to government plan, within a short time the army and the local militia were called out to patrol the area and encircle churches and chapels, since the white population, intensely suspicious of the Christian ideologies of human brotherhood, vented their anger on the enslaved and on the churches and chapels that had attracted their membership. Wesleyan and Baptist ministers were attacked, their churches destroyed. Even the Moravians were subjected to hostile scrutiny, and one of their missionaries almost hanged. The arson continued past Christmas into the new year, and even later in 1832 there were lingering acts of murder and arson in several parishes, not only in the western end of the island but also in the north. These events marked the most serious attack against the slave system in Jamaica, resulting in 307 being killed in field skirmishes and as many executed. Fourteen whites had been killed and twelve wounded.[22] The debacle helped hasten the British Parliament's decision in 1833 to declare the abolition of slavery in 1834, even though this declaration was to be the start of a modified system of continued enslavement called Apprenticeship, which was intended to last till 1840. In any event, the entire system was abolished in 1838.

Although Archibald declined to join in a widespread and (what may have seemed to him at a distance from the organizers) ill-defined thrust for freedom, he nevertheless pursued what was considered the "legal" means of gaining his own emancipation. Having paid off the colored Monteaths, he now used his free status to turn down offers of employment in managerial-type positions on nearby estates in favor of working full time for the Moravian Church. For a fee of twelve pounds per annum he rendered his services to the Church as an assistant to the mission establishment, thus serving not only his immediate church community but all the mission stations that the Moravians had established in the west of the island: "wherever there was need of help, he was ready to work, and the appearance of his portly figure, mounted on his pony, was hailed with joy by old and young."[23] He preached at prayer meetings in huts and at church at some of the Sunday services, visited the sick, and counseled those in family or neighborhood disputes. He gave part of his land for a school building, since by January 1839 he had bought from Nancy Monteath fifteen acres of land on which he built a home, described three decades later as "a good two-storied house."[24]

He had thus extricated himself from the confinements of slavery but had substituted a form of freedom that bound him to the tenets and practices of the Moravian Church. The Moravian Brethren had sprung up out of the Reformation in fifteenth-century Moravia and Bohemia, western provinces of the Czech lands in central Europe. Facing Catholic persecution, they had withdrawn to Germany where they won the hospitality of the Lutheran Count Nicholas Ludwig von Zinzendorf in Saxony on whose lands they established an egalitarian settlement and devised their organizational structures and theological positions. By the early eighteenth century they began to spread their doctrines overseas, mainly among the Inuit [Eskimos] and Native Americans of North America and the Khoi-San of South Africa. By 1732 they sent out missionaries to the Danish islands of the Caribbean (St. John, St. Croix, and St. Thomas, today's US Virgin Islands). By December 1754 they dispatched three missionaries to Jamaica specifically to minister to the enslaved. This mission did not begin to flourish until the early 1800s, and it enlarged its scope with schools in the 1820s.[25]

Archibald's religious affiliation with the Moravians strengthened his moral fiber but also led him into condemning dancing, secular merriment, and religious beliefs associated with African and African-Christian forms of worship. This discrepancy was produced by the difficulty of delinking religious from cultural ideas, and Archibald had been removed from his natal environment too early to have learned enough of his society's religious ideas and practices to have clung to them in his later years. Yet he understood sufficient of his lineage and the social significance of the *ichi* marks he would have borne on his forehead had he not been abducted to strive for excellence in the tasks he was given or willingly chose to undertake. He begins his narrative with assertions of his Igbo identity and his parentage and that of his maternal grandfather, and it is clear that he saw his life as a series of achievements, in keeping with the high standards of his ancestral heritage.

But as a metanarrative critique, one notes that Archibald himself did not initiate or write his life story. True, he narrated its episodes, but he most likely had not participated in their compilation, their sequencing, or their selection. One missionary commented on his love of recounting stories about his life, but the biography as we have it was not his own composition.[26] This means that the ultimate purpose of the narrative was shaped by others, and it was a purpose closely linked to the desire of the Church to portray a life worthy of emulation by its membership, a life that had been spent in dedication to the mission of the Church. The amanuenses were prepared to give details of Archibald's African experience as it no doubt established his alterity for their reading public: he gives his and his parents' names, the name of the Igbo Creator-god, Chukwu, the crops his community farmed; and he dedicated ample space to the description of the scarification rite undergone by boys of aristocratic lineage. By contrast, however, the voyage from Africa is conveyed through generalizations, both because the ghostwriters sought to suppress the harrowing and unsavory and because a shorthand vocabulary for slave-ship experience had already been established in anti-slavery literature through phrases like "wretched figures," "acute bodily suffering," "cries pressed from them," and "dreadful scene." By contrast, the story of Catherine Mulgrave's passage from Luanda in west-central Africa to the Caribbean specifies places and persons they saw on the way, the death of certain enslaved passengers, and the suffering of the mulatto woman whom the captain kept in his cabin.[27] And there are the details in the fragmentary story of Florence Hall, another Igbo, who speaks of the stripping of beaded loin-coverings from the bodies of young girls once they were on board.[28] Monteath's story says nothing of the mode of transportation by which he was carried from the port city where he landed to his new owner's property at the other end of the island. The story says nothing about the various types of work he did, apart from the fact that he was a playmate for the colored Monteath children. What were the entertainments of himself and his friends, and which were those he participated in before his church life began and after? The story omits discussion about his agricultural practices on his private plot of land while still enslaved or on his fifteen-acre property he acquired as a free man. It only speaks of his yam cultivation in the context of his farming on a Sunday and the epiphany he once experienced when he realized that he ought not to break the day of rest. Furthermore, all these omissions testify to how his conversion narrative structured contextual details about his life to focus on the Christian lessons the Moravians wanted their readers to absorb. The story is silent about the punishments he received and those that he dispensed as a driver. It is also silent about his wife, apart from her name and the date of his marriage; was her mothering of only one known child the result of infertility, miscarriages, or infants born live that died soon after birth? Similarly, we have no idea about her character other than that she was a committed Christian; we do not know what sort of a husband Archibald made or the nature of his family life. How did he relate to his daughters, his grandchildren, his sons-in-law?

These omissions could in part have been due to Archibald's own vetting of his experiences, either because he wanted to show himself to the missionaries in a light that would gain their approval or because he had figured out the nature of the topics that would grab their interest. But one also suspects that his amanuenses exercised their own judgment about the topics that appealed to them and that would appeal to their readership as well. Thus the extant narrative gives today's reader a portrait of Archibald and some idea of his character traits: dogged persistence, energy, courage, intelligence, and his optimism. But we can never be certain that the amanuenses had not excised points of view that he held and episodes he had mentioned or even that they were able to comprehend the complexity of the subject whom they sought to project. In any case, similar processes of filtering and selection would have been exercised by Archibald himself had he the inclination, the drive, the command of continuous composition that were needed to produce an autobiography. Archibald shows himself, then, as a man who exercised choice at many junctures of his life. But his biography also reveals the various forms of "imperial encirclement"[29] to which his life was subjected, the several ways in which circumstance constrained him, whether in Igboland or in the island to which fate brought him, Jamaica.

NOTES

1. Nri includes towns like Nri, Awka, Nsukka, Ihiala, Ebenebe, Nnewi, Orlu, and Udi.

2. See M. Angulu Onwuejeogwu, *Social Anthropology of Africa: An Introduction* (London: Heinemann, 1975), 44–46.

3. The first published version was in German in 1864, the English version of which appeared in another Moravian Church magazine in 1865 and as an appendix to a book on Christianity in Jamaica in 1867. The fourth version is an 1853 original English manuscript and is lodged at the Moravian Archives in Bethlehem, Pennsylvania. See Maureen Warner-Lewis, *Archibald Monteath: Igbo, Jamaican, Moravian* (Kingston, JM: University of the West Indies Press, 2007), 9–10.

4. The last three letters of his surname on the gravestone are obliterated but, as in the memoir, the name is spelled "Monteith." Archibald, however, spelled his name "Monteath," the form in which his master John and his immediate ancestors spelled theirs. By the mid-nineteenth century, however, the "ei" spelling was being adopted by John's brothers in Scotland and also by John's sons in Jamaica. The 1800 date on the gravestone is speculative, as is the date 1799 given in the memoir, and later writers have disputed this time line. See Warner-Lewis, *Archibald Monteath*, 41.

5. Such as negotiating peace between communities; the cleansing, dissolution, and removal of shrines and markets; the conferment of the *ọzọ* title; the ordination of ritual and political officials; the cleansing of persons who had broken

taboos; and the promotion of fertility, especially yam growth. See Onwuejeogwu, *Social Anthropology*, 44–46.

6. S. D. Behrendt, David Eltis, and David Richardson, "The Bights in Comparative Perspective: The Economics of Long-Term Trends in Population Displacement from West and West-Central Africa to the Americas before 1850," 3 (paper presented at the Summer Institute, "Identifying Enslaved Africans: the Nigerian Hinterland and the Creation of the African Diaspora," York University, Toronto, 1997).

7. John Elliott, O-1 Diary of New Carmel, September 1, 1837, Moravian Archives, Jamaica Archives, Spanish Town, Jamaica.

8. The fact that he had few children—two are claimed in the biography—may well be due to the need of the amanuenses to present Archibald in as favorable a light as could be tolerated by their church readership as well as to the appallingly high infant mortality rate under slavery.

9. Jamaica Archives, 1B/11/8/6, vol. 2. Parish Register, St. Elizabeth, Baptisms, Not White.

10. An excellent example is Thomas Thistlewood. See Douglas Hall, *In Miserable Slavery: Thomas Thistlewood in Jamaica, 1750–86* (London: Macmillan, 1989; Kingston, JM: University of the West Indies Press, 1999); and Trevor Burnard, *Mastery, Tyranny, and Desire: Thomas Thistlewood and His Slaves in the Anglo-Jamaican World* (Kingston, JM: University of the West Indies Press, 2004).

11. For discussion of slave-naming practices as exhibited in the Monteath material, see Warner-Lewis, *Archibald Monteath*, 240–43.

12. See Warner-Lewis, *Archibald Monteath*, 93–117. For exposition on the nexus between trans-Atlantic slavery and European economic advancement, see, *The Atlantic Slave Trade*, ed. Joseph E. Inikori and Stanley L. Engerman (Durham, NC: Duke University Press, 1992); and Joseph E. Inikori, *Africans and the Industrial Revolution in England* (Cambridge: Cambridge University Press, 2002).

13. Late eighteenth-century land rents for Arnmore and Powside amounted to Scottish £355.6s.8d, while Kep brought in £118. By contrast, William Douglas of Castle Douglas collected £882 for Castle Douglas and seven other properties. See Loretta R. Timperley, ed., *A Directory of Landownership in Scotland c. 1770* (Edinburgh: Scottish Record Society, 1976), 117, 195.

14. Attorneys hired and fired overseers and bookkeepers, decided on the purchase of slaves, bought plantation supplies, arranged for shipment of produce, and advised on investment prospects. See Alan Karras, *Sojourners in the Sun: Scottish Migrants in Jamaica and the Chesapeake, 1740–1800* (Ithaca, NY: Cornell University Press, 1992), 65. See also Barry Higman, *Plantation Jamaica, 1750–1850: Capital and Control in a Colonial Economy* (Kingston, JM: University of the West Indies Press, 2005), 41–91.

15. Island Record Office, Registrar General's Department, Twickenham Park, Jamaica. Old Deeds 507, f. 140; Old Deeds 451, f. 147.

16. The existence of black overseers has been recorded by Augustus Hardin Beaumont in 1836. See Richard Sheridan, "The Role of the Scots in the Economy and Society of the West Indies," in *Comparative Perspectives on Slavery in New World Plantations*, ed. Vera Rubin and Arthur Tuden (New York: New York Academy of Sciences, 1977), 101.

17. In 1822 a case was brought against Nancy attempting to levy on her eleven slaves. See Public Record Office, London, T71/1440, f. 576.

18. Jamaica Archives, 1B/11/8/6, vol. 3. St. Elizabeth Parish Register, Marriages.

19. A subgroup of the Igbo with a militaristic and entrepreneurial philosophy.

20. Femi Kolapo, "Trading Ports of the Niger-Benue Confluence Area, c. 1830–1873," in *Ports of the Slave Trade (Bights of Benin and Biafra)*, ed. Robin Law and Silke Stickrodt (Stirling, UK: Centre of Commonwealth Studies, University of Stirling, 1999), 108.

21. See Warner-Lewis, *Archibald Monteath*, 282–82, 299.

22. See Verene Shepherd and Ahmed Reid, "Rebel Voices: Testimonies from the 1831–32 Emancipation War in Jamaica," *Jamaica Journal* 27, nos. 2–3 (2004): 54–63; and Michael Craton, *Testing the Chains: Resistance to Slavery in the British West Indies* (Ithaca, NY: Cornell University Press, 1982).

23. Editor, "Memoir of Br. Archibald Monteith," *Periodical Accounts Relating to the*

Missions of the Church of the United Brethren 25 (1865), 433.

24. Augustus Clemens, "Report of Visits to Some Missionary Stations in Jamaica," *Periodical Accounts* 24 (1861), 161.

25. John H. Buchner, *The Moravians in Jamaica* (London: Longman, Brown., 1854); and Beverly Prior Smaby, *The Transformation of Moravian Bethlehem* (Philadelphia: University of Pennsylvania Press, 1988).

26. See Clemens, "Report of Visits," 161; and Editor, "Experiences of a Former Slave in Jamaica," in Warner-Lewis, *Archibald Monteath*, 267.

27. See Maureen Warner-Lewis, "Catherine Mulgrave's Unusual Transatlantic Odyssey," *Jamaica Journal* 31, nos. 1–2 (2008): 32–43.

28. See Florence Hall, "Memoirs of the Life of Florence Hall." Ms. fragment. The Historical Society of Pennsylvania Library, ca. 1800.

29. Phrase culled from George Lamming, *Conversations: George Lamming: Essays, Addresses and Interviews, 1953–1990*, ed. Richard Drayton and Andaiye (London: Karia Press, 1992), 202.

17 IGBO INFLUENCES ON MASQUERADING AND DRUM-DANCES IN THE CARIBBEAN

Robert W. Nicholls

> The Christmas and New Year Eves have been solemnized in West End by making these entire nights hideous with tom-tom rattle and yelling. The dwellers in this town . . . could only lie helplessly awake till morning, forced to listen wide-eyed to an almost continuous roar of barbarous drumming and howling. . . . Could the noisy rites of human sacrifice and cannibal feasts to the fetish of Eboe of Dinka or Corromantee on the West African Coast be more appalling to the ears?
>
> —*THE ST. CROIX AVIS* (1901)

This portion of a letter by "A Watcher Against His Will," was published in the January 3, 1901, issue of *The St. Croix Avis*, a Virgin Islands newspaper. The racist rant against the Christmas merry making of African descendents picks out the Igbo of Nigeria and the Cromanti of Ghana for singular disdain. The slurs are typical of this period when opponents of African-style drum-dances were in fighting mode and were rallying the local establishment for a final onslaught against Bamboula dances. The Igbo were tied to Bamboula by the use of the transverse "Ebo drum" and by a notion of what Uchendu describes as "transparent living," whereby wayward individuals, especially administrators, were mocked by masquerades or shamed in songs.[1] The "dark continent" cliché, which uses Virgin Islanders' African heritage against them, had been fostered previously in the December 28, 1872, Editorial of the *St. Thomas Tidende* newspaper, which repudiated the "bambola dance" [*sic*] as a "remnant of barbarism . . . [which] might be very appropriate in Ujiji of the Nile, which Dr. Livingstone delights in exploring" (Livingston died in 1873).[2] The Editorial of the November 22, 1890, *Tidende*, advocated wiping out Bamboula because it is "used mainly as a channel of open lampoonery. . . . By disbanding the troupes those composing them would be forced to seek other and better forms of amusement."[3] The vitriolic attacks of the Virgin Islands establishment led to the decline of the Bamboula as a viable African-style folk expression early in the twentieth century. Other Igbo influenced cultural traits, however, have fared better.[4]

This chapter explores the role of diffusion in the development of Caribbean music and masquerading, and traditions are analyzed in the light of possible antecedents in West Africa and Western Europe. The term "Afro-Creole," however, recognizes that within the West Indies, people of African descent have been in the majority. In the British West Indies, the Afro-Creole prototype of masquerading, like the Creole dialect, emerged at the outset of the plantation economy. Masquerading was recorded by Hans Sloane in Jamaica in the 1680s and probably extends back to the beginning of slavery in Barbados, St. Kitts-Nevis, Antigua, and Montserrat, where the early Jamaican planters and slaves migrated from.[5]

Caribbean masquerading emerged from a fusion of styles, and some early nineteenth-century writers noted the similarities with European masquerades. While Lewis described John Canoe in Jamaica as a "Merry Andrew," Scott compared it to a "Jack Pudding" and also to a "Jack-in-the-Green."[6] Belisario drew a Jamaican Jack-in-the-Green in 1836 whereby palm fronds substituted for conventional British greenery.[7] During Christmas 1839, Gurney saw "a merry-andrew" during a "negro Saturnalia" in St. Thomas in the Virgin Islands.[8]

Caribbean Creolisms might be viewed on a sliding scale between African and European poles, with Quadrille gravitating toward the European end while the Mocko Jumbie is closer to the African end of the continuum. The European heritage was also evident in Maypole and in hero-combat Mummer's plays such as King George and the Dragon, or David and Goliath. Due to the preponderance of African descendents, African influences have impacted the region significantly, and where European influences have been incorporated, African aesthetic sensibilities have been applied. Africanist and Diasporan scholars tend to focus on African traits. Burton, for example, argues that the early Jonkonnu with bull horns "is clearly a neo-African or indigenized, rather than creolized, cultural form."[9]

Bilby points out that within the initial process of creolization, "blending occurred not only between European and African traditions but also within the varied traditions of a multitude of African ethnic groups."[10] Discussing overlapping call-and-response singing, polymeter, and other African musical survivals, Bilby states:

> One of the most interesting things about these neo-African traditions is that although they remain essentially African in every respect, most of them must be seen as syncretic (blended) New World creations, for with few exceptions they are not traceable in their entirety to any specific region or ethnic group in Africa.[11]

One reason for this blending was due to the fact that although newly arrived Africans could, and did, identify with fellow members of their ethnic group, as Crahan and Knight emphasize:

> Reconstitution of any specific ethnic group overseas did not necessarily re-create the original conditions for the propagation of the basic African culture in all its authentic dimensions. For we are not dealing with free individuals in families, but with slaves in slavery.[12]

In any case, Douglas Chambers offers a caveat and suggests that the search for one-to-one transfers of African traits is tenuous at best:

> Like "Jonkonnu" in Jamaica, "Jumbie" (even Mocko Jumbie) may have been Creolisms, not just randomly made up by slaves out of nothing. African slaves, I argue, generally drew on what they knew to create what they needed in New World situations. Creolisms therefore were most often a combination of the familiar and the functional. The point should not be to look for one-to-one transfers of "traits" but to look at ancestral forms (in this case, dancing, masking and collective performance) in specific culture-areas as "resources" on which slaves drew in order to adapt to the conditions of slavery in particular places in the Americas.[13]

Among Africans who contributed to Caribbean music, dance, and masquerading, this chapter focuses on the Igbo and reviews historical evidence from the Igbo and their neighbors in southeastern Nigeria. Of necessity, the early contributions of the Mandinka, Mende, and other peoples of the Upper Guinea region are also discussed. Crahan and Knight found that as a result of certain aspects of the supply-and-demand cycle for slaves, the Caribbean experienced an influx of "ethnic and culturally cohesive cohorts and allowed for the establishment of certain societal norms to which later arrivals, regardless of their customs would have to conform."[14] From 1526 to 1640, Caribbean slaves came primarily from Senegambia, Guinea-Bissau, Sierra Leone, Cameroon, and Angola. There was a steady increase of Akan groups from the Gold Coast into the Caribbean from 1655 to 1807. However, after 1776, Gold Coast slave shipments were outnumbered by those from the Bight of Biafra.[15]

Large numbers of Igbo were not included in the earliest slave shipments, but in due course they were nevertheless able to take their place among the African nations that performed

Big Drum-dances, for example, in Carriacou. The Akan of the Gold Coast contributed significantly to Caribbean culture and they engineered a number of rebellions. Their contributions to masquerading, however, were minimal, because "masquerades are not now, and probably were never, products of Akan societies."[16] In contrast, the Igbo inherited a flourishing masquerade tradition, and their subsequent arrival reinvigorated preexisting masquerades. They were able to adopt the indigenous prototypes and adapt them to better reflect Igbo aesthetics. A similar process occurred with the songs and dances of Gombay and Bamboula. The best educated guess of most scholars is that the precursor of these drum-dances was established by the first wave of slaves from Angola and Congo early in the Colonial era. The drum-dances are quintessentially African and would seem familiar to subsequently arriving slaves. They were readily embraced by the Igbo, whose drum, along with the frame drum, became the trademark of Gombay.

THE IGBO IN THE CARIBBEAN

Some of the earliest mention of the Igbo in the Caribbean lists them among various enslaved African groups. They are either mentioned explicitly or implied by origins of shipments, for example, Bight of Biafra. Sometimes they are lumped together with Ibibio and smaller neighboring groups from the Nigeria-Cameroon borderland. The arrival of enslaved Africans was observed in the central Windward Islands by Sir William Young, governor of Tobago. In an entry dated December 16, 1791, he states:

> The ships came from distinct districts and with people of different nations on board: The Pilgrim of Bristol, with 370 Eboes [Igbos] from Bonny. The Colus of Liverpool with 300 Windward Negroes from Baffa [*sic*]. The Anne of Liverpool, with 210 Gold Coast Negroes from Whydah.[17]

Igbos are specifically identified in Young's list, while "Baffa" might be Biafra. In the early literature, tribal designations are often ambiguous. Some are current today while others are archaic. Writing about the Virgin Islands, the missionary C. G. A. Oldendorp lists recognizable names such as Fula, Mandinga (Upper Guinea), Akkran, Fante (Ghana), Ibo, Karabari, and Mokko [*sic*] (Nigeria) along with more obscure names. He states, "The Ibo, friends of the Karabari [Kalabari], possess a vast land which lies in the interior of Africa. The Mokko also share a border with Karabari."[18]

In eighteenth-century Jamaica, British slaveholder Bryan Edwards (1794) appraised African ethnicities for their productive worth. While recognizing that the different Gold Coast (Akan) peoples were "engaged in perpetual warfare [with] many of the captives taken in battle"[19] (i.e., mainly warriors); he goes on to compare the "fierce and savage manners of the Koromantyn Negroes" to "the timid and desponding temper of the Eboes [*sic*]."[20] Edwards felt differences in music styles were indicative of ethnic temperaments. He noted how gentle Igbo music was in contrast to fiery Asante (Koromante/Cromanti) music. He states, "Their tunes in general are characteristic of their national manners; those of the Eboes being soft and languishing; of the Koromantyns heroick and martial [*sic*]."[21] Is it possible that the progressions in minor sixths that A. M. Jones observed in Igbo music, which provides gentle and reflective musical sequences, were evident during this early period?[22]

Writing of Jamaica in the eighteenth century, Moreton (1790) reproduces the text of a chorus sung in vernacular.

> If we want for go in a Ebo
> Me can't go there!
> Since dem tief [thieve] me from a Guinea
> Me can't go there![23]

Edwards suggested that Igbo captives had a tendency to suicide. He states, "the great objection to the Eboes as slaves, is their constitutional timidity, and despondency of mind; which are so great as to occasion them very frequently to seek, in a voluntary death, a refuge from their own melancholy reflections."[24] However, Edwards further explains, "but if their confidence be once obtained, they manifest a great fidelity, affection, and gratitude, as can reasonably be expected from men in a state of slavery."[25] Writing of Carriacou, at the southern tip of the Grenadines, McDaniel discusses a patois song collected in the mid-nineteenth century by Pearse (1956). McDaniel states:

> The transplanted African often believed that at death his spirit would take flight and cross the ocean to join his brotherhood and ancestors. This piece . . . suggests the longing for homeland and the ultimate form of rebellion in suicide often realized by the Igbo.
>
> Oyo, Mama, Bel Louise oh,
> Nu kai alé na Gini pu
> Korwé pawa mwé!
> Lame bawé mwé
> We shall go to Africa to meet
> my parents!
> The sea bars me.[26]

On the *Tombstone Feast: Funerary Music of Carriacou* album, there is a track entitled "Igbo ginade-o," which means "Granadian Igbo." Grenada is the island immediately to the south of Carriacou. In patois, the song's refrain, "Ba t'ni mama; ba t'ni papa," translates as "I have no mother; I have no father." Although such laments are typical of enslaved people, it is somewhat of an enigma because "it is a song of migration, loneliness, and hopelessness, but it is danced with fervor and exuberance."[27] This sheds a new light on Edwards's characterization of the Igbo as a "languishing" people.[28]

Many African ethnic groups continued their musical traditions in the New World, and an instrument was identified in the seventeenth century that has parallels in Igboland. In 1688, Sloane saw dancers in Jamaica who wore leg and wrist rattles that were shaken in time with an instrument that seems like a kind of idiophonic pot drum. Sloane states that the musician "makes a sound on the mouth of an empty gourd or jar with his hand."[29] This musical style was known as "Jenkoving" in Jamaica and "Jinkgouing" in Barbados and is described as clapping of hands on the mouth of two jars.[30] This musical technique is similar to playing the Udu musical pot, an Igbo rhythm instrument. The Udu is an unusual clay instrument shaped like a spherical gourd with a protruding hollow neck and an approximately two-inch-diameter hole in the side of the pot. Like a slit-drum, it is classed as a concussion idiophone; but unlike the slit-drum, which is beaten with sticks, it is played by alternately beating each hole with the flattened palm of each hand. This produces a rhythmic gulping sound, not unlike the *dundun* talking drum of the Yoruba. Known as Otah-ubah (literally pot-drum) among the Igede, who are northern neighbors to the Ezza and Izzi Igbo, it is heard to good effect on *The Igede of Nigeria* CD.[31] It is also known as Kimkim among Ibibio people and has now spread throughout north central Nigeria, especially within Christian church ensembles.[32] It might be anticipated that the "Jenkoving" of the seventeenth century produced similar gulping rhythms.

AFRICAN NATION DANCES

During interludes in their work routines, it was usual for Africans in the Caribbean to congregate to dance and make music, and this provided a spectacle for sightseers. The eighteenth-century Igbo diarist, Olaudah Equiano, witnessed celebrations in Jamaica in which "different nations of Africa meet and dance after the nature of their own country."[33] When the Englishman, Thomas Thistlewood, first landed in Kingston, Jamaica (ca. 1750), he wandered "to the westward of the Town to see Negro Diversions—odd Music, Motions, etc. The Negroes of Each Nation by themselves [*sic*]."[34] African nation dances occurred throughout the Caribbean but gradually died out as the slave population became indigenized. In a few remote locations such as Carriacou they have continued virtually until today.

African nation dances occurred in New Orleans, and this reinforces the idea that the city belongs more to the Caribbean than to the American mainland. Louisiana was not part of the United States until the Louisiana Purchase of 1803. Due to general disinterest and less paternalism on the part of former French and Spanish planters, African traits survived in Louisiana longer than elsewhere in the United States. Throughout the latter half of the eighteenth and the first half of the nineteenth century, transplanted Africans held impressive dance festivals at Congo Square, New Orleans, on Sundays. Originally a ceremonial ground of the Oumas Indians, Congo Square was a large open field, situated where Beauregard Square is today. More than five hundred Africans formed separate dance rings, and they attracted twice that number of spectators.

Tribal groupings were represented by the different clusters of onlookers, musicians, and dancers, "each nation taking their place in different parts of the square . . . the Minahs would not dance near the Congos, nor the Mandringos near the Gangas."[35] Brown (1860) listed Congo Square ethnic groups as "Kraels [Creoles], Minahs, Congos and Mandringas, Gangas, Hiboas, and Fulas [*sic*]."[36] This list included savannah groups, Mandinkas and Fulani (Mandringas and Fulas) and forest groups, Congos, and Igbos (Hiboas).

In Benjamin Latrobe's report, two orchestras were described. One orchestra had a square membrane drum, the typical gombay drum that came to be transplanted from the Caribbean to Sierra Leone and Ghana; and a wooden instrument that is recognizably a slit-drum as used by forest people such as Igbos and Congos. It was described as "a block cut into something in the form of a cricket bat with a long deep mortice down the center. This thing made a considerable noise being beaten on the side by a short stick."[37] Historical evidence shows that the native Taino people that inhabited some Caribbean islands in pre-Columbian times used a hollow log slit-drum.[38] However, although it is common in Central and West African forest areas, reports of transplanted Africans using this instrument in the Caribbean have not surfaced.

Ethnic identification existed in Jamaica as late as the 1820s–1830s, for Kelly observed at Christmas: "The Mangolas, the Mandingoes, the Eboes, the Congoes, etc., [*sic*] formed into exclusive groups . . . [and each performed] the music and songs . . . peculiar to their country."[39] Because of its remote location, small size, and high proportion of blacks to whites, the island of Carriacou retained nation dances longer than elsewhere. These were performed in Big Drum rituals in the twentieth century and continue in a tourist diluted form into the twenty-first century. They were recorded by musicologist Alan Lomax in 1962. The names of the African nations indicate the regions in West Africa from which Carriacou people trace their ancestry. According to McDaniel, these are shown in table 17.1.

The African regions of Upper Guinea, Gold Coast, Biafra, and Central Africa are represented, and three of the above nine groups are from the Bight of Biafra. Although "Moko" is now defunct as an ethnic designation, in the literature the Moko have been associated with the Igbo.[40] Nevertheless, Oldendorp discovered that the Moko name for God is "Abassi," and that their numbers, one, two, three, four, are "kia, iba, ita, inan."[41] This shows that the Moko were speaking Efik, the language of Ibibio groups of the Calabar region. Territory labeled "Moko" appears on the map in Baikie's *Narrative of an Exploring Voyage* (1856). It is some fifty miles northeast of Calabar in the area occupied today by various Ekoi groups. Jones confirms that "[Ibibio] provided an unduly large proportion of the slaves shipped from the Bight of Biafra in the eighteenth century."[42] It is conceivable that the Moko were, as Douglas Chambers suggests, "Ekoi (Yako) and, taken as slaves from Calabar may have included Ogoni and Okrika."[43]

The liner notes of the *Carriacou Calaloo* album state, "Nation dances have distinct rhythmic patterns associated with each ethnic group. These form a sociomusical code, offering extra-musical information on Carriacou history and peoples."[44] Track 21 of the *Tombstone Feast: Funerary Music of Carriacou* album is a Moko song entitled "C'est mwe, Nani Moko" ("I am Nani Moko"), which, sung in patois, is the recurring refrain of this song. The song belongs to the Moko Yegéyéyé nation. According to Pearse, the Moko of Carriacou split into two groups.[45] The Moko Bangé became sophisticated townspeople, while the Moko Yegéyéyé remained country folk. For McDaniel,

TABLE 17.1 Carriacou African ancestry

Nation	*Region*	*Modern country*
Cromanti	Gold Coast	Ghana
Igbo	Bight of Biafra	Nigeria
Manding	Senegambia, Mali	Senegambia, Mali
Temne	Sierra Leone	Sierra Leone, Liberia
Kongo	Congo, Central Africa	Republic of Congo
Chamba	Bight of Biafra	Nigeria
Moko	Bight of Biafra	Nigeria, Cameroon
Arada	Ardra, Dahomey	Benin Republic
Banda	Gold Coast or Congo	Ghana/Central Africa

Source: Lorna McDaniel, *The Big Drum Ritual of Carriacou* (Gainesville: University Press of Florida, 1998), 38.

"the evolving nature of class is evident in the Moko Bangé dance, a *bakra* (white people's) dance where everybody dances in the ring together instead of in ones or twos as in the other nation dances."[46] In contrast, the Moko Yegéyéyé is more African in style and danced singly. Similar developments occurred with Igbo dances, which expanded to include Scotch Igbo and Jig Igbo, the "jig" being a British and Irish heel-and-toe dance. McDaniel states, "As new peoples such as the Scotch Igbo entered the society, a new racial classification as well as a new dance style was invented."[47]

Of the six African Nation tracks on the *Carriacou Calaloo* album, two are Igbo. "Igbo Le Le" is performed by a female lead vocalist with a "chac-chac" shaker, accompanied by a female chorus and three male drummers. It has a repetitive call-and-response refrain, "Igbo Le Le, Oh, le, wo yo," which hints at ancient hocketing choral techniques of African equatorial forest regions.[48] On the *Tombstone Feast: Funerary Music of Carriacou* album, Track 10 is entitled "Iama Diama Igbo Lé-Lé." The liner notes state:

> As in most songs of the Ibo group, the text invokes the name of the [supposed] Ibo god Ibo Lélé, here called by his full title—Iama (or Ianman Dianma) Igbo Lélé. The proud phrase "Ayen ba ka fé Igbo" ("Nothing can harm the Igbo") also occurs in most Ibo songs. The word polin is still obscure.
>
> Chorus: Iama Diama Igbo Lé-Lé, Iama
> Leader: C'est mwe negess Igbo
> Chorus: Iama Diama Igbo Lé-Lé, Iama
> Leader: C'est mwe polin Igbo
> Chorus: Iama Diama Igbo Lé-Lé, Iama
> Leader: Ayen ba ka fé Igbo!
> Translation:
> Iama Diama Igbo Lé-Lé, Iama
> I am an Ibo woman
> Iama Diama Igbo Lé-Lé, Iama
> I am a polin Ibo
> Iama Diama Igbo Lé-Lé, Iama
> Nothing can hurt the Ibo! [*sic*].[49]

JONKONNU WITH BULLHORNS

Although different masquerades have existed in the Caribbean, the affinity between them suggests that a common thread of ideas existed between the various islands during both the pre- and postemancipation eras. In the area of masked dancing, "John Canoe" or "Jonkonnu" became a generic name for a widely dispersed assortment of masquerades in Jamaica, Tortola, Belize, Bahamas, and even North Carolina during the antebellum era. One of the earliest was recorded in Jamaica and wore a pair of spreading bull horns and parallels the John Bull, Red Bull, and Wild Bull masquerades of the Leeward Islands. The description of the "John Connu" mask (ca. 1760s) by planter-historian Edward Long is often quoted:

> In the towns, during the Christmas holidays, they have several tall or robust fellows, dressed up in grotesque habits, and a pair of ox-horns on their head, sprouting from

> the top of a horrid sort of visor, or mask, which about the mouth is rendered very terrific with large boar tusks. The masquerader, carrying a wooden sword in his hand, is followed with a numerous crowd of drunken women, who refresh him frequently with a cup of aniseed-water, whilst he dances at every door, bellowing out John Connu.[50]

Long's description is singularly important because he names two African groups that he identified with masquerading. He states, "In 1769, several new masks appeared; the Ebos [Igbo], the Pawpaws [an Ewe related group, described as Ewe-Fon], etc, having their respective Connus, male and female, who were dressed in a very laughable style."[51] Unfortunately, Long's silence regarding the ethnic groups implied by his "etc" is deafening. As is common in West Africa, the songs performed for the John Canoe dance consisted of short perfunctory refrains:

> This character . . . was attended thro' the town by a great number of negroes, beating old canisters, or pieces of metal, singing "ay, ay John Canoe" in the time expressed by three quavers and two semiquavers, but with little inflexion of the voice: the word "ay, ay," being frequently repeated like a chorus.[52]

It is worthy of note that the scary visor mask had two prominent adornments: a spreading ox horn headdress and boar tusks around the mouth. In the literature, the John Connu horns are often emphasized more than the tusks. In Africa the use of real horns is much less frequent than masks that include carved wooden horns. The use of headdresses with a pair of real horns (as opposed to a cluster) is generally limited to some groups in the arid northeast region of Ghana, such as the Bulsa, Kassena, Moba, and Frafra, where they symbolize manhood and are used by hunters' societies.[53] Masks with real cattle horns also feature in the initiation rituals of various Mande people in the Upper Guinea region, including the Bamana of Mali and the Mandinka and Jola of Senegambia.[54] These groups arrived in the Caribbean early in the slavery era.

IGBO HORNED MASKS

Among the Igede and the Igbo, horns have martial connotations and are also associated with hunting. Horns are blown, for example, to orchestrate the Ohafia War Dances. Within a masking genre in Igboland there may be several types of masks. Each type has a specific appearance, costume, dance, drum rhythms and music, and rules of behavior.[55] Some of the Mmanwu masks documented by Eli Bentor have real cow horns, though they are not identified as either bulls or bush cows.[56] The Caribbean Bull masks sometimes encompassed the whole cranium, but no comparable practice has been discovered in Upper Guinea; however, some Igbo Mgbedike masquerades wore the skull and horns of a bull instead of a face mask when they performed at the Afo New Yam Festival in the village of Umuokwara, in the Akokwa area just to the west of Arondizuogu. Mgbedike masquerades have clappers made out of dried pods tied to their costumes, resulting in a rattling sound when they move. The masks often have large teeth and carry machetes and must be restrained by handlers.[57]

A bull-horned Mwanwu masquerade from the Njima Club of Arondizuogu danced in a shaggy costume and a checkered apron at Oror, Arochukwu, on January 5, 1988, during the burial ceremony of the Eze Aro, the traditional ruler of Arochukwu (Plate 15).[58] The Njima masquerade club was established in 1972 to restore the masking culture of Arondizuogu following the Nigerian civil war. They once performed for President Shehu Shagari at the opening of a large hotel owned by an Arondizuogu man in Abuja; club members also performed at the burial of Muslim politician Shehu Aminu Kano in Kano in 1983. During Arondizuogu's annual Ikeji Festival, the bull-horned Njima masquerade included paying homage to an ofo tree (*Detarium senegalense/elastica*).[59]

Another masking genre, Okonko (Plate 18), differs from Mmanwu in that the Mmanwu costume must cover all parts of the body, while Okonko often leaves the hands and legs bare.[60] Okonko masquerades are often adorned with horns, and the heads of some, like the masquerades of the Nri-Akwa of the Northwest corner of Iboland documented by Boston, are topped by multiple animal horns, which are normally hunting trophies; that is, "narrow pointed horns of various kinds of antelope." These composite masks consist of a helmet made of a cylinder of coiled grass coated with a "thick black gum . . . [which] provides modeling material for the features and a cement for fixing the horns, teeth, hair and decorative rows of red seeds."[61] Although not representing particular ancestors, the Nri-Akwa consider the masquerades as *mmo* spirits of the dead.[62] Tufts of raffia adorn the wrists and ankles of Okonko, and some wear bulky raffia costumes topped by antelope horns and a semi-concealed cloth mask with the eyes and nose outlined with cowry shells (Plate 19).[63] On the first day of the Okonko festival of Umuowa, the masqueraders will circle the market five times. During Okonko festivals in Isu Njaba near Nkwerre, musicians who accompany masquerades comprise a large number of men rapping horns with sticks as percussion instruments. Eight days later, a particularly secretive masquerade will come out during the night and walk along the boundaries of the community to mark the end of the festival.[64] Unlike the Jola and Mande horned masks, there are no historical records confirming the antiquity of the Igbo horned masks, such as would suggest they existed during the eighteenth century when enslaved Igbo were transported to the Caribbean.

TUSKS

A 1797 description of the Jamaican Jonkonnu is pertinent; it states, "The Negroes have their droll, which, however it may be dressed is always called a John Canoe; a whimsical character . . . Sometimes they wear two faces . . . usually they have but one, which is often rendered hideous by beards and boar's tusks."[65] In this account of the masquerade, there is the suggestion of janus masks and a description of a bearded mouth embellished, yet again, with boar's tusks. The tusks might indicate an Igbo influence. Apart from the false-face masks of the Dan of Liberia that feature tumors and other disfigurements, masks rendered hideous by tusks are unusual in West Africa.[66] However, tusked masks do appear among the Igbo. For example, the mouth of an Igbo mask in the Nigerian Museum in Lagos is distorted by the addition of five crooked teeth and tusks. It hails from a village northeast of Onitsha and is composed of a basketry helmet plastered with gum and has a dozen or so horns of wild animals covering the top of its head and is decorated with red seeds.[67]

Light and dark, female and male Okoroshi masks perform in the Owerri region during the annual six-week masking season that heralds the New Yam festival. The Igbo, like the Kalabari, the Igede, and others in southern Nigeria, traditionally celebrate an annual New Yam Festival with music, dance, and masquerading. It is enacted to "foster productivity of both fields and women."[68] The spirits that dwell in Okoroshi masks purify the community and remove all evil and negativity from the village so that the next year begins fresh and clean. There are "two classes of Okoroshi masks, white or light colored masks and dark ones. While, the small light masks, carved with refined delicate features, manifest female spirits, the larger dark masks, often carved with grotesque features, manifest male spirits" and represent danger and mystery.[69] Visona et al. state:

> Near the end of the season, several ritually powerful, "heavy" dark masks come out often with an entourage of male followers carrying clubs and singing dirges about war and conquest. . . . Most have strongly distorted, enlarged features, perhaps with snaggle teeth.[70]

Visona et al. include a photograph of a dark wooden apelike mask collected at Nwaozo (ca. 1960) named Chimpanzee. It has a distorted mouth with large snaggle teeth consisting mostly of bleached scallop shells and a protruding tusk that extends up the right cheek almost as far as the eye.[71] Cole and Aniakor include a photograph of an Okorishi Odu mask in the Nigerian National Museum at Lagos. Carved in wood by Anozie (ca. 1948), its distorted mouth displays snaggle teeth and a pair of tusks.[72]

LIGHT MASKS

The Nri-Akwa *mmo* masks also have female counterparts that "represent traditional Ibo ideas of beauty and feminine character."[73] Known to art collectors as "white face masks" or "maiden spirit masks," around Onitsha they are called *agbogho mmwanu* (literally "unmarried girl"). These female masks appear during the main festival of the year, held early in the dry season when harvesting is almost over, or during the feast of the earth spirit, Ane, which occurs later in the dry season. They can also perform at funerals and in connection with male initiation. Nearly all the neighbors of the Igbo have versions of the light/dark, beauty/beast masks, yet it is uncommon beyond this area. Although appearing within the same festival, light and dark masks rarely appear together.

While the tusked John Canoe mask can be equated to the dark beast masks, the light Igbo masks can be compared to the wire mesh masks, which are painted in light colors and are ubiquitous throughout the Caribbean. It is sometimes assumed that because the mesh masks were pale they were meant to represent Caucasians. It should be remembered, however, in Africa, spirits are usually believed to be white or colorless. The Igbo *agbogho mmwanu* and similar white masks in the southeastern region, which indicate maiden spirits, is an example, while the Poro society initiations of the Dan in Liberia where novices are painted with white clay to symbolize they are temporarily dead, is another. Against this, Virgin Islander, Ethel McIntosh says that some of the local masks were deliberately painted pink with blue eyes as a means of subtly satirizing the white population.[74] Undoubtedly some of these masks poked fun at Europeans, but that was to be expected because everything and everyone else were also lampooned during the Christmas and New Year festivities.[75]

MOCKO JUMBIE

The Mocko Jumbie is a stilt-dancing masquerade that is found throughout the Caribbean but particularly identified with the US Virgin Islands. Two early reports of stilt masquerades in the Caribbean come from St. Vincent, an Anglophone island in the central Windward Islands. The first report of a "Moco-Jumbo" signifies a Mandinka heritage.[76] The second report actually identifies the performer as an Igbo who is assisted by some of Igbo soldiers of a "negro regiment."[77] The latter doubtless belonged to the British West India Regiment stationed in St. Vincent.

William Young describes Christmas 1791 and a stilt dancer called "Moco-Jumbo" who was wearing a "false head" [mask] and, accompanied by musicians and swordsmen, roamed the streets assuming the "antic terrible" and entertaining passersby.[78] A footnote probably added by editor Bryan Edwards identifies the "Moco-Jumbo" with the "Mumbo Jumbo of the Mendengoes [Mandinkas]."[79] He is probably correct in this assumption, because Young concluded the Christmas season with a feast and was entertained by visiting slaves who danced to the music of a "balafo [*sic*]."[80] A *balafon* is a wooden xylophone used by Mandinka and neighboring people.[81] Robert Dirks also describes the Mocko Jumbie as "a Mandingo import."[82] In light of the discussion below of Gombey more than thirty years later and Bamboula more than half a century later, Young's description of the drum-dance is worth noting. The dancers were "dressed in the highest beauism, with muslin frills, high capes, and white hats." The women wore "handkerchiefs folded tastefully about their heads and gold ear-rings and necklaces." In due course, "about a dozen girls, began a curious and most lascivious dance, with much grace as well as action; of the last plenty in truth."[83]

Charles Williams Day's report, published in 1852, describes an Igbo stilt dancer whose costume combines African and European elements (cowrie shells and grenadier's cap). The stilt dancer is not referred to as a Mocko Jumbie, but simply as "De Jumbee" or "De

Jumpsa-man." However, Day does explain, "'De jumbee' was of course an imitation of the genuine" (i.e., mock):

> One evening in Kingston (St. Vincent) I witnessed a "Willy" or jumbee dance, got up as an exhibition by an African Ebo [Igbo] negro. . . . De Jumpsa-man' was assisted by some of the Ebo soldiers of the negro regiment stationed here. . . . The Jumpsa-man was . . . stilts six feet high, fastened to his feet. . . . He was dressed in a guernsey-frock and long striped trousers, made very wide, which concealed his feet. His face was covered with a mask of scarlet cloth, ornamented with cowrie shells; and having a huge wig and beard, with a grenadier's hairy cap on his head, he looked unearthly. The dance consisted of various contortions of the body, sufficiently droll. . . . [He] alternately amused and frightened the women for twenty minutes.[84]

Construing "Mocko Jumbie" to mean "the Jumbie of the Moko," is an intriguing interpretation. However, this rationale does not exist within the Virgin Islands collective memory. Although many different stilt masquerades are explored in Robert W. Nicholls, "The Mocko Jumbie of the U.S. Virgin Islands: History and Antecedents," two potential but disparate prototypes are highlighted. These are the Laniboy masquerade of the Toma, Guerzé, and Kissien people of Guinea and the similar Dan masquerade versus the Ekeleke masquerade of the western Igbo of the Kwale area of Nigeria, nearby southern Edo communities, and the Western Urhobo communities of the Niger Delta.[85] Many different stilt masquerades are found in the Upper Guinea region, but despite the abundance of masquerades in Igboland, there are surprisingly few reports of stilt masquerades, and those that exist tend to have stilts that are much shorter than those associated with Mocko Jumbies, and few represent a viable prototype. A possible exception is Ekeleke.

In his article, Nicholls suggests that a provenance for the Mocko Jumbie in the upper-Guinea region seems more plausible than an origin in southeastern Nigeria.[86] Although Young does not describe the costume, Day describes the masquerade as wearing striped trousers, which are commonplace among the stilt masquerades of the Upper Guinea Region.[87] It is of interest that a 1919 photograph of a Mocko Jumbie wearing a suit with bold vertical stripes in Port of Spain, Trinidad, appears in Nunley and Bettelheim.[88] Regarding the derivation of the name Mocko Jumbie, the word "Jumbie," is commonly understood by Virgin Islanders to refer to a ghost or spirit and is likely derived from the word "zumbi," of the Kimbundu of the Congo, meaning a departed spirit. "Mocko," on the other hand, appears to be a compound term with multiple meanings. The idea of the masquerade as a "sham jumbie" and "derider of jumbies" seems to prevail in most Virgin Islander's minds, but interpretations as a "mumbo jumbo," "sorcerer," and even "bogey man," are also available. Like the Upper Guinea masquerades that dispel witchcraft, the Caribbean Mocko Jumbie is believed to drive out bad spirits and generally bring beneficence. The facts do not appear to support an interpretation that the masquerade is derived from a Moko prototype. Although this study of southeastern Nigerian stilt masquerades is limited, most, like Ekeleke, fulfill other purposes than warding off evil spirits. There is a need for further research in this area.[89]

ADOPTION AND ADAPTATION

What then can explain "De Jumbee" performed by an Igbo? The Igbo are tied to the Mocko Jumbie genre by Day's 1852 report.[90] Could Day's example illustrate a process of Igbo performers adopting and modifying a Mandinka prototype? And might not the same process of adoption and adaptation be at play with Jonkonnu, whereby the bull horn mask characteristic of the Upper Guinea region amalgamated with similar Igbo genres and added Igbo tusks around the mouth? Again, with the exception of the Dan, whose masks may feature broken jaws with hideous protruding teeth, the research has not revealed any such tusks on the horned masks of Mande peoples. It seems that Igbo individuals in the Caribbean partook of established masquerades that they encountered and transformed them to some extent and moved them forward. The process of adoption and adaptation is in line with the idea that once established the aesthetics of a Creole masquerade type remains somewhat constant. Although modified and embellished by subsequent waves of enslaved West Africans, the established template would not be drastically reformulated or abandoned and replaced by something completely different.

The act of adopting and modifying is in accordance with the traditional character of the Igbo, and this native ingenuity has been formed historically. Classical social anthropological and historical accounts of Igbo society describe it as "stateless" and "acephalous." Historically, these are the "uncaptured peasantry" that Goren Hyden refers to.[91] Horton argues that the decentralized familial basis of segmentary societies produce individuals with a great deal of personal autonomy.[92] Igbo are known as great innovators and entrepreneurs.

Douglas Chambers warns us that it may not be possible to discern one-to-one transfers of African traits. Instead, he suggests that it is better to "look at ancestral forms (in this case, dancing, masking, and collective performance) in specific culture-areas as 'resources' on which slaves drew in order to adapt to the conditions of slavery."[93] Accordingly, the remainder of this chapter goes beyond a comparison of costume characteristics and looks instead at levels of understanding within a given society, in this case the Igbo, and the philosophies and dispositions for social living that they brought to the Caribbean.

SOCIOPOLITICAL FUNCTIONS

It is apparent that music, dance, and masquerading can provide the means to achieve particular sociopolitical ends. The fierceness of some masquerades is apparent in Visby-Petersen's description of horned masquerades in a St. Thomas Christmas parade (ca. 1892). It can be observed, however, that the blackened nakedness of the performers is not typical of the Virgin Islands but seem more akin to the Jab Jab Molasses of Trinidad and Grenada who daub their bodies with grease or molasses and threaten to smear onlookers:

> The pitch black negroes are quite naked except for a loincloth to which the devil's tail is fastened. Big horns are attached to their foreheads. . . . A strong rope, held by a muscular negro, is fastened to the waist of each devil, so that he will not endanger the crowd.[94]

The behavior of these and other ferocious masquerades can be compared to G. I. Jones's description of a masquerade performance in the Northern Igbo village of Amobia, whereby "the fierce characters had ropes or chains around their waists which were held by burly attendants to prevent them from attacking the crowd."[95]

To underscore its unpredictable nature, the John Bull of Antigua was accompanied by a whipman who would lash the masquerade to make him angry. George "Pope" Farrell's costume consisted of a banana shaggy skirt and a heavily padded burlap blouse to protect him from the lashes. Nevertheless, Pope bares whip scars from previous encounters.[96] Many elders in the Virgin Islands remember the Bull and how it chased children with its chain dragging on the ground as if it had broken loose from its grapnel. For example, Schrader remembers Smokey Joe of Bethlehem in the guise of the Bull.[97]

Certain Caribbean masquerades used their intimidating presence as a means of modifying behavior, particularly among children. Visby-Petersen, in her report of a Mocko Jumbie in St. Thomas (ca. 1892), talks of "the traditional 'Mumbo-Jumbo' or Mukka Jumbe . . . [who did] an insane dance on tall stilts. . . . This bogeyman, the 'Mumbo-Jumbo,' is always performed by a man."[98] Her reference to the Mocko Jumbie as a "bogeyman," is significant because, unlike its arcane function of dispelling bad spirits and attracting good ones ("Mumbo Jumbo"); "bogeyman" refers the more pragmatic function of social control. Leona Watson admits she wet herself at the age of eight when she first saw Marshall the Mocko Jumbie. Her grandfather had told her that masquerades are "the spirits of our ancestors," while her mother threatened, "If you don't behave, I'll bring Marshall the Mocko Jumbie."[99]

SOCIAL CONTROL

With regard to masquerades fulfilling particular sociopolitical functions, some African and European practices relative to the use of masquerades for social regulation were reproduced in the Caribbean. Masquerades used as vehicles for behavior modification have been part of the traditional landscape in much of West Africa. For the acephalous Igbo, masquerades were most often attached to men's societies, some of which had regulatory functions, implementing sanctions against individuals who violated communal norms. The degree to which masquerades penetrated the actual governance of West African communities varied from ethnic group to ethnic group. Kasfir states:

> In the Dan country of Liberia and Ivory Coast . . . the mask system penetrated the social system, rather than remaining its symbolic counterpart. Masks personified and carried out real political roles from the judgment of criminals to the settlement of land disputes. This also happened in southeastern Nigeria and Cameroon.[100]

Here, again, similarities between Dan and ethnic groups in southeastern Nigeria are apparent. Referring to Igbo masking, Visona et al. state:

> Before 1900 and early in the colonial era, powerful masked spirits, deputized by councils of elders, frequently had broad governmental authority, policing, fining, judging, and even occasionally executing criminals. Most of these roles were taken over by British colonial authorities; after the recognition of Nigerian independence in 1960 they passed to the Nigerian government. Yet some masks radiate an aura of power even today, and many still have locally effective regulatory roles.[101]

There follows two examples of masquerades that enforce law and order or settle disputes. In the mid-1970s, I was accustomed to visit a village in Mbano, Imo state, Nigeria. The settlement had a landmark, a huge *iroko* tree, possibly 150 feet high. It was earmarked to be cut down by the local landowner but this was prevented. At the behest of the community, the local *mmo* masquerade applied spiritual injunctions by circling the tree and performing protective rites.[102] Ottenberg confirms that Afikpo Igbo masquerades such as *okpa* can still wield coercive power. He states:

> A devout Christian, annoyed by an *okpa* playing in front of his house, violated secret-society rules by trying to drag the masquerader away. The next day dozens of *okpa* from all over Afikpo tore the man's house down (and those of neighbors as well) and killed his animals. . . . The police took no action.[103]

Within European agrarian communities in preindustrial times, masquerades operated as vehicles for social regulation much as they did in West Africa. For example, Alford maintains that the horned masquerade known as the "Ooser" of Melbury Osmond in Dorset, England, could be "brought out for the punishment of village wrongdoers in a Skimmington or Rough Music."[104] At Christmas, in parts of Germany, the compassionate St. Nicholas is accompanied by an authoritarian "Knecht Ruprecht . . . who is dressed in skins, or straw, and looks very fierce."[105] The "good children get cakes for saying their prayers; the bad ones are beaten with ash-bags."[106] These children would eventually become covered in ash, which is funeral wake adornment in much of West Africa. It is of interest that during Christmas and New Year festivities in St. Thomas, those venturing out without costumes were dashed with flour or confetti and become costumed anyway.[107]

In Styria (Eastern Austria), the "Krampus" goes round the village with St. Nicholas. He "is shaggy, has a goat mask and horns, cloven hooves and a long tail, rattles his chains, and brandishes a bundle of birch twigs . . . to punish naughty children."[108] In Malmo, Sweden, a decree of 1695 banned the "Julbuck," the Christmas buck, from performing because it "frightened children and caused pregnant women to lose their babies."[109] In Antigua, the John Bull masquerade mirrored regulatory Old World functions at Christmas when he would visit various houses and be told to "run" any child who had been naughty, a bed wetter being a prime target. Usually the warning alone was enough. William Richardson says that when he performed as a Mocko Jumbie in St. Kitts-Nevis, parents would sometimes ask him to chase a naughty child, and often adults as well as children would run.

COMMUNAL CRITIQUES

Igbo segmentary societies were inherently democratic because decisions were not imposed by autocratic external rulers; instead, local consensus was pursued. In her examination of Ubakala women's Nkwa dance-plays, Hannah juxtaposes the Igbo's "egalitarian distaste for assertive authority" to "the norm of bringing things into the open."[110] She describes Nkwa as "a political forum of coercion in a shame oriented society."[111] In his discussion of the Igbo, Uchendu outlines a notion he describes as "transparent living" (i.e., rendering invisible behaviors visible), a technique that sometimes leads to irreverence and mockery.[112]

Visona et al. state that the regulatory roles of masquerades include providing "models of ideals" and "satirizing unacceptable behavior."[113] For example, Ottenberg discusses the popular adult Okumkpa masquerade of the Afikpo Igbo, which provides

> a humorous and satiric calypso-like adult performance . . . [where] a variety of masquerades sang and acted out humorous and scurrilous events that had occurred in the community within the past year. The masquerades impersonate and named individuals, ridiculing them, often making moral comments on their behavior.[114]

Ottenberg's use of the term "calypso" is apposite because the device of "transparent living" was used throughout the Caribbean to instigate change, whereby errant individuals were mocked by masquerades or shamed in songs. The busiest time for lampooning in the British West Indies was Christmas and New Year. Depictions of recognizable personages appeared in Jamaica. Michael Scott states:

> The John Canoe, who was the workhouse driver, was dressed up in lawyer's cast-off gown and bands, black silk breeches, no stockings or shoes, but with sandals of bullock's hide strapped on his . . . feet, a small cocked hat on his head, to which were appended a large cauliflower wig, and the usual white false face, bearing a very laughable resemblance to Chief-Justice S_____, with whom I happened to be personally acquainted.[115]

To guard against negative repercussions from Caribbean planters and administrators, rather than name persons, messages were usually encoded in metaphor and double entendre. Using such devices, masquerades indirectly poked fun at the establishment and lampooned figures of authority. Earnest social commentators often had to disguise themselves as comedians. In the Virgin Islands, for example, Albert Halliday's portrayal of a pompous cleric, Parson Darknight, who read from a ledger held upside down, included profound insights within otherwise nonsensical diatribes.[116]

Christmas was grafted onto an older Yuletide festival celebrating the rebirth of the sun during the Winter Solstice. In Europe, Yuletide pageants featured antlers, horns, and animal skin costumes. Although given over to revelry, on a deeper level, renewal rituals are profoundly spiritual and most societies have annual transitions of some kind. The Igbo and others in southern Nigeria traditionally celebrate New Year in their annual New Yam Festival, which is celebrated with music, dance, and masquerading, an example being Okorishi discussed above. Enacted to renew the fertility of the soil, the festival combines elements of purification and thanksgiving and includes the New Yam blessings, special family feasts, speeches, and discussions.

In the Caribbean, the slaves' Christmas revels were described as "Bacchanalia" or "Saturnalia." Saturnalia is an Ancient Roman agricultural festival that was held during December. During its limited duration, it was characterized by a symbolic reversal of power relations, whereby the meek appeared mighty and the mighty appeared meek. Joseph Tuckerman (1837) described the Christmas and New Year's activities of St. Croix, Virgin Islands, 1836–1837 as a "complete Saturnalia." He states:

> The houses of the proprietors of slaves are thrown open; and long processions of slaves decked in silks and in showy white muslins, and with banners and music, enter at will the habitations to which they determine to go, obtain undisputed possession, are served with cakes and wine by their owners, or by others upon whom they may call, and dance till they may be disposed to depart.[117]

In his book, *Black Saturnalia*, Robert Dirks notes, "Christmas meant setting aside the very premise of inequality upon which relations normally rested and replacing it with a cordial and sportive, if at times somewhat tense, egalitarianism."[118] He further states, "If those who ran the estates were not fully committed to the spirit of the bacchanal, at least they were aware of having to deal with an 'overheated boiler' and were prepared to bend every effort toward making sure it did not explode."[119] As if to emphasize that the Saturnalia was simply a temporary inversion of social distinctions, Tuckerman concludes somberly, "but their liberty expired with the day. They slept, and were again slaves." Dirks maintains that the annual revelry constituted "a symbolic representation of the slaves' world view . . . [which] gave voice to an illiterate and therefore historically mute folk."[120] Although the masquerading and Christmas songs were often viewed simply as a spectacular form of entertainment, through parody and satire, they served as a vehicle for social commentary and protest.

THE IGBO DRUM

A discussion of drums provides a segue from masquerades depicted as vehicles of behavior modification to song texts that serve a similar function. Just as the Igbo have been identified above with male Caribbean masquerades, the inclusion of the Igbo drum in Gombay identifies the Igbo with mixed-gender drum-dances such as Bamboula and Gombay that feature satirical songs. References to the "Igbo drum" appear in the Caribbean literature. In his account reproduced below, Cynric Williams distinguishes between a "gombay" drum and an "ebo drum" (Igbo drum) and describes dancers performing "a sort of pyrrhic [war dance] before the ebo drummer."[121]

Williams states that the "ebo drum [is] made out of a hollowed tree with a piece of sheepskin stretched over it."[122] Edwards describes the "Goombay" in a similar fashion as "a rustic drum; being formed of the trunk of a hollow tree, one end of which is covered with a sheepskin."[123] With this concurrence in description, one might expect the terms Gombay and Igbo drum to be used interchangeably and, sure enough, Lewis tells of a dance group whose drums "consisted of Gambys (Eboe drums), Shaky-skekies [maracas] and kitty-katties [*sic*]."[124] (The latter is "a flat piece of board" that is beaten with two sticks.) Although Lewis refers to gombay drums as Igbo drums, Williams distinguishes between them. Most often "gombay drum" refers to a square frame drum (or bench drum), which eventually crossed back over the Atlantic to Sierra Leone in 1800 with repatriated Maroons. Subsequently, the drum and the name spread throughout West Africa.[125] Oldendorp provides an early description of frame drums in Antigua that "consisted of small square boxes over which skins have been stretched."[126]

Nissen, in his report of Virgin Islands dances in 1831, however, describes a "Gombee" drum as "a small barrel, the bottom of which is taken out [and] a goat skin is drawn over the rim."[127] Many such descriptions of Caribbean drums exist in the literature and may not seem remarkable. Indeed, the standard drum of southeastern Nigeria is a hollowed log with a skin at one end. It is significant, however, because a consideration of the Igbo drum helps differentiate between masquerades who parade through the streets and Bamboula performers who are based in a fixed location. While the former use European-style drums and sometime Creole frame drums, the latter use the Igbo drum. The term Gombay is treated rather loosely in the literature and sometimes describes a stationary group and sometimes a perambulating group. Bolton provides a description of a "Gomby parade" in Bermuda, and a letter to the editor of the January 8, 1856, *St. Croix Avis* newspaper talks of "the laboring populations . . . [who] go in bands along the street with the Gumbee."[128] From Garde's report of Gombay at Christmas (ca. 1851) in St. Thomas, it is clear that a stationary Gombay group is able, at a whim, to become a perambulating group: "Sometimes they interrupt the dance to walk about in the streets in a crowd singing in front of the houses of all the dignitaries, and their songs always contain something about these people."[129] However, the band that instigated the "Gumbee Confrontation" in Christiansted in 1852 was a fixed location group, and that, in part, was the problem.

In the literature, the drums of the early Jonkonnu are not described in detail, but the portable fife and drum bands, based on European military models or their Hausa-Fulani counterparts that invariably accompanied the Bull and other masquerades in the British West Indies, were not of the single-skin Igbo drum variety, which is beaten with bare hands. Instead, a bass drum and a "kettle" or "kittle" drum, with skins at both ends, were suspended from the neck or waist of the rhythm and lead drummer, respectively. While the bass drum is struck with a padded beater on a stick, conventional drumsticks are used with the kettle drum. The Caribbean kettle drum has no resemblance to the kettle drum used in European orchestras. In today's usage, the term "kettle drum" is often used interchangeably with "snare drum," although it lacks the "snare" (cords stretched across one skin to increase reverberation). Belisario's sketch, "Band of the Jaw-Bone John Canoe" shows a perambulating group that includes two drummers with drums suspended from their necks.[130] One beats a frame drum with his hands, while the other has a large double-ended European drum suspended from his neck, which he beats with padded sticks.

Regarding the drums used for stationary drum-dances such as Bamboula, although some drums were relatively small, others were very large. Garde describes Gombay music of St. Thomas (ca. 1851): "The music consists of a huge drum, which is beaten . . . with the flat of the hands."[131] The "Igbo drum" described above can be held between the knees in a sitting position or squatted on. Belisario's sketch, "French Set Girls,"[132] shows drummers seated on large transverse drums, which they beat with their hands. Pinckard depicts the stationary method of playing a transverse drum:

> [The drummer is] sitting on the body of the drum, as it lies lengthwise upon the ground, beats . . . the sheep skin . . . with his hands and heels, and . . . [another musician is] sitting upon the ground at the other end . . . beats upon the wooden sides of it with two sticks.[133]

Hearns's account from Martinique adds to this description: "The skilful player straddles the drum and plays upon it with the finger-tips of both hands simultaneously. Occasionally, the heel of the naked foot is pressed lightly or vigorously against the skin at one end so as to produce changes of tone."[134] The use of "catta sticks" beaten on the drum's body appears in Leif's description of the huge "Ka drum" of Bamboula dancers in St. Thomas. Such transverse drums are distributed throughout the Caribbean including Jamaica and the French West Indies. Regarding the catta stik (kata tik in Jamaica), it has not been traced to a particular African antecedent. Ken Bilby suggests that they "are probably Kongo-related (or related to other Central African traditions). The word kata, I believe, has been traced fairly reliably to Kikongo or neighboring languages."[135]

On December 24, 1852, Christmas Eve, it was a stationary Gombay group that sparked off the confrontation between "Gumbee dancers" and the militia in Christiansted, St. Croix, which "led to bloodshed and loss of human life." This, in turn, resulted in the militia being disbanded as a result of their overreaction. On December 30, 1852, Virgin Islands' Governor Birch was prompted to write a letter of explanation to the Danish Colonial Office in which he differentiated between street parades and the stationary Gombay bands:

> The lower part of the population in the towns is accustomed to spend Christmas and New Year's Eve with amusements consisting partly of street parades accompanied with boisterous music and singing; partly in dancing to the sound of an instrument called the Gumbee, a peculiar kind of drum presumed to be of African origin. . . . On St. Thomas . . . the drumming has in recent years been directed to the outskirts of town.[136]

Probably the parades' perambulatory aspect rendered them more transitory and less disturbing than drum-dances that remained in one spot. Subsequently, pressure to quell boisterous music and dance in the Virgin Islands increased but seems to have been aimed more at African drum-dances such as Gombay and Bamboula, with their biting song texts, than it was at masquerading. In contrast to the drum-dances, the establishment appeared at times to tacitly encourage masquerading. In 1872, Haynes wrote: "The Danish governor . . . this year permitted the privilege of masquerading, wisely concluding that this gratification of vanity would prevent the riot . . . of former occasions."[137]

SHAMING IN SONG

Songs fulfill various purposes for the Igbo and other West Africans. They serve as mnemonic devices; they teach, test, and store information; relay history; instill pride and solidarity; comment on local news; provide a medium for thinking through ideas; and critique local action and personages. Singing is frequently coextensive with dance and not many songs are performed in an immobile position. During dance performances, singers often enjoy a special license for social commentary. In his discussion of Igede song texts, Ogede saw the breadth of discourse enjoyed by the Ihih women's association of the Igede and refers to "the widespread phenomenon in many parts of Africa where criticism is tolerated in song where it would not be tolerated elsewhere."[138] The threat of being derided publicly is an effective means of encouraging conformity to social norms. Such songs can be considered redressive because it is intended that listeners pay heed and correct objectionable behavior. The songs are thus directed at creating behavioral change.

For transplanted Africans in the Caribbean, the annual Saturnalia provided the appropriate occasion for dances and songs that focused on local news and scandals. Bilby states:

> The use of song for social commentary has been so widely reported in the Caribbean that one must consider this a pan-Caribbean phenomenon. The topical song, relying for its effect on such devices as double entendre, irony, and veiled allusions, is a Caribbean specialty.[139]

Edwards noted that Jamaican slaves possessed oratorical gifts, a "talent of ridicule and derision, which is exercised not only against each other but also not infrequently, at the expense of their owner or employer."[140] Using ciphers or language codes that were developed in slavery, subjects of a contentious nature contained indirect allusions, which rendered the meaning obscure to outsiders. During Christmas festivities, many Europeans and elites were perturbed to find themselves the topic of songs without being sure whether they were flattering or derisive.

GOMBAY AND BAMBOULA

There are two descriptions of drum-dances, Gombay in Jamaica by Cynric Williams (1826) and Bamboula in St. Lucia by Henry Breen

(1844), which are similar in many ways and are worth comparing. Both Gombay and Bamboula were distributed widely throughout the Caribbean. They both demonstrate the role of song and dance as a social tool. It should be noted that Breen uses the terms Bamboula and Belair as coextensive; while Bamboula refers to the dances, Belair refers to the songs.

Williams describes a slave celebration of Christmas and Boxing Day on a Jamaican estate in 1823. He includes a description of an Igbo and African style libation as follows: "He poured a few drops on the ground, and drank off the rest to the health of his master and mistress." Williams explains that on receiving a glass of punch, "the negroes have a custom of performing libations when they drink, a kind of first-fruit offering."[141]

Boxing Day performances included a Jonkanoo in the form of a house ghost, which at that time was beginning to supplant the Jonkanoo with bull horns:

> A man dressed up in a mask with a grey beard and long flowing hair, who carried the model of a house on his head. . . . The house is an emblem of Noah's ark and that Jonkanoo means the sacred boat. . . . The Jonkanoo is . . . chosen for his superior activity in dancing.[142]

Williams describes a musical ensemble composed of "gombays, bonjaws [prob. banjoes], and an ebo drum" that he saw the previous evening, Christmas Day, and the dances that were performed:

> They assembled on the lawn before the house with their gombays, bonjaws, and an ebo drum. . . . They divided themselves into parties to dance, some before the gombays, in a ring, to perform a bolero or a sort of love dance. . . . Others performed a sort of pyrrhic [war dance] before the ebo drummer, beginning gently and quickly quickening their motions, until they seemed agitated by the furies.[143]

Rather than being "dressed down" and disguised in rough attire like an animal masquerade, dancers enhanced themselves and wanted to be seen. The gombay dancers' costumes show that they were "dressed up" and adopting metropolitan and mainstream styles:

> They were all dressed in their best; some of the men in long-tailed coats, one of the gombayers in old regimentals; the women in muslins and cambrics with colored handkerchiefs tastefully disposed round their heads, and earrings, necklaces and bracelets . . . in profusion.[144]

Breen's description of a Bamboula Dance in St. Lucia is markedly similar to the previous account. Again the performers are dressed extravagantly. The male dress is comparable to "that commonly worn by gentlemen in England or France." The females wore a striped skirt of silk or satin and an "embroidered bodice trimmed with gold and silver tinsel." The headdress is composed of a "madras handkerchief, erected in a pyramid or a castle." Gold earrings are worn and there is similarly a profusion of necklaces, bracelets, and bouquets.[145]

Breen begins with the location: "The dancers proceed at sunset to the place appointed for the bamboula. A circle is formed in the center of some square or grass plot. . . . Flags and banners richly emblazoned . . . and bearing characteristic legends in gilt letters, are seen fluttering in the air." Breen continues, "On one side appear four or five Negroes quite naked down to the waist, and seated on their tam tams. These together with some timbrels, compose the orchestra." Breen's description of the "tam tam" shows the similarity to the Igbo drum: "The tam tam is a small barrel covered at one end with a strong skin. To this placed between his legs, the Negro applies the open hand and fingers, beating time to the belair with the most astonishing precision."[146]

At a given point the dancers enter the circle and the chanterelle begins a refrain:

> The groups of dancers advance in all directions, the darkness of night disappears before the blaze of a thousand flambeaux. . . . Now the chanterelle, placing herself in front of the orchestra, gives a flourish . . . then repeats a verse of the belair: the dancers take

> up the refrain, the tam tams and timbrels strike in unison and the scene is enlivened by a succession of songs and dances.[147]

Although delivered in a call-and-response style, the song texts are now more elaborate than the short ostinato refrains that accompanied masquerades.[148]

In different islands the chanterelle is known variously as chantwell or chanteuse, and sometimes the prima donna, and is, according to Breen, "the most important personage next to the sovereignty [dance royalty] . . . upon [her] devolves the task of composing their Belairs, and of reciting them at their public dances."[149] He describes Belairs as

> A sort of pastoral in blank verse, adapted to a peculiar tune or air. . . . Some are exquisitely melodious. . . . The Belairs turn generally on the praises of the respective societies. . . . [Their own compared to competitors] the good qualities, both physical and mental, of individual members; the follies and foibles of the opposite party.[150]

A "philippic" is defined as a public act of denouncing, characterized by harsh and often insulting language. Within the Jamaican Gombay dance, Williams observed that "the merriment became rather boisterous as the punch operated, and the slaves sang satirical philippics against their master, communicating a little free advice now and then."[151] According to Oliver, the chantwells or prima donnas of the Virgin Islands had dual roles, they were entertainers and they were also the voices of the people.[152] La Motta states:

> To the beat of the Bamboula drums a storyteller would evoke a chant, improvising lyrics based on a given topic. . . . The drumhead [Bamboula] functioned as the eyes and ears of the community. It was a means of communication, comment and criticism, a local scandal-sheet taken off the tongues of the masses. . . . They were . . . dusted with scorn and ridicule.[153]

Historically in the Virgin Islands, women "Cariso" singers were paramount dispensers of commentary in song, but as Christmas approached men such as Ciple who accompanied his songs on a tin can or Albert Halliday in his various getups would recount the local scandals of the preceding year in songs and speeches. Furthermore, most, but not all, Calypsonians are male. Both before and after Emancipation, Afro-Creole music and dance facilitated nonverbal and verbal communication between various classes and ethnic groups, and served as vehicles for intergroup communication and negotiation.

DECLINE OF THE BAMBOULA

We have now come full circle, back to where we began: the end of the nineteenth century in the Virgin Islands. At that time, the establishment's patience was wearing thin and pressure was being applied to the street revels, more so against Bamboula, with its overt African characteristics, than against masquerading. The Gombay had long since vanished from the Virgin Islanders' collective memory. Bamboula dances were boisterous and viewed by Europeans as overtly sexual; the ribald lyrics of some songs also offended their delicate sensibilities. Elites were particularly irritated by the singing of philippics by stationary groups in town. Local newspapers were at the forefront of the condemnation. The Editorial of the December 15, 1880, *St. Thomas Tidende*, condoned intervention by police and military:

> The Bomboola nuisance [*sic*], with its attendant disorders, seems to be reviving, as the preliminary singing meetings are being kept up in . . . "Savannah" [Savan] and "Back of All," where the troupes congregate nightly and render the neighborhood uncomfortable with the most indecent songs. Last night a row ensued . . . until the Police intervened, and with the assistance of the Military guard from the barracks, made some arrests.[154]

The Editorial of the November 22, 1890, *Tidende*, pointed out, however, that satirical songs were as likely to praise individuals as lambaste them: "It is not a rule, however, that individuals . . . are ridiculed or scandalized; in many cases it is just the other way, but whether the nature of the song be emulative or derogatory, it . . . [is] an unwarrantable license that peoples' names be handled with such levity." Despite this, the Editorial pondered the question, "whether dragging an individual's name and character into sing song and holding them up to public obloquy is a tolerable or harmless, kind of amusement.[155]" Opting for censorship the establishment clamped down and Bamboula dwindled. In the twentieth century, Miss Clara and the Southside Bamboula dancers kept the genre alive up until the St. Thomas Carnivals of the 1950s. By this time, however, it was more a form of parade entertainment than a viable folk form. Since 2006, St. Thomians have annually danced Bamboula within a reenactment of the Coal Women's Strike of 1892 that was led by Bamboula Queen Coziah.

This chapter discusses Igbo influences on masquerading and drum-dances in the Caribbean and suggests that because the Igbo inherited a thriving musical tradition, their arrival in the Caribbean reinvigorated preexisting masquerades and drum-dances. Jonkonnu and other masquerades of the eighteenth century would have seemed familiar to the Igbo from their experience of New Yam Festivals. The evidence suggests that they adopted the prototypes and modified and transformed them to better reflect Igbo aesthetics. In the case of the Mocko Jumbie, an Igbo adoption of a Mandinka prototype took place in the Caribbean. A similar process occurred with the songs and dances of Gombay and Bamboula. Drum-dances were probably established early by the first wave of slaves from Angola and Congo, but Young's report of dancers in 1791, executing a "lascivious dance" to the music of a *balafon* with "handkerchiefs folded tastefully about their heads and gold ear-rings and necklaces," shows that the early prototype was being shaped by Upper Guinea influences.[156] Drum-dances were readily embraced by the Igbo, whose "Igbo drum," along with the frame drum, became the trademark of Gombay.

The act of adopting and modifying is in accordance with the traditional character of the Igbo, and this native ingenuity is a feature that has been formed historically. Horton and others have shown that the decentralized familial basis of segmentary societies produce individuals with a great deal of personal autonomy.[157] Indeed, Igbo are known as great innovators and their entrepreneurialism is recognized globally. Moreover, the idea of dressing up in finery is enjoyed by the Igbo and their willingness to embrace cosmopolitan styles has been inculcated by their Nigerian heritage.

Although music and dance are often thought of as simply a catharsis or entertainment, historically in the Caribbean they encoded complex cultural messages related to continuity and change and made the local ideology salient to the populace. Normative aspects were important and masquerades were utilized as vehicles of social control and behavior modification. Through parody and satire, songs directed at creating behavioral change can be considered redressive because the intent is that listeners pay heed and correct objectionable behavior. Sometimes they served as a vehicle for social protest and this impetus was especially strong during the annual Saturnalia.

Turner coined the term "social drama" to describe redressive processes that enable society to evaluate itself and effect affirmations or adjustments.[158] Hanna suggests that the Nkwa dance-play of the Ubakala Igbo meets the criteria of social drama. She states, "The nkwa may communicate the breach, foment the crisis, ameliorate the conflict (or at least hold it in suspension so that it is visually present, viewable, and ponderable), and proclaim the schism or celebrate the reintegration."[159] The processes of social drama are often at work during the collective performances described in this chapter. By manifesting the symbolic themes operant in a Caribbean community, music, dance, and masquerading not only provided a means of communication between the various classes, but also served as a transactional media that enabled affirmations or adjustments. Turner further argues that certain cultural phenomenon can be considered as "protostructure," a creative source of new behavior and structure that offers a latent system of alternatives and reminds individuals and groups of their responsibilities.[160] The context in which such redressive measures operate is one where play (music and dance) becomes non-play (sociopolitical transformation), and in Hanna's terms "message and reality merge."[161] The Gumbee dancers' confrontation of 1852 in the Virgin Islands is one of the more extreme examples of a social transformation resulting from Christmas festivities.

The evidence suggests that the Igbo vigorously entered into collective performance in the British West Indies with all its inherent sociopolitical implications. In the Virgin Islands, in the nineteenth century, the establishment brought strong social pressures to bear against the street revels and especially criticized Bamboula with its overt African characteristics, boisterous nature, and controversial lyrics. Although Bamboula dwindled, social commentaries in song persist to some extent in Quelbe and scratch band traditions. Other cultural manifestations such as masquerading and Quadrille fared better and are still performed today.

The Igbo readily embraced cosmopolitan styles and the Jig Igbo in Carriacou exemplifies their adoption of the mainstream milieu. Moreover, in Carriacou, a new Scotch Igbo category of Big Drum emerged. For McDaniel, this represents not simply a "new dance style" but "a new racial classification" and "a new people."[162] Although during the early colonial era, it was common to identify Africans in the Caribbean by ethnic designations, as new arrivals ceased, tribal labels diminished. Over time the various cultural contributions of the different African ethnicities blended and are best described as Neo-African or New World creations.

NOTES

1. Victor C. Uchendu, *The Igbo of Southeast Nigeria* (New York: Holt, 1965).

2. The *St. Thomas Tidende* was known in Danish as the *St. Thomae Tidende.* It was a semiweekly newspaper published in both Danish and English by J. Englund, in St. Thomas, VI.

3. Robert W. Nicholls, *Old-Time Masquerading in the U.S. Virgin Islands* (St. Thomas: Virgin Islands Humanities Council, 1998), 84.

4. The US Virgin Islands; St. Thomas, St. Croix, and St. John, were formerly the Danish West Indies until the United States bought them in 1917. They are now administered as a US territory. The British Virgin Islands are to the east.

5. See Hans Sloane, *A Voyage to the Islands of Madera, Barbados, and Jamaica* (London: B. M., 1707), 1:46–48.

6. Matthew G. Lewis, *Journal of a West Indian Proprietor* (London: John Murrey, 1834), 51; Michael Scott, *Tom Cringle's Log* (Edinburgh: William Blackwood, 1836), 250.

7. Isaac Mendes Belisario, *Sketches of Character in Illustration of the Habits, Occupation, and Costumes of the Negro Population in the Island of Jamaica* (1838; repr., Hanapepe, Hawaii: Kauai Fine Arts, 1939).

8. Joseph John Gurney, *A Winter in the West Indies: Described in Familiar Letters to Henry Clay, of Kentucky* (London: J. Murray, 1840), 26. Within the heterogeneity of Creole aesthetics, multiple influences can often be at play. For example, in Britain during the late eighteenth and the nineteenth century, the Christmas Bull reemerged as a popular form of Mumming at Yuletide, particularly among those West Country populations from whom many Middle Passage sailors were drawn. They were also documented in the Scottish Highlands and South Wales. The coincidence of bull masquerading emerging in the Caribbean and reemerging in Britain at the same time is unlikely to be accidental, and the Caribbean may have been exerting the major influence.

9. Richard D. E. Burton, *Afro Creole: Power, Opposition, and Play in the Caribbean* (Ithaca, NY: Cornell University Press, 1997), 65.

10. Kenneth M. Bilby, "The Caribbean as a Musical Region," in *Caribbean Contours*, ed. Sidney W. Mintz and Sally Price (Baltimore, MD: Johns Hopkins University Press, 1985), 183.

11. Bilby, "The Caribbean as a Musical Region," 187. With regard to African retentions, it is generally true that those cultural traits that arrived late in the slavery era were more likely to retain observable Africanisms than those that were established early and subsequently

modified. For example, late-arriving Yoruba "indentured servants" established the worship of Orissas in Trinidad and the Yoruba similarly impacted Bahia in Brazil. Fon traditions of voodoo were consolidated in Haiti. By the same token, the Abakua masquerade of Cuba is akin to the Ekpe leopard society masquerade of the Efik and Ejagham. See Judith Bettelheim, "Negotiations of Power in Carnaval Culture in Santiago, de Cuba," *African Arts* 24, no. 2 (1991): 66–75; Peter Manuel, *Caribbean Currents: Caribbean Music from Rumba to Reggae* (Philadelphia, PA: Temple University Press, 1995), 26; Ivor Miller, "Cuban Abakua Chants: Examining New Linguistic and Historical Evidence for the African Diaspora," *African Studies Review* 14, no. 1 (2005): 23–58.

12. Margaret E. Crahan and Franklin W. Knight, *Africa and the Caribbean: The Legacies of a Link* (Baltimore, MD: Johns Hopkins University Press, 1979), 10.

13. Douglas Chambers, personal correspondence, May 17, 1997.

14. Crahan and Knight, *Africa and the Caribbean*, 11.

15. Monica Schuler, "Akan Slave Rebellions in the British Caribbean," *Savacou* 1, no. 1 (1970): 373–86; Philip M. Sherlock, *West Indian Nations: A New History* (Kingston: Jamaica Publishing House, 1973). It is significant whether a trait has roots in Senegambia or Cameroon because these areas are indicative of wider cultural regions. Upper Guinea groups may possess Sudano-Sahelian influences or inherit the legacy of the ancient empires of Ghana, Mali, and Songhai, whereas forest groups may be more representative of the locally based, segmentary societies. See Melville J. Herskovits, *Man and His Works: The Science of Cultural Anthropology* (New York: Knopf, 1995), 191. In his map of cultural areas of Africa, Herskovits positions Senegambia in the "Western Sudan" region and southeastern Nigeria and the Cameroon in the northwestern "Congo Area," with the "Guinea Coast" area in between.

16. René A. Bravmann, "Gur and Manding Masquerades in Ghana," *African Arts* 13, no. 1 (1979): 44–51, 98.

17. William Young, "A Tour Through the Islands of Barbados, St. Vincent, Antigua, Tobago and Grenada in 1791 and 1792," in *History, Civil and Commercial, of the British Colonies in the West Indies*, ed. Bryan Edwards (London: Whittaker, 1807), 3:269.

18. C. G. A. Oldendorp, "A Caribbean Mission: History of the Mission of the Evangelical Brethren of the Caribbean Islands of St. Thomas, St. Croix, and St. John," ed. Johann Jakob Bossard, trans. by Arnold R. Highfield and Vladimir Barac (1770; Ann Arbor, MI: Karoma, 1987), 167.

19. Bryan Edwards, *The History, Civil and Commercial, of the British Colonies in the West Indies* (London: John Stockdale, 1794), 2:797.

20. Ibid., 797.

21. Ibid., 111.

22. A. M. Jones, *Africa and Indonesia: The Evidence of the Xylophone and other Musical and Cultural Factors* (Leiden, NL: Brill, 1971).

23. J. B. Moreton, *Manners and Customs in the West India Islands* (London: Richardson, 1790), 153.

24. Edwards, *The History, Civil and Commercial*, 74.

25. Ibid.

26. Lorna McDaniel, "The Concept of Nation in the Big Drum Dance of Carriacou, Grenada," *Musical Repercussions of 1492: Encounters in Text and Performance*, ed. Carol E. Robertson (Washington, DC: Smithsonian, 1992), 400–401.

27. Lorna McDaniel and Donald R. Hill, *Tombstone Feast: Funerary Music of Carriacou.* Cambridge, MA: Rounder Records, 2001. Music CD with liner notes.

28. Edwards, *The History, Civil and Commercial, of the British Colonies*, vol. 2.

29. Sloane, *A Voyage to the Islands.*

30. Charles Leslie, *A New and Exact Account of Jamaica* (Edinburgh, UK: Fleming, 1739), 326; and Flora Spencer, *Crop-Over: An Old Barbadian Plantation Festival* (Bridgetown, Barbados: Commonwealth Caribbean Center, 1974), 4.

31. Robert W. Nicholls, *The Igede of Nigeria* (Chapel Hill, NC: Music of the World, 1991), track 13.

32. D. W. Ames and K. A. Gourlay, "Kimkim: A Women's Musical Pot," *African Arts* 11, no. 2 (1978): 56–64; Abashiya Magaji Ahuwan, "Clay as a Creative Media: A Survey of the Kimkim Musical Instrument from South Kaduna," in *Diversity of Creativity in Nigeria: A Critical Selec-*

tion from the Proceedings of the 1st International Conference on the Diversity of Creativity in Nigeria, ed. Bolaji Campbell (Ife, Nigeria: Department of Fine Arts, Obafemi Awolowo University, 1992), 143–52.

33. Olaudah Equiano, *The Life of Olaudah Equiano; or Gustavus Vassa, the African* (1789; repr., New York: Negro Universities Press, 1969), 209.

34. D. Hall, *In Miserable Slavery, Thomas Thistlewood in Jamaica, 1750–1786* (New York: Macmillan, 1989), 12.

35. *Daily Picayune*, October 12, 1879, cited in Jerah Johnson, *New Orleans' Congo Square* (New Orleans: Louisiana Landmark Society, 1995).

36. William Wells Brown, *My Southern Home: The South and Its People* (Boston: A. G. Brown, 1880; Gloucester, Gloucestershire, UK: Dodo Press, 2009), 93.

37. Benjamin Latrobe, *Journal of Latrobe*, ed. J. H. B. Latrobe (1819; New York: Oxford University Press, 1969).

38. Irving Rouse, *The Rise and Decline of the People Who Greeted Columbus* (New Haven, CT: Yale University Press, 1996), 6.

39. James Kelly, *Voyage to Jamaica* (Belfast, IE: Wilson, 1838), 21.

40. Edward Long, *The History of Jamaica* (London: T. Lowndes, 1774), 2:424; Leonard Barrett, *The Sun and the Drum: African Roots in Jamaican Folk Tradition* (Kingston, Jamaica: Sangster's Books, 1979), 113; and John Thornton, *Africa and Africans in the Making of the Atlantic World, 1400–1680* (New York: Cambridge University Press. 1992), xxvi.

41. Oldendorp, *A Caribbean Mission*, 203, 205.

42. G. I. Jones, *The Art of Eastern Nigeria* (New York: Cambridge University Press, 1984), 174.

43. Personal correspondence, May 19, 1997.

44. Lorna McDaniel and Donald R. Hill, *Carriacou Calaloo*. Cambridge, MA: Rounder Records, 1999. Music CD with liner notes.

45. Andrew Pearse, *The Big Drum Dance of Carriacou*. New York: Folkways Ethnic Library, 1956.

46. McDaniel, "The Concept of Nation," 401.

47. Ibid., 408.

48. McDaniel and Hill, *Carriacou Calaloo*, track 29.

49. Ibid., track 10.

50. Long, *The History of Jamaica*, 2:424.

51. Ibid., 2:424–25.

52. Ibid., 2:424.

53. Soulay Ousman, personal communication, March 20, 2003.

54. Peter Mark, *The Wild Bull and the Sacred Forest: Form, Meaning, and Change in Senegambian Initiation Masks* (New York: Cambridge University Press, 1992).

55. Robert W. Nicholls, *The Jumbies' Playing Ground: Old World Influences on Afro-Creole Masquerades in the Eastern Caribbean* (Jackson: University Press of Mississippi, 2012), 154–56.

56. Eli Bentor, personal communication, February 12, 2012.

57. Ibid.

58. A bull-horned Mwanwu masquerade from the Njima Club of Arondizuogu dancing during the burial ceremony of the Eze Aro at Oror, Arochukwu, on January 5, 1988. Photo by Eli Bentor.

59. Ibid.

60. This horned Okonko mask with a body stocking costume comes from Umodim village in Imo. The antelope horns show the connection to hunting, March 12, 1988. Photo by Eli Bentor.

61. J. S. Boston, "Some Northern Ibo Masquerades," *The Journal of the Royal Anthropological Institute of Great Britain and Ireland* 90, no. 1 (1960): 54–65, 58.

62. Ibid., 58.

63. An Okonko masquerade wearing a bulky raffia costumes topped by antelope horns performs at the Okonko festival in Isu Njaba, Umuowa, Imo, March 12, 1988. Photo by Eli Bentor.

64. Eli Bentor, personal communication, February 12, 2012.

65. Anonymous, "Characteristic Traits of the Creolian and African Negroes in Jamaica," *The Colombian Magazine* (April–October 1797), in Roger D. Abrahams and John F. Szwed, *After Africa: Extracts from British Travel Accounts and Journals of the Seventeenth, Eighteenth, and Nineteenth Centuries Concerning the Slaves, Their Manners, and Customs in the British West Indies* (New Haven, CT: Yale University Press, 1983).

66. Priscilla Hinckley, *To Dance the Spirit: Visitors Guide to Exhibition of Liberian Art*

(Cambridge, MA: Peabody Museum, Harvard University, 1987).

67. Ekpo Eyo, *Guide to the Nigerian Museum in Lagos* (Lagos: Associated Press of Nigeria, 1980), 29.

68. Monica Blackmun Visona, Robin Poyner, Herbert M. Cole, and Michael D. Harris, *A History of Art in Africa* (Upper Saddle River, NJ: Prentice Hall, 2001), 292.

69. Ibid., 290.

70. Ibid., 291.

71. Ibid.

72. Herbert M. Cole and Chike C. Aniakor, *Igbo Arts: Community and Cosmos* (Los Angeles: Museum of Cultural History, University of California, 1984), 191.

73. Boston, "Some Northern Ibo Masquerades," 54–65.

74. Personal interview, July 9, 1995.

75. Mesh masks can claim both West European and West African ancestry. Discussing nineteenth-century carnivals in Nice, France, Annie Sidro, "Carnival in Nice," *The World and I: A Chronicle of Our Changing Era* 2, no. 2 (1987): 454–63, explains that flower petals, candy-sugar confetti, plaster, and baker's flour was liberally thrown around. This also occurred in the Caribbean. Therefore, "one had to be . . . protected . . . from flour and plaster dust. To spare one's face, one had to wear a wire-meshed mask similar to a fencer's" (459). Relative to Africa, Michel Huet, *The Dance, Art and Ritual of Africa* (New York: Pantheon, 1978) reports that the masks worn by Kono and Dan stilt dancers in the Upper Guinea region are made of "a net of palm-tree fiber" (27).

76. Young, "A Tour Through the Islands of Barbados," 275.

77. Charles William Day, *Five Years' Residence in the West Indies* (London: Colburn, 1852), 1:53.

78. Young, "A Tour Through the Islands of Barbados," 258.

79. See Bryan Edwards's footnote on p. 258 of William Young, "A Tour Through the Islands of Barbados, St. Vincent, Antigua, Tobago, and Grenada in 1791 and 1792," in *History, Civil, and Commercial, of the British Colonies in the West Indies*, ed. Bryan Edwards (London: Whittaker, 1807), 3:241–84.

80. Ibid.

81. Ibid., 258–59.

82. Roberts Dirks, *The Black Saturnalia: Conflict and Its Ritual Expression on British West Indian Slave Plantations* (Gainesville: University of Florida Press, 1987), 5.

83. Young, "A Tour Through the Islands of Barbados," 259.

84. Day, *Five Years' Residence in the West Indies*, 53.

85. Cole and Aniakor, *Igbo Arts*; Wilson Perkins Foss, "The Arts of the Urhobo Peoples of Southern Nigeria" (PhD dissertation, Yale University, 1976); and Philip M. Peek, "Isoko Arts and their Mocko Jumbie of the U.S. Virgin Islands: History and Antecedents," *African Arts* 32, no. 3 (1999): 49–61, 94–95.

Nicholls, "The Mocko Jumbie of the U.S. Virgin Islands: History and Antecedents," *African Arts* 32, no. 3 (1999): 49–61.

See Young, "A Tour Audiences," *African Arts* 13, no. 3 (1980): 58–60. See also Nicholls, "The Mocko Jumbie," 49–61, 94–95.

86. Nicholls, "The Mocko Jumbie," 49–61.

87. See Young, "A Tour Through the Islands of Barbados"; and Day, *Five Years' Residence in the West Indies*, 241–84.

88. John Nunley and Judith Bettelheim, *Caribbean Festival Arts: Each and Every Bit of Difference* (Seattle: University of Washington Press, 1988), 92.

89. Stilts are not unique to the Caribbean or to Africa. They were worn by shepherds in France and hop twiners in Britain, and stilt walkers also appeared in European circuses. However, Mocko Jumbie performer, Alli Paul, uses the term stilt "dancers" to differentiate Mocko Jumbies from stilt "walkers" that appear in European circus rings (personal communication, July 10, 1995).

90. Day, *Five Years' Residence in the West Indies*, 85.

91. Goran Hyden, *Beyond Ujamaa in Tanzania: Underdevelopment and an Uncaptured Peasantry* (Berkeley: University of California Press, 1980).

92. Robin Horton, "Stateless Societies in the History of West Africa," in *History of West Africa*, vol. 1, ed. J. F. A. Ajayi and M. Crowder (London: Longmans, 1971).

93. Douglas Chambers, personal correspondence, May 17, 1997.

94. Thora Visby-Petersen, *St. Thomas Tropeminder Fra De Vestindiske Oer*, trans. by Poul Erik Olsen (Copenhagen: Aarhus, 1917), 26.

95. G. I. Jones, *The Art of Eastern Nigeria* (New York: Cambridge University Press, 1984), 60.

96. George Farrell, personal communications, November 13, 2003.

97. Richard A. Schrader, *Notes of a Crucian Son* (Fredriksted, St. Croix, VI: Antilles Graphics, 1989), 64.

98. Visby-Petersen, *St. Thomas Tropeminder Fra De Vestindiske Oer*, 26.

99. Leona Watson, personal communication, August 9, 1996.

100. Sidney L. Kasfir, "Masquerading as a Cultural System," in *West African Masks and Cultural Systems*, ed. Sidney L. Kasfir (Tervuren, BE: Musée Royal de L'Afrique Centrale, 1988), 7.

101. Visona et al., *A History of Art in Africa*, 290.

102. Robert W. Nicholls, "Igede in the Twentieth Century: Modernity Impacts on Traditional Life-Styles in Tribal Nigeria," *The World and I: A Chronicle of Our Changing Era* 2, no. 7 (1987): 527–28.

103. Simon Ottenberg, "We Are Becoming Art Minded: Afikpo Arts 1988," *African Arts* 22, no. 4 (1989): 58–67, 88.

104. Violet Alford, *The Hobby Horse and Other Animal Masks* (London: Merlin Press, 1978), 59.

105. Christina Hole, *A Dictionary of British Folk Customs* (London: Paladin Grafton, 1978), 70.

106. Alford, *The Hobby Horse*, 116.

107. Philip Rhymer, personal communication, July 16, 1996.

108. E. C. Cawte, *Ritual Animal Disguise* (London: Folklore Society, 1978), 201.

109. Alford, *The Hobby Horse*, 120.

110. Judith Lynne Hanna, *To Dance is Human: A Theory of Nonverbal Communication* (Chicago, IL: University of Chicago Press, 1987), 172.

111. Hanna, *To Dance is Human*, 173.

112. Uchendu, *The Igbo of Southeast Nigeria*.

113. Visona et al., *A History of Art in Africa*, 290.

114. Simon Ottenberg, "Emulation in Boys' Masquerades: The Afikpo Case," in *Playful Performers: African Children's Masquerades*, ed. Simon Ottenberg and David A. Binkley (New Brunswick, NJ: Transaction, 2006).

115. Michael Scott, *Tom Cringle's Log* (Edinburgh: William Blackwood, 1836).

116. Nicholls, *Old-Time Masquerading*, 35.

117. Joseph Tuckerman, cited in Nicholls, *Old-Time Masquerading*, 169.

118. Dirks, *The Black Saturnalia*, ix.

119. Ibid., 189.

120. Ibid., xiii.

121. Cynric A. Williams, *A Tour Through the Island of Jamaica, from the Western to the Eastern End, in the Year 1823* (London: Hunt and Clarke, 1826).

122. Ibid., 22.

123. Bryan Edwards, *The History, Civil and Commercial, of the British Colonies in the West Indies* (London: John Stockdale, 1794), 2:84.

124. Lewis, *Journal of a West Indian Proprietor*, 74.

125. John Collins, "Gumbay Drums of Jamaica in Sierra Leone" (paper presented at the 12th Triennial Symposium on African Art (ACASA), Marriott Frenchman's Reef Resort, St. Thomas, US Virgin Islands, April 27, 2001).

126. Oldendorp, *A Caribbean Mission*, 264.

127. Johan Peter Nissen, *Reminiscences of a 46 Years' Residence in the Island of St. Thomas, in the West Indies* (Nazareth, PA, 1838), 164–65.

128. H. Carrington Bolton, "Gombay, a Festival Rite of Bermudian Negroes," *The Journal of American Folklore* 3, no. 10 (1890): 222–26.

129. H. F. Garde, *Paa Orlogstopgt Til Vestindien for 100 Aar siden. Breve fra H. G. F. Garde 1851–52, 1867–68 og 1872–73*, trans. Leif Caludann-Larsen (Copenhagen, DK, 1962).

130. Belisario, *Sketches of Character in Illustration of the Habits*.

131. Garde, *Paa Orlogstopgt Til Vestindien for 100 Aar siden*.

132. Plate 7, Isaac Mendes Belisario, *Sketches of Character in Illustration of the Habits, Occupation, and Costumes of the Negro Population in the Island of Jamaica* (Kingston, JM, 1938; reprint Hanapepe, HI: Kauai Fine Arts, 1998).

133. George Pinkard, *Notes on the West Indies*, vol. 1 (London: Longman, 1806).

134. Hearns's (1878) cited in Earl Leaf, *Isles of Rhythm* (New York: A. S. Barnes, 1948), 140–41.

135. Personal correspondence, July 26, 2007.

136. Nicholls, *Old-Time Masquerading*, 77.

137. S. B. Haynes, "The Danish West Indies," *Harper's New Monthly Magazine* 44 (January 1872): 200–202.

138. Ode S. Ogede, "Counters to Male Domination: Images of Pain in Igede Women's Songs," *Research in African Literature* 3 (1994): 117.

139. Bilby, "The Caribbean as a Musical Region," 201.

140. Edwards, *The History, Civil and Commercial, of the British Colonies*.

141. Williams, *A Tour Through the Island of Jamaica*.

142. Ibid.

143. Ibid.

144. Ibid.

145. Henry H. Breen, *St. Lucia: Historical, Statistical, and Descriptive* (London: Longman, Brown, and Green, 1844).

146. Ibid.

147. Ibid, 197.

148. Ibid.

149. Ibid.

150. Ibid.

151. Cynric A. Williams, *A Tour Through the Island of Jamaica, from the Western to the Eastern End, in the Year 1823* (London: Hunt and Clarke, 1826).

152. Cynthia Oliver, "St. Croix Dancing: The Contemporary and Historical Path of Dance on the U.S. Virgin Island of St. Croix" (MA thesis, Gallatin Division of New York University, 1995), 74.

153. Bill La Motta, "Bamboula to Soul: A Long Musical Journey," *The Daily News* (St. Thomas, VI), August 1, 1975.

154. Nicholls, *Old-Time Masquerading*, 84.

155. *St. Thomas Tidende*, Editorial, November 11, 1890, 84.

156. Young, "A Tour Through the Islands of Barbados."

157. Horton, "Stateless Societies."

158. Victor W. Turner, "Commentary on Arts, Values, and Social Action Session" (American Anthropological Association Meeting, Houston, 1977).

159. Hanna, *To Dance is Human*, 172.

160. Victor W. Turner, *Drama, Fields, and Metaphor: Symbolic Action in Human Society* (Ithaca, NY: Cornell University Press, 1974).

161. Hanna, *To Dance is Human*, 137.

162. McDaniel, "The Concept of Nation," 408.

18 THE AFRO-CARIBBEAN DIASPORA IN REVERSE AND ITS IMPLICATIONS FOR THE DEVELOPMENT OF CHRISTIANITY AND EDUCATION IN IGBOLAND, SOUTHEASTERN NIGERIA, 1895–1925

Waibinte E. Wariboko

Igboland, during the period under review, encountered and responded to immense political, economic, sociocultural and religious forces of change. These encounters and responses were demonstrated, among others, through these episodic and epoch-making events: the "Aro Expedition"[1] of 1891–1892 undertaken to incorporate the area into the evolving colonial state in Southern Nigeria; the appearance, among other anti-European movements, of the Ekumeku Society[2] in Southern Nigeria between 1893 and 1910; the penetration of European trading companies, following the emasculation and eventual elimination of African coastal middlemen,[3] into the primary producing communities of southeastern Nigeria; the renewed attempt of the Church Missionary Society (CMS) Niger Mission under Bishop Herbert Tugwell, the successor of Bishop Samuel Crowther, to enthrone whiteness over blackness in Igboland through the concerted efforts of Afro-Caribbean and European missionaries;[4] and the final amalgamation in 1914 of the protectorates of Southern and Northern Nigeria to create the present geopolitical entity called Nigeria.[5]

Igbo receptivity to Christianity has to be perceived and constructed within the context of the above developments. Simon Ottenberg had argued that the Igbos, as compared with other major sociolinguistic groupings in Nigeria such as the Yoruba, were "probably most receptive to culture change, and most willing to accept Western ways"[6] following the intervention of the extraterritorial, tripartite forces of change—the colonial state, Christian missionaries, and European trading companies—in their internal affairs. E. A. Ayandele, in *The Missionary Impact on Modern Nigeria*, has articulated a similar sentiment about the Igbo-speaking peoples.

> In statistical terms and in the desire to appropriate all the material and social opportunities that missionary enterprise could afford, it is the Ibo people who have responded most enthusiastically to Christianity. By 1910 the number of Christian adherents in Eastern Nigeria had outstripped that in the area west of the Niger [home to the Yoruba-speaking peoples]. In 1910 there were 18,500 in the former and 17,000 in the latter. Ten years later the figures stood at 514,395 and 260,500 for Eastern and Western Nigeria respectively. In the present decade [1960] there are about four million Christian adherents in Eastern Nigeria, as opposed to about a million in the west of the Niger.[7]

Adaptability to external forces of change in the aftermath of the trans-Atlantic trade in enslaved Africans, as portrayed by Ottenberg and Ayandele, is a pervasive and enduring theme in Igbo historiography across the Atlantic. When compared with other enslaved African groups such as the Yoruba and the Akan-speaking peoples, the enslaved Igbo-speaking Africans (as indicated in the following section) had also arguably demonstrated greater willingness and readiness to embrace change in the plantation societies of the New World. This chapter is about some of the most critical catalysts of change that were either ignored or given very superficial references by scholars[8] interested in reconstructing Igbo responses to Christianity and education: the Afro-Caribbean missionaries. These missionaries, driven by a sense of race-belonging to contribute to the ongoing process of culture change in Igboland under the auspices of the CMS Niger Mission, enthusiastically responded to the back-to-Africa campaign.

In its own self-interest, the management of the Church Missionary Society at Salisbury Square in London, including the Church of England in Jamaica and the Niger Mission under Bishop Tugwell in Southern Nigeria, had endorsed some of the objectives articulated by the back-to-Africa black protagonists in the New World. This was because, in their perception, such objectives were capable of transforming the benighted continent culturally. Given that thinking, it is pertinent to discuss the back-to-Africa movement and its underpinning ideological motives. Before delving into that discussion, including the internal circumstances within the CMS Niger Mission that led to the recruitment of Afro-Caribbean missionaries and their engagement in Igboland, it is germane to make some very brief comments on the "genealogical" connection between the African-Caribbean diaspora and Igboland.

IGBOLAND AND THE PEOPLING OF THE AFRICAN-CARIBBEAN DIASPORA: A GENERAL OVERVIEW

There are, according to J. Derrick, "between 70 and 100 million people of mainly black African descent" permanently residing outside of the ancestral continent today; and, of these persons, approximately 20 million "live in the West Indies and on the Caribbean mainland, including 5 million in Haiti, the main stronghold of African culture in the New World after Brazil."[9] Although enslaved Africans and their descendants gave birth to this formation and also facilitated and influenced its demographic and cultural growth, voluntary immigrants from various African ethnicities began joining this nascent black Atlantic community immediately after the 1838 emancipation of slaves in the Caribbean. M. E. Thomas has noted, for example, that "some 7, 500 immigrants had come voluntarily from Africa to Jamaica"[10] between 1840 and 1865.

Regarding enforced relocation to the New World, however, it has been shown that the greatest victims of the trans-Atlantic trade in enslaved Africans from the Bight of Biafra were the Igbo-speaking populations who lived in the hinterland of the Eastern Niger Delta middleman trading states: Bonny [Ibani], New Calabar [Elem Kalabari], and Nembe-Brass, including the Efik-speaking middleman trading state of Old Calabar.[11] Douglas Chambers,[12] for example, has argued that enslaved Igbo-speaking peoples constituted about 80 percent of the estimated 1.7 million enslaved Africans that reached the New World from the Bight of Biafra between 1470 and 1860; and a substantial proportion of these enslaved Igbo-speaking Africans, he also noted, were initially sold to planters in the British Caribbean and North American plantation societies. Although chronologically limited to the nineteenth century, table 18.1 lends some credence to the view expressed above because it also shows that Igbo-speaking peoples represented more than 50 percent of the enslaved Africans in Trinidad, St. Lucia, St. Kitts, Berbice, and Anguilla.

As table 18.1 shows, the contingent of enslaved Igbo-speaking Africans in Trinidad at the beginning of the nineteenth century was by no means negligible. M. Warner-Lewis, without the benefit of this table, had earlier come to a similar opinion in *Guinea's Other Suns*:

> Apart from the Igbo, a number of ethnic groups from southeastern Nigeria seem to have been present in the island, among them the Ijo /ijo/ from the Niger Delta and the Ibibio /bibi/ from between the Cross and Niger Deltas. However, the Ibibio seems another name for the Moko /moko/ from Calabar near the Niger Delta whose memory survives in the word moko-jumbi which refers to the masquerade who walks on stilts and in the phrase 'the vengeance of Moko'—an unrelenting punitive force. The presence of the Sobo, which survives in the place-name Sobo village in La Brea and in the pejorative term 'Sobo woman,' further reinforces the possible numerical impact of the south-

TABLE 18.1 African ethnicities from the Bight of Biafra on British West Indies registration lists, 1813–1827

Location	*Igbo*	*Moko*	*Ibibio*	*Other*	*Total*
Trinidad (1815)	2,826	2,240	371	21	5,520
	51.8%	40.6%	6.7%	.04%	
St. Lucia (1815)	894	291	59	6	1,250
	71.5%	23.3%	4.8%	.5%	
St. Kitts (1815)	440	164	—	4	608
	72.4%	27.0%		.05%	
Berbice (1819)	111	64	—	7	182
	61.0%	35.2%		3.8%	
Anguilla (1827)	4	2	—	—	6
	66.7%	33.2%			
Total	4,312	2,529	371 (?)	38	7,566
	57.9%	33.4%	5.0%	.005%	

Source: Hall, Slavery and African Ethnicities, 139.

> eastern Nigeria and Niger Delta ethnic complex on Trinidad society. The Sobo are the Urhobo, a southern subgroup of the Benin Edo peoples.[13]

However, notwithstanding the contingent of enslaved Africans traceable to southeastern Nigeria, the present Creole sociocultural landscape of Trinidad is predominantly reflective of ethnic identities and religious practices traceable to the enslaved Yoruba-speaking peoples of southwestern Nigeria.

Finally, although there are no figures for Jamaica, we know from other narrative sources that enslaved Igbo-speaking Africans also constituted part of the plantation workforce in this Caribbean island; and there is some evidence, however scanty, to suggest that they also contributed to the evolving Creole culture in the island. John Tharp, the proprietor of several estates in Jamaica, including Good Hope, Wales, Lansquinet, and Potosi, had a particular preference for enslaved Igbo-speaking slaves; and, according to his biographer, "there were 3,002 slaves on all of the Tharp estates"[14] at the beginning of the nineteenth century. Many Trelawny planters in Jamaica, according to the same source just cited,[15] also owned Igbo-speaking slaves. The enslaved Igbo-speaking Africans, as this excerpt from Rev. Walter Brown indicates, left an indelible imprint in the formation of *patois*—one of the Atlantic Creole languages of the Caribbean spoken mainly in Jamaica.

> The Ibo language is a fascinating study. The sort of English or Jamaica dialect [*patois*] commonly heard in our streets in Jamaica contains many Ibo words. For example, *unu* for you, *soso* for only, and *okro* a corruption of *okwuba*. The presence of these and other words in our every day speech seems to indicate that a large proportion of our people [Afro-Jamaicans] are descendants of the Ibos.[16]

The biography of an Igbo-speaking enslaved African, Archibald Monteath, who contributed immensely to the propagation of Christianity in Jamaica during the mid-nineteenth century, is another sterling illustration of the contributions of Igbo-speaking enslaved Africans to the emergent Creole societies in the African-Caribbean diaspora.[17] Monteath, it could also be argued, exemplified Igbo receptivity to change in the New World. C. J. Korieh, in "African Ethnicity as a Mirage?: Historicizing the Essence of the Igbo in Africa and the Atlantic Diaspora," has noted that "From a transatlantic perspective, when compared with the cultural continuities and ethnic identities of other African groups [such as the Akan and Yoruba] the Igbo seem difficult to identify," despite the "sheer size" of their contingent in the peopling of the New World diaspora.[18] Korieh's assertion could be rephrased slightly differently for the purpose of this chapter: among other factors, Igbo cultural continuities and ethnic identities "seem difficult to identify" because, unlike the Akan and the Yoruba, they had responded more readily and willingly to the overwhelming forces of change in the New World slave-using plantation societies.

THE BACK-TO-AFRICA MOVEMENT AND THE RECRUITMENT OF AFRO-CARIBBEAN MISSIONARIES BY THE CMS NIGER MISSION

The genesis of the scheme to recruit black West Indian missionaries could be attributed to several interrelated factors on both sides of the Atlantic. For the purpose of the chapter, however, I will discuss two factors: the back-to-Africa movement that induced black West Indians to apply for missionary job vacancies in the continent; and the internal circumstances and thinking within the CMS Niger Mission that created the specific demand for black West Indian missionaries after the demise of Bishop S. Crowther in 1891.

The back-to-Africa movement was built around one ideological pillar: race. Informed by race consciousness and belonging, it was intended, among other aims, to work for the cultural "regeneration" and education of the benighted populations in the continent. With education and conversion to Christianity the movement believed that the continent could gain the respect and admiration of the civilized world. It also believed that, having gained that respect and admiration, the overall image of black people in the New World could be enhanced. "Blacks [in the New World] felt compelled," E. P. Skinner has argued, "to rehabilitate Africa and African peoples in their own eyes and in the eyes of the world so that by extension both they and that continent would be saved."[19]

Among the leaders of thought in this movement, such as E. W. Blyden, W. E. B. Du Bois, and S. Williams, there was the essentialist presumption that race united the descendants of Africa in the New World and those in the ancestral homeland. Blyden believed that "The exiled Negro . . . has a home in Africa. Africa is his, if he will. He may ignore it. He may consider that he is divested of any right to it; but this will not alter his relations to that country, or impair the integrity of his title."[20] Based on this reasoning, Blyden urged all those willing to undertake the civilizing mission to Africa, especially teachers and missionaries, to roll "back the appalling cloud of ignorance and superstition which overspreads the [continent]."[21]

These views, predicated on the essentialist notion of race, were not different from those of Williams of Trinidad, the founder of the Pan-African Association in 1897. That Association, among other goals, was founded to unite "the African world into one solid body which would be strong [to] fight on behalf of Africa."[22] In pursuit of this aim, Williams traveled throughout the West Indies at the beginning of the twentieth century establishing several branches of the Association in order to foster and promote the preexisting sense of Africa consciousness and race belonging among the Afro-Caribbean populations. Williams and his allies, including Du Bois, were cognizant of the potential material benefits to be derived from the educational and industrial programs of European missionary organizations; but they were unequivocally critical of the alliance being forged between these missionary organizations and the emergent colonial state to enhance the exploitation of the human and natural resources of the continent. This was how Du Bois put it: "Let not the cloak of Christian missionary enterprise be allowed . . . to hide the ruthless economic exploitation and political downfall of less developed nations."[23] "There is no evidence that [European] Christianity," Blyden also commented like Du Bois, "would have been less unscrupulous in their dealings with the natives of Africa, than they have been with the natives of America, of Australia, [and] of New Zealand."[24] These depressing and sarcastic commentaries, which were in part informed by the selfish economic motives that propelled the European scramble for Africa in the last quarter of the nineteenth century, illustrated the profound unease these back-to-Africa activists, scholars, and publicists felt about European missionaries and the emergent colonial state as instruments for the development of the continent. Hence they campaigned tirelessly for the "regeneration" of Africa through the missionary efforts of its own sons and daughters in the New World.

The British imperial government, including the Church Missionary Society at Salisbury Square in London and the Church of England in Jamaica, also embraced the assumption that race united the descendants of Africa in the New World and those in the continent; and, in their own ideological self-interests, they also promoted the back-to-Africa movement. By 1840, for example, Lord John Russell of the Colonial Office had drawn attention to the role that the British government expected West Indians to play in the "regeneration" of Africa in the aftermath of the trans-Atlantic trade in enslaved Africans: "It appears to H M Government that on one hand, men of African birth who have been trained in civilization and instructed in Christianity in Jamaica, or Barbados, would be the best teachers of the Negro Race in Africa itself."[25] Given all of these prevailing sentiments the Church of England in Jamaica—the body that ultimately worked in concert with Salisbury Square in London and the Niger Mission in Southeastern Nigeria to recruit Afro-Caribbean missionaries—began to portray the British civilizing mission to West Africa before its Afro-Caribbean adherents as a special arena of black activity within the Anglican Communion. To enthuse and encourage the Afro-Caribbean people to perceive the evangelization of Africa as their special task, the Church of England in Jamaica argued thus: "Many of you, to whom this appeal comes, can do what others [Europeans], who have tried, cannot do; and it seems that unless there is a grand response made by those in the West Indies, this extensive region of Africa will continue dark, and indeed may grow yet darker."[26] Persuaded by this race-oriented thinking, the Church of England in Jamaica began to prepare black Jamaicans for their missionary projects in West Africa; and in 1896, the year Tugwell initiated recruitment discussions with the Church of England in Jamaica, three black Afro-Jamaican missionaries were sent to the Rio Pongas Mission in Guinea-Conakry, West Africa. The other name of the Rio Pongas Mission—"The Mission from the sons and daughters of Africa in the West Indies to Africa"—is very instructive: it underscored the extent to which the ideological sentiments of race-belonging and Africa consciousness were being propagated by the Church of England in Jamaica in order to recruit its Afro-Caribbean followers for the civilizing missions to West Africa.[27]

Before proceeding further it is pertinent to pose this critical question: what internal and immediate circumstances prompted Tugwell, after the demise of Crowther, to turn to the West Indies for recruitment around the end of the nineteenth century? To fully understand the circumstances that gave rise to this situation, it is necessary to provide this background information. Under the episcopacy of Samuel A. Crowther, a Yoruba by birth and an ex-slave, the CMS Niger Mission had utilized missionary personnel drawn almost entirely from among the recaptives of Sierra Leone. The idea of "indigenous church" or "native agency," which informed the administrative and evangelical operations of the Niger Mission under Crowther and his Sierra Leonean recaptive missionaries, was the brainchild of Henry Venn, the secretary of the CMS from 1841 to 1872.[28] There was, however, some opposition to this arrangement from the outset; and, after the demise of Venn, that opposition signaled its intention not to continue with the administrative structure of the Niger Mission as it had hitherto been.

Within the secular hierarchy of the Niger Mission, this meant restoring to Europeans some of the administrative powers previously vested in Crowther and his team of Sierra Leonean workers. Before very long the relationship between these Europeans and their African colleagues in the Niger Mission had strained irreparably. These strains came most visibly to the open when a European-dominated committee was appointed to investigate a report on the finances of the Niger Mission. That committee made very damaging and brutal allegations of huge financial improprieties by Crowther's lieutenants, including his son, Archdeacon Dandeson C. Crowther. Other charges brought against these African agents were: overindulgence in alcoholic beverages, poor work ethics and indiscipline, adultery, and licentiousness.

Based on these charges, some of which were unproven and untrue, the committee recommended the dismissal and disconnection of nearly all of the Sierra Leonean agents from the Mission. These events, later referred to as the "Niger purge," coincided with the rising tide of African resistance against the British invasion and occupation of Southern Nigeria.

This background of rising African nationalism in part made it possible for Crowther and his allies, including many educated and politically minded African elites within and outside of the church, to perceive and interpret the purge as an exercise designed to portray Africans as unfit for rational leadership. Encouraged by his ideologically driven supporters, Crowther began to consider separation from the Church of England. However, he died in 1891 before he could implement the proposed separation plan. After his demise the CMS, to the chagrin of Crowther's ideological supporters, announced that no African would be appointed to succeed him as the bishop of the Niger Mission. As a result, Bishop J. S. Hill was directed by Salisbury Square to manage the affairs of the Mission before the appointment of Bishop H. Tugwell in 1894—the man who initiated the scheme for the recruitment of Afro-Caribbean missionaries. The appointment of Tugwell, now seen and interpreted by the protagonists of secession as a deliberate attempt to deny the African any rights in the leadership of his church, finally broke the camel's back, and in 1892, under the auspices of D. C. Crowther, the supporters of the late bishop formed the Niger Delta Pastorate Church. This whole episode and its effects, known as the "Niger Crisis" or the "Delta Revolt,"[29] marked a watershed in the evangelization of Southeastern Nigeria by the CMS Niger Mission.

Faced with the opposition led by D. C. Crowther, including the shortfall in missionary personnel precipitated by the dismissal of the Sierra Leonean clergymen and teachers employed by the late bishop, Tugwell turned to the West Indies for recruitment. This was because, as the events leading to the "Revolt" might have shown, the decades of trust and confidence that Salisbury Square reposed in Sierra Leoneans and their spiritual fitness for missionary work in West Africa had been severely damaged. However, even before the death of Crowther and the secession, the CMS leadership at Salisbury Square in London had debated whether West Indians were "a more hopeful bridge between Europe and Africa than an indigenous recaptive [Sierra Leonean] population." The preference for black West Indians was predicated on the reasoning that they had been "long uprooted from Africa . . . and thus were less likely to lapse into Africa's unredeemed past."[30] S. Crowther had disagreed fundamentally with this position, and, with the support of Venn, Salisbury Square was persuaded to accept his own position. He perceived recaptive Africans as representing "the best hope, and the last chance, of securing [Christianity's] future" in the continent. Rejecting the earlier pro-West Indian argument, he "suggested that . . . their alleged proximity to European culture and, correspondingly, their alienation from African culture, was a weakness, not an advantage."[31] However, with the passing of Crowther and Venn, the policy reorientations taking place within Salisbury Square and the Niger Mission, including the imposition of formal colonialism in West Africa, the internal and external circumstances became auspicious for the recruitment, training, and deployment of twenty-eight black West Indians from 1896 to 1925 by the Niger Mission.

Some members of this nascent Afro-Caribbean missionary workforce were sent to mission-stations in southern and northern Nigeria outside of Igboland. For this chapter, however, we could identify with the following Afro-Caribbean missionaries and the Igbo-speaking communities set out in table 18.2.

This homecoming, as illustrated by the presence of these Afro-Caribbean missionaries in the aforementioned Igbo-speaking communities, could be interpreted as a fulfillment of the political and philosophical prediction of Blyden arguably:.

> God has his designs upon that vast land [Africa]. . . . The branch torn away from the parent stem in Africa, by our ancestors, was brought to America—brought by Divine permission—in order that it might be

TABLE 18.2 Afro-Caribbean missionaries in Igboland

Names	*Igbo Communities*	*Duration*
Walter E. Blackett	Onitsha and Awka	1899–1924
W. William White	Awka	1902–1903
S. M. Binger	Obusi and Onitsha	1902–1907
Catherine A. Hive	Onitsha	1904
Mabel Richards	Onitsha	1904
J. B. Stewart	Awka, Onitsha, and Asaba	1905–1922
Walter L. Brown	Nnewi, Asaba, and Awka	1905–1924
Reuben A. Llewellyn	Awka	1905–1924
John Wright	Okwuzu and Asaba	1904–1910
A. Franklin	Umuleri and Agulu	1906
Thomas Jennings	Nri and Agulu	1910
Thomas Edward Mackay	Onitsha and Owerri	1913–1921

> engrafted upon the tree of the Cross. It will return in part to its own soil, not by violence or deportation, but willingly, and borne on the wing of faith and charity.[32]

Given these sentiments, including other factors not worth detailing here, these missionaries were required to "make Africa the sphere of their life's work"[33] by Salisbury Square. As Sidney Smith, the secretary of the Niger Mission, also put it: they were expected to settle down permanently in Africa and visit the Caribbean occasionally.[34]

THE ACTIVITIES AND CONTRIBUTIONS OF AFRO-CARIBBEAN MISSIONARIES IN THE NIGER MISSION TO THE DEVELOPMENT OF EDUCATION AND CHRISTIANITY IN IGBOLAND

Owing to space constraint, I will confine the discussions to three preeminent Afro-Caribbean missionaries whose activities contributed substantially to the growth and development of education and Christianity in Igboland: Blackett, Brown, and Mackay. In 1899 Blackett arrived in Onitsha and was required immediately "to take the oversight of an educational institution" located "in the old CMS compound, Onitsha";[35] in addition, he was advised to put the necessary plans in place for the establishment of a boarding school for boys in Onitsha. "The education to be given in this institution," Blackett and his European supervisor, J. N. Cheetham, were told, "will be quite plain, corresponding to that given in standards 1–VII of an English board school."[36] In 1902, as a result of Blackett's perceived competence and sense of responsibility, the Executive Committee of the Niger Mission decided "to place the responsible charge of the work in Onitsha Town in his hands."[37] As an inspector of schools, Blackett became responsible for the running and organization of the following institutions: Christ Church Primary, Onitsha; Christ Church Nursery School, Onitsha; Holy Trinity, Asaba; St. Andrews School, Obosi; and St. Immanuel's School, Umuaroli.[38] Between 1907 and 1918 Blackett was administratively responsible for the smooth running of fifty primary schools in the Onitsha district, including twenty "combined schools."[39]

The enormous increase in the number of schools under his superintendence represented the phenomenal rapid growth of education in Igboland at the beginning of the twentieth century. This is also borne out by these comments from the secretary of the Niger Mission, Sidney Smith, in 1917: "[During Blackett's tenure] as Inspector and Examiner of CMS Day Schools, the pupils . . . have increased from about 500 [including Nembe-Brass and Northern Nigeria] to 18, 229 in the Ibo-speaking districts alone."[40] Given Blackett's enormous managerial responsibilities and the experiences he had acquired over the years, he was appointed as a member of the Elementary Education Subcommittee of the Niger Mission—a body responsible for the formulation, implementation, and coordination of policies pertaining to all primary schools owned and operated by the CMS Niger Mission in southern and northern Nigeria. Other members of this committee—all Europeans—were: S. R. Smith (chairman), Miss Warner, Rev. G. T. Basden, and J. N. Cheetham.[41]

As an educational administrator cum evangelist, Blackett sought to correct the perception that "women are mere menials and objects of lust, a play thing to be thrown aside at any time and for any cause." To alleviate the plight of women, he advocated for educational policies that would emphasize "the great importance of having female teachers . . . as torch bearers of the true light to their fellow creatures now sitting in darkness and in the region of the shadow of death."[42] After thirteen years of working with the above policy-making body, Blackett received this commendation from the Executive Committee: "As a member of the CMS Education Board, he helped to formulate the 'School Code'; and in 1919, he also worked to bring about the syllabuses of the CMS schools in line with those of the colonial government of southern Nigeria."[43]

For the purpose of proselytizing, the Niger Mission divided Igboland into five administrative zones or districts at the beginning of the twentieth century: the western, eastern, central, northern, and southern zones. Missionaries were required, under the "Pupil Teachers Itineration Programme," to proselytize on monthly basis with the assistance of Igbo-speaking pupil teachers drawn from the Awka Training Institution. Under this program, Blackett headed a team of Igbo-speaking pupil teachers—James, Simeon, and Isaiah—to propagate the gospel at Okwuzu and Umuleri in the western missionary district between 1900 and 1903. In the northern zone S. M. Binger, another West Indian, proselytized at Okwuzu-Oba, Izi, and Igbolo with Igbo-speaking pupil teachers Hezekiah, Matthew, and Timothy.[44] Before the end of 1903, according to the Executive Committee of the Niger Mission, the proselytizing endeavors of Blackett in the western district had started to produce impressive dividends.

> At Emmanuel's Church, as a result of Mr. Blackett's work, assisted by Mr. T. Agusiobi [an Igbo catechist], church and class attendances had largely improved. . . . The financial condition of this Church was much more satisfactory, and in addition to their contributing to class fees towards the support of their teacher, they had also undertaken to provide food for the support of a missionary agent at Nkwele-Ogidi.[45]

In addition to the work at Emmanuel's Church, Blackett was "practically in charge of the Bishop Crowther Memorial Church at Ontisha" between 1903 and 1917 as a senior catechist and lay reader. Sidney Smith, the European parson officially in charge of the Bishop Crowther Memorial Church, had this to say about the proselytizing capabilities of Blackett in 1917: "I have had many opportunities of hearing his addresses and sermons and they are very good indeed in every way, except in length."[46] Persuaded by these personal qualities, Blackett was ordained by the Niger Mission on St. Paul's Day, February 25, 1920.[47]

Walter L. Brown, another Afro-Caribbean missionary with a prodigious record of achievement, worked in the Igbo-speaking communities of Nnewi, Asaba, and Awka. Nnewi, according to Brown, was his "home in Africa" because it was "intimately associated with the infancy of [his] mission life, and [grew] in importance as [he] advanced in years."[48] Brown, like Blackett and Binger before him, led a band of pupil teachers on proselytizing campaigns. In 1908, for example, campaigns were conducted at Agulu, Ujalle, Ikelionwu, and Oko; and, according to Brown, "It was the seeds sown then and after which sprang up . . . to produce settled Christian congregations" in these areas.[49] Brown's lasting legacy to the Nnewi Christian community included, among others, the construction of school and church buildings—for example, the St Mary's Church—with funds donated by philanthropists in Jamaica between 1912 and 1915. With these facilities in place, coupled with the vigorous proselytizing campaigns pursued under the auspices of the "Pupil Teachers Itineration Programme," Christianity at Nnewi began to grow in leaps and bounds; for example, from thirty-five stations in the district at the end of

1914, the number increased to forty-five at the beginning of 1917.[50]

In 1915 Brown was appointed to act as assistant superintendent and assistant inspector of schools in the Asaba district. These comments from the secretary of the Niger Mission, Rev. Sidney Smith, provide a good summary of Brown's evangelical and secular endeavors and accomplishments in that district:

> I am greatly indebted to Mr. W.L Brown who is not only looking after the interest of schools in the Asaba district as inspector but is in charge of all the accounts as treasurer of the sustentation fund. He is also responsible for the superintendence of the 12 stations outside of the Asaba district.[51]

The Asaba district, taken as whole, consisted of twenty stations, with a day school attached to each station. According to Brown, he covered two hundred and fifty miles every month to do the work required in these mission-stations: conducting services, preaching, and examining candidates for baptism.[52]

Given this level of enterprise, industry, and dynamism, including the departure on furlough of Rev. G. S. Basden, the European superintendent in charge of the Awka district, Brown was elevated to the rank of acting superintendent of that district after his ordination on January 25, 1922. Here is Brown's account of his routine secular and evangelistic activities between 1922 and 1924, as acting superintendent of the Awka missionary district:

> There are sixty-four stations which I have to supervise and I have already made several tours and visited over fifty of them [between June and November 1921] preaching, administering baptisms, performing marriages, admitting catechumens, investigating and settling disputes, conducting examination of various candidates and seeing after a dozen and one other things which are incidental to missionary work.[53]

There were only eight mission stations within the Awka district in 1912; at the end of 1914, however, they had "increased to twenty-three, with over 2,000 adherents."[54] Between 1914 and 1921, as the above testimony attributed to Brown reveals, the stations had increased to sixty-four. This impressive and phenomenal growth rate, as shown in Onitsha, Nnewi, Asaba, and Awka, reflected the general sociocultural transformation that was taking place in Igboland.

The narrative from Owerri and Egbu, where Thomas E. Mackay worked as the coordinator and inspector of schools and churches, could provide yet another solid illustration of the pivotal role of Afro-Caribbean missionaries in the aforementioned sociocultural transformation. Egbu, the southernmost mission-station in the Igbo-speaking area, was previously under the superintendence of Archdeacon T. J. Dennis and his wife—two towering European pioneer missionaries of the Niger Mission. Mackay, after being in Onitsha from 1913 to 1916, was assigned to supervise the Egbu-Owerri district after the death of Archdeacon Dennis. The establishments in this district included 136 mission-stations, 10 "Central Schools," 84 "Lower Schools," and 42 "Vernacular Schools"; 9,200 pupils were enrolled in these schools and, instructively, 1,080 of all those enrolled were girls.[55] Afro-Caribbean missionaries, as Brown once put it, believed that "It was only by the influence and teachings of the church that women may hope to occupy their rightful positions" in society.[56]

In 1919, along with the secular work of inspecting and supervising these schools, Mackay prepared 229 persons for baptism, admitted 320 persons to the catechumenate, assisted in conducting 16 marriages, and sold 3,500 union cards and almanacs as part of a planned fundraising activity.[57] Aside from maintaining and sustaining existing mission-stations and schools, Mackay also built new ones. In 1919 seventeen new stations were opened, while four unviable ones were shut down. To man these new stations twenty-six agents were recruited as teachers and catechists. By 1920, according to Mackay, "the work had progressed . . . and there were over 154 stations—though the [official CMS] register shows only 151—in this large district."[58] Finally, these comments from Mackay, like those of Brown cited previously, portrayed the commitment of Afro-Caribbean missionaries to the CMS civilizing mission in Igboland: "Sometimes I am moving among the people without break for nearly three months; and the more I move about the more I get to understand a people to whom I desire to do good, and the better I get to understand their language and customs."[59]

In 1956, about three decades after the demise of the West Indian project, the Bishop of the Niger Delta Diocese, the Rt. Rev. C. J. Patterson, commended the Church of England in Jamaica for its role in the growth and development of Christianity in southern Nigeria through the activities and accomplishments of the Afro-Caribbean missionaries discussed. Part of that commendation goes thus: "Nor must the part of the West Indian missionaries be forgotten. The memory of what they did in the latter years of the nineteenth century and the early years of the twentieth lives on in the Niger Diocese today."[60] Fully to appreciate these black West Indians, who were propelled by a sense of Africa consciousness, it is necessary to relate their endeavors to the overall achievements of the Niger Mission during the episcopacy of Bishop Herbert Tugwell.

Tugwell, as noted earlier, had inaugurated the scheme to salvage the Niger Mission from collapsing after the "Niger Delta Revolt" and the subsequent loss of the Sierra Leone market for the recruitment of African agents as teachers, catechists, and parsons. At its sixtieth anniversary to mark the commencement of missionary work at Onitsha in July 1918, the Niger Mission stated that in 1899—the year the first West Indian, Blackett, joined the Niger Mission—there were only five hundred pupils in all of the CMS schools in Igboland, including Nembe-Brass and Northern Nigeria. Before the end of 1920, however, the demand for Western education in the evolving colonial state of Nigeria, particularly among the Igbo-speaking populations, had grown in leaps and bounds. In 1918, about twenty years after the commencement of the West Indian scheme, the number of pupils had increased to 22,155. Among these, 20,237 were males, while females amounted to 1,918. The figures for 1918, which showed an increase of 3,500 over that recorded for 1917, amply illustrated the tremendous annual growth rate in enrollment.[61] In addition to school enrollment, 22,625 persons were baptized before the demise of the scheme; and the number of communicants similarly increased from 660 in 1906 to 4,103 in 1916.[62] These developments, according to Tugwell, "give occasion for much rejoicing, but caused no little amount of concern to the [European] missionaries in view of the dearth of qualified [indigenous] teachers and [parsons]."[63] It is against this background that we can appreciate the significance of the back-to-Africa movement: the presence of black West Indian schoolmasters, catechists, and parsons remedied the shortfall in the amount of qualified non-European personnel needed by the CMS Niger Mission to successfully pursue the goals of the civilizing mission in Igboland during the period under review.

NOTES

1. J. U. J. Asiegbu, *Nigeria and Its British Invaders, 1851–1920* (New York: Nok, 1984), 235–58.

2. J. C. Anene, *Southern Nigeria in Transition, 1885–1906* (Cambridge: Cambridge University Press, 1966), 240–49.

3. W. I. Ofonagoro, *Trade and Imperialism in Southern Nigeria 1881–1929* (New York: Nok, 1979), 95–190.

4. W. E. Wariboko, *Ruined by "Race": Afro-Caribbean Missionaries and the Evangelization of Southern Nigeria, 1895–1925* (Trenton, NJ: Africa World Press, 2007).

5. T. N. Tamuno, *The Evolution of the Nigerian State: The Southern Phase, 1898–1914* (London: Longman, 1972), 339–52.

6. S. Ottenberg, "Ibo Receptivity to Change," in *Continuity and Change in African Cultures*, ed. W. R. Bascom and M. J. Herskovits (Chicago, IL: University of Chicago Press, 1959), 130–43.

7. E. A. Ayandele, *The Missionary Impact on Modern Nigeria, 1842–1914: A Political and Social Analysis* (London: Longman, 1966), 343.

8. Wariboko, "Overview of Current Literature," in *Ruined by "Race,"* 13–17. The discussions

in this chapter are largely based and derived from *Ruined by "Race,"* including other materials obtained while doing the archival research connected to its production.

9. J. Derrick, *Africa's Slaves* (New York: Schocken, 1975), 110–11.

10. M. E. Thomas, *Jamaica and Voluntary Laborers from Africa, 1840–1845* (Gainesville: University Press of Florida, 1974), 199.

11. G. M. Hall, *Slavery and African Ethnicities in the Americas* (Kingston, JM: Ian Randle, 2006), 126–43.

12. D. B. Chambers, "'My own nation': Igbo Exiles in the Diaspora," *Slavery and Abolition* 8, no. 1 (1997): 72–97.

13. M. Warner-Lewis, *Guinea's Other Suns: The African Dynamic in Trinidad Culture* (Dover, MA: Majority Press, 1991), 16.

14. D. A. Dunkley, "The Legacies of John Tharp, 1744–1804" (MA research paper, University of the West Indies at Mona, 1997), 72.

15. Dunkley, "The Legacies of John Tharp, 1744–1804," 133.

16. W. L. Brown, "News from the Missionary Front: Nigeria," *Jamaica Diocesan Gazette and Church Magazine* (November 1919).

17. M. Warner-Lewis, *Archibald Monteath: Igbo, Jamaican, Moravian* (Kingston, JM: University of the West Indies Press, 2007).

18. C. J. Korieh, "African Ethnicity as Mirage?: Historicizing the Essence of the Igbo in Africa and the Atlantic Diaspora," *Dialectical Anthropology* 30 (2006): 91–118.

19. E. P. Skinner, "The Dialectic Between Diasporas and Homelands," in *Global Dimensions of the African Diaspora* ed. E. J. Harris (Washington, DC: Howard University Press, 1993), 22.

20. V. Y. Mudimbe, *The Invention of Africa* (Indianapolis: Indiana University Press, 1988), 105.

21. E. W. Blyden, *Christianity, Islam and the Negro Race* (1888; repr., Baltimore, MD: Black Classic Press, 1994), 47.

22. T. Martin, *The Pan-African Connection: From Slavery to Garvey and Beyond* (Dover, MA: Majority Press, 1985), 11–12.

23. J. A. Langley, *Pan-Africanism and Nationalism in West Africa, 1900–1945* (Oxford: Clarendon Press, 1978), 28.

24. Mudimbe, *The Invention of Africa*, 126.

25. Quoted in P. D. Curtin, *The Image of Africa: British Ideas and Actions, 1780–1850* (Madison: University of Wisconsin Press, 1964), 419.

26. "The Young Men and Women in the West Indies: A Call," *Jamaica Churchman* 26 (October 1901): 20.

27. W. E. Wariboko, "West Indian Church in West Africa: The Pongas Mission among the Susus and Its Portrayal of Blackness, 1851–1953," in *Missions, States, And European Expansion in Africa*, ed. C. J. Korieh and R. C. Njoku (New York: Routledge, 2007), 167–86.

28. W. R. Shenk, *Henry Venn—Missionary Statesman* (New York: Orbis Books, 1983).

29. G. O. M. Tasie, *Christian Missionary Enterprise in the Niger Delta, 1864–1918* (Leiden, NL: Brill, 1978), 83–135.

30. L. Sanneh, "The CMS and the African Transformation: Samual Ajayi Crowther and the Opening of Nigeria," in *Church Mission Society and World Christianity*, ed. K. Ward and B. Stanley (Grand Rapids, MI: Eerdmans, 2000), 85.

31. Sanneh, "The CMS and the African Transformation," 86.

32. Blyden, *Christianity, Islam and the Negro Race*, 115.

33. G3A3/1905/102, "Employment of West Indian Missionary Agents in West Africa."

34. G3A3/1917/12, Sidney Smith to G. T. Manley, April 7, 1917.

35. G3A3/1899/121, T. J. Dennis to Rev. F. Baylis, October 16, 1900.

36. Ibid.

37. G3A3/1902/42, "An Adjoined Meeting of the Executive Committee held on Thursday, 27 February 1902."

38. G3A3/1903/63, W. E. Blackett to the Secretary, Niger Mission, "Schools' Report for January 1903."

39. G3A3/1918/29, "Women's Conference: Minutes and Reports," July 1918.

40. G3A3/1917/41, Sidney Smith to G. T. Manley, June 12, 1917.

41. G3A3/1916/15, Niger Mission Minutes II, July–November 1915.

42. W. E. Blackett, Onitsha: Missionary Work in West Africa, *Jamaica Times*, Kingston, April 4, 1903.

43. G3A3/19/49, "Niger Mission: Minutes of the Executive Committee," July 1919.

44. G3A3/1903/52, Herbert Tugwell, "Programme of Itineration," April 1903.

45. G3A3/1903/54, Executive Committee Meetings, January 23–February 8, 1903.

46. G3A3/1917/4,. Sidney Smith to G. T. Manley, June 12, 1917.

47. G3A3/1920/13, Niger Mission: Minutes of the Executive Committee, February 1920.

48. W. L. Brown, "At Work in West Africa," *Jamaica Times*, Kingston, October 6, 1917.

49. "The Jamaican in Africa: Mr. Brown Reviews Two Years Work," *Jamaica Times*, Kingston, June 19, 1915.

50. "The Jamaican in Africa."

51. G3A3/1918/29, "Education Board: Minutes of Meeting held 3 July 1918."

52. G3A3/1921/28, Niger Mission Executive Committee Minutes, March 21, 1921.

53. "From H. Herbert Simpson and Mrs. A. H. Simpson to the Editor," *Jamaica Diocesan Gazette and Church Magazine*, November 12, 1921.

54. "The Jamaican in Africa."

55. G3A3/1919/49, Executive Committee Minutes (Appendix One), July 1919.

56. "The Jamaican in Africa."

57. Executive Committee Minutes (Appendix One), July 1919.

58. "From Our Own Missionary: T. E. Mackay," *The Jamaican Diocesan Gazette and Church Magazine*, July 20, 1920.

59. Ibid.

60. *Jamaica Diocesan Magazine* 30, no. 4 (April 1956): 20–21.

61. G3A3/1918/24, "Niger Mission Statistics."

62. G. O. M. Tasie, *Christian Missionary Enterprise in the Niger Delta*, 259.

63. "Advance in Western Equatorial Africa," *Jamaica Diocesan Gazette and Church Magazine* (May 1917).

19 THE MAKING OF IGBO ETHNICITY IN THE NIGERIAN SETTING

COLONIALISM, IDENTITY, AND THE POLITICS OF DIFFERENCE

Raphael Chijioke Njoku

This chapter examines the emergence of Igbo identity and how the evolution of exclusionary politics under colonial rule engendered a conflictual pattern of ethnic structures and ethnonationalism in postcolonial Nigeria. The politics of exclusion began with the establishment of British colonial rule and the introduction of Western education in the early twentieth century. Among other things, Western education led to the rise of a new class of lettered elite who were exposed to the attractions of neopolitical and neocapitalist systems. The new world order, established on fault lines of domination and exploitation, pitched the Igbo elite against their neighbors in a heated struggle for access to power and pursuit of economic self-interests. The educated Igbo leaders, like their peers elsewhere in Africa, found writing and political speeches instrumental for mass mobilization and survival in the new sociopolitical milieu. The result was a gradation of a pattern of conflict at both the regional and national levels, which robbed the precolonial patterns of intergroup relations of its benevolent aura of innocence. Soon after independence in 1960, interelite struggles for power and privileges coalesced to produce the Nigerian Civil War (1967–1970). Since the end of the war, the place of the Igbo in the Nigerian federation has remained a debate that elucidates fear, bitterness, ethnonationalism, and violence. There is a widely shared belief among Nigerians that the "Igbo problem" must be duly addressed for the nation to move forward.

IGBO IDENTITY IN THE "AGE OF INNOCENCE" (CA. BEFORE 1900)

The term "innocence" is adopted here to exemplify the nature of Igbo identity in the period before 1900. Without suggesting that precolonial eastern Nigeria was a haven of peace, one would however assert that the various independent Igbo villages bordering non-Igbo communities to the Northern, Southern, Eastern, and Western Regions shared more fluid intercommunity relations with their neighbors. Though the Igbo could be delineated as a linguistic/cultural group during the precolonial period, Igbo consciousness was not sharply perceived in relation to their non-Igbo-speaking neighbors until colonial intrusion of the late nineteenth and early twentieth centuries. The precolonial relations were devoid of a "pan-Igbo" versus "pan-Ibibio" or "pan-Efik," or pan-Igala consciousness. The Igbo Village Group (a collection of small villages that share common history of origin and rituals) was rather "a nation" apart from both the other Igbo Village Groups and bordering non-Igbo communities. The areas distinguished as Igboland today was part of a broader eastern Nigerian commonwealth composed of people tied together by reciprocal economic, cultural, and social relationships.

Scholarly opinions, however, are divided on whether there was a concept of the "Igbo" as a cohesive and "self-conscious" group in the precolonial era. This controversy gained popularity following the influential work of colonial anthropologists Daryll Forde and G. I. Jones, *The Ibo and Ibibio-speaking Peoples of South-Eastern Nigeria.*[1] Forde and Jones divided the Igbo country into five cultural zones: Onitsha or Northern Igbo, Owerri or Southern Igbo, Western Igbo, Cross River or Eastern Igbo, and Northeastern Igbo.[2] The authors based their classifications on observable minor cultural variations among the various sub-Igbo groups, resulting from their geographical proximity to their non-Igbo neighbors. To the east are found the Afikpo, Abiriba, Bende, Ohafia,

Edda, Unwana, Ndoki, and Arochukwu communities, whose aspects of social institutions are identical with those of their Ibibio and Efik neighbors. To the western banks of the Niger River are found the Onitsha, Anioma, Umunede, Oguta, and Ossomari, who borrowed some aspects of their political and cultural institutions from their Edo neighbors. To the northern fringes are found the Nsukka and Nri, who have had long-standing cross-cultural relations with their Idoma and Igala neighbors. To the south are the Obosima, Ohaji, Elele, and Egbema communities, who share many cultural institutions with their Ijo neighbors.[3] In light of this, Forde and Jones concluded that the precolonial Igbo, who lived in independent villages, "are a single people in the sense that they speak a number of related dialects . . . but were not politically unified." Therefore the Igbo hardly perceived themselves as a nation in the modern sense.[4]

Extending this view, James Coleman argued in his 1958 seminal study, *Nigeria: Background to Nationalism*, that there was no preexisting pan-Igbo identity and that this evolved in the colonial setting, acquiring an innovative dimension by the mid-1930s when Dr. Akanu Ibiam, the first Igbo missionary doctor, completed his medical program in Scotland and returned home to join the leadership of the nascent Igbo State Union in Lagos.[5] The inaugural meeting of the pan-Igbo Union was formally launched in Lagos in June 1936, and similar associations were founded in other major cities in Nigeria.[6] The declared main purpose of the union was to move forward the Igbo people chiefly in the field of education.[7] Coleman's work is important because it identified the colonial urban center, in a sense a diaspora social milieu, as a platform for ethnic inventions in colonial Nigeria. In her magisterial study of the Igbo in 1976, Elizabeth Isichei reaffirmed the previous studies with the assertion that Igbo ethnic identity was first articulated by the Igbo diasporas: "A sense of Pan-Igbo identity came only when its people left Igboland—an experience first imposed by the slave trade or when colonial conquest and rule violently extended the categories through which the Igbo perceived their world."[8]

Indeed, the ample evidence of the autobiography of Igbo-born ex-slave Olaudah Equiano, *The Interesting Narrative of the Life of Olaudah Equiano*, first published in 1789, provides historians with the earliest attempt, in the modern era, to articulate and contest a sense of Igbo identity as opposed to the "Other"—or what Equiano qualified as "primitive Europe."[9] Equiano's graphic and prideful description of his "Eboe" (i.e., Igbo) life and customs in the eighteenth century mirrors similar accounts by Archibald Monteath, an Igbo-born "Aniaso" in 1799 and enslaved in Jamaica from around 1802.[10] Similar mentions of the Igbo or *Heebo* (as it appeared in early slave trade) as a cultural group exist in the documented memoirs of early European visitors to the Bight of Benin and Biafra. Both Duarte Pacheco Pereira, a fifteenth-century Portuguese sea captain and geographer, and John Grazilhier, who made a voyage to Old Calabar in 1699, wrote about the "Hakbous [Igbo] Blacks" in their separate memoirs.[11] Thus, we understand the origins of pan-Igbo ethnic identity, like Pan-Africanism, as an ideology that gained relevance in the diaspora and gradually infiltrated the ancestral homeland.

Meanwhile, those who contend that a pan-Igbo identity was a reality prior to colonialism have similarly cited the same writings and memoirs left by the ex-slaves and other foreign visitors.[12] John Reader has argued, for instance, that in "Nigeria, although broad cultural identities—pan-Igbo, pan-Hausa, and pan-Yoruba had emerged before the missionaries and British administration arrived to make their mark on the social landscape, they did not correspond to the colonial notion of static tribal identities."[13] While this might be the case for the Hausa and Yoruba who lived under centralized polities, the precolonial Igbo society was different, and indeed the precolonial sense of *Igboness* was quite different from what later evolved in the colonial setting. The proto pan-Igbo identity, whether articulated in the diaspora or at home was, at best, akin to a dormant volcano with potentials for a more aggressive and violent activities. The lava of Igbo consciousness alongside those of their major opponents erupted with the introduction and expansion of Western socioeconomic and political institutions. In light of the primordialist paradigm, the point here is that the Igbo is primordial to the Nigerian colonial state. Colonialism stirred up the Igbo to a new form of consciousness that appealed to a shared history, language, geography, and such cultural symbols as religion, totemic, and/or figural emblems. Igbo identity was therefore imposed, invented, appropriated, and anchored on certain preconceived characteristics—particularly language and culture.

Culturally heterogeneous, Igbo precolonial institutions and value systems were products of a combination of indigenous practices with borrowings from the non-Igbo communities with whom they have had centuries of cultural relations, including trade, war, and marriage alliances.[14] Through a symbiotic fusion and friction, the precolonial Igbo communities to the east borrowed age-grade and masquerade institutions from their Ibibio and Efik neighbors. Those on the western banks of the Niger and the northern fringes of Nsukka areas borrowed and adapted aspects of monarchical political ideas (suitable to the Igbo temperament) from their Edo and Idoma/Igala neighbors, respectively.[15] In exchange, as some studies have shown, the Igbo lend to their neighbors some aspects of religious rituals connected with agriculture, kinship practices, and exercise of oracular authority.[16]

The symbiosis of cross-cultural borrowings and fertilization of ideas therefore hinders a rigid imposition of Igbo, Efik, Igala, or Idoma identities. It is noteworthy that the meaning of the word "Igbo" has been variously contested as representing the "the people," "slaves," and "Forest dwellers." Even the Ibibio were once distinguished as "Kwa Ibo" by the Europeans.[17] One can further cite *West African Countries and Peoples* published in 1868 by Africanus Horton, a Sierra Leonean resident of Igbo parentage, as an evidence of a benignited Igbo ethnicity. In his work, Horton, a Christian missionary apologist and African patriot, demonstrated more concerns with the wider African identity than a narrower Igbo or Creole identity, as he used terms like "savage" and "barbarous" to describe the conditions found among the native populations, including his Igbo.[18] Generally, the Igbo community that emerged in Sierra Leone in the nineteenth century did not put their ethnicity above the Pan-African ideology despite the fact that they founded the Freetown Igbo Union in 1860 with William Henry Pratt as President.[19]

Until the late 1950s, the Aro Igbo, who share several common cultural traditions with their Calabar and Ekoi neighbors, hardly saw themselves as Igbo. Perhaps William Balfour Baikie (1824–1864), a nineteenth-century Scottish naval doctor who visited the Niger and the Delta in the 1850s and encountered the Igbo, provides a fair sense of how the precolonial Igbo perceived themselves: "In Igbo each person hails . . . from the particular district where he was born, but when away from home, all are Igbos."[20] The emerging sense of identity expanded under colonial rule, and it would be interesting to examine how these innovations played out in the colonial Igbo/Nigerian setting.

WESTERN EDUCATION AND IGBO IDENTITY IN A COLONIAL SETTING

Between the end of the Berlin Conference in 1885 and roughly 1904, the European imperial powers had seized control of most African territories. As the colonial forces attempted to pacify their newly acquired colonies, the Christian missionaries campaigned for new souls for Christ Jesus. The goals of the evangelists and colonial officials converged in the need to provide the crucial security for stability in the colonies. Part of this concerned teaching the African to read and write—skills required not only to interpret the Bible but also to help equip the learner with the ability for colonial service at the subordinate levels.[21] It is therefore crucial to reaffirm that the sites of ethnic struggles were created with the entrance of Western education and writing from around 1900. Western education is tied to the preparation of the individual for survival in the modern socioeconomic and political order. The ability to speak and write equips the individual with the power to communicate one's ideas, shape and reshape public opinions, and to mobilize a segment of the population or, in this case, an ethnic base for political and social actions.

With the exception of Onitsha, where the Church Missionary Society led by Bishop Samuel Ajayi Crowther (ca. 1809–1891) landed in the 1850s, the first mission schools were introduced in the Igbo hinterlands in the early 1900s following the military conquest of the area. In places like Lagos, Abeokuta, and Calabar, the missionaries founded schools as early as between 1841 and 1891.[22] British military operations in the face of pockets of resistance continued in the Igbo area until 1917, and by the second decade of the twentieth century, the Presbyterians, Protestants, Methodists, Qua Iboe, and Catholics were operating schools in the Igbo heartland. Pieces of evidence from both the Roman Catholic and Protestant sources suggest that between 1900 and 1912, the number of baptized Catholics grew from 2,450 to 32,781. The typical school attendance also rose from 156 to 5,421. The Protestant Mission alone recorded an increase in school attendance from an insignificant 5 in 1900 to an average attendance of 142.7 by 1912.[23]

Distinct from the outcasts, slaves, and other classes of marginalized groups, the free-born in Igbo society approached Western education with reservations in the first decade of colonial rule because the Christian values it carried challenged the values of Igbo indigenous life. Their cautious attitude gradually changed to a wider acceptance of "certain aspects" of Western education like reading, writing, and handling money.[24] The major reason for the change in attitude was because mission education prepared the individual for entry into such lucrative positions as colonial interpreters, catechists, messengers, teachers, and clerks. As would be explained below, the new opportunities for occupational mobility defined entry into the neocapitalist and neopolitical order as the indigenous society transformed. Those born in this period—as exemplified with the careers of Nnamdi Azikiwe (1904–1996), the first indigenous Governor-General of Nigeria; Sir Louis Mbanefo (1911–1977), the first lawyer from eastern Nigeria; and Chief Dennis Osadebe (1911–1995), the first Premier of Mid-Western state, and their peers—embraced mission education in order to gain employment and influence in the new colonial order.

The popular proclivity toward Western education as a ladder for social progress and the ethnicity it generated challenged the primordialist dictum that Africans think tribally and act likewise, hence the persistent crises of nation states in the continent. The evidence of this study reveals that ethnicity is an instrument for political and economic bargaining. As Anthony Enahoro, a First Republic elite figure who attended the famous King's College Lagos, recalls:

> From the moment when as "fags" we stepped within the school portals, we were informed that we now had honor of belonging to Nigeria's foremost institutions and must behave and comport ourselves and that we are the elite of Nigerian school population. We were assured that King's College (King's or K. C. for short) was the country's only public school—and the college was established to produce gentlemen of political learning. . . .[25]

Such hegemonic ideology inculcated at King's College was commonly encountered at other colonial schools. By the 1920s, official and missionary records reveal that there were 3,533 primary schools with 218,610 pupils in southern Nigeria.[26] In this period also, more Igbo young men left for locations far removed from their home environment—like Calabar, Port Harcourt, Onitsha, Enugu, Kano, and Lagos. The incentive for migration remained the quest for education, civil service employment, and business opportunities. David Abernethy underlines that the intensity of the drive for education was sharply high among the Onitsha and the Owerri Igbo.[27] Yet, the mid-1920s was remarkable as a time when a handful of adventurous Igbo young men were beginning to migrate overseas to obtain higher education because no institution of higher learning was established in their country. Dr. Nnamdi Azikiwe was one of the prominent Igbo young men who left for America in the mid-1920s for studies. His return to Nigeria in 1937 helped inspire younger people like Mbonu Ojike, Kingsley Mbadiwe, Okechukwu Ikejiani, and

Nwafor Orizu to travel overseas for university education.[28] By the late 1940s and the early 1950s, some of these adventurous men were returning home to constitute the core-educated elite and champions of African nationalism and Nigerian independence.[29]

Consumed with the enthusiasm to use their newly acquired knowledge of the wider world for the salvation of their homeland from alien domination, some of these figures quickly went into colonial or missionary service. Others who had the means either established schools or media houses and/or political parties to pressure the colonialists to effect changes in the political and economic administrations of the colony. The influence of the emergent elite would not have been very well organized and effective without their studied ability to communicate nationalist ideals and thoughts through their speeches and writing.

WRITING

Ample studies, including those by Terence Ranger and Leroy Vail, have established strong links among literacy, ethnogenesis, and the rise of ethnic identities and conflict in modern African politics.[30] These studies contend that the educated African elite were attracted to ethnic ideologies in order to garner a political base for themselves and to create ethnic models that would easily fit into the colonial notion of statehood. In a paper entitled "Missionaries, Migrants and the Manyika: The Invention of Ethnicity in Zimbabwe," Ranger painted a graphic historical picture of how the various evangelizing missions built, sustained, and entrenched tribal differences in Zimbabwe with the *introduction of writing*. The ability to write helped native sons and daughters construct local histories with such categories as "clever tribes" and less-privileged rivals as stereotypes of marginality and differentiation of groups.[31]

In relation to the Igbo, it was the British colonial scholars like G. T. Basden, P. A. Talbot, M. D. W. Jeffreys, Margaret Green, and C. K. Meek who originally assumed the task of establishing the Igbo origins as a critical element of colonial administration. As Talbot explicated in the foreword to his book, *The Peoples of Southern Nigeria*, first published in 1926, the major objective of his work was "an attempt to classify the tribes and sub-tribes and to define their boundaries."[32] Part of the clarification encompassed unraveling the puzzle of Igbo origins, understanding Igbo sociocultural institution, and harmonizing Igbo dialects into a central Igbo vernacular.

On the question of Igbo origin, although the celebrated Equiano had in 1789 argued that the Igbo were a branch of the Jews and that Christianity, which civilized barbarian Europe, was a Jewish culture, it was the colonial scholars who would popularize this externalist view and elevate it as part of the grander Hamitic literature.[33] For instance, Sir Herbert Richmond Palmer considered the religious and ritual practices of Igbo communities like the Aro and the Nri, and argued in a memo, dated 1921, that the Aro and the Nri had Hamitic blood in their veins and were therefore superior to their neighbors. The author claims that it was under their leadership that the highest character of Igbo culture evolved.[34] This form of ethnohistory is the tool of identity construction, the construction of "We" as opposed to "They," or what Benedict Anderson has described as "imagined communities."[35] Central to this is the development of a readership to the emerging form of literature.

Similarly, the Very Rev. G. T. Basden, an ethnolinguist, examined certain constructions in Igbo language and concluded that Igbos originated from Israel. Among other things, Basden argued that the Igbo word *uburu* sounds like "Hebrew," thus concluding that Igbo culture probably evolved under the influence of the Levitical Code.[36] M. D. W. Jeffreys, who specialized in Igbo ethnography and ethnohistory, also traced the origin of the Igbo to Egypt, especially when he considered characteristics of Nri-Awka part of Igboland. Jeffrey was primarily interested in the dual nature of Igbo social structure—a situation that reminds one of the divisions of ancient Egypt into upper and lower entities.[37] Future Igbo-born scholars would capitalize on this pool of Hamitic ideology to claim that the Igbo are superior to their neighbors. Such ethnohistories would lead to tensions—especially when their major rivals, the Yoruba and the Hausa, had constructed similar chauvinistic legends of origin. Both the Bayajidda (prince from Baghdad) legend of the Hausa and the Oduduwa legend among the Yoruba imagined precolonial ethnogenesis for the various groups, claiming that the forebearers of the two different groups migrated from Baghdad and Egypt, respectively.[38]

Yet one cannot understate the power of language in forging of group consciousness. From the very first beginning, the European missionaries operating in Onitsha town on the west banks of the Niger have demonstrated enthusiasm in studying the local tongue as a realistic means of communicating the Christian gospel to the Africans. Generally, the Europeans considered a vernacular Bible as crucial to the progress of Christianity; hence the Church Missionary Society (CMS) missionaries began work in earnest on several dialects with the hope of creating one generally acceptable Igbo tongue.[39] Eventually, a collaborative effort among the various Christian missions resulted in six different dialects: Isuama, Onitsha, Bonny, Unwana, Union Ibo, and the Onitsha Adapted Ibo Union.[40] Despite the enthusiasm of the CMS to propagate the Igbo vernacular as a language of classroom instruction, the government did not come out openly to support this venture until the "Joint Memorandum" of 1926 issued by the Lieutenant-Governor, S. P., and Director of Education E. R. J. Hussey.[41] Two years later, with the help of a German linguist, Professor Diedrich Hermann Westermann, a reputed authority on African languages, a plan of action was developed.

After a tour of Nigeria in 1929, Westermann recommended development of a new orthography for both Igbo and Efik as a standard for African languages.[42] Following this, a central dialect for all Igbos was adopted and in 1929 Dr. Ida Caroline Ward immediately started work on the Igbo language project at the University of London. After several tours of the Igboland and despite the influence of Onitsha dialect—thanks to a huge number of its educated elite, Dr. Ward recommended the Owerri dialect as the basis for standardization.[43] She followed this up with her book *An Introduction to the Igbo Language* published in 1936.[44]

Nonetheless, it is important to assert that while an Igbo orthography was been developed and a central Igbo dialect encouraged, most parents rather preferred that their children were educated in the English language. To most Igbo, English was the language of power. This perhaps reflected on the publication of pamphlets now known as the Onitsha Market Literature (OML) whose titles sold between three and four thousand copies. The pamphleteers, most of whom were students of mission schools, became part of the first group of Africans to write local histories of Igbo people. These native sons and daughters were writing in the 1930s when the interests of the colonial scholars and administrators were gradually declining, having unraveled the Igbo puzzle, and thus helped strengthened colonial administration. It was also in the 1930 that Nnamdi Azikiwe, then a student in America, authored his ethnohistorical essays, among them "Nigerian Political Institutions" (1929), and "Fragments of Onitsha History" (1930).[45]

All these initiatives constituted the background on which the development of an Igbo orthography and language as a marker of ethnic consciousness was sequestered. As a basis for an academic tradition, the development of Igbo orthography was continued by Igbo scholars. When Pita Nwana wrote his *Omenuko: Official Orthography Edition* in 1933, it became the first Igbo novel.[46] In 1949, F. C. Ogbalu founded the Society for Promoting of Igbo Language and Culture (SPILC) with one of its goals to continue the quest for a "Union Ibo" or "Central Igbo." The late 1940s and early 1950s coincided with the homecoming of some notable Igbo individuals who had received degrees overseas and founded media houses and/or political parties to push not only for changes in the political and economic administrations of the colony but also for decolonization. Their ideologies and visions for Nigeria were articulated and contested in the urban centers of colonial Nigeria, which served as a nursery bed for both political learning and actions.

URBANIZATION

Although not everyone living in the colonial cities was literate, the urban dwellers frequently made contact with the Europeans, gained entry into new jobs, explored new opportunities for business or trade, read newspapers, and joined ethnic-based unions, labor unions, and nationalist parties. The urban centers were the melting pots of modernity, the arenas where the fruits of the mission education impregnated inventiveness and identity consciousness. In the townships individuals from diverse cultural and ideological orientations mingled and competed for privileges and positions. The rural-urban migrants—whether Igbo, Yoruba, Urhobo, Efik, Ijo, or Ibibio—brought to the cities those aspects of their village culture, which could accommodate the challenging demands of the new environment, including the very popular lineage/improvement organizations.

Peter Ekeh has argued persuasively that under colonialism the notion of kinship was considerably expanded into the construction of ethnic groups.[47] Indeed, the Nigerian colonial cities witnessed a profusion of an expanded and complex practice of kinship belongingness. This was not limited to the Igbo alone. In their attempts to create the modern man and modern communities, ethnic unions were also established by the other groups like Calabar, Ibibio, Urhobo, Edo, and Efik—most of them with subnationalities that sponsored the overseas education of indigenous sons.[48] For example, for their overseas education, Dr. A. Esien received a scholarship from Oron Union, and Dr. E. Udoma was sponsored by the Ibibio State Union.[49]

The foremost of the Igbo lineage organizations in colonial Nigeria was founded in about 1920.[50] In the township, the smallest Igbo "lineage" was the Village Group, and this expanded fictional kinship network or "brotherhood" provided the basis for organizing group activity.[51] The lineage organizations later flowered into formal patriotic and improvement unions, eventually becoming a defining part of Igbo life and culture in the third and fourth decades of the colonial era.

For the Igbo, like their neighbors, these organizations served as forums of mobilization and communal expressions. Even though membership in the Igbo lineage/improvement unions were hypothetically voluntary, the truth is that individuals who declined to identify with kin were perceived as social and ethnic renegades.[52] For the Afikpo Association, "membership shall only be terminated by death, permanent insanity or expulsion."[53] The ethnic organizations also pressured its members to make financial contributions to community projects. By 1946, the unions had secured the colonial government's approval to collect dues and fines under the Land Perpetual Succession Ordinance. This ordinance enabled ethnic unions to provide many of the social amenities that were lacking in both the urban and local areas.[54] The colonial government encouraged and supported the growth of ethnic unionism because their activities better served the state formation theory that in the natural order of human progression, clans will give way to tribes, and that in turn to nation states. The colonial authorities welcomed the village unions as they served to facilitate the evolutionary process of nationhood.[55]

More importantly, the Igbo Unions were symbols of cultural identity in the cities where it was easy for the individual to lose his identity. For instance, the Owerri and Onitsha ethnic associations erected public halls for hosting meetings, dances, fun fairs, marriage and birth feasts, and farewell and reception ceremonies especially for newly arrived members and college graduates returning home from overseas.[56] In fact, for its cultural celebrations, an "Igbo Day" was set aside for jubilation and festivity. During the celebrations, members were awarded titles symbolic of the progress a person had made in his community. Each Igbo Improvement Union presented its dance and masquerades at this festival.[57] Such cultural programs helped the Igbo maintain their cultural heritage and develop ethnic consciousness. For politics, it would mean that the village unions would align their support for one of their kind—thus making party politics assume the nature of communal rather than individual affairs.

The ethnic unions often meddled in national politics as both pressure groups and power arbiters. For instance, between 1949 and 1957, when the authority of Oba Adele II of Lagos was challenged by the House of Docemo, the Egbe Omo Oduduwa heavily leaned toward Oba Adele. The Igbo State Union, at several instances, tried to play the role of a peacemaker in the NCNC, as was the case of the party crisis of 1952–1953, when some party officers rebelled against the authority of Dr. Azikiwe.[58] It was apparent then that the political activities of the ethnic unions were contributing to the politics of tribalism and exclusive/inclusive political culture. This was more apparent when Chief Samuel Ladoke Akintola (1910–1966), the Action Group Deputy and later Premier of Western Region in 1959 (following his party's request that he swaps post with Chief Awolowo), declared that "the aims and objectives of the Egbe and the Action Group are as inseparable as wine and water."[59] The politics of cultural pluralism ran the entire gamut of socioeconomic and political life, including the Ivory Tower. For instance, in 1965, the leadership of the University of Lagos changed hands from Dr. Eni Njoku, an Igbo, to Dr. S. O. Obiobaku, a Yoruba, thus contributing more fracture between the ethnic unions.

Thus far it has been demonstrated how the dominant visions and goals of the Igbo colonial elite, like their peers from the other groups, were shaped by their exposures to Western education and other imported institutions. The creation of Igbo ethnic history and orthography soon followed. As instruments of ethnic construction, the elite helped prepare the Igbo for group cooperation in the cities where the new socioeconomic and political opportunities were mostly available. The cities served as the arena for intergroup competition and conflict, the melting pot of modernity as determined by the spread and entrenchment of European-style neocapitalist and neopolitical systems. The new order evolved on the global stage with the Age of European Discovery from ca. 1500 to ca. 1830s. It is the socioeconomic and political culture inherent in the new world order that brought about the rise of ethnogenesis in colonial Africa.

THE NEOCAPITALIST/NEOPOLITICAL AND THE POLITICS OF ETHNIC IDENTITY AND CONFLICT

The terms *neocapitalism* and *neopolitical practices* are used here as paradigmatic tools to make a distinction between the quasi-capitalist modes of production/exchange in precolonial societies from the more sophisticated and often criminalized version that evolved with the ascension of European dominance on the global stage. Neocapitalism thus defines the structures of the modern state system founded on imperial culture of domination, extraction, big business, big government, and nationalist thinking. The new system that breeds social discontents and conflicts redefined the concepts of nobles and peasants, masters and servants, and rich and poor and entrenched inequalities among individuals and nations. Africa was gradually being integrated into the emergent world system until the era of colonial rule when the pace of integration hastened and was institutionalized through Western education, urbanization, foreign travels, international trade networks, and informal agencies of socialization such as the news media, family networks, political parties, and peer and religious groups. As the activities of the African urban dwellers would reveal, in the emergent system, individuals and states are driven by a ravenous quest for wealth, power, luxury, titles, and all that these entail. It is therefore normal that competitions for neocapitalist indulgences are rife with conflicts along individual/group interests. Chief Obafemi Awolowo, a maverick Yoruba politician summed it up in 1968 with his association of the system with greed, selfishness, or naked self-interest, concluding that "the system is bound to generate secular social disequilibrium in the society."[60]

Chief Awolowo was both a key player and observer in the Nigerian political setting from the 1940s to the period of Civil War (1967–1970), when the aspirations of African nationalism he had espoused along with his peers exploded into a deadly conflict. Awolowo's comments, although inspired by Marxism, capture the contexts in which new ideas and new ways of doing things transformed intra-ethnic and interethnic relations in colonial Nigeria. The modern world system would, in this context, define a long period of transition in which the usual mechanisms of reward within a social system proved so ineffective from the point of view of so many important social actors that a major restructuring of the economy and structures of power begins to occur.[61]

The gradual but consistent constitutional changes from the interwar years are typical of responses to the exertions of the neocapitalism/neopolitical restructuring/transitional phase in Nigerian/African politics, while new actors like the African educated elite positioned themselves as stakeholders. The Nigerian Youth Movement (NYM) (formerly the Lagos Youth Movement), founded in 1937, is typical of the new stakeholders' preparations. The movement provided an umbrella under which the emergent elite articulated their political interests. Until 1937, no Igbo politician was visible in national politics dominated by the Saros resident in Lagos and the Yoruba educated elite. Dr. Azikiwe's emergence in the mid-1930s would transform the political scenario, tilting the balance on the side of the Igbo.[62]

The NYM broke up in 1941 after some altercations between Dr. Azikiwe and Chief Awolowo over Chief Samuel Akinsanya (Azikiwe's loyalist) and Ernest Okoli (Awolowo's henchman). Following the 1944–1947 constitutional changes, under Sir Arthur Richards, a major opening was created through which the emergent nationalist leaders announced their presence on national politics. It was also over this period in 1946 that Azikiwe became the national president of the Igbo State Union. The National Council of Nigeria and Cameroon (NCNC), launched in 1944 under the leadership of Herbert Macaulay and Azikiwe as President and Secretary, respectively, soon became the most popular nationalist party.[63] The party used the *West African Pilot* and the *Comet* newspapers owned by Azikiwe as its house organs.[64] In a statement that appeared in the *West African Pilot* in 1949, and perceived by his rivals as controversial, Azikiwe urged the Igbo not to shy away from the leadership responsibility of the region.[65] Commenting on the advantages these tabloids conferred on the owners, Enahoro stated that "Dr. Azikiwe appeared to possess the advantage of being his own master as well as being better equipped professionally, more popular and colorful and more responsive to the mood and temper of the time than his rivals."[66] Here we see the strength of Western education, writing, and the power of discourse as instruments of hegemonic construction.

The Egbe Omo Oduduwa, a Yoruba cultural association, was launched by Chief Awolowo and his allies in London in 1945.[67] The Egbe was imported to Nigeria in 1948, first as a counter hegemonic association opposed to the Igbo State Union. When the Egbe was transformed and officially named the Action Group (AG) party in 1951, it became the staunchest rival to the NCNC.[68] The *Daily Service* newspaper, edited by Ernest Okoli, served as AG's mouthpiece. Early in 1944, the *Daily Service* predicted "an era of wholesome rivalry among the principal tribes of Nigeria [Hausa, Yoruba, and Ibo]."[69] In a direct declaration of what he saw as the Yoruba role in Nigerian politics, Sir Adeyemo Alakija, the president of the Egbe, aptly predicted in 1948 that "The big tomorrow is the future of our children. . . . How they will hold their own among other tribes of Nigeria. . . . How the Yorubas will not be relegated to the background in the future."[70]

The recent developments were followed by the formation of the Northern People's Congress (NPC) as the political party of the Northern Region following the promulgation of the Macpherson Constitution in 1951. The stated motto of the NPC was "One north, one people, irrespective of region, rank or tribe."[71] Three years earlier, the Hausa-Fulani leaders had openly voiced their apprehension over the likely domination of the north by the more educated Christian south, comprising the East and West. Abubakar Tafawa Balewa, who later became the first Prime Minister of independent Nigeria, expressed concern over the migration to the north of educated southerners, whose presence threatened to displace northerners in the colonial civil service.[72] Because southerners had more Western-educated people, the editor of the *Gaskiya Ta Fi Kwabo* newspaper warned in an article published in February 1950 that if the British granted Nigeria early independence, the southerners would take the places of Europeans in the North:

> It is the Southerner who has the power in the north. They have control of the railway stations; of the Post Offices; of Government Hospitals; of the canteens; the majority employed in the Kaduna Secretariat and in the Public Works Department are all Southerners.[73]

Prior to 1951, the northern political elite had been relatively quiet on national politics apparently because of the paucity of university graduates of northern origin. As the drive for independence increased, however, the north began to position itself in order to challenge the political clots of the Igbo and Yoruba. The leader of NPC was the same as the spiritual leader of the Hausa-Fulani, the Sarduana of Sokoto Alhaji Ahmadu Bello. While the goal of the NPC was the attainment of self-government for Nigeria and the introduction of a permanent federal constitution, it aimed to study and preserve their cultures and carry out reforms to make them capable of meeting modern conditions. The NPC also aimed to educate the northerners to accept the leadership of the NPC and to support its candidates for elections to the regional legislatures and to local councils. It also planned the nurturing of minds of the northerners in a genuine love for the region and all that is northern, and a special reverence for religion, law and order, and the preservation of customs and traditions.[74]

It is noteworthy that the institutionalization of ethnic hegemonies and counterhegemonies in forms of political parties were taking place in the 1950s when more Igbo migrants (civil servants, businessmen, and other professionals, and their families) were expanding into other parts of Nigeria, particularly Lagos, Kano, Jos, and other regions. It was not a mere coincidence therefore that the first major acts of violence against the Igbo communities in the Northern Region were occurring at this time. Although an anti-Igbo riot had flared up earlier on in Jos in 1945, the riot that began on May 8, 1953, in the northern city of Kano was revealing in the sense that the Igbo had little or nothing to do with the cause of northern anger. The trouble started on the floors of the Federal House of Representatives in Lagos where Chief Enahoro had moved a motion for Nigeria's independence in 1956. The northern leaders opposed the motion with the argument that the country was not yet ready for independence.[75] After one of the sessions, Alhaji Bello, the leader of the northern delegation, was booed as he was leaving the Federal House by the Lagos press corps who were outraged by the Alhaji Bello-led opposition to the proposal for independence in 1956. This act of disrespect for the northern leader drew the anger of northern citizens who had spoken against the British amalgamation of the Northern and Southern Protectorates in 1914. Thus, when Chief S. L. A. Akintola embarked on an ill-advised tour of Kano in May to address the crowd on the matter, word had already spread concerning the treatment of the northern Premier by the southerners—the most visible in Kano being the Igbo.

The bloody riot of 1953 revealed that the difficult task of getting the three diverse regions to work harmoniously in any closely knit federation. It thus became necessary to revisit the Macpherson Constitution in order to make provisions for greater regional autonomy; larger and more representative legislatures with wider powers in the regions and at the center emerged.[76] The revised constitution made provisions for a Council of Ministers comprising eighteen members: twelve Nigerians and six official members. The Council of Ministers had equal representation from each region and the nomination of members was done by the regional legislatures. Also, a House of Representatives with 142 members was created. Nigerians occupied 136 seats. At the regional level, the House of Assembly continued in each region with a House of Chiefs in the Northern and Western Regions. The power to make laws (subject to reference to the governor) on a limited number of subjects, mainly to do with local matters, resided with the regional legislatures.[77]

The impact of the constitution on the political development of the country cannot be overemphasized. One was the entrenchment of ethnic politics, with the emphasis placed on regional politics by the constitution. While the AG and NPC represented Western and

Northern Regional interests, respectively, the NCNC, in spite of its nationalist pretensions, tended toward the Eastern Region. Its operation was obviously affected by the activities of it rivals. In the subsequent election held under the new constitution, the NCNC won a majority of seats in the east, while the AG and the NPC won similarly in the west and north, respectively.[78] This showed that ethnic politics had taken the center stage in the evolution of Nigeria's political order.

Another result of the 1953 riots that impacted the new constitution is that the north wanted the central government to deal with foreign affairs and customs—meaning that such matters as defense and parastatals should be regionalized. The London conference of July 1953, which was convened to find a solution to the crisis, reached the following agreements. Nigeria should have a federal constitution, that is, one in which certain specific powers would reside with the federal government, while all others not specifically allowed to the center (residual powers) would become the prerogative of the regions. There were also specific concurrent powers, shared by the center and the regions.[79] The issue of self-government was left flexible, with the understanding that any region that so wished could have it in 1956, provided that the self-governing region would not attempt to undermine the federal system. The question of total independence in 1956 was set aside to the relief of the northern delegation.[80] The conference, which continued in Lagos in 1954, also resolved issues on Lagos as a federal territory and that on revenue allocation.

These conferences resulted in the Lyttleton Constitution of 1954. The landmark of the new constitution was that it marked the inauguration of a truly federal structure in Nigeria's political development. The constitution also stipulated that members of the national legislature were to come through direct election, with the exclusion of the north. Another significant resolution of the constitution was that the leader of the majority party in any of the Houses should head the government. The individual would have the responsibility to recommend those to be considered for ministerial posts by the governor—the representative of the British Crown.[81]

DECOLONIZATION AND THE ENTRENCHMENT OF ETHNIC POLITICS

The ongoing structural, demographic, and sociopolitical changes prior to independence present an ample setting for assessing the problems of identity and ethnicity in Nigeria. As Coleman notes, by the early 1950s, the population of Igbos in Lagos increased from 264 to 26,000. In the Northern Provinces there were fewer than three thousand Igbos in 1921, but by 1951 the number had increased to more than one hundred twenty thousand.[82] These figures become more meaningful when it is realized that most of the Igbo immigrants were attracted by the availability of wage employment and trading opportunities in the urban centers. Actually by 1946, Igbo clerks, artisans, traders, and laborers constituted a sizable minority group in every urban center of Nigeria and the British Cameroons. The demographic changes in the ethnic structure of the various regions came with its social problems to the immigrants, the host communities, and the political system.

Azikiwe's leadership of the Igbo State Union from 1948 to 1952 became a topic of controversy because one of his arch rivals, Chief Awolowo, perceived his speeches and writings within the organization as attempts to consolidate Igbo hegemony in Nigeria. Calling Azikiwe "an unabashed Ibo jingoist" in his autobiography published in1960, Awolowo paraphrased and distorted Azikiwe's address to the Igbo Union in 1949 in order to score some political points.

> It would appear that the God of Africa has specially created the Ibo to lead the children of Africa from the bondage of the ages. . . . The marital prowess of the Ibo nation at all stages of human history has enabled them not only to conquer others but also to adapt themselves to the role preserver. . . . The Igbo nation cannot shirk its responsibility.[83]

A closer read of the original speech by Dr. Azikiwe reveals that Chief Awolowo purposely distorted the speech by adding phrases that completely took Azikiwe's intentions out of context. The relevant section of the original speech of June 25, 1949, by Azikiwe reads as follows: "It would appear that God has specially created the Ibo people to suffer persecution and to be victimized because of their resolute will to live. Since suffering is the label of our tribe, we can afford to be sacrificed for the ultimate redemption of the children of Africa."[84] In the same paragraph is found the exact words and context of Azikiwe's speech directed to the British colonial authorities and the humiliating colonial policies against the Igbo. But "instead," Azikiwe continued, "there is a record to show that the marital prowess of the Ibo, at all stages of human history, has enabled them not only to survive persecution, but to adapt themselves to the role thus entrusted upon them by history, of preserving all that and most noble in African culture and tradition."[85] Chief Awolowo substituted these lines with these inflammatory lines: "*the marital prowess of the Ibo nation at all stages of human history has enabled them not only to conquer others but also to adapt themselves to the role preserver. . . . The Igbo nation cannot shirk its responsibility. . . .*"[86]

As the evidence shows, the theme, context, and intentions of Azikiwe's 1949 speech, cited by Awolowo as a proof of Igbo designs for hegemonic control, were invented by the Yoruba politician. Chief Awolowo further charged that

> It was clear from [those] statements and from the general political and journalistic manoeuvres [*sic*] of Dr. Azikiwe over the years that his great objectives was to set himself up as a dictator over Nigeria and to make the Ibo nation the master race. It would appear according to his reckoning that the only obstacle in the path of his ambition was the Yoruba intelligentsia, and these must be removed.[87]

Even though Azikiwe denied these charges and considered them a personal threat to his person, the Igbo Union declared that any threat to Azikiwe was a threat to the entire Igbo group and that the Union stood to his defense. The concern here is not to dwell more on these charges but to note that similar perceptions that demonized the Igbo as colonialists, arrogant, aggressive, and greedy emerged from a culture of stereotyping with the active participation of the British colonial officials. As Azikiwe had underscored in the same controversial 1949 address, "Socially, the British has not been sparing in describing us as 'the most hated in Nigeria.' In this unholy crusade, the *Daily Mirror*, *The Times*, *The Economist*, *News Review* and the *Daily Times* have been in the forefront. . . . Needless to say that today, both in England and in West Africa, the expression 'Ibo' has become a word of opprobrium."[88]

From this period on, the political ambition of the Igbo elite was dogged by the rise of a more aggressive counterhegemonic ethnic consciousness and exclusive political linings. The immediate manifestation of this trend was felt in the 1953 elections in Lagos, the federal capital city whose politics was first perceived by the nationalists as a "No Man's Land," and a model of truly national political community whose residents were drawn from different parts of the country. Although located in Yoruba territory previously, politics of the city of Lagos were dominated by the better organized NCNC led by Dr. Azikiwe. With the rise of rival political parties, the NCNC came to be regarded as an Igbo party simply because Azikiwe was an Igbo. The truth is that there were some high-ranking non-Igbo politicians like H. O. Davis who shared the aspiration that the multiethnic and cosmopolitan reputation of Lagos and its pluralistic politics should be preserved. Davis had expressed his belief in an article in the *Daily Times* of January 18, 1950, that "it will be a pity if the genius of the country is stultified by narrow representation of Lagos in the Western Region."[89]

But Chief Awolowo did not share this sentiment. The politics of Lagos (and indeed the Western Region) was dominated by the NCNC, and Awolowo was bent on breaking that influence. He criticized his comrades and rivals who considered Lagos a neutral territory, objecting to the view that "only those who lived within its confines should essay [*sic*] to lead the country."[90] Awolowo campaigned seriously to abrogate the Lagos Town Council (LTC) system even though he was not a Lagos resident. Eventually the LTC was dissolved, and the city capital was merged with the Western Region in 1953 under the Macpherson Constitution.[91]

As a result of the dissolution of the LTC, which had elected Mbonu Ojike, an Igbo, its deputy mayor in 1950, and the Azikiwe's loses in the Western Region's elections, the Igbo elite were momentarily forced to shift their political base from Lagos to the Eastern Regional Government headquarters in Enugu. The Eastern Regional House soon became an arena for individual and group rivalry and the struggle for power and resource control in the east. The major protagonists in the east were in the NCNC led by Dr. Azikiwe versus Ikoku's National Independent Party (NIP) and Eyo Ita's National Democratic Party (NDP).[92] The bone of contention was the removal of Professor Eyo Ita as leader of Government Business in order to make way for Azikiwe in Eastern Region's leadership. The crisis in the Eastern Region continued up to the eve of independence, even after Dr. Azikiwe and some of his cohorts had returned to the federal level in 1957. The truth is that the Azikiwe-Ita conflict affected the relationship between the Igbo and the Eastern Region's minorities.

THE ROAD TO INDEPENDENCE AND AFTER, 1957–1967

Another constitutional conference in 1957 struggled to strengthen out some knotty issues surrounding self-rule in a postcolonial government. While the Western and Eastern Regions opted for 1957 as date for self-rule, the North opted for 1959. The delegates at the conference also agreed that in each of the self-governing regions, there would also be a premier or leader of government business who would preside over an all-African cabinet chosen by him. The ministers in both the regions and the center would be directly responsible to their respective legislatures. The conference further agreed that there would be a coalition government if the necessity were to arise. In the prevailing spirit of national unity, it was unanimously agreed that the Prime Minister under the new constitution would form a government with ministers from the entire three main political parties—NPC, NCNC, and AG. Universal adult suffrage was also agreed on, except that it was not extended to women in the North. This was to respect the Islamic injunctions with regard to women's participation in politics.

While the big three ethnic groups dominated political activities in the various regions, there was no concerted efforts to meet the political demands of the minority groups scattered across the various regions. With the prospects for independence getting brighter, the minorities in the various regions increased their agitation for separate autonomy within the federal system. As stated in the Willink Commission's Report of 1957–1958, "The movement for a Rivers State began after the constitutional conference of 1953, when the Council of Rivers Chiefs prepared a memorandum for the resumed conference of 1954; as in the case of the COR State."[93] To the minorities, the influences of the three major groups were overbearing and suffocating. After a commission under a British Judge, Sir Henry Willink, was set up to look at the problem, the report of the commission was reviewed at the 1958 constitutional conference.[94] The AG and NCNC, both of which asked for the breaking up of Nigeria into more subunits for a more realistic federal system, reluctantly accepted the Willink Commission's recommendation that the Niger Delta area (part of the proposed and anticipated Calabar-Ogoja-Rivers, or COR, state) be designated a "special area" to make sure it was not ignored.[95] The North totally opposed the idea of more states. The British authorities, however, considered the creation of new substates at that point in time could delay the handover date for self-rule, since these new states would have to be adequately set up before independence for the entire country would be granted. On this ground, it was taken for granted that the fears of the minorities would be more conveniently addressed by writing the fundamental human rights listed by the commission in the new Nigerian constitution. It was, however, unfortunate that the minority issue could not be properly tackled before Nigeria's independence in 1960 because the problem resurfaced soon after independence and would contribute to the demise of the First Republic.[96]

Given the spirit of compromise demonstrated on various issues raised at the 1957 and 1958 conferences by Nigerian politicians, the British were obliged to grant total political authority to what they considered mature leaders. The reassurance was the agreement of the three major political parties to form a national government under Sir Tafawa Balewa. In December 1959, federal elections to an enlarged House of Representatives were held. Also, members of a new senate were appointed. The results of the 1959 federal elections saw none of the parties winning an absolute majority to gain control of the House of Representatives. A coalition government between the NPC and the NCNC was arranged. The NPC, which polled the highest vote in the elections, became the senior partner in the coalition. The parties came to an agreement that Alhaji Tafawa Balewa of NPC should become the Prime Minister while Dr. Nnamdi Azikiwe, leader of the NCNC, became President of the Senate. The AG under Chief Awolowo's leadership chose to be on the opposition side.[97]

With independence on October 1, 1960, Dr. Azikiwe first served as senate president and eventually succeeded Sir James Robertson as the first indigenous Governor-General of the federation and its new head of state from October 1, 1963. Dr. Azikiwe assumed the title of President and Sir Balewa remained Prime Minister.[98]

Nigeria's First Republic triregional federal system left the minorities feeling uncomfortable. Consequently, minorities' demands for separate government became popular all over the country. In 1963–1964, the minorities in western Nigeria were granted a separate region (Mid-Western Region), thereby increasing the number of regions to four. The small concession failed to placate the increasing minorities' protestations against majority domination. Making the situation worse was the fact that the big ethnic groups (Hausa-Fulani, Igbo, and Yoruba) fought among themselves for the control of the center. Through their policies and actions, the alliance government between the NPC and the NCNC demonstrated intolerance toward the opposition party, the Action Group. In response, politics in the Western Region soon became a serious source of threat to national unity. On January 15, 1966, the first military coup stopped the obvious breakdown of law and order in the country.

The period following the demise of the First Republic was the most trying period in Nigeria's political history, in which the country faced numerous problems. The execution of the January coup left a dangerous impression that its leaders, mainly from the Igbo tribe, were out to exterminate the Hausa-Fulani-led First Republic government in order to establish Igbo political ascendancy. This suspicion arose from the fact that while prominent politicians and top military officers of northern origin in the First Republic were killed during the coup, those from the east escaped unhurt.[99] Hausa-Fulani and Igbo differences worsened when the succeeding Igbo-led military government hurriedly adopted a unitary system of government as a substitute for the preexisting federal structure. A unitary system meant free competition for the available opportunities in the country—a system in which the northerners were at a disadvantage, given their poor level of (Western) education then. Federalism guaranteed separate educational and employment policies for each region. According to Claude Phillips, while the import of the coup left the impression among most other ethnic groups that "the Igbo has gained everything and lost nothing,"[100] Decree No. 34, which abolished the federal system instituting a single system of public administration, helped raise these suspicions.[101] The North therefore threatened to secede from the federation.

A counter *coup d'etat* in July 1966 was followed by several months of mutinies against Igbo officers across the country. Civilian casualties recorded about fifty thousand, as the North prepared to proclaim "The Republic of the North."[102] Hostilities in the North spread to other ethnic groups of eastern origin, hence Colonel Emeka Ojukwu, the Eastern Region's military governor, had to ask all non-Easterners to leave the region, since their safety could no longer be guaranteed following reported cases of revenge in that region.[103]

Northern leaders, however, reconsidered the bid for secession because of two major economic considerations: (1) the pursuance of secession would amount to self-denial of access to the strategic southern seas, and (2) the region would be cut off from the promising new oil wealth in the Southeast.[104] Desperate efforts to stave off war included an Ad Hoc Constitutional Review Conference (in September 1966), during which the East insisted on the inclusion of the right to secede in the constitution, and the Aburi talks in January 1967 at the behest of Ghana's military leader General Ankara—but all failed.[105] On May 27, 1967, the federal government partitioned the four regions in Nigeria into twelve substates in order to destabilize Biafra's cohesion.[106] The East was carved into three substates. Apart from granting eastern minorities a long-sought autonomy, Port Harcourt, a predominantly Igbo city, was left outside the Igbo state. To the Igbo, this decision was considered an open challenge to secede.[107] Col. Ojukwu proclaimed his Biafran nation on May 30, 1967. On July 6, 1967, federal troops began a campaign to stop Biafra.[108] The rebellion eventually took the armed forces thirty months to overcome, leaving in its wake more doubts over Nigeria's oneness.

POST–CIVIL WAR NIGERIA AND THE IGBO

Particularly under the military regime of Gen. Yakubu Gowon, who was overthrown in 1975, post–Civil War Nigeria has seen efforts aimed at strengthening the basis of unity in the federal system. To his credit, Gowon promoted a program of reconstruction and national unity that went a long way toward mending some of the wounds of the Civil War. Since the 1980s, Nigeria has expanded the number of its substates from twelve to thirty-six in order to ameliorate the fear of domination of one group by another and to provide the opportunity for full realization of the political, economic, and social growth of each state and to bring government nearer to the people, and to minimize conflicts between states and within states.[109]

Despite these initiatives, the overall effort at political reintegration of the Igbos has been undermined by the climate of suspicion and fear of a potential rise of Igbo political power. The Igbo have tried unsuccessfully to bid for the presidency since the end of the Civil War but the other groups appear not to be impressed with this ambition. At the center of the crisis is the problem of structure and stereotyping. According to Barrington Moore, the nature of interaction between groups in society, that is, the whole social groups and primarily "structures of power," explains democratization processes.[110] Structures of power could be seen as the particular interrelationships of certain structures—economic, social, and political—as they gradually change through history, providing constraints and opportunities that drive political elite along a historical trajectory. The stereotyping of the Igbo as aggressive, dangerous, and so on, mostly favor the Hausa-Fulani and the Yoruba—thus entrenching an imbalance in both the ethnic and class structures of power. There is little likelihood that other ethnic groups would support the Igbo demand for federal control any time soon. Generally viewed as colonialists, the Igbo appear as the most resented group in Nigeria. Arthur Nwankwo puts it succinctly when he contends that Nigerians of all other groups will probably achieve consensus on no other matter than their common resentment of the Igbo.[111] Yet, unless the vilification and marginalization of the Igbo ends, Nigerian politics will continue to be troubled by alliance-making and suicidal institutional sabotages that have been the bane of the previous administrations.

This chapter focused on the dynamics of Igbo identity formation in colonial Nigeria and how this was shaped by the entrance of Western education, colonial administration, and the propensity for power and domination. Colonial rule introduced the Igbo and their neighbors to the new neopolitical and neocapitalist order of domination and exploitation. The attractions of socioeconomic self-interests turned out to be the markers of difference and forces of identification and stereotyping between groups and individuals. Indeed, modern manifestations and character of ethnicity were more or less the direct reflection of the new dynamics of categories introduced by the imperial agents in Africa. By contextualizing this paper in the idiom of the invention paradigm, I have resist the temptation to allow it to get in the way of a fully historical treatment of colonial hegemony and of a fully historical treatment of the African participation and initiative in innovating customs. The Igbo developed their consciousness in contexts that were imagined, invented, imposed, and also appropriated. In other words, the process of ethnicization was characterized by active and tacit involvement of local actors for specific individual and group advantages. Among these actors were the educated elite, hence Anthony Smith contends that nationalism is articulated through appeal to local history and culture. The argument goes that once this appeal is successfully packaged and magnified, images of national history and cultural emblems have strong potentials for developing into ethnic consciousness and separatist agitations.[112] This exemplar tends to accentuate the role of the educated elite to the rise of ethnic consciousness. The elite approach to interpreting ethnic consciousness is controversial because it denies agency to subaltern groups and simplifies both the processes of national consciousness and the dynamics of neocapitalism as the function of elite whims and caprices. One would rather argue that both elite and subaltern roles are critical in the construction of ethnic or national consciousness. Thus, combining subaltern and elite roles in the process of identity formation and ethnic mobilization, as demonstrated here, produced a richer perspective on the making of Igbo ethnicity in the colonial Nigerian setting.

NOTES

I owe a lot of gratitude to Professor Emeritus Michael Vickers and Professor Ogechi Anyanwu who kindly read the first drafts of this paper and provided crucial perspectives.

1. Daryll Cyril Forde and G. I. Jones, *The Ibo and Ibibio-speaking Peoples of South-Eastern Nigeria* (London: The International African Institute, 1950).

2. Ibid., 10, 28–57.

3. See Nigerian National Archives Kaduna (hereafter NNAK), File No. 15911 vol. 1, Tribes of Nigeria (i) Inter-Relations (ii) Arochukwu, Jukun, etc.; and National Archives Ibadan (hereafter NNAI), CSO 26/240, File No. 29380, Milne Report on Ogboli Group of Nsukka Division (n.d.).

4. Forde and Jones, *Ibo and Ibibio-speaking Peoples*, 4.

5. James S. Coleman, *Nigeria: Background to Nationalism* (Berkeley: University of California Press, 1958), 340.

6. Nigerian National Archives Enugu (hereafter NNAE), C 632, RIVPROF 2/1/87, Activities of Village Unions (1947); C 633, RIVPROF 2/1/87, Native Authorities and clan unions (1947).

7. NNAE, OP 3029, ONDIST 12/1/2094, Ibo State Union matters affecting (1949).

8. Elizabeth Isichei, *A History of the Igbo People* (New York: St. Martin's Press, 1976): 19–20.

9. Olaudah Equiano, *The Interesting Narrative of Olaudah Equiano, or Gustavus Vassa, the African, Written by Himself*, vol. I (London: Author, 1789), 5, 43.

10. Rev. Joseph Horsfield Kummer, "Archibald John Monteath: Native Helper and Assistant in the Jamaica Mission at New Carmel," *Transactions of the Monrovian Historical Society* 21, no. 1 (1966): 29–51.

11. Duarte Pacheco Pereira, *Esmeraldo de situ orbis (edicao de Raphael Eduardo de Azevado Basto)* (Lisbon: National Press, 1892), 72–84; and John [Jean] Barbot, "Mr. John Grazilhier's Voyage from Bandy to New Calabar," in *A Collection of Voyages and Travels*, ed. Awnsham Churchill (London: Churchills, 1746): 5:380–81.

12. This argument has propped up in academic circles such as the Igbo Studies Association Meeting, Howard University, Washington, DC, April 2–3, 2004; and the African Studies Association Meeting, San Francisco, CA, November 16–19, 2006.

13. John Reader, *Africa: A Biography of a Continent* (New York: Alfred A. Knopf, 1997), 615.

14. See A. E. Afigbo, *The Age of Innocence: The Igbo and their Neighbors in Precolonial*

Times: Ahiajioku Lectures 1981 (Owerri, NG: Ministry of Information and Culture, 1981), 346; *Ropes of Sand: Studies in Igbo History and Culture* (Nsukka, NG: UNN and Oxford University Press, 1981), esp. chaps. 2 and 3; and "Igbo Origins and Migration," in *Groundwork of Igbo History*, ed. A. E. Afigbo (Lagos, NG: Vista Books, 1992), 21–23.

15. Raphael Chijioke Njoku, *African Cultural Values: Igbo Political Leadership in Colonial Nigeria* (New York: Routledge, 2006), 18.

16. NNAE, File No. AD 635 vol. I ARODIV 3/1/55, Aro Confederation Report by H. F. Mathews (1945); Aro Origin and the Basis of Widespread Aro Influence (1927); ARODIV 20/1/15, Aro Sub-tribe (1947). See also NNAK, 15911; and NNAI, CSO 26/240.

17. See Forde and Jones, *Ibo and Ibibio-speaking Peoples*, 9.

18. James Africanus Horton, *West African Countries and Peoples* (1868; repr., Edinburgh: Edinburgh University Press, 1969), 172–75.

19. Christopher Fyfe, *Africanus Horton: 1830–1883: West African Scientist and Patriot* (London: Ashgate, 1993), 49–50, 79–80; Ahanotu, "Igbo Union," 173.

20. William Balfour Baikie, *Narrative of an Exploring Voyage Up to the Rivers Kuora and Binue: Commonly Known as the Niger and Tsadda in 1854* (1856; repr., London: Routledge, 1966), 51–2; 307; Isichei, *Igbo People*, 20.

21. NNAE, 805, BRASDIST 10/1/169, Cooperation between the colonial Administration in Africa and the Missionary Bodies (1947).

22. See Dalhousie University Library, C. A2/065, Yoruba Mission (microfiche reel 73): Letters, Journals and Reports of Rev. Thomas Babington Macaulay (1852–77).

23. C.M.S. G3/A3/0, S. R. Smith, Annual Letter (Dec. 7, 1912); C.M.S. G3/A3/0, J. Cheetham's Annual Letter (Dec. 5, 1911); C.M.S. C.A. 3/037, Taylor's Journal Entry for June 25, 1863 (1863).

24. For an engaging discussion on this, see Elizabeth Isichei, "Seven Varieties of Ambiguity: Some Patterns of IGBO response to Christian Missions," *Journal of Religion in Africa* 3, no. 2 (1970): 209–27; and David Abernethy, *The Dilemma of Popular Education* (Stanford, CA: Stanford University Press, 1969), 62.

25. Anthony Enahoro, *Fugitive Offender* (London: The Camelot Press, 1965), 52.

26. See Abernethy, *Education*, 62; and P. Amaury Talbot, *The Peoples of Southern Nigeria* (1926; repr., London: Frank Cass, 1969), iv, 9–10, 100–108.

27. Abernethy, *Education*, 62. For a similar comment, see Bishop Shanahan, cited in *John P. Jordan, Bishop Shanahan of Southern Nigeria* (1942; repr., Onitsha, NG: Elo Press, 1971), 82.

28. See Nnamdi Azikiwe, *My Odyssey: An Autobiography* (1970; repr., Ibadan, NG: Spectrum Books, 1999), 53–77.

29. See *West African Pilot* (Lagos) (hereafter *WAP*), January 16, 1947; *WAP*, January 20, 1947; *WAP*, July 15, 1955 (front page article); and *WAP*, February 26, 1948.

30. Terence Ranger, "The Invention of Tradition in Colonial Africa," in *The Invention of Tradition*, ed. Terence Ranger and E. Hobsbawn (Cambridge: Cambridge University Press, 1983), 211–62; Terence Ranger, "The Invention of Tradition Revisited: The Case of Colonial Africa," in *Legitimacy and State in Twentieth-Century Africa: Essays in Honour of A.H.M. Kirk-Greene*, ed. Terence Ranger and Olufemi Vaughan (London: Macmillan, 1993), 62–111; and Leroy Vail, ed., *The Creation of Tribalism in Africa* (Berkeley: University of California Press, 1989), 1–20.

31. Ranger, "Missionaries, Migrants and the Manyike," 118.

32. Talbot, *Peoples of Southern Nigeria*, vi.

33. Equiano, *Interesting Narrative*, 30–40.

34. NNAE, Palmer, H. R. ARODIST 1/7/33, Aro People (Memo dated 1/5/21 by Palmer H. R.).

35. See Benedict Anderson, *Imagined Communities. Reflections on the Origin and Spread of Nationalism* (1983; rev. ed., London: Verso, 2006).

36. G. T. Basden, "Notes on the Ibo Country and Ibo People of Southern Nigeria," *The Geographical Journal* 39 (1912): 241–47; *Among the Ibos of Nigeria: A Description of the Primitive Life, Customs and Animistic Beliefs of the Igbo People of Nigeria* (1921; repr., London: Frank Cass, 1966), see particularly 212–22.

37. NNAE, EP.8766 Vol. II; CSE 1/85/4596A; CSE 1/85/228, M. D. W. Jeffreys, Awka Division Anthropological Report (1931). See also M. D. W. Jeffreys, "Ibo Warfare," *Man* 56 (1956): 77–79.

38. See, for example, Samuel Johnson, *The History of the Yoruba, from the Earliest Times to the Beginning of the British Protectorate*, ed. D. O. Johnson (1921; repr., London: Routledge and Kegan Paul, 1966).

39. As a common issue, in 1897, for instance, *The Lagos Weekly Record* of June 5, 1897, had called on the Henry Carr, the Inspector of Schools, to promote vernaculars as mediums of classroom instructions.

40. Dmitri van den Bersselaar, "Creating 'Union Igbo': Missionaries and the Igbo Language," *Africa* 67, no. 2 (1977): 273–95. See also Dmitri van den Bersselaar, "The Language of Igbo Ethnic Nationalism," *Language Problems and Language Planning* 24, no. 3 (2000): 125.

41. NNAI, CSO 2616303, A Joint Memorandum by the Lieutenant-Governor, S. P., and the Director of Education, S. P., January 1926.

42. National Archives Kew, CO 583 166/582, Annual Report on the Education Departments, Northern Provinces and Colony and Southern provinces for the Year 1928 (Lagos, 1929); NAE, OG 903, OGPROF 2/1/353, Phonetic Orthography (1931–1952).

43. NNAE, OB 853, OBUBDIST 4/1/349, Native languages and Dialects (1949–1950); OG 903, OGPROF 2/1/353, Phonetic Orthography (1931–1952); OP2348, ONDIST 12/1/2348, Igbo Dialect—report by Mrs. Ida Ward.

44. Ida Caroline Ward, *An Introduction to the Ibo Language* (Cambridge: Heffer and Sons, 1936), xi, 7; Ida C. Ward, "A Linguistic Tour in Southern Nigeria," *Africa* 8, no. 1 (1935): 90–97.

45. Ben A. Azikiwe, "Nigerian Political Institutions," *The Journal of Negro History* 14, no. 3 (1929): 328–40; Fragments of Onitsha History," *The Journal of Negro History* 15, no. 4 (1930): 474–97.

46. Pita Nwana, *Omenuko: Official Orthography Edition* (1933; repr., Ikeja, NG: Longman, 1963).

47. Peter P. Ekeh, "Colonialism and the Two Publics in Africa: A Theoretical Statement," *Comparative Studies in Society and History* 17 (1975): 91–112.

48. NNAE, C 632, RIVPROF 2/1/87, Activities of Village Unions (1947); C 633, RIVPROF 2/1/87, Native Authorities and clan unions.

49. J. S. B. Ikpe, "Ibibio Union 1928–1938 Anniversary Celebration 28 April, 1928, Uyo, 1928. See also NAE, 6385, PHDIST 7/1/87, Ibibio Union: Matters relating to (1947). Austin M. Ahanotu, "The Role of Ethnic Unions in the Development of Southern Nigeria: 1916–66," in *Studies in Southern Nigerian History*, ed. B. I. Obichere (London: Frank Cass, 1982), 163–64.

50. Ahanotu, "Ethnic Unions," 156.

51. See Eghosa E. Osaghae, *Trends in Migrant Political Organizations in Nigeria: The Igbo Union in Kano* (Ibadan, NG: IFRA, 1994); and Audrey C. Smock, *Ibo Politics: The Role of Ethnic Unions in Eastern Nigeria* (Cambridge, MA: Harvard University Press, 1971).

52. NNAE, C 632, RIVPROF 2/1/87, Activities of Village Unions (1947); C 633, RIVPROF 2/1/87, Native Authorities and clan unions.

53. *Afikpo Town Welfare Association Constitution, March 20, 1950* (Afikpo, 1952), 14–15.

54. For details, see NAE, C 632, RIVPROF 2/1/87, Activities of Village Unions (1947); and C 633, RIVPROF 2/1/87, Native Authorities and Clan Unions; and E. P. Onyeaka Offodile, "Growth and Influence of Tribal Unions," *The West African Review* 18, no. 239 (August 1947): 937.

55. Henrika Kuklick, *The Savage Within: The Social History of British Anthropology* (Cambridge: Cambridge University Press, 1991), 218.

56. NNAE, C 632, RIVPROF 2/1/87, Activities of Village Unions (1947); C 633, RIVPROF 2/1/87, Native Authorities and clan unions.

57. Ibid.; and NNAE, EP 13192, CSE 1/85/6539, Matters relating to and similar organizations (1937).

58. See *WAP*, February 4, 1953 (front page report); and *WAP*, January 17, 1952.

59. Minutes of the Ninth Annual General Assembly of the Egbe Omo Oduduwa, Ijebu-Remo, December 17–19, 1956.

60. Obafemi Awolowo, *The People's Republic* (Ibadan, NG: Oxford University Press, 1968), x.

61. Immanuel Wallerstein, *The Modern World System II: Mercantilism and the Consolidation of the European World-Economy 1600–1750* (New York: Academic Press, 1974), 7.

62. NNAK, CO 583/317/4, Activities of Dr. N. Nnamdi Azikiwe, Nigerian Nationalist Leader (1950–1951).

63. NNAE, OG 3335, OGPROF 2/1/2826, National Council of Nigeria and the Cameroons (NCNC) (1946–1951).

64. For details on the emergence of these parties, see NNAE, OG 3335, OGPROF 2/1/2826, Matters relating to (1946–1951). For a complete list of newspapers printed in colonial eastern Nigeria, see NAE, File No. 3265, ONDIST 20/1/1481, Newspapers in Eastern Provinces (1950–1951).

65. *WAP*, July 6, 1949.

66. Enahoro, *Fugitive Offender*, 65–66.

67. NNAE, 8633, PHDIST 10/1/1448, Action Group (1952).

68. Ibid.

69. *Daily Service* (Lagos), October 17, 1944, 2.

70. Minutes of the first inaugural conference of the Egbe Omo Oduduwa, June 1948, as cited in Coleman, *Nigeria*, 346.

71. Schwarz, *Nigeria*, 103. The Sarduana perceived his main mission in Nigerian politics as that of preserving the religious traditions of the emirate.

72. *Legislative Council Debates*, Nigeria, March 4, 1948, 227; quoted in Coleman, *Nigeria*, 361.

73. Editorial, *Gaskiya Ta Fi Kwabo*, February 18, 1950; cited in *Report on the Kano Disturbances of May 1953* (Kaduna, NG: Northern Regional Government, 1953), 43.

74. Azikiwe, *Development of Political Parties*, 18–19.

75. NNAK, CO 554/965, Position of ex-officio members of the Northern Region Executive Council of Nigeria 1956–1957; NNAI, NC/B10, Records of Proceedings of the Nigerian Constitution Conference held in London in July and August (1953); see appendix on Self-Government in (1956), 125–37.

76. NNAI, NC/B12, Records of Proceedings of the Resumed Conference on Nigerian Constitution (1954).

77. NNAI, NC/B10, Records of Proceedings of the Nigerian Constitution Conference held in London in July and August (1953).

78. NNAE, OG 3335, OGPROF 2/1/2826, National Council of Nigeria and the Cameroons (NCNC) (1946–1951).

79. NNAI, NC/B12, Records of Proceedings of the Resumed Conference on Nigerian Constitution (1954).

80. NNAI, NC/B10, Records of Proceedings of the Nigerian Constitution Conference held in London in July and August (1953), esp. the appendix on Self-Government in (1956), 125–37.

81. NNAI, NC/B12, Records of Proceedings of the Resumed Conference on Nigerian Constitution (1954).

82. Coleman, *Nigeria*, 334.

83. Obafemi Awolowo, *Awo: The Autobiography of Chief Obafemi Awolowo* (Cambridge: Cambridge University Press, 1960), 172 (italics mine).

84. Nnamdi Azikiwe, A Presidential Address at the Igbo State Assembly held at Aba on Saturday June 25, 1949.

85. Ibid.

86. Awolowo, *Awo: The Autobiography*, 172 (italics mine).

87. Ibid.

88. Azikiwe, Address at the Igbo State Assembly, June 25, 1949.

89. H. O. Davis, *Daily Times*, January 1950.

90. Awolowo, *Awo: An Autobiography*, 154.

91. See *WAP*, February 11, 1953; and *WAP*, July 19, 1952.

92. NNAE, 4715, CALPROF 7, 1/2424, National Independence Party (1953–1954).

93. NNAK, CO 957, Willink Commission, 1957–1958, chap. 7, para. 14.

94. Ibid.; NNAK, CO554/1634, Nigeria (Constitution) (Amendment No. 2) Order-in-Council 1958.

95. NNAK, CO 957, Willink Commission, 1957–1958, esp. chap. 7, 46–47.

96. Ibid.

97. NNAK, CO 554/1564, Provisions in Constitution for transition of Nigeria independence, 1959.

98. NNAK, FO 371/146838, Appointment and Inauguration of Dr. Nnamdi Azikiwe as Governor-General (1960).

99. Claude S. Phillips, "Nigeria and Biafra," in *Ethnic Separatism and World Politics*, ed. Frederick L. Shiels (Lanham, MD: University Press of America, 1984), 166.

100. Ibid., 168; Stokke, *Nigeria: An Introduction*, 48.

101. NNAK, DO 195/426, Death of General Ironsi GOC (General Officer Commanding) Nigerian Army (1965–1966).

102. NNAK, PREM 13/1041, Nigeria. Political Situation in Nigeria: deaths of Sir Abubakar; and General Ironsi; coup d'etat; part 3 (Oct. 1966).

103. See NNAK, FCO 65/1362, Position of Colonel Ojukwu, former rebel leader of Biafra (1973).

104. Schwarz, *Nigeria*, 210; Stokke, *Nigeria: An Introduction*, 53.

105. NNAK, FCO 38/214–221, Record of peace talks between Nigeria and Biafra (1968).

106. NNAK, FCO 23/182, Nigeria and Biafra (1968).

107. Schwarz, *Nigeria*, 230.

108. NNAK, FCO 23/182, Nigeria and Biafra (1968).

109. Shehu Musa Yar'Adua, "Nigeria in Transition (a critical examination of the main political economic and social aspects of the Nigerian society)," *Report of the Seminar on Nigeria in Transition* (Kaduna, NG: Government Press, 1979), 7.

110. Barrington Moore, *The Social Origins of Dictatorship* (London: Allen Lane, 1967), 413–70.

111. Arthur Nwankwo, *The Igbo Leadership and the Future of Nigeria* (Enugu, NG: Fourth Dimension Publishers, 1985), 9.

112. Anthony D. Smith, "The Ethnic Sources of Nationalism," in *Ethnic Conflict and International Security*, ed. Michael Brown (Princeton, NJ: Princeton University Press, 1993), 28; John L. Comaroff, "Of Toteism and Ethnicity: Consciousness, Practice, and the Signs of Inequality," *Ethnos* 52 (1987): 301–23.

20 ETHNICITY AND THE CONTEMPORARY IGBO ARTIST

SHIFTING IGBO IDENTITIES IN THE POST–CIVIL WAR NIGERIAN ART WORLD

Sylvester Okwunodu Ogbechie

IGBO ETHNICITY AND ULI REVIVALIST AESTHETICS

The Uli-revivalist movement of the Nsukka School is the most ideological manifestation of modern art to appear in Nigeria in the postcolonial period.[1] This movement adopts the Igbo Uli body and mural painting tradition as a conceptual framework for contemporary practice. It also represents a distinct mode of identification for specific contemporary Nigerian artists who are mainly of Igbo origin. By circumscribing their artistic practice within the parameters of identifiable Igbo aesthetic and conceptual systems, these artists defined a distinctive space of representation in their art and self-representation, which provides much material for study by historians of contemporary African art.

The contemporary Igbo artist and educator Christopher Uchefuna Okeke is widely credited with developing the conceptual framework and pedagogical environment in which the Uli revivalist ideology evolved. Other dominant figures of this movement include V. C. Amaefuna, Chike Aniakor, Obiora Udechukwu, Tayo Adenaike, El Anatsui, and Ndidi Dike. All of them are Igbo, with the exception of Adenaike, a Yoruba, and El Anatsui, an Ewe from Ghana, both long domiciled in Igbo environments. Ever since 1970, when Uche Okeke instigated this ethnic ideal of contemporary practice at the University of Nigeria, the Uli-revivalist movement has developed into a categorical mode of self-representation, an aesthetic and political platform on which an Igbo identity is defined for these artists.

This inclination toward an identity formation based on ethnicity—the idea, for example, of a distinct "Igbo" form of contemporary Nigerian art—raises questions about the terminology and criteria of analysis in contemporary African art history. As Richard Thompson noted:

> Ethnic processes . . . have been relatively recent historical creations of colonialism and imperialism and the subsequent post-colonial period in which primordial communities have become integrated into new and often unstable state structures. Thus, there is little that is "traditional" or pre-modern about ethnic differences in Africa . . . they are part and parcel of a contemporary world and perform critical functions for the combined evolution of that world.[2]

Beyond the immediate problem of using inappropriate forms of identification to analyze the Nsukka artists, the recourse to ethnicity in the discourse suggests too strongly a transfer of redundant terms of identification from the field of traditional African art studies into the arena of contemporary art. This implies that an insistence on the validity of ethnic identification as a mode of classifying contemporary African artists manifests that earlier insistence on an "African" identity for African artists in the twentieth century.

The analysis below focuses on the implications of adopting ethnicity as a mode of defining contemporary practice in Nigerian art by reviewing how this tendency played out in the Nsukka School. It evaluates the historical origins of Igbo identity and its intersection with contemporary politics in the Nigerian civil war, and then investigates the ideological nature of such notions of identity within the spaces of practice of specific contemporary Nigerian artists of Igbo (and non-Igbo) origin. By postulating a shift in Igbo identity in post–civil war Nigeria, several assumptions already circumscribe the boundaries of this analysis. The first assumption deals with the historical question of the nature of Igbo identity within the political entity defined as Nigeria. This entity was formulated by British colonial intervention into the structure of indigenous social, political, and cultural entities. The new entity formed from this intervention was imbued by fiat with political authority and a national structure whose origins are embedded in European paradigms of the nation state. The second assumption concerns the notion of a shifting Igbo identity, which implies a normative space/process of Igbo ethnic identification grounded in biological or social processes of which a deviation in contemporary aesthetic practices becomes identifiable and against which it can be measured and compared. The third assumption concerns the spatiotemporal concept of a "post–civil war Nigeria" and the history of political interaction between the Igbo and other ethnic constituents of the Nigerian polity. This history exhibits enough cultural and psychological structure that affects the articulation of Igbo ethnic identity and the material culture/production of contemporary Igbo artists.

Questions about the above assumptions do not minimize the need for investigation into processes of Igbo identity formation within the Nigerian political and cultural environment. Rather, they compel recognition of the functions such narratives serve in the articulation of contemporary Nigerian cultural and political identities. Since nothing was more concrete than one's identity as an Igbo in the tumultuous period of civil war conflict between 1967 and 1970 in Nigeria, Igbo ethnicity in post–civil war Nigeria articulates an ethnic awareness of specific historical occurrences. The pursuit of ethnically oriented aesthetics in contemporary Nigerian art reflects a distinctive social and cultural understanding of this history. The following analysis of contemporary Igbo ethnic identity thus investigates the relationship between ethnic awareness, self-representation, and the production of material art and artifacts within the social space of the modern Nigerian nation.

IGBO ETHNICITY: HISTORY AND THEORY

Artistic practice as an aspect of material production serves as a site for interrogating notions and expressions of Igbo ethnic identity within larger sociocultural imperatives. If art concretizes a society's symbol systems in visual imagery, one of its major modes of cognition is the larger sphere within which specific worldviews validate consensual notions of norms and alterity in individual societies. Concern with this larger sphere marks the external boundaries of any analysis of ethnicity and artistic identity; within it, a focus on certain aspects (the notion of Igbo identity, for example) becomes possible only as a matter of expediency.

Ethnic behaviors are "those human behaviors that are, at a minimum, based on cultural or physical criteria in a social context in which these criteria are relevant to the possibility of self-actualization by specific social and cultural units."[3] Ethnicity thus deals with processes by which human beings classify themselves and other peoples into identifiable categories. It also focuses on the processes by which cultural significance or meaning is attached to these classifications, and the degree to which certain social orders allocate social positions and roles based on such criteria. The historical fact of the struggle between the Igbo and other ethnic groups in Nigeria led to one of Africa's most intense postcolonial civil wars (the 1967–1970 Nigerian/Biafran war). The notion of an Igbo identity in the post–civil war era thus carries with it the historical affect of a contemporary attempt at self-definition engendered by that war. This history intersected with political and social factors that eventually bred a conflict within which definitions of Igbo ethnic identity were further honed. The subsequent drive for Igbo ethnic identity was not recourse to autonomous modes of inscription based on biological differences between Igbo peoples and "others." Instead, it was a forceful attempt to gain the "freedom to be self determining in an emerging world order that threatens to deny such freedom."[4] This shift in conceptual focus moves attention from sociobiological or primordialist definitions of ethnicity. It redefines ethnic identities as a function of changes in the material and metaphysical circumstances of actors within specific social spaces.[5] Although Igbo societies have long made indigenous distinctions between themselves and strangers, these distinctions were not always been based on ethnic differences. Rather they were based on cultural and linguistic differences. This fact affirms that "the conception of ethnicity is an ideological framework for Africa constructed in the West"[6] rather than a strict mode of indigenous definition of self and social identity.

The records of the earliest European explorers to Africa attest to the historical presence of the Igbo as a social and cultural unit of the West African subregion. Beyond the arrival of these essentially foreign elements in the late fifteenth century, the presence of a historically verifiable Igbo culture in this region can also be inferred from archaeological discoveries made by Thurstan Shaw in Igbo-Ukwu in the Anambra region of Eastern Nigeria.[7] According to Shaw, more than one hundred sixty-five thousand beads were found at Igbo Ukwu, a site he dated to the ninth century AD. Shaw lists the following sources for the Igbo Ukwu beads hoard: India (Carnelian beads, which may have been reworked locally, typical of ancient Asiatic beads), Egypt (Kilwa-Indian trade-wind beads), and Europe (striped beads of possible Venetian/Mediterranean origin). Other archaeologists who matched Igbo Ukwu bead-types to known archetypes from these cultures validate Shaw's identification of these beads as foreign items. Igbo Ukwu archaeology provides a historical basis for postulating Igbo ethnicity based on shared cultural forms and symbols, such as those that appear on the precolonial artifacts found at the site. The problem raised by the presence of beads from Asia in the Igbo-Ukwu horde is still unresolved. However, they imply connections between the Igbo and their neighbors because these beads probably made their way into Igboland through regional processes of trade and economic exchange. Ultimately, the vast bead hoard attests to Igbo-Ukwu participation in a transnational trade network that spanned three continents.

The cultural value placed on these discoveries by advocates of an ancient pedigree for the Igbo was enormous, in light of similar epochal discoveries in Northern Nigeria (the Nok culture) and in Western Nigeria (Ife bronze and terra-cotta images) earlier in the twentieth century. These separate archaeological findings were used by each of the three major Nigerian ethnic groups—Igbo, Yoruba, and Hausa—to legitimize their claim to political and cultural supremacy in the modern Nigerian State. In addition, the cultural narratives of different societies within "Igboland" indicate an awareness of initial processes whereby the notion of a distinct Igbo identity was developed primarily as a mode of distinction between *ndi olu* (foreigners, strangers, etc.) and *ndi Igbo*. Studies by G. T. Basden, Adiele Afigbo, Elizabeth Isichei, Angulu Onwuejeogwu, Don Ohadike, Donatus Nwoga, and many others indicate that it is possible to postulate a diverse area of social and cultural practice in which shared cultural features defined an ethnic identity identifiable as distinctly Igbo.[8] For example, Onwuejeogwu adopts the anthropological concept of "culture area" to define Igbo culture. He locates within specific conceptual parameters certain themes that allow him to develop a mode of classification for this ethnic group. He concludes that the people living within the Igbo culture area speak the same language and possess shared patterns of social organization, an identical concept of the cosmos and similar cultural traditions.[9]

Based on a study of the relationship between Igbo peoples and their physical environment, Adiele Afigbo evaluates the origins of the Igbo as an ethnic group and the processes whereby they arrived at the locations they now occupy. Afigbo's analysis presents a thinly veiled evolutionary notion of cultural development that began with proto-Igbo dispersal from its parent Kwa linguistic subfamily in the fifth and fourth millennia BC. He suggests that this dispersal gave rise to increasing sophistication in agricultural, social, and cultural practices owing to interaction with the Edo, Igala, Ijo, Yoruba, and Cross River peoples, which subsequently produced a distinctive Igbo culture as its end result.[10] Afigbo and other scholars explain Igbo identity in terms of the development of Igbo "culture" but decline to interrogate the idea of an ethnic identification in which vast differences in locale-specific responses to social, cultural, cosmological, and ritual issues bring the entire notion of a monolithic Igbo identity into question. Most notable in this respect is the ideological schism among the Igbo societies on opposite sides of the River Niger. The Western Igbo are regarded as very distant (and perceived as culturally inferior) relatives of the central and eastern Igbo; the supposed kinship between these different regions of Igboland only emerge forcefully during political moments when Igbo ethnicity is invoked as a rallying force against the machinations of other ethnic groups. This is especially true for the Hausa, whom Igbos perceived as antagonistic political rivals. In fact, Don Ohadike notes that although all Igbo groups speak a fundamentally common language, have similar political and social institutions, and share a common cultural heritage, their cultural practices reveal identifiable differences. He suggests that we should speak of Igbo cultures in the plural because of local variations arising from cultural isolation and interclan relationships.[11]

The question of Igbo ethnic identity is not restricted to an issue of its efficacy within the West African region. Identifiable manifestations of Igbo culture appear in the African diaspora. This includes the case of Olaudah Equiano's documented sojourn in England in the eighteenth century and the cultural revivalism of Igbo slaves resettled in Sierra Leone in the mid-eighteenth century after the abolition of slavery.[12] The volume of slave trade from different ports in the Bight of Biafra also ensured that large numbers of Igbo peoples who were captured and sold into slavery from the fifteenth century onward are represented in the development of African diaspora cultures. Evidence of their vital resistance to slavery abounds in the historical record. One famous and poignant example concerns the events of *Ibo Landing* in which Igbo captives drowned themselves at Dunbar Creek, on St. Simon Island, off the coast of Georgia (currently home to their Gullah descendants) to escape enslavement. Their relative marginalization in African diaspora discourses, against the valorization of Yoruba and Kongo diasporization, stems from a comparative paucity of scholarship into the Igbo diaspora population rather than an absence of viable communities that trace their descent from Igbo ethnic groups.

The cultural matrix of Igbo populations in precolonial Nigeria indicates that multiple cultural and social identities were amalgamated to produce Igbo ethnicity in colonial and postcolonial Nigeria. The incidence of British colonial rule in the closing years of the nineteenth century played a major role in this development. Colonial anthropologists were baffled by the complexity of Igbo culture and its apparent resonance with Jewish Talmudic customs. They thus sought to demonstrate a correlation between these two disparate traditions. For example, G. T. Basden, using textual evidence provided by Richard F. Burton, argues for a common Egyptian source for specific Igbo and Jewish customs like circumcision to explain the coincidences between Igbo and Jewish sociocultural observances. Percy Amaury Talbot links the Igbo veneration of Ala (Ani, Ana, Ale depending on dialect) to the Egyptian worship of Isis (Ast/Auset) and the Cretan earth goddess and her snakes.[13] This attempt to trace Igbo origins to foreign (Middle Eastern) sources reflects the diffusionist theories of that era. It is less credible today in light of archaeological evidence that Igbo peoples have occupied their current location for a very long time.

The amalgamation (on behalf of the British Colonial Administration) of the Northern and Southern protectorates by Frederick Lugard in 1914 was a decisive point in the constitution of contemporary Igbo ethnic identity.[14] This amalgamation impacted the emergence of an ethnically defined artistic practice by Igbo artists under colonial rule and in the postcolonial era. The development of a distinctly nonindigenous mode of practice in the sphere of Igbo art occurred within the period of colonial rule. It began with the introduction of European methods of formal academic art instruction into Nigeria at the beginning of the twentieth century with Aina Onabolu (1888–1973) as its first documented Nigerian exponent. The art world within which contemporary Nigerian artists operate today—both inside the country and internationally—derives mostly from the introduction of a capitalist economy and the integration of indigenous African societies into a capitalist world-system. In the realm of politics, the immediate result of this integration was a struggle for position within the new social and political spaces. In the realm of "culture," it took the form of a transformation of established modes of material production through an initial transformation of the identity and role of the artist in this new dispensation. The changes thus engendered make it necessary to distinguish between processes for self-representation based on ethnic identity and those based on cultural identity.

Ethnic identity relates to biologically rooted notions of inclusion and exclusion in socially identifiable (if not socially coherent) groups. Within this frame of reference, and in spite of any criticism of such essentialist attitudes, inclusion in an ethnic category seems to imply mostly that one either belongs on the basis of genealogical descent or one does not belong at all. In this sense, analysis of Igbo ethnic identity might suggest an investigation into processes of self-representation adopted by artists of Igbo origin. This definition, applied to the Nsukka School, automatically excludes many of the artists most relevant to the development of this particular artistic tradition. The development of cultural identity, on the other hand, implies a conscious adoption of ideological concepts, which guides modes of practice for a group of people and defines their interaction within distinct social spaces. This conception of identity is fluid and tends to include and exclude individuals on bases other than that of biological descent. One may thus speak of contemporary Igbo artists but only if that description refers both to artists of Igbo ethnic origin and those artists whose art pursues stated ideological objectives based on Igbo aesthetics.[15]

THE NSUKKA SCHOOL AND ULI REVIVALIST AESTHETICS

The Nsukka School of the University of Nigeria, Nsukka (UNN) was the principal site where an idea of specific Igbo ethnicity played out in the visual arts. The formation of indigenous art schools and universities in Nigeria in the 1960s was a nationalist project arising from the imminent demise of the British colonial project in one of its prime African colonies. African nationalists of that era perceived universities as an indispensable tool for achieving a decolonized sensitivity and national pride. The founding of the University of Nigeria coincided with Nigerian independence. It was named after the country and its project made coincident with the national history of Nigeria. It advocated a humanist cultural orientation focused on engendering a political and social empowerment for the Nigerian nation, hence its overriding nationalist ideals.[16] Its principal goal was to create an institution capable of linking the country's educational system to the concerns of its social, political, and cultural environments, and thereby provide a functional basis for a modern Nigerian social order.[17] Its academic model was a blend of the "land-grant college ideal of the United States with the classical concept of universities adapted to the changing circumstances of contemporary Nigerian society."[18]

The founding mandate of the University of Nigeria was an ideological call to arms, reflected in its motto, "to restore the dignity of man," and its Pan-African exhortation to defend the inalienable right of Africans to social equality, economic security, political freedom, and religious tolerance in the postcolonial and global world order. The place of art and culture in this scheme was further emphasized by a humanities program established in the 1961–1962 academic year, whose goals were to reflect the nationalistic aspiration, independence, self-reliance, and authenticity of Nigeria. Sir Eric Ashby, a prominent member of the commission that established the university, asserted that "the future of Nigeria is bound up with the future of Africa, and Nigeria's past lies in African history and folklore and language. It should be the first duty of Nigerian Universities, therefore, to foster the study of African history and antiquities, its languages, its societies, its rocks and soils, vegetation and animal life."[19] Nigeria's first president, Nnamdi Azikiwe, a great advocate of the new institution, saw the humanities as central to actualizing the philosophy and ideals of the university.

If the humanities were central to actualizing the philosophy and ideals of the university, fine arts were expected to play a major role in this process because the colonial government often asserted its racial superiority by claiming that Africans did not have aesthetic comprehension and were incapable of producing decent art.[20] Soon after the university was founded, the Enwonwu College of Fine Arts was established to rise to this challenge. Named for Ben Enwonwu (1918–1994), an internationally famous Igbo artist and Art Adviser to the Federal Government of Nigeria, the art school was staffed by a diverse body of American and Nigerian instructors including the famous Nigerian painter, Akinola Lasekan (1916–1974).

The ideological impetus circumscribing its activities meant that the University of Nigeria was more involved with national events than any other comparable Nigerian institution of higher learning. One such pivotal event was the Nigerian/Biafran civil war of 1967–1970. Pogroms against the Igbo in many parts of Nigeria (especially brutal in Northern Nigeria) led to a mass return of Igbo peoples to their ancestral homelands and an attempt to secede from the Nigerian polity under the banner of the Republic of Biafra.[21] A comparative mass exodus of non-Igbo citizens from eastern Nigeria occurred when the military governor of the region announced in October 1966 that he could no longer guarantee the safety of non-Igbos.[22] During the war, Nigerian soldiers especially targeted the university since it was considered the intellectual hub of the Biafran resistance. At the end of the war, most of the university's structural and intellectual edifices stood in ruins.[23]

The civil war truncated the first stage of the university's history and its impact was devastating since the University of Nigeria had gone out of its way to demonstrate a national rather than sectarian outlook. The war transformed UNN from a national university into an Igbo university so that by the end of the war, it was largely populated by Igbos and catered to Igbo issues. This development has not been reversed since then. Non-Igbo student enrollment increased in the decades after the war only to plummet again as Nigerian institutions became increasingly reorganized along ethnic lines in the 1980s and 1990s.

In 1970 after the war ended, Uche Okeke was appointed to head the reconstituted Enwonwu College of Fine Arts. The university's unique history provided a fertile ground for Uche Okeke's experiments in Uli aesthetics, which he had integrated into his art since his days as a student at Nigerian College of Aviation and Technology (NCAST) in Zaria. Its Pan-Africanist founding mandate and the traumatic ethnic reconfiguration of the institution made UNN ripe for Uche Okeke's ideological focus on an aesthetic system based on ideals of Igbo ethnicity. Okeke turned an ideological paradigm of "Natural Synthesis" that emerged in Zaria in 1958 as a nationalist critique of the colonial institution's anglocentric pedagogy into a (not altogether unjustified) focus on militant ethnicity in post–civil war Nigerian art. He gathered a wide group of Igbo intellectuals to his cause and, in two decades, he and his students established Uli revivalist aesthetics as a major ideological paradigm in contemporary African art. Uli art was a traditional body and mural painting tradition practiced by women in Igbo societies well into the colonial era. Uche Okeke and other contemporary Nigerian artists applied the aesthetic logic of Uli painting to a contemporary context of art practice principally dominated by male artists.[24]

The Nigerian/Biafran civil war fractured an uneasy Nigerian nationalism and created a resort to militant ethnicity in contemporary Nigerian art. Subsequently, several ideological formations based on affirmations of ethnic imagery and symbolism emerged in the country after 1970. In eastern Nigeria, artists reconfigured indigenous Igbo aesthetics and body-painting traditions into a format of contemporary practice with focus on social and political concerns. A similar concern with Yoruba identity in western Nigeria produced an ideological movement known as *Onaism*, located at the University of Ife (now Obafemi Awolowo University). At the Ahmadu Bello University in Zaria in Northern Nigeria, artists reconfigured the calligraphic orientation of Islamic art into a conceptual framework for contemporary abstract painting. At the University of Benin, arts and culture of the historical Edo Kingdom of Benin provided a comparable conceptual framework for interpretations of the modern aesthetic experience. Yaba Polytechnic, located in Lagos, largely privileged the style of pictorial verisimilitude pioneered by Aina Onabolu, pioneer modern Nigerian artist. These ideological formations enabled analysis of contemporary Nigerian art in terms of school styles such as "the Nsukka School," "the Ife School," and the "Yaba School."

The above analysis is necessary for proper understanding of practice and pedagogy in the Enwonwu School of Fine Arts of the University of Nigeria, an ideological project now collectively identified as the "Nsukka School."[25] The period from 1970 to 1985 is documented in the university's archives as a "period of reconstruction." This period can also be associated with the Nsukka School's active construction of an artistic identity based on an appeal to Igbo ethnicity.

WORDS AND WORKS

How does the idea of Igbo identity play out in the visual images of specific artists in the contemporary era? The politics of representation in the modern Nigerian nation demanded novel approaches to subjectivity and identity formation. This is compounded by the fact that notions of identity are more implied than inscribed in the imagery employed by modern Nigerian artists. Placed between their ideological utterances and their maneuvers for better visibility in the political and cultural arena, analysis of specific works by contemporary Nigerian artists may enable us identify the processes by which ideological posturing translates into significant images in their search for artistic identity. The following section therefore looks at the material production of Igbo artists both in the historical and contemporary era in order to evaluate how specific elements in each phase bore the burden of articulating Igbo identity. It begins with historical expressions of Igbo aesthetics.

Thurstan Shaw's excavations at Igbo-Ukwu in the Anambra region unearthed evidence of a divine kingship tradition and exquisite bronze objects, indicating a long history of Igbo artistic practice. Among the Anambra Igbo, the *Ijele* masquerade epitomized the aesthetic ideal of Igbo culture, both in its striking visual image and its physical beauty. The representations of *Ijele* today reveal a major shift in the nature of material production in Igbo culture. Compared to its original context, *Ijele* in its contemporary assemblage by both Igbo and Western artists show how Western conceptions of art and authorship redefine the meaning of creative endeavors in Igbo art. The authorship ascribed to a single individual in the contemporary times is opposed to the collective production (under the supervision of master artists) of the precolonial times. The concept of *Ijele* and its visual representation was developed and refined over several centuries, and this concept properly belongs to the various Igbo communities who produced and used this masquerade for various ritual purposes. In this sense, the *Ijele* in context is a work of art with major social, economic, and political overtones whereas the representation of *Ijele* by Mike Chukwukelu is simply a work of contemporary art that borrows the iconic image of *Ijele* for its visual structure. The first image is sacred whereas the second is resolutely secular. Nevertheless, both types of *Ijele* reflect the ideal of superior creativity that is the foundation of Igbo aesthetics.

Among the Anambra Igbo, the mythical Badunka, the epitome of the artist/craftsman, is invoked in Uli art as a conceptual framework for engagement with the creative processes. Badunka's mastery of material and symbolic form finds ultimate expression in the Uli symbols of the Earth deity Ala (variously Ani or Ana). The python, symbolic animal of this deity, is revered in Uli art because of its beautiful bodily markings and grace of movement, in addition to its status as a preeminent entity in the natural world. The form of the python is wrapped around the superstructure of the *Ijele* masquerade. Thus enabled, *Ijele* becomes a physical manifestation of the python's grace and efficacy, a material presentation of its society's social and cosmological ethos. Hence, as an Igbo proverb affirms, "the eye that beholds *Ijele* beholds the ultimate spectacle."

The conception of spectacular performance points to Igbo definitions of artistic practice (*Ikwa Nka*) as a process of *embodiment* in which the creative persona operates as a conduit channeling prodigious and usually unpredictable amounts of energy from the realm of the supernatural into the realm of the living. In this context, the artist is not only a master of physical forms defined as the concrete manifestation of abstract paradigms through objects realized in wood, metal, and other media, he is also a master of conceptual form and a ritual expert attuned to the invincible forces that guide his interaction with the realms of the supernatural. Thus Igbo peoples call an artist *Omenka* and recognize him/her as one who mediates the above interchange of ideals. Adepts are called *DiNka* (literally, masters of art), and the artworks thus produced are invested with meanings extending beyond their physical nature and immediate functions. In terms of the Ijele masquerade, the idea of "spectacle" (*ihe nkiri*) and "sublimity" (*ihe di egwu*: that which evokes awe) signifies an aesthetic of transcendence, an understanding of material form as a liminal stage in the evocation of supernatural forces. Exhibitions such as *Magiciens de la Terre* institute magic and mysticism—with attendant ideas of trickery and sleight of hand—as a determinant of artistic identity for the contemporary African artist. Through this, they displace the conscious adoption of forms and concepts by African artists in favor of a mythicized response to form. The mastery of form and symbolism that enabled such personages as Badunka to be celebrated as Omenka is displaced in favor of an interpretation of African art as the simplistic responses of simple-minded individuals to overwhelming physical and spiritual forces.

The Igbo Ukwu artifacts obviously predate any Igbo interaction with European ideas. Likewise, a mural painting tradition based on Uli symbols also appears to predate the colonial period, although its conflation with Mbari architecture in the Owerri region implies a response to the colonial incursion. Mbari rituals employed locally made ceramic objects (also named Mbari) as integral elements of Mbari architecture. In the colonial period, imported porcelain plates (commonly called "china," attesting to their source) replaced these ceramic objects. Their subsequent prevalence in Mbari architecture suggests a reconfiguration of existing indigenous practice.

The Ikenga ritual complex is one of the most important cultural practices found among Igbo peoples. Ikenga embodies a moral and ethical code and illustrates the liminality inherent in individual existence on the interface between multiple dimensions of the living, the dead, and the unborn. A male Igbo installs an Ikenga to affirm responsibility to himself and his society. The attendant need to understand symbolic forms encoded in the structure of the Ikenga object often directs the individual to seek knowledge of his society's symbol systems through systematic study and initiation.

Like the Ikenga, the *Ọzọ* tradition is widespread in Igboland, although it is by no means pervasive. Initiation into this society marks an individual's ascent into positions of overt power and authority. The art forms utilized as official insignia by the *Ọzọ* are also symbolic codes potent enough in their ability to designate meaning that one might view them as visual texts. The textuality of the image is here manifest in its inscriptions of physical and symbolic form. In precolonial Igbo society, the residence of an *Ọzọ* titled man is decorated with sculpture (carved doors and objects of power) and mural paintings using Uli symbols. The integration of mural painting, sculpture, and architecture in this context shows that Igbo cultures rely heavily on visual images as a means of archiving memory. The *Ọzọ* titleholder reaffirms his role in the community by a lavish use of highly revered images that define a sacred space of interaction around him in addition to circumscribing the kind of activities that may take place within that space. The importance of doors as points of interaction between private and public domains, and between sacred and secular spaces, is suggested in the collage of carved doors installed in the compound. Flamboyant or restrained in their motifs, each image projects distinctive ideas about specific domestic or ritual environments.

The above sample of institutions and material objects illustrates that Igbo societies are defined by shared cultural, ritual, political, and social practices. The colonial experience heightened the pace of change in these societies as well as the nature of its material and symbolic forms. Artists who developed during this period exhibited marked reactions to the introduction of European academic methods of art production. Of these pioneering artists, Benedict Chukwukadibia Enwonwu (1918–1994) was perhaps the most successful and definitely the most famous.[26] Enwonwu's professional practice marked the appearance of artists of Igbo origin in the field of modern African art. His ethnicity was not in doubt—he was an Igbo from Onitsha—but his forms suggest that his notion of artistic identity was not based solely on identification with his ethnic origins. In his quest for artistic identity, Enwonwu gravitated toward a quintessential African art form—masquerades and masking figures. His adoption of masquerades and dance as metaphors suggests an attempt at self-definition in new spaces of practice. Enwonwu put his art in the service of politics and nationalism and combined forms from Igbo, Edo, and Yoruba cultures to create a Nigerian national artistic synthesis. His principal themes drew on Igbo ethnic and cultural ideas. However, in sculptures like *Sango* (1964), Enwonwu adopted a Yoruba metaphysical personage as a metaphor for new physical and social reality of electricity. This transformation of indigenous concepts of power and affect into motifs and images for contemporary art later informed the ideological project of members of the Zaria Art Society, which codified Enwonwu's prescriptions on art into the ideology of "Natural Synthesis." Uche Okeke was a leader of the Zaria Art Society, which functioned from 1958 to 1962. All members of this organization were students at the Nigerian College of Arts, Science, and Technology (NCAST) in Zaria.

In 1956, Enwonwu was commissioned to produce a portrait of Queen Elizabeth II of England. He completed the sculpture in 1957 and unveiled it to wide acclaim. The Queen's portrait marks the limits of Enwonwu's formal academic orientation. In this work, Enwonwu engaged the politics of representation in the confrontation between a colonial subject and the personification of the colonial empire.[27] Subsequently his art returned to explorations of Igbo cultural identity and culminated in a series of powerful artworks focused on the Onitsha masquerade pantheon. By the time Enwonwu died in 1994, he was regarded as a major pioneer and one of Africa's greatest artists.

Igbo artists who were active in the colonial period were Eke Okaybulu, S. A. O. Chukwuegu, and C. C. Ibeto, among a growing list by the time Nigeria became independent in 1960. The initial postindependence surge of fraternization among Nigerian artists and writers saw several attempts to create an "authentic" artistic identity in the newly independent state. The Mbari movement, one of the more prominent, advocated a Pan-African sensibility that was expressed in its search for a definable postcolonial identity. An art market revolving around expatriate patrons developed with its center(s) in the embassies of previous colonial overlords: Britain, France, Germany, Italy, and the United States. Expatriates, who often instigated and supported distinct art forms and movements, dominated the art market. Their involvement in propagating specific types of art and their attempts to set the standards by which the new African art was judged, became a point of contention among contemporary Nigerian artists and art historians. The most glaring example of this kind of culture brokerage was the 1962 Oshogbo art movement instituted by Ulli Beier, Susan Wenger, and Georgina Beier around a core of Yoruba artists. Ulli Beier's contention that the products of these Oshogbo artists manifested a repressed (hence retrievable) Yoruba sensibility marks the emergence of a notion of artistic identity based on ethnicity in modern Nigerian art.[28]

The Nigerian civil war broke up the fraternal consciousness propagated by the Mbari movement. Igbo peoples were at the core of the Secessionist State of Biafra, and as such, Igbo identity became a very important and imperiled designate. It unified several societies to resist the genocide perpetrated against the Igbo, yet was imperiled since whole segments of Igbo political and cultural units were in danger of decimation. Exhibitions of Biafran art in

Germany showcased the works of Igbo artists such as Uche Okeke, Simon Okeke, and Obiora Udechukwu. Uche Okeke's "mythical realism" adopted Igbo deities and folktales (especially Ala) as central motifs in his art thus extending Enwonwu's transfiguration of indigenous metaphysical entities into concepts expressing contemporary social reality. Indigenous Igbo practices became important motifs for artists of Igbo origin in the period after the civil war. The post–civil war Nsukka School (at this time, the term mainly designated the art school of the University of Nigeria) developed the style of "social realism." This style was first used to chronicle the debilitating effects of the civil war on Igbo people. It later developed into a sweeping indictment of national profligacy in the 1970–1980 oil-boom era, during which its unceasing critique of social ills found maturity in the art of Obiora Udechukwu. In 1972 Obiora Udechukwu and Bons Nwabiani held a joint exhibition in Lagos, thus bringing an interest in contemporary interpretations of Igbo art and culture, honed by the experience of the civil war, to the Nigerian art scene. In a series of exhibitions hinged on interpretations of the Uli tradition, artists from the Nsukka School increasingly came to be identified with Igbo aesthetics and motifs. In the Nsukka School itself, interest in these forms intensified because instructors like Chike Aniakor, V. C. Amaefuna, and Ola Oloidi insisted that their students study Igbo art and societies.

Obiora Udechukwu is a principal figure of the Nsukka School both for his pedagogy and professional practice. The quintessential linear form of his mature art shows influences from Uli, Nsibidi, Islamic calligraphy, the stylized figuration of the Khatoum school (notably in the work of Ibrahim El Salahi), and Chinese calligraphy.[29] Udechukwu's austere ink-and-wash line drawings defined the canonical Uli style for much of the 1980s until the early 1990s when he returned to experiments with color. Then he produced such paintings as "What the Weaver Wove" (acrylic, 1992) in which he attempted a synthesis of his formalistic orientation. His notion of the artist as a weaver suggests that the art object, as well as formation of artistic identity, is a work in progress that depends on deft manipulation of diverse strands of experience. The loom and threads are invoked here as a representation of modern Nigerian art's spaces of practice, the context of interaction between the individual artist and subjective environments, which forms the contextual parameters of the production of subjectivity but does not contain it completely.

Several notable artists who are not of Igbo ethnicity aided principal developments in Uli revivalist aesthetics. For example, El Anatsui, a Ghanaian, brought elements of Ewe sculptural traditions into Nsukka School sculpture practice, thus establishing a completely identifiable substyle in Nsukka School art. His chainsaw sculpture technique has been much appropriated by sculptors in this environment, and his general principles of composition and installation art have found their way into the work of several Nsukka artists. In his early artworks, Anatsui used the architectonic logic of West African strip-woven cloth to create distinctive sculptures inscribed with ideographic images. Anatsui's late style of installation art, which uses copper wire and metal strips to create large wall hangings of haunting beauty, are now the most globally recognized product of the Nsukka School. It is notable that the artist continues to reside in Nsukka despite his frenetic global presence.

Tayo Adenaike, a Yoruba from Western Nigeria, is another Nsukka School artist who uses Uli aesthetics as a format to create paintings themed around Yoruba and Igbo folktales, critiques of Nigerian political attitudes, and general philosophical issues. His dedicated pursuit of the watercolor idiom and the spontaneity that characterized traditional Uli aesthetics establishes him as an important figure in the development of this tradition. Stylistically, his early work reflects influences derived from a period of tutelage and long-term association with Obiora Udechukwu. His mature style is distinctive, poignant, and unmistakably personal.

The Nsukka School style reflects a humanist aesthetic in keeping with the orientation of the University of Nigeria as defined above. Consequently, an inclination toward figuration persists in the works of artists from the Nsukka School. Their subject matter addresses issues of social concern structured within a focus on Igbo mythoforms.[30] Among artists like Tony Nwachukwu, a combination of figuration and the pictographic/ideographic forms of Uli and Nsibidi art produced new stylistic platforms for painting. The work of Chijioke Onuora is important in this respect for his eclectic use of African art images and orientation to mixed media. Although largely unrecognized in the critical evaluation of Nsukka School art, Chijioke Onuora maintains an Nsukka School heritage of expressive drawing, calligraphy, and signature experiments with mixed-media batik paintings. Likewise, Olu Oguibe's early art depended heavily on his use of Uli aesthetics, although his style has changed radically since he began a self-imposed exile, first in the United Kingdom, and subsequently in the United States, since 1990. Barthosa Nkurumeh broke ground as the first Nsukka artist whose principal medium was printmaking. Although Nsukka artists regularly produce prints, Nkurumeh's devotion to this medium elevates his work far above any comparable development in the Nsukka School. He has also successfully exported his printmaking into the international arena, where he is still one of the few artists to sustain ongoing experimentation in Uli principles of representation.

The paucity of female artists in the list above indicates a major point of contention in narratives of Nsukka School art, especially considering that Nsukka artists appropriated a quintessential female Igbo art form for a male-dominated contemporary art practice. This has prompted critics like Nkiru Nzegwu to decry the marginalization of female artists in Nsukka School narratives.[31] In this respect, it is proper to acknowledge the immense contributions of Ndidi Dike to the ideological project of the Nsukka School. Ndidi Dike has been at the center of a contentious debate concerning the legacy of tutelage on artistic practice and the role of gender on her creativity and self-representation since she emerged as a professional studio artist in the late 1980s. These issues arise from her background as a student of El Anatsui, whose innovations in sculpture shaped her initial explorations in this medium. Dike trained as a painter at the University of Nigeria and only started to work as a sculptor after she left the institution. She appropriated sculptural techniques from the institutional style developed by Anatsui while redirecting her production to specific concerns about her position as a female artist within this tradition. Dike's mature sculpture continues to focus on such issues and, as such, she is often marginalized in a narrative that locates artistic excellence solely within the heroics of a male-dominated pantheon of Uli revivalists. Dike's artworks and her role as Nigeria's leading female sculptor and installation artist thus create dissonance in Nsukka School narratives. Her professional career so far and numerous solo exhibitions indicate that she should be considered a principal figure of the Uli revivalist movement.[32] Other visible female Nsukka artists include Chinwe Uwatse, Nenna Okorie, and Marcia Kure.

The history of the Nsukka School in modern Nigerian art has been established by the reflexivity brought to bear on their own practice by Nsukka artists and the series of exhibitions that defined the orientation of this ideological project in relation to some of its most famous artists. The true achievement of the Nsukka School is to have developed an ideology powerful enough to sustain several generations of artists. Close examination of Nsukka School art reveals that its appeal to ethnicity derives in part from a definable historical impetus, in this case, the Nigerian/Biafran conflict of 1967–1970. The ensuing ideology provided the University of Nigeria with a focus for its reconstruction efforts after the war and provided its artists with a conceptual framework that normalized Igbo concerns within the ideological spaces of the institution and its art school. As with all modernist ideologies, the production of a canonical interpretation of this phenomenon (by Ogbechie and Ottenberg, among others) suggests that the Uli revivalist ideology of the Nsukka School is already historical as the artists involved move further into the international arena and younger artists map new formalistic and conceptual frameworks.

Nsukka School art provides a model of how ethnic concerns can have an overriding impact on artistic expression and an excellent example of how a focused ideological position can strengthen institutional and individual creativity. This is evident in the manner that principal impulses within the art of key individuals (Udechukwu in painting, Anatsui in sculpture and installations, and art criticism in the case of Ola Oloidi) have been transformed into major movements by the multiplier effects of followership. As Simon Ottenberg concludes in his study on Nsukka School art, many of the artists involved have become influential artists and critics well established in the international discourses of art, art history, and art criticism.[33] Their success in the international arena suggests that the Nsukka School was cognizant of its multiple heritages and flexible enough to allow for individual modifications in artistic responses to aesthetic and critical issues. In this sense, the ethnic orientation of Uli revivalist aesthetics bespeaks a contingent rather than essentialist ideal of Igbo ethnicity.

The appeal to Igbo culture as a basis for contemporary art is an important aspect of Nsukka School aesthetics. Nonetheless, it does not transform their art into a specifically Igbo art because these artists also partake in a modern Nigerian identity engendered by the modernization process and are now fully integrated into global art discourses. "Modern in this case speaks less of temporal locations in the sense of what is most recent; rather, it means, in philosophy as well as in art, a notion of strategy and style and agenda."[34] It is in this latter context that one needs to search for the uniqueness of the Nsukka Uli revivalist movement in order to relate their ethnic orientation to wider issues of social change and political and aesthetic autonomy in the fractious politics of the modern Nigerian State.

NOTES

1. This essay was first presented at the *Rethinking Igbo Art and Culture: African Initiatives in Knowledge* Symposium, Emory University, Atlanta, October 1, 1995.

2. Richard H. Thompson, *Theories of Ethnicity: A Critical Appraisal* (New York: Greenwood Press, 1989), 100. Thompson's uncritical and unreflective usage of terms like "underdeveloped," and "primordial communities," undermines his analysis of sociobiological and primordialist theories of ethnicity, although his general line of argument provides an effective theoretical framework.

3. Thompson, *Theories of Ethnicity*, 11. The differences between the Igbo and members of other ethnic groups in Nigeria are more cultural than physical. Long-range historical processes of inter-ethnic relations invalidate any understanding of these societies as self-contained autonomous units within which unalterable biological "natures" impose essential differences in behavior and culture.

4. Thompson, *Theories of Ethnicity*, 62. For the theory of ethnicity as a reflection of the capitalist world system propagated by Immanuel Wallerstein (critiqued in Thompson, *Theories of Ethnicity*, 107–39), see Immanuel Wallerstein, *The Capitalist World-Economy* (Cambridge: Cambridge University Press, 1979), 165–230.

5. Anthony Giddens, *The Constitution of Society: Outline of a Theory of Structuration* (Berkeley: University of California Press, 1984), 1–40. Giddens defines "social space" as an arena of interaction within which consensually validated notions of norms and alterity work to define processes of inclusion and exclusion. Such an arena has fluid boundaries and the identity affected by individuals within such spaces is understood in terms of multiplicity and multivalency. For additional analysis of the constitution of ethnic identity, see Thomas Spear and Richard Waller, eds., *Being Maasai: Ethnicity and Identity in East Africa* (London: James Curry, 1993), 1–16.

6. Aidan Campbell, *Western Primitivism, African Ethnicity: A Study in Cultural Relations* (London: Cassell, 1997), 6.

7. See Thurstan Shaw, *Igbo Ukwu: An Account of Archaeological Discoveries in Eastern Nigeria* (Evanston, IL: Northwestern University Press, 1970); see also Timothy Insoli and Thurstan Shaw, "Gao and Igbo Ukwu: Beads, Interregional Trade, and Beyond," *African Archaeological Review* 14, no. 1 (1997): 1–15. Shaw provides information on the Igbo-Ukwu excavation and the controversy over the resultant dates attributed to the artifacts that were unearthed (contested dates range from c. 500 BC to 500 AD).

8. G. T. Basden, *Among the Igbos of Nigeria* (London: Frank Cass, 1966); A. E. Afigbo, *Ropes of Sand: Studies in Igbo History and Culture* (Nsukka: University of Nigeria Press, 1981); Elizabeth Isichei, *A History of the Igbo People* (London: Macmillan, 1976); Donatus Nwoga, *The Supreme God as Stranger in Igbo Religious Thought* (Mbaise, NG: Hawk Press, 1984); Don C. Ohadike, *Anioma: A Social History of the Western Igbo People* (Athens: Ohio University Press, 1994).

9. M. Angulu Onwuejeogwu, "The Igbo Culture Area," in *Igbo Language and Culture*, ed. F. C. Ogbalu and Emmanuel Nolue Emenanjo (Ibadan, NG: Oxford University Press, 1975), 1–10. Onwuejeogwu's analysis combines socio-biological and primordialist approaches in an attempt to present the Igbo as a historically and culturally coherent ethnic group.

10. Adiele Afigbo, "Prolegomena to the Study of the Culture History of the Igbo-speaking Peoples of Nigeria," in *Igbo Language and Culture*, ed. Ogbalu and Emenanjo, 28–53. Adiele suggests that Igbo identity is not fixed and that its contemporary manifestation displays processes of identification differing radically from earlier notions given the exigencies of contemporary environmental factors.

11. Ohadike, *Anioma*, 28.

12. See Joanna Brooks, ed., *The Interesting Narrative of Olaudah Equiano or Gustavus Vassar, the African, Written by Himself* (1794; Chicago, IL: Lakeside Press, 2004). Authors who claim that he was an American born in South Carolina have recently challenged the veracity of Equiano's narrative; for the general outline of this alternative theory, see Vincent Carretta, "Olaudah Equiano or Gustavus Vassa? New Light on an Eighteenth-Century Question of Identity," *Slavery and Abolition*,20, no. 3 (1999): 96–105. For an analysis of manifestations of African culture in the diaspora, see Robert Farris Thompson, *Flash of the Spirit: African And African American Art and Philosophy* (New York: Random House, 1983). See Kenneth Onwuka Dike, *Trade and Politics in the Niger Delta 1830–1895* (Oxford: Clarendon Press, 1956), for a detailed analysis of the economic interaction between the Igbo and their neighbors (including the Europeans) before the advent of active colonization. Michael Echeruo discusses the activities of "migrant" Igbo societies on the West-African Coast and in England in "A Matter of Identity," in the 1979 *Ahiajoku* Lecture (Owerri, NG: Imo State Ministry of Information, Culture, Youth and Culture, 1979).

13. Ohadike, *Anioma*, 3. The references cited are Richard Burton, *Wanderings in West Africa* (New York: Dover, 1991); Percy Amaury Talbot, *The Peoples of Southern Nigeria: A Sketch of their History, Ethnology, and Languages, with an Abstract of the 1921 Census*, 4 vols. (London: Oxford University Press, 1926).

14. The institution of colonial rule differed in its modes of operation as well as political and economic interests, from the economic relationship developed between Igbo societies and the Europeans since the early days of the slave trade. Colonialism marks a more militant attitude to the exploitation of a subject dominion by the colonizing entity. See Elizabeth Isichei, *The Igbo People and the Europeans: Genesis of a Relationship to 1906* (London: Faber and Faber, 1973).

15. It is not possible to isolate "Contemporary Igbo art" as a specific form of practice in modern Nigerian art although one can argue for the ideological inscription of an idea of Igbo identity within the objectives of the Nsukka School. However, it is undeniable that Igbo artists are among the most accomplished and internationally famous modern Nigerian artists.

16. For a comprehensive evaluation of the ideological project of the University of Nigeria, see Emmanuel Obiechina, Chukwuemeka Ike, and John A. Umeh, eds., *The University of Nigeria, 1960–1985: An Experiment in Higher Education* (Nsukka: University of Nigeria Press, 1986), 104. The university's scholarship has been very self-reflexive and the above book provides the best compendium of scholarship on various aspects of the school at that time, written by UNN faculty members, national historians and its alumni. Authors cited in connection with UNN history are taken from the book unless otherwise noted.

17. B. I. C. Ijomah, "The Origin and Philosophy of the University," in Obiechina et al., *The University of Nigeria* .

18. "Background of Philosophy Animating Principles" (First Meeting of Provisional Council

with Dr. Nnamdi Azikiwe as Chairman, March 3, 1960). *University of Nigeria, Nsukka Graduate Album, 1963–1966* (Annual Publication of the University of Nigeria, 1967), 9.

19. Sir Eric Ashby, "Post-School Certificate and Higher Education in Nigeria" (University Commission Report, 1960), in Obiechina et al., *The University of Nigeria.*

20. Ola Oloidi evaluates the impact of this colonial rhetoric on the art and activities of Nigeria's pioneer modern artist Aina Onabolu (1888–1963). See Ola Oloidi, "Constraints on the Growth and Development of Modern Nigerian Art in the Colonial Period," *Nsukka Journal of the Humanities* 5, no. 6 (June/December 1989): 28–51.

21. For a personal account of the Nigeria/Biafra Civil War, see Chinua Achebe, *There Was a Country* (New York: Penguin, 2012).

22. V. Chukwuemeka Ike, *The University and the Nigerian Crises: 1966–1970*, in Obiechina et al., *The University of Nigeria*, 27–52. Ike notes that "the quit order did not affect the Ika Igbo of Mid-Western Nigeria" (35), thus demonstrating the general perception of Western Igbo peoples as societies of marginal Igbo identity by their eastern Igbo compatriots.

23. For an account of the Nigerian/Biafran conflict, see Eghosa E. Osaghae, Ebere Onwudiwe, and Rotimi T. Suberu, eds., *The Nigerian Civil War and Its Aftermath* (Ibadan, NG: John Archers, 2002).

24. See Nkiru Nzegwu, "Crossing Boundaries: Gender Transmogrification of African Art History," *Ijele: Art eJournal of the African World* 1, no. 1 (2000), http://www.ijele.com. Nzegwu criticizes the dearth of female artists in narratives of modern Nigerian art. There are several factors responsible for this tendency. The curricula framework devised for Nigerian colonial art education was gendered along Victorian ideals that relegated females to domestic arts (textiles, decorative arts etc). Although the University of Nigeria graduated large numbers of female artists, many left art practice to pursue other interests. Nevertheless, Nzegwu argues correctly that prominent female Nsukka School artists such as Ndidi Dike have been marginalized in the discourse.

25. Nsukka School artists and critics were prolific in documenting their own practice. For a bibliography of such publications, see Simon Ottenberg, *New Traditions from Nigeria: Seven Artists of the Nsukka Group* (Washington, DC: Smithsonian Institution Press, 1997), 281–97.

26. For a definitive account of Ben Enwonwu's professional career, see Sylvester Ogbechie, *Ben Enwonw: The Making of an African Modernist* (Rochester, NY: University of Rochester Press, 2006).

27. See Sylvester Okwunodu Ogbechie, "Contested Vision: Ben Enwonwu's Portraits of Queen Elizabeth II," *Ijele: Art eJournal of the African World* 1, no. 2 (2000), http://www.ijele.com.

28. For Beier's account of the Oshogbo experiment, see Ulli Beier, *Thirty Years of Oshogbo Art* (Bayreuth, DE: Iwalewa, 1991).

29. For examples of Obiora Udechukwu's art, see *Obiora Udechukwu: Selected Sketches 1965–83* (Lagos, NG: National Council for Arts and Culture, 1984).

30. For a review of artworks from the Nsukka School, see Sylvester O. Ogbechie, *HOMAGE: ArtGrads UNN exhibition* (Nsukka, NG: ArtGrads UNN, 1991).

31. Nkiru Nzegwu, "Subverting the Power of Masculinity," in, *Issues in Contemporary African Art*, ed. Nkiru Nzegwu (Binghamton, NY: ISSA, 1998), 117.

32. Simon Ottenberg included Ada Udechukwu rather than Ndidi Dike in *New Traditions from Nigeria: Seven Artists of the Nsukka School* (Washington, DC: Smithsonian Institution Press, 1997) and exhibition on Nsukka School art, a decision that has subsequently generated much controversy. Ada Udechukwu trained as a poet and took up painting under the influence of her husband, Obiora Udechukwu. Ndidi Dike, on the other hand, is a formally trained graduate of the Nsukka School and arguably its leading female exponent of Uli revivalist aesthetics. Ottenberg's decision to incorporate Ada Udechukwu into a formal history of the Nsukka School was thus problematic, although it can be ratified on the basis of her creative experiments and two documented exhibitions in textile design.

33. Ottenberg, *New Traditions from Nigeria*, 281–96.

34. Arthur Danto, *After the End of Art: Contemporary Art and the Pale of History* (Princeton, NJ: Princeton University Press, 1997), 8.

21 ỌSỌNDU

PATTERNS OF THE IGBO QUEST FOR JESUS POWER

Ogbu U. Kalu

All over Igboland, in urban and rural communities, the chorus rings out:

> Jesus power, super power
> Jesus power, super power
> Mami Wata power, nonsense powers
> Ogboni power, powerless power

And so the diatribe against non-Christian sources of power will be excitedly recited, raising the hands up to the sky when mentioning "Jesus power," and bending to touch the ground when mentioning the dusty defeat of non-Christian sources of power. This popular chorus is only one among many that assert that "*Jesus don win again, kpata, kpata e go win again!*" This particular chorus in Pidgin English has been adapted by politicians for the anticipated electoral victories of their political parties. The rapid growth of Christianity in contemporary Africa has been shaped by charismatic Pentecostal spirituality that has creatively engaged popular culture. The movement that became unstoppable from the 1970s has, after a period of resistance and opposition from mainline churches, charismatized the religious landscape and the mainline churches. All churches have broadened the space for charismatic spirituality as an encapsulation strategy. But this is a characteristic of the southern globe.

In Nigeria, the charismatic movement did not only affect the Igbo of southeastern Nigeria. As Matthew Ojo's *End-Time Army* demonstrates, it was very strong in southwestern Nigeria in the early 1970s. Richard Burgess in his *Nigeria's Christian Revolution* traces the roots in Igboland to the Nigerian Civil War period.[1] By the mid-1970s, bands of intrepid young people from secondary schools and universities in southern Nigeria moved into the Muslim communities of northern Nigeria, disrupting the religious compromise that had been established between Muslims, colonial government, and missionaries from the defeat of the Sokoto Caliphate. In contemporary Nigeria, the charismatic Christian flow has connected with the charismatic spirituality in indigenous worldviews, making it difficult to explain the model of conversion in any particular region as a differentiated phenomenon. Even more problematic is that all religions are growing; religion has exploded so vigorously into the public space that Nigeria faces a contentious religious pluralism. Therefore, this reflection focuses on the period before the charismatic movement got the wind under its sail in 1970.

In his book *Missionary Impact on Modern Nigeria*, Emmanuel Ayandele asserts that the "collapse of pagandom" in Igboland was more astonishing and widespread than in the rest of the country; that Christianity came earlier to the Yoruba communities in southwestern Nigeria but made faster progress in the southeast; that this fact needed to be explained. As he puts the matter,

> In statistical terms and in the desire to appropriate all the material and social opportunities that missionary enterprise could afford, it is the Ibo people who have responded most enthusiastically to Christianity.[2]

It appeared that the missionary enterprise enjoyed a huge success in one region of the country and betrayed the Igbo receptivity to change. Beyond this, Ayandele points to the Islamic factor in Nigerian history. Islam moved into northern Yorubaland after the Usman dan Fodio jihad (1804). The jihadist forays into northern Yorubaland and the routes in the kola nut trade mapped the encounter. Thus, in spite of the contours of resistance by various Yoruba subethnic groups, Yorubaland acquired a degree of Islamic presence that escaped the forest belts of Igboland. Islamic presence in Igboland has remained peripheral in urban areas and centered on commercial contacts in cattle and sheep trade. Northerners in Igboland tend to reside in areas demarcated as *Ama Awusa* (Hausa quarters). It does not matter that many of these may be Fulani. Similarly, the southerners resident in the North live in secluded *sabon gari* (strangers' quarters) located on the outskirts of their walled towns.

Why did the Igbo abandon the gods of their fathers in such a hurry? Certain issues are important here: (1) whether the Igbo gods beat a hasty retreat or were just embattled by the onward march of Christian soldiers; (2) the comparison with the fortunes of Jesus power among the Yoruba of southwest Nigeria; and (3) the periodization in the discussion. Since the goal of this reflection is to review the discourses that have been deployed to explain the patterns of Igbo conversion to Christianity, it should be necessary to pay attention to the Yoruba case study for two reasons: Yoruba historiography provides a guiding as well as a comparative perspective. The nationalist historiography of the Ibadan School that Ayandele exemplified is endangered by contemporary sectarian historiography as each ethnic group strives for its version of history. Doing history in Nigeria demands that scholars connect the stories of various subnationalities and paint the large canvas of the religious landscape of the entire nation. As Ayandele queried in the pages of *African Notes* in 1969, "how truly Nigerian is our Nigerian history?" He accused the elite of using historical scholarship to balkanize the nation.[3] I shall, therefore, use the contributions of David Laitin and John Peel to briefly explore the comparative Yoruba data.

David Laitin's *Hegemony and Culture: Politics and Religious Change among the Yoruba* argues that the Yoruba tend to value land above religious divides, and easily accommodate different religious traditions. "Yoruba political calculations have been consistently based on the exploitation of ancestral city fissures." He contrasts this with the Hausa/Fulani of the north who use religion as markers of identity especially when confronting outsiders. They abandon their indigenous religions and use Islam as the rallying cry.[4] Embedding the politics of difference in the womb of religious passion has immense political consequences. Other scholars have exploited this argument to argue that the Yoruba demonstrate the highest values of religious coexistence. Members of the same family could function as leaders in Muslim, Christian, or indigenous religious traditions. As Akin Akinade has argued in his article, "Islamic Challenges in African Christianity," the pattern of Christian-Islamic dialogue in Yorubaland should serve as a model for the contemporary discussion.[5]

An important analysis of religious change in Yorubaland that helps our reflection on patterns of conversion in Igboland is John Peel's *Religious Encounter and the Making of the Yoruba*.[6] Its contributions to African historiography are many but especially its keen eye to methodology and the problem of reconstructing the past from fragments of evidence. As he puts it, the challenge is not only about the nature of the sources but also "lies in how to blend the three narrative themes which are pertinent to it: the missionary endeavor, colonization, and endogenous development of African societies."[7] He constantly returns to the problem of lenses and images, sources and their interpretation, as well as the quest to reinsert contemporary religious history into its primal roots.

This concern comes out clearly in the structure of the book: after the introductory chapter that explores the key concerns, the next three chapters provide the sociopolitical backdrop comprising the nineteenth-century Yoruba wars and an overview of the politics in an "age of confusion." This highlights the interplay in the politics of difference operating within communities and in their interactions with others. The engine that moved the politics in such communities consisted of the triad of power, status, and wealth. One looked in vain for Laitin's emphasis on land. These are followed by perceptive analyses of the traditional religion of an African people because religion serves as the substratum of the political superstructure. Both reinforce each other. Peel's profile of the indigenous religion breaks from Geoffrey Parrinder's pyramid structure. Yoruba indigenous religions are "congeries of cultic practices, actuated by some common principles but varying a great deal over space and over time."[8] Politics and religion are not merely the "surrounds" for sociological analysis; rather the cultural discourse and thick cultural descriptions are important for analyzing the patterns of a community's appropriation of Christianity. Worldviews or "culture postures" describe the lenses, presuppositions, and allegiances deployed in making meaning, explaining realities, and domesticating new religious structures, symbols, and experiences.

Peel, therefore, achieved two goals: (1) to show that before "Christianity arrived in the 'high noon' (*osan gangan*) of Yoruba religious history, it not only came into an open and dynamic system of belief and practice, but found there were currents with which it could swim and hope to turn its own way"[9]—the contest of worldview maintenance is emphasized; and (2) to provide the counterfoil for explaining the pattern of religious change by privileging "local cult complex" instead of pan-Yoruba-wide pantheon and giving the *orisa* prominence of place as the main form in which Yoruba religion was realized in daily lives. The problem for interpreters of the gospel would, therefore, be less on the Supreme Being and more on the *orisa*. This method helps in showing why different subgroups responded to the gospel differently. Peel canvasses five modes of appropriation ranging from euhemerist arguments through restoration, evolution, and anticipation to prophecy.[10] But before dealing with conversion, Peel uses a *historical* discourse to reconstruct the insertion of the gospel that combines the patterns of vertical and horizontal expansion. Mission, he affirms, "is a certain kind of power in the land, a power both specific and limited." Power contexts are structures, and one could tell the story of the people who set up and managed the structures, their goals, motivations, strategies, and relationship with other power nodes such as the colonial government and local rulers of towns and kingdoms. Peel employs the cost-benefit model in explaining the pragmatist-driven relationship between evangelizers and the evangelized caught in the flux of colonial political turmoil. He analyzes the complex contexts of regional politics and the ambiguities that suffused the missionary project. The *instrumentalist* discourse in religious change asserts that communities respond to the new religious change agent because of the political, economy, and its social consequences. Religion is often an instrument or one of the means of adjustment. The patterns of adjustment could be underscored with biographical portraits of the personalities, white and black, but especially, the African pastors such as the first homegrown priests and the Saro returnees.

The core assertion of the *cultural* discourse is that during the process of horizontal expansion, when the "roots" of the gospel confront the "soil" of the community's beliefs, practices and cultures, those who own the land will react. The heartbeat of evangelization evokes responses. This is significant for bringing the core of missionary theology and hermeneutics back into the center of doing church history and into the epicenter where religious interaction occurs. People reacted to both the method of evangelism (especially the triumphalism) and to the challenge of the gospel to the interior of primal worldview that underpinned practices. One could imagine the scene in Eleta market where the pastor preached to a hundred people and a woman interjected by praising her deity, *Ori*, and probably rejected the uninformed rebuttal that "*ori* is merely made of cowries"![11] What did she think about the doctrines of transgression, redemption, and last things though she may have heard of heaven and hell from Muslims? Indeed, Peel explored "the conceptual bridgehead offered to Christianity by the prior religious, ethical and cosmological influence of Islam."[12] The implication is that church historiography must not yield the grounds easily to sociological analysis but be attentive to the *religious* discourse on the power of the message in the conversion process. In spite of many hurdles, argues Peel, the power of the message and the labors of the indigenous messengers won some attention as the Yoruba contextualized Christianity in a mutual assimilation manner that Peel characterizes with the metaphor of Christian leaf and Yoruba soap, *ewe* and *ose*. "The history of Yoruba Christianity" he wrote, "has not proceeded evenly, but by challenge and reaction, by lulls and revivals."[13] The revivals include the insurgence of the Aladura movement in 1918–1919 and the patronage of naked faith concept of the Faith Tabernacle by mid-1920s. Since this group did mission only through the Post Office, their early devotees deserted them for the British Apostolic church, and this movement later produced the Christ Apostolic Church, a harbinger of modern Pentecostalism.[14] The pace and direction of the growth of the African-instituted churches raises the ancillary matter as to why certain ethnic groups (the Zulu, Luo, and Yoruba) have been such great religious innovators.

After multidimensional and multidisciplinary perspectives that surveyed the historical, cultural, instrumentalist, and religious discourses, Peel brings the core argument to a head. Having profiled the Yoruba people through time and shown the patterns of religious encounter, he argues that the local agency put a stamp on the Christianity that emerged and provided the dynamic substance to the notion of a shared Yoruba identity in such a manner that Christianity and cultural nationalism became integral. Peel insists that reference to the Yoruba as "Aku" in Sierra Leone did not make it back to Nigeria; rather, the label "Yoruba," which the Muslims had applied to the Oyo, became encrusted in the Bible translation as an identity for the whole race and took on a national task of its own! Ironically, Christianity had a deeper effect among the Yoruba than among the Igbo precisely because the Union Igbo Bible (1917) was not the dialect of any Igbo subculture, was not organic, and did not serve in producing an Igbo identity.

The reassertion of the force of local agency in responding to global processes and in gestating the resources of external change agents informs the title of my book, *Embattled Gods: The Christianization of Igboland*.[15] The gods of the Igbo, like the gods of many other Nigerian ethnic groups, were embattled but unconquered. We shall argue that pagandom did not collapse among Igbo communities in the way that Emmanuel Ayandele had imagined. Indeed, two rival schools oppose the hegemony or collapse discourse: Eurocentric revisionists point to the complex nature of culture-contacts; the tendency toward worldview maintenance by all parties; contests between rival narratives; ambiguous relationships with colonial officers and policies; the plurality of voices within the missionary enterprise, including European champions of indigenous cultures; and the exigencies of the mission fields that compelled massive readjustment of strategies and goals. They challenge the relationship between commerce and providentialism and evangelical piety as the motor of the missionary enterprise.

Scholars from the Global South privilege the power of indigenous worldviews in the patterns of appropriation of the gospel, indigenous agency, choices empowered by the translation/vernacularization project, multiple modes of appropriations, and especially the effect of charismatic spiritualities such as the prophetic movement of Garrick Braide (1914–1918) and the Aladura movement that arose from the interior of African religions in reshaping the face of Christianity in Africa. They argue that charismatic religious genius resulted in "Christianities" and new theologies ranging beyond missionary ideals. Education that served as the strongest agent of missionary reshaping of the African world produced unintended consequences by breeding nationalists and arming them with the logic against colonial and missionary control, the tools for reading the Bible, and the possibilities of new ecclesiology and theology.

OSONDU: DISCOURSES IN IGBO CONVERSION

The Igbo image the art of living or the passage through life as a long journey that at death will be continued through the ancestral world. To protect, sustain, and enhance the quality of the journey through the human world, individuals and communities literally run to powerful sources to garner the resources for long life with dignity (*nka na nzere*). Since this is a preoccupying endeavor, life itself is often imagined as a race, a long-distance race, a pursuit that involves perseverance, struggle, and quest for the power and resources that ensure sustainability for a person or community. This is *oso-ndu*, the race of life (*oso=race; ndu=life*). Underneath lurks a precarious vision of the human world that is invested by evil forces to thwart the cherished goal of a prosperous life. But providentially, the cosmos also possesses a number of munificent supernatural forces and spirits that protect and deliver: deities that could empower a person to triumph. One such deity is the *ikenga*, the ram-headed deity that strengthens the right hand and communes with the *chi*, the individual god of fate and destiny. Other spiritual forces are connected to each node in the rites of passage from birth through death to reincarnation and to each sector of the agricultural cycle, from locating the farming sites, through planting and harvesting of vegetables, to new yam harvest. Some of the deities inhabit the sky; the earth has human spirits, the earth deity, patron/guardian spirits responsible for professions, nature spirits inhabiting the physical features of the landscape, and evil spirits. Marine spirits are like daughters of the earth deity. Ancestors live in the earth beneath from where they sometimes visit the human world as masquerades and sometimes return permanently through a process of reincarnation. Individuals and communities run to these spiritual forces with sacrifices and rituals to garner power. Thus, conversion refers to turning away from primary allegiances and relationships with these gods to other higher powers such as Jesus Christ after whom Christians are named. It is the problem exploring the religious changes that may occur within the religious worldviews and practices of individuals and communities triggered by either internal forces or from the encounter with external religious agents. Jesus power or Christianity is only one of the sites to which Igbo people ran in the quest to harness power for the race of life. This chapter explores five discourses that explain the direction of the quest: ecological/culturalist, imaginative/intellectualist, historical, instrumentalist, and religious.

HISTORY, ECOLOGY, AND RELIGIOUS CHANGE: THE CULTURAL DISCOURSE

The relationship between Church history and the ecosystem needs to be spelled out because, in the effort to give the discipline a methodological identity, attention to the ecosystem is crucial. People live and are nurtured by the resources of the environment. Indeed, cultures are hewn from the rocks of challenges that the ecological system poses for a community. The argument simply asserts that the structure of the ecology determines a community's economic structure and food security; the agricultural cycle is woven around the economic activities; the major rituals and festivals celebrate the agricultural cycle; the cultural structures and values emerge as attempts to respond to the challenges in the ecosystem; and the poverty that afflicts Africa is directly connected to lack of attention to ecological ethics. The environment poses a challenge and the community constructs a worldview that unravels the riddle of the universe. It must address and reflect the specific nature of the challenge by probing their inner experience. People forge culture in the encounter with and effort to tame their environment and harness its resources for the nurture of that community. Worldviews therefore underpin cultures. A culture is the powerful expression of the creativity of the human spirit, the engine that moves civilization, and the substance of history. It is becoming axiomatic that the nurture, mobilization, and utilization of a community's resources for the enhancement of life are all dependent on the core values embedded in the worldview of the people and especially the ecological ethics emanating from that worldview. If, for instance, there is a shift from anthropocentric view of the world into a more organic one that perceives the ecosystem as a shared psychic space, the purview, questions, and method in doing history will change. History will cease to be an interpretation of the human past, but an interpretation of the relationships of humans to themselves as well as to animals and other beings, sentient or nonsentient.

Thus, the geographical location of Igboland was crucial for its church history. Since Igboland is not bounded by the Atlantic Ocean, it required a number of expeditions tracing the River Niger in 1841, 1854, and 1857 before a viable access could be gained. Accessibility is important in the church histories of communities: those communities located on the waterfront came into earlier and consistent contact with external change agents, while those in the hinterland made late contacts. Often, young teachers from the coastal communities served as teachers and pastors and paraded the coastal cultures as being superior. This factor becomes important when it is realized that the Igbo did not perceive themselves as one people but as different groups emerging from different migratory routes, raising the question about the emergence of an Igbo identity. For instance, the theory that Nri is the cradle of Igbo culture is a myth arising from the early contact and enculturation of northwestern Igboland with European culture and its bearers—traders and missionaries.

Thus, a viable reconstruction compels the culture area approach. A culture area is defined as a geographical delineation of an area that has the same dominant and significant culture traits, complexes, and patterns. The advantages of this approach include the depth of data collection, comparative perspectives on why the gospel permeated some parts of Igboland more than others, and interpretation of the nonreligious factors that explain the patterns of vertical and horizontal expansion of Christianity.[16]

Igbo culture areas or complexes include:

- The western culture theatre: Asaba, Ika, and Ndokwa (Delta Igbo);
- Northwest: north and south Niger flood plain, Onitsha, Idemili, Aguata, Nri, and Awka (Anambra state);
- Northern: Awgu, Enugu, Nsukka, and Abakiliki (Enugu state and part of Ebonyi state);
- Central-i: Orlu, Owerri, Nkwere, and Ideato; Central-ii: Mbano, Mbaise, Etiti, and Okigwe (Imo state);
- Southwest: Ohaji, Egbema, Oguta, Ndoni, and Ikwerre (parts of Imo and Rivers states);
- South: Ngwa, Asa, Etche, and Ukwa (Abia state);
- Eastern: Umuahia-Ikwuano, Bende, Ohafia, Afikpo, and Aro (parts of Abia and Ebonyi states).[17]

The above structure points to the cultural axes that explain the differentiated patterns of responses to the gospel among Igbo communities.

For Church history, ecology is central to the biblical definition and task of the church. First, geography, values, and culture of a community not only are challenged by the power of the gospel but they, too, determine the community's response because the community struggles to contextualize the gospel to fit its needs. For instance, rich agricultural and sedentary communities are more resistant to the gospel or any change agent than those with commercially driven economies. It is the old concept of open and closed societies. Thus, communities in the northern and southern flood plains of the River Niger enjoyed a fertile terrain and a rich agricultural life and remained resistant to Christianity in spite of location on the waterfront. The soil pattern and density of population drove the rest of the northwest into early migrations and long-distance trade in search of resources. The Igbo Ukwu excavations by Thurstan Shaw showed that the precolonial northwestern Igbo traded in the upper Benue River with the Jukun. Further evidence comes from the Edda-Afikpo culture complex in eastern Igboland, where the existence of the *isi ji* ritual for initiation into manhood stood at the door of the culture and barred acceptance of Christianity because any young man who does not perform the pilgrimage to the shrine of *Alusi Edda* cannot marry or function as a male in the society.

The concept adds that the tensile strength of indigenous customs remains stronger in centralized societies than among segmentary societies. The Igbo have a few centralized political systems in Onitsha and Oguta; therefore, the predominantly segmentary nature of Igbo political organization and its republican spirit encouraged individualism and competition. Competing religious denominations exploited this as rival chiefs and rival neighboring communities invited missionaries from different denominations. Such invitations soon became markers of status. For instance, in 1912, Obi Ejeshi, the chief of Ezedibia-Emekuku in central Igboland, blocked the access of schoolchildren who attended school in neighboring Egbu-Owerri, where the Church Missionary Society (CMS) missionaries first settled. He appealed to the rival Roman Catholics to open a school and Father Feral jumped at the opportunity. Since the students at Egbu read an Igbo primer entitled *Azu Ndu* ("*Fresh Fish*"), the chief advised the students to change their diet to dry fish.[18] Thus, the ecology could determine the pattern of reception and domestication of the Christian gospel.

Second, the major challenges to the Church's faithful witness arise from worldview, ecology, and human problems (such as poverty) that emerge from the environmental challenges. These compel stewardly diaconic response by the churches.

Third, African Christianity is rooted in the African worldview because people expect the gospel to answer questions raised in the interior of the worldview—regarding, for example, witchcraft and sorcery, ancestral curses and blessings, and power of spiritual forces. Indigenous religious leaders found large swaths of resonance between the biblical worldview and the Igbo worldview. This is not surprising because the Igbo claim to share common origins with the Hebrews. Historians must pay due attention to worldviews in explaining the patterns of conversion or religious change in the race of life because African worldviews tend to be religious cosmologies that determine responses to new religious agents, either as an extension of the innate spiritual desires and hopes of the people or as challenges. New religious movements source their problems, idioms, and answers from this fountain.

RELIGION AND WORLDVIEWS: THE INTELLECTUALIST DISCOURSE

Robin Horton emphasized the import of worldviews as an intellectual ordering of reality that aids explanation, prediction, and control of space-time events. He perceived a relationship between African and Western scientific thought patterns; that a worldview is like theory building and, therefore, a "quest for the unity underlying apparent diversity; for the simplicity underlying apparent complexity and for order underlying disorder; for the regularity underlying apparent anomaly." It does more as it brings into causal relationship wider vistas of reality and everyday life. He demonstrated the assertion with Kalabari worldview, showing that the fears, hopes, and religious ardor of the Kalabari could easily be understood by a close look at three basic kinds of forces: ancestors, heroes, and water-spirits. Appreciating the idiom of their "mystical" thinking may not only solve the riddle of "primitive mentality," which bothered Levy-Bruhl, but also explain the factors of the mental matrix of the community that assists them in surviving in their ecosystem. They could link events in the visible, tangible (natural effects) to their antecedents in the same world (natural causes).[19]

Worldview is the hermeneutic, the cultural lens through which human experiences are explained. Horton argued that religious change emerges from the enlargement of scale; as people migrate out of their small-scale, village, culture areas (microcosm) to more complex urban environments or other cultures (macrocosm), their local deities that sustained the microcosmos lose power because new needs become compelling, creating an openness toward new, empowering religious ideas and symbols. Thus, religious change could be traced through changes in the worldviews that are replicated in social structures.

Igbo indigenous cultures share worldviews with other African cultures that serve as reservoirs of indigenous knowledge. They are stored in proverbs and folk myths. Myths of origin abound, explaining how the world came into existence. One of these imagines the world as a sacred egg, at once fragile, enfolding, and nurturing. Its sacred origin imbues it with a sacral order, which, when understood and followed, ensures a miracle—as this seemingly fragile frame has the capacity to sustain so many and so much activity.[20] From such myths people begin to construct how and why things are the way they are. Explanation aids prediction of space-time events and this, in turn, enables control. Myths of origin are, therefore, the vehicles of worldviews and differ among the ethnic groups who inhabit West Africa. A common structure underlies all of them and they share a deep level of meaning. Each is couched in religious, numinous terms: creation was the act of a Supreme Being utilizing the services of subaltern gods. The divine origin confers a sacred shroud on the created beings and social order.

People, therefore, construct a moral order, with a certain rhythm, to explain, predict, and control space-time events in their ecosystem. A worldview is a mental construct that empowers action and endows rhythm and meaning to life processes. It is the foundation of customs, social norms, and law. Worldviews are embedded in the people's experience and are enacted in their cultures. This can be illustrated with one major cultural feature, the masking tradition, which is very important in the rituals, festivals, aesthetics, and plastic arts. Masqueraders of semisavanna, grassland communities such as in northern Igboland tend to be clothed in dry grass. Some look like moving bundles of grass. Among the forest-zone dwellers of southern and central Igboland, the masqueraders leap out of the bushes as followers caparison with leaves and branches. Among the riverine communities in the Niger Delta, the masqueraders, wearing masks depicting various kinds of fish, arrive in canoes. The community dances to the waterfront, welcomes them with a chorus into the village, and the celebration begins. At dusk, they are led back to the beach. As they paddle off, the people wave and cry for the departing ancestors. The crux of the cultural form is that the masqueraders *are* ancestors; they *are* the gods as guests to the human world. With their arrival, the seen and the unseen worlds meet; the living and the living dead reunite even if for a brief period. The resonance is strong with Owu cultural form of the Kalabari.

Various anthropologists have sought to capture the nuances of worldview: some call it "mind-world" and explore the differences between Western and non-Western mindworlds. The ethnologist, Edward Sapir, termed it "the unconscious patterning of behavior in society . . . the way a people characteristically look outward on the universe." He noted that a people's worldview comprises patterns of thought, attitude toward life, conceptions of time, a mental picture of what ought to be, a people's understanding of their relationship to unseen things and to the order of things, and their view of self and others. Paul G. Hiebert organizes the content of worldview into three categories: cognitive, affective, and evaluative. These refer to the abstract ideas, interpersonal structures, and ethical values. Charles Kraft underscores the place of values in a worldview as "the culturally structured assumptions, values and commitments underlying a people's perception of reality." They are "deep-level bases from which people generate surface-level behavior."[21] Therefore, concludes Marguerite Kraft, worldviews

> affect how people perceive self, the in-group to which they belong, outsiders, nature around them and non-human world . . . [and] makes it possible for people to feel comfortable in their environment. . . . Worldview is a picture of what is and ought to be, and it provides the motivation for behavior and gives meaning to the environment.[22]

Worldview is, indeed, as John Grim explains, "a story of the world which informs all aspects of life among a people, giving subsistence practice, artistic creation, ritual play and military endeavor a significant content."[23] Like the rest of culture, it can be unconsciously learned and deliberately transmitted. It could become encrusted into customs, safe in the womblike warmth of the sacred egg, but it is not a static concept. No matter how resistant it might be to the battering forces of change, the shell chips away as the process of reconfiguration and reconstruction begins with new experiences and challenges.

This reflection is based on a survey of the gods of various culture areas of Igboland. For instance, I catalogued 615 gods located within the three-dimensional perception of space and typologized them into seven categories, as shown in table 21.1.

TABLE 21.1 Typology of Igbo gods

Space	*Number*	*Percentage*
SKY		
Oracular	17	2.7
LAND		
Nature	61	9.91
Earth deity	59	9.59
Guardian/patron	76	12.35
Spiritual force	151	24.45
MARINE		
Water deities	135	21.19
ANCESTRAL WORLD		
Ancestors	116	18.86
Total	615	100

If we prioritized the three of the most prominent deities in each culture area, the foci of religious ardor will become clearer:

Culture Area	*Dominant Deities*
WEST	water, spirit force, ancestral
NORTHWEST	spirit force, water, nature
NORTH	spirit force, ancestral, nature
CENTRAL-I	water, ancestral, spirit force
CENTRAL-II	nature, ancestral, earth deity
SOUTH	spirit force, ancestral, earth deity
EAST	spirit force, water/guardian spirit (tied), ancestral[24]

The conclusion is that each culture area of Igboland prioritizes its religious concerns differently. Communities weave covenants with these gods and develop elaborate rituals for garnering power to run the race of life. When the gospel comes into a culture area it must contend with the gods that rule over the affairs of that culture area. This is why worldviews are important: they enable the historian to reconstruct the power encounter in the horizontal expansion of the gospel, that is, when the gospel ethics seek to transform the indigenous beliefs and values of a community. The Garrick Braide agents displayed this most acutely as they came into southern Igboland in 1918, burning oracular deities among the Ngwa while singing a chorus declaring that *Jesus abiala, ekwensu agbagho oso!* (*Jesus has come and the devil has run away!*)[25]

But it is also known that communities, like individuals, could preserve their indigenous religion by creating a center secured with symbols of cultural identity and developing a periphery where the negotiation with the new religious agent takes place. Thus, in the west, northwest, and central Igboland, the major ritual symbols and festivals preserve the allegiance to water deities who give wealth and confer social status. Indeed, a cult of water of deities (Mami Wata) that gives wealth has dominated the culture areas in spite of early contact with external change agents who came through the River Niger. In a similar manner, the entire northeastern Igboland is divided into *Odo* and *Omabe* subculture areas based on their ancestral deities, *Omabe* and *Odo*. A major controversy occurred in the *Odo* axis in 1989 when the indigenes insisted that all Christian churches should close their doors at the climax of the *Odo* festival that fell on a Sunday.[26] Nature spirit is so strong in that axis that people are named after hills and shrines, and the sun has shrines on hills from where they lick up sacrifices for the Supreme Being. Missionaries wondered why Igbo converts still resort to indigenous priests without realizing that all over Igboland, people believe in holding some medicinal symbols that have been imbued with power for enhancing and protecting life—just as popular Catholicism uses icons of saints. The spirit force featured prominently in all culture areas in the taxonomy of Igbo deities.

In a section of central Igboland, the earth deity is so prominent that her shrine has become a major artistic center as devotees built sculptures that celebrate her munificence. But the emphasis arises from land scarcity and the need for divine arbitration over land disputes. After a church is established, the community reaches a compromise whereby the church does not attack the festivals and rituals or customs that succor the political economy and moral foundation of the community. These are called *omenala* (*ome n'ala*—the things that are done to secure the land). For instance, everyone knows that when a masquerade is pursuing someone and the person runs into the church premises, the masquerade does not trespass into the church compound. Similarly, the guardians of the village rituals do not expect the church members to attack the ritual calendar. Conversion as compromise suffered hiccups between the years 1920 and 1950 when the frequency of clashes between missionaries and indigenous leaders over culture increased. Most controversies centered on the rites of passage and rituals celebrating the agricultural cycle. From December 1949 through January 1950, matters came to a head in a major conflict when church members in eastern Igboland who had been members of the *Ekpe* secret society betrayed the secrets during a Bible class. Infuriated communities burned schools and churches in Bende District. The District Officer intervened and blamed the church members. The colonial government's cultural policy was more concerned with maintaining public order than with the Christian diatribe against demonic cultures and superstitions.[27] This explains the discussions in the literature about the continuity of Igbo values after conversion and ambiguities in Igbo conversion.

THE HISTORICAL DISCOURSE: MISSIONARY NARRATIVE AND VERTICAL EXPANSION

The historical discourse examines the home bases of missionaries: motives, policies strategies, recruitment, and funding. The ideology of mission was embedded in these factors. In the conversion process, the method of doing evangelization was often more important than what was said. The tendency toward a transplantation ideology emerged from the racism and triumphalism that characterized the colonial project and overrule. Missionaries were children of their age. Indeed, it was voluntarism that created flexible missionary projects because protagonists could operate outside the control of denominations to raise funds from all segments of the public. Buoyed with mass appeal and funding, a missionary had more initiative and reported to only the home board rather than to the official church. Biographies are important because the force of personality and career track (black and white) are essential for reconstructing the insertion of the gospel and the vertical expansion of Christian presence into Igboland. Each denomination sported individuals who changed the shape of their denominational presence. The color of the missionary agent was important in conversion: in some communities, people admired the black agent; in others, the presence of a white person was a status symbol.[28]

The first aspect of historical discourse is an eye to periodization: Christianity became important in Igboland from the twilight of the nineteenth century and was just entering the hinterland when World War I broke out. The impact of that war catalyzed the quest for education, and World War II reshaped both geopolitics and opportunities for indigenous agency. The Nigerian/Biafran Civil War (1967–1970) scrambled the religious landscape by disrupting the structures of the mainline churches and creating a heightened charismatic spiritual need. Later, charismatic spirituality and the translation of the Bible reared new indigenous agents and challenged the old missionary structures that had consolidated through its former pupils who now held power in the postcolonial state. New Christianities emerged in the anvil of the encounter among the gospel, Igbo cultures, and new life experiences.

To backtrack to an earlier period, the impact of the slave trade vitiated the missionary enterprise. The geographical location of Igboland meant that the Portuguese missionaries of the period before the nineteenth century did not make contact with the Igbo directly. Middlemen provided the abundance of Igbo slaves. The Aro of the eastern Nigerian culture theatre were the chief commercial agents of the nefarious trade. When abolitionism moved the engine of mission, many recaptives returned to Yorubaland from Sierra Leone as pastors, traders, colonial officers, and advisors to local chiefs. The Igbo in Sierra Leone chafed for such opportunities: they even contributed money and tried a failed expedition before the Church Missionary Society succeeded in 1857 to establish in Onitsha on the Niger River using a band of ex-slaves from Sierra Leone. Some were Igbo but who had lost both the language and culture, unlike many Yoruba returnees, including the famous Samuel Ajayi Crowther, who became a bishop in 1864 and supervised the

Niger mission from Lagos.[29] The failure of the Niger Mission has become a matter of debate because the investigation in 1891 was unfair to Crowther and smacked of racism. The CMS replaced the leadership with young British men with a strong Keswick-Evangelical spirituality. The Igbo and riverine ethnic groups seceded to form the Niger Delta Church.

The French Holy Ghost fathers came to Onitsha in 1885.[30] Felix Ekechi's *Missionary Rivalry* argues that it was the rivalry among European nations (typified by the Berlin Conference of 1885 where they partitioned Africa into colonies) and competition between the CMS and Spiritans that decided the pace, direction, and character of missionary vertical expansion. Rivalry was aided by the militarized "pacification" exercise to establish Western judiciary and administrative system, legitimate trade in palm oil and other raw materials, and Christianity as a civilizing agent. The British raided communities in Igbo hinterland in the attempt to dislodge the Aro slave-trading middlemen in 1901–1902. Pacification opened the hinterland for a variety of other British missionaries to come into Igboland—the Jamaican and Scottish Presbyterians, British Primitive Methodists, Welsh, Qua Iboe Mission, and American Lutherans. By 1911, in the aftermath of the Edinburgh Conference, the Protestants started annual conferences and delimited Igboland into zones of operation for each mission to avoid rivalry. By 1914, many Igbo communities, except those in inaccessible hinterland, were just making their first contacts with Christianity.

World War I drastically reshaped the interior of African Christianity. Some District Officers warned about a renaissance of secret societies as an antiwhite bonding. Colonial governments dreaded the competition to rational administrative structures by religious power nodes as secret societies, cults, and oracles. Beyond rumors that the colonial governments were about to collapse, the war further heightened tension within African communities because it required the services of recruits and porters and gave the local chiefs extraordinary powers to mobilize able-bodied men. Some men escaped into the bush to avoid recruitment; others devised the subterfuge of conversion and moved into missionary enclaves/stations in large numbers—to the initial delight of missionaries. Soon all devices collapsed as missionaries themselves were compelled to engage in the affray.

The world wars severely disrupted the structure and moral economy of the missionary enterprises in Africa. Germans lost territories and mission stations. The Presbyterians in Calabar were sent to take over Basle missions in southwest Cameroon and Gold Coast. Untoward geopolitical forces such as rumors of war, wars, economic collapse/depression, political instability, and the rise of anti-Christian communist and totalitarian ideologies were followed by seven wearisome years of World War II. These devastated missionary presence and structures by 1945. Yet, by the end of World War II, Christianity in Igboland had grown in the wake of missionary absence and indigenous leadership. Some missionary groups contemplated massive restructuring and downsizing in recognition of the new-fangled self-confidence of the "younger churches."

Ironically, missionary structures showed a high degree of resilience in the interwar years as "internationalism" became a new war cry that spurred young university students into the mission fields. Indeed, a process of domesticating Christian values intensified between 1919 and 1950. The process was aided by two other factors, namely, an outbreak of an ecumenical spirit detectable in various assemblies of the International Missionary Council and in the formation of national councils of churches in African countries. Christian Council of Nigeria (CCN) was first formed in the southeast in 1934 and consolidated in the southwest by 1944. Between 1960 and 1965, Anglicans, Methodists, and Presbyterians negotiated to unite.[31] But it was education and its mass appeal that rescued the missionary enterprise and ensured its recovery after the World War I.

In nineteenth-century Yorubaland, an Africanist movement, Ethiopianism, mobilized African discomfort with colonialism and white monopoly of power in the church. Beyond giving voice, some resorted to exit from missionary churches to found the Native African churches. Typical is Mojola Agbebi, who broke away from the Baptist church in 1888.[32] Ethiopianism had little effect on Igboland. Similarly, when Africans showed a stronger charismatic initiative with a wave of African indigenous churches, especially during the influenza epidemic of 1918, Aladura churches failed to wean Igbo people from the mainline churches until during the Civil War period (1967–1970).[33] The earliest or classical Aladura emerged from mainline churches by recovering the pneumatic resources of the translated Bible. Later, new forms appeared that had no linkage with missionary churches. They institutionalized quickly into churches and equally deployed traditional symbols as the classical core but to a greater degree. Soon differences appeared based on the dosage of traditional religion in the mix: some *messianic* leaders claimed to be one or the other of the Trinity; the *revivalistic* ideologically promoted the significance of indigenous religion by privileging the resonance with Christian symbols; the *vitalistic* tapped occult powers; and the *nativistic* remained as indigenous cults, borrowing Christian symbols and paraphernalia. Thus, many forms operate beyond the pales of Christianity. Some worship on Sundays while others worship on Saturdays as Sabbatharians; some are political while others are safe religious havens for the brutalized Africans.

The Igbo perceived the movement as a Yoruba phenomenon patronized by Yoruba indigenes working in the eastern region. A pioneer Aladura church in Igboland is "Odozi Obodo," founded by Madam Agnes Okoh (1905–1995) in 1947. The Odozi Obodo merged with the Christ Apostolic Church between 1950 and 1975. The church is interesting because it grew under an illiterate woman; it is located in Onitsha (the headquarters of the Anglicans and Roman Catholics since 1854), in Igboland, where the African Instituted Churches (AICs) have been confronted by stiff opposition from the mainline churches. Odozi Obodo liturgy is charismatic and utilizes indigenous culture. Madam Agnes Okoh, the founder, insisted on divine healing and contested Western medicine.[34] Except for the revivalistic genre like Godianism led by Chief K. O. K. Onyioha, the Igbo showed little creativity but patronized messianic forms that originated among Ibibio and Cross River communities. The Igbo were more prominent in the foundation of the sabbatharian Aladura movement that could be traced to Dede Keke Lolo of Akwete. From 1920, the Faith Tabernacle from Philadelphia emerged in Igboland, became strong from 1925 through the patronage of palm oil traders along the Imo River, and has endured to the present.

Interpreters image the Aladura variously as signals of African Christian initiative and contribution to World Christianity; African theological response to missionary gospel with immense creativity on the gospel-culture interface; a poignant reaction to colonial Christianity; a religion of the oppressed resembling cargo cults; the quest for belonging, safe havens amidst white racism; an emergent syncretistic spirituality that exploits the schismatic character of Protestantism; the religious stroke in nascent political nationalism; and succor to displaced peoples amid increased urbanization. Obviously, the surge was aided by the translation of the message into indigenous languages. which renewed interest in those elements that missionary message ignored or muted. These churches mined the Old Testament resonance with indigenous worldviews. Their astounding popularity engendered persecution.

It should be noted that there were three different types of charismatic responses to the gospel message in these times. First was the prophetic movement characterized by individual prophets, such as Garrick Braide from Bakana in the Niger Delta, who burst into prominence in 1914 but was quickly incarcerated by the colonial government and died in 1918. His disciples continued the task. Second was the African Instituted Churches. Third, other charismatic flares occurred within mainline churches; for instance, among the Qua Iboe church in Ibibioland, Nigeria, in 1927. Five young men of the Faith Tabernacle in Umuahia spoke in tongues, were expelled, formed the Church of Jesus Christ in 1934, and invited the Assemblies of God, who took them over in 1939. The evangelical transcontinental tours of American evangelists such as Billy Graham buoyed the spirits of the young

Africans before the decolonization blues of the 1960s. This is the background to the charismatic wind that blew prominently from the 1970s among young people.

Soon after World War I, missions reorganized, brought back some German-speaking priests, and exploited the unsettled circumstances to steal bases and expand. Throughout this period, the "bush school" (or the village schools) became the mascot of missionary presence. Schools were used as a means of evangelization, rivalry, civilizing project, legitimization of colonial industrial policy, vertical expansion into rural areas, and domestication of Christian values. One had to be literate to read the catechism and sing the salvation hymns. School and church shared space and significance. Those who did not attend Sunday school were caned in the school on Mondays. Debate ranged around the curricula, level of education, use of indigenous personnel, governments' roles, and the relationship between education and evangelism. Some missionaries resisted the expansion of school apostolate whereas others saw it as the means to capture the future generation, especially the education of the girl-child. Missionaries perceived education as an investment good, not a consumer good. They hated the pretensions of educated Africans. Therefore, curricula should be confined to assisting them to cope within their cultural milieu, acculturate the values of the change agents, serve as intermediaries between Western and traditional societies, and mediate colonial civilizing policies and instruments. Industrial missions held much promise. The colonial government was more concerned about the quality of education and broader curricula than the missions wanted and, therefore, employed grants-in-aid and inspectorate system as instruments of control.

Missionaries concentrated on teacher training and primary schools. There were only a few secondary and grammar schools until the 1940s, when some indigenous entrepreneurs funded secondary education. The Igbo paid for the foundation of Denis Memorial Grammar School, Onitsha—the first Igbo grammar school—in 1925. Sometimes, communities would provide the infrastructure while missions supplied the personnel. Africans instigated much of the expansion: those returning from the war or from mines and plantations urged the presence of schools as a sign of development, acquisition of white power, solving the riddle of the paper that talked, and coping mechanism for the new times. Communities built the school and house for a teacher and even put a deposit toward the salary. Competing missions exploited intercommunal rivalry while the District Officers delimited areas of operation. Rapid expansion compelled the use of poorly trained teachers.[35]

Agitation for university education after the World War II induced government concern for secondary education. Government instituted the Phelps-Stokes Commission Report that showed off the capability of the brilliant Ghanaian, Dr. J. E. K. Aggrey (1875–1927). But its reliance on Booker T. Washington's approach met with African criticism: that it limited the ranges of African access to education. In this period, the number of young Africans studying overseas for the "golden fleece" increased. Dr. Emmanuel Onwu, Dr. Akanu Ibiam, and a host of Igbo young men traveled to Scotland, Britain, and the United States, where Lincoln University bred a number of nationalists such as Dr. Nnamdi Azikiwe, Dr. Mbonu Ojike, and Dr. Ozumba Mbadiwe. These individuals would become the agitators of the post-1945-era nationalist struggles in Nigeria. Either the wars' experiences opened people's eyes to the power of white technology or the onslaught of the years on traditional cultures finally took its toll. It could also be that the new patterns of exploitation weakened primary resistance and gave way to a mass movement to Christianity that further intensified in the wake of youthful charismatism of the 1970s and has continued unabated. The literature has recaptured the large roles played by indigenous agents and also the strongly charismatic nature of indigenous response. These combined with vernacularization and the appeal of education to explain the vertical expansion of Christianity in Igboland.

The appeal of the gospel must be nuanced because when the gospel spread to the villages, the encounter of gospel and culture created disquiet. In towns, urbanization expanded with serious moral implications. Thus, in spite of mass movement, a spectrum of responses appeared as the guardians of the ancestral calabash struck back in persecutions. Indeed, some of the patrons of church and school did not convert because it was education that they sought for their progenies. Novelists have captured this mood more accurately. Ironically, indigenous agents bore the brunt of missionary expansion: chiefs invited and patronized missions; and communities raised the funds to pay teachers, built the school houses, and furnished porters, evangelists, interpreters, house-servants, and co-pastors.

THE INSTRUMENTALIST DISCOURSE

The *instrumentalist* discourse argues that religious changes are responses to changes in the mundane realm, influenced by the rapid and untoward changes in their sociopolitical and economic environment; that changes in the social structure explain religious change. Caroline Ifeka-Moller states the case sufficiently to see its limits:

> Conversion to mission Christianity . . . was most in evidence . . . in and around certain communities of the oil palm belt. Villages which experienced intensive change went over rapidly, and in large numbers, to the mission churches and then to the Aladuras. Mass conversion was a consequence of these social changes: incorporation into the new world economy, the imposition of new political roles under the colonial system, and a growing realization among the inhabitants of those communities that they had failed to obtain the rewards promised by acceptance of these radical changes. Christianity promised a new kind of power, the power of the white man, which people could use to discover the secret of his technological superiority.[36]

The model shows the utility of building the "surround" or social milieu of conversion. But the argument that people accepted the new dispensation discounts the patterns of indigenous resistance. In fact, there were two levels of conversion: to mission churches and to exit into charismatic churches. The same explanation cannot hold true for both. There is evidence of a counterdirection in the linkage between wealth, disappointment, and religious affiliation. New wealth, as in the case of Brass in the Niger Delta, made it possible for the indigenous elite to patronize Christianity. They donated generously toward new infrastructure. When the middlemen were displaced by new colonial policy, the people resorted to *iguana*, the indigenous religion that worships the crocodile.[37]

In the complex relationship between Igbo communities and missionaries, Christianity equipped individuals and communities to participate in the colonial political economy—to acquire the skills for confronting modernity and the right attitude of hope and optimism in the face of poverty and other life-threatening conditions. The instrumentalist discourse explores the psychological, economic, and social (especially gender) dimensions of indigenous responses to Christianity. Education, for instance, served as the strongest instrument of conversion because it was used to indoctrinate and socialize converts into the values (represented as civilization) of the new religion. For missionaries, education was a means of evangelization, and charitable institutions were built in the heat of rivalry. For the converts, the new religion enhanced social mobility and status and brought wealth and capacity to serve as interpreters of the new dispensation. Some entrepreneurs gained the warrant chieftaincy from colonial officers even when they lacked local legitimacy. Missionaries served as diplomats in the relationship between communities and the colonial officers. Some argue that it was a game of mutual deceit, that Christianity was manipulated as an instrument because adherence was more important than deep-level faith development. This explains the tendency to exit from mission churches when charismatic churches beat their drums and promised to heal the sick based on a deeper religious commitment. Bishop Shanahan is alleged to have concluded that it took seven generations to make one true convert. But he was rewarded when an Igbo, Father Tansi, joined the monastery in Britain.[38] Elizabeth Isichei and Cyril Okorocha proposed a generational analysis of the patterns of conversion: that the first generation of the Igbo responded differently from the second generation in the postcolonial period while the response in the contemporary period has its specific features in a context where the churches no longer control education or access to health care.[39] The instrumentalist discourse invites an analysis of the connection between the growth of Christianity in contemporary Igboland and the collapse of economies, long years of military rule, legitimacy crises, and the corruption of the political elite—untoward forces that have catalyzed increased violence and social crimes.

PILGRIMS AND STILL NATIVES: THE RELIGIOUS DISCOURSE

As churches lose the control of charitable institutions and the gospel contends with attacks from the state and other competing religious and secular institutions and ideologies, the religious discourse argues that purely religious dimensions of conversion are important. The power of the word and a certain measure of religious genius empowered the appropriation of the gospel in such a manner that the gospel answers questions confronting the Igbo—as individuals, communities, and as a racial group. The gospel is like a pilgrim living off the resources of the cultures that he encounters. It is also indigenous or native expressing itself in the languages, idioms, and cultures of the world. As communities convert or turn their cultures and inner selves to the sunlight of the gospel, they are renewed and yet judged by the mandates of the gospel. Christ is in every culture and judges all cultures. The quality of conversion is, therefore, a function of the quality of dialogue in the encounter.

The religious discourse enables the historian to show that Christian theologies vary and matter in the explanation of the growth of the movement because the messages attract. It enables a phenomenological, eidetic exploration, especially because the concept of a systematic theology has been thrashed in postmodernist discourse. Theology is no longer a reified enterprise but simply human reflection on the relationship of God-in-Christ to human beings and to the world of nature through his *agape* (love) and the power of the Holy Spirit. Every theology reflects its contextualized location. The resources of the reign of God are being experienced among us but the fullness has not been revealed. Each generation and each cultural context should continuously reflect on the meaning of the presence of the reign of God among the human communities, both globally and locally. Religious change in contemporary Igboland reflects the achievements of theological development, especially in its oral forms, as people quest for power of life. Oral theology is endowed with indigenous initiative—creativity in hermeneutics that explores the resonances between the Bible and indigenous traditions and that leaps into appropriation of the text for immediate needs. It is endowed with creative use of language and the homilectical power of evangelists and local catechists untrammeled by the logic of schooled theologians. Contemporary Igboland is characterized by new charismatic movements that perceive themselves to be the beneficiaries of the increasing revelations of divine wisdom and resources. Each receiving context must dialogue and question the validity of the given "truth" that the missionaries proffered. The public visibility of the new Christianity and its unstoppable growth needs our final attention. Many commentators agree that the growth is connected to its consumption of media resources, popular culture, and the marketability of religion.

POPULAR CULTURE, MEDIA, AND THE MARKETABILITY OF RELIGION

To end the reflection from where we started: how did *osondu*, the past Igbo quest for vitality in life, generate the contemporary Christian landscape? A number of directions are optional. One could be a reflection on how Igbo republicanism created a competitive space for the patronage of many varieties of Christianity and explains the famous notion that the Igbo are highly receptive to change. The Igbo image of life as a struggle (*ndogha*) accentuates the quest for power. For instance, in recent times, some born-again Christians burn the shrines of their communities because these impede the struggles of the members to prosper. Anthropologists bemoan the removal of markers of cultural identities and compare the Igbo Christians to Yorubas, who will tolerate the icons of the cultural past. Why are the Igbo so willing to let the ancestral marks to be erased? It could be because the Igbo experiences within the Nigerian state may have sharpened the notion of struggling to survive amid the hostile responses from other ethnic groups.

A second direction is to pick one key feature of contemporary Christianity that encapsulates a wider range of forces. Here, we shall argue that Christian media consumption has created a heightened public visibility that may belie the depth of conversion. Burning of idols has been an old strategy of Christian penetration of Igbo communities. Resistance to the bonfire has remained a sign of the tensile strength of the indigenous religious and political culture. The most successful attack on Igbo religion is found in the growing media industry, especially Nollywood's film and video industry.

Specifically, how does the charismatic movement, as the fastest growing Christian form, deploy media technology and popular culture in its missionary strategy against Igbo indigenous religion? A caveat should be entered that media has its own culture and spirit that could ensure that religion is, in turn, reshaped and repackaged by both popular culture and media technology. Therefore, historiographical question is: given the fact that media technology has an innate culture and that popular culture is driven by a different spirit, how can the media technologies serve as resources and challenges in evangelism and representation?

First, we explore four models of the relationship between religion and popular culture. The *religion in culture* model emphasizes the use of religious themes, languages, images, characters, and subjects in film or music, sport, or television. It props the rebuttal that entertainment appears crucial for the survival of religion in the marketplace of culture. It is an acculturating pathway for touching youthful audiences who are already enmeshed, wired in the electronic culture, and bored with the equally packaged institutional religion. Religion and popular culture must be meshed to attract the youths, just as mainline churches experiment with new liturgies and music. Others note the *popular culture in religion* model, evident in initiatives that employ the tools, strategies, resources, language, and media of popular culture for the purposes of transmitting particular faith traditions and communities. This model images the primary goal of media as an enabling, valorized strategy for making disciples and proffer advice on how to counter its dangerous dimensions. Another model deploys the *popular culture as religion* model to argue that the secular corporate interests have taken over spirituality to subvert individuals and seduce them into consumerism, that advertisements utilize religious cultural cachet and brand names to associate products with personal fulfillment, inner peace, happiness, and success in relationships. Management efficiency is packaged as religious paths to enlightenment. A fourth model, *religion and popular culture in dialogue*, sees both as linked and requiring mutual accountability. The dialogue is more compelling because of critical scholarship on the popular culture in religion model.

Second, it is argued that the contours and emphases within the charismatic movements changed in each decade from the 1970s and that access to mass media is a feature of the 1980s. The media landscape has also changed character in two time frames: before the 1980s and after the 1980s.

Third, as the use of media technology became important during the 1980s, the charismatic movements interacted with popular culture and deployed the various media: newspaper, pamphlets, book publication, advertisement, television, radio, music, and dance.[40] Since American televangelism aroused great interest, the impact of this global cultural flow cannot be ignored. Yet we reject the alleged Americanization of the hooks and corners of Igboland because of the power of indigenous knowledge and resilient local identities. The forms of local appropriation, initiative. and creativity contest the Americanization impulse.

Fourth, all analyses of religious change must recognize that *ọsọndu* is a race that takes different directions; it is like a quest in a dank forest where people carve many pathways. The explosion of theosophic religions in Igboland is an example: Grail Message, Eckankar, and Freemasonry lodges have found enthusiastic devotees, especially among the professional elite. Someone quipped that the Igbo discovered these pathways in the attempt to gain entry into brotherhoods that reopened the professional associations and businesses after the Civil War. This leaves us pondering how the process of readjustment to the trauma, scars, and stigma of the Nigerian/Biafran Civil War (1967–1970) informs the contours of religious change among the Igbo of southeastern Nigeria.

NOTES

1. Matthew Ojo, *End-Time Army* (Trenton, NJ: Africa World Press, 2006); Richard Burgess, *Nigeria's Christian Revolution: The Civil War Revival and Its Pentecostal Progeny (1967–2006)* (Eugene, OR: Wipf and Stock, 2008).

2. Emmanuel A. Ayandele, *Missionary Impact on Modern Nigeria* (London: Longman, 1966), 34.

3. Emmanuel A. Ayandele, "How Truly Nigerian is our Nigerian History?" *African Notes* 5, no. 2, (1969): 19–35.

4. David Laitin, *Hegemony and Culture: Politics and Religious Change among the Yoruba* (Chicago: University of Chicago Press, 1986), 132. See also Olufemi Richard Vaughan, "Political Ethnicity in Western Nigeria: Chieftaincy, Communal Identities, and Party Politics," in *The Transformation of Nigeria*, ed. Ade Oyebade (Trenton, NJ: Africa World Press, 2002), 435–62.

5. Akin Akinade, "Islamic Challenges in African Christianity," in *African Christianity: An African Story*, ed. Ogbu U. Kalu (Trenton, NJ: Africa World Press, 2006), 103–22.

6. John Peel, *Religious Encounter and the Making of the Yoruba* (Bloomington: Indiana University Press, 2000).

7. Ibid., 2.

8. Ibid., 121.

9. Ibid., 122.

10. Ibid., 295.

11. Ibid., 157.

12. Ibid., 194.

13. Ibid., 313.

14. Ogbu U. Kalu, "Doing Mission Through the Post Office: The Naked Faith People of Igboland, 1920–1960," *Neue Zeitschrift fur Missionwissenschaft* 56, no. 4 (2000): 263–80; Abi Olowe, *Great Revivals, Great Revivalist—Joseph Ayo Babalola* (Houston, TX: Omega Publishers, 2007).

15. Ogbu U. Kalu, *Embattled Gods: The Christianization of Igboland, 1841–1991* (Lagos and London: Minaj Publishers, 1995; repr., Trenton, NJ: Africa World Press, 2003).

16. Ogbu U. Kalu, *Clio in a Sacred Garb: Christian Presence and African Responses, 1900–2000* (Trenton, NJ: Africa World Press, 2008), 23–56.

17. The creation of states may have scrambled the culture areas and all communities are not listed.

18. Kalu, *Embattled Gods*, 195. See also I. R. A. Ozigbo, *Roman Catholicism in Southern Nigeria, 1885–1930: A Study in Colonial Evangelism* (Onitsha: NG: Etukokwu Press, 1988).

19. R. Horton, *The Patterns of Thought in Africa and the West* (Cambridge: Cambridge University Press, 1993).

20. See, Ogbu U. Kalu, "Precarious Vision: The African Perception of His World," in *Readings in African Humanities: African Cultural Development*, ed. Ogbu U. Kalu (Enugu, NG: Fourth Dimension Publishers, 1978), chap. 3.

21. P. G. Hiebert, *Anthropological Insights for Missionaries* (Grand Rapids, MI: Baker Books, 1985), 46; Charles H. Kraft, *Christianity with Power: Your Worldview and Your Experience of the Supernatural* (Ann Arbor, MI: Vine Press, 1989), 20, 182; D. G. Mandelbaum, ed., *Selected Writings from Edward Sapir in Language, Culture and Philosophy* (Berkeley: University of California Press, 1958), 548.

22. Marguerite G. Kraft, *Worldview and the Communication of the Gospel* (Pasadena, CA: William Carey, 1995), 21.

23. M. E. Tucker and J. A. Grim, eds., *Worldviews and Ecology* (Lewisburg, PA: Bucknell University Press, 1993), 42.

24. See Kalu, *Embattled Gods*, 29–52, for details.

25. Ogbu U. Kalu, "Waves From the Rivers: The Spread of Garrick Braide Movement in Igboland, 1914–1934," *Journal of the Historical Society of Nigeria* 8, no. 4 (June 1977): 95–110.

26. Ogbu U. Kalu, "The Dilemma of Grassroots Inculturation of the Gospel," *Journal of Religion in Africa* 25 (February 1995): 48–72.

27. Ogbu U. Kalu, "Missionaries, Colonial Government and Secret Societies in Southeastern Igboland, 1920–1950,"*Journal of the Historical Society of Nigeria* 9, no. 1 (December 1977): 75–90; Ogbu U. Kalu, "Formulation of Cultural Policy in Colonial Nigeria," in *Tradition and Modern Culture*, ed. Edith Ihekweazu (Enugu, NG: Fourth Dimension Publishers, 1985), 125–38.

28. Ogbu U. Kalu, "Color and Conversion: The White Factor in Christianization of Igboland, 1857–1970," *Missiology* 18, no. 1 (Jan. 1990): 61–74.

29. See their letter, London: CMS Archives, CA1/024, The Onitsha Country in Sierra Leone to the Parent Committee 20/AO/1858. John Christopher Taylor moaned that as an Igbo, he should have led the Niger Mission. He contributed immensely in Bible translation into Igbo language. However, the Ibo Union Bible was later produced by T. J. Dennis with the assistance of Igbo people from eight dialect areas.

30. The Spiritans grew so rapidly that in 1972; a Province of Nigeria was erected that soon surpassed the French Province and ranks as the most populous Spiritan province worldwide. Bishop Shanahan's personality in building the Spiritans in Igboland looms large. Felix Ekechi, *Missionary Enterprise and Rivalry in Igboland, 1857–1914* (London: Frank Cass, 1972).

31. Ogbu U. Kalu, *Divided People of God: Church Union Movement in Nigeria, 1875–1966* (New York: NOK, 1978).

32. Ogbu U. Kalu, "Ethiopianism in African Christianity," in *African Christianity: An African Story*, ed. Ogbu U. Kalu (Trenton, NJ: Africa World Press, 2007), 227–43. See also Toyin Falola ed., *Dark Webs: Perspectives on Colonialism in Africa* (Durham, NC: Carolina Academic Press, 2005), 137–60.

33. Ogbu U. Kalu, "*Ndi Afe Ocha*: The Early Aladura of Igboland, 1925–1975," in *Christianity and Social Change in Africa: Essays in Honor of J. D. Y. Peel*, ed. Toyin Falola (Durham, NC: Carolina Academic Press, 2005), 335–60.

34. Thomas Oduro, *Christ Holy Church International: The Story of an African Independent Church* (Minneapolis, MN: Lutheran University Press, 2007).

35. Ogbu U. Kalu, "Education and Change in Igboland, 1857–1967," in *Groundwork of Igbo History*, ed. A. E. Afigbo (Lagos, NG: Vista Books, 1992), chap. 19.

36. Caroline Ifeka-Moller, "White Power: Social-Structural Factors in Conversion to Christianity in Eastern Nigeria, 1921–1966," *Canadian Journal of African Studies* 8, no. 1 (1974): 55–72, see 61–62.

37. E. A. Ayandele, "The Missionary Factor in Brass, 1875–1900: A Study in Advance and Recession," *Bulletin for the Society of African Church History* 2, no. 3 (1967): 259–75.

38. Elizabeth Isichei, *Entirely for God: Life of Father Tansi* (London: Macmillan, 1980).

39. Elizabeth Isichei, "Seven Varieties of Ambiguities: Some Patterns of Igbo Response to Christian Missions," *Journal of Religion in Africa* 3, no. 3 (1970): 198–213; C. C, Okorocha, *The Meaning of Religious Conversion in Africa: The Case of the Igbo of Nigeria* (Aldershot, UK: Averbury, 1987). See Chinedu N. Ubah, "Religious Change Among the Igbo during the Colonial Period," *Journal of Religion in Africa* 18 (1988): 71–91; Frank Salomone, "Continuity of Igbo Values after Conversion," *Missiology* 3 (January 1975): 33–43.

40. Ogbu U. Kalu, *African Pentecostalism: An Introduction* (New York: Oxford University Press, 2008), 103–22.

SELECTED BIBLIOGRAPHY

Abernethy, David. *The Political Dilemma of Popular Education: An African Case*. Stanford, CA: Stanford University Press, 1969.

Achebe, Chinua. *Arrow of God*. London: Heinemann, 1960.

———. *Morning Yet on Creation Day: Essays*. London: Heinemann, 1975.

———. *No Longer at Ease*. London: Heinemann, 1962.

———. *Once There Was a Country: A Personal History of Biafra*. London: Penguin, 2012.

———. *Things Fall Apart*. London: Heinemann, 1956.

Achebe, Chinwe. *The World of Ogbanje*. Enugu, NG: Fourth Dimension Publishers, 1986.

Achebe, Nwando. "Balancing Male and Female Principles: Teaching about Gender in Chinua Achebe's *Things Fall Apart*." *Ufahamu: A Journal of the African Studies* 29, no. 1 (2002): 121–43.

———. *Farmers, Traders, Warriors and Kings: Female Power and Authority in Northern Igboland, 1900–1960*. Portsmouth, NH: Heinemann, 2005.

———. "Igo Mma Ogo: The Adoro Goddess, Her Wives and Challengers—Influences on the Reconstruction of Alor-Uno, Northern Igboland, 1890–1994." In "Revising the Experiences of Colonized Women." Special Issue, *Journal of Women's History* 14, no. 4 (2003): 83–104.

———. "When Deities Marry: Indigenous 'Slave' Systems Expanding and Metamorphosing in the Igbo Hinterland." In *African Systems of Slavery*, edited by Stephanie Beswick and Jay Spaulding, 105–33. Trenton, NJ: Africa World Press, 2009.

Acholonu, Catherine Obianju. "The Home of Olaudah Equiano: A Linguistic and Anthropological Search." *Journal of Commonwealth Literature* 22 (1987): 5–16.

———. *The Igbo Roots of Olaudah Equiano*. Owerri, NG: Ata Publications, 1989.

Adams, John. *Remarks on the Country extending from Cape Palmas to the River Congo: Including Observations on the Customs and Manners of the Inhabitants. With an Appendix Containing an Account of the European Trade with the West Coast of Africa*. London: G. & W., 1823.

———. *Sketches Taken during Ten Voyages to Africa, between the Years 1786 and 1800; including Observation on the Country between Cape Palmas and the River Congo; and Cursory Remarks on the Physical and Moral Character of the Inhabitants*. London: G. and W. B. Whittaker, 1822.

Afigbo, A. E. *The Abolition of the Slave Trade in Southeastern Nigeria, 1885–1950*. Rochester, NY: University of Rochester Press, 2006.

———. *The Age of Innocence: The Igbo and their Neighbors in Pre-colonial Times: Ahiajioku Lectures 1981*. Owerri, NG: Ministry of Information and Culture, 1981.

———. "The Aro Expedition of 1901–1902: An Episode in the British Occupation of Igboland." *Odu, A Journal of West African Studies* 7 (1972): 3–27.

———. "The Eclipse of the Aro Slaving Oligarchy of South-Eastern Nigeria, 1901–1927." *Journal of the Historical Society of Nigeria* 6, no. 1 (1971): 3–23.

———, ed. *Groundwork of Igbo History*. Lagos, NG: Vista Books, 1992.

———. "Igbo-Efik Relations in Historical Perspective." In *The Efiks and Their Neighbours: Historical Perspectives*, edited by Okon E. Uya, 140–66. Calabar, NG: CAT Publishers, 2005.

———, ed. *The Image of the Igbo*. Lagos, NG: Vista Books, 1991.

———. "The Nineteenth Century Crisis of the Aro Slaving Oligarchy in South-Eastern Nigeria." *Nigeria Magazine* 110–12 (1974): 66–73.

———. "Nsukka Communities from Earliest Times to 1951." In *The Nsukka Environment*, edited by G. E. K. Ofomata, 24–39. Enugu, NG: Fourth Dimension Publishers, 1978.

———. "Prolegomena to the Study of the Culture History of the Igbo-speaking Peoples of Nigeria." In *Igbo Language and Culture*, edited by F. Chidozie Ogbalu and E. Nolue Emenanjo, 28–53. Ibadan, NG: Oxford University Press, 1975.

———. "Revolution and Reaction in Eastern Nigeria: 1900–1929." *Journal of the Historical Society of Nigeria* 3, no. 3 (1966): 539–51.

———. *Ropes of Sand: Studies in Igbo History and Culture.* Nsukka, NG: UNN and Oxford University Press, 1981.

———. *The Warrant Chiefs: Indirect Rule in Southeastern Nigeria, 1891–1929.* London: Longman, 1972.

Afikpo Town Welfare Association Constitution. Afikpo, Nigeria, March 20, 1950.

Aguwa, Jude C. U. *The Agwu Deity in Igbo Religion: A Study of the Patron Spirit of Divination and Medicine in an African Society.* Enugu, NG: Fourth Dimension Publishers, 1995.

Ahanotu, Austin M. "The Role of Ethnic Unions in the Development of Southern Nigeria: 1916–66." In *Studies in Southern Nigerian History*, edited by B. I. Obichere. London: Frank Cass, 1982.

Aird, Sheila. "The Forgotten Ones: Enslaved Children and the Formation of a Labor Force in the British West Indies." PhD diss., Howard University, 2006.

Alagoa, Ebiegberi Joe. "The Development of Institutions in the States of the Eastern Niger Delta." *Journal of African History* 12 (1971): 269–78.

———. *A History of the Niger Delta: An Historical Interpretation of Ijo Oral Tradition.* Ibadan, NG: Ibadan University Press, 1972.

———. "Ke, the History of an Old Delta Community." *Oduma* 2 (1974): 4–10.

———. "Long-Distance Trade and States in the Niger Delta." *Journal of African History* 11, no. 3 (1970): 319–29.

———. "Oral Tradition and Archaeology: The Case of Onyoma." *Oduma* 1 (1974): 10–12.

———. *The Small Brave City State.* Ibadan, NG: Ibadan University Press, 1964.

Alford, Violet. *The Hobby Horse and Other Animal Masks.* London: Merlin Press, 1978.

Allan White to James Rogers & Co. January 27, 1793, C107/6.

America, Facsimili of 1627 Edition. Bogotá, Empresa Nacional de Publicaciones, 1956.

Anderson, Benedict. *Imagined Communities. Reflections on the Origin and Spread of Nationalism.* 1983; rev. London: Verso, 2006.

Andrew's Life Story (lebenslauf) in the Moravian Archives, Bethlehem, Pennsylvania, dated March 13, 1779.

Anene, J. C. *Southern Nigeria in Transition, 1885–1906.* Cambridge: Cambridge University Press, 1966.

Anonymous. "Aenwijsingese van diversche Beschrijvingen van de Noort-Cust van Africa," f. 10v, Journal of a voyage to the Rio Reale, February 1652; f. 11v, notes on customs at the "Calbary River or River Reale." In *West Africa in the Mid-Seventeenth Century: An Anonymous Dutch Manuscript*, edited by Adam Jones. Atlanta, GA: African Studies Association, 1995.

Anozie, F. N. "Onyoma and Ke: A Preliminary Report on Archaeological Excavations in the Niger Delta." *West African Journal of Archaeology* 6 (1976): 89–99.

Anstey, Roger. "The Slave Trade of the Continental Powers, 1760–1810." *Economic History Review* 30 (1977): 259–68.

Archivio "De Propaganda Fide." (Rome) Scritture riferite nelli Congressi, Africa, Congo, etc. vol. 2, f. 480v, Francesco da Monteleone to Propaganda Fide, 25 April 1691.

———. Scritture riferite nelli Congressi, Africa, Congo, etc, vol. 2, f. 553, Francesco da Monteleone to Propaganda Fide, 19 March 1692.

Arinze, Francis. *Sacrifice in Igbo Religion.* Ibadan, NG: Ibadan University Press, 1970.

Arnold, James. "Account of a Voyage to the Coast of Africa by James Arnold, 24 March 1789," BT 6/11 (no folio number).

Ashby, Sir Eric. "Post-School Certificate and Higher Education in Nigeria." University Commission Report, 1960.

Asiegbu, J. U. J. *Nigeria and Its British Invaders, 1851–1920*. New York: Nok, 1984.

Astley, Thomas. *A New General Collection of Voyages and Travels*, 4 vols. London, 1743–1747.

Austen, Ralph A. "The Slave Trade as History and Memory: Confrontations of Slaving Voyage Documents and Communal Traditions." *William and Mary Quarterly* (2001): 229–44.

Austen, Ralph A., and Jonathan Derrick. *Middlemen of the Cameroons River: The Duala and their Hinterland, c.1600–c.1960*. Cambridge: Cambridge University Press, 1999.

Austen, Ralph A., and K. Jacobs. "Dutch Trading Voyages to Cameroon, 1721–1759: European Documents and African History," Annales de la Faculté des lettres et sciences humaines, Université fédérale du Camerones/de Yaounde, 2 (1974): 47–83.

Awolalu, J., and P. Dopamu. *West African Traditional Religion*. Ibadan, NG: Onibonoje Press, 1979.

Awolowo, Obafemi. *Awo: The Autobiography of Chief Obafemi Awolowo*. Cambridge: Cambridge University Press, 1960.

———. *Path to Nigerian Freedom*. London: Faber and Faber, 1947.

———. *The People's Republic*. Ibadan, NG: Oxford University Press, 1968.

Ayandele, E. A. *The Missionary Impact on Modern Nigeria, 1842–1914: A Political and Social Analysis*. London: Longman, 1966.

Azikiwe, Ben A. "Fragments of Onitsha History." *The Journal of Negro History* 15, no. 4 (Oct. 1930): 474–97.

———. "Nigerian Political Institutions." *The Journal of Negro History* 14, no. 3 (July 1929): 320–40.

Azikiwe, Nnamdi. *Address at the Igbo State Assembly*, June 25, 1949.

———. *My Odyssey: An Autobiography*. 1970; reprint Ibadan, NG: Spectrum Books, 1999.

———. A Presidential Address at the Igbo State Assembly held at Aba on Saturday June 25, 1949.

Baikie, William Balfour. *Narrative of an Exploring Voyage Up the Rivers Kwóra and Bínue in 1854*. London: John Murray, 1856.

Barbot, John [Jean]. *A Description of the Coasts of North and South-Guinea; and of Ethiopia Interior, Vulgarly Angola; Being a New and Accurate Account of the Western Maritime Countries of Africa*. London: Churchill, 1732.

———. "Mr. John Grazilhier's Voyage from Bandy to New Calabar." In *Churchill's Voyages and Travels*. Vol. 5, *A Description of the Coasts of North and South Guinea*. London: Churchills, 1746.

———. "'Ten Percent' Trader with English Connections." In *Barbot on Guinea: The Writings of Jean Barbot on West Africa, 1678–1712*. Vol. 1 and 2, edited by P. E. H. Hair, Adam Jones, and Robin Law. London: Ashgate, 1992.

Barclay, James. *The Voyages and Travels of James Barclay, Containing Many Surprising Adventures and Interesting Narratives*. Dublin, Ireland: n.p., 1777.

Bascom, William R. *Sixteen Cowries: Yoruba Divination from Africa to the New World*. Bloomington: Indiana University Press, 1980.

Basden, G. T. *Among the Ibos of Nigeria: A Description of the Primitive Life, Customs and Animistic Beliefs of the Igbo People of Nigeria*. 1921; reprint London: Frank Cass, 1966.

———. *Among the Ibos of Nigeria: An Account of the Curious and Interesting Habits, Customs and Beliefs of a Little Known African People by One Who Has for Many Years Lived Amongst then on Close and Intimate Terms*. London, 1921.

———. "Notes on the Ibo Country and Ibo People of Southern Nigeria," *The Geographical Journal* 39 (1912): 241–47.

Bastian, Misty L. "'The Demon Superstition': Abominable Twins and Mission Culture in Onitsha History." *Ethnology* 40, no. 1 (2001): 13–27.

Beck, Jane C. "The West Indian Supernatural World: Belief Integration in a Pluralist Society." *Journal of American Folklore* 88, no. 349 (July–September 1975): 235–44.

Beckford, William, jun. *Remarks upon the Situation of Negroes in Jamaica, Impartially Made from a Local Experience of Nearly Thirteen Years in that Island*. London: Egerton, 1788.

Behrendt, Stephen D. "Human Capital in the British Slave Trade." In *Liverpool and Transatlantic Slavery*, edited by David Richardson, Suzanne Schwarz, and Anthony Tibbles.

66–97. Liverpool, UK: Liverpool University Press, 2008.

———. "Markets, Transaction Cycles, and Profits: Merchant Decision Making in the British Slave Trade." *William and Mary Quarterly* 58 (2001): 171–204.

Behrendt, Stephen D., David Eltis, and David Richardson. "The Bights in Comparative Perspective: The Economics of Long-Term Trends in Population Displacement from West and West-Central Africa to the Americas before 1850," 3. Paper presented to the Summer Institute "Identifying Enslaved Africans: The Nigerian Hinterland and the Creation of the African Diaspora," York University, Toronto, 1997.

Behrendt, Stephen D., and Eric J. Graham. "African Merchants, Notables and the Slave Trade at Old Calabar, 1720: Evidence from the National Archives of Scotland." *History in Africa: A Journal of Method* 30 (2003), 37–61.

Behrendt, Stephen D., A. J. H. Latham, and David Northrup, eds. *The Diary of Antera Duke, an Eighteenth-Century African Slave Trader*. Oxford: Oxford University Press, 2010.

Beier, Ulli. *Thirty Years of Oshogbo Art*. Bayreuth: Iwalewa, 1991.

Bell, Malcolm, Jr. *Major Butler's Legacy: Five Generations of a Slaveholding Family*. Athens: University of Georgia Press, 1987.

Bellegarde-Smith, Patrick, ed. *Fragments of Bone: Neo-African Religions in a New World*. Urbana: University of Illinois Press, 2005.

Ben-Amos, Paula, and John Thornton. "Civil War in the Kingdom of Benin: Continuity or Social Change, 1689–1732." *Journal of African History* 42 (2001): 353–76.

Benezet, Anthony. *Some Historical Account*. London, 2nd ed., 1788.

Bentor, Eli. Personal communication, February 12, 2012.

Bergad, Laird W. *Fé Iglesias García, and María del Carmen Barcía, The Cuban Slave Market, 1790–1880*. Cambridge: Cambridge University Press, 1995.

Berlin, Ira. *Many Thousands Gone: The First Two Centuries of Slavery in North America* Cambridge, MA: Harvard University Press, 1998.

Bersselaar, Dmitri van den. "Creating 'Union Igbo': Missionaries and the Igbo Language." *Africa* 67, no. 2 (1977): 273–95.

———. "The Language of Igbo Ethnic Nationalism," *Language Problems & Language Planning* 24, no. 3 (Summer 2000): 123–47.

Beverly Prior Smaby. *The Transformation of Moravian Bethlehem*. Philadelphia: University of Pennsylvania Press, 1988.

Biblioteca del Palacio (Madrid). MS 722, Juan de Santiago, "Brebe relacion delo sucedide a doce Religiosos Cappuchinos . . ." (MS of 1648), ff. 143–45; a published summary in Giovanni Antonio Cavazzi da Montecuccolo, *Istorica Descrizione de' tre regni Congo, Matamba ed Angola* (Bologna, 1687), Book V, para. 121 (mod. ed. and Portuguese translation, Graziano Maria [Saccardo] da Leguzzano, *Descrição Histórica dos três reinos, Congo, Matamba e Angola* [2 vols., Lisbon, 1965]).

Bilby, Kenneth M. "The Caribbean as a Musical Region." In *Caribbean Contours*, edited by Sidney W. Mintz and Sally Price, 181–218. Baltimore, MD: Johns Hopkins Press, 1985.

Blackett, W. E. "Onitsha: Missionary Work in West Africa," *Jamaica Times*, Kingston, April 4, 1903.

Blount, Roswell C., and Efiong Ben Attah. *A Brief History of the Nsukka Area*. Nsukka: University of Nigeria, June 1963.

Bluett, Thomas. *Some Memoirs of the Life of Job, the Son of Solomon the High Priest of Boonda in Africa*. London, 1734.

Blyden, E. W. *Christianity, Islam and the Negro Race*. Originally published in 1888; reprint Baltimore, MD: Black Classic Press, 1994.

Boahen, Adu A. "The States and Cultures of the Lower Guinean Coast." In *UNESCO General History of Africa. Africa from the Sixteenth to the Eighteenth Century*, edited by B. A. Ogot. Berkeley: University of California Press, 1992.

Bosman, Willem. *Naukeurige Beschryving van de Guinese Goud-, Tand-, en Slave Kust*. Utrecht, DE,1704.

———. *A New and Accurate Description of the Coast of Guinea*. London, 1705.

Bowser, Frederick. *The African Slave in Colonial Peru, 1524–1650*. Stanford, CA: Stanford University Press, 1974.

Brandon, George. *Santeria from Africa to the New World: The Dead Sell Memories* Bloomington: Indiana University Press, 1993.

Bravmann, René A. "Gur and Manding Masquerades in Ghana." *African Arts* 13, no. 1 (November 1979): 44–46.

Brown, Carolyn A. "Testing the Boundaries of Marginality: Twentieth-Century Slavery and Emancipation Struggles in Nkanu, Northern Igboland, 1920–29." *Journal of African History* 37, no. 1 (1996): 51–80.

Brown, Carolyn A., and Paul E. Lovejoy, eds. *Repercussions of the Atlantic Slave Trade: The Interior of the Bight of Biafra and the African Diaspora*. Trenton, NJ: Africa World Press, 2011.

Brown, Soi-Daniel W. "From the Tongues of Africa: A Partial Translation of Oldendorp's Interviews." *Plantation Society in the Americas* 2, no. 1 (1983): 37–61.

Brown, W. L. "At Work in West Africa." *Jamaica Times*, Kingston, October 6, 1917.

———. "News from the Missionary Front: Nigeria." *Jamaica Diocesan Gazette and Church Magazine*, November 1919.

Bucer, Henry. "The Atlantic Slave Trade and the Gabon Estuary: The Mpongwe to 1860." In *Africans in Bondage: Studies in Slavery and the Slave Trade*, edited by Paul E. Lovejoy. Madison: University of Wisconsin Press, 1986.

Buchner, John H. *The Moravians in Jamaica*. London: Longman, Brown and Co., 1854.

Buisseret, David. "Slaves arriving in Jamaica, 1684–92." *Revue Française d'Histoire d'Outre-Mer LXIV* (1977): 85–88.

Burnard, Trevor. "The Atlantic Slave Trade and African Ethnicities in Seventeenth-Century Jamaica." In *Liverpool and Transatlantic Slavery*, edited by David Richardson, Suzanne Schwarz, and Anthony Tibbles, 138–63. Liverpool, UK: Liverpool University Press, 2008.

———. "E Pluribus Plures: African Ethnicities in Seventeenth and Eighteenth Century Jamaica," *Jamaican Historical Review* 21 (2001): 8–22, 56–59.

———. *Mastery, Tyranny & Desire*. Chapel Hill: University of North Carolina Press, 2004.

Burnside, Madeleine, ed. *Spirits of the Passage*. New York: Simon and Schuster, 1997.

Burton, Richard D. E. *Afro Creole: Power, Opposition, and Play in the Caribbean*. Ithaca, NY: Cornell University Press, 1997.

———. *Wanderings in West Africa*. New York: Dover, 1991.

Byrd, Alexander X. *Captives and Voyagers: Black Migrants across the Eighteenth-Century British Atlantic World*. Baton Rouge: Louisiana State University Press, 2008.

———. "Eboe, Country, Nation, and Gustavus Vassa's Interesting Narrative." *William and Mary Quarterly* 63 (2006): 123–48.

C107/59. "Sales of Two Hundred and Two Slaves Imported in the Ship African Queen." March 10, 1793.

C107/59. Sales of 342 Slaves Imported in the ship Jupiter . . ." July 3, 1793.

C107/7. Francis Grant to James Rogers, December 1788, Box 2.

C107/9. Francis & Robert Smyth to James Rogers, February 22, 1788, C107/8.

C107/9. Francis Grant to James Rogers, August 4, 1789; Francis Grant to James Rogers, October 10, 1789.

CA2/065. Yoruba Mission (microfiche reel 73): Letters, Journals and Reports of Rev. Thomas Babington Macaulay, 1852–1877.

Cabral, Marino, J. Incháustegui Reales Cedulas y Correspondencia de Gobernadores de Santo Domingo. *De la Regencia del Cardenal Cisneros en Adelante*, 5 vols. Madrid, ES: 1958.

Cabrera, Lydia. *Anaforuana: Ritual y símbolos de la iniciación en la sociedad secreta Abakuá*. Madrid, ES: Ediciones R., 1975.

———. *La Sociedad Secreta Abakuá: Narrada Por Viejos Adeptos*, rev. ed. Miami, FL: Collección del Chicherekú, 1970.

Campbell, Aidan. *Western Primitivism, African Ethnicity: A Study in Cultural Relations*. London: Cassell, 1997.

Campbell, Alan F. C. "Missionary Activity in the Kingdom of Warri to the Early Nineteenth Century." *Journal of the Historical Society of Nigeria* 2 (1960): 1–24.

Captain Forsyth to James Rogers, July 9, 1792, C107/13.

Caron, Peter. "'Of a Nation Which the Others Do Not Understand': Bambara Slaves and African Ethnicity in Colonial Louisiana,

1718–60." *Slavery and Abolition* 18, no. 1 (1997): 98–121.

Carretta, Vincent, ed. *Equiano, The African: Biography of a Self-Made Man*. Athens: University of Georgia Press, 2005.

———. *The Interesting Narrative and Other Writings*. New York: Penguin Putnam, rev. ed. 2003.

———. "More New Light on the Identity of Olaudah Equiano or Gustavus Vassa." In *The Global Eighteenth Century*. Edited by Felicity Nussbaum, 226–35. Baltimore, MD: Johns Hopkins University Press, 2003.

———. "Olaudah Equiano or Gustavus Vassa?: New Light on an Eighteenth-Century Question of Identity." *Slavery and Abolition* 20 (1999): 96–105.

Carrington, Selwyn H. H. *The Sugar Industry and the Abolition of the Slave Trade, 1775–1810*. Gainesville: University Press of Florida, 2002.

Cate, Margaret Davis. *Early Days of Coastal Georgia*. St. Simons Island, GA: Fort Frederica Association, 1955.

———. *Our Todays and Yesterdays: A Story of Brunswick and the Coastal Islands*. Brunswick, GA: Glover Bros., 1926.

Cawte, E. C. *Ritual Animal Disguise*. London: Folklore Society, 1978.

Chambers, Douglas B. "*Biafran African Runaways in 18th-Century Jamaica and Saint-Domingue*." TMs. Historical Society of Nigeria, Southeast Zonal Conference, Abia State University, February 2013.

———. "The Black Atlantic: Theory, Method, and Practice." In *The Atlantic World, 1450–2000*, 151–74, edited by Toyin Falola and Kevin D. Roberts. Bloomington: Indiana University Press, 2008.

———. "Eboe, Kongo, Mandingo: African Ethnic Groups and the Development of Regional Slave Societies in Mainland North America." International Seminar, "The History of the Atlantic World," Harvard University, September 3–11, 1996.

———, ed. *Enslaved Igbo & Ibibio in America: Runaway Slaves and Historical Descriptions*. Enugu, NG: Jemezie Associates, 2013.

———. "Ethnicity in the Diaspora: The Slave Trade and the Creation of African 'Nations' in the Americas." *Slavery and Abolition* 22 (2001): 25–39.

———. "'He Gwine Sing He Country': Africans, Afro-Virginians and the Development of Slave Culture in Virginia, 1690–1810." PhD diss., University of Virginia, 1996.

———. *The Igbo Diaspora in the Era of the Slave Trade*. Glassboro: NJ: Goldline and Jacobs, 2014.

———. "Igbo Women in the Early Modern Atlantic World: The Burden of Beauty." In *Olaudah Equiano and the Igbo World: History, Society, and Atlantic Diaspora Connections*, edited by Chima J. Korieh, 311–31. Trenton, NJ: Africa World Press, 2008.

———. "The Links of a Legacy: Figuring the Slave Trade to Jamaica." In *Caribbean Culture: Soundings on Kamau Brathwaite*, edited by Annie Paul. Kingston, JM: University of the West Indies Press, 2007.

———. *Murder at Montpelier: Igbo Africans in Virginia*. Jackson: University Press of Mississippi, 2005.

———. "The Murder of Old Master Madison in 1732: A Local Event in Atlantic Perspective." *The Maryland Historian* 28 (2003): 10–19.

———. "'My Own Nation': Igbo Exiles in the Diaspora," *Slavery and Abolition* 18, no. 1 (1997): 72–97.

———. Personal correspondence, May 17, 1997.

———. "The Significance of Igbo in the Bight of Biafra Slave-Trade: A Rejoinder to Northrup's 'Myth Igbo,'" *Slavery and Abolition* 23, no. 1 (2002): 101–20.

———. "Tracing Igbo into the African Diaspora." In *Identifying Enslaved Africans: The "Nigerian" Hinterland and the African Diaspora*, edited by Paul Lovejoy. London: Continuum, 2000.

———. "The Transatlantic Slave Trade to Virginia in Comparative Historical Perspective, 1698–1778." In *Afro-Virginian History and Culture*, edited by John Saillant, 3–28. New York: Garland, 1999.

Chubb, L. T. *Ibo Land Tenure*. Ibadan, NG: Ibadan University Press, 1961.

Chuku, Gloria. "From Petty Traders to International Merchants: A Historical Account of Three Igbo Women of Nigeria in Trade and

Commerce, 1886 to 1970." *African Economic History* 27 (1999): 1–22.

———. "Gender and Innovation: Farming, Cooking, and Palm Processing in the Ngwa Region, South-Eastern Nigeria, 1900–1930." *Journal of African History* 25, no. 4 (1984): 411–27.

———. *Igbo Women and Economic Transformation in Southeastern Nigeria, 1900–1960*. New York: Routledge, 2005.

———. "Igbo Women and Political Participation in Nigeria, 1800s–2005." *International Journal of African Historical Studies* 42, no. 1 (2009): 81–103.

———. "Olaudah Equiano and the Foundation of Igbo Intellectual Tradition." In *The Igbo Intellectual Tradition: Creative Conflict in African and African Diaspora Thought*, edited by Gloria Chuku, 33–66. New York: Palgrave Macmillan, 2013.

———. "The Rise and Fall of Aro Business Oligarchy from 15th Century to 20th Century." MA thesis, Department of History, University of Port Harcourt, Nigeria, 1989.

———. "Women and the Complexity of Gender Relations." In *Nigeria in the Twentieth Century*, edited by Toyin Falola. Durham, NC: Carolina Academic Press, 2002.

———. "Women in the Mid-19th and Early 20th-Century Palm Oil Trade in *Igboland, Nigeria*." Paper presented at the 43rd Annual Conference of the African Studies Association, Nashville, TN, November 16–19, 2000.

Chukwu, Hannah Eby N. "African Cultural Values: The Significance of Igbo Oral Forms in Selected Carinnean Poetry." In *Olaudah Equainao and the Igbo World: History, Society and Atlantic Diaspora Connections*, edited by Chima J. Korieh. Trenton, NJ: Africa World Press, 2009.

Clapperton, Hugh. *Journal of a Second Expedition into the Interior of Africa*. London: J. Murray, 1829.

Clarkson, Thomas. *An Essay on the Slavery and Commerce of the Human Species, Particularly the African: In Three Parts*. London: J. Phillips, 1786.

Clemens, Augustus. "Report of Visits to Some Missionary Stations in Jamaica." *Periodical Accounts* 24 (1861).

CMS. G3/A3/0. S. R. Smith, Annual Letter (Dec. 7, 1912); C. M. S. G3/A3/0, J. Cheetham's Annual Letter (Dec. 5, 1911); C. M. S. C. A. 3/037, Taylor's Journal Entry for June 25, 1863 (1863).

CMS/CA 1 M7. Report of the West Africa Mission, 1834, by the Rev. J, Raban, 155; Pine, Annual Report, 1847.

Coleman, James S. *Nigeria: Background to Nationalism*. Berkeley: University of California Press, 1958.

Collins, John. "Gumbay Drums of Jamaica in Sierra Leone." Paper presented at the 12th Triennial Symposium on African Art (ACASA), Marriott Frenchman's Reef Resort, St. Thomas, US Virgin Islands, April 27, 2001.

Colonial Office, CO267/204, Acting-Governor [Benjamin] Pine's Annual Report on the Colony of Sierra Leone for 1847.

Comaroff, John L. "Of Toteism and Ethnicity: Consciousness, Practice, and the Signs of Inequality." *Ethnos* 52 (1987): 301–23.

Conniff, Michael L., and J. Davis Thomas. *A History of the Black Diaspora*. New York: St. Martin's Press, 1994.

Cornell, Stephen E., and Douglas Hartmann. *Ethnicity and Race: Making Identities in a Changing World*. Oaks, CA: Pine Forge Press, 2006.

Cornwall Chronicle. St. George Workhouse (1816), incarcerated February 2, 1816.

Costanzo, Angelo. "The Narrative of Archibald Monteith, a Jamaican Slave," *Callaloo* 13, no. 1 (1990): 115–30.

Cottman, Michael. *The Wreck of the Henrietta Marie: An African American Journey to Uncover a Sunken Slave Ship's Past*. New York: Crown, 1999.

Courlander, Harold. *The Drum and the Hoe: Life and Lore of the Haitian People*. Berkeley: University of California Press, 1960.

Crahan, Margaret E., and Franklin W. Knight. *Africa and the Caribbean: The Legacies of a Link*. Baltimore: Johns Hopkins University Press, 1979.

Craton, Michael. "Jamaican Slave Mortality: Fresh Light from Worthy Park, Longville and the Tharp Estates." *Journal of Caribbean History* 3 (1971): 3.

———. *Testing the Chains: Resistance to Slavery in the British West Indies*. Ithaca, NY: Cornell University Press, 1982.

Cronje, S. *The World and Nigeria*. London: Sidgwick and Jackson, 1972.

Crowther, Samuel, and John C. Taylor. *The Gospel on the Banks of the Niger: Journals and Notices of the Native Missionaries Accompanying the Niger Expedition of 1857–1859* [1859]. London: Dawsons of Pall Mall, 1968.

Cugoano, Quobna Ottobah (Stuart, John). *Thoughts and Sentiments on the Evil and Wicked Traffic of the Slavery and Commerce of the Human Species*. London, 1787.

Curtin, Philip D. *Africa Remembered. Narratives by West Africans from the Era of the Slave Trade*. Madison: University of Wisconsin Press, 1967.

———. *The Atlantic Slave Trade: A Census*. Madison: University of Wisconsin Press, 1969.

———. *The Image of Africa: British Ideas and Actions, 1780–1850*. Madison: The University of Wisconsin Press, 1964.

———. "Nutrition in African History," *Journal of Interdisciplinary History* 14, no. 2 (1983): 371–82.

Da Morro, Francesco and Francesco da Monte Cassiano. "Relazione sulla missione de San Tome," ca. 1707. In *Le Missione a Benin e Warri nel XVII Secolo*, edited by Vittorion A. Salvadorini, 294; Archivio "*De Propangada Fide.*" Acta, vol. 81, f. 277, Francesco da Collevecchio to Propaganda Fide, May 12, 1711.

Daily Service (Lagos), October 17, 1944.

Daniel, Jack, and Milford Jeremiah. "Makin' a Way Outa No Way: The Proverb Tradition in the Black Experience." *Journal of Black Studies* 17, no. 4 (1987): 482–508.

Danto, Arthur. *After the End of Art: Contemporary Art and the Pale of History*. Princeton, NJ: Princeton University Press, 1997.

Dapper, Olfert. *Description de l'Afrique*, French trans. Amsterdam: Wolfgang, Waesberge, Boom & van Someren, 1686.

———. *Naukeurige Beschrijvinge van Africa gewesten*. Amsterdam, 1668, 2d ed. 1676), 135–8. Leers, Pertinent Beschryvinge, 312–13; "Aenweijsinge," ff. 10v, 11v.

Darwin, Major, Walter Egerton, Dr. Falconer, and A. E. Kitson. "Southern Nigeria: Some Considerations of its Structure, People, and Natural History: Discussion." *The Geographical Journal* 41, no. 1 (1913): 34–38.

Davies, K. G. *The Royal African Company*. London: Longmans, 1957.

Davis, David Brion. *The Problem of Slavery in the Age of Revolution, 1770–1823*. Ithaca, NY: Cornell University Press, 197.

Davis, H. O. *Daily Times*. January 1950.

Dayrell, E. "Further Notes on 'Nsibidi Signs' with their Meanings from the Ikom District, Southern Nigeria," *The Journal of the Royal Anthropological Institute* 14 (1911): 521–40.

Dayrell, Elphinstone. "Some 'Nsibidi' Signs." *Man* 10 (1910): 113–14.

De Castelblanco, Mendez. "Relaçao." In *Monumenta Missionaria Africana.* Edited by Antonio Brásio, 6:471. Lisbon: Agencia Geral do Ultramar, 1958.

De Sandoval, Alonso. *Naturaleza, policia sagrada i profana, costumbres i ritos, disciplina i catechismo Evangelico de todos Etiopes*. Seville, 1627, mod. ed. with modernized spelling Angel Valtierra, Bogota, 1956.

De Verteuil, Anthony. *Seven Slaves and Slavery: Trinidad, 1777–1838*. Port of Spain, TT: Scrip–J Printers Limited, 1992.

Derbyshire Record Office, D239 M/E 16753–16754, "West Indian Papers," *Plantations of William Perrin and William Philip Perrin, Correspondence of the Jamaican Attorneys*, January 10, 1773.

Derrick, Jonathan. *Africa's Slaves Today*. New York: Schocken Books, 1975.

Dike, Kenneth Onwuka. *Trade and Politics in the Niger Delta, 1830–1885; An Introduction to the Economic and Political History of Nigeria*. Oxford: Clarendon Press, 1956.

Dike, Kenneth Onwuka, and F. I. Ekejiuba. *The Aro of South-Eastern Nigeria, 1650–1980: A Study of Socio-Economic Formation and Transformation in Nigeria*. Ibadan, NG: Ibadan University Press, 1990.

Diptee, Audra A. "African Children in the British Slave Trade during the Late Eighteenth Century." *Slavery and Abolition* 27, no. 2 (2006): 183–96.

———. *From Africa to Jamaica: The Making of an Atlantic Slave Society, 1775–1807*. Gainesville: University Press of Florida, 2010.

———. "Imperial Ideas, Colonial Realities: Enslaved Children in Jamaica, 1775–1834." In *Children in Colonial America*, edited by James Marten. New York: New York University Press, 2007.

Dirks, Robert. *The Black Saturnalia: Conflict and Its Ritual Expression on British West Indian Slave Plantations*. Gainesville: University Press of Florida, 1987.

Donnan, Elizabeth. *Documents Illustrative of the Slave Trade to America*, Vol. II. New York: Octagon Books, 1965.

———. "The Slave Trade into South Carolina before the Revolution." *American Historical Review* 33 (1927–28): 816–17.

Doster, Stephen, ed. *Voices from St. Simons: Personal Narratives of an Island's Past*. Winston-Salem, NC: John F. Blair, 2008.

Dunkley, D. A. "The Legacies of John Tharp, 1744–1804." MA research paper, UWI-Mona Campus, 1997.

Dunn, Richard S. *Sugar and Slaves: The Rise of the Planter Class in the English West Indies, 1624–1713*. Chapel Hill: University of North Carolina Press, 1972.

Echena, Bridget. Interview by author, tape recording, Nrobo, Enugu State, Nigeria, October 3, 1998.

Echeruo, Michael. "A Matter of Identity" in the 1979 Ahiajoku Lecture. Owerri, NG: Imo State Ministry of Information, Culture, Youth and Culture, 1979.

Editor. "Memoir." Periodical Accounts Relating to the Missions of the Church of the United Brethren 25 (1865).

Editorial, Gaskiya Ta Fi Kwabo, February 18, 1950.

Edwards, Bryan. *The History, Civil and Commercial, of the British Colonies in the West Indies*. London, 1793.

Edwards, Paul. "Introduction." In *The Life of Olaudah Equiano. Or Gustavus Vassa, the African*, xix–xx. London: Dawsons of Pall Mall, 1969.

Edwards, Paul, and Rosalind Shaw. "The Invisible Chi in Equiano's 'Interesting Narrative.'" *Journal of Religion in Africa* 19 (1989): 146–56.

Ejikeme, Anene. "Subterfuge and Resistance: A History of Infanticide in Onitsha." In *Power and Nationalism in Modern Africa*, edited by Toyin Falola and Salah M. Hassan, 155–68. Durham, NC: Carolina Academic Press, 2008.

Ekechi, Felix. "Igbo Response to British Imperialism: The Episode of Dr. Stewart and the Ahiara Expedition, 1905–1916." *Journal of African Studies* 1, no. 2 (1974): 145–57.

———. "Merchants, Missionaries and the Bombardment of Onitsha, 1879–89: Aspects of Anglo-Igbo Encounter." *The Conch* 5, 1 and 2 (1973): 61–81.

———. *Missionary Enterprise and Rivalry in Igboland, 1857–1914*. London: Frank Cass, 1972.

Ekeh, Peter P. "Colonialism and the Two Publics in Africa: A Theoretical Statement." *Comparative Studies in Society and History* 17 (1975): 91–112.

Ekejiuba, Ifeoma F. "The Aro System of Trade in the Nineteenth Century," *Ikenga* 1, no. 1 (1972): 10–18.

———. "Omu Okwei, the Merchant Queen of Ossomari: A Biographical Sketch." *Journal of the Historical Society of Nigeria* 3, no. 4 (1967): 633–46.

Ekwe Nche Organization. "Leadership in Igbo Society: Analysis, Challenges and Solutions." http://www.biafraland.com/leadership_Igbo%20Identity.rtf. December 12, 2004.

Elliott, John. O-1 Diary of New Carmel, September 1, 1837. Moravian Archives, Jamaica Archives, Spanish Town, Jamaica.

Eltis, David. "The British Transatlantic Slave Trade before 1714: Annual Estimates of Volume and Direction." In *The Lesser Antilles in the Age of European Expansion*, edited by Robert L. Paquette and Stanley L. Engerman. Gainesville: University Press of Florida, 1996.

———. *Economic Growth and the Ending of the Transatlantic Slave Trade*. Oxford: Oxford University Press, 1987.

———. "Ethnicity in the Early Modern Atlantic World." Paper presented at the Harriet Tubman Seminar, York University, January 26, 1999.

———. *The Rise of African Slavery in the Americas*. Cambridge: Cambridge University Press, 2000.

———. "The Slave Trade in Nineteenth-Century Nigeria." In *Studies in the Nineteenth-Century Economic History of Nigeria*, edited by Toyin

Falola and Ann O'Hear. Madison: University of Wisconsin Press, 1998.

Eltis, David, Stephen D. Behrendt, David Richardson, and Herbert S. Klein, eds. *The Trans-Atlantic Slave Trade: A Database on CD-ROM*. Cambridge: Cambridge University Press, 1999.

Eltis, David, and Stanley L. Engerman. "Fluctuations in Sex and Age Ratios in the Transatlantic Slave Trade, 1663–1864." *Economic History Review* 46 (1993): 308–23.

———. "The 'Numbers Game' and Routes to Slavery." *Slavery and Abolition* 18, no. 1 (1997): 1–15.

———. "Was the Slave Trade Dominated by Men?" *Journal of Interdisciplinary History* 23, no. 2 (Autumn 1992): 237–57.

Eltis, David, Paul E. Lovejoy, and David Richardson. "Slave-Trading Ports: Towards an Atlantic-Wide Perspective." In *Ports of the Slave Trade* (Bights of Benin and Biafra). Papers from a Conference of the Centre of Commonwealth Studies, University of Stirling, June 1998, edited by Robin Law and Silke Strickrodt. Stirling, UK: Centre for Commonwealth Studies, 1999.

Eltis, David, and David Richardson. "The Dutch in the Atlantic World: New Perspectives from the Slave Trade with Particular Reference to the African Origins of the Traffic." In *Extending the Frontiers*, edited by David Eltis and David Richardson, 119, 141, 244. New Haven, CT: Yale University Press, 2008.

———. "A New Assessment of the Transatlantic Slave Trade." In *Extending the Frontiers: Essays on the New Transatlantic Slave Trade Database*, edited by David Eltis and David Richardson. New Haven, CT: Yale University Press, 2008.

———. "Prices of African Slaves Newly Arrived in the Americas, 1673–1865: New Evidence on Long-Run Trends and Regional Differentials." In *Slavery in the Development of the Americas*, edited by David Eltis, Frank D. Lewis, and Kenneth L. Sokoloff. Cambridge: Cambridge University Press, 2004.

———. "Productivity in the Transatlantic Slave Trade." *Explorations in Economic History* 32 (1995): 465–84.

———. "West Africa and the Transatlantic Slave Trade: New Evidence on Long Run Trends." *Slavery and Abolition* 18, no. 1 (1997): 16–35.

Emecheta, Buchi. *The Slave Girl*. New York: George Braziller, 1977.

Enahoro, Anthony. *Fugitive Offender*. London: The Camelot Press, 1965.

Engerman, C. F., L. Stanley, and B. W. Higman. "The Demographic Structure of the Caribbean Slave Societies in the Eighteenth and Nineteenth Centuries." In *General History of the Caribbean*. Vol, III, *The Slave Societies of the Caribbean*, edited by Franklin W. Knight. London: UNESCO/Macmillan, 1997.

Equiano, Olaudah. *The Interesting Narrative of Olaudah Equiano, or Gustavus Vassa, the African, Written by Himself*, vol. I. London: Author, 1789.

Evans, Freddi Williams. *Congo Square: African Roots in New Orleans*. Lafayette: University of Louisiana at Lafayette Press, 2011.

Eze, Ejike Omowo. Anthony Interview by author, tape recording, Adani, Enugu State, Nigeria, November 20, 1998.

Eze, J. O. N. "Population and Settlement." In *Nsukka Division: A Geographical Appraisal*, edited by P. K. Sircar. Nsukka: University of Nigeria, Annual Conference of the Nigerian Geographical Association Proceedings, 1965.

Eze, Katherine Faull. "Self-Encounters: Two Eighteenth-Century African Memoirs from Moravian Bethlehem." In *Crosscurrents: African Americans, Africa, and Germany in the Modern World*, edited by David McBride, LeRoy Hopkins, and C. Aisha Blackshire-Belay, 29–52. Columbia, SC: Camden House, 1998.

Eze, Paulinus I. "Numu Kwome, Mother of Obukpa People." Diploma, Department of Religion, University of Nigeria, Nsukka, June 1984.

Ezeh, Peter Donatus. "Igbo Traditional Religion in the Life of the People of Obukpa, Nsukka Local Government Area." BA thesis, Department of Religion, University of Nigeria, Nsukka, June 1984.

Ezema, Emmanuel Francis. "The Traditional Beliefs and Practices in Ibagwa-Ani Town in Nsukka Local Government Area of Enugu State." Diploma, Department of Religion, University of Nigeria, Nsukka, June 1995.

Ezema, Samuel Francisco. "A History of Edem, Nsukka From the Earliest Times to 1910." BA thesis, Department of History, University of Nigeria, Nsukka, June 1977.

Ezeugwu, Roseline. "Shrines in Igboland and Its Significances [*sic*] to African Traditionalist [*sic*]: A Case Study of Nsukka Area." Diploma, Department of Religion, University of Nigeria, Nsukka, June 1994.

Falconbridge, Alexander. *An Account of the Slave Trade on the Coast of Africa*. 1788; New York: AMS Press, 1973.

Falola, Toyin. *Colonialism and Violence in Nigeria*. Bloomington: Indiana University Press, 2009.

Falola, Toyin, and Matt D. Childs, eds. *The Yoruba Diaspora in the Atlantic World* Bloomington: Indiana University Press, 2005.

Fischer, David Hackett. *Albion's Seed: Four British Folkways in America*. New York, 1989.

Forde, Daryll, ed. *Efik Traders of Old Calabar, Containing the Diary of Antera Duke 1785–88*. Oxford: Oxford University Press, 1956.

Forde, Daryll, and G. I. Jones. *The Ibo and Ibibio-speaking Peoples of South-Eastern Nigeria*. London: International African Institute, 1950.

"Francesco da Leone to Secretary of Propaganda Fide, 29 September 1691." In *Monumenta Missionaria Africana*, edited by Antonio Brásio, 14:271. Lisbon: Agencia Geral do Ultramar, 1958.

Francklyn, Gilbert. *An Answer to the Reverend Mr. Clarkson's Essay*. London, 1789.

Frazier, Franklin E. *Negro Church in America*. New York: Schocken, 1963.

———. *The Negro Family in the United States*. 1939; revised and abridged, New York: Dryden Press, 1948.

———. "The Significance of the African Background." In *Americans from Africa: Slavery and Its Aftermath*, edited by Peter I. Rose. New York: Atherton, 1970.

Fyfe, Christopher. *Africanus Horton: 1830–1883: West African Scientist and Patriot*. London: Ashgate, 1993.

———. *A History of Sierra Leone*. Oxford: Clarendon Press, 1962.

———, ed. *Sierra Leone Inheritance*. London: Oxford University Press, 1964.

G3A3/1899/121. T. J. Dennis to Rev. F. Baylis, October 16, 1900.

G3A3/19/49. "Niger Mission: Minutes of the Executive Committee," July 1919.

G3A3/1902/42. "An Adjoined Meeting of the Executive Committee held on Thursday, 27 February 1902."

G3A3/1903/52. Herbert Tugwell, "Programme of Itineration," April 1903.

G3A3/1903/54. Executive Committee Meetings, January 23–February 8, 1903.

G3A3/1903/63. W. E. Blackett to the Secretary, Niger Mission, "Schools' Report for January 1903."

G3A3/1905/102. "Employment of West Indian Missionary Agents in West Africa."

G3A3/1916/15. Niger Mission Minutes II, July–November 1915.

G3A3/1917/12. Sidney Smith to G. T. Manley, April 7, 1917.

G3A3/1917/41. Sidney Smith to G. T. Manley, June 12, 1917.

G3A3/1918/24. "Niger Mission Statistics."

G3A3/1918/29. "Education Board: Minutes of Meeting held 3 July 1918."

G3A3/1918/29. "Women's Conference: Minutes and Reports," July 1918.

G3A3/1919/49. Executive Committee Minutes (Appendix One), July 1919.

G3A3/1920/13. Niger Mission: Minutes of the Executive Committee, February 1920.

G3A3/1921/28. Niger Mission Executive Committee Minutes, March 21, 1921.

Geary, Patrick, J. *The Myth of Nations: The Medieval Origins of Europe*. Princeton, NJ: Princeton University Press, 2002.

Geggus, David. "The French Slave Trade: An Overview," *William and Mary Quarterly* 58 (2001): 119–38.

———. "Sex Ratio, Age and Ethnicity in the Atlantic Slave Trade: Data from French Shipping and Plantation Records." *Journal of African History* 30 (1989): 23–44.

Georgia Writers' Project. Work Projects Administration [WPA]. *Drums and Shadows: Survival Studies Among the Georgia Coastal Negroes*. 1940; reprint Athens: University of Georgia Press, 1986.

Giddens, Anthony. *The Constitution of Society: Outline of a Theory of Structuration*. Berkeley: University of California Press, 1984.

Gomez, Michael A. "The Anguished Igbo Response to Enslavement in the Americas." In

Repercussions of the Atlantic Slave Trade: The Interior of the Bight of Biafra and the African Diaspora, edited by Carolyn A. Brown and Paul E. Lovejoy, 103–18. Trenton, NJ: Africa World Press, 2011.

———, ed. *Diasporic Africa*. New York: New York University Press, 2006.

———. *Exchanging our Country Marks Transformation of Identities in the Colonial and Antebellum South*. Chapel Hill: University of North Carolina Press, 1998.

———. "A Quality of Anguish: The Igbo Response to Enslavement in America." In *Trans-Atlantic Dimensions of Ethnicity in the American Diaspora*, edited by Paul Lovejoy and David Trotman, 82–95. London: Continuum, 2003.

Grainger, James. *An Essay on the More Common West-India Diseases*. London, 1764.

———. *The Sugar-Cane*. A Poem. London, 1764.

Great Britain, Parliamentary Papers 1825.

Green, M. M. *Ibo Village Affairs*. New York: Frank Cass, 1964.

Griffin, Patrick. *The People with No Name: Ireland's Ulster Scots, America's Scots Irish, and the Creation of a British Atlantic World, 1689–1764*. Princeton, NJ: Princeton University Press, 2001.

Gronniosaw, James, Albert, Ukawsaw. *A Narrative of the Remarkable Particulars in the Life of James Albert Ukawsaw Gronniosaw, an African Prince, as Related by Himself*. Bath, 1772.

Hair, P. E. H., Adam Jones, and Robin Law, eds. *Barbot on Guinea: The Writings of Jean Barbot on West Africa 1678–1712, Hakluyt Society*, 2 vols., Series II, vols. 175–76. London: Hakluyt Society, 1992.

Hair, P. E. H., and Robin Law. "The English in Western Africa to 1700." In *The Oxford History of the British Empire*. Vol. 1, *The Origins of Empire*, edited by Nicholas Canny. Oxford: Oxford University Press, 1998.

Hall, Douglas. *In Miserable Slavery: Thomas Thistlewood in Jamaica, 1750–1786*. 1989; Kingston, JM: University of the West Indies Press, 1999.

Hall, Gwendolyn Midlo. "Africa and Africans in the African Diaspora: The Uses of Relational Databases." *American Historical Review* 115, no. 1 (February 2010): 136–50.

———. *Africans in Colonial Louisiana: The Development of Afro-Creole Culture in the Eighteenth Century*. Baton Rouge: Louisiana State University Press, 1992.

———. "African Women in Colonial Louisiana." In *The Devil's Lane: Sex and Race in the early South*, edited by Catherine Clinton and Michele Gillespie, 247–62. New York: Oxford University Press, 1997.

———. Afro-Louisiana History and Genealogy, 1719–1820 [CD-ROM]. Baton Rouge: Louisiana State University Press, 2000. Available online at http://www.ibiblio.org/laslave.

———. *Slavery and African Ethnicities in the Americas*. Kingston, JM: Ian Randle, 2006.

Hamilton, James. *Negro Plot. An Account of the Late Intended Insurrection among a Portion of the Blacks of the City of Charleston, South Carolina*. Boston, MA: Joseph W. Ingraham, 1822.

Hanna, Judith Lynne. *To Dance Is Human: A Theory of Nonverbal Communication*. Chicago, IL: University of Chicago Press, 1987.

Harms, Robert. *The Diligent: A Voyage Through the Worlds of the Slave Trade*. New York: Basic Books, 2001.

Harris, Joel Chandler. *Uncle Remus: His Songs and His Sayings*. New York: Appleton, 1880. Reprinted in *The Complete Tales of Uncle Remus*, comp. Richard Chase. Boston: Houghton Mifflin, 1955.

Hartle, D. D. "Archaeology in Eastern Nigeria." *Nigeria Magazine* 93 (June 1967): 134–43.

Hastings, Adrian. *The Church in Africa, 1450–1950*. Oxford: Clarendon Press, 1994.

Haynes, S. B. "The Danish West Indies." *Harpers New Monthly Magazine* 44 (January 1872): 200–202.

Haywood, Linda, M., ed. *Central Africans and Cultural Transformations in the American Diaspora*. Cambridge: Cambridge University Press, 2002.

Heath, Barbara. "Space and Place within Plantation Quarters in Virginia, 1700–1825." In *Cabin, Quarter, Plantation: Architecture and Landscapes of North American Slavery*, edited by Clifton Ellis and Rebecca Ginsburg. New Haven, CT: Yale University Press, 2010.

Henderson, Richard N. *The King in Every Man: Evolutionary Trends in Onitsha Society and*

Culture. New Haven, CT: Yale University Press, 1972.
Herskovits, Melville. *The Myth of the Negro Past*. New York: Harper and Brothers, 1941.
Higman, B. W. *Slave Population and Economy in Jamaica, 1807–1834*. Cambridge: Cambridge University Press, 1976.
Higman, Barry. *Plantation Jamaica, 1750–1850: Capital and Control in a Colonial Economy*. Kingston, JM: University of the West Indies Press, 2005.
Hildebrand, Jennifer. "'Dere Were No Place in Heaven for Him, An' He Were Not Desired in Hell': Igbo Cultural Beliefs in African American Folk Expressions," *Journal of African American History* 91, no. 2 (2006): 127–52.
Hobsbawm, Eric J. *Nations and Nationalism since 1780*. Cambridge: Cambridge University Press, 1990, 2nd ed. 1992.
Hobsbawm, Eric J., and Terence Ranger, eds. *The Invention of Tradition*. Cambridge: Cambridge University Press, 1983.
Hole, Christina. *A Dictionary of British Folk Customs*. London: Paladin Grafton Books, 1978.
Holloway, Joseph E. "'What Africa Has Given America': African Continuities in the North American Diaspora." In *Africanisms in American Culture*, edited by Joseph E. Holloway. Bloomington: Indiana University Press, 2005.
Horsfield, Joseph, Rev. "Archibald John Monteath: Native Helper and Assistant in the Jamaica Mission at New Carmel," edited by Vernon H. Nelson, *Transactions of the Monrovian Historical Society* 21, no. 1 (1966): 29–51.
Horton, James Africanus. *West African Countries and Peoples*. 1868; reprint Edinburgh, 1969.
Horton, W. R. G. "The Ohu System of Slavery in a Northern Ibo Village-Group," *Africa* 24, no. 4 (1954): 311–35.
Howard, Philip A. *Changing History: Afro-Cuban Cabildos and Societies of Color in the Nineteenth Century*. Baton Rouge: Louisiana State University Press, 1998.
Howe, Stephen. "Historiography." In *Ireland and the British Empire*, edited by Kevin Kenny. New York: Oxford University Press, 2004.
Ifemisia, Chieka. *Traditional Humane Living among the Igbo: An Historical Perspective*. Enugu, NG: Fourth Dimension Publishers, 1979.
Igbafe, Philip. "Western Igbo Society and Its Resistance to British Rule: The Ekumeku Movement, 1898–1911." *Journal of African History* 12, no. 3 (1971): 441–59.
Ikpe, J. S. B. "Ibibio Union 1928–1938 Anniversary Celebration 28 April, 1928," Uyo, 1928.
Ilogu, Edmund C. *Christian Ethics in an African Background: A Study of the Interaction of Christianity and Ibo Culture*. Leiden, NL: Brill, 1974.
"Imquiriçam que se tyrou nesta Ilha de SantÃtonjo sobre a nao dos armadores da Ilha de Santomé, que foy a Benj este ano de bcxbj (19 November 1516)." In *Monumenta Missionaria Africana*, edited by Antonio Brásio, 1:494–95. Lisbon: Agencia Geral do Ultramar, 1958.
Inikori, Joseph E. "The Development of Entrepreneurship in Africa: Southeastern Nigeria during the Era of the Transatlantic Slave Trade." In *Black Business and Economic Power*, edited by Alusine Jalloh and Toyin Falola, 41–79. Rochester, NY: University of Rochester Press, 2002.
———. "The Sources of Supply for the Atlantic Slave Exports from the Bight of Benin and the Bight of Bonny (Biafra)." In *De la traite a l'esclavage Actes du Colloque international sur la traite des Noirs, Nantes*, edited by Serge Daget (France: CRHMA, 1985).
Inniss, Tara. "From Slavery to Freedom: Children's Health in Barbados, 1823–1838." *Slavery and Abolition* 27, no. 2 (2006): 251–60.
Interview with Augustine Ntehe, male priestess of Anunje. Augustine Ntehe, interview by author, tape recording, Adani, Enugu State, Nigeria, November 20, 1998.
Interview with Ichie Anago Okoye, 1912–2002.
Interview with Ichie Okoye Mmefu at Nri, December 2003. Chambers Field Notes (II).
Isichei, Elizabeth. "Historical Change in Ibo Polity: Asaba to 1885." *Journal of African History* 10, no. 3 (1969): 421–38.
———. *A History of the Igbo People*. New York: St. Martin's Press, 1976.
———. "Ibo and Christian Beliefs: Some Aspects of a Theological Encounter." *African Affairs* 68, no. 271 (1969): 121–34.
———. *The Igbo People and the Europeans: Genesis of a Relationship* to 1906. London: Faber and Faber, 1973.

———. *Igbo Worlds: An Anthology of Oral Histories and Historical Descriptions*. Philadelphia, PA: Institute for the Study of Human Issues, 1978.

———. "Seven Varieties of Ambiguity: Some Patterns of IGBO Response to Christian Missions." *Journal of Religion in Africa* 3, no. 2 (1970): 209–27.

Island Record Office. Registrar General's Department, Twickenham Park, Jamaica. Old Deeds 507, f. 140; Old Deeds 451, f. 147.

Langley, J. A. *Pan-Africanism and Nationalism in West Africa, 1900–1945*. Oxford: Clarendon Press 1978.

Jamaica Archives. 1B/11/8/6 vol. 2. Parish Register, St. Elizabeth, Baptisms, Not White.

———. 1B/11/8/6 vol. 3, St. Elizabeth Parish Register, Marriages.

Jamaica Churchman. "The Young Men and Women in the West Indies: A Call." No. 26, October 1901.

Jamaica Diocesan Gazette and Church Magazine. "Advance in Western Equatorial Africa." May 1917.

———. Correspondence "From H. Herbert Simpson and Mrs. A. H. Simpson to the Editor." November 12, 1921.

———. Correspondence "From Our Own Missionary: T. E. Mackay." July 20, 1920.

Jamaica Diocesan Magazine 30, no. 4 (April 1956).

Jamaica Times. "The Jamaican in Africa: Mr. Brown Reviews Two Years Work." Kingston, JM, June 19, 1915.

James Jones to Lord Hawkesbury, July 26, 1788.

James Maud to James Rogers, July 30, 1786 (Antigua).

James, C. L. R. *The Black Jacobins: Toussaint L'Ouverture and the San Domingo Revolution*. New York: Vintage Books, 1963.

Jeffreys, M. D. "Ibo Warfare." *Man* 56 (1956): 77–79.

John Cunningham to James Rogers, April 20, 1792, C107/6.

Johnson, James. Quarterly Reports, C. M. S. Archives CAI/0123.

Johnson, Jerah. *Congo Square in New Orleans*. New Orleans: Louisiana Landmarks Society, 1995.

Johnson, Samuel. *The History of the Yoruba, from the Earliest Times to the Beginning of the British Protectorate*, edited by D. O. Johnson. 1921; reprint London: Routledge and Kegan Paul, 1966.

John Taylor Letter to Simon Taylor, August 7, 1793, Taylor/14, Letterbook A.

Jones, Cecily. "'If this be living I'd rather be dead': Enslaved Youth, Agency and Resistance on an Eighteenth Century Jamaican Estate." *The History of the Family* 12 (2007): 92–103.

———. "'Suffer the Little Children': Setting a Research Agenda for the Study of Enslaved Children in the Caribbean Colonial World." *Wadabagei* 9, no. 3 (2006): 7–25.

Jones, G. I. "Olaudah Equiano of the Niger Ibo." In *Africa Remembered. Narratives of Africans from the Era of the Slave Trade*, edited by Phillip Curtin, 60–98. Madison: University of Wisconsin Press, 1967.

———. *Report on the Position, Status and Influence of Chiefs and Natural Rulers in the Eastern Region of Nigeria*. Enugu, NG: Government Printer, 1957.

———. *The Trading States of the Oil Rivers: A Study of Political Development in Eastern Nigeria*. London: Oxford University Press for the International African Institute, 1963.

Jordan, John P. *Bishop Shanahan of Southern Nigeria*. 1942; reprint Onitsha, NG: Elo Press, 1971.

Joseph, Richard A. *Democracy and Prebandalism in Nigerian Politics*. Cambridge: Cambridge University Press, 1987.

Kalu, Ogbu. *Embattled Gods: Christianization of Igboland, 1841–1991*. Lagos, NG: Mina Publishers, 1996.

Karras, Alan. *Sojourners in the Sun: Scottish Migrants in Jamaica and the Chesapeake*, 1740–1800. Ithaca, NY: Cornell University Press, 1992.

Kasfir, Sidney L. "Masquerading as a Cultural System." In *West African Masks and Cultural Systems*, edited by Sidney L. Kasfir. Brussels: Musee Royal de L'Afriquw, Tervuren, Belgium, 1988.

Kenny, Kevin. "Diaspora and Comparison: The Global Irish as a Case Study." *Journal of American History* 90 (2003): 134–62.

Klein, Herbert S. *African Slavery in Latin America and the Caribbean*. New York: Oxford University Press, 1986.

———. *The Atlantic Slave Trade*. Cambridge: Cambridge University Press, 1999.

Klein, Herbert S., and Stanley L. Engerman. "Slave Mortality on British Ships 1791–1797." In *Liverpool, the African Slave Trade, and Abolition*, edited by Roger Anstey and P. E. H. Hair, 117–18. Liverpool: Historical Society of Lancashire and Cheshire, 1976.

Klein, Herbert S., Stanley L. Engerman, Robin Haines, and Ralpsh Shlomowitz. "Transoceanic Mortality: The Slave Trade in Comparative Perspective." *William and Mary Quarterly*, 58 (2001): 93–118.

Kloza, Daniel. "African Origins of Igbo Slave Resistance in the Americas." In *Olaudah Equiano and the Igbo World: History, Society, and Atlantic Diaspora Connections*, edited by Chima J. Korieh, 349–68. Trenton, NJ: Africa World Press, 2009.

Koelle, Sigismund W. *Polyglotta Africana*. London: Church Missionary House, 1854.

Kolapo, Femi J. "The Canoe in Nineteenth Century Lower Niger and the Delta." In *The Aftermath of Slavery: Transitions and Transformations in Southeastern Nigeria*, edited by Chima Korieh and Femi Kolapo, 75–114. Trenton, NJ: Africa World Press, 2007.

———. "The Igbo and their Neighbours during the Era of the Atlantic Slave Trade." *Slavery and Abolition* 25 (2004): 114–33.

———. "Trading Ports of the Niger-Benue Confluence Area, c. 1830–1873." In Law and Stickrodt, *Ports of the Slave Trade. Bights of Benin and Biafra*, edited by Robin Law and Silke Stickrodt, 96–121.

Korieh, Chima J. "African Ethnicity as Mirage?: Historicizing the Essence of the Igbo in Africa and the Atlantic Diaspora." *Dialectical Anthropology* 30 (2006): 91–118.

———, ed. *Olaudah Equiano and the Igbo World: History, Society and Atlantic Diaspora Connections*. Trenton, NJ: Africa World Press, 2009.

Kuklick, Henrika. *The Savage Within: The Social History of British Anthropology*. Cambridge: Cambridge University Press, 1991.

Kulikoff, Allan. "The Origins of Afro-American Society in Tidewater Maryland and Virginia, 1700 to 1790." *William and Mary Quarterly* 35 (1978): 226–59.

Laird, Macgregor, and R. A. K. Oldfield. *Narrative of an Expedition into the Interior of Africa by the River Niger*, Vol. 2. London: R. Bentley, 1837.

Lambert, Sheila, ed. House of Commons Sessional Papers of the Eighteenth Century. Wilmington, DE: Scholarly Resources, 1975.

Lamming, George. "Conversations: George Lamming: Essays, Addresses and Interviews, 1953–1990" edited by Richard Drayton and Andaiye. London: Karia Press, 1992.

Lander, Richard, and John Lander. *Journal of an Expedition to Explore the Course and Termination of the Niger with a Narrative of a Voyage Down that River to Its Termination*, Vol. 2. New York: J. & J. Harper, 1832.

Landers, Jane G., ed. *Against the Odds: Free Blacks in the Free Societies of the Americas*. London: Frank Cass, 1996.

———. *Black Society in Spanish Florida*. Urbana: University of Illinois Press, 1999.

Latham, A. J. H. "Currency, Credit and Capitalism on the Cross River in the Pre-Colonial Era." *Journal of African History* 12 (1971): 599–603.

———. *Old Calabar 1600–1891: The Impact of the International Economy upon a Traditional Society*. Oxford: Clarendon Press, 1973.

Law, Robin. "Ethnicity and the Slave Trade: 'Lucumi' and 'Nago' as Ethnonyms in West Africa." *History in Africa* 24 (1997): 205–19.

Law, Robin, and Paul E. Lovejoy, eds. *The Biography of Mahommad Gardo Baquaqua: His Passage from Slavery to Freedom in Africa and America*. Princeton, NJ: Markus Wiener, 2003.

Leers, Arnout. *Pertinente Beschriyvinge van Africa . . . getrokken en vergadert uyt Reysboeken van Johannes Leo Africanus*. Rotterdam, 1655.

Leers, Pertinent Beschryvinge, 312–13; "Aenweijsinge," ff. 10v, 11v.

Legislative Council Debates. Nigeria, March 4, 1948, 227.

Leslie, Charles. *A New and Exact Account of Jamaica*. Edinburgh: Fleming, 1739.

Lewis, Marvin A. *Ethnicity and Identity in Contemporary Afro-Venezuelan Literature: A Culturalist Approach*. Colombia: University of Missouri Press, 1992.

Lewis, Matthew. *Journal of a West India Proprietor, Kept during a Residence in the Island of Jamaica*, edited with an introduction and Notes by Judith Terry. 1834; Oxford: Oxford University Press, 1999.

"License to the Moradores of São Tomé, December 11, 1493." In *Monumenta Missionaria Africana*, edited by António Brásio. 1st series, 15 vols. Lisbon, 1952–1988.

Littlefield, Daniel C. *Rice and Slaves: Ethnicity and the Slave Trade in Colonial South Carolina*. Baton Rouge: Louisiana State University Press, 1981.

Locke, John. *An Essay Concerning Human Understanding and other Philosophical Writings*, edited by Peter H. Niddich London: Clarendon Press, 1979.

Long, Edward. *The History of Jamaica*. London, 1774.

Look. Des Moines, Iowa. November 26, 1968.

Lorena, Walsh. *From Calabar to Carter's Grove: The History of a Virginia Slave Community*. Charlottesville: University Press of Virginia, 1997.

Lovejoy, Paul E. "The African Diaspora: Revisionist Interpretations of Ethnicity, Culture and Religion under Slavery." *Studies in the World History of Slavery, Abolition and Emancipation* II, 1 (1997). January 21, 2002. http://www2.hnet.msu.edu/~slavery/essays/esy9701love.html (October 9, 2002).

———. "Autobiography and Memory: Gustavus Vassa, alias Olaudah Equiano, the African." *Slavery and Abolition* 28 (2006): 317–47.

———. "The Children of Slavery—The Transatlantic Phase." *Slavery and Abolition* 27 (2006): 197–217.

———. "Identifying Enslaved Africans: Methodological and Conceptual Considerations in Studying the African Diaspora." Paper presented at the conference "Identifying Enslaved Africans: The 'Nigerian Hinterland' and the African Diaspora," York University, Toronto, 1997.

———. *Transformations in Slavery: A History of Slavery in Africa*. Revised edition Cambridge: Cambridge University Press, 2000.

———. "The Volume of the Atlantic Slave Trade: A Synthesis." *Journal of African History* 23 (1982): 473–501.

———. "The Yoruba Factor in the Trans-Atlantic Slave Trade." Unpublished ms.

Lovejoy, Paul E., and Jan S. Hogendorn. "Slave Marketing in West Africa." In *The Uncommon Market: Essays in the History of the Atlantic Slave Trade*, edited by Henry E. Gemery and Jan S. Hogendorn, 213–35. New York: Academic Press, 1979.

———. *Slow Death for Slavery: The Course of Abolition in Northern Nigeria, 1897–1936*. Cambridge: Cambridge University Press, 1993.

Lovejoy, Paul E., and David Richardson. "Anglo-Efik Relations and Protection against Illegal Enslavement at Old Calabar, 1740–1807." *In Fighting the Slave Trade: West African Strategies*, edited by Sylvane Diouf. Athens: Ohio University Press, 2003.

———. "From Slaves to Palm Oil: Afro-European Commercial Relations in the Bight of Biafra, 1741–1841." In *Maritime Empires: British Imperial Maritime Trade in the Nineteenth Century*, edited by David Killingray, Margarette Lincoln, and Nigel Rigby. New York: Boydell, 2004.

———. "The Initial 'Crisis of Adaptation': The Impact of British Abolition on the Atlantic Slave Trade in West Africa, 1808–1820." *From Slave Trade to 'Legitimate' Commerce: The Commercial Transition in Nineteenth-Century West Africa*, edited by Robin Law. Cambridge: Cambridge University Press, 1995.

———. "Letters of the Old Calabar Slave Trade, 1760–1789." In *Genius in Bondage: Literature of the Early Black Atlantic*, edited by Vincent Carretta and Philip Gould. Lexington: University Press of Kentucky, 2001.

———. "'This Horrid Hole': Royal Authority, Commerce and Credit at Bonny, 1690–1840." *Journal of African History* 45, no. 3 (2004): 363–92.

———. "Trust, Pawnship, and Atlantic History: The Institutional Foundations of the Old Calabar Slave Trade." *American Historical Review* 104 (1999): 333–55.

Lovejoy, Paul E., and David V. Trotman. "Enslaved Africans and their Expectations of Slave Life in the Americas: Towards a Reconsideration of Models of 'Creolisation.'" In *Questioning Creole: Creolisation Discourses in Caribbean Culture*, edited by Verene A. Shepherd and Glen L. Richards, 67–91. Kingston, JM: Ian Randle, 2002.

———. "Introduction: Ethnicity and the African Diaspora." In *Trans-Atlantic Dimensions of Ethnicity in the African Diaspora*, edited by Paul E. Lovejoy and David V. Trotman, 1–8. London: Continuum, 2003.

Lugard, F. D. *Political Memoranda*. 1919; 3rd ed. London: Frank Cass, 1966.

Lynch, Hollis R. *Blyden to Rev. Henry Venn (C.M.S.), Selected Letters of Edward Wilmot Blyden*. Millwood, NY: Kto Press, 1978.

Lynn, Martin. *Commerce and Economic Change in West Africa: The Palm Oil Trade in the Nineteenth Century*. Cambridge: Cambridge University Press, 1998.

Macgregor, J. K. "Some Notes on Nsibidi." *The Journal of the Royal Anthropological Institute of Great Britain and Ireland* 39 (1909): 209–19.

"Malhorquim, Auto of António." In *Monumenta: Missionaria Africana*, edited by Antonio Brásio, 9:328 (July 24, 1645). Lisbon: Agencia Geral do Ultramar, 1958.

Manfredi, Victor. "Philological Perspectives on the Southeastern Nigerian Diaspora." *Contours: A Journal of the African Diaspora* 2, no. 2 (2004): 239–87.

Mann, Kristin. "Shifting Paradigms in the Study of the African Diaspora and of Atlantic History and Culture." *Slavery and Abolition* 22, no. 1 (2001): 6–10.

Manning, Patrick. *Slavery and African Life: Occidental, Oriental and African Slave Trades*. Cambridge: Cambridge University Press, 1990.

Manuel, Barcia. *Seeds of Insurrection. Domination and Resistance on Western Cuban Plantations, 1808–1848*. Baton Rouge: Louisiana State University Press, 2008.

Manuel, Peter. "Music, Identity, and Images of India in the Indo-Caribbean Diaspora." *Asian Music* 29, no. 1 (1997/1998): 18–35.

Martin, Susan. *Palm Oil and Protest: An Economic History of the Ngwa, South-Eastern Nigeria, 1800–1980*. New York: Cambridge University Press, 1988.

———. "Slaves, Igbo Women and Palm Oil in the Nineteenth Century." In *From Slave Trade to "Legitimate" Commerce: The Commercial Transition in Nineteenth-Century West Africa*, edited by Robin Law, 172–94. Cambridge: Cambridge University Press, 1995.

Martin, Tony. *The Pan-African Connection: From Slavery to Garvey and Beyond*. Dover, MA: Majority Press, 1985.

Mascuch, Michael. *Origins of the Individualist Self: Autobiography and Self-Identity in England, 1591–1791*. Cambridge: Polity Press, 1997.

Matthews, John. *A Voyage to the River Sierra-Leone, on the Coast of Africa; Containing an Account of the Trade and Productions of the Country, and of the Civil and Religious Customs and Manners of the People; in a Series of Letters to a Friend in England. By John Matthews, Lieutenant in the Royal Navy; During his Residence in that Country in the Years 1785, 1786, and 1787*. London, 1788.

McCall, John. *Dancing Histories: Heuristic Ethnography with the Ohafia Igbo*. Ann Arbor: University of Michigan Press, 2000.

———. "Portrait of a Brave Woman." *American Anthropologist* 98, no. 1 (1996): 127–36.

McDaniel, Lorna, and Donald R. Hill. *Carriacou Calaloo*. Cambridge, MA: Rounder Records, 1999. Music CD with liner notes.

McNeill, Hector. *Observations on the Treatment of the Negroes, in the Island of Jamaica, Including some Account of their Temper and Character, with Remarks on the Importation of Slaves from the Coast of Africa*. In a letter to a Physician in England, from Hector McNeill. London: Printed for G. G. J. and J. Robinson, and J. Gore, Liverpool, 1788.

Mebuge-Obaa, Prince P.N., II. "An Oral History Research Project: History of Scarification (Tattoo) in Nri." TMs., May 1, 2002.

Meek, C. K. *Law and Authority in a Nigeria Tribe: A Study of Indirect Rule*. London: Oxford University Press, 1937.

Memoirs of the late Captain Hugh Crow of Liverpool. London: *Longman*, Rees, Orme, Brown, & Green, 1830.

"Memórias da Academia das Ciéncias de Lisboa." *Classe de Ciénca*. 20 (1977):7–75, Separata by Centro de Estudos de Cartografia Antiga,

99 (1977), also found with original foliation of MS in *Monumenta Missionaria Africana*, edited by António Brásio. 15 vols. Lisbon, 1952–1988.

Metuh, Emefie Ikenga. *Comparative Studies of African Traditional Religions*. Onitsha, NG: IMICO, 1987.

———. *God and Man in African Religion*. London: Geoffrey Chapman, 1981.

Miller, Ivor L. *Voice of the Leopard: African Secret Societies and Cuba*. Jackson: University Press of Mississippi, 2009.

Miller, Joseph. "The Significance of Drought, Disease and Famine in the Agriculturally Marginal Zones of West-Central Africa." *Journal of African History* 23, no. 1 (1982): 17–61.

Mintz, Sidney, and Richard Price. *An Anthropological Approach to Afro-American Past: A Caribbean Perspective*. Philadelphia: Institute for the Study of Human Issues, 1976.

———. *The Birth of African-American Culture*. Boston: Beacon Press, 1992.

Minutes of the 9th Annual General Assembly of the Egbe Omo Oduduwa, Ijebu-Remo, December 17–19, 1956.

Minutes of the first inaugural conference of the Egbe Omo Oduduwa, June 1948.

Moore, Barrington. *The Social Origins of Dictatorship*. London: Allen Lane, 1967.

Moore, David. "Of a 17th Century Slave Ship: Historical and Archaeological Investigations of 'The Henrietta Marie.'" PhD diss., East Carolina University, 1989.

Moráguez, Oscar Grandío. "The African Origins of Slaves arriving in Cuba, 1789–1865." In *Extending the Frontiers*, edited by David Eltis and David Richardson, 119, 141, 244. New Haven, CT: Yale University Press, 2008.

Moravian Archives, Bethlehem. Biography of Andrew the Moor; Biography of Joshua, 1761.

Morgan, Kenneth. "Liverpool's Dominance in the British Slave Trade, 1740–1807." In *Liverpool and Transatlantic Slavery*, edited by David Richardson, Suzanne Schwarz and Anthony Tibbles, 66–97. Liverpool, UK: Liverpool University Press, 2008.

Morgan, Philip D. "The Cultural Implications of the Atlantic Slave Trade: African Regional Origins, American Destinations, and New World Developments." *Slavery and Abolition* 18 (1997): 122–42.

———. *Slave Counterpoint: Black Culture in the Eighteenth-Century Chesapeake and Lowcountry*. Chapel Hill: University of North Carolina, 1998.

Morgan, W. B. "Farming Practice, Settlement Pattern and Population Density in Southeastern Nigeria." *Geographical Journal* 121, no. 3 (1955): 320–33.

Morrish, Ivor. *Obeah, Christ, and Rastaman: Jamaica and Its Religion*. Cambridge: James Clark, 1982.

Mudimbe, V. Y. *The Invention of Africa*. Indianapolis: Indiana University Press, 1988.

Mullin, Michael. *Africa in America: Slave Acculturation and Resistance in the American South and the British Caribbean, 1736–1831*. Urbana: University of Illinois Press, 1992.

Munro MacFarlane to James Rogers, September 4, 1792, C107/5.

Nadel, S. F. "The Kede: A Riverain State in Northern Nigeria." In *African Political Systems*, edited by M. Fortes and E. E. Evans-Pritchard. London: Oxford University Press, 1940.

Nationaal Archief Nederland (formerly Algemeen Rijksarchief), 8, f. 245, Jan Maurtis to Herren XIX, 22 October 1639.

———. Oude West Indische Compagnie 56, no. 3 (no pagination) description of African trade to Brazil in 1641.

National Archives, Kew. CO 583, 166/582, Annual Report on the Education Departments, Northern Provinces and Colony and Southern provinces for the Year 1928. Lagos, 1929.

———. John Goodrich to James Rogers, April 9, 1793.

———. John Goodrich to James Rogers, December 30, 1792.

———. John Goodrich to James Rogers, January 11, 1793.

———. John Goodrich to James Rogers, January 24, 1793.

———. John Goodrich to James Rogers, June 15, 1793.

———. John Goodrich to James Rogers, March 5, 1793.

———. "Sales of 342 Slaves Imported in the Ship Jupiter . . . July 3rd 1793." All letters are in the C107/59 series, National Archives, Kew Gardens (London, UK). The C107 series (Chancery Records).

National Archives of Barbados, Recopied Deed Books, RB 3/1, p. 202. Contract of Nicholas Crispe of London Samuel Chrispe and John Wood of London merchants, last day of February 1642, assuming here that the English yacht bound for Barbados that the Dutch factor on São Tomé observed passing the island sometime in 1641, OWIC 57, Journal of Jan Claesz Cock, May 8, 1642 [Journal runs from December 2, 1641].

Niane, D. T. "Relationships and Exchanges among the Different Regions." In *UNESCO General History of Africa. Africa from the Twelfth to the Sixteenth Century*, edited by T. Niane. Berkeley: University of California Press, 1984.

Nicholls, Robert W. "Igede in the Twentieth Century: Modernity Impacts on Traditional Life-Styles in Tribal Nigeria." *The World and I: A Chronicle of Our Changing Era* 2, no. 7 (1987): 527–28.

———. *The Jumbies' Playing Ground: Old World Influences on Afro-Creole Masquerades in the Eastern Caribbean*. Jackson: University Press of Mississippi, 2012.

———. *Old-Time Masquerading in the USVI*. St. Thomas: Virgin Islands Humanities Council, 1998.

Nigerian National Archives Enugu. 4715, CALPROF 7, 1/2424, National Independence Party (1953–1954).

———. 6385, PHDIST 7/1/87, Ibibio Union: Matters relating to (1947).

———. 805, BRASDIST 10/1/169, Co-operation between the colonial Administration in Africa and the Missionary Bodies (1947).

———. 8633, PHDIST 10/1/1448, Action Group (1952).

———. Aro Origin and the Basis of Widespread Aro Influence (1927).

———. ARODIV 20/1/15, Aro Sub-tribe (1947).

———. AW 546, AWDIST 2/1/363, Udorie (Girl) of Aro-Nanka—Whereabout of, 1932.

———. C 632, RIVPROF 2/1/87, Activities of Village Unions, 1947.

———. C 633, RIVPROF 2/1/87, Native Authorities and clan unions, 1947.

———. C.P. 2039-CALPROF 3/1/1928, File No. M.P. no. P.C. 1/1/1931 of June 15, 1931.

———. CSE 1/85/228, M. D. W. Jeffreys, Awka Division Anthropological Report, 1931.

———. EP 13192, CSE 1/85/6539, Matters relating to and similar organizations, 1937.

———. EP.8766 vol. II; CSE 1/85/4596A.

———. File No. 3265, ONDIST 20/1/1481, Newspapers in Eastern Provinces, 1950–1951.

———. File No. AD 635 vol. I ARODIV 3/1/55, Aro Confederation Report by H. F. Mathews, 1945.

———. H. F. Matthews, Government Anthropologist in his Reports on the Aro, see the file A.D. 635 on Aro Sub-tribes in the National Archives, Enugu, Nigeria.

———. OB 853, OBUBDIST 4/1/349, Native languages and Dialects (1949–1950); OG 903, OGPROF 2/1/353, Phonetic Orthography (1931–1952).

———. OG 3335, OGPROF 2/1/2826, Matters relating to (1946–1951). For a complete list of newspapers printed in colonial eastern Nigeria.

———. OG 3335, OGPROF 2/1/2826, National Council of Nigeria and the Cameroons (NCNC) 1946–1951.

———. OG 903, OGPROF 2/1/353, Phonetic Orthography, 1931–1952.

———. OP2348, ONDIST 12/1/2348, Igbo Dialect—report by Mrs. Ida Ward.

———. OP 3029, ONDIST 12/1/2094, Ibo State Union matters affecting, 1949.

———. Palmer, H. R. ARODIST 1/7/33, Aro People (Memo dated 1/5/21 by H. R. Palmer).

———. RIVPROF 2/1/24, C.136, No. 217/Vol. 3/210/09 by S. P. George on February 4, 1935.

———. RIVPROF 8/5/47, Rex vs. Ebube Dike of Nkwerre Charged with Kidnapping.

Nigerian National Archives Ibadan. CSO 1/3, Southern Nigeria Dispatches to the Colonial Office, No. 361, July 29, 1903.

———. CSO 2616303, A Joint Memorandum by the Lieutenant-Governor, S. P., and the Director of Education, S. P., January 1926.

———. CSO 26/240, File No. 29380, Milne Report on Ogboli Group of Nsukka Division (n.d.).

———. NC/B10, Records of Proceedings of the Nigerian Constitution Conference held in

London in July and August (1953); see appendix on Self-Government in (1956), 125–37.
———. NC/B12, Records of Proceedings of the Resumed Conference on Nigerian Constitution, 1954.
Nigerian National Archives Kaduna. CO 554/1564, Provisions in Constitution for transition of Nigeria independence, 1959.
———. CO 554/965, Position of ex-officio members of the Northern Region Executive Council of Nigeria, 1956–1957.
———. CO 583/317/4, Activities of Dr. N. Nnamdi Azikiwe, Nigerian Nationalist Leader (1950–1951).
———. CO 957, Willink Commission, 1957–1958; CO554/1634, Nigeria (Constitution) (Amendment No. 2) Order-in-Council, 1958.
———. DO 195/426, Death of General Ironsi GOC (General Officer Commanding) Nigerian Army (1965–1966).
———. FCO 23/182, Nigeria and Biafra (1968).
———. FCO 38/214–221, Record of peace talks between Nigeria and Biafra (1968).
———. FCO 65/1362, Position of Colonel Ojukwu, former rebel leader of Biafra (1973).
———. File No. 15911 vol. 1, Tribes of Nigeria (i) Inter-Relations (ii) Arochukwu, Jukun, etc.
———. FO 371/146838, Appointment and Inauguration of Dr. Nnamdi Azikiwe as Governor- General, 1960.
———. PREM 13/1041, Nigeria. Political Situation in Nigeria: Deaths of Sir Abubakar; and General Ironsi; coup d'etat; part 3 (October 1966).
Njaka, Elechukwu N. *Igbo Political Culture.* Evanston, IL: Northwestern University Press, 1974.
Njoku, Akuma-Kalu J. "'There's got to be a tortoise in it': Lore as the Conceptual Focus of Igbo Folklore." *Southern Quarterly* 46, no. 4 (2009): 159–72.
Njoku, Raphael Chijioke. *African Cultural Values: Igbo Political Leadership in Colonial Nigeria, 1900–1966.* New York: Routledge, 2006.
———. "Igbo Slaves and the Transformation of the Niger Delta." In *The Aftermath of Slavery: Transitions and Transformations in Southeastern Nigeria*, edited by Chima Korieh and Femi Kolapo, 70–99. Trenton, NJ: Africa World Press, 2007.
———. "Meanings of Igbo Masks and Carnivals of the Black Diaspora." In *Migrations and Creative Expressions in Africa and the African Diaspora*, edited by Toyin Falola, Niyi Afolabi, and Aderonke A. Adesanya, 257–78. Durham, NC: Carolina Academic Press, 2008.
Noah, M. E. "Social and Political Developments: The Lower Cross Region." In *A History of the Cross River Region*, edited by M. B. Abasiattai. Enugu, NG: University of Calabar Press, 1990.
Noble, Donald R., Jr. Introduction to *The Valley of Shenandoah: Or, Memoirs of the Graysons*, by George Tucker, xx–xxxi. Chapel Hill: University of North Carolina Press, 1970.
Nora, Pierre. "Between Memory and History: Les Lieux de Mémoire." *Representations* 26 (1989): 7–25.
Northrup. David. *Africa's Discovery of Europe, 1450–1850.* New York: Oxford University Press, 2002.
———. "The Compatibility of the Slave and Palm Oil Trades in the Bight of Biafra." *Journal of African History* 17 (1976): 353–84.
———. "The Growth of Trade among the Igbo before 1800." *Journal of African History* 13, no. 2 (1972): 217–36.
———. "The Ideological Context of Slavery in Southeastern Nigeria in the 19th Century." In *Ideology of Slavery and Africa*, edited by Paul E. Lovejoy, 101–22. Los Angeles, CA: Sage, 1981.
———. "Igbo and Myth Igbo: Culture and Ethnicity in the Atlantic World, 1600–1850." *Slavery and Abolition* 21 (2000): 1–20.
———. "Nineteenth-Century Patterns of Slavery and Economic Growth in South-Eastern Nigeria." *International Journal of Historical Studies* 12, no. 1 (1979): 1–16.
———. *Trade without Rulers: Precolonial Development of Southeastern Nigeria.* Oxford: Clarendon Press, 1978.
———. "West Africans and the Atlantic, 1550–1800." In *The Oxford History of the British Empire Companion Series: Black Experience and the Empire*, edited by Philip D. Morgan and Sean Hawkins. Oxford: Oxford University Press, 2004.
Nsugbe, Philip O. *Ohafia: A Matrilineal Ibo People.* Oxford: Clarendon Press, 1974.

Nwala, Uzodinma. "Some Reflections on British Conquest of Igbo Traditional Oracles, 1900–1924." *Nigeria Magazine* 142 (1982): 25–35.

Nwana, Pita. *Omenuko: Official Orthography Edition*. 1933; reprint Ikeja, NG: Longman, 1963.

Nwankwo, Arthur. *The Igbo Leadership and the Future of Nigeria*. Enugu, NG: Fourth Dimension Publishers, 1985.

Nwoga, Donatus. *The Supreme God as Stranger in Igbo Religious Thought*. Mbaise, NG: Hawk Press, 1984.

Nwokeji, G. Ugo. "African Conceptions of Gender and the Slave Traffic." *William and Mary Quarterly* 58, no. 1 (2001): 47–68.

———. "The Atlantic Slave Trade and Population Density: A Historical Demography of the Biafran Hinterland." *Canadian Journal of African Studies* 34, no. 3 (2000): 616–55.

———. "The Biafran Frontier: Trade, Slaves and Aro Society, 1750–1905." PhD diss., University of Toronto, 1999.

———. "The Slave Emancipation Problematic: Igbo Society and the Colonial Equation." *Comparative Studies in Society and History* 40, no. 2 (1998): 318–55.

———. *The Slave Trade and Culture in the Bight of Biafra: An African Society in the Atlantic World*. Cambridge: Cambridge University Press, 2010.

Nwokeji, G. Ugo, and David Eltis. "Characteristics of Captives Leaving the Cameroons for the Americas, 1822–37." *Journal of African History* 43 (2002): 191–210.

Nwuduaku, Nkwonto. *Oral history, Enugwu-Ukwu*. In *Igbo Worlds: An Anthology of Oral Histories and Historical Descriptions*, edited by Elizabeth Isichei, 30–34. London: Macmillan, 1977.

Nzegwu, Nkiru. "Crossing Boundaries: Gender Transmogrification of African Art History." *Ijele: Art eJournal of the African World* 1, no. 1 (2000), http://www.ijele.com.

Nzewunwa, Nwanna. *The Niger Delta: Aspects of its Prehistoric Economy and Culture*. Cambridge: Cambridge University Press, 1980.

———. *The Niger Delta: Prehistoric Economy and Culture*. Oxford: Cambridge Monographs in African Archaeology 1, B.A.R. International Series 75, 1982.

Nzimiro, Ikenna. *Studies in Ibo Political Systems: Chieftaincy and Politics in Four Niger States*. Berkeley: University of California Press, 1972.

Obadele-Starks, Ernest. *Freebooters and Smugglers: The Foreign Slave Trade in the United States after 1808*. Fayetteville: University of Arkansas Press, 2007.

Obiechina, Emmanuel, Chukwuemeka Ike, and John A. Umeh, eds. *The University of Nigeria, 1960–1985: An Experiment in Higher Education*. Nsukka: University of Nigeria Press, 1986.

Occasional Paper No. 6. Centre of Commonwealth Studies, University of Stirling, 1999.

Ochogu, Prince, Mebuge-Obaa, P. N. II. "Age Grade/Group (Oral History Project Report)." TMs., December 7, 2003.

Offodile, E. P. O. "Growth and Influence of Tribal Unions," *The West African Review* 18, no. 239 (August 1947): 937.

Ofonagoro, W. I. *Trade and Imperialism in Southern Nigeria 1881–1929*. New York: Nok, 1979.

Ogbali, Obeta. Attama of Iye-Ojah. Interview by author, tape recording, Ogurugu, Enugu State, Nigeria, September 16, 1998.

Ogbechie, Sylvester Okwunodu. *Ben Enwonw: The Making of an African Modernist*. Rochester, NY: University of Rochester Press, 2006.

———. "Contested Vision: Ben Enwonwu's Portraits of Queen Elizabeth II." *Ijele: Art eJournal of the African World* 1, no. 2 (September 2000). http://www.ijele.com.

———. *HOMAGE: ArtGrads UNN Exhibition*. Nsukka, NG: ArtGrads UNN, 1991.

Ogede, Ode S. "Counters to Male Domination: Images of Pain in Igede Women's Songs." *Research in African Literature* 3 (1994): 105–20.

———. "The Igbo Roots of Olaudah Equiano." *African: Journal of the International African Institute* 16 (1991): 138–41.

Oguagha, Philip, and Alex Okpoko. *History and Ethnoarchaeology in Eastern Nigeria: A Study of Igbo-Igala Relations with Special Reference to the Anambra Valley*. Oxford: B.A.R., 1984.

Ogude, Steve E. "Facts into Fiction: Equiano's *Narrative* Reconsidered." *Research in African Literatures* 13 (1982): 30–43.

Ohadike, Don C. *Anioma: A Social History of the Western Igbo People*. Athens: Ohio University Press, 1994.

———. "The Decline of Slavery Among the Igbo People." In *The End of Slavery in Africa*, edited by S. Miers and R. Roberts, 437–61. Madison: University of Wisconsin Press, 1988.

———. *The Ekumeku Movement: Western Igbo Resistance to the British Conquest of Nigeria, 1883–1914*. Athens: Ohio University Press, 1991.

———. "'When Slaves Left, Owners Wept': Entrepreneurs and Emancipation among the Igbo People." *Slavery and Abolition* 19, no. 2 (1998): 189–207.

Okafor, Chinyere. "From the Heart of Masculinity: Ogbodo-Uke Women's Masking." *Research in African Literatures* 25, no. 3 (1994): 7–17.

Okere, Linus C. *The Anthropology of Igbo Food in Rural Igboland, Nigeria*. Lanham, MD: University Press of America, 1983.

Okigbo, Bede. *Plants and Food in Igbo Culture and Civilization, Ahiajoku Lecture*. Owerri, NG: Ministry of Information and Culture, 1980.

Okonjo, Kamene. "The Dual-Sex Political System in Operation: Igbo Women and Community Politics in Midwestern Nigeria." In *Women in Africa: Studies in Social and Economic Change*, edited by Nancy Hafkin and Edna G. Bay, 45–58. Stanford: Stanford University Press, 1976.

———. "Nigerian Women's Participation in National Politics: Legitimacy and Stability in an Era of Transition." Working Paper no. 221, Michigan State University, July 1991.

Okoye, Ichie Anago. Interview (April 2002), in *Mebuge-Obaa* II. TMs., May 1, 2002.

Okpewho, Isidore. *The African Diaspora: Origins and New World Identities*. Bloomington: Indiana University Press, 1999.

Okuku Oli. "(1846–1854): Tradition and Modernisation in Nri," Vol. II [Pamphlet, Eze Nri Enweleana II, n.d., ca. 1989], 9.

Oldendorp, Christian Georg Andreas. *Historie der caribischen Inseln Sanct Thomas, Sanct Crux und Sanct Jan, inbesondere der dasigen Neger und der Mission der evangelischen Brüder under denselben*. Modern Edition. Gudrun Meier, Stephan Palmié, Peter Stein, and Horst Ulbricht. 4 vols, Berlin, 2000–2002.

———. *History of the Mission of the Evangelical Brethren on the Caribbean Islands of St. Thomas, St. Croix, and St. John*. Edited by Johann Jakob Bossard and translated by Arnold R. Highfield and Vladimir Barac. Ann Arbor, MI: Karoma, 1987.

Oloidi, Ola. "Constraints on the Growth and Development of Modern Nigerian art in the Colonial Period." *Nsukka Journal of the Humanities* 5, no. 6 (June/December 1989): 28–51.

Onuwuejeogwu, Angulu M. *An Igbo Civilization: Nri Kingdom and Hegemony*. Benin: Ethiope, 1981.

———. "The Igbo Culture Area." In *Igbo Language and Culture*, edited by F. Chidozie Ogbalu and E. Nolue Emenanjo, 1–10. Ibadan, NG: Oxford University Press, 1975.

———. *The Social Anthropology of Africa: An Introduction*. London: Heinemann, 1975.

Onwumechili, Cyril Agodi. *Igbo Enwe Eze: The Igbo Have No Kings. The 2000 Ahiajoku Lecture*. Owerri, NG: Ministry of Information, 2000.

Onyeneke, A. J. *A Short History of Uzuakoli by Students of the Methodist College, Uzuakoli, under the Direction of A. J. Fox*. London: Oxford University Press, 1964.

Onyeneke, A. O. *The Dead Among the Living: Masquerades in Igbo Society*. Nimo, NG: Holy Ghost Congregation, Province of Nigeria and Asele Institute, 1987.

Original Acts, Pointe Coupée Parish, May 1787, document no. 1571, Vente d'esclave, Monsanto to LeDoux.

Oriji, John. "Oracular Trade, Okonko Secret Society and the Evolution of Decentralized Authority among the Ngwa-Igbo of Southeastern Nigeria." *Ikenga* 5, no. 1 (1981): 35–52.

———. "A Re-Assessment of the Organization and Benefits of the Slave and Palm Produce Trade amongst the Ngwa-Igbo." *Canadian Journal of African Studies* 16, no. 3 (1982): 523–48.

———. "The Slave Trade, Warfare and Aro Expansion in the Igbo Hinterland." *Transafrican Journal of History* 16 (1987): 151–66.

———. *Traditions of Igbo Origin: A Study of Pre-Colonial Population Movements in Africa*. New York: Peter Lang, 1990.

Ortiz, Fernando. *Los Bailes y El Teatro De Los Negros En El Folklore De Cuba*. 1951; 2nd ed. La Habana, Cuba: Editorial Letras Cubanas, 1981.
———. *Hampa afro-cubana: Los negros esclavos; Estudio sociológico y de derecho público*. La Habana, Cuba: Revista Bimestre Cubana, 1916.
———. *Los Instrumentos de la Musica Afrocubana*. Vol. V, *Los pulsativos, los fricativos, los insuflativos, y los aeritivos*. Habana, Cuba: Cardenas y Cia, 1955.
Osaghae, Eghosa E. *Trends in Migrant Political Organizations in Nigeria: The Igbo Union in Kano*. Ibadan, NG: IFRA, 1994.
Osaghae, Eghosa E., Ebere Onwudiwe, and Rotimi T. Suberu, eds. *The Nigerian Civil War and Its Aftermath*. Ibadan, NG: John Archers, 2002.
Ottenberg, Simon. *Double-Descent in an African Society: The Afikpo Village-Group*. Seattle: University of Washington Press, 1968.
———. "Ibo Oracles and Intergroup Relations." *Southwestern Journal of Anthropology* 14, no. 3 (1958): 295–317.
———. "Ibo Receptivity to Change." In *Continuity and Change in African Cultures*, edited by W. R. Bascom and M. J. Herskovits, 130–43. Chicago, IL: University of Chicago Press, 1959.
———. *New Traditions from Nigeria: Seven Artists of the Nsukka School*. Washington, DC: Smithsonian Institution Press, 1997.
———, ed. *The Nsukka Artists and Nigerian Contemporary Art*. Washington, DC: The Smithsonian National Museum of African Art, 2002.
———. "We Are Becoming Art Minded: Afikpo Arts 1988." *African Arts* 22, no. 4 (August 1989): 58–88.
Palmer, Colin A. *The First Passage: Blacks in the Americas*, 1520–1617. New York: Oxford University Press, 1995.
———. *Human Cargoes: The English Slave Trade to Spanish America, 1700–1739*. Urbana: University of Illinois Press, 1981.
Parker, Isaac. Minutes of the Evidence Taken before the Select Committee. Public Records Office. *Publications of the House of Commons*, 1/84.
Pavich-Lindsay, Melanie, ed. *Anna: The Letters of a St. Simons Island Plantation Mistress, 1817–1859*, 326–27. Athens: University of Georgia Press, 2002.
Peel, J. D. Y. *Religious Encounter and the Making of the Yoruba*. Bloomington: Indiana University Press, 2000.
Pereira, Duarte Pacheco. *Esmeraldo de Situ Orbis* (edicao de Raphael Eduardo de Azevado Basto. Lisbon, PT: National Press, 1892.
Philip, Rhymer. Personal communication, July 16, 1996.
Phillips, Claude S. "Nigeria and Biafra." In *Ethnic Separatism and World Politics*, edited by Frederick, L. Shield. Lanham, MD: University Press of America, 1984.
Phillips, Ulrich Bonnell. *American Negro Slavery: A Survey of the Supply, Employment and Control of Negro Slavery*. Baton Rouge: Louisiana State University Press, 1918; reprint 1966.
Picayune Daily, New Orleans, October 12, 1879.
Pinkard, George. *Notes on the West Indies*, Vol. 1. London: Longman, 1806.
Postma, Johannes Menne. *The Dutch in the Atlantic Slave Trade, 1600–1815*. Cambridge: Cambridge University Press, 2008.
Powell, Timothy. "Summoning the Ancestors: The Flying Africans' Story and Its Enduring Legacy." In *African American Life in the Georgia Lowcountry: The Atlantic World and the Gullah Geechee*, edited by Philip Morgan, 253–80. Athens: University of Georgia Press, 2010.
Public Record Office, London. CO 388/10.
———. CO 520/12, Southern Nigeria Dispatches to the Colonial Office, July 7, 1901.
———. T71/1440, f. 576.
Ranger, Terence. "The Invention of Tradition in Colonial Africa." In *The Invention of Tradition*, edited by Terence Ranger and E. Hobsbawn. Cambridge: Cambridge University Press, 1983.
———. "The Invention of Tradition Revisited: The Case of Colonial Africa." In *Legitimacy and the State in Twentieth Century Africa: Essays in Honour of A. H. M. Kirk Greene*, edited by Terrence Ranger and Olufemi Vaughan, 62–111. Hampshire, UK: Macmillan, 1993.
Ransom, John Crowe, ed. *I'll Take My Stand: The South and the Agrarian Tradition by Twelve Southerners*. New York: Harper, 1930.

Reader, John. *Africa: A Biography of a Continent.* New York: Knopf, 1997.

"Rey de Calabar to Francesco da Monteleone (22 September 1692). In *Monumenta Missionaria Africana*, edited by Antonio Brásio, 14:224. Lisbon: Agencia Geral do Ultramar, 1958; "Francesco da Monteleone to Giuseppe Maria da Busseto (10 July 1692)."

Richardson, David. "Background to Annexation: Anglo-African Credit Relations in the Bight of Biafra, 1700–1891." In *From Slave Trade to Empire: Europe and the Colonisation of Black Africa 1780s–1880s*, edited by Olivier Pétré-Grenouilleau, 47–66. London: Routledge, 2004.

———, ed. *Bristol, Africa and the Eighteenth-Century Slave Trade to America.* Vol. 1, *The Years of Expansion 1698–1729.* Bristol Record Society's Publications, xxxviii. Gloucester, UK: Bristol Record Society, 1986.

———. "Profits in the Liverpool Slave Trade: The Accounts of William Davenport, 1757–1784." In *Liverpool, the African Slave Trade, and Abolition*, edited by Roger Anstey and P. E. H. Hair. Liverpool: Historical Society of Lancashire and Cheshire, 1976.

———. "Slave Exports from West and West-Central Africa, 1700–1810: New Estimates of Volume and Distribution." *Journal of African History* 30 (1989): 1–22.

———. "Slavery and Bristol's 'Golden Age.'" *Slavery and Abolition* 26 (2005): 35–54.

Robertson, David. *Denmark Vesey.* New York: Knopf, 1999.

Romans, Bernard. *A Concise Natural History of East and West Florida.* New York, 1775.

Royal Gazette, June 23–30, 1781, and November 10–17, 1781.

Rubin, Arnold. "Review of Frank Willett, Life in the History of West African Sculpture." *African Notes* 6, no. 2 (1971): 113–23.

Rucker, Walter C. *The River Flows On; Black Resistance, Culture, and Identity Formation in Early America.* Baton Rouge: Louisiana State University Press, 2006.

Ryder, A. F. C. *Benin and the Europeans*, 1485–1891. London: Prentice Hall, 1969.

Samford, Patricia M. *Subfloor Pits and the Archaeology of Slavery in Colonial Virginia.* Tuscaloosa: University of Alabama Press, 2007.

Samuel Richards to James Rogers, June 21, 1788, C107/9.

Sanneh, L. "The CMS and the African Transformation: Samual Ajayi Crowther and the Opening of Nigeria." In *Church Mission Society and World Christianity*, edited by K. Ward and B. Stanley. Grand Rapids, MI: Eerdmans, 2000.

Schrader, Richard A. *Notes of a Crucian Son.* St. Croix, VI: R. A. Schrader, 1989.

Schuler, Monica. "Akan Slave Rebellions in the British Caribbean." *Savacou* 1, no. 1 (1970): 373–86.

Scott, Michael. *Tom Cringle's Log.* Edinburgh: William Blackwood, 1836.

Sertima, Ivan Van. *They Came Before Columbus.* New York: Random House, 1976.

Shaw, Thurstan. "Gao and Igbo Ukwu: Beads, Interregional Trade, and Beyond." *African Archaeological Review* 14, no. 1 (1997): 1–15.

———. *Igbo Ukwu: An Account of Archaeological Discoveries in Eastern Nigeria.* London: Faber and Faber, 1970.

———. *Unearthing Igbo-Ukwu.* Oxford: Oxford University Press, 1977.

Shenk, W. R. *Henry Venn—Missionary Statesman.* New York: Orbis Books, 1983.

Shepherd, Verene, and Ahmed Reid. "Rebel Voices: Testimonies from the 1831–32 Emancipation War in Jamaica." *Jamaica Journal* 27, nos. 2/3 (2004): 54–63.

Sheridan, Richard B. "The Role of the Scots in the Economy and Society of the West Indies." In *Comparative Perspectives on Slavery in New World Plantations*, edited by Vera Rubin and Arthur Tuden, 94–106. New York: New York Academy of Sciences, 1977.

———. *Sugar and Slavery: An Economic History of the British West Indies, 1623–1775.* Baltimore, MD: Johns Hopkins University Press, 1974.

Sherlock, Philip M. *West Indian Nations: A New History.* Kingston: Jamaica Publishing House, 1973.

Skinner, E. P. "The Dialectic between Diasporas and Homelands." In *Global Dimensions of the African Diaspora*, edited by E. J. Harris. Washington, DC: Howard University Press, 1993.

Sloane, Hans. *A Voyage to the Islands of Madera, Barbados, and Jamaica*, Vol. 1. London: B. M., 1707.

Smith, Anthony D. "The Ethnic Sources of Nationalism." In *Ethnic Conflict and International Security*, edited by Michael Brown. Princeton, NJ: Princeton University Press, 1993.

Smith, William. *A New Voyage to Guinea*. London, 1744; 2nd ed. 1745.

Smock, Audrey C. *Ibo Politics: The Role of Ethnic Unions in Eastern Nigeria*. Cambridge, MA: Harvard University Press, 1971.

Sparks, Randy J. "The Two Princes of Calabar: An Atlantic Odyssey from Slavery to Freedom." *William and Mary Quarterly* 59 (2002): 555–84.

———. *The Two Princes of Calabar: An Eighteenth-Century Atlantic Odyssey*. Cambridge, MA: Harvard University Press, 2004.

Spear, Thomas, and Richard Waller, eds. *Being Maasai: Ethnicity and Identity in East Africa*. London: James Curry, 1993.

Spencer, Flora. *Crop-Over: An Old Barbadian Plantation Festival*. Barbados: Commonwealth Caribbean Center, 1974.

Stampp, Kenneth M. "Between Two Cultures." In *Americans from Africa: Slavery and Its Aftermath*, edited by Peter I. Rose. New York, Atherton Press, 1970.

Stanfield, James Field. *Observations on a Voyage to the Coast of Africa, in a Series of Letters to Thomas Clarkson, by James Field Stanfield, Formerly a Mariner in the African Trade*. London, 1788.

Stein, Robert Louis. *The French Slave Trade in the Eighteenth Century: An Old Regime Business*. Madison: University of Wisconsin Press, 1979.

Stein, Stanley. *Vassouras: A Brazilian Coffee County, 1850–1900*. Princeton, NJ: Princeton University Press, 1985.

Sutton, J. E. G. "Igbo-Ukwu and the Nile." *African Archaeological Review* 18, no. 1 (2001): 49–62.

Talbot, Percy Amaury. *The Peoples of Southern Nigeria: A Sketch of their History, Ethnology, and Languages, with an Abstract of the 1921 Census [4 volumes]*. London: Oxford University Press, 1926.

———. *Tribes of the Niger Delta: Their Religions and Customs*. London: Sheldon Press, 1932.

Tamuno, T. N. *The Evolution of the Nigerian State: The Southern Phase, 1898–1914*. London: Longman, 1972.

Tasie, G. O. M. *Christian Missionary Enterprise in the Niger Delta*, 1864–1918. Leiden, NL: Brill, 1978.

Teelucksingh, Jerome. "The 'Invisible Child' in British West Indian Slavery." *Slavery and Abolition* 27, no. 2 (2006): 237–50.

Thesée, François. *Les Ibos De L'Amelie: Destinée d'une Cargaison de Traite Clandestine á la Martinique* (1822–1838). Paris: Editions Caribeénnes, 1986.

Thomas, Clarkson. *The Substance of the Evidence of Sundry Persons on the Slave-Trade, Collected in the Course of a Tour Made in the Autumn of the Year 1788*. London, 1789.

Thomas, Hoobler. *Toussaint L'Ouverture*. New York: Chelsea House, 1990.

Thomas, M. E. *Jamaica and Voluntary Laborers from Africa, 1840–1845*. Gainesville: University Press of Florida, 1974.

Thompson, Richard H. *Theories of Ethnicity: A Critical Appraisal*. New York: Greenwood Press, 1989.

Thompson, Robert Farris. *Flash of the Spirit: African and Afro-American Art and Philosophy*. New York: Vintage Books, 1983.

Thornton, John. *Africa and Africans in the Making of the Atlantic World, 1400–1800*. Cambridge: Cambridge University Press, 1992; rev. ed. 1998.

Thorp, Daniel B. "Chattel with a Soul: The Autobiography of a Moravian Slave." *The Pennsylvania Magazine of History and Biography* 112 (1988): 433–51.

Time, August 23, 1968.

Timperley, Loretta R., ed. *A Directory of Landownership in Scotland c. 1770*. Edinburgh: Scottish Record Society, 1976.

Uba-Mgbemena, Asonye. "The Role of Ífò in Training the Igbo Child." *Folklore* 96, no. 1 (1985): 57–61.

Uchendu, Victor C. *The Igbo of Southeast Nigeria*. New York: Holt, Rinehart and Winston, 1965.

———. "'Kola Hospitality' and Igbo Lineage Structure." *Man* 64, no. 53 (1964): 47–50.

———. "Slaves and Slavery in Igboland, Nigeria." In *Slavery in Africa: Historical and Anthropological Perspectives*, edited by Suzanne Miers and Igor Kopytoff. Madison: University of Wisconsin Press, 1977.

Udechukwu, Obiora. *Obiora Udechukwu: Selected Sketches 1965–83*. Lagos, NG: National Council for Arts and Culture, 1984.

Ugwu, Aniemeka Michael. "Some Aspects of the History of Obukpa Town Before 1960." BA thesis, Department of History, University of Nigeria, Nsukka, June 1984.

Ugwu, Anthony O. "A Pre-Colonial History of Obukpa." BA thesis, Department of History, University of Nigeria, Nsukka, June 1980.

Ugwuoke, Igwebueze. Interview, 1996.

Universitetsbiblioteket Uppsala, L 123, f. 62, "Handel op alle de kuste van Africa van Cap: Spartell tott Cab: Bona Esperanca," the trading list is on ff. 63v–65.

Unugwu, Interview by author, tape recording, Okpara Nrobo, Enugu State, Nigeria, November 1, 1998.

Usoro, Eno J. *The Nigerian Oil Palm Industry*: (Government Policy and Export Production, 1906–1965). Ibadan, NG: Ibadan University Press, 1974.

Utazi, John. Interview by author, tape recording, Ajuona, Adani, Enugu State, Nigeria, November 20, 1998.

Uwadiegwu, Innocent Chiturugo. "Sister Ngozi of Alor-Uno and the Removal of the Dreaded Adoro Deity." BA thesis, University of Nigeria, Nsukka, February 2003.

Vail, Leroy, ed. *The Creation of Tribalism in Africa*. Berkeley: University of California Press, 1989.

Van den Boogart, Ernst, and Pieter C. Emmer. "The Dutch Participation in the Atlantic Slave Trade, 1596–1650." In *The Uncommon Market: Essays on the Atlantic Slave Trade*, edited by Henry A. Gemery and Jan S. Hogendorn, 359–60. New York: Academic Press, 1979.

Vanony-Frisch, Nicole. "Les esclaves de la Guadeloupe a la fin de l'ancien régime." *Bulletin de la Société d'Histoire de la Guadeloupe* (1985): 63–64.

Vanstory, Burnette. *Georgia's Land of the Golden Isles*. Athens: University of Georgia Press, 1956.

Vasconcellos, Colleen. "And a Child Shall Lead Them?: Slavery, Childhood, and African Cultural Identity in Jamaica, 1750–1838." PhD diss., Florida International University, 2004.

Visona, Monica Blackmun, Robin Poyner, Herbert M. Cole, and Michael D. Harris. *A History of Art in Africa*. New York: Harry N. Abrams, 2001.

Wallerstein, Immanuel. *The Capitalist World-Economy*. Cambridge: Cambridge University Press, 1979.

———. *The Modern World-System II: Mercantilism and the Consolidation of the European World-Economy, 1600–1750*. New York: Academic Press, 1974.

Walsh, Lorena S. "The Chesapeake Slave Trade: Regional Patterns, African Origins, and Some Implications." *William and Mary Quarterly* 58, no. 1 (2001): 139–70.

———. *From Calabar to Carter's Grove: The History of a Virginia Slave Community*. Charlottesville: University Press of Virginia, 1997.

Ward, Ida Caroline. "*A Linguistic Tour in Southern Nigeria*." Africa 8, no. 1 (1935): 90–97.

———. *An Introduction to the Ibo Language*. Cambridge: Heffer and Sons, 1936.

Wariboko, Waibinte E. "New Calabar: The Transition from Slave- to Produce-Trading and the Political Problems in the Eastern Delta, 1848–1891." In *Ports of the Slave Trade*, edited by Robin C. Law and Silke Strickrodt, 153–68. Stirling, UK: University of Stirling, 1999.

———. *Ruined by "Race": Afro-Caribbean Missionaries and the Evangelization of Southern Nigeria, 1895–1925*. Trenton, NJ: Africa World Press, 2007.

———. "West Indian Church in West Africa: The Pongas Mission among the Susus and Its Portrayal of Blackness, 1851–1953." In *Missions, States, and European Expansion in Africa*, edited by Chima J. Korieh and Raphael Chijioke Njoku, 167–86. New York: Routledge, 2007.

Warner-Lewis, Maureen. *Archibald Monteath: Igbo, Jamaican, Monrovian*. Kingston, JM: University of the West Indies Press, 2007.

———. *Guinea's Other Suns: The African Dynamic in Trinidad Culture*. Dover, MA: Majority Press, 1991.

Wax, Darold, D. "Preferences for Slaves in Colonial America." *Journal of Negro History* 58 (1973): 371–401.

West African Pilot (Lagos, Nigeria), January 20, 1947.

———. February 11, 1953.
———. February 17, 1952.
———. February 26, 1948.
———. February 4, 1953.
———. January 16, 1947.
———. July 15, 1955.
———. July 19, 1952.
———. July 6, 1949.

Whitford, John. *Trading Life in Western and Central Africa*, 2nd ed. London: Frank Cass, 1877; reprint 1967.

Wilson, Ellen, Gibson. *The Loyal Blacks*. New York: G. P. Putnam's Sons, 1976.

Wolf, Eric R. *Europe and the People without History*. Berkeley: University of California Press, 1982.

Wondji, C. "The States and Cultures of the Upper Guinea Coast." In *UNESCO General History of Africa*. Vol. V, *Africa from the Sixteenth to the Eighteenth Century*, edited by B. A. Ogot, 368–98. Berkeley: University of California Press, 1992.

Work Projects Administration. *Georgia: A Guide to Its Towns and Countryside, American Guide Series*. Athens: University of Georgia Press, 1946.

Yar'Adua, Shehu Musa. "Nigeria in Transition: A Critical Examination of the Main Political Economic and Social Aspects of the Nigerian Society)." Report of the Seminar on Nigeria in Transition. Kaduna, NG: Government Press, 1979.

Young, William. "A Tour Through the Islands of Barbados, St. Vincent, Antigua, Tobago and Grenada in 1791 and 1792." In *History, Civil and Commercial, of the British Colonies in the West Indies*, Vol. 3, edited by Bryan Edwards. London: Whittaker, 1807.

Zorzi, Alessandro. "Informatiõ hauuto jo Alexandro da Portogalese. 1517. Venecia," f. 140. Edited and published by Francisco Leite de Faria and Avelino Teixeira da Mota in "Novidades Náuticas e ultramarinas numa informação dada em Venezia em 1517."

CONTRIBUTORS

Nwando Achebe, PhD, is Professor of History, Michigan State University. She received her PhD from the University of California, Los Angeles, in 2000. Achebe served as a Ford Foundation and Fulbright-Hays Scholar-in-Residence at The Institute of African Studies and History Department of the University of Nigeria, Nsukka, in 1996 and 1998, respectively. Her research interests involve the use of oral history in the study of women, gender, sexuality, and power in Nigeria. Her first book is *Farmers, Traders, Warriors, and Kings: Female Power and Authority in Northern Igboland, 1900–1960* ((2005). Professor Achebe's second book, *The Female King of Colonial Nigeria: Ahebi Ugbabe* (2011) is a full-length critical biography on the only *female* warrant chief and "king" in all of colonial Nigeria, and arguably British Africa. The writing was funded by a generous grant from the Wenner-Gren Foundation.

A. E. Afigbo, PhD (1939–2009), was reputed to be the leader in the study of Nigerian history. On various subjects such as the Igbo, slavery, colonial history, nation-building, and others, his publications define the fields and have been cited in thousands of works by others. For his achievements as scholar/teacher, the Nigerian federal government conferred on him the Nigerian National Merit Award, the highest academic honor in Nigeria. Professor Afigbo was a first-rate historian who published in the leading journals, contributed to major books, evaluated manuscripts for publication, and shaped the direction both of African studies and the academy at large. He was active in promoting education and African studies for more than thirty years. Professor Afigbo led many research teams, organized important projects in Africa, and interacted with local and international communities. With solid achievements in ethnography, history, and other disciplines, Afigbo's work is truly interdisciplinary. His creative ideas and opinions remain highly valued by publishers, journal editors, and students alike.

Vincent Carretta, PhD, is Distinguished Professor in the Department of English at the University of Maryland, College Park. He recently added a Guggenheim Fellowship to his treasure trove of awards, fellowships, and grants. He has produced astounding and truly original research into the literary lives of the eighteenth-century Atlantic world. Carretta has written many groundbreaking books, especially on early African American literature. Among notable scholarly editions are several that have become classroom staples, including *Olaudah Equiano's The Interesting Narrative and Other Writings* (2003), *Philip Quaque's Correspondence* (2010), *Quobna Ottobah Cugoano's Thoughts* and *Sentiments on the Evil of Slavery* (1999), *Phillis Wheatley's Writings* (2014), and *Unchained Voices: An Anthology of Black Authors in the English-Speaking World of the Eighteenth Century* (2005). Perhaps best known for the widely read *Equiano, the African: Biography of a Self-Made Man* (2007), Carretta's investigation into the life of Olaudah Equiano has remapped the recent critical discourse for early African American writing. Carretta's most recent book is *Phillis Wheatley: Biography of a Genius in Bondage* (2014). He is now working on an edition of *Letters of the Late Ignatius Sancho, an African* (London, 1782).

Douglas B. Chambers, PhD, is Associate Professor of History at the University of Southern Mississippi. He is a cultural historian of "Atlantic Africa" with research interests in the Igbo Diaspora and comparative slavery in the Americas. Chambers is the author of more than twenty scholarly essays and four other books, including *Murder at Montpelier: Igbo Africans in Virginia* (2005) and *Enslaved Igbo and Ibibio in America: Runaway Slaves and Historical Descriptions* (2013). He served as the executive editor of the *Southern Quarterly* from 2005 to 2011. In 2005, Professor Chambers was honored with a traditional Igbo chieftaincy title *Okwulu Nri Oka Omee, Ife Umunna Umunri*, by the Umunri Royal Family Association, Obeagu, Nri, Nigeria. His other major research project is *Documenting Runaway Slaves*, a collaborative effort to compile runaway slave advertisements in historical newspapers from the U.S. South and the Caribbean.

Gloria Chuku, PhD, is Professor of Africana Studies with a specialty in African history, Affiliate Professor of Gender and Women's Studies, and Affiliate Professor of the Language, Literacy, and Culture graduate program at the University of Maryland, Baltimore County. Her research has focused primarily on Igbo history and culture; gender studies; women and the political economies of Nigeria and Africa; ethnonationalisms and conflicts in Nigeria; intellectual history; and slavery, slave trade and African Diaspora. Professor Chuku is the editor of *The Igbo Intellectual Tradition: Creative Conflict in African and African Diasporic Thought* (2013) and author of *Igbo Women and Economic Transformation in Southeastern Nigeria, 1900–1960* (2005). She has also published more than forty scholarly articles in peer-reviewed international journals and multiauthored volumes. She is currently working on a book manuscript: *Confronting the Silences: Gender, Ethnicity, and the Biafra-Nigeria War.*

Hannah Chukwu, PhD, holds graduate degrees from the University of Nigeria, Nsukka, and the University of Saskatchewan, Saskatoon. As an Associate Professor, she taught English for Academic Purposes for several years at the University of Nigeria, Nsukka. As a Fulbright scholar at the University of Wisconsin, Madison, she pursed a comparative study of black women's writings. She continues to write and publish in this field with various articles in journals and anthologies. Her other passion is in the field of Teaching English as a Second Language (TESL). She worked with immigrant and refugee professionals for several years with a community-based organization and, as a consultant, with the provincial government. She supervised three ESL programs in Saskatoon. She is a creative writer who has published several poems and written a play that was performed in 2012. Her novel, *Just for Mercy* (Mercy Series Book 1) is published in 2016. She is currently working on a collection of short stories and Mercy Series Book 2. She has several book projects such as African cultural values in the diaspora and a curriculum for Teaching English as a Second Language in Nigerian universities.

Audra A. Diptee, PhD, is Associate Professor in the Department of History at Carleton University. She is also cross-appointed to the Institute of African Studies. Her research covers common themes in both Africa and the Caribbean and explores issues related to children and childhood, gender, historical consciousness, slavery, and race relations. She has published work in each of these areas including a monograph, edited works, and several articles.

Toyin Falola, PhD, is Frances and Sanger Mossiker Chair in the Humanities and University Distinguished Teaching Professor, University of Texas at Austin. He is the recipient of over twenty lifetime career awards, including six honorary doctorates. He has written and edited more than one hundred books, including *The Yoruba Diaspora in the Atlantic World* (2005).

Gwendolyn Midlo Hall, PhD, is Professor Emerita of History at Rutgers University, where she taught Latin American and Caribbean history. She received a BA and MA in history from the University of the Americas in 1962 and 1963, respectively, and her doctorate in Latin American history from the University of Michigan in 1970. Her books include *Social Control in Slave Plantation Societies: A*

Comparison of St. Domingue and Cuba (1971) [paperback 1996]; *Africans in Colonial Louisiana: The Development of Afro-Creole Culture in the Eighteenth Century* (1992) [paperback 1995]; *Africans in the Americas: Continuities of Ethnicities and Regions* (2001), and *Ethnicity and Race: Slavery and Freedom in French, Spanish, and Early American Louisiana, 1720–1820* (in preparation). Dr. Hall received numerous awards for *Africans in Colonial Louisiana*, including the John Hope Franklin Prize, the Elliott Rudwick Prize, the Willie Lee Rose Prize, and the Theodore Saloutos Memorial Book Award. She is also the editor of *Love, War, and the 96th Engineers (colored): The New Guinea Diaries of Captain Hyman Samuelson During World War II* (1995) [paperback 2000] and *Databases for the Study of Afro-Louisiana History and Genealogy, 1699–1860* (2000), a CD-ROM publication. Professor Hall is an elder of the African Heritage Studies Society and a Guggenheim Fellow. In 1997, she was appointed Chevalier dans l'Order des Arts et des Letters by the government of France and, in 1994, she was the Louisiana Endowment for the Humanities Humanist of the Year.

Ogbu U. Kalu, PhD (1942–2009), was Henry Winters Luce Professor of World Christianity and Mission, McCormick Theological Seminary at the time of his death. He served as a faculty member at McCormick Theological Seminary in Chicago from 2001 to 2009. He also served as the Director of the Center for Global Ministry. Professor Kalu was respected internationally for his scholarship and church leadership, and his death is a great loss to many around the world as a great scholar and teacher. He was an active member of the Society for Pentecostal Studies for several years and was a prominent scholar of Pentecostalism in Africa. He authored or edited sixteen books, including *Power, Poverty and Prayer: The Challenges of Poverty and Pluralism in African Christianity, 1960–1996* (2006), *History of the Chistianity in West Africa* (1981), and *African Christianity: An African Story* (2007). He also edited and published more than 150 articles in journals and volumes. In October 2008, Kalu was honored at the 26th annual Association of Third World Studies meeting as one of two winners of the Toyin Falola Award for the best book on Africa published during 2007–2008. This was for his *African Pentecostalism: An Introduction* (2008).

Chima J. Korieh, PhD, teaches African History at Marquette University, Milwaukee, Wisconsin. He holds a doctorate in African History from the University of Toronto, Canada. He completed a prestigious British Academy Visiting Fellowship at Oxford University, Oxford, UK (2007/2008). He has authored many articles and essays in journals, books, and encyclopedias. His publications include *The Land Has Changed: Studies in Agrarian Change, Gender, and Society in Eastern Nigeria* (2010) and twelve edited books.

Paul E. Lovejoy, PhD, is Distinguished Research Professor, Department of History, York University, and holds the Canada Research Chair in African Diaspora History. He is a Fellow of the Royal Society of Canada and was the Founding Director of the Harriet Tubman Institute for Research on the Global Migrations of African Peoples. Formerly a member of the UNESCO "Slave Route" Project (Section du dialogue interculturel), he has published more than twenty-five books, including *Transformations in Slavery* (3rd ed., 2011). He is coeditor of *African Economic History* and General Editor of the Harriet Tubman Series on the African Diaspora, Africa World Press. In 2007 he was awarded an Honorary Degree, Doctor of the University, University of Stirling; in 2009 he received the President's Research Award of Merit at York University. He is also the recipient of the Distinguished Africanist Award from the University of Texas at Austin (2010), the Life Time Achievement Award from the Canadian Association of African Studies (2011), and the Teaching Award from the Faculty of Graduate Studies, York University in (2012). He is currently completing a book, *Equiano's World: A Biography of Gustavus Vassa (c. 1742–1797).*

Kenneth Morgan, PhD, is Professor of History at Brunel University, Uxbridge, Middlesex, England. He was educated at the University of

Leicester; New College, Oxford; King's College, Cambridge; and the University of Pennsylvania. He has published widely on slavery, the slave trade, and the eighteenth-century Atlantic commercial world. Professor Morgan is the editor of *The Bright-Meyler Papers: A Bristol-West India Connection, 1732–1837* (2007). His books include *Bristol and the Atlantic Trade in the Eighteenth Century* (1993), *Slavery, Atlantic Trade and the British Economy, 1660–1800* (2000), and *Slavery and the British Empire: From Africa to America* (2007).

Robert W. Nicholls, PhD, was born and raised in Britain. He obtained a BA in Art at London's Central School of Art and Design, an Art Teachers Certificate from University of London Institute of Education, and a MEd, and a PhD in African Studies from Howard University in 1992. Nicholls joined the faculty of the University of the Virgin Islands in 1993, where he is currently a tenured professor in the College of Arts and Social Sciences. He prepared a successful bid for the University of the Virgin Islands to host the 12th Triennial Symposium on African Arts sponsored by the Arts Council of the African Studies Association (ACASA), which was held in April 2001 to coincide with the Virgin Islands Carnival. Previously, Nicholls spent several years as faculty of Ahmadu Bello University in Nigeria, where he conducted research on the expressive culture of the Igede people. Much of Nicholls's academic career has been devoted to exploring linkages between the folklore of West Africa and that of the African Diaspora; for example, Nicholls has researched masquerading and tree lore in the Eastern Caribbean and has published books and numerous articles on both. Nicholls is author of *The Jumbies' Playing Ground: Old World Influences on Afro-Creole Masquerades in the Eastern Caribbean* (2012) and *Remarkable Big Trees in the U.S. Virgin Islands: An Eco-heritage Guide to Jumbie Trees and Other Trees of Cultural Interest* (2006). Nicholls has also produced music CDs, including *The Igede of Nigeria*, sixteen selections of traditional music (1991); *Trojan Presents Mod Ska: Forty Original Ska Anthems from 1962–67* (2012); and *Boogie Chillen: Early Mods First Choice Vinyl* (2013).

Raphael Chijioke Njoku, PhD, Professor at Idaho State University was a first-class honors graduate of the University of Nigeria, Nsukka, and Nigeria's 16th Rhodes Scholar-elect. He received a doctorate in Political Science from Vrije University, Belgium, in 2001, and a doctorate in African history from Dalhousie University, Canada, in 2003. His research specialty is African history and African politics. He is the author of *Culture and Customs of Morocco* (2005) and *African Cultural Values: Igbo Political Leadership in Colonial Nigeria 1900–1966* (2006) and is coeditor of *Missions, States, and European Expansion in Africa* (2007), *War and Peace in Africa* (2010), *Africa and the Wider World* (2010), and *The History of Somalia* (2013). Njoku has also published forty-two scholarly articles in international journals and edited volumes. Some of his awards include the Distinguished Research Award in the Category of Social Sciences (2009), Indiana University Library Residency Award (2009), Victor Olurunsola Endowed Research Award (2007), and the Schomburg Center award for Research in Black Studies (2006–2007). Njoku is currently the Chair of the Department of Global Studies and Languages at ISU.

Sylvester Okwunodu Ogbechie, PhD, specializes on the arts and visual culture of Africa and its Diasporas, especially in terms of how art history discourses create value for African cultural patrimony in the age of globalization. He is the author of *Ben Enwonwu: The Making of an African Modernist* (2008, winner of the 2009 Herskovits Prize of the African Studies Association for best scholarly publication in African studies), *Making History: The Femi Akinsanya African Art Collection* (2011), and editor of *Artists of Nigeria* (2012). He is the director of Aachron Knowledge Systems, and founder and editor of *Critical Interventions: Journal of African Art History and Visual Culture*. Professor Ogbechie organized and coordinated the First International Nollywood Convention and Symposium (Los Angeles, June 2005) that evaluated new media in contemporary African Visual Culture from the perspective of the internationally acclaimed Nigerian Video Film Industry. He subsequently founded the Nollywood Foundation in 2006 to formalize study and research of this phenomenon and produced annual international Nollywood conventions from 2005 to 2009. Ogbechie has received several fellowships, grants, and awards for his work from the Getty Research Institute, American Academy in Berlin, Rockefeller Foundation, Institute for International Education, Smithsonian Institution, and a consultancy for the Ford Foundation. He was the 2010 Consortium Professor of the Getty Research Institute and served as guest editor for a History of Photography special issue on African Photography. His current project focuses on the politics of cultural patrimony debates as it affects demands for the repatriation of African cultural patrimony held in Western museums and institution. His research is widely published, and he has lectured and consulted on African and African Diaspora arts for major museums in the United States, Europe, Africa, and Asia.

John Thornton, PhD, received his doctorate in African history in 1979, and after stints at the University of Zambia, Allegheny College, the University of Virginia, and Millersville University he joined the Boston University faculty in the fall 2003. His specializations include Africa and Atlantic History as well as world history. He is the author of *The Kingdom of Kongo: Civil War and Transition, 1641–1718* (1983); *Africa and Africans in the Formation of the Atlantic World, 1400–1680* (1992); *The Kongolese Saint Anthony: Dona Beatriz Kimpa Vita and the Antonian Movement, 1684–1706* (1998); *Warfare in Atlantic Africa, 1500–1800* (1999); and in 2007, with Linda Heywood, published *Central Africans, Atlantic Creoles, and the Foundation of the Americas* (2007), which won the Melville J. Herskovits Prize that year. His latest book is *A Cultural History of the Atlantic World, 1350–1820* (2012).

Waibinte E. Wariboko, PhD, is Professor of African history and Deputy Dean of graduate studies for the Faculty of Humanities and Education at the Mona Campus of the University of the West Indies in Jamaica. Between August 2007 and July 2009, he was the Head of the Department of History and Archaeology at the Mona Campus. He has authored numerous book chapters and journal articles as well as the following books: *Planting Church-Culture at New Calabar: Some Neglected Aspects of Missionary Enterprise in the Eastern Niger Delta, 1865–1918* (1998); *Ruined By "Race": Afro-Caribbean Missionaries and the Evangelization of Southern Nigeria, 1895–1925* (2005); and *Race and the Civilizing Mission: Their Implications for the Framing of Blackness and African Personhood, 1800–1960* (2010).

Maureen Warner-Lewis, PhD, is Professor Emerita of African-Caribbean Language and Orature in the Department of Literatures in English, University of the West Indies, Mona, Jamaica, where her teaching specializations were West Indian, African, and Oral Literatures. Her research on African cultural and linguistic retentions in the Caribbean resulted in the publication of *Guinea's Other Suns* (1991), *Yoruba Songs of Trinidad* (1994), *Trinidad Yoruba* (1996, 1997), *Central Africa in the Caribbean* (2003), and *Archibald Monteath* (2007).

INDEX